The Unlevel Playing Field

SPORT AND SOCIETY

Series Editors
Benjamin G. Rader
Randy Roberts

A list of books in the series appears at the end of this book.

The Unlevel *Playing Field*

A Documentary History
of the African American
Experience in Sport

DAVID K. WIGGINS

and

PATRICK B. MILLER

UNIVERSITY OF ILLINOIS PRESS
URBANA AND CHICAGO

670 6903

Library of Congress Cataloging-in-
Publication Data
The unlevel playing field : a documentary
history of the African American
experience in sport / David K. Wiggins
and Patrick B. Miller.
p.   cm. — (Sport and society)
ISBN 0-252-02820-1 (cloth : alk. paper)
1. Discrimination in sports—United
States—History.
2. African American athletes—History.
I. Wiggins, David Kenneth, 1951–   .
II. Miller, Patrick B. III. Series.
GV706.32.U65   2003
796'.089'96073—dc21   2002014269

To Edwin Bancroft Henderson, Wendell Smith,
Sam Lacy, and a generation of racial reformers
who endowed African American sport with
special meaning and enlisted black athletic
achievements in a larger crusade

CONTENTS

3
Parallel Institutions: Black Sports between the World Wars

4

The Quest for Racial Reform: Affirmation and Protest in the Sporting Realm, 1920s and 1930s

5

African American Athletes and Democratic Principles: Interpreting the Desegregation of Sport, 1940s and 1950s

6

Sport, the Civil Rights Movement, and Black Power, 1960s and 1970s

7

Progress, Protest, and Alienation in the Sports Factory, 1970s and Beyond

8

Black Cultural Commentary: Race Relations and Sport at the Turn of the Twenty-first Century

PREFACE

Sometimes it begins simply: while carefully turning the brittle pages of a college year-book assembled a century ago, you discover a certain photograph. The composition is simple, and the athletes portrayed may or may not have seen themselves as making history. Yet now, the image speaks compellingly to race pride and the struggle for success in America's national pastimes.

Or perhaps you walk away from reading an editorial printed in a journal of uplift and assimilation, only to realize hours—or days—later how insistently, though often in the most subtle and sophisticated terms, African American activists have enlisted black triumphs in sports in a broad-based civil rights crusade throughout much of the twentieth century.

The process of discovery might have begun with the cranking of the handle of a microfilm machine, or during a session with a former athlete's autobiography, or after taking notes on an article written by a news reporter, educator, or social commentator, whose explorations of athletic competition elaborate the larger meanings of popular culture. The documents illuminating various dimensions of black identity as well as the long, complex stories about race relations in sport originate in many sources.

For our part as historians, we recall hours of reading archival materials from the vast holdings of the Moorland-Spingarn Research Center at Howard University, conversations among the scholars-in-residence at the Schomburg Center for Research in Black Culture in Harlem, and investigations of the resources at the National Archives and the Library of Congress, just as we remember isolated references—here and there—to a poem in a book review that ostensibly had nothing to do with sport, or to a news clipping sent by a colleague or friend.

One by one, the documents we found seemed to animate particular moments, then increasingly an entire era in the long history of the African American experience in sporting competition. Both of us had read through the *Crisis,* the journal of the National Association for the Advancement of Colored People (NAACP), as well as *Opportunity,* the organ of the National Urban League, even as we had reviewed the pages of such short-lived but provocative periodicals as *Voice of the Negro* and *The Messenger.* Our reading in black newspapers was facilitated by the many reels of microfilm that constitute the Tuskegee Institute News Clipping File, laboriously compiled over the course of seven decades and, fortuitously for us, indexed to sport. Still, we had not imagined at the outset of this undertaking a decade ago that we would find both Booker T. Washington and W. E. B. Du Bois holding forth on the significance of Jack Johnson in African American culture, or for that matter Marcus Garvey and Richard Wright suggesting ways to reckon with the phenomenon of Joe Louis. And it would not be until the last phase of our research that we would find fascinating commentaries on the subject of basketball published by bell hooks and Nikki Giovanni.

At many points we wanted to test some of our ideas about the ways that black intellectuals, educators, and social reformers have often assessed sport as an integral part of African American culture and consciousness—as a critical ingredient in the quest for equal opportunity in America and as an emblem of cultural nationalism. Included in this process were numerous conversations with other scholars, sometimes at conferences on sport history, southern history, and American studies, and at a meeting sponsored by the Association for the Study of Afro-American Life and History (ASALH), as well as at a presentation at the Chicago Seminar on Sport and Culture. Over the years, we encountered an increasing number of people who were less interested in the final score of a football game, or an athlete's record, or the rankings of a team, or the split-second timing of a gold medal performance than in the larger significance of athletic competition in the history of American race relations. We have been encouraged by the support of those who discern the difference between what is customarily presented on the sports page and how that news helps shape the meanings of athletics within a broader social landscape and historical context.

It has not been enough, though, to revise or correct the early histories of black participation in sport, or to expand upon *A Hard Road to Glory,* Arthur Ashe's admirable compendium devoted to the contributions of African Americans to a variety of national pastimes. We have not endeavored to tell every story, exalt every hero, or map all the barriers and breakthroughs during the crusade for racial justice. More expansively, we believe our project lines up in many respects with Lawrence Levine's *Black Culture and Black Consciousness,* as a way of amplifying African American voices as they defined significant elements of racial solidarity and at the same time suggested the terms within which integration would eventually be celebrated. Another model appears in Gerald Early's essays in *The Culture of Bruising.* Although we might contend that our *own* notions of what can be called "muscular assimilationism" and a "strenuous cultural nationalism" add significant elements to the study of the African American experience, we are also keenly aware that we owe a debt to many other scholars for inspiring our research and refining the ways we think about the sporting realm, black identity, and race relations in the United States.

Regrettably, we were not able to tap all the sources that speak to the richness and variety of the African American experience in sport. Conspicuously absent from this volume are impressive works of journalism that we had selected from *Ebony, Jet,* and *Negro Digest.* Without explanation, the publisher of those magazines denied permission for republication. Although some other individuals and business agencies did not specifically prohibit the use of significant historical materials, the price tags they set effectively made some documents unavailable.

Then again, there remain many lenses on the formation of the black community—and on such themes as sports entrepreneurship and activism. The current editors of *Opportunity* and the *Chicago Defender* have helped us expand the scope of this project. The tracking of documents began in archives and numerous research libraries, and we were blessed—there is no better word—to have worked with archivists such as Renée

McKinney at Spelman College and Donna Wells at the Moorland-Spingarn Library at Howard University, as well as specialists at the Amistad Research Center at Tulane University in New Orleans, at Tougaloo College, and at Fisk University. Likewise, the staffs at West Virginia State University, Amherst College Archives, Brown University Library, Hampton University, the University of Pennsylvania Archives, the library at Bradley University, the Oberlin College Archives, and the Schomburg Center for Research in Black Culture attended swiftly and thoroughly to our phone calls, e-mails, faxes, and letters. Perhaps our most memorable expedition was one we took together in May 1996 to Tuskegee University. With the guidance of the archivist, Cynthia Wilson, we spent the better part of three days studying collections that had been amassed for a century and more, and we came away from that research adventure not only with copies of photos and documents and with fresh perspectives for the book; we also departed in awe of the rich materials—testifying to a significant tradition of African American hope and endeavor stretching far beyond the playing fields—that we had briefly held in our hands.

The Nevada Historical Society; the Baseball Hall of Fame Library in Cooperstown, New York; the Keeneland Library in Lexington, Kentucky; and the Basketball Hall of Fame in Springfield, Massachusetts, were generous with their time and efforts as we attempted to match themes and documents, texts and images. John Vernon at the National Archives found important photographs to illustrate the text; so did Steve Gietshier of the *Sporting News*. Richard Newman at the W. E. B. Du Bois Institute at Harvard University helped us locate Sondra Kathryn Wilson, the executor of the James Weldon Johnson estate.

Scholars from as far away as Finland and friends from as long ago as our high school years showed us new sources and thus offered some innovative ways of examining the meanings with which many African Americans endowed their participation in the sporting realm. Lonnie Bunch, Jerry Gems, David Zang, Jeffrey Sammons, Andrew Ritchie, Michael Lomax, Mikko Hyvärinen, Susan Rayl, C. Robert Barnett, Calvin H. Sinnette, John Carroll, Karl Lindholm, Bill Schutte, Eugene Friedman, C. Keith Harrison, Robert Pruter, Dan Lerner, Pamela Grundy, Patrick Hill, Edwin Redkey, Susan Bandy, J. Thomas Jable, Bill Baker, Richard Pierce, Rita Liberti, Daniel Nathan, and Johanna X. K. Garvey all offered suggestions about documents that might be useful and in some cases sent us texts that they had used in writing their own works. Craig Lloyd, the biographer of Eugene Bullard, not only described the many dimensions of his own research; he also put us in touch with Richard K. Reid, Bullard's grandson, who graciously permitted us to quote from Bullard's unpublished memoir and to print a fabulous illustration, both of which speak to the early history of the African American expatriate experience in Paris. Together, these people played an instrumental role in helping us document the profound impact of black athletes on American society as well as the destructive effects of long-standing and pervasive racism in the athletic domain and beyond.

At critical junctures, we counted on Paul Spickard, Charles Martin, Benjamin Rader, and Randy Roberts to help us clarify broader substantive points or to reconceive some of the issues that inform the work. Larry Malley—a friend for many years—offered sage advice about the assembly of richly textured and often sensitive materials, then again about the publishing business in general. We also owe a huge debt of gratitude to Charles Petit for his support of our work—indeed his understanding of its many dimensions—

and his expertise in copyright law. For his part, our editor, Richard Wentworth, helped mark some of our paths through the thicket of the permissions process. We were also assisted in many wonderful ways by Carol Betts, our copy editor. Her efforts have improved this volume considerably.

A number of works that appear in this book were generously contributed in the larger interest of expanding scholarship in the field of African American studies. Gerald Early, Henry Louis Gates Jr., Lloyd V. Hackley, and Marian E. Washington simply expressed their interest in the project and wanted to see the book published; O. K. Davis and Rick Rocamora likewise donated their work. At the same time, other commentators abetted the process of making their ideas available to a larger audience. Ultimately perhaps no person has been more involved in expediting the completion of this book than Wayne Wilson. From his offices at the Amateur Athletic Foundation in Los Angeles, Wayne has served as liaison to prominent ex-athletes and sports figures whose stories we wanted to tell; he has also helped us enormously in finding photographs that fit our project.

Colleagues and friends from our respective universities should also be thanked profusely. Steven Riess, June Sochen, and Gregory Singleton of the history department at Northeastern Illinois University kindly read the list of contents and offered valuable suggestions about the meanings of sport in terms of ritual and representation as well about today's culture of celebrity. Simply stated: between her computer and her telephone, Margie Greif administered technological problems into oblivion, thus keeping this project—and probably many others—lively from day to day. At the NEIU library, Debbie Siegel handled dozens of requests for printed sources, then dealt graciously with her counterparts at other colleges and universities when we had spent rather too much time with the materials we had borrowed. At George Mason University, Susan J. Pufnock was indispensable in typing hundreds of pages of photocopied material while Valerie Block scanned sundry documents that have ultimately made their way into our text. Bill Fleming and Marianne Chase offered many valuable observations about how libraries and presses handle acquisitions and copyright.

Throughout the endeavor, Brenda Wiggins has been both astute and wonderfully patient as we grappled with the choice of documents, selection of photographs, and overall format of the book. This project would not have been so rewarding or come to fruition without her unwavering support.

Ultimately, we envision many additions to our scholarship. In fact, we encourage readers to offer items that will contribute new perspectives, new ideas, and new material for future editions of the book. The dedication of this volume has the past in mind: we want to pay respect to a tradition in sportswriting that firmly embraced ideals for a better future for African Americans. With the future in mind, we harbor a similar vision— that there will be sufficient evidence to allow us a new title for the next edition, a book that speaks further, and perhaps fully, to equality and opportunity in the athletic realm and beyond.

ACKNOWLEDGMENTS

Grateful acknowledgment is made to the various individuals and publishers for permission to reprint the following documents in this collection:

Excerpt from "National American Tennis Association Championships," by Gerald Norman, *Opportunity* 6 (October 1928): 306–7. Reprinted by permission of the National Urban League.

Letter from J. Elmer Reed to Art Carter, March 5, 1942, Art Carter Collection, Moorland-Spingarn Research Center, Howard University. Reprinted by permission of the Moorland-Spingarn Research Center, Howard University.

"Cum Posey Is No More," by Frank A. Young, *Chicago Defender*, April 13, 1946. Reprinted by permission of the *Chicago Defender*.

"Tribune Girls Settle Fuss on Court with Bennett's 5," *Chicago Defender*, March 24, 1934. Reprinted by permission of the *Chicago Defender*.

Excerpt from "Nation Eyes Lincoln and Howard Game," *Chicago Defender*, December 2, 1922. Reprinted by permission of the *Chicago Defender*.

Excerpt from Hildrus A. Poindexter, *My World of Reality: An Autobiography* (Detroit: Balamp Publishing, 1973), 33–36. Copyright © 1973 by Balamp Publishing Co. Reprinted by permission of Balamp Publishing Co.

Excerpt from James Weldon Johnson, *Black Manhattan* (New York: Knopf, 1930), 59–64. Reprinted by permission of Dr. Sondra Kathryn Wilson.

"Free Fantasia: Tiger Flowers," by Robert Hayden, in *Robert Hayden: Collected Poems,* ed. Frederick Glaysher (1975; New York: Liveright/Norton, 1985), 130. Copyright © 1975 by Robert Hayden. Used by permission of Liveright Publishing Corporation.

Excerpt from "All Blood Runs Red," unpublished memoir by Eugene Bullard, quoted in P. J. Carisella and James W. Ryan, *The Black Swallow of Death: The Incredible Story of Eugene Jacques Bullard, the World's First Black Combat Aviator* (Boston: Marlborough House, 1972), 70–71, 207. Reprinted by permission of Richard K. Reid.

"The 100 Meters Finals at the Olympics," by Herbert Henegan, *Crisis* 40 (November 1933): 262. Reprinted by permission of the Crisis Publishing Co. Inc.

Excerpt from "Race and Runners," by W. Montague Cobb, *Journal of Health and Physical Education* 7 (January 1936): 3–7, 52–56. Reprinted with permission from the *Journal of Health and Physical Education,* a publication of the American Alliance for Health, Physical Education, Recreation, and Dance, 1900 Association Drive, Reston, Virginia 20191.

Excerpt from "High Tide in Harlem: Joe Louis as a Symbol of Freedom," by Richard Wright, *New Masses,* July 5, 1938, 18–20. Copyright © 1938 by Richard Wright. Reprinted by permission of John Hawkins and Associates, Inc.

Excerpt of letter from Willis P. Armstrong to Arthur Carter, October 5, 1941, including Armstrong's poem "A Toast to Joe Louis," Art Carter Collection, Moorland-Spingarn Research Center, Howard University. Reprinted by permission of the Moorland-Spingarn Research Center, Howard University.

Excerpt of letter from James D. Carr to William H. S. Demarest, June 6, 1919, Special Collections and University Archives, Rutgers University Libraries. Reprinted by permission of Special Collections and University Archives, Rutgers University Libraries.

"Citizens Suspect Segregation Move in Recreation Center," *Chicago Defender,* November 13, 1931. Reprinted by permission of the *Chicago Defender.*

Letter from Charles H. Houston to Eleanor Patterson, November 28, 1938, NAACP papers, Moorland-Spingarn Research Center, Howard University. Reprinted by permission of the Moorland-Spingarn Research Center, Howard University.

Excerpt from "The Negro Athlete and Race Prejudice," by Edwin Bancroft Henderson, *Opportunity* 14 (March 1936): 77–79. Reprinted by permission of the National Urban League.

"That Old Southern Accent," by Roy Wilkins, *New York Amsterdam News,* October 23, 1936. Reprinted by permission of the *New York Amsterdam News.*

Excerpt from "Has Professional Football Closed the Door?" by Williams A. Brower, *Opportunity* 18 (December 1940): 375–77. Reprinted by permission of the National Urban League.

"Jackie Robinson on Trial," by Walter White, *Chicago Defender,* April 26, 1947. Reprinted by permission of the *Chicago Defender.*

Excerpt from "American Integration, Black Heroism, and the Meaning of Jackie Robinson," by Gerald Early, *Chronicle of Higher Education,* May 23, 1997, B4–B5. Reprinted by permission of the author.

Excerpt from "*Society:* Status Without Substance," by E. Franklin Frazier, from his *Black Bourgeoisie* (New York: Free Press, 1957), 207–8. Reprinted with the permission of Scribner, a division of Simon and Schuster. Copyright © 1957, 1962 by Macmillan Publishing Company.

Excerpt from "Harlem Globetrotters," by Nelson George, from his *Elevating the Game: The History and Aesthetics of Black Men in Basketball* (New York: Simon and Schuster, 1992), 41–42, 47–51. Copyright © 1992 by Nelson George. Reprinted by permission of Harper Collins Publishers.

Excerpt from "Racial Integration in the Field of Sports," by Rufus Clement, *Journal of Negro Education* 23 (1954): 222–30. Reprinted by permission of the *Journal of Negro Education.*

"Photos Taught a Lesson," by Adam Buckley Cohen, *Los Angeles Times,* October 20, 2001. Reprinted by permission of the author.

"The Skies Refused to Fall," by Andrew W. Ramsey, *Indianapolis Recorder,* March 26, 1955. Reprinted by permission of the *Indianapolis Recorder.*

Excerpt from "What Now," by Althea Gibson, from her *I Always Wanted to Be Somebody* (New York: Harper, 1958), 157–59. Reprinted by permission of the Althea Gibson Foundation.

Excerpt from "On the Road in the South, 1960," by Chet Walker, from Chet Walker with Chris Messenger, *Long Time Coming: A Black Athlete's Coming of Age in America* (New York: Grove Press, 1995), 77–82. Copyright © by Chet Walker. Reprinted with permission of the Carol Mann Agency.

Excerpt from "Rebellion at Cal," by A. S. "Doc" Young, *Chicago Defender,* February 1, 1968. Reprinted by permission of the *Chicago Defender.*

Excerpt from "Mounting the Revolt," by Harry Edwards, from *The Revolt of the Black Athlete* (New York: Free Press, 1969), 38–43. Reprinted with the permission of the Free Press, a division of Simon and Schuster, Inc. Copyright © 1969, 1979 by The Free Press.

Excerpts from "Why Negroes Should Boycott," by Tommie Smith, and "Why They Should Not," by Ralph Boston, *Sport,* March 1968, 40–41, 42–43, 68–69. Reprinted by permission of *Sport* magazine.

Excerpt from "The Fight: Patterson vs. Liston" (1963), by James Baldwin, *The Nugget,* February 1963. Copyright © 1963 by James Baldwin. Copyright renewed. Reprinted by arrangement with the James Baldwin Estate.

"The Muhammad Ali–Patterson Fight," by Eldridge Cleaver, excerpt from *Soul on Ice* (New York: McGraw-Hill, 1968), 91–94. Copyright © 1968 by Eldridge Cleaver. Reprinted by permission of the McGraw-Hill Companies.

Excerpt from "James Gregory: Grambling's First White Player," by Eddie Robinson with Richard Lapchick, from *Never Before, Never Again: The Stirring Autobiography of Eddie Robinson* (New York: St. Martin's, 1999), 134–39. Copyright © 1999 by Eddie Robinson and Richard Lapchick. Reprinted by permission of St. Martin's Press, LLC.

Excerpt from "We Need to Educate Our Athletes," by Lloyd V. Hackley, *Black Collegian* 13 (April/May 1983): 35–37. Reprinted by permission of the author.

Excerpt from "Black Women in Sports: Can We Get off the Track," by Marian E. Washington, *Proceedings of the Seventy-seventh Annual Meeting of the National Collegiate Physical Education Association for Men* (Chicago: University of Illinois at Chicago, 1974), 42–44. Reprinted by permission of the author.

Excerpt from "In America's National Pastime . . . White is the Color of the Game off the Field," by Frank Robinson, *People Weekly,* April 27, 1987, 46, 51. Copyright © 1987 Time Inc. All rights reserved. Reprinted by permission of Time, Inc.

Excerpt from *Out of Bounds,* by Jim Brown with Steve Delsohn (New York: Kensington, 1989), 47–52. Copyright © 1989 by Jim Brown with Steve Delsohn. Reprinted by permission of Kensington Publishing Company.

Excerpt from *The Best That I Can Be: An Autobiography,* by Rafer Johnson and Philip Goldberg (New York: Doubleday, 1998), 182–83, 188–91, 238, 241, 243–52. Copyright © 1998 by Rafer Johnson. Used by permission of Doubleday, a division of Random House, Inc.

"A Team's True Colors," by David Aldridge, *Washington Post,* December 16, 1995, A1–A8. Copyright © 1995, the *Washington Post.* Reprinted with permission.

Excerpt from "Calvin Hill Interview," by David W. Zang, *Journal of Sport History* 15 (Winter 1988): 334–55. Reprinted by permission of the author.

"On the Court, In the World," by Margo Jefferson, *New York Times,* June 13, 1993, Sec. 7, pp. 11, 28–29. Copyright © The New York Times. Reprinted with permission.

"Delusions of Grandeur," by Henry Louis Gates Jr., *Sports Illustrated,* August 19, 1991, 78. Reprinted by permission of the author.

"We've Got to Be Strong: The Obstacles Facing Black Women in Sports Have Scarcely Diminished with Time," by Anita DeFrantz, *Sports Illustrated,* August 12, 1991, 77. Copyright © 1991, Time, Inc. all rights reserved. Reprinted courtesy of *Sports Illustrated.*

"Left Behind," by Welch Suggs, *Chronicle of Higher Education,* November, 30, 2001. Copyright © 2001, *The Chronicle of Higher Education.* Reprinted with permission.

Excerpt from "Dreams of Conquest," by bell hooks, *Sight and Sound* 5 (April 1995): 22–23. Reprinted by permission of *Sight and Sound.*

Excerpt from "Be Like Mike? Michael Jordan and the Pedagogy of Desire," by Michael Eric Dyson. Copyright © 1993 from *Cultural Studies* by Michael Eric Dyson. Reproduced by permission of Taylor and Francis, Inc., <http://www.routledge-ny.com>.

Excerpt from "Playing Dennis Rodman," by John Edgar Wideman. Copyright © 1996 by John Edgar Wideman, first published in *The New Yorker,* April 29–May 6, 1996, 94–95. Reprinted by permission of the Wylie Agency.

"Iverson's Posse," by Nikki Giovanni, *Blues: For All the Changes* (New York: Morrow, 1999), 82–84. Copyright © 1999 by Nikki Giovanni. Reprinted by permission of HarperCollins Publishers, Inc.

"History in Black and White," by Michael Wilbon, *Washington Post,* April 15, 1997, B1–B2. Copyright © 1997 the *Washington Post.* Reprinted with permission.

"NFL's Silent Majority Afraid to Force Change," by William C. Rhoden, *New York Times,* January 29, 1999, D1–D2. Reprinted by permission of the *New York Times.*

Excerpt from "New Deal Makes Venus Richest Female Athlete," *Jacksonville Free Press,* January 10, 2001. Reprinted by permission of the *Jacksonville Free Press.*

Excerpt from "The Next Millennium," by Kenneth Shropshire, *In Black and White: Race and Sports in America* (New York: New York University Press, 1996), 142–46, 157–59. Reprinted by permission of New York University Press.

Excerpt from "Performance and Reality: Race, Sports, and the Modern World," by Gerald Early, *The Nation,* August 10–17, 1998, 11–18. Reprinted by permission of the author.

"The Decline of the Black Athlete: An Interview with Harry Edwards," by Dave Leonard, *ColorLines* 30 (April 2000): 20. Reprinted by permission of *ColorLines.*

The Unlevel Playing Field

INTRODUCTION

In the first of her many autobiographical writings, Maya Angelou described the significance of the career of Joe Louis for the people in her hometown during the depths of the Great Depression and the high tide of Jim Crow. *I Know Why the Caged Bird Sings* contains many insights about race relations in the South of the 1930s, but among its most dramatic passages is Angelou's evocation of one of Louis's early bouts, a compelling image of how many African Americans perceived their victories and defeats in sport. Angelou recalled an occasion during her childhood when black farmers and workers entered tiny Stamps, Arkansas, gathering around a store radio and filling rows of chairs, stools, and overturned boxes to listen to the long-awaited contest. This was an experience marked by shared values and ideals. Angelou remembers that at one point, when Louis was forced against the ropes and seemed to be losing, paralyzing dread gripped those around her. It was not just another boxer in trouble, she declares. "It was our people falling. It was another lynching: Yet another Black man hanging on a tree. One more woman ambushed and raped. A Black boy whipped and maimed. It was hounds on the trail of a man running through slimy swamps. It was a white woman slapping her maid for being forgetful. . . . We didn't breathe. We didn't hope. We waited."

That breathless passage—full of tension—stands for many of the other documents assembled here. What black people could accomplish in athletic competition has always represented something more—further contributions to what has often been conceived as the pageant of American history, larger statements about the travails and triumphs of black Americans since the era of slavery and beyond. This collection of articles, essays, and verse is intended to evoke, just as Angelou endeavored to capture, the *meanings* of the African American experience in sport. It is at once a chronicle of significant athletic events and the accomplishments of numerous black sporting heroes and a gathering of impressions, observations, and assessments by African American commentators about the roles sport has played in the larger history of race relations in the United States. To provide a systematic account of championships won or records set, numerous historians have scrutinized myriad sports pages for batting averages or points scored or the fastest times for the 100-meter dash. Other scholars have conducted exhaustive research on such themes as the desegregation of major league baseball or of intercollegiate athletics and then have written compellingly about the relationship between sport and racial reform. In sum, a considerable body of richly detailed and insightful scholarship helps form the basis for the narrative we have shaped, as well as the various interpretations we have made, concerning the African American experience in the realm of sport. This study is an attempt to link the ideas of many specialists in sport studies, as well as social history and cultural commentary, to broader patterns of development in

African American history, specifically the campaign by black Americans to become full participants in the social, economic, and political life of the nation.

Here we tell the stories of Jack Johnson, Joe Louis, Jesse Owens, Jackie Robinson, Muhammad Ali, and Michael Jordan; we also chronicle the exploits of Althea Gibson, Wilma Rudolph, Jackie Joyner-Kersee, and Venus and Serena Williams. In sum, we have included documents that discuss the lives and careers of numerous black champions, though certainly there are many more stars whose stories are inspirational than can be included in just one volume. We have also been particularly concerned with institutional developments, such as the ways that Jim Crow was imposed in the realm of sport and the means by which racial reformers challenged and eventually triumphed over long-standing patterns of segregation. At the same time, this book seeks to illuminate a vital dimension of black culture—expressed in Negro League baseball and the traditions and rivalries that characterized athletic competition at what we now call Historically Black Colleges and Universities (HBCUs)—and some of the controversies triggered by the pursuit of excellence in sport at the expense of other cultural forms and social programs. In every instance possible, *The Unlevel Playing Field* examines the meaning of sport from the perspectives of African American participants and observers. Thus it is not only the stories themselves but also the larger themes about African American history and race relations that have been our major points of reference. Black history and sport history come together here to add a significant dimension to American history, writ large.

––––––––

Deriving principally from black sources, the book begins in the antebellum era with the relatively few accounts available from African Americans about their lives in slavery or as free people of color. The enormous hardships faced by blacks within the confines of "the peculiar institution" and the racism prevailing north of slavery meant that there was scant opportunity for the pursuit of play, games, and sport. The slave narratives—a distinctive genre within and forceful contribution to American literature—offer little information on the subject, nor does the emerging African American press in the North, although those sources are also suggestive about the vitality of black culture. After emancipation, the opportunity for blacks to participate in a more expansive sporting realm was gradually circumscribed, by custom and by law, as segregation became more deeply rooted throughout the nation. Though some African Americans succeeded in winning championships—as boxers and jockeys, for instance—during the late nineteenth and early twentieth centuries, the vast majority of black people were excluded from mainstream organizations and broad-based municipal associations and were thus compelled to create their own sporting institutions. Those newly formed leagues and teams expressed a richly textured African American culture. If they did not always flourish in financial terms, that was principally because they were established within the context of widespread economic dislocation among black Americans generally. But sport created a sense of shared values and aspirations; it helped shape a spirit of community.

By the early twentieth century an increasingly energetic black press thoroughly covered sporting accomplishments and adopted a stance that would soon become the policy of the most prominent black advocates of uplift and activism. African American sportswriters, including those who wrote for the *Crisis* and *Opportunity*, consistently celebrated black achievement in sport while at the same time denouncing racism and discrimination in the realm of athletics. This notion, perhaps best captured in the phrase "muscular assimilationism," was enlisted as a significant element in the campaign for civil rights. If "sportsmanship" and "fair play" could be achieved in national pastimes, then ideally such notions could be extended to all walks of life. Such programs for racial reform were devised to bring about the demise of Jim Crow, and African American commentators on sport were exceedingly articulate about the ways they hoped to use the playing fields as a platform for social mobility and to enlist athletic triumph in the quest for equal opportunity in America.

Within this strategy of appeal, black champions such as Joe Louis and Jesse Owens—then later such figures as Jackie Robinson and Wilt Chamberlain, Althea Gibson, and Bill Russell—became important symbolic figures in the crusade, yet it was African American activists more than anyone else who initiated the erasure of the color line in sport. Ultimately, during the critical years of civil rights mobilization, an increasing number of athletes themselves helped showcase racism in the United States, for all the world to see. The transformation of the 1968 Olympic Games into a stage for black protest bore witness to one of the ways that sport was further insinuated into broad-based programs for racial justice. At the same time, when Cassius Clay renamed himself Muhammad Ali and became an outspoken critic of many American social conventions as well as of U.S. foreign policy, he demonstrated that blacks did not speak with one voice about integration and the prospects for the future. Indeed, he showed that a strenuous cultural nationalism was attractive to many African Americans.

While the last several decades have been marked by enormous progress with regard to the desegregation of the playing fields, the process was never simple or uncontested. As a consequence, many of those who were pioneers in breaking the color line in sports have looked back on their ordeal with considerable bitterness. For other black athletes and activists, more concerned with problems of the present or in setting up programs for the future, the relationship between sport and society remains enormously significant. Whether they are discussing the images projected by the most prominent black men and women in sport or the connections between athletics and academics at institutions of higher education, African American commentators continue to emphasize the power of the sporting experience to transform larger patterns of culture and consciousness. At the same time, there is no other way to characterize black commentary on sport than as vigilant; there is no room for complacency or self-congratulation. And whether articulated from the corridors of Ivy League universities or from the street corners of cities like Chicago, black activism must contend with the invidious distinctions that still mark the racial landscape.

Such considerations have informed not only our selection of documents for this book but also much of its emphasis on the middle part of the twentieth century. First, it has been the *commentary* on the broader meanings of sport, variously elaborated by black intellectuals and racial reformers, as much as the achievements by African American athletes themselves, that has challenged mainstream society to live up to ideals of equality and opportunity. We have scant knowledge of any athletic prowess that W. E. B. Du Bois or Richard Wright might have possessed, yet when Du Bois made sporting accomplishment a substantial part of *Crisis* coverage under his editorship, or when Wright described the symbolic value of Joe Louis's victory over the German Max Schmeling, they made ringing statements about the meaning of sport for African Americans. It may be just as important to emphasize that it was during the interwar era specifically that such notions as "muscular assimilationism" were devised as a means of making claims about American democracy and at the same time expressing enormous pride in black cultural achievement. Significantly, these were complementary rather than rival dimensions of African American consciousness and social commitment. And such mutually reinforcing notions were articulated not only at the highest levels of competitive sport but also by local activists, who sought to establish municipal playgrounds, recreation areas, and robust high school athletic programs.

The events that followed the era of Jackie Robinson did not line up in a clear pattern of progress toward the advancement of civil rights and racial justice; neither have all black commentators stood in agreement about the ideal role of sport in American culture. But even as we chronicle more recent breakthroughs or contemporary debates about race relations in the sporting realm, it is essential to keep in mind the historical context. Today, most Americans probably do not watch every stride of a black athlete in an Olympic final for its racial impact. Neither do we scrutinize every stroke made by Venus Williams or Tiger Woods as a means of transforming prevailing conceptions of race relations in America or of altering public policy. But as Maya Angelou reminds us in her description of the Joe Louis fight, there was a time when many African Americans did just that. Ideally, this book will help renew interest in the stories of struggle from the past, just as it may help frame some questions about race relations in sport—and well beyond the athletic domain—for the future.

1

Antebellum Ordeals: Slavery, Sport, and the Prospects of Freedom

Introduction

The pervasiveness of slavery in antebellum America and the depth of oppression facing free people of color, North and South, were the principal elements in the shaping of African American history before 1860. Black culture included song and dance, sacred rituals, and communal ceremonies that can be traced back to African sources; what is more, the mingling of cultural forms from Africa, Europe, and the Americas helped create variegated musical traditions, as well as distinctive religious practices. Yet the historical record remains relatively sparse with regard to folkways that can be explicitly linked to the black experience in organized athletic competition. Critically, slave narratives emphasized the labor regime of "the peculiar institution"—an ordeal of constant physical exhaustion. During the constitutional crises and moral crusades that made abolitionism a revolutionary appeal to human rights, any accounts by African Americans about their participation in sporting endeavors would not have loomed large in the popular consciousness.

By the era of the Civil War, approximately four million blacks in the United States were held as slaves; another half million might claim the status of freedmen, but racism and discrimination plagued their lives as well. So it is difficult to discuss athletics in any modern sense, or to abstract patterns of leisure and recreation from the desperate lives led by the mass of African Americans. This point cannot be stressed enough. Though we might speak about the expansiveness of black culture—how a particular sermon or a song bore witness to the hopes as well as the travail of bondsmen—there was precious little opportunity for African Americans to make pastimes out of physical activity, or to organize games and sport. For it was the fundamental objective of chattel slavery to direct blacks' strength and energy to labor in the fields or around the plantation house.

The institution of slavery, in fact, compelled the vast majority of African Americans to "steal" time for leisure and recreation, just as they stole a certain kind of knowledge when they learned to read and write. The daily reality for most slaves was intensive labor from sunup often past sundown; meager housing, clothing, and portions of food; inadequate medical attention; and always the threat of the lash. Yet historical assessments of slave religion demonstrate the richness and complexity of African American spirituality and the innovativeness of the enslaved in finding time for worship. As described by folklorists, the same patterns seem to have prevailed when bondsmen and women adapted the work regimen into something broader, more expressive of their beliefs and ideas. In such a way, slave songs and dances, as well as the occasional foray into a game, a match, or a race, were physical expressions of black culture and consciousness, embodiments of a world that was *not* bound to the labor system that their masters had created.

Significantly, the documents that lie at the center of this part of the present study do not reveal in enormous detail how slaves participated in physical competition or devised for themselves various kinds of play or games. They do, however, speak to the creativity of individuals as well as to the diverse forms of solidarity within the slave community. They suggest how strength and autonomy could be exhibited as a source of pride. Wrestling and running were rather basic activities, while hunting served the useful purpose of providing food. Nevertheless, many elders commented on the energy of slave youth when it came to tests of skill, speed, and stamina. Even though these accounts approach leisure and recreation from different perspectives, virtually all speak to the ways slaves expanded their universe through music and dance, through rituals that combined physical exertion and celebration, and through rhythms and phrases that often recalled their African heritage. Here were testaments to a vibrant culture—even as it was forced to measure itself within the constraints of chattel slavery. The competition of corn shucking, for instance, clearly aided masters in getting their labor force to move speedily, but that competition also opened out, at least partly, to an element of play. The teams organized by masters and overseers thus were exploitative in every way but one. Black men and women, young and old, self-consciously created something festive from their labors.

That a few slaves were able to escape work in the fields by displaying impressive skills as athletes offers yet another example of how a subject people seized on every opportunity to make their way out of forced servitude. Because there are so few accounts of jockeys, boxers, wrestlers, or runners (or those who trained cocks to fight—in yet another traditional pastime within the plantation South), students of the slave experience need to be wary of generalizing about those who used their physical talents to win their freedom. Antebellum southern life revolved around economic matters, principally the growth and sale of cotton, or sugar, or rice. The overwhelming majority of slaves toiled in the fields or performed jobs that kept the farms and plantations in operation.

At the same time, we must consider recreation within a larger dynamic; the subtleties of "paternalism" on the part of masters served *their* larger purposes. With this notion in mind, Frederick Douglass raised a cautionary voice in describing some aspects of leisure activities sanctioned for slaves; he portrays them not as liberating but as debilitating. His interpretation of "holiday times" as a mechanism of social control can well be juxtaposed to the ways dancing and drinking, as well as games and other forms of physical exertion, expressed slave consciousness and culture through the language of the body.

Finally, the documents regarding pastimes within slavery are framed here by two others. The first highlights the brief, troubled life of Tom Molineaux, the first great black boxer. His career—marking his passage from slavery to freedom and then to celebrity as an athlete—is especially important because it would later serve as a touchstone, a founding fact, in a long litany of African American triumph in sporting competition. Amos Webber's account of a diverse program of athletic events characterizing a Thanksgiving Day celebration held by a black regiment in the Union army may be more significant still. For this story opens out to the activities fashioned by an expanding northern population of free people of color during the antebellum era. In the time they spent away from work, African American laborers created rituals and festivals of their own, just as they surely participated—when they were allowed—in more organized mainstream sports. Negro election day and the Pinkster celebrations of New York City carried with them a carnival-like atmosphere, one in which African Americans sought relief from their status as sweated labor and offered an ebullient, thus countervailing, view of themselves and their position in a largely segregated, increasingly racist society. In those events, African Americans in the North demonstrated the same kind of race pride and esprit suggested by Webber's description of black soldiers during the Civil War.

Games and sport played a very small role in the African American experience during the antebellum era. The paucity of accounts by and about black athletes is thus significant in its own right. Before emancipation, there were few playing fields available for black Americans. That would change in the aftermath of the Civil War, though what African Americans encountered then—and not just in the realm of sport—was an unlevel playing field.

1. Tom Molineaux, Black Pioneer in Sport

The first of the legendary black boxers in American history, Tom Molineaux, was praised by the famous English chronicler of early prizefighting, Pierce Egan, as "the tremendous man of colour." Sadly, though, sportsmen in the boxer's own country were indifferent to his talent and success across the Atlantic. The historical record of Molineaux's early life is sketchy at best, presumably lost forever. Secondary sources generally claim that Molineaux was born a slave in either Virginia or Maryland in 1784 and gained his freedom after winning a boxing match for his master, who had wagered heavily on the contest. Legend also has it that Molineaux came from a family of rugged bare-knucklers. Regardless of the accuracy of these accounts, we know that by the early part of the nineteenth century Molineaux was a free man who traveled to London, where he trained as a boxer under the tutelage of Bill Richmond, an American-born free black who instructed young fighters in the "pugilistic sciences" at his own Horse and Dolphin Tavern. As the historian Elliott Gorn describes the scene, Molineaux then fought several important bouts in 1810, his strength and acumen astonishing the Englishmen who followed "the manly art."*

Molineaux's exploits of 1810 included a long, heroic, though ultimately losing match to the English champion Tom Crib. His impressive victories over other opponents, though, still made him the principal challenger to Crib. Thus at the end of the year he issued a formal challenge, reprinted in the London press, for a rematch. That is the first of the documents that follow. The second derives from Pierce Egan's impressions of the fighter Molineaux— as a man of color, as a foreigner—doubly then, a threat to notions of English virility and national honor. Egan's account of the rematch, on September 28, 1811, suggests the importance of the bout: perhaps as many as twenty thousand were attracted to Thistleton Gap, outside of London; the marquis of Queensberry and various lords and knights of the realm mingled with gamblers, tavern keepers, butchers, weavers, and, of course, pickpockets at the event. Though it can be read as an early specimen of sports journalism, the Boxiana *piece also revealed the breadth and depth of British patriotism during the age of revolution and the Napoleonic wars. In the event, the fray was a bloody one and yet again a defeat for Tom Molineaux, who lost to Crib in eleven grueling rounds. After the bout, Molineaux fought a number of matches over the next several years. But by most accounts, the sporting culture also involved considerable dissipation. Such an existence can take a swift and early toll, and so it was with Tom Molineaux, who died on August 4, 1818.*

---

* The best appraisal of the career of Molineaux and its context can be found in Gorn, *The Manly Art,* 19–22, 34–36, 50–51 ("man of colour" quote appears on p. 36); see also Brailsford, *Bareknuckles,* 53–65; Goodman, "The Moor vs. Black Diamond"; Cone, "The Molineaux-Cribb Fight, 1810."

To Mr. thomas crib.

St. Martin's-street, Leicester-square, Dec. 21, 1810.

Sir,—My friends think that had the weather on last Tuesday, the day upon which I contended with you, not been so unfavourable, I should have won the battle; I therefore, challenge you to a second meeting, at any time within two months, for such sum as those gentlemen who place confidence in me may be pleased to arrange.

As it is possible this letter may meet the public eye, I cannot omit the opportunity of expressing a confident hope that the circumstance of my being of a different colour to that of a people amongst whom I have sought protection will not in any way operate to my prejudice. I am, Sir,

Your most obedient humble Servant,
T. MOLINEAUX

Witness, J. Scholfield.

"Molineaux Challenges Crib," *London Times*, December 25, 1810.

Tom Molineaux, the first African American sporting hero (Mezzotint by John Young after Thomas Douglas Guest, c. 1810, courtesy National Portrait Gallery, Smithsonian Institution)

Egan's *Boxiana:*

TOM MOLINEAUX:
The hero who to live in story,
In search of honour dares to roam,
And reaps a crop of fame and glory—
This is the warrior's harvest home.

UNKNOWN, unnoticed, unprotected, and uninformed, the brave Molineaux arrived in England—descended from a warlike hero, who had been the conquering pugilist of *America,* he felt all the animating spirit of his courageous sire, and left his native soil in quest of glory and renown—the British nation, famed for deeds in arms, attracted his towering disposition, and his ambitious spirit prompted him with an ardent desire to enter the lists with some of her most distinguished Champions—distance created no obstacles, nor the raging seas were no impediment to his heroic views, and, like the daring adventurer, who suffers nothing to thwart his purposes, the object of his wishes were gained, and he, at length, found himself in the most enviable capital in the world, London—a perfect stranger, a rude, unsophisticated being, who, resting upon his pugilistic pretensions to excellence, offered himself to the notice of the public, the patron of those gymnastic sports, which, from their practice and support, have instilled those principles of valour into her hardy sons, producing exploits by land and sea, that have not only added greatness, but given stability to the English character.

MOLINEAUX came as an open and bold competitor for boxing fame, and who challenged the proudest heroes to the hostile combat—such declaration was manly, fair, and honourable, and entitled to every respect and attention among the pugilistic circles—but it has been objected to MOLINEAUX, that he was too ambitious, by threatening to wrest the laurels from the English brow, and planting them upon the head of a foreigner—if so, dearly he has paid for his temerity; but if his claims to pugilism were of that first-rate quality which they have been represented, the greater honour was attached to the conquest of such a formidable hero. . . .

MOLINEAUX, at all events, must rank high as a scientific pugilist; and it is said, that if he could receive punishment equal to the manner in which he *serves it out,* it would be almost impossible for any one to stand long against him. In height, about five feet nine inches; weighing between thirteen and fourteen stone, and twenty-eight years of age; inferior to none in point of courage and *bottom;* and considered a most excellent two-handed fighter. Full of fight, he exchanges *hits* with great alertness, and stops with considerable dexterity. Remarkably civil and unassuming in his demeanor, considering his want of education, MOLINEAUX has rendered himself to the *Fancy,* if not a decided favorite, at least an object of considerable attention. To *Richmond,* he is undoubtedly indebted for a considerable portion of that superior pugilistic science which he possesses. . . .

[The REMATCH:]

First round: A minute elapsed in sparring, when the CHAMPION made play right and left, and put in a right-handed blow on the body of the *Moor,* who returned a feeble hit on his opponent's *nob*. A rally now commenced, in which a few blows were exchanged, and *Molineaux* received a hit in his throat, which sent him down, though not considered clean.

Second: The *claret* was perceived to issue first from the mouth of *Crib*, upon commencing this round. A most terrible rally took place by mutual consent, when the *Champion* planted with his right hand a severe body hit, which was returned on the head by Molineaux with his left flush. They both fought at half-arm's length for superiority, and about six good hits were exchanged, when they closed, and in a trial of strength, *Crib* was thrown. Five to two on the *Champion*.

Third: In the last rally the right eye of *Crib* was almost *darkened*; and another now commenced equally as ferocious, after sparring to obtain wind, in which it was perceived the *Moor* was defective, when the *Champion* put in a most tremendous *doubler* in the body of *Molineaux*, and who, notwithstanding he was hit away, to the astonishment of every one, renewed the rally in that determined manner, as to create considerable agitation among those persons who had betted the odds. There was a marked difference in their method of fighting; *Crib* hit right and left at the head and body, while the *Moor* aimed at the *nob* alone, and with much judgment planted several dexterous flush hits, that impaired the eye-sight of *Crib*, and his mouth bled considerably. This rally continued a minute and a half, and in closing the *Champion* received a heavy fall. The superiority of the *Moor's* strength was evinced by his grasping the body of *Crib* with one hand, and supporting himself by the other resting on the stage; and in this situation threw *Crib* completely over upon the stage, by the force of a cross-buttock. To those not *flash*, the mere appearance of things appeared in favor of the *Moor*; but the fortitude of the *Champion* stayed his friends, although the betting had got down seven to four.

Fourth: *Molineaux's* wind could not be depended upon; and the head of *Crib* was terrific; and although he was bleeding from every wound, he smiled with confidence, and rallied in the first style of manliness. A number of good blows were exchanged: *Crib milling* away at the body, and *Molineaux punishing* the head. Crib went down from a trifling blow, and betrayed symptoms of weakness. No variation in the betting.

Fifth: *Molineaux* commenced a rally, and the punishment was truly dreadful on both sides; but the *Moor* had the best of it, and the *Champion* fell from a hit, and received another in the act of falling, which occasioned some difference of opinion, but the umpires decided it to be correct, as the hands of *Crib* were at liberty.

Sixth: *Molineaux* from want of wind, lunged right and left, but gained nothing by it, and stopped with neatness the right hand of the *Champion*. *Crib* now gave the *Moor* so severe a blow in the body with his right hand, that it not only appeared to *roll him up*, but seemed as if he had completely knocked the wind out of him, which issued so strong from his mouth like smoke from a pipe, that he was literally gasping for breath. On renewing a rally, he behaved quite frantic, and seemed bewildered as to what manner he should conduct himself—afraid of his opponent's *punishment*, he dared not go in, although wishing do to do, and capered about in an extravagant manner, to the derision of *Crib* and the spectators, hit short and was quite abroad;

when the *Champion* pursued him round the stage with great success, and concluded the round by a full-length hit, which laid the *Moor* prostrate. Five to one on *Crib*.

Seventh: *Molineaux* quite furious ran in on an intemperate rally, and gained a trifling advantage; but *Crib punished* him as severe as can be described, about the neck and jugular; and after the expiration of a minute, the *Moor* fell from weakness.

Eighth: *Molineaux*, still desperate, rallied, but his blows were too short; when *Crib nobbed* him in fine style, and *fibbed* him most dreadfully till he fell, the *Champion* having got his head under his arm. All betters.

Ninth: It was so evident which way the battle would now terminate, that it was "*Lombard Street to a China Orange*," *Crib* as the conqueror. The *Moor* in running in, had his jaw broke, and he fell as if dead, from a tremendous left-handed blow of the *Champion. Molineaux* did not come to his time by a full half a minute—but *Crib* wished that the Spectators should fully witness his superiority in giving away this chance—dancing about the stage, when he ought to have been proclaimed the conqueror: and went in again, knocking him nearly down, and then up again, and then *levelled* him.

Tenth: It was with the utmost difficulty that *Molineaux* could be brought from the knee of his second, and then it was only to add to the severe *milling* which he had received; but the *Moor* still game, made a desperate though unsuccessful effort, and fell from great distress

Eleventh: *Crib* had given another *chance* away respecting time, but the *Moor* was in a state of stupor, his senses having been completely *milled* out of him; and upon receiving a *floorer,* he was unable to be got from it—when victory was announced in a sort of Scotch reel by *Gulley* and *Crib,* elated with success, that the applause was tumultuous in the extreme.

Pierce Egan, *Boxiana, or Sketches of Ancient and Modern Pugilism* (London: G. Smeeton Publishers, 1812), 316–17, 325–26, 363–66.

2. Frederick Douglass / "Holiday Times"

The lives of the vast majority of slaves in the antebellum South were spent in hard work from dawn to evening darkness and often were characterized by cruelty and inhumane treatment. Slaves were, however, typically granted holidays throughout the year, which gave them some relief from the normal plantation regime. Although this custom varied from farm to plantation and by geographical location, slaves were often given time to celebrate Christmas, the Fourth of July, Thanksgiving, and Easter. Of these holidays, the slaves looked forward to Christmas more than any other since it provided them with the opportunity to visit friends and relatives on other plantations, hunt in nearby woods, engage in general merrymaking and frivolity, and enjoy the dinner and dance typically given by the planter and his family.*

---

* For insight into holidays and the general pattern of leisure among slaves on Southern plantations, see Genovese, *Roll, Jordan, Roll,* 566–84; King, *Stolen Childhood,* 43–65; Abrahams, *Singing the Master,* esp. 83–106; Stampp, *The Peculiar Institution,* 168–70, 172, 365–66.

The significance of the Christmas holidays to the maintenance of the plantation regime was not something the ordinary slave probably even considered. Other than detailing the specific activities they engaged in and how enjoyable it was to be excused from labor and have the time to be with friends and family, the surviving record seems to indicate that slaves did not expound on the implication of the Christmas holidays to themselves or other members of their community. Neither the autobiographies published by former slaves nor the Works Progress Administration (WPA) narratives (interviews conducted during the 1930s) speak in much detail about the meaning of such recreation for bondsmen.

One major exception to this general rule was Frederick Douglass, an escaped slave from Baltimore who became the foremost black abolitionist of the era. A writer and orator of enormous intellectual power and ultimately of considerable influence, Douglass voiced opposition to the evils of "the peculiar institution" and provided financial assistance to fugitive slaves and the use of his home in Rochester, New York, as the headquarters of the local underground railroad. In the following selection from his autobiography, Douglass maintains that slaveholders granted Christmas holidays out of purely selfish reasons rather than from any genuine interest in the welfare of their bondsmen. Slaveholders used the Christmas holidays as a safety valve, he argues; in hegemonic terms, they encouraged their bondsmen to drink excessively and to participate in "only those wild and low sports peculiar to semicivilized people" so they would not be pushed to the brink of hopelessness and engage in insurrection. In truth, writes Douglass, the Christmas holidays were a fraud perpetrated by slaveholders who were concerned only with their own survival and the perpetuation of the inhumane and oppressive institution.* Douglass's interpretation, while not universally accepted, has drawn the attention of historians of slavery. Eugene Genovese, for instance, in Roll, Jordan, Roll: The World the Slaves Made, *argues that Douglass was correct in thinking that holidays helped curb thoughts of insurrection by slaves but was wrong in believing it resulted from slaves' being forced "into triviality and self-degradation." In Genovese's view, leisure time in general helped to curb rebellious impulses among slaves because it allowed them to create a sense of community among themselves and to sustain certain well-defined arrangements with the white planter and his family.***

———   ———

The days between Christmas Day and New Year's were allowed the slaves as holidays. During these days all regular work was suspended, and there was nothing to do but to keep fires and look after the stock. We regarded this time as our own by the grace of our masters, and we therefore used it or abused it as we pleased. Those who had families at a distance were expected to visit them and spend with them the entire week. The younger slaves or the unmarried ones were expected to see to the animals and attend to incidental duties at home. The holidays were variously spent. The sober

---

* Douglass also spoke out on the hypocritical nature of the Fourth of July celebrations on southern plantations. "What to the American slave is your Fourth of July?" writes Douglass. "I answer, a day that reveals to him more than all other days of the year, the gross injustice, and cruelty to which he is the constant victim." Quoted in Meltzer, *In Their Own Words*, vol. 1, 23–25.

** Genovese, *Roll, Jordan, Roll*, 580.

Frederick Douglass
(National Archives)

thinking, industrious ones would employ themselves in manufacturing corn-brooms, mats, horse-collars, and baskets, and some of these were very well made. Another class spent their time in hunting opossums, coons, rabbits, and other game. But the majority spent the holidays in sports, ball-playing, wrestling, boxing, running, footraces, dancing and drinking whisky, and this latter mode was generally most agreeable to their masters. A slave who would work during the holidays was thought by his master undeserving of holidays. There was in this simple act of continued work an accusation against slaves, and a slave could not help thinking that if he made three dollars during the holidays he might make three hundred during the year. Not to be drunk during the holidays was disgraceful.

The fiddling, dancing, and "jubilee beating" was carried on in all directions. This latter performance was strictly southern. It supplied the place of violin or other musical instruments and was played so easily that almost every farm had its juba beater. The performer improvised as he beat the instrument, marking the words as he sang so as to have them fall pat with the movement of his hands. Once in a while among a mass of nonsense and wild frolic, a sharp hit was given to the meanness of slaveholders. Take the following for example:

> We raise de wheat,
> Dey gib us de corn;
> We bake de bread
> Dey gib us de crust;
> We sif de meal,
> Dey gib us de huss;
> We peel de meat,
> Dey gib us de skin;
> And dat's de way
> Dey take us in;
> We skim de pot,
> Dey gib us de liquor,
> And say dat's good enough for nigger.
> Walk over! walk over!
> Your butter and de fat;
> Poor nigger, you can't get over dat!
>   Walk over—

This is not a bad summary of the palpable injustice and fraud of slavery, giving, as it does, to the lazy and idle the comforts which God designed should be given solely to the honest laborer. But to the holidays. Judging from my own observation and experience, I believe those holidays were among the most effective means in the hands of slaveholders of keeping down the spirit of insurrection among the slaves.

To enslave men successfully and safely it is necessary to keep their minds occupied with thoughts and aspirations short of the liberty of which they are deprived. A certain degree of attainable good must be kept before them. These holidays served the purpose of keeping the minds of the slaves occupied with prospective pleasure within the limits of slavery. The young man could go wooing, the married man to see his wife, the father and mother to see their children, the industrious and money-loving could make a few dollars, the great wrestler could win laurels, the young people meet and enjoy each other's society, the drinking man could get plenty of whisky, and the religious man could hold prayer-meetings, preach, pray, and exhort. Before the holidays there were pleasures in prospect; after the holidays they were pleasures of memory, and they served to keep out thoughts and wishes of a more dangerous character. These holidays were also used as conductors or safety-valves to carry off the explosive elements inseparable from the human mind when reduced to the condition of slavery. But for these the rigors of bondage would have become too severe for endurance, and the slave would have been forced to a dangerous desperation.

Thus they became a part and parcel of the gross wrongs and inhumanity of slavery. Ostensibly they were institutions of benevolence designed to mitigate the rigors of slave-life, but practically they were a fraud instituted by human selfishness, the better to secure the ends of injustice and oppression. Not the slave's happiness but the master's safety was the end sought. It was not from a generous unconcern for the slave's labor, but from a prudent regard for the slave system. I am strengthened in this opinion from the fact that most slaveholders liked to have their slaves spend the holidays in such manner as to be of no real benefit to them. Everything like rational enjoyment was frowned upon, and only those wild and low sports peculiar to semicivilized people were encouraged. The license allowed appeared to have no other object than to disgust the slaves with their temporary freedom, and to make them as glad to return to their work as they had been to leave it. I have known slaveholders resort to cunning tricks, with a view of getting their slaves deplorably drunk. The usual plan was to make bets on a slave that he could drink more whisky than any other, and so induce a rivalry among them for the mastery in this degradation. The scenes brought about in this way were often scandalous and loathsome in the extreme. Whole multitudes might be found stretched out in brutal drunkenness, at once helpless and disgusting. Thus, when the slave asked for hours of "virtuous liberty," his cunning master took advantage of his ignorance and cheered him with a dose of vicious and revolting dissipation artfully labeled with the name of "liberty."

Frederick Douglass, "Holiday Times," from his *Life and Times of Frederick Douglass: His Early Life as a Slave, His Escape from Bondage, and His Complete History* (New York: Collier Books, 1962), 145–48.

3. Francis Fedric / "A Corn Shucking"

Many of the slaves' pastimes in the antebellum South were closely linked with rural customs and influenced by the type of work done on individual plantations. Planters often turned corn shuckings, log rollings, hog killings, quilting bees, and sometimes even cotton picking into grand social gatherings for themselves and their slaves. These gatherings, which usually included different material incentives, lavish dinners, and all-night dances, might be fondly anticipated by slaves for the festivities that followed the intense labor. In sources such as the WPA narratives and published autobiographies, many slaves remembered these gatherings as the most enjoyable times of the year, in some cases even outranking the Christmas holidays in popularity and interest.*

In the following account, Francis Fedric, a former slave who had spent his years in bondage in Virginia and Kentucky, recalls the corn-shucking celebration ("A Bee it is called") organized by one of the large planters. He renders in rich detail the gathering of the corn, the selection of captains for the shucking itself, and the songs that accompanied the celebration. The meaning of the celebration, as described by Fedric, has generally attracted little attention from students of the slave experience. One scholar, however, who has done an in-depth analysis of the corn-shucking celebration is Roger Abrahams, the noted folklorist from the University of Pennsylvania. In his Singing the Master: The Emergence of African American Culture in the Plantation South, *Abrahams offers an innovative interpretation of the corn-shucking ritual, arguing that the event allowed slaves an opportunity for self-expression and a means to mock and ridicule the planter. Through such activities as the corn shuckings, slaves actively resisted the plantation regime without depriving "themselves of their*

---

* For examples see the various volumes of Rawick, *The American Slave;* Fisk Collection, *Unwritten History of Slavery;* Yetman, *Voices from Slavery;* Blassingame, *Slave Testimony.*

A corn shucking (Library of Congress)

African cultural heritage" or adhering "to the behaviors and performance patterns of their masters."* At one level, Abrahams contends, slaves developed a distinctive cultural style through the corn-shucking ceremony that influenced both white minstrel and vaudeville shows and paradoxically today's African American performance styles.

——————

In harvest time, thirty or forty years ago, it was customary to give the slaves a good deal of grog, the masters thinking that the slaves could not do the hard work without the spirits. A great change has taken place now in this respect; many of the planters during harvest give their slaves sixpence a day instead of the whiskey. The consequence is there is not a fifth of the sickness there was some years ago. The country is intensely hot in the harvest-time, and those who drank grog would then want water; and, having got water, they would want grog again; consequently, they soon either were sick or drunk. All round where I dwelt the sixpence was generally substituted for the spirits; the slaves are looking better, and there are fewer outbreaks in the fields. In the autumn, about the 1st of November, the slaves commence gathering the Indian-corn, pulling it off the stalk, and throwing it into heaps. Then it is carted home, and thrown into heaps sixty or seventy yards long, seven or eight feet high, and about six

———————————

* Abrahams, *Singing the Master,* xxii.

or seven feet wide. Some of the masters make their slaves shuck the corn. All the slaves stand on one side of the heap, and throw the ears over, which are then cribbed. This is the time when the whole country far and wide resounds with the corn-songs. When they commence shucking the corn, the master will say, "Ain't you going to sing any tonight?" The slaves say, "Yers, sir," one slave will begin:—

"Fare you well, Miss Lucy.

ALL: John come down de hollow."

The next song will be:—

"Fare you well, fare you well.

ALL: Weell ho. Weell ho.

CAPTAIN: Fare you well, young ladies all.

ALL: Weell ho. Weell ho.

CAPTAIN: Fare you well, I'm going away.

ALL: Weell ho. Weell ho.

CAPTAIN: I'm going away to Canada.

ALL: Weell ho. Weell ho."

One night Mr. Taylor, a large planter, had a corn shucking, a Bee it is called. The corn pile was 180 yards long. He sent his slaves on horseback with letters to the other planters around to ask them to allow their slaves to come and help. On a Thursday night, about 8 o'clock, the slaves were heard coming, the corn-songs ringing through the plantations. "Oh, they are coming, they are coming!" exclaimed Mr. Taylor, who had been anxiously listening some time for the songs. The slaves marched up in companies, headed by captains, who had in the crowns of their hats a short stick, with feathers tied to it, like a cockade. I myself was in one of the companies. Mr. Taylor shook hands with each captain as the companies arrived, and said the men were to have some brandy if they wished, a large jug of which was ready for them. Mr. Taylor ordered the corn-pile to be divided into two by a large pole laid across. Two men were chosen as captains; and the men, to the number of 300 or 400, were told off to each captain. One of the captains got Mr. Taylor on his side, who said he should not like his party to be beaten. "Don't throw the corn too far. Let some of it drop just over, and we'll shingle some, and get done first. I can make my slaves shuck what we shingle to-morrow," said Mr. Taylor, "for I hate to be beaten."

The corn-songs now rang out merrily; all working willingly and gaily. Just before they had finished the heaps, Mr. Taylor went away into the house; then the slaves, on Mr. Taylor's side, by shingling, beat the other side; and his Captain, and all his men, rallied around the others, and took their hats in their hands, and cried out, "Oh, oh! fie! for shame!"

It was two o'clock in the morning now, and they marched to Mr. Taylor's house; the Captain hollering out, "Oh, where's Mr. Taylor? Oh, where's Mr. Taylor? all the men answering, "Oh, oh, oh!"

Mr. Taylor walked, with all his family, on the verandah; and the Captain sang,

"I've just come to let you know.

MEN:	Oh, oh!
CAPTAIN:	The upper end has beat.
MEN:	Oh, oh!
CAPTAIN:	But isn't they sorry fellows?
MEN:	Oh, oh, oh!
CAPTAIN:	But isn't they sorry fellows?
MEN:	Oh, oh, oh!
CAPTAIN:	But I'm going back again.
MEN:	Oh, oh, oh!
CAPTAIN:	But I'm going back again.
MEN:	Oh, oh, oh!
CAPTAIN:	And where's Mr. Taylor?
MEN:	Oh, oh, oh!
CAPTAIN:	And where's Mr. Taylor?
MEN:	Oh, oh, oh!
CAPTAIN:	And where's Mr. Taylor?
MEN:	Oh, oh, oh!
CAPTAIN:	I'll bid you, fare you well,
MEN:	Oh, oh, oh!
CAPTAIN:	—For I'm going back again.
MEN:	Oh, oh, oh!
CAPTAIN:	I'll bid you, fare you well.
	And a long fare you well.
MEN:	Oh, oh, oh!"

They marched back, and finished the pile. All then went to enjoy a good supper, provided by Mr. Taylor; it being usual to kill an ox, on such an occasion; Mr., Mrs., and the Misses Taylor, waiting upon the slaves, at supper. What I have written cannot convey a tenth part of the spirit, humour, and mirth of the company, all joyous—singing, coming and going. But, within one short fort-night, at least thirty of this happy band were sold, many of them down South, to unutterable horrors, soon to be used up. Reuben, the merry Captain of the band, a fine, spirited fellow, who sang, "Where's Mr. Taylor?" was one of those, dragged from his family. My heart is full when I think of his sad lot.

Francis Fedric, "A Corn Shucking," from his *Slave Life in Virginia and Kentucky; Or Fifty Years of Slavery in the Southern States of America* (London: Wertheim, Macintosh, and Hunt, 1863), 47–51.

4. Solomon Northup / "Patting Juba"

Dancing was an integral part of slave life in the plantation South. A central feature of almost every holiday celebration, Saturday night party, and impromptu social gathering on the plantation, dancing was an extremely important cultural activity for slaves of both sexes and all ages and backgrounds. It was characterized, as Melville Herskovits, Lawrence

Levine, and other scholars have suggested, by more distinctive elements of African culture than any other activity brought to the new world.* Unlike the more sedate minuets, European reels, and schottishes often performed by the planter and his family, slave dancing was similar to what could be found on the west coast of Africa in that it was distinguished by "its propulsive, swinging rhythm," "its flexed, fluid bodily position," and "its emphasis upon flexibility and improvisation."**

Here, Solomon Northup, a slave who wrote one of the most detailed and well-known recollections of plantation life, describes the slave dance known as "patting juba." A dance of African origin, which has most often been mentioned in conjunction with a West Indies dance of competitive skill, patting juba, as described by Northup, featured a special routine of slapping the hands, knees, thighs, and body in a rhythmic pattern accompanied by a variety of songs. Perhaps more than any other dance on the plantation, patting juba provided a visible example of the importance slaves attached to improvisation and freedom of individual expression. It was also a dance, like so many others in the slave quarters, accompanied by secular songs used by slaves to express some of their innermost feelings. Although Northup claimed that "patting" was "accompanied with one of those unmeaning songs, composed rather for its adaptation to a certain tune or measure than for the purpose of expressing any distinct idea," it is clear from other contemporary materials that the songs performed along with this dance were used by slaves to communicate with one another, comment on the mannerisms of whites, and express their own fears and desires.

———————

On that particular Christmas I have now in my mind, a description whereof will serve as a description of the day generally, Miss Lively and Mr. Sam, the first belonging to Stewart, the latter to Roberts, started the ball. It was well known that Sam cherished an ardent passion for Lively, as also did one of Marshall's and another of Carey's boys; for Lively was lively indeed, and a heart-breaking coquette withal. It was a victory for Sam Roberts, when, rising from the repast, she gave him her hand for the first "figure" in preference to either of his rivals. They were somewhat crest-fallen, and, shaking their heads angrily, rather intimated they would like to pitch into Mr. Sam and hurt him badly. But not an emotion of wrath ruffled the placid bosom of Samuel, as his legs flew like drum-sticks down the outside and up the middle, by the side of his bewitching partner. The whole company cheered them vociferously, and, excited with the applause, they continued "tearing down" after all the others had become exhausted and halted a moment to recover breath. But Sam's superhuman exertions overcame him finally, leaving Lively alone, yet whirling like a top. Thereupon one of Sam's rivals, Pete Marshall, dashed in, and, with might and main, leaped and shuffled and threw himself into every conceivable shape, as if determined to show Miss Lively and all the world that Sam Roberts was of no account.

Pete's affection, however, was greater than his discretion. Such violent exercise

---

* See Herskovits, *Myth of the Negro Past*, 76; Levine, *Black Culture and Black Consciousness*, 16–17.
** Levine, *Black Culture and Black Consciousness*, 16.

took the breath out of him directly, and he dropped like an empty bag. Then was the time for Harry Carey to try his hand; but Lively also soon out-winded him, amidst hurrahs and shouts, fully sustaining her well-earned reputation of being the "fastest gal" on the bayou.

One "set" off, another takes its place, he or she remaining longest on the floor receiving the most uproarious commendation, and so the dancing continues until broad daylight. It does not cease with the sound of the fiddle, but in that case they set up a music peculiar to themselves. This is called "patting," accompanied with one of those unmeaning songs, composed rather for its adaptation to a certain tune or measure, than for the purpose of expressing any distinct idea. The patting is performed by striking the hands on the knees, then striking the hands together, then striking the right shoulder with one hand, the left with the other—all the while keeping time with the feet, and singing, perhaps, this song:

"Harper's creek and roarin' ribber
Thar, my dear, we'll live forebber;
Den we'll go to de Ingin nation,
All I want in dis creation,
Is pretty little wife and big plantation.

Chorus: Up dat oak and down dat ribber,
          Two overseers and one littler nigger."

Or, if these words are not adapted to the tune called for, it may be that "Old Hog Eye" is—a rather solemn and startling specimen of versification, not, however, to be appreciated unless heard at the South. It runneth as follows:

"Who's been here since I've been gone?
Pretty little gal wid a josey on.
      Hog Eye!
      Old Hog Eye,
      And Hosey too!
Never see de like since I was born,
Here come a little gal wid a josey on.
      Hog eye!
      Old Hog Eye!
      And Hosey too!"

Or, may be the following, perhaps, equally nonsensical, but full of melody, nevertheless, as it flows from the negro's mouth:

"Ebo Dick and Jurdan's Jo,
Them two niggers stole my yo'.

Chorus: Hop Jim along,
          Walk Jim along,
          Talk Jim along, &c.

Old black Dan, as black as tar,
He dam glad he was not dar.

Hop Jim along," &c.

During the remaining holidays succeeding Christmas, they are provided with passes, and permitted to go where they please within a limited distance, or they remain and labor on the plantation, in which case they are paid for it. It is very rarely, however, that the latter alternative is accepted. They may be seen at these times hurrying in all directions, as happy looking mortals as can be found on the face of the earth. They are different beings from what they are in the field; the temporary relaxation, the brief deliverance from fear, and from the lash, producing an entire metamorphosis in their appearance and demeanor. In visiting, riding, renewing old friendships, or perchance, reviving some old attachment or pursuing whatever pleasure may suggest itself, the time is occupied. Such is "southern life as it is," three days in the year, as I found it—the other three hundred and sixty-two being days of weariness and fear, and suffering, and unremitting labor.

Solomon Northup, "Patting Juba," from his *Twelve Years a Slave: Narrative of Solomon Northup, A Citizen of New York Kidnapped in Washington City in 1841 and Rescued in 1853 from a Cotton Plantation Near the Red River in Louisiana* (Buffalo: Derby, Orton, and Mulligan, 1853), 213–20.

5. Benny Dilliard / "Preachin' and Baptizin'"

Slave children spent much of their time nurturing those younger than themselves and performing such chores as carrying water to the field hands, cleaning up the yards, fetching wood, tending the family garden, and feeding the livestock. They also engaged, however, in the simple pleasures of eating, conversing, and playing with their companions. When permitted, slave children might enjoy roaming the fields and woods within the borders of their home plantation, visiting neighboring plantations, and hunting and fishing with their fathers during the evening hours. They also danced, played various games, and tested their strength and physical prowess through impromptu athletic contests. The fellowship attained during these occasions offered a rare means of furnishing slave children with feelings of security. Their play activities were, moreover, a way for them to assure themselves of their own self-worth, the manner in which their individuality was asserted and maintained, and the medium through which they learned the values and mores of the adult world. At some level, play both isolated them from and initiated them into the complicated workings of slavery; before they personally experienced the full imposition of the system, they might enact some of the features that marked the plantation hierarchy as well as many of the methods of cultural assertion that their parents had devised.*

In the following account, Benny Dilliard, an ex-slave who spent his childhood on a Georgia plantation, describes the "make-believe preachin' and baptizin'" he and his playmates

---

* For insights into the play of slave children, see King, *Stolen Childhood*, 43–65; D. Wiggins, "The Play of Slave Children."

organized. This account provides just one example of the role playing that slave children found so significant in their lives. Like all young people, slave children wished to be grown up and yearned to be wanted, needed, and a useful part of the adult world. It was natural for them to recreate that world using themselves as the leading characters. There were several distinguishing features about the imitative play of slave children, most notably their tendency to reenact those events they found most troubling and those most crucial to older members of the slave quarter community. Unable always to comprehend the world around them, slave children attempted thereby to solve that problem as well as to relieve their particular anxieties and fears. This helps explain, then, the frequency in which they conducted simulated church activities, funerals, and slave auctions.

———

Us would have make-believe preachin' and baptizin' and de way us would sing was a sight. One of dem songs us chillun loved de best went lak dis:

> "Why does you thirst
> By de livin' stream?
> And den pine away
> And den go to die.
> Why does you search
> For all dese earthy things?
> When you all can
> Drink at de livin' spring,
> And den can live."

When us started playin' lak us was baptizin' 'em, us th'owed all us could ketch right in de crick, clothes and all, and ducked 'em. Whilst us was singin':

> "Git on board, git on board
> For de land of many mansions,
> Same old train dat carried
> My Mammy to de Promised Land."

Benny Dilliard, "Preachin' and Baptizin'," from George Rawick, ed., *The American Slave: A Composite Autobiography* (Westport, Conn.: Greenwood, 1972), supp. 1, vol. 12, 290.

6. William Green / "Becoming a Race Rider"

The participation of African Americans in sport began during the days of slavery. Southern planters often used their most trusted and talented slaves in ancillary positions or as athletes in a variety of sports. Although their names were not always known or have been permanently lost from the historical record, the evidence is clear that slaves were utilized as

Slave jockey with the racehorse Wagner (*American Turf Register*, July 1843, Keeneland Library, Lexington, Kentucky)

oarsmen in local boat races, as assistants in hunting excursions, as horse trainers and jockeys, and as boxers, wrestlers, and runners in various competitions. These slaves held a privileged position in the plantation community, sometimes traveling to distant parts of the South to compete. They were granted a more flexible work schedule and other favors by their masters, and they realized a higher degree of status among their fellow slaves.* It has even been contended by some scholars that these slaves (the boxer Tom Molineaux being the most prominent example) actually were granted their freedom because of their athletic victories.**

In the following account, William Green, a former slave on Maryland's Eastern Shore, recalled becoming a jockey for his master. One of the few slave jockeys to leave personal accounts, Green explains that he remained a "race rider" until his apparent religious conversion convinced him, with his master's blessing, to quit the horse-racing business. Green lived just north of early America's "race horse region" and was merely one in a long line of slave jockeys who had competed in one of the oldest of all sports. From approximately the mid-seventeenth century to the early years of the nineteenth, the center of horse racing was the North Carolina–Virginia border and many of the jockeys were slaves who rode against black as well as white riders, were sometimes paid for their services, and traveled with their owners to different tracks for matches. The career pattern for many of these slave jockeys was to become full-time trainers (apparently some of them had actually assumed the dual role of

---

* See Farish, *Journal and Letters of Philip Vickers Fithian,* 202; Steward, *Twenty Two Years a Slave,* 45; Blassingame, *Slave Testimony,* 392; Mallory, *Old Plantation Days,* 19.

** See Betts, *America's Sporting Heritage,* 334; A. S. Young, *Negro Firsts in Sports,* 20–22; Grombach, *The Saga of Sock,* 45–46, 261–62.

jockey-trainer) once their riding days were over. These positions carried a level of trust and involved responsibilities that typically characterized the lives of free men rather than those held in bondage. *

At the age of eight or nine years I was taken from my mother, who had until this time been permitted to retain me, and brought to the great house as the servants call the residence of the master, to wait upon master; and from that time I entered upon a new scene of my life. However, I got along very well. My master, being a very easy man to please and his demands being quite reasonable, I found but little difficulty in pleasing him. I remained with him from nine years old until I was about twenty, in the situation of body-servant. He then took me to be a race rider. He kept a great number of fine noble horses, with a number of race horses; and being of the right size for a rider, he took me to ride races. I remained in this employment until the Lord, as I humbly trust, was pleased to pardon my sins for Christ's sake and riding races being now repugnant to my feelings, and my master being quite a conscientious man in some things, though not enough so in others, would not make me continue that business.

William Green, "Becoming a Race Rider," from his *Narrative of Events in the Life of William Green (Formerly a Slave) Written by Himself* (Springfield, Mass.: L. M. Gurnsey, 1853), 4.

7. Amos Webber Reports on Thanksgiving Field Day

At first glance, Amos Webber's account of the Thanksgiving Day recreations of his Civil War regiment might not appear to be a notable document for the study of the social and cultural history of black Americans; it seems merely a listing of more-or-less athletic events, winning contestants, and prizes awarded. But set in context, it conveys a strong argument against the notion of African American physical weaknesses and docility that lent itself to assertions of white racial superiority. Indeed, above all else Webber's letter suggests the enormous vitality of the black soldiers in his unit, their "fitness" for the many tasks involved in liberating the South from slavery and winning the Civil War.

If we consider the observations of Thomas Wentworth Higginson, Webber's remarks take on added meaning. A leading advocate of physical training during the antebellum period, Higginson was also a radical abolitionist and one of the "secret Six" who funded the antislavery crusades of John Brown. During the war, Higginson served as a colonel of a black regiment and took the opportunity to comment on his troops. Thus, he might have been expected to praise black soldiery; yet Higginson used the same disparaging terms as the majority of his white countrymen. "In speaking of the military qualities of blacks," he declared, "the only point where I am disappointed is . . . their physical condition. . . . I think that neither their physical nor moral temperament gave them that toughness, that obstinate purpose of living,

---

* See Hotaling, *The Great Black Jockeys*, esp. 9–37.

which sustains the more materialistic Anglo-Saxon." Set against Higginson's assertions, the foot racing, turkey shooting, and jig dancing of Webber's compatriots of the Fifth Massachusetts Cavalry offer a corrective to the prevailing view of their energy and abilities. In fact, one out of every ten Union soldiers and one out of every four sailors in Yankee blue were African Americans. In all, 188,000 blacks served and sacrificed during the Civil War.*

———————

Permit me to inform you of the doing on Thanksgiving Day in and about the Fifth Massachusetts Cavalry camp. It was the first holiday that we have witnessed during the eleven months in service. Our officers determined to have some sport most congenial to the feelings of their men, and a sumptuous turkey dinner for each Company; wines excepted.

> *PROGRAMME OF THE DAY*
> Reveille—Full Bank, 10 A.M.
> Horse Race, for officers, at 12 o'clock P.M.
> Thanksgiving Dinner
> Sack Race, 1-1/2 o'clock
> 1st prize, 1 turkey; 2d prize, bale of tobacco.
> Climbing Greased Poles; 2 o'clock
> 1st prize, 1 goose; 2d prize, plug of tobacco.
> Foot Race; 2-1/2 o'clock
> 1st prize, pair of gauntlets; 2d prize, pair of spurs.
> Wheelbarrow Race; 3 o'clock
> One prize—a box of Cigars
> A Jog Dance—Prize, a pair of Mexican spurs.
> A greased pig will be let out every half hour.
> Music by the band at intervals during the exercises.
> Committee: Maj. H[enry] P. Bowditch of the 2d Battalion;
> C[harles] C. Parsons, Captain of Co. D;
> F[rederick] G. Parker, Assistant Surgeon in Hospital

The day proved as clear and fine as an autumn day in the North, and all got ready to see the events of the day as it was ushered in bright and clear. According to the programme, the exercises commenced at 12 o'clock. The officers entered the course for the race, and after a spirited run, Lieut. [Curtis] Whittemore's horse won the race.

> Dinner—The turkey dinner was served up to each Company in fine style. I noticed Cos. C, D, and E had a large table spread out in the Co.'s street, about 40 feet long, and the men were all seated around the table, eating away for life, on turkeys, oysters, turnips, onions, bread without butter, etc.

---

* See Higginson, *Army Life in a Black Regiment,* 72, 246. See also Borish, "The Robust Woman." On racial ideologies during the period, see Fredrickson, *The Black Image in the White Mind.* Regarding African American contributions to the Union effort, see "Black Liberators," in Litwack, *Been in the Storm So Long,* 64–103.

Sack Race—The parties entered for the race with their heads just out of the sack. It was a laughable affair to see them jumping along for the prize. Sergt. Wm. Holmes, Co. G, won the 1st prize; David White, Co. E, the 2d.

Greased Poles—There were two greased poles. On the top of one hung the goose; on the other a plug of tobacco. After many attempts, John Miller, Co. M, succeeded in getting the tobacco; others failed and left the goose high and dry.

Foot Race—1st prize won by William D. Cooper; 2d by Boyd Hude, both of Co. E.

Wheelbarrow Race—Won by Peter Smith of Co. D.

Turkey Shooting—The following men shot a turkey for their prize: Sergt. Wm. Holmes, Co. G; Corp. David Walker, Thos. Bell, Westley Rhoades, all of Co. I; Franklin Jennings of Co. B, and another whose name I could not learn.

Jig Dance—Prize won by Richard Holes, Bugler of Co. A.

Pig Chase—One caught by Alexander Ware, Co. H; one by Alexander Davis, Co. D, and by others, names unknown.

Second Foot Race—The officers and visitors, being anxious to see the sport of another Foot Race, soon made up a donation for the prizes. 1st prize, Sergt. James Treadwell, Co. M, $25.00; 2d prize, James C. Greenly, Co. G, can turkey; 3d prize, James Moulton, Co. D, box of collars and $4.75.

Second Jig Dance—Corp. Ray of Co. E received $5.00 and $4.00 2d prize on the first Jig Dance.

Thus the day was well spent in sport and pleasure to their satisfaction. During the time, Capt. [Horace] Welch of Co. C was recipient of a handsome sabre, two scabbards and a silk sash, all neatly finished. It was presented to the Captain by Sergt. John Davis (Orderly Sergeant) in an eloquent speech. The Captain lifted his hat and responded in a brief manner.

The event was well spent, to the enjoyment of all. The band poured forth volumes of music from their great horns, during the day and evening, for which they received great credit.

The Chief Bugler of the regiment, Sergt. Rueben Huff, was recipient of a handsome cavalry jacket and sabre-belt, presented to him by the buglers of the regiment as a token of respect to their Chief.

Amos Webber reports on "the doings" of the Fifth Massachusetts Cavalry, Point Lookout, Maryland, November 26, 1864, *Weekly Anglo-African*, December 17, 1864. This document derives from Edwin S. Redkey, ed., *A Grand Army of Black Men: Letters from African-American Soldiers in the Union Army, 1861–1865* (Cambridge: Cambridge University Press, 1992), 119–21.

2

Striving for Success: African American Athletes in the Early Period of Jim Crow, 1865–1915

Introduction

During the fifty years after Appomattox, African Americans expressed their hopes that out of the ashes of the Civil War a biracial democracy might be forged throughout the nation. After the ratification of the Fourteenth and Fifteenth Amendments, an increasing number of freedmen became involved in electoral politics—principally in the party of Lincoln—just as they strived to establish educational institutions and publicly supported hospitals and sanitariums in the war-torn South. What they hoped would occur during Reconstruction was a redistribution of land and fair compensation for their labor as the means of establishing themselves as full participants in the political, economic, and social life of the Union. For some black Americans who came of age during and after the war, that ideal included the chance to display their physical prowess in athletic competition.

Emancipation did not translate into equal opportunity, however, and formal freedom was unaccompanied by substantial changes in the economic system. In the South, cotton remained king, and former slaves—instead of being granted a parcel of their own land and the means to farm it—were set to work as wage laborers, then as sharecroppers and tenants. Eventually the convict leasing system would also become a building block in the "new" southern racial and economic order. Significantly, too, African American service and sacrifice in the war persuaded all too few northern whites to treat blacks with greater respect. Racism and the color line did not follow geographical contours or the boundaries that had divided North and South during the conflagration. The era of Reconstruction and the years that followed were thus a time of enormous hope for the mass of African Americans who had survived slavery and armed conflict. But that period—what many historians agree was the "nadir"—also bore witness to the anguish and alienation of many black Americans. Beyond such occurrences as the founding of the Ku Klux Klan and everyday acts of terrorism perpetrated against black Americans, beyond the statistics recording lynchings, the disfranchisement of black men, and the formalization of segregation, lay the doctrine of white supremacy. The 1896 Supreme Court decision in *Plessy v. Ferguson,* sanctioning Jim Crow, like the racial massacres that took place in Wilmington, North Carolina; Atlanta, Georgia; and Springfield, Illinois, were devastating in their own ways. Yet the prevailing images within the dominant culture—from minstrelsy to the specter of the black-beast rapist—so relentlessly cast African Americans as abjectly inferior or socially threatening that the long-term psychic damage of such cultural violence would be incalculable.

It is against this stark backdrop that blacks, South and North, created institutions for themselves and struggled still to be included in the social mainstream. First, they built churches and established agencies for uplift and self-help: penny banks and life insurance companies, organizations for mutual assistance, and community associations that endeavored to ensure that the water they drank was safe, that their children could attend school, or that they would be buried with dignity. Concern about the larger public sphere was virtually unwavering during the early years; the entrepreneurial spirit remained strong among many black Americans, even if resources were scarce, and even in the face of overwhelming white hostility to black business initiatives. Where they could,

African Americans resisted the drawing of the color line, especially in the North. The story of the Pythian baseball team of Philadelphia and its petition to join a statewide sporting organization, like the protest against discrimination made by Weldy Wilberforce Walker, attests to the desire to be a part of what soon would be called the *national* pastime. When such contests against Jim Crow were lost, black Americans showed ingenuity in establishing more of their own institutions.

Although there was a wide-ranging controversy over the means and ends of black education during this era, many of the colleges and universities of the South, for instance, established a curriculum that paralleled the course offerings of the most eminent institutions of higher education of the North. As a result, the transition from Fisk to Harvard by W. E. B. Du Bois was apparently seamless in intellectual terms; likewise the move from Virginia Normal and Industrial to Amherst (and ultimately Harvard Law School) by William Henry Lewis. Activities outside the regular curriculum followed the same pattern, and by the turn of the twentieth century, black colleges, large and small, boasted football, baseball, and basketball teams (women's sports as well as men's teams) in addition to choral groups and poetry societies. The black baseball teams of the North were similarly organized along the same principles as their white counterparts. They clearly represented race pride and community solidarity, but in playing by the same rules as "organized" baseball, they effectively demonstrated that their founders were awaiting their chance to compete, without regard to race, on a level playing field. Such sentiments would be articulated in much broader terms, with reference to civil rights and

Hampton women at basketball, ca. 1905 (Courtesy Hampton University Archives)

constitutional law, by those who spoke for the Niagara Movement and the emergent National Association for the Advancement of Colored People (NAACP), founded in 1909.

Throughout this era, a significant number of African Americans distinguished themselves as athletes and became racial heroes when their exploits were elaborated in the black press. Jockeys such as Isaac Murphy dominated the early history of the Kentucky Derby, and boxers such as George Dixon and Peter Jackson won numerous bouts—including interracial contests. But just as the color line was drawn in professional baseball, it extended to other sports, and opportunities dwindled for black athletes. The telling story of the champion sprint cyclist "Major" Taylor, who felt compelled to compete in Europe to make a living in the athletic world, suggests the anguish of these athletes, rebuked and scorned by white America. Ultimately, though, a hero emerged in the figure of Jack Johnson, who reigned as heavyweight champion of the world from 1908 until 1915. Johnson stood as a symbol of race pride. Outside the ring, he also defied the mores and conventions of mainstream America, and that part of his career drew commentary from two of the leading figures of turn-of-the century racial reform. According to Booker T. Washington, race men, including athletes, needed to be respectable men. For W. E. B. Du Bois, Johnson's powerful presence in the athletic arena was a more complicated matter. As champion, Jack Johnson had become part of a sporting heritage that extended back to Greek antiquity, Du Bois maintained. The heroic dimension of that sporting phenomenon threatened white people precisely because it inspired African Americans.

A

THE PROBLEM OF EXCLUSION

1. The Color Line in Organized Baseball

One of the earliest and most prestigious black baseball teams in America was the Pythian Base Ball Club of Philadelphia. Founded in 1866 by the political activist Octavius Catto and three other leading black Philadelphians, the Pythians consisted of four teams fielded from the upper crust of African American society. With Catto playing shortstop and serving as captain and John Cannon leading the team in both pitching and hitting, the club established a reputation for its superior baseball skills. The Pythians played other black teams from Philadelphia, including the Excelsiors, who were actually considered the oldest black club in the city; they also entertained well-known black baseball nines from Chicago, Brooklyn, Washington, D.C., and Harrisburg, Pennsylvania. In 1871, the Pythians played for the unofficial "Colored Championship of the United States," in a series against the Mutuals of Washington, D.C. Like other elite organizations, the Pythians, until their apparent dissolution following the 1872 season, instilled a sense of pride among all blacks while at the same time reinforcing class distinctions within the African American community in Philadelphia. Through baseball and the social activities of the club, the Pythians stood out as racial representatives while marking themselves off from the lower and middling classes in the African American community. *

The following document is a letter from a member of the Pythians who had served as a delegate in 1867 to the Pennsylvania State Convention of Base Ball Players. Addressed to the president and members of the club, the letter provided details explaining the ultimate decision to withdraw the Pythians' application for admission to the convention since the organization had already drawn the color line. The Pythians' inability to be admitted to the group foreshadowed the pattern of exclusion of black teams from white organized leagues and associations at both the amateur and professional levels of the sport. Although black clubs occasionally competed against whites in exhibition games, they could never secure official sanction from white organizations intent on maintaining racial segregation in America's national pastime.

---

* Details on the Pythians can be gleaned from Jable, "Sport in Philadelphia's African-American Community, 1865–1900," 160–65; Reed, "Not by Protest Alone"; Lane, *Roots of Violence in Black Philadelphia*, 52, 54; idem, *William Dorsey's Philadelphia and Ours,* esp. 305–6, 323; Kirsch, *The Creation of American Team Sports,* esp. 125–26, 150–52, 166, 212.

Philadelphia, Dec. 18th, 1867

To the President & Members of the Pythian B.B.C.
Gentlemen:

The delegate appointed by this Club to represent them in the Pa. State Convention of Base Ball Players which met at Harrisburg on the 16th of Oct. last, respectfully reports that on the night of the 5th of Oct. he proceeded to Harrisburg and put up at the Lochul House where he met Messrs. Hayhurst and Ellis of the Athletic B.B.C. and other delegates to the Convention. The next morning he proceeded to the Court House where the Convention assembled and was introduced by Mr. Hayhurst to President Rose, Sec. Domer and others. On the Convention being called to order, and the roll called, Messrs. Evans Rogers, Saml Hayhurst and Wm. Cramer, were appointed a Com. on Credentials. Whilst this Com. were making up this report the delegates clustered together in small groups to discuss what action might be taken on the admittance of the Pythians' delegate, and your delegate himself was waited on by Sec. Domer who stated that he and Mr. Hayhurst had both been discussing the matter of our admittance, and canvassing the other delegates, and tho' they and the President were in favor of our acceptance, still the majority of the delegates were opposed to it and they would advise me to withdraw my application, as they thought it were better for us to withdraw than to have it on record that we were black balled. This your delegate declined to do, and waited for the Com. to report, which they shortly did and reported favorably on all the credentials presented to them save that of the Pythian which they purposely left out of their general report. On their report being read a resolution was hastily passed and Mr. Ellis quickly springing to his feet moved that the Com. be discharged. Your delegate was about to say that as they had not finished their business they ought not to be discharged when Mr. Rodgers arose and said that there was one other credential in their hands which they were bound to report, from the Pythian B.B.C. a colored organization from Philadelphia, and they had presented it alone, that the Convention might take such action on it as they should deem fit. It having been read by the Secretary, Mr. Ellis moved that it be laid on the table, which motion was seconded by at least two thirds of the Convention, and but for the timely interference of Messrs. Rogers (of the Bachelor Club of this city) and Hayhurst, Mr. Ellis' motion would have passed. These gentlemen begged that as there were but a few delegates present (some 20 in all) that the matter be deferred till evening when in all probability there would be a larger no. present, and they thought if unfair that the few present should take the responsibility of rejecting a delegate (for so the most of them seemed disproved) when perhaps a greater proportion of those present in the evening would be in favor of this acceptance. To this Mr. Ellis and Mr. Rogers of the Chester Club, the mover and seconder of the motion to table agreed together with the rest of the delegates. The Convention then proceeded the adoption of a Constitution. . . .

After the adjournment in the morning the members of the Convention clustered around your delegate and whilst all expressed sympathy for our club, a few only such as Messrs. Hayhurst, Domer, Rose Stimel of the Chestnut St. Theater, and Rogers of the Batchelors expressed a willingness to vote for our admission, while numbers of others openly said that they would in justice to the opinion of the clubs they represented be compelled, tho against their personal feelings, to vote against our admission. Messrs. Hayhurst and Domer again requested the withdrawal of our credentials and were seconded in their request by most of the members. As your delegate did not feel at liberty to do this whilst there was any hope what ever of admission, he telegraphed home for instructions and received word to "fight if there was a chance." When evening came the delegates were in number about the same as in the morning and as there seemed no chance for anything but being black balled, your delegate withdrew his application, and rec'd. from Mr. Domer the Sec. a pass home over the Phila. Central R.R.

Before closing this already too lengthy report your delegate feels bound to state that *all* the delegates seemed disproved to show their sympathy and respect for our club by showing him every possible courtesy and kindness. While at dinner Messrs. Hayhurst and Rogers and others invited him to attend the base ball match that was to be played that afternoon in company with them which was accepted. And on the road and at the match, your delegate cannot speak so highly of the kind attentions which these gentlemen showed him and their expression of friendship from our club.

"Pythians Seek Admission to Pennsylvania State Convention of Base Ball Players," December 18, 1867, Leon Gardiner Collection, Box 8G, Historical Society of Pennsylvania.

2. Weldy Wilberforce Walker / "Why Discriminate?"

A number of African Americans participated in predominantly white professional baseball during the latter half of the nineteenth century. Although excluded from the National Association or the National League, African Americans competed alongside white players on teams in various parts of the country. According to Benjamin Rader, there were upwards of fifty-five African American players on integrated professional teams between 1883 and 1898. * *Included among this group were Moses Fleetwood Walker and his brother, Weldy, who played in 1884 with Toledo of the American Association—which at that time had major league status.*

In the following selection from The Sporting Life *of March 14, 1888, Weldy Wilberforce Walker chastised the leaders of the Tri-State League for what he thought was their decision to exclude African Americans from participation. The sharpness with which Weldy criticized the Tri-State League for its supposed racial slight was not unique to him or his brother, Moses. In 1884, Weldy, along with a family friend, Hannibal Lyons, brought suit against a roller rink in Steubenville, Ohio, for its exclusion of African Americans. In 1889, Moses, along with a friend, filed suit against a Detroit restaurant for denying them service. He also apparently filed suits against hotels that refused him accommodations.*

Eventually, both brothers became so disillusioned with the racial discrimination in America that they became involved in the African colonization movement that was popular among some African Americans around the turn of the century. They edited for an indeterminate length of time a black newspaper, The Equator, *and Moses wrote a 1908 trea-*

---

* Rader, *Baseball*, 51. See also Tygiel, *Baseball's Great Experiment*, 10–16; Lucas and Smith, *Saga of American Sport*, 269–71.

Oberlin 1881 baseball team, with Moses Fleetwood Walker, seated at left, and Weldy Wilberforce Walker, standing, second from right (Courtesy Oberlin College Archives)

tise, Our Home Colony: A Treatise on the Past, Present, and Future of the Negro Race in America, *in which he advocated a return to Africa for black Americans.**

———————

An Appeal to the Tri-State League by a Colored Player

W. W. Walker, a well-known colored player, requests THE SPORTING LIFE to publish the following open letter to the president of the Tri-State (late Ohio) League:

Steubenville, O., March 5

Mr. McDermitt, President, Tri-State League—Sir: I take the liberty of addressing you because noticing in THE SPORTING LIFE that the "law permitting colored men to sign was repealed, etc.," at a special meeting held at Columbus, Feb. 22, of the above-named League of which you are the president. I concluded to drop you a few lines for the purpose of ascertaining the reasons of such an action.

I have grievances, and it is a question with me whether individual loss subserves the public good in this case. This is the only question to be considered—both morally

---

* The best source of information on the Walker brothers is Zang's biography, *Fleet Walker's Divided Heart.* See also M. Walker, *Our Home Colony.*

and financially—in this, as it is, or ought to be, in all cases that depend upon the public for success—as base ball. I am convinced beyond doubt that you all, as a body of men, have not been impartial and unprejudiced in your consideration of the great and important question—the success of the "National game."

The reason I say this is because you have shown partiality by making an exception with a member of the Zanesville Club and from this one would infer that he is the only one of the three colored players—Dick Johnson, alias Dick Malo, alias Dick Noyle, as THE SPORTING LIFE correspondent from Columbus has it; Sol White, of the Wheelings, whom I must compliment by saying was one, if not the surest hitter in the Ohio League last year, and your humble servant, who was unfortunate enough to join the Akrons just ten days before they "busted."

It is not because I was reserved and have been denied making my bread and butter with some club that I speak; but it is in hopes that the action taken at your last meeting will be called up for reconsideration of your next.

The law is a disgrace to the present age, and reflects very much upon the intelligence of your last meeting and casts derision at the laws of Ohio—the voice of the people—that say all men are equal. I would suggest that your honorable body, in case that black law is not repealed, pass one making it criminal for a colored man or woman to be found in a ball ground.

There is now the same accommodation made for the colored patron of the game as the white, and the same provision and dispensation is made of the money of them both that finds its way into the coffers of the various clubs.

There should be some broader cause—such as want of ability, behavior, and intelligence—for barring a player than his color. It is for these reasons and because I think ability and intelligence should be recognized first and last—at all times and by everyone—I ask the question again, why was the law permitting colored men to sign repealed, etc.?

Yours truly, Weldy W. Walker

Weldy Walker, "Why Discriminate?" *The Sporting Life,* March 14, 1888.

B

HEALTH, RECREATION, AND SPORT IN THE POSTBELLUM ERA

3. W. E. B. Du Bois / "The Problem of Amusement"

After Emancipation, the most pressing concern for the mass of freedmen and women was economic survival. While many African American leaders, such as Frederick Douglass, emphasized education and political engagement, others, such as Booker T. Washington, urged black self-help as well as withdrawal from electoral politics and from legal action against racism and segregation. With this swirl of rival ideals as a backdrop, W. E. B. Du Bois first entered the scene as a historian (in The Suppression of the African Slave Trade to the United-ed States of America, *1896), then as a sociologist of the northern urban scene (*The Philadelphia Negro, *1899).* It is from his exhaustive research in the largest African American community in the North that Du Bois articulated his concerns about recreation and amusement among youth in the black metropolis.*

"The Problem of Amusement" is an essay in the Emersonian mode, and in this respect it anticipates the meditations that would soon thereafter form the chapters of Souls of Black Folk *(1903). Here, Du Bois argues that conditions in northern cities do not resemble the situation in the southern countryside; the perils are more numerous and varied, he alleges. He then goes on to suggest that, historically, the most significant institution in the black community—the church—had often contributed to the problem by denouncing out of hand anything that would have helped relieve the stresses of everyday life for black workers in the North; his example of billiards and his reference to the Young Men's Christian Association (YMCA) movement are telling in this context. Ultimately, Du Bois argues that recreation is essential to individual happiness and social order. He asserts that the church must encourage healthy amusements and organize them when it could. He then suggests that other social agencies (settlement houses and the YMCA) could also serve the needs of black city-dwellers for rational recreation.***

The essay by Du Bois not only engaged the founding doctrines of the playground move-

---

* For background, see Meier, *Negro Thought in America;* see also, Lewis, *W. E. B. Du Bois,* 179–92; Katz and Sugrue, *W. E. B. Du Bois, Race and the City.*

** In another part of the essay, Du Bois speaks to the needs of southern youth, as well as to the role of the schools and the importance of sport in the formation of character. "And yet, unless [a] school does amuse, as well as instruct those boys and girls, and teach them how to amuse themselves, it fails of half its duty and it sends into the world men and women who can never stand up successfully in the awful moral battle which Negro blood is today waging for humanity. Here again athletic sports must in the future play a larger part in the normal and mission schools of the South, and we must rapidly come to the place where the man all brain and no muscle is looked upon as almost a big a fool as the man all muscle and no brain; and when the young woman who cannot walk a couple of good country miles will have few proposals of marriage."

*ment, which formed a critical element in Progressive Era municipal reform; it also deftly juxtaposed traditional notions of moral and spiritual guidance by the black church with modern sociology, the notion of a "safety valve" for youthful energies. In this regard and others, Du Bois makes points that would be elaborated by scholars of the urban experience throughout the twentieth century. What is more, his fears and hopes would be raised again a century later by black social commentators such as Harry Edwards—speaking to the role of family and church, recreation and sport in ending the dislocation of black Americans in the cities. (See document 14 in the final part of this book.)**

I wish to discuss with you somewhat superficially a phase of development in the organized life of American Negroes which has hitherto received scant notice. It is the question of the amusements of Negroes—what their attitude toward them is, what institutions among them conduct the recreations, and what the tendency of indulgence is in amusements of various sorts. I do not pretend that this is one of the more pressing of the Negro problems, but nevertheless it is destined as time goes on to become more and more so; and at all times and in all places, the manner, method, and extent of a people's recreation is of vast importance to their welfare.

I have been in this case especially spurred to take under consideration this particular one of the many problems affecting the Negroes in cities and in the country because I have long noted with silent apprehension a distinct tendency among us, to depreciate and belittle and sneer at means of recreation, to consider amusement as the peculiar property of the devil, and to look upon even its legitimate pursuit as time wasted and energy misspent. . . .

When now a young man has grown up feeling the trammels of precept, religion, or custom too irksome for him, and then at the most impressionable and reckless age of life, is suddenly transplanted to an atmosphere of excess, the result is apt to be disastrous. In the case of young colored men or women, it is disastrous, and the story is daily repeated in every great city of our land, of young men and women who have been reared in an atmosphere of restricted amusement, throwing off when they enter city life, not one restriction, not some restrictions, but almost all, and plunging into dissipation and vice. This tendency is rendered stronger by two circumstances peculiar to the condition of the American Negro: the first is his express or tacit exclusion from the public amusements of most great cities; and second, the little thought of fact that the chief purveyor of amusement to the colored people is the Negro church, which in theory is opposed to most modern amusements. Let me make this second point clear, for much of the past and future development of the race is misunderstood from ignorance of certain fundamental historic facts. Among most people the primitive sociological group was the family or at least the clan. Not so among American Negroes: every vestige of primitive organization among the Negro slaves was destroyed by the slave ship; in this country the first distinct voluntary organization of

---

* See also Reed, *W. E. B. Du Bois and American Political Thought*; Gaines, *Uplifting the Race*.

Negroes was the Negro church. The Negro church came before the Negro home, it antedates their social life, and in every respect it stands to-day as the fullest, broadest expression of organized Negro life. . . .

We are so familiar with churches, and church work is so near to us, that we have scarce time to view it in perspective and to realize that in origin and functions the Negro church is a broader, deeper, and more comprehensive social organism than the churches of white Americans. The Negro church is not simply an organism for the propagation of religion; it is the centre of the social, intellectual, and religious life of an organized group of individuals. It provides social intercourse, it provides amusements of various kinds, it serves as a newspaper and intelligence bureau, if supplants the theatre, it directs the picnic and excursion, it furnishes the music, it introduces the stranger to the community, it serves as lyceum, library, and lecture bureau—it is, in fine, the central organ of the organized life of the American Negro for amusement, relaxation, instruction, and religion. To maintain its preeminence the Negro church has been forced to compete with the dance hall, the theatre, and the home as an amusement-giving agency; aided by color proscription in public amusements, aided by the fact mentioned before, that the church among us is older than the home, the church has been peculiarly successful, so that of the ten thousand Philadelphia Negroes whom I asked, "Where do you get your amusements?" fully three-fourths could only answer, "From the churches." . . .

Under such circumstances two questions immediately arise: first, Is this growing demand for amusement legitimate? And, can the church continue to be the centre of amusements?

Let us consider the first question; and ask, What is amusement? All life is rhythm—the right swing of the pendulum makes the pointer go around, but the left swing must follow it; the down stroke of the hammer welds the iron, and yet the hammer must be lifted between each blow; the heart must beat and yet between each beat comes a pause; the day is the period of fulfilling the functions of life and yet the prelude and end of day is night. Thus throughout nature, from the restless beating of yonder waves to the rhythm of the seasons and the whirl of comments, we see one mighty law of work and rest, of activity and relaxation, of inspiration and amusement. We might imagine a short sighted philosopher arguing strongly against the loss of time involved in the intermittent activities of the world—arguing against the time spent by the hammer in raising itself for the second blow, against the unnecessary alternate swing of the pendulum, against sleep that knits up the ravelled sleeve of care, against amusements that reinvigorate and recreate and divert. With such a philosophy the world has never agreed, the whole world today is organized for work and recreation. Where the balance between the two is best maintained we have the best civilization, the best culture; and that civilization declines toward barbarism where, on the one hand, work and drudgery so predominate as to destroy the very vigor which stands behind them, or on the other hand, where relaxation and amusement become dissipation instead of recreation.

I dwell on these simple facts because I fear that even a proverbially joyous people like the American Negroes are forgetting to recognize for their children the God-given right to play; to recognize that there is a perfectly natural and legitimate demand for amusement on the part of the young people, and that no people can afford to laugh at, sneer at, or forcibly repress the natural joyousness and pleasure-seeking propensity of young womanhood and young manhood. Go into a great city today and see how thoroughly and wonderfully organized its avenues of amusements are; its parks and play grounds, its theatres and galleries, its music and dancing, its excursions and trolley rides represent an enormous proportion of the expenditure of every great municipality. That the matter of amusement may often be overdone in such centres is too true, but of all the agencies that contribute to its overdoing none are more potent than undue repression. Proper amusement must always be a matter of careful reasoning and ceaseless investigation, of nice adjustment between repression and excess; there is not a single means of amusement from church socials to public balls, or from checkers to horse racing that may not be carried to harmful excess; on the other hand it would be difficult to name a single amusement which if properly limited and directed would not be a positive gain to any society; take, for instance, in our modern American society, the game of billiards; I suppose, taken in itself, a more innocent, interesting, and gentlemanly game of skill could scarcely be thought of, and yet, because it is today coupled with gambling, excessive drinking, lewd companionship, and late hour, you can hear it damned from every pulpit from San Francisco to New York as the straight road to perdition; so far as present conditions are concerned the pulpit may be right, but the social reformer must ask himself: Are these conditions necessary? Was it not far sighted prudence for the University of Pennsylvania to put billiard tables in its students' club room? Is there any valid reason why the YMCA at Norfolk should not have a billiard table among its amusements? In other words, is it wise policy to surrender a charming amusement wholly to the devil and then call it devilish? . . .

But in . . . truth, properly conceived, properly enunciated, there is nothing incompatible with wholesome amusement, with true recreation—for what is true amusement, true diversion, but the re-creation of energy which we may sacrifice to noble ends, to higher ideals, while without proper amusement we waste or dissipate our mightiest powers? If the Negro church could have the time and the opportunity to announce this spiritual message clearly and truly; if it could concentrate its energy and emphasis on an encouragement of proper amusement instead of on its wholesale denunciation; if it could cease to dissipate and cheapen religion by incessant semireligious activity then we would, starting with a sound religious foundation, be able to approach the real question of proper amusement. For believe me, my hearers, the great danger of the best class of Negro youth today is not that they will hesitate to sacrifice their lives, their money, and their energy on the altar of their race, but the danger is lest under continuous and persistent proscription, under the thousand little annoyances and petty insults and disappointments of a caste system, they lose the divine faith of their fathers in the fruitfulness of sacrifice; for surely no son of the nineteenth century has heard more plainly the mocking words of "Sorrow, cruel fellowship!"

W. E. B. Du Bois, "The Problem of Amusement," *Southern Workman* 27 (September 1897): 181–84.

4. Samuel Archer and J. B. Watson on Football at Southern Black Colleges

Many African American educators—as well as white college authorities—embraced the athletic creed, which posited that sports developed character and the traits of true leadership. Thus in 1901 the catalog of Wiley College announced that "athletic sports are not only allowed, but encouraged." At that small school in Marshall, Texas, institutional policy also stressed the notion "that the best education is that which develops a strong, robust body as well as other parts of the human makeup."*

The 1892 football competition in North Carolina matching Biddle (now Johnson C. Smith) and Livingstone was the first black intercollegiate contest on record for the sport. Within two years Howard and Lincoln as well as Tuskegee Institute and Atlanta University had commenced what would become celebrated rivalries, and by the turn of the twentieth century, Morgan College, Atlanta Baptist (now Morehouse College), and Virginia Union had also entered the intercollegiate athletic fray. By 1906 and 1907, when the following articles were written, fascination with the sport infused campus culture from Wilberforce, in Ohio, to Talladega, Alabama. In the first selection here, Samuel Archer—who was a professor at Atlanta Baptist as well as the first coach of the team—highlights the character-building dimension of intercollegiate football, while in the second, J. B. Watson expands upon the development of the sport at various southern schools. Both authors allude to the storm over intercollegiate football at the time. In fact, this was a tumultuous period in the history of college football. In 1905 and during the next several years, white college officials inveighed against the abuses of football, specifically its corruption by professional coaches as well as its violence. Though a few of those educational leaders called for the abolition of football, the majority advocated reform, and following the model of other Progressive Era regulations—one part exhortation, one part admonition, one part rules—the forerunner of the National Collegiate Athletic Association (NCAA) was established in 1905. Significantly, the Colored Intercollegiate Athletic Association (CIAA) would be founded in 1912.** The articles by Archer and Watson both appeared in the Voice of the Negro *(known simply as* The Voice *when Watson's essay was published), which was established in Atlanta in 1904 to engage social issues as well as developments in art and culture. During its three years of publication, this journal embraced the platform of the Niagara Movement and offered critical commentary on race relations. Violence on the northern college football fields was noteworthy, it asserted, but a far greater outrage lay in the number of lynchings in the South.†*

---

* Wiley College Catalog, 1901, quoted in Heintze, *Private Black Colleges in Texas*, 171.

** On the football crisis of 1905, see R. Smith, *Sports and Freedom*, 191–208; Watterson, "The Gridiron Crisis of 1905." On the development of sport in the Black South, see Miller, "To 'Bring the Race Along Rapidly.'"

† Regarding the short, troubled history of the journal, see Harlan, "Booker T. Washington and the *Voice of the Negro*"; Daniel, *Black Journals of the United States*.

Samuel Archer

Football in our schools has been played under conditions that were very favorable for the development of the strong and aggressive in union with the gentle and the just. From the beginning the squads in the various institutions have been under the direct control of some member of the faculty who could enter enthusiastically into the sport to give proper emphasis to each element of the game and to eliminate every feature inimical to health, detrimental to learning, and demoralizing to character. The relationship which exists between the member of the faculty and the team is poorly expressed by the word coach. There is all the solicitous care of the trainer for the perfect physical conditions which is fundamental in the game, but the motive is not to make a powerful cog in a powerful machine; it goes beyond this and touches on all sides the well-being of the individual.

That we have a genuine fidelity to the English idea of "sport for sport's sake" is due to the fact that men of strong personality,—who command and inspire respect everywhere, impart knowledge of the game. There is no need to stoop to questionable methods of defense or offense for the worth of the coach does not in any sense depend upon victory nor does he jeopard[ize] his bread and butter by a series of defeats on the gridiron. The ideal has been to train faithfully, to practice daily, to play hard, to win fairly and honestly, and, if need be, lose cheerfully to superior brawn and brain. The victories that have come at the sacrifice of honor and person have been few. It is called a sad ending to win in one direction and lose in another. Teams have not played simply to win. Truly enough the victory was eagerly and earnestly sought but not as the end. Victory has been rather the pleasing and agreeable incident in the game. There is no record of a team that has cancelled a game simply because it could not win.

Thus hedged about the game has been remarkably free from serious accidents, unsportsmanlike conduct and professionalism. Concerning accidents and clean sport in the schools, a keen observer of the game, who has had a wide experience with football East, West, and South says, "I have never known such clean football and so few injuries during the past fifteen years, as during the last two years in Negro colleges." The splendid brute and the slugging bully have never been in evidence, this alone is sufficient to reduce accidents to a minimum. It will be a decided loss—a step backwards to countenance professionalism in any form. . . . The college man ordinarily has a high sense of honor and is very sensitive about fair play and acts that are not sportsmanlike. If left to himself he will insist on the principle,—first a gentleman, then an athlete.

We need not nor do we desire to avoid the present discussion of football. Most of the charges made against the game are general and might well apply to any of the sports that appeal to young and vigorous manhood. The dearth of specific charges makes the outcry savor much of the hysterical and the unwarranted attention, which the incidental features of the game have received, partakes too much of cant. . . .

S. H. Archer, "Football in Our Colleges" *Voice of the Negro* 3 (March 1906): 199–205.

J. B. Watson

Often we are too prone to forget that what we call college spirit is the real college itself and that this lives in the hearts of men and not in bricks and mortar. Whatever unifies this spirit is desirable, for it preserves and fosters the college. . . .

Perhaps Howard, Fisk, and Shaw are the most representative colored colleges in athletics in the country. They have played the game of football longer and their teams have traveled more extensively and played harder schedules. Prof. C. C. Cook of Howard writes that football in that university has the cheerful support of both faculty and students, and that in his opinion it benefits the body and mind as no other sport does. One of the most enthusiastic supporters of football in our colleges is President Thirkield of Howard, [who] has been connected with institutions for the higher education of Negroes for nearly a quarter of a century, and his opinion should be of more than passing worth. Among other things he says: "The students have entered with great heartiness into the several games. They have made a splendid record. The games have been free from all roughness and rowdyism. They have contributed to the heightening of the moral spirit as well as to the physical development of the students."

Fisk University has played football successfully for twelve years and has taken uniformly high rank. Last season under the new rules she broke all former records by carrying out the hardest schedule ever undertaken by a colored college.

Few schools have had such conspicuous success at football as Shaw University. The university has played the game for ten years, during the first four of which her goal line was never crossed. Prof. C. R. Frazer now feels that it would be a decided loss to Shaw to have football abolished in that institution. President Meserve believes that football quickens the mental faculties and develops courage.

Knoxville College was never more enthusiastic over the game than at present. President McGranahan is highly in sympathy with it and his faculty and students are with him. Knoxville is noted for clean play.

Atlanta Baptist College has played the game seven years, in only one game, during the first five years of which did her teams have the sensation of crossing another school's goal line. In 1905 the tide turned. This year the Baptist college made a total of eighty-nine points against Clark University, Atlanta University and Talladega College, while these teams never once threatened her goal. The season of 1906 left this college without a defeat and with but two touchdowns against her. In this season she scored forty-six points against Talladega, Fisk, and Meharry Medical College.

Football has had a remarkably good effect on the student of this little college. Here is a solidarity seldom formed in any school. President Hope credits football largely with this good spirit. He also states that it has made discipline easy and has helped the scholarship and health of the college. The vast majority of players here are among the best students in college and are most active in other college activities. . . .

As to what school holds the championship of the whole South among the colored teams there can be little more than conjecture. . . . There has never been, to my knowledge, a game between the two sections of the South, and there is absolutely no way of telling how the matter stands between Atlanta Baptist, Shaw and Howard.

There is a move on foot at present, however, to have them try conclusions in the season of 1907. . . .

The indications are that football has come to stay, and, with this prospect, steps should be taken to place it on the highest possible basis and in proper relations to other college activities. I feel safe in saying that in nearly every case where football has failed, it has done so because of a lack of proper faculty oversight. . . .

An institution in demand now is an Intercollegiate Athletic Association affecting all the colleges of the whole South. With intercollegiate organization many evils connected with the choice of officials and the playing of games could be done away with and the whole matter of college athletics given a higher tone. It does not necessarily mean that every college in such an organization must play every other college. The purpose of an athletic association is not alone to afford opportunity for comparison of strength, but rather it is to bring colleges into helpful association.

The outlook for the season of 1907 is very bright. The leading colleges are already making up their schedules and the prospects are that we shall see more than the usual number of "big" games played by clean sportsmen.

J. B. Watson, "Football in Southern Negro Colleges," *The Voice* 4 (May 1907): 165–69.

5. William Clarence Matthews / "Negro Foot-ball Players on New England Teams"

A small number of outstanding African American athletes participated in college sport on predominantly white university campuses during the latter stages of the nineteenth century and early part of the twentieth. Such men as George A. Flippen of Nebraska, George M. Chadwell of Williams College, William Washington and Moses Fleetwood Walker of Oberlin, William Tecumseh Sherman Jackson of Amherst, and William Henry Lewis of both Amherst and Harvard were true scholar-athletes who successfully balanced great sport performances with academic achievements. Although their home lives varied to some extent, these scholar-athletes typically came from upper-middle-class families who placed extraordinary emphasis on education and culture. For most, their informal education began in the home, where parents made sure that books, music, and art constituted an important part of everyday life. They prepared for careers in medicine, law, politics, and other prestigious professions by initially attending a well-known public school, a private academy in New England, or an historically black college in the South. Once this stage of their education was complete, they matriculated at one of the more racially liberal colleges in the North where they could compete in intercollegiate sport while receiving the high-quality education essential to enter professions that would confirm their upper-middle-class status.*

The following document details the careers of several African Americans who compet-

---

* For information on African American athletes on predominantly white university campuses at the turn of the century, see D. Wiggins, "Prized Performers"; Berryman, "Early Black Leadership"; R. Smith, *Big-Time Football at Harvard,* esp. 8–9, 74, 119; Chalk, *Black College Sport,* esp. 1–36, 140–96.

William Clarence
Matthews (*McClure's
Magazine*, 1905)

*ed in sport at New England colleges around the turn of the twentieth century. The article
is perhaps most significant in that its author, William Clarence Matthews, was one of those
athletes. Born in Selma, Alabama, in 1877, Matthews first attended Tuskegee Institute before Booker T. Washington arranged for him to be educated at the well-known Massachusetts prep school Phillips Academy, Andover. In his four years at Andover (1896–1901),
Matthews became one of the school's top students and starred in football. After graduating, he enrolled in Harvard where for five years he was one of college sports' greatest all-
around athletes, distinguishing himself especially in baseball as the school's slick fielding
and hard-hitting shortstop. Like many other African American athletes on predominantly
white university campuses at this time, however, Matthews suffered the pangs of racial discrimination, at least twice being held out of baseball games against southern institutions
because of their refusal to compete against schools with black players. After departing
Harvard, Matthews played one season of baseball for Burlington, Vermont, in the Northern League, and then later took his law degree from Boston University, which prepared him*

for a number of influential governmental positions, including service as assistant to the attorney general of the United States. *

———————

During the past ten years, foot-ball has come to occupy a very important place in most Negro institutions of learning. The game, though still crudely played by most of the southern institutions, holds the same interest and excitement that it does for the under-graduates of Yale and Harvard. The Negro schools have the game minus the business of foot-ball. In Yale, Harvard or Princeton the player has to undergo the strictest discipline, which comes under the general head of "training." This element, which by the way is very essential to the best development, is eliminated in the Negro schools and partly accounts for the lack of foot-ball ability. Every team must be built upon strict business principles and conducted in the same manner, or the result of the season's work will be unsatisfactory.

There is no reason why such teams as Shaw, Lincoln, Tuskegee, Hampton, Fisk, Talladega, Atlanta and Meharry could not cope with the best small colleges in New England. The great difference between the two types is the lack of business methods on the one hand, and the use of these same methods on the other. Negroes have shown their ability in more than one instance to cope successfully with the best players in the country. Out of the eleven greatest football players the country has ever produced, Mr. Walter Camp has chosen W. H. Lewis as the greatest centre-rush. This is a remarkable fact when we realize that the proportion of Negroes who have played on college teams has been very small. It is well to say just here that Mr. Lewis is the most expert foot-ball authority in the United States to-day. His treatise on foot-ball has never been outdone. He is considered by Mr. Camp as the brainiest man in the foot-ball world. It was through Mr. Lewis that the Harvard system of foot-ball was worked out and perpetuated.

Harvard

Mr. Lewis was the first Negro to play on a Harvard "varsity" foot-ball team. It was on that famous team that "Bert" Waters captained, when each man wore a red leather suit. Since that time, only two colored men have played on Harvard teams in championship games; these men were Howard Lee of Boston and W. C. Matthews of Montgomery, Alabama. So much has been written of late about this latter player that we will not say more about him here.

J. T. Jones of Old Point Comfort, Virginia, has been for five years a prominent member of the Harvard "varsity" squad, playing in many of the games. Jones was considered one of the best tackles that ever played at his "prep" school—Exeter. He is considered one of the strongest, as well as best developed men in the university. He was one of the most likely candidates for end-rush during the past season until an injured ankle put him out of the running.

———————

* For information on Matthews's life and career, see: Chalk, *Black College Sport*, esp. 11–17; Lindholm, "William Clarence Matthews"; idem, "William Clarence Matthews: 'The Jackie Robinson of His Day,'" in Rutkoff, *Cooperstown Symposium*, 25–42.

Williams College

During the championship game between Williams and Dartmouth, the playing of [Earnie] Marshall of Williams was the occasion for much enthusiastic cheering. The honors for Williams that day were shared, equally, by Marshall and the Williams captain. More than once, when every other attempt failed, Marshall would plow through the heavy Dartmouth line for fifteen and twenty yards at a time. These gains were remarkable when we remember that Dartmouth had one of the heaviest and strongest teams in the country, while Williams' was very light. Marshall's position was right-tackle. He prepared for college at Exeter, where he was captain of the foot-ball team last year being the only man of African descent to hold such a position at Exeter. While captain of Exeter, he defeated Andover, the rival preparatory school, in a very decisive victory. Marshall is a Freshman at Williams and comes from Baltimore. Other than Marshall, there is only one Negro in college at Williamstown.

Massachusetts Agricultural College

The majority of New England institutions give every man a fair and equal chance to make the teams and if he proves himself worthy, they accord him all the honors they have to bestow. This point is forcibly illustrated in the case of [William H.] Craighead, who was this past season elected captain of the Massachusetts Agricultural College foot-ball team, commonly known as the Amherst "Aggies." Next year will be Craighead's fourth year on the team. He plays tackle and is one of the most aggressive, as well as most consistent players in any of the small colleges. Before going to Amherst, Craighead was a student at Cornell, where he played foot-ball and rowed on the Freshman crew. One of the remarkable things about the Amherst "Aggies" team is, that during the past season they were coached by the famous Negro player, "Matt" Bullock, who played end on the four best teams Dartmouth ever had. Bullock turned out a team for Amherst "Aggies" this year which surpassed anything they have had for the past ten years. While a player at Dartmouth, Bullock was considered one of the best ends in the East. Though light, he was aggressive and faithful in every particular. This fact probably accounts for the rare popularity which he has maintained among all who know him.

Amherst

Another end who has proved himself a valuable man in foot-ball is Shannon from Amherst College. During the past season Amherst has shown remarkable strength on the gridiron, and one of their star players was Shannon. It will be remembered that last year Amherst defeated Columbia, and the year before overcame Harvard by a score of 6 to 0. A Negro who wins a place on such a team certainly has the requisites for a niche in our Foot-ball Hall of Fame.

Colby College

A friend of mine who had been traveling down in Maine, during the past summer, told me that he noticed on the telegraph posts and on board fences the name of Watkins. Watkins weighs about 160 lbs., and is 5 feet 7 inches; yet he is one of the most remarkable half-backs in the Maine league. Bates, Bowdoin and the University of Maine know Watkins well and appreciate his wonderful performances for their rival college, Colby. Charlie Watkins prepared for college at Phillips Academy, Andover, Mass., where he played on the foot-ball team and ran the quarter-mile on the track team. When he went to Waterville, Maine, to attend Colby College, he soon became a popular idol and all that was necessary to draw a crowd to a game or a track meet, was to say Watkins would compete. It is this popularity which accounts for the appearance of his name in prominent places.

The Colby team, on which Watkins plays, is coached by "Tony" Harris, an old ex-player of Tufts College at Medford, Massachusetts. Harris has coached Colby for two years and has had considerable success. He was a hard player while at Tufts and was considered one of the best players on the team.

William Clarence Matthews, "Negro Foot-ball Players on New England Teams," *Colored American Magazine* 9 (March 1905): 130–32.

6. Thomas J. Clement / "Athletics in the American Army"

African Americans served in the western territories as both infantrymen and cavalry soldiers following Reconstruction. Dispatched by the United States government to help prevent disputes between Indians and white settlers, African American soldiers served in four black regiments, the Twenty-Fourth and Twenty-Fifth Infantries, and the Ninth and Tenth Cavalries. These soldiers, while certainly not immune from the racism so prevalent in American society during this period, held jobs that were vastly superior to many of those found in civilian life. In addition to being provided decent clothing, housing, and pay for their services, African American soldiers realized a degree of status and sense of pride in their country not experienced by others in the black community. They were similar to fighting men everywhere, however, in that the irregular rhythm of military life provided them periods of leisure and ample opportunity to participate in sport and recreation.*

The following document recounts the athletic programs engaged in by the soldiers of the Tenth Cavalry. Perhaps most notable was the intense competition and variety of athletic contests organized by the soldiers. They played football, organized intertroop baseball games as well as contests against neighboring town teams, and held field days that included baseball games, track-and-field events, wrestling matches, horse races, tent-pitching contests, and tugs-of-war. Evidently, these activities were arranged by an athletic committee composed of officers of the regiment.

———   ———

* Information on the lives of African American soldiers in the Western territories can be gleaned from Durham and Jones, *The Negro Cowboys;* W. Katz, *The Black West;* Leckie, *The Buffalo Soldiers;* Carroll, *The Black Military Experience;* Fletcher, *The Black Soldier and Officer;* idem, "The Black Soldier Athlete in the United States Army."

There are many people who have the absurd idea that the life of a soldier is chiefly one of hardships and inconsistencies; and I venture to assert that six tenths of the moderately educated of the eighty millions of Americans to-day have a surprisingly small knowledge of the conduction of the regular Army, which stands for the assertion of American honor and the protection of the "Stars and Stripes." Tracing history from the Spartans and Greeks down to the modern American, we find in all the world's great contests a triumph of the robust and hardy over the weak and untrained. The respective armies of the Greeks and Spartans at Marathon and Thermopylae present a striking example of the well disciplined and hardened soldier who may be out-numbered but never outclassed. The same lesson is learned from the sturdy little Japanese in their struggle against the gigantic but untrained Russians. The results of their athletic training are plainly seen in the fortitude with which they withstand the hardships inevitable in war.

Since the 10th Cavalry has been back in the States from Cuba, and the Philippines, and under the command of its present Colonel, J. A. Augur, there has been a keen and unprecedented interest taken in athletics. From the most excellent showing made by the regiment during the Department meet at Fort Riley, Kansas, in 1903, until now, there has been steady progress in athletic endeavors among the different troops. Especially is this improvement noted during the base ball season, and on field days, when the rival squadrons and troops compete for athletic honors. Although we were defeated in the final game of base ball when Troop K was playing the different teams of the Department at Fort Riley, we returned home highly elated just the same. We had defeated the teams from Fort Leavenworth and Fort Riley, shutting Leavenworth out by a score of 5 to 0; and were only beaten by the 25th Infantry team, the only colored regiment there besides the 10th Cavalry.

We get more and more encouragement every year in our athletic work. Field days are set apart during the spring and summer and the competitors are rewarded for their excellence by money prizes, athletic banners for their organizations and the hearty applause of their comrades; and the squadron sentiment and competition makes the interest all the more keen. It might be well to mention some of the features of the Field Day, that contribute to the sport, for the benefit of some of the outside people who are not familiar with the "manners and customs" of the regular Army. Aside from the regular individual contest, such as the hundred yard dash, 220 yard hurdle race, the broad and high jump, etc., a good part of the field day exercises consist of team work. Mounted wrestling teams (4 men to a team) from troops or squadrons, meet on bare-back horses and wrestle to dismount their opponents; tent pitching teams (8 men each) for alacrity in performance, this exercise being more of a troop competition than that of the squadron; and of course I could not leave out the "tug-of-war," which amongst us of the Cavalry branch, is contested on bare-back horses. Another of the most interesting and exciting of the day's event is the horse race,—something equally exciting among soldiers and civilians. The day is generally wound up by a game of base ball between the squadrons. The points of the day are summed up between the troops and at the end of the season the troop having made the most points during the season is awarded an athletic banner.

During the summer season we have a regular base ball league, and each troop, the band and hospital corps, have scheduled games, which are played on the dates set apart by the Athletic Committee of the regiment, composed of officers; and at the end of the season the team having the highest percentage of winning games is presented with a pennant. Besides these games we have the pleasure of meeting many of the outside teams, since our post team, made up as it is of the best of them all, is of excellent calibre, and plays quite a few games with neighboring towns. This fall quite an interest has been manifested in foot ball, another great athletic sport. . . . The "K" Troop team . . . has been most successful in its athletic efforts. The writer has the honor to be its Captain and right half back. We have been defeated but once this season, and then only by the small score of 5 to 0.

Thanksgiving was celebrated by a game between gridiron exponents of "B" and "K" Troops. The result was a surprise to many who thought that "K" Troop would have a walk a-way, but we found "B" Troop to be a foe worthy of our steel. It was one of the fiercest engagements between knights of the pigskin ever witnessed by soldiers. Our friends from the 1st Squadron fought with stubborn aggressiveness but the steady retaliation of the heavy "Ks" held the score to 10-10.

Before the appearance of this article we shall have had a great time during the holidays, a season always enjoyed by the soldiers. Our new gymnasium will have been completed before then. After its completion we shall hope for greater accomplishments, because of better opportunities, than we have ever had in indoor athletics.

Thomas J. Clement, "Athletics in the American Army," *Colored American Magazine* 8 (1905): 21–29.

7. Sol White / "Managers Troubles"

Sol White was one of the most important individuals in the history of black baseball. John Holway, a chronicler of black baseball, has noted that "if Rube Foster was the father of black baseball, then Sol White was the grandfather."* Jerry Malloy, another authority on the Negro Leagues, describes White as "black baseball's first historian" and "also one of its earliest 'lifers.'"** Born in 1868 in Bellaire, Ohio, White supposedly got his first taste of organized baseball in 1883 when he played for his hometown Bellaire Globes, an integrated amateur club that included on its roster the future president of the American League, Byron Bancroft "Ban" Johnson. Following his stint with the Globes, White embarked on a long career as a player, manager, or administrator with several professional teams. In 1887 he joined the Pittsburgh Keystones in a black league that included such clubs as the New York Gorhams, Boston Resolutes, Philadelphia Pythians, and Lord Baltimores. He spent the 1889 season with the Gorhams, played the following year with New York in the integrated Eastern Interstate League, and then beginning in 1891 and extending over the entire decade, played for a number of famous teams, including the Cuban Giants, Big Gorhams, Page Fence Giants, Cuban X-

---

* See Holway, *Blackball Stars*, 1.
** Malloy, *Sol White's History of Colored Base Ball*, xxi.

The Philadelphia Giants, with Sol White (back row, fourth from the right) (National Baseball Hall of Fame Library, Cooperstown, N.Y.)

Giants, and Columbia Giants. In 1902 White was hired by H. Walter Schlichter and Harry Smith, two white Philadelphia sportswriters, to manage the Philadelphia Giants, one of the most dominant teams on the East Coast for some eight years. White managed the Lincoln Giants in 1911 but after dissolution of the team returned to Bellaire, where he worked in some unknown capacity for nearly a decade. He returned to baseball in 1920 as secretary of the Columbus, Ohio, team in Rube Foster's newly created Negro National League (NNL), managed the Cleveland Browns of the NNL in 1924, and two years later assumed his last position in baseball as coach of the Newark Stars of the Eastern Colored League. He spent the last years of his life in New York City where he died in 1955 at the age of eighty-seven.

The following is taken from White's 1907 book on the history of black baseball, Sol White's Official Base Ball Guide. *Edited and published by H. Walter Schlichter, the book was later described as "part fund-raising effort, advertising brochure, team hype, and celebration of black baseball, and throughout an implicit and explicit challenge to racism." In the selection here, White alludes to the difficulties of managers in black baseball. Because of the more loosely organized structure of their league, players kept jumping from one club to another looking for better financial opportunities. In addition, White claims in an apparent moment of wishful thinking, that the "funny man in colored base ball is becoming extinct." This assertion would prove inaccurate because black baseball continued to have some players and select teams that performed comedy routines, a fact that sparked spectator interest while at the same time perpetuating the stereotypical views whites had of African Americans.**

---

* The later description of White's book comes from the dust jacket of Malloy, *Sol White's History of Colored Base Ball.* For brief discussions of the comedy and performance styles in black baseball, see Rogosin, *Invisible Men,* 141–50; Chadwick, *When the Game Was Black and White,* Tygiel, *Baseball's Great Experiment,* 18–19.

——— ——

To deal with the question from an independent stand-point, it is found more difficult to handle a team in that respect than when a member of a league, under the National agreement. Rules laid down by league teams are easily enforced; from the fact that players in the minor organizations have aspirations to shine as stars in the major leagues and consequently cannot afford a reckless disregard of the rules to compel them to keep in condition for first-class ball playing. Once in the big league they have a horror of being relegated to the minors, which creates a greater respect for the rules.

In this day and time, when colored base ball teams are numerous and each striving for supremacy, the colored manager's path is not one of sunshine. With twelve or fourteen men under his command, twelve or fourteen different minds and disposi-tions to control and centre on the intricate points of play: with no National League of baseball clubs behind the rules and regulations, with the many complaints of players and threats of quitting ringing in his ears day after day, he passes many a sleepless night and will often ask for that "Patience he needs."

To guard against such contingencies, managers should be careful in selecting players to compose a team. A player of mediocre ability who is a willing and hard worker and easily handled, is far better in every respect to a team than one of rare ability with so much self-importance as to create a feeling of antipathy among his fellow players.

It will be found that 80 per cent of these self-important players think so well of their individual reputations, that an error or misplay on their part during a game is liable to make them lose their nerve.

It is the man with the nerve that gets there, but in base ball there are two kinds of nerve. One kind is on the outside and the other on the inside. For a winner, the inside nerve is the best every time. A "four-flusher" will make all kinds of noise with his mouth, but when it comes to a test on the ball field, will develop a "yellow streak" a yard long. The ball player with the nerve on the inside does but little talking about what he is going to do, but just watch this man when it comes to the game depending on quick action and he is invariably there.

Managers should possess gray matter and have up-to-date ideas. They should ac-quire a full understanding of the game and strive to instill it into the heads of his play-ers. There is a general weakness among colored players that mitigates to a great extent against their success on the diamond; that is, their lack of knowledge and understand-ing of the playing rules. The rules should be thoroughly understood as games have been won and lost where the deciding play depended on the interpretation of a rule.

They should aim to blend the team into a highly polished and magnificent ma-chine. The play itself is a science, if that term may be applied to sport. Compared to town ball or other old fashioned games, it suggests the present day harvesting engine and its prototype, the scythe.

The attitude of the spectators, or as they are popularly called "fans," has changed at about the same rate as the game. Formerly they were content with being amused and the game developed comedians like Abe Harrison and Bill Joyner. But now they demand faultless play. Genuine diversion is as scarce as the green carnation. Rugged, callous, fearless though he be, the player seldom volunteers any original fun-making on the field, or on the coaching-line, lest the "fans" take it amiss.

Not that the spectator is unwilling to be amused! He goes to the game with that hope and intention—so eager for amusement, indeed, that if a player somersaults on a wet field, or another doffs his cap with a sly, unwonted grimace, after making a great catch, it provokes Heaven-splitting laughter.

On the other hand, mighty and bitter is the reward of wrath visited upon one who by lack of vigilance, activity or quickness brings disaster upon his team.

The funny man in colored base ball is becoming extinct. Where every man on a team would do a funny stunt during a game back in the eighties and early nineties, now will be found only one or two on a team who essays to amuse the spectators of the present day. Monroe, third baseman of the Royal Giants of Brooklyn, is the leading fun-maker of the colored profession of to-day. His comic sayings and actions while on the field, together with his ability as a fielder, hitter and runner has earned for him a great reputation as a ball player. Joyner, of Chicago, draws a salary for fun-making alone. Pop Watkins, Gordon and Best of the Genuine Cuban Giants, are the other present day comedians of the diamond.

The majority of colored ball players are now carefully watching the scientific points of the game with a mind to perfect team work, base running, bunting, place hitting and every other department of the game is studied and discussed by the leading colored players which, if continued, will enable them, in the course of a few years, to cope successfully in every particular with the leading teams of the country.

Sol White, *Sol White's Official Base Ball Guide: History of Colored Base Ball* (Philadelphia: H. Walter Schlichter, 1907), 67–74.

8. "Baseball among the Fairer Sex Coming into Prominence"

Information on the patterns of sport among African American women around the turn of the twentieth century is limited. Due to the lack of primary source materials and serious research studies, much of the sporting life of African American women during this period in American history is unknown and open to speculation. The secondary materials that are available, however, make it apparent that upper-class African American women at this time resembled their white counterparts in that they participated in a world of conspicuous leisure characterized by exclusive clubs and such outdoor amusements as croquet, archery, horseback riding, tennis, golf, and bicycling. Young, middle-class African American women gained access to early forms of physical education and athletic programs at such historically black colleges as Howard, Spelman, Fisk, and Lincoln (Missouri). Still other African American women participated in sport and recreational activities offered by settlement houses, city playgrounds, the Young Women's Christian Association (YWCA), and other programs of the Progressive Era. A smaller number of more rebellious African American women, *moreover, defied conventions by participating in sports commonly identified as male, such as shooting, long-distance walking, and baseball.* *

The following column from the Indianapolis Freeman *of 1908 announced the organization of women's baseball teams in Springfield, Ohio, and Louisville, Kentucky. The article is interesting for a number of reasons, including the genuine enthusiasm shown for women's sport, evidence of racial pride, and the comparisons made between white and black women athletes. This latter topic is of particular significance in that it reflects an important theme in the sports pages of black newspapers. Because of racial segregation in sport during the first half of the twentieth century, black newspapers continually drew parallels between black and white athletes so as to both encourage black athletes and prove their worth in a society that doted on the notion of Negro inferiority. Black newspapers were, of course, in an enviable position because they had direct access to black athletes and entrepreneurs. They were the source of information on sport for many African Americans and could point out the inequities in sport and the larger American society without fear of retribution.* **

———————

Efforts are being made to get the fairer sex interested in athletics. This line of pleasure has been practically neglected or overlooked by the women of our race. The men have acquired fame, wealth and health in all lines of the athletic and sporting world. Why not the women? Our neighbors' wives and daughters (white) take interest in athletics, and why not those of our race? Athletics are not copyrighted: they are at the disposal of each and every one. To some degree last summer tennis was taken up by the fair ones of this city, and there promises to be more interest manifested in the coming season. A good thing. Push it along. Take up athletics girls: take physical exercise: get interested in the games of the field, diamond, and in other pastimes of the like. Enjoy life as it is: don't make it what it isn't or what it should not be.

In Springfield, O., there has been organized a baseball team, not composed of the rugged ball players that have monopolized the spherical game, but composed of girls: nothing better could be done along this line; nothing better could be done to make the game clean sport; nothing better could be done to abolish the physical inability and make healthy our women. Modesty? Well, that has caused the failure of more women than anything else known. Modesty should be possessed 'tis true, by men as well as by women, but it can be carried to an extreme, as can timidness. Take up the game girls in your town. Learn the game of baseball in all of its phases: know it from start to finish.

Louisville should have a girls' baseball team, as she has about the best woman baseball expert in the country in the person of Mrs. Henry Newboy. Every one should take interest and give encouragement to the promotion of girls' baseball teams.

———————

* For sources of information on African American women athletes during this period, see Captain, "Enter Ladies and Gentlemen of Color"; Cahn, *Coming on Strong*, esp. 12–30.

** For information on the relationship between the black press and sport, see D. Wiggins, "Wendell Smith"; idem, "The 1936 Olympic Games in Berlin"; Simons, "Jackie Robinson and the American Mind"; Williams, "Sportswomen in Black and White."

Springfield, O., has organized a baseball team of girls to take the diamond next season under the leadership of Mrs. Sarah S. Brooker. A number of other Ohio and Indiana cities have fallen in line, several games have been arranged, and it is probable that an Ohio-Indiana League will be formed by May 1, which is the beginning of the baseball season for girls. An effort is also being made by promoters of baseball to form an eight-team league in some of the larger cities to be known as the Colored American League for Girls. Information regarding same can be had by addressing President C. L. Mayberry, 1712 North Limestone Street, Springfield, O., or Manager (Mrs.) Sarah S. Brooker, 813 East Front Street, same city.

President C. L. Mayberry, of the Springfield, O., girls' baseball team, is very anxious for the promotion of the new project, and is devoting much time and labor to send it on the road to success. Mr. Mayberry is prompted to have colored girls organized into baseball teams from the fact that he believes colored girls can do, and do just as well, if not better, in some cases, what the white girls can do. He wants to create enough enthusiasm in athletic circles to get on foot a league for girl players for the season of 1909. He has the following to say in reference to colored girls playing baseball:

"I know that you are aware there is but little that the girls of our race can find to do, and I feel that if this project can be made a success, and I am sure it can, it will be opening fields for our girls which have hitherto been totally closed. Why not our girls? Why wait until the white girls have worn all of the 'new' off, and then start, as we have done in so many other things? I feel that it is high time for us to begin to be original in some things at least, and to start some things ourselves, and not wait until the white man or woman, as the case may be, gets tired and throws it aside, and then we take it up. I believe that if this is encouraged by men of influence and men of means, it will mean worlds to our girls."

Louisville, Ky—Mr. and Mrs. Henry Newboy are training their baseball club for next season. They expect to have a strong club. Mrs. Newboy is an expert at the game, and practices with the club. The club meets every Sunday morning at the residence of Mr. Newboy, who is manager. Mrs. Newboy is secretary. There are very few women, especially colored women, who even understand a game of baseball when they see it played, to say nothing of taking a part in a game. But Mrs. Newboy understands and can play baseball and enjoys the diamond duel. But it is just a question of a few months until women will ask no odds on the game.

"Baseball among the Fairer Sex Coming into Prominence," *Indianapolis Freeman,* December 26, 1908.

C

BLACK ATHLETIC HEROES AT THE TURN OF THE CENTURY

9. Isaac Murphy, the Great Lexington Jockey

There were a number of outstanding African American jockeys during the latter half of the nineteenth century. Partly because a racing tradition had been established during the days of slavery and owners of race horses continued to attach less importance to their riders than to their horses, black jockeys were able to capitalize—bit by bit—on their athletic prowess, ultimately establishing national reputations. By the turn of the twentieth century, however, their spreading fame prompted a harsh reaction. Thereafter the practice of segregation—sometimes encoded in the law—eliminated most of them from competition. Included among this group were such well-known jockeys as Abe Hawkins, Willie Simms, Isaac Murphy, James "Soup" Perkins, and Shelby "Pike" Barnes.

Perhaps the most famous of these jockeys was Murphy, a rider whose exploits have been recounted extensively in the secondary literature.* Born Isaac Burns in Fayette County, Kentucky, in 1861, Murphy eventually took the surname of his grandfather, Green Murphy, an auctioneer and bellringer from Lexington. Beginning his riding career in 1875, Isaac Murphy would become the first jockey to win three Kentucky Derbys. He also placed first in the famous American and Latonia Derbys four and five times, respectively, and had an overall winning record of 44 percent, proving victorious on 628 of his 1,412 mounts. His success on the track earned him a yearly salary estimated between $15,000 and $20,000, allowing him to purchase expensive real estate and to acquire his own stable of horses. He died on Lincoln's birthday in 1896, at the age of thirty-five. It was less than five months after his last race. Decades later—in 1955—Murphy would become the first jockey elected to the National Racing Hall of Fame in Saratoga Springs, New York. In the following interview, published in the Lexington Leader *in 1889, Murphy recalled his early days in racing and his various triumphs on the track. The interview took place a year prior to what may be Murphy's most famous triumph, a victory aboard Salvator in a much-publicized match race at Sheepshead Bay, New York, against the highly regarded jockey "Snapper" Garrison and his horse Tenny. The interview provides some intriguing details into Murphy's early riding career and his approach to the sport of horse racing.*

——— ———

———

* See D. Wiggins, "Isaac Murphy,"; Hotaling, *The Great Black Jockeys,* 239–75; Borries, *Isaac Murphy.*

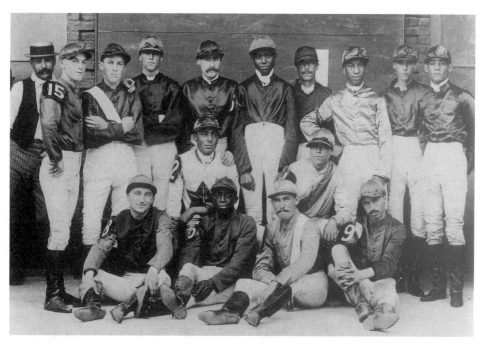

Isaac Murphy (left, middle row) with a group of jockeys, 1891 (Courtesy Keeneland Library, Lexington, Kentucky)

"It is pleasant for me to recall the past. Its months and years, no matter what the future may have in store for me, will always be the happiest of my life. I look back to them with delightful memories and keen enjoyment. I would gladly live over the old days, as they were filled with the sunshine of success, in which few shadows ever fell."

How Isaac Began

"It was in 1874, when fourteen years old, that I first entered the training stable of Williams & Owings, then at the Lexington track. I commenced as an exercising boy and weighed seventy pounds." Isaac had to laugh as he thought of himself in those old days. "Somebody has said, and it has almost become recognized as a fact among those who care anything about it, that my first public mount was a win, the race being the Bluegrass Stakes at Louisville, September 21, 1876. My horse, Springbranch, won 'tis true, but it wasn't the first time I had been the leader passing the judges. The year before, 1875, I rode several races at the Crab Orchard track, this State, and one of them I won on Glentina. That was my first victory on a regular track. I had a mount on Lady Greenfield at the same place previous to that on Glentina, which was a losing one, but the event marked the real beginning of my jockey life, as it was the first race I was ever in on such a course. At Crab Orchard I rode at seventy-four pounds, which is the lightest I ever reached; yet during the seasons of 1876, '77, and '78, I was down to ninety-five pounds, and occasionally a little under."

Good Words for an Early Mount

"My first big stake victory, however, was on Vera Cruz in the St. Leger at Louisville in the fall of 1877," and Isaac once more smiled. "I have often thought of that day. Success made me very happy. But before the St. Leger winning, and in addition to the stakes following the Glentina and Springbranch victories, I won the Cumberland Stakes at Nashville with Vera Cruz, the Filly Stakes at Lexington with Fonwitch, and the Viley Stakes at the same place with Vera Cruz. The last three races were run in 1877, and I have always thought that I should have won the Kentucky Derby that year also had not Vera Cruz, my mount, been left at the post. Vera Cruz was a superior race horse, but never sound, and when this is considered, his career was all the more remarkable. I rode him in the Breckinridge Stakes, at Baltimore, the same year, and on election day at Jerome Park, beating St. Martin and Barricade in a special sweepstakes. With the exception of Checkmate, the son of Virgil and Regan, [sic] was the best horse I rode during my engagement with Williams & Owings, which ceased in 1878."

Reaching the Top

"Then I signed to ride for the late J. W. Hunt Reynolds, in whose employ I remained until his death, which occurred in 1880. Even then I continued to ride for his widow, now the wife of the turfman and breeder, Colonel L. P. Tarlton, until engaged to Mr. Corrigan, in the winter of 1884. During the years 1878 and until 1884 I rode many cracks and captured my share of important events—in fact, this was one of the most successful periods of my career. When my engagement with Mr. Corrigan terminated in 1885, I signed with Mr. E. J. Baldwin, and have remained in his employ ever since. In regard to this year I have not yet entered into an agreement to ride for any particular stable, but if I do not don the colors of the California turfman I will in all probability ride for the Dwyer Brothers. My relations with Mr. Baldwin, however, have been so pleasant that I dislike to sever my connections with his stable, notwithstanding inducements offered for my services by several prominent Eastern racing firms." . . .

Emperor of Norfolk Best of All

"But good as Freeland, Leonatus and Checkmate were, and good as were Falsetto, Glenmore, Volante, Kingston, Troubadour, Blue Eyes, General Harding, Luke Blackburn, and other cracks ridden by me, I consider Emperor of Norfolk the best horse I ever rode, taking everything into consideration. I tell you he was a wonder, and when in the best condition I have yet to see the horse that, in my opinion, could defeat him. Mr. Thomas, the trainer of Mr. Baldwin's stable, worked him a trial at Nashville last spring, before shipping him to Brooklyn, and he beat Volante as if he had been a selling plater, giving him weight in addition to the three years' difference in age. When we landed in Brooklyn, Sir Dixon just purchased by the Dwyer Brothers for a long price, and Raceland, Mr. Belmont's great colt, were all the rage, and when the Emperor started against them in the Brooklyn Derby, the Eastern Turfmen were of the opinion that he and Prince Royal would have the empty honor of fighting for third place. I laid with him in an easy position until the head of the stretch was reached, and then sent the Emperor to the front, and he won without the semblance of an effort." . . .

When Isaac Was in Danger

"I do not know of a jockey who has ridden so many races as I have that has been so fortunate in escaping injury. I never had but one horse to fall with me in a race, and in that instance I was only slightly hurt and able to ride in the last event on the same day. It was at St. Louis, on June 11, 1884, I was on Bonnie Australian, and along the backstretch Revoke, who was running in front of me, fell, and my horse went over him. Another horse (General Custer) struck me in the side as he passed; but he did not hurt me much, as I was able to drag Fishburn, who was riding Revoke and was badly injured, through the fence, and remained by his side until medical aid arrived. For a long time after a shiver ran through me when I recalled the accident, as had General Custer come a little closer he would have struck me square in the head. I was very careful for many days after; but such an accident is of the unavoidable kind, and if it is to happen there is no way to prevent it."

The Surprise of Isaac's Life

"Of course, like every jockey, my career has been full of surprises, but when I won the American Derby in 1886, at Chicago on Silver Cloud, I can safely say I was never more surprised in my life. I was running in the ruck on the back stretch when the notion just struck me I would send him to the front if that was possible, as neither Mr. Baldwin nor Mr. McClelland, the trainer, had any idea he had the ghost of a chance to win, nor did I think so. As I raised on him I drew the whip and struck him twice, and before the other jockeys could realize it, I was ten lengths in the lead. They at once set

Currier and Ives lithograph of the Futurity Race, Sheepshead Bay, Long Island, 1883 (Library of Congress)

sail for us, but Silver Cloud was a race horse, at least that day, and drawing away at every stride won one of the easiest of races by a dozen lengths or more. The book-makers cleaned up everything on that race, as I honestly believe there was not $25 bet on Silver Cloud, while Ben Ali, Blue Wing and several of the other starters were heavi-ly backed. In this connection I recall that I have been remarkably successful, in that race, the American Derby, as in the five times it has been run I have won it four times, with Modesty, Volante, Silver Cloud and Emperor of Norfolk respectively, and I should have won it when C. H. Todd captured it, as I could have piloted Miss Ford to victory, but by Mr. Baldwin's orders I rode her stable companion, Goliath. Miss Ford lost by a head, while I never could get Goliath near the front, and he ultimately finished among the badly beaten members."

Took All the Races

"My most successful day's ride was at Detroit, on July 4, 1879, when I won the entire programme of four events with Checkmate, Enquiress, and Glenmore, the latter win-ning twice that day. In the same year at St. Louis I rode the three winners in one day—Solicitor, Checkmate and Shortline, and might have swept the deck on that occasion also had I had a mount in the last race."

How He Suffered Unjustly

"I have been exceedingly fortunate in keeping the respect of starters and racing offi-cials, and thus avoiding the ban of suspension with but one single exception. That took place at Cincinnati at the old Chester Park in 1878, and in that instance I was in no wise to blame and for months paid the penalty of another's misdeeds. I was riding Class-mate in a race and a boy started to cross me, not only cutting me out, but running the risk of injuring both the mare and myself. As it was it knocked the mare to her knees, but I soon pulled her together and was quickly in the race again. Another boy, Link Gross, who was in the race, was also jostled by the same daring rider, and, Link's tem-per getting the best of him he struck the offending lad in the face. The blood spurted on my shirt, and when the latter claimed foul against me and brought the charge of my having hit him, the officials looked at the shirt and blood, and putting more faith in that circumstantial evidence than in my denial, disqualified Classmate for the head, fined me $25 and suspended me for one year. Mr. Edgar Johnson was the presiding judge on that occasion, and after finding out to his satisfaction that I had told him the truth, he exerted his influence to have me reinstated and later on apologized for his hasty action, which cost me considerable at that time, as I was then only a poor lad, and the money I earned by riding was all I had to live on."

Lucky Isaac

"Since that time I have learned year after year, and my annual salary has been much as that of the members of President Harrison's Cabinet. Outside of my salary Mr. Bald-win has given me $1,000 extra every time I have won the American Derby for him, and my extra mounts each year bring me on an average as much as my salary."

I believe my percentage of wins to the number of mounts is the best on record in this country, as since my first race in 1875, I have ridden in 1,087 races, 411 of which I have won. The value of the stakes and purses I have no way to estimate, but as I have scored victories in almost every nook and corner of America, and my name appears in all the lists of important races, I know it must be an enormous sum."

Proud of His Calling

"I am as proud of my calling as I am of my record, and I believe my life will be recorded a success, though the reputation I enjoy was earned in the stable and in the saddle. It is a great honor to be classed as one of America's greatest jockeys."

Isaac Murphy: "Biographical Sketch of the Great Lexington Jockey," *Lexington Leader,* March 20, 1889.

10. Marshall "Major" Taylor, Champion Sprint Cyclist

Marshall Walter "Major" Taylor was an internationally famous bicycle racer during the latter years of the nineteenth century and early stages of the twentieth century. Born to Gilbert Taylor and Saphronia Kelter on the outskirts of Indianapolis in 1878, Taylor dropped out of school after the eighth grade and began working for the Hay and Willits Bicycle Company where he performed trick-riding exhibitions to attract customers. A short time later he was hired as the personal valet and company messenger for George Munger, a prominent bicycle racer and manufacturer. Munger, recognizing the enormous potential of Taylor as a bicyclist, gave him important training tips and advice on racing. In 1896, just a year after relocating to Worcester, Massachusetts, with Munger and following several amateur victories on the track, Taylor was triumphant in his first professional race, a half-mile handicap win in Madison Square Garden against Eddie Bald, the reigning American sprint champion. Three years later Taylor captured the world one-mile sprint championship at the Queen's Park track in Montreal, Canada. In 1901, he traveled across the Atlantic for a triumphant four months of racing, a trip owing as much to America's continued racial discrimination as to the enormous popularity of bicycling in France specifically, and Europe more generally. Taylor returned to Europe for several more years of racing and also spent two seasons in Australia where he defeated many of the world's best riders. He retired from competitive racing in 1910, having established numerous world records, netting some $75,000 in winnings, and earning an international reputation over a sixteen-year career. Taylor was far less successful in his postracing career, failing at several business ventures and suffering the disintegration of his marriage. For many years he was also frustrated by his inability to find a publisher for his autobiography. He died of a heart attack in 1932 at a Cook County hospital charity ward in Chicago.*

The following accounts include a description of one particularly brutal incident in which Taylor was attacked after a bumping incident during a race. Another article offers a brief

---

* The definitive study on Taylor is Ritchie's *Major Taylor.* See also Taylor's autobiography, *The Fastest Bicycle Rider in the World.* Additional information can be gleaned from Grant, "Marshall Walter Taylor"; Palmer, "The Fastest Man on Wheels"; and Lucas, "The World's Fastest Bicycle Rider."

Marshall "Major" Taylor
depicted on the cover of
a French cycling maga-
zine, March 1901 (Cour-
tesy Andrew Ritchie)

assessment of the racial climate in the cycling world. Here, too, Taylor discusses his racing strategy. He explains that he was forced to ride in front in each of his races or otherwise be hemmed in at the back of the pack by conspiring white riders intent on denying him victory. This account provides a brief glimpse of the racial antagonism and overt discrimination experienced by Taylor on the track. His autobiography, countless cycling reports, and Andrew Ritchie's Major Taylor: The Extraordinary Career of a Champion Bicycle Racer *shed light on the experiences shared by Taylor with other African American athletes of the period. Racial episodes both within competition and beyond the sporting arena caused considerable heartache. For his part, Taylor was never able to shake off physical assaults and the indignities he suffered when he was banned from races in the southern states or forced to stay in segregated hotels and eat in segregated restaurants. Taylor's story offers another reminder that despite their many successes as athletes, black people still dwelled in a highly racist society.*

Taunton, Mass., Sept. 23—The bicycle races held here today in connection with the Bristol county fair were well attended but the spectators were not well pleased with the action of some of the riders in the one-mile open race.

In getting away, there was a bad mix-up. Tom Butler crossed the tape first with Maj. Taylor second and W. E. Becker third.

After the riders had crossed the tape, Becker wheeled up behind Taylor and grabbed him by the shoulder. The colored man was pulled off his wheel and thrown to the ground. Becker choked him into a state of insensibility and the police were obliged to interfere.

It was fully 15 minutes before Taylor recovered consciousness and the crowd was on the point of assaulting Becker when the police put an end to the trouble.

Becker maintains that Taylor crowded him into the fence during the race. Becker was disqualified and the race was run over again, Tom Butler winning.

"Choked Taylor," *Boston Globe*, September 24, 1897.

It would have been sufficiently disgraceful had the participants been of the same color; the fact that the alleged "victim" was a colored man, and the only one now prominent as a racing man in this country, but complicates the difficulty. It is such incidents as these that bring discredit on a sport whose promoters have strenuously endeavored to keep it clean and honest. . . .

There appears to be no doubt about the facts in the case, and the Racing Board will have no difficulty in reaching a decision, but unfortunately the decision will not cure the evil. The defendant, Becker, who assaulted Taylor, will undoubtedly be punished with a lengthy term of suspension, which he richly deserves. . . .

. . . Late reports chronicle a significant ending of the Taylor-Becker episode. Instead of the lengthy suspension which was expected, Chairman Mott [of the governing association] availed himself of a rule which has been little utilized and fined Becker $50. Whether this may be regarded as partial vindication for Becker or not, it was still more significant when the racing men took up a collection among themselves at Trenton, where the news was received, and paid Becker's fine at once, so that he was not deprived of participation in the day's races. The riders insisted their action was not a proof of their enmity toward Taylor because of his color, but on account of their belief that his foul riding caused Becker to lose his temper and act as he did at Taunton.

Bicycling World, October 1, 1897, 4.

Taylor is now most anxious to right himself with the men against whom he must compete, but how to go about it he does not know. Failing in his laudable efforts, it is his intention to follow good advice given him last spring and go to France, where a colored man is never looked down upon. Major Taylor may be a competitor in the French races another season, thereby removing the friction in racing matters in this country, which his presence has made throughout the season. The white men claim that it is not fear of his prowess and ability that brings about the present opposition, but a doubt exists if the white men are wholly honest about this. Taylor is a great rider, of that there can not be the slightest doubt. He is also a daring rider and the first of his class to ever show championship form in the present-day fast company and there is a fear that his presence in the races may excite other colored riders to such admiration that more of his race will want to compete. Taylor's trip to France would end the discussion, and no one appreciates this more than the colored man. One thing is certain, the meet directors will regret his going, for he proves an excellent drawing card and his entry is eagerly sought.

Bearings, October 14, 1897, 903–4.

"I am having my troubles if anyone should ask you, and the fact that I do not look so white as some of them is yet evident. I am riding faster this year than I was last, and that has saved me a good many times. I simply ride away from the rest of the bunch and do not give them a chance to pocket me, which is so disagreeable to a rider, and makes it impossible to win a race. It always falls to my lot to set the pace, and this I always do to save any mix-ups which might occur if I remained in the bunch and gave someone else the chance of setting the pace. And it is not always pleasant to have to push out in the lead and give the men their work to do, for though I am stronger than ever I was, still it tells on a rider at the finish and takes a whole lot of strength. But it cannot be helped, and it must be done if I want to win, and by that you see I ride the race from the crack of the pistol till the finish, making a clear raceway through the course. That is the way I have won all my races this season, and I suppose that the thing must be kept up till the end. There are some of the riders who have shown me more consideration, but the rest are just about as bad as they ever were."

Marshall Walter "Major" Taylor, "Racism on the Track," *Worcester Telegram,* July 27, 1898.

11. George Dixon's Long Career in Boxing

George Dixon was one of the great black boxers of the late nineteenth century, capturing titles in both the bantamweight and featherweight divisions. Born in Halifax, Nova Scotia, in 1870, Dixon became a permanent resident of Boston after moving with his parents to that city at the age of eight. He first became interested in boxing at about the age of fourteen when he witnessed an exhibition match between two local fighters at the Boston Music Hall. Armed with a newfound interest in the sport, the five-foot three-inch Dixon, who would become popularly known as "Little Chocolate," embarked on a boxing career that encompassed some eight hundred fights during twenty years in the ring. He garnered international acclaim in 1890 when he knocked out the English featherweight champion, Nunc Wallace, in the eighteenth round at the famous Pelican Club in London. He captured the American featherweight championship from Cal McCarthy in Troy, New York, on March 31, 1891, avenging a seventy-round draw with McCarthy just a year earlier in Boston. In 1892, Dixon participated in a famous three-day pugilistic festival at the Olympic Club in New Orleans that included his featherweight championship bout against Jack Skelly, a lightweight championship fight between Jack McAuliffe and Billy Myer, and a heavyweight championship bout pitting James

J. Corbett against the "Boston Strong Boy," John L. Sullivan. Dixon's fight with Skelly was a decisive victory for "Little Chocolate" and so enraged the already racially antagonistic white citizens of New Orleans that interracial bouts were not permitted in the city until well into the next century. Dixon's last major bouts were a loss by knockout to Joseph "Terrible Terry" McGovern in 1900 at the Broadway Athletic Club in New York City and both a draw and a fifteen-round loss by decision to Abe "The Little Hebrew" Attell in 1901. Dixon finally retired from the ring in 1906 and died three years later.*

The following account provides a brief description of Dixon's victory over Cal McCarthy in 1891. This fight was particularly significant to Dixon because it earned him the featherweight championship he was to retain for some nine years. Far more important to remember from an historical standpoint, however, is that Dixon's fight with McCarthy was just one of many he had with white boxers. Although his contests with white fighters could inflame racial prejudices, as evidenced in New Orleans after the Skelly fight, Dixon was more fortunate than black boxers in the heavier divisions in that he was better able to secure fights with white boxers because his smallish size mitigated fears about interracial matches. Unlike black heavyweights, who carried the symbolic burden of race and thus were largely forced to fight one another, Dixon and other black fighters from the lower weight divisions were able to secure bouts with white boxers and fight for championships. Interracial bouts would eventually become common in all weight divisions as promoters played on the public's fascination with racial contrasts to create more interest and draw more fans.**

——— ———

Cal McCarthy of Jersey City, who has for over two years been the featherweight champion of America, tonight surrendered the title to George Dixon, the colored boxer of Boston, who has also won the featherweight of England.

The contest took place in the ring of the Troy Bicycle Club on Federal Street under the auspices of the Troy Crib Club. Seats were built about the building and were capable of accommodating 3,000 persons. There was an outside ring for the seconds and timekeepers, and a gong for recording of "time" all in the much approved fashion. Both men, with the handlers, arrived early this morning. They were weighed this afternoon, and McCarthy tipped the beam at 114; Dixon—115—the limit.

Gathering on the Clang

The sports from the neighboring towns began to pour into Troy before noon. By nightfall Troy contained a couple of thousand men who did not live here. Almost all of them arrived in the hope of getting into the hall by hook or crook, certainly not by paying the $10 admission.

At 7 o'clock the doors about the ring on Federal Street were surrounded, and an

---

* For background information on Dixon, see Henderson, *The Black Athlete*, 25–29; Somers, *The Rise of Sports in New Orleans,* 179–83; J. P. Davis, "The Negro in American Sports," 780–81. Some additional information can be gleaned from Dixon's primer, *A Lesson in Boxing.*

** Important discussions about racial symbolism in boxing can be found in Early, *Tuxedo Junction,* 115–23; Sammons, *Beyond the Ring,*33–34, 114–17; idem, "Boxing as a Reflection of Society"; Capeci and Wilkerson, "Multifarious Hero"; Edmonds, "The Second Louis-Schmeling Fight"; Roberts, *Papa Jack.*

hour later the thoroughfare in front was covered. At 7:45 nearly every seat was occupied and it was estimated that $15,000 had been paid for tickets.

Dixon entered the ring at 10:10 and received a great big cheer. Tom O'Rourke, M. J. Slattery, of Providence, and Howie Hodgkins were with him. McCarthy entered the ring five minutes later and by the way the crowd yelled, it was easy to see that the white boy was the favorite in the hearts of the spectators.

With the Jerseyman were Jack McAuliffe, the lightweight champion, Billy Madden and Tom Collins of Jersey City. When he got his outer clothing off McCarthy appeared in a pair of short blue drawers and black shoes. There was nothing about his appearance to indicate that he had not done his training work faithfully, except a trifling shallowness about the skin. Dixon wore besides his dark brown shoes, simply a pair of brief white trunks. The colored boy showed his fine condition at a glance.

The Fight Begins

The men shook hands and then proceeded to fight for a $4,000 purse of which the loser was to get only $200. Dixon had the best of the fight throughout, and it is generally believed that he could have ended the fight in the third or fourth round had he been so disposed. The colored man delivered a terrible knock-out blow in the second round, which completely dazed the Jerseyman, and he never completely recovered from its effects.

The fight continued for twenty-two rounds when Dixon, by severely punishing the Jerseyman's face and stomach, so completely used him up that he was unable to go out for the twenty-third round, and the referee gave the fight to Dixon.

"A Colored Man Wins the Championship of America," *Richmond Planet*, April 4, 1891.

12. Peter Jackson and the Elusive Heavyweight Championship

*Peter Jackson, the imposing black boxer from Australia via the island of Saint Croix, Virgin Islands, first came into prominence when he defeated Tom Lees for the Australian championship in 1886, at Jack Foley's White Horse Saloon in Sydney. The bout, which was a grueling thirty-round fight, established Jackson as a legitimate contender in pugilistic circles. Unfortunately, Jackson was unable to secure any contests immediately following his match with Lees because of the lack of other high-quality fighters in Australia at the time, and the fact that some boxers, including the well-known fighter Jack Burke, refused to enter the ring with the new Australian champion because of his color. As a result, Jackson decided to travel to America in 1888 to seek matches with this country's outstanding fighters, most notably, John L. Sullivan, the heavyweight champion of the world.** [*]

Jackson was never able to secure a fight with Sullivan because the "Boston Strong Boy"

---

[*] For biographical information on Jackson see Hales, *Black Prince Peter;* D. Wiggins, "Peter Jackson."

Peter Jackson, ca. 1890
(Courtesy Bill Schutte)

always refused to cross the color line. The Australian fighter was, however, able to arrange bouts over the next several years with some of the world's great boxers from both America and England. In 1891, Jackson fought a famous sixty-one–round fight against James J. Corbett at the California Athletic Club in San Francisco, a match that ended in a draw but would ensure Corbett a title fight with Sullivan. In 1892, Jackson garnered perhaps his greatest ring triumph, a tenth-round knockout of Frank Slavin at London's National Sporting Club. Boxing historians have ranked the bout as one of the most brutal ever fought in England. The following selection from the Cleveland Gazette *announced Jackson's return to New York City approximately six months after his fight with Slavin and provides a brief interview with the fighter on various subjects. Not surprisingly, Jackson was asked about a possible rematch with Corbett, who had just captured the heavyweight championship from Sullivan in New Orleans. In customary fashion, Jackson claimed he would not challenge Corbett but would love to fight the new heavyweight champion to settle the question of who was the best boxer.*

———————

Peter Jackson, the heavy-weight pugilist, was among the passengers on the steamship Teutonic, which arrived last week Thursday morning. The giant's appearance did not create a favorable impression to the critical observers. He did not look like the Jackson of old. His eyes were somewhat sunken and had deep circles around them that extended almost to his prominent cheek bones. He was as bright and cheerful as ever, however. He was perfectly willing to talk about anything that the reporters did not want him to talk about. He has all, if not more, of his old suavity of manner, and is as excessively polite as ever.

He appeared to be anxious to fight Corbett again. He smiled when asked about Goddard's draw having been said to be really a victory for Goddard. He was as diplomatic as ever, but did not appear to be the man physically that he was when he made his first bow to a metropolitan audience. He has acquired a stoop of the shoulders that he did not have before. His step is not as distinct in fact, he looks to be fully ten years older than he was three years ago. Parson Davies, Jackson's manager, was perfectly satisfied with his appearance. He is of the opinion that with a few days' rest after the rough sea passage, Jackson will be himself again. Several farewell dinners were tendered to Jackson before he left England, and it may be that the dinners were a trifle too heavy for Jackson's digestive organs. Jackson is fond of the good things of this world. He has enjoyed life thoroughly since he gained an easy victory over Slavin.

When the Teutonic entered her dock Jackson was on the upper deck chatting with a number of friends. He was dressed in a black suit of English broadcloth, a sealskin vest, silk hat, Piccadilly collar and patent leather shoes. His mustache is quite long and military looking. After leaving the ship he was driven to the Occidental hotel on the Bowery, where quarters had been engaged for him by Tom O'Rourke. A reporter was one of the party which accompanied him to the hotel. After Jackson had adjusted some personal business he began to speak of his experiences across the water.

"We had a very rough trip across," he said. "A pleasant feature, however, was the entertainment provided by Wilson Barrett for the benefit of the seamen of the ship. It was a big success and yielded many dollars to the men. I was treated finely by the passengers and am very grateful for their courtesy toward me. I would like to have remained in England, as I was so well treated, but business demanded my presence in New York."

"After I fought Slavin I had a grand time. It was one continual round of pleasure. Almost every day I received invitations from friends to participate in enjoyable affairs and accepted. I remember one occasion when I was out hunting when a lady of English aristocracy appeared before me. She did not know who I was and at once began plying me with questions. She asked me whether I had heard of a colored pugilist by the name of Peter Jackson. I said that I certainly had. And is he such a great fighter as they say he is? asked the lady. I simply replied that I believed so. Finally she was told that I was Peter Jackson. She was very much surprised." . . .

[The reported asked,] "Were you surprised when Corbett defeated Sullivan?"

"No: Corbett is a good man. However, I am willing to meet him at any time. I never challenge anybody. If he wants to meet me again, I will accommodate him. I consider my draw with him a disgrace, and I will not be satisfied until we settle the question of supremacy."

When asked what he thought of Goddard, Jackson said that the Barrier man was not a bad pugilist by any means. He smiled when told that Goddard had claimed the championship of the world.

In speaking of Slavin, Jackson said that he was game to the core. "He's not an easy man to defeat by any means," he continued. "He can hit as hard as any of them. When I left London he was running two public houses and is doing well. Pony Moore, Mitchell's father-in-law, set Frank up in business."

Before he left London he received from a number of friends a costly diamond ring. He also carried with him a few valuable canes, which were presented to him by the employees of the hotels where he stopped.

Jackson would not express an opinion upon the result of the fight between Godfrey and Choynski. He said that he would be present at the battle, but would not be in Choynski's corner.

The fighter's future plans have not as yet been mapped out. After spending a few weeks in this city he will probably return to San Francisco. He expressed his willingness more than once to battle at the Coney Island Athletic club.

"Champion Jackson," *Cleveland Gazette,* November 5, 1892.

13. William Henry Lewis: Uplifting the Race

William Henry Lewis won accolades as an outstanding college football player and coach at the turn of the twentieth century, then went on to become a prominent lawyer and politician. Born to freed slaves in Berkeley, Virginia, in 1868, Lewis first attended Virginia Normal and Industrial School in Petersburg, Virginia, and then traveled north to Massachusetts where he became a famous "center-rush" first on the Amherst, then on Harvard football teams. His leadership skills and athletic abilities were such that Lewis was selected captain of the Amherst squad, then again (at least for one game) at Harvard. Not only was he chosen to Walter Camp's prestigious All-American teams in 1892 and 1893, but authorities on the gridiron game later ranked him as the dominating player at his position for the entire decade.

After taking his law degree from Harvard, Lewis combined his efforts as a fledgling lawyer with part-time work as a football coach for his alma mater in Cambridge. (With a few exceptions, the collegiate coaching system at the time placed alumni standouts, like Lewis, at or near the center of the autumn sporting ritual. The age of the full-time, professional coach would soon follow, but it would not include black sportsmen until the end of the twentieth century.) For his part, Lewis was a great strategist and student of the game, authoring a book, Primer of College Football *(1896); an essay on how to develop a football team in Casper Whitney's journal,* Outing *(1902); and a chapter on line play in Walter Camp's* How to Play Football *(1903).*

Deeply involved in African American politics, Lewis played a significant role in the conflict between Booker T. Washington and W. E. B. Du Bois at the turn of the century. His influence

William Henry Lewis (with football) and Amherst teammates, 1891. William Tecumseh Sherman Jackson stands directly behind Lewis. (Courtesy Amherst College Archives and Special Collections)

and abilities resulted in his appointment as United States attorney for Boston (1903–6). More important still, he held the post of assistant attorney general of the United States during the Taft administration (1911–13) and as such he was the highest-ranking African American in the federal government. He died in Boston in 1949 at the age of eighty-one.*

Here, in a dispatch from the AME Zion Quarterly Review, Lewis is extolled as a significant representative of the race. His accomplishments as a player and coach distinguish him, the report asserts, as someone who has already demonstrated excellence in a highly regarded endeavor. These achievements, like those of Roscoe Conkling Bruce, Harvard's champion debater, signify that blacks can master any field and compete at any level, if only given the opportunity. Proudly describing Lewis's role in Harvard's stunning football victory, the article is noteworthy as an early evocation of the importance of athletic success—as a means of uplift and assimilation—for many racial reformers

———————

Mr. W. H. Lewis, coach of the Harvard foot-ball team is to day the most famous football strategist in America. The success of the Harvard eleven in their contest with that

* For information on Lewis see Wade, *Black Men of Amherst;* Ewing, "William H. Lewis"; R. Smith, *Big-Time Football,* esp. 8–9; Oriard, *Reading Football,* 232–33; Chalk, *Black College Sport,* esp. 140–141, 144–147, 149–150. On Lewis's place in the African American political landscape, see Meier, *Negro Thought in America;* Lewis, *W. E. B. Du Bois.*

of the University of Pennsylvania, on Soldiers Field, Cambridge, last Saturday, by a score of seventeen to five, settled that fact for all time. It was admitted by every foot-ball expert in the East that the Pennsylvania team was the strongest and should win easily. The betting was ten to seven in favor of Pennsylvania. And yet with a weak and crippled team Harvard was overwhelmingly victorious. And why? Because W. H. Lewis, the colored coach had studied the methods of the Pennsylvania system and mastered them. He devised a system of defence which completely blocked Pennsylvania's team and made it almost impossible for them to score. Every time a colored man masters any honorable profession or science and pursues it to success he makes the condition of his people that much better.

Foot-ball to day is a science. Men spend years in devising and perfecting systems of play. It is very flattering to have Mr. Lewis with his system and a weak team defeat the Pennsylvania system with a strong team. Mr. Lewis is the son of a Baptist minister of Portsmouth, Virginia, and has earned his high standing at the Boston bar and in the foot-ball world solely upon his merits. Being a graduate of Harvard College and coming in contact daily with the leading people of the East he has a wonderful opportunity to impress himself upon the community and make a good impression for his race. This he has done and is doing. With all of his success his naturally "big head" has not been swelled, and when his merits are mentioned is as modest as a school girl. Ordinarily we would sorrow for Penn's defeat; but as it is we rejoice with Harvard because her success is the triumph of her colored coach William H. Lewis. . . .

The civilized world holds in high respect the trained and successful athlete. The best of the colleges of the world encourage athletics as a means of strengthening and adding to the health of students and of stimulating their mental powers at the same time. . . .

Mr. Lewis is a past master in the art of playing foot-ball and managing a foot-ball team. The proud Anglo-Saxon admits that his superior has not appeared on the athletic field. We honor him the more because he has rendered himself indispensable to the success of the great Harvard team, Harvard College standing at the head of all American seats of learning. Our race is proud of him because in all his success he stands for us, and the higher he goes in the physical field of athletics or the mental field of law or literature, he must necessarily open the way for others, and lift us all up at the same time.

Young Roscoe Conkling Bruce has also won high honors at Harvard College in being selected to represent that renowned institution in an oratorical contest with Princeton College, and remarkable to say he won the contest. In the face of such positive evidences of race capacity how can it be reasonably argued that the race will never amount to anything. It would really seem the chief trouble is the race is amounting to too much.

"Lewis' Great Work," *AME Zion Quarterly Review* 10 (October–December 1900): 63–64.

14. "Papa Jack": In the Ring and Out

Jack Johnson was one of the most controversial athletes in history. Heavyweight champion of the world from 1908 to 1915, Johnson lived life on his own terms without any apparent fear of danger or death. He became a hero to large segments of the African American community for both his ring triumphs and his refusal to acquiesce to the dominant white culture. On the other hand, many whites, and some blacks as well, viewed Johnson with disdain because of his arrogance, dissipation, and violation of the prevailing racial etiquette. His three marriages to white women and his illicit relationships with many others were considered his most serious transgressions. These sexual unions, established during one of the most racially oppressive periods in American history, eventually resulted in Johnson's 1913 conviction for violating the Mann Act, which forbade the transportation of women across state lines for illicit purposes.* Johnson eventually spent a year in the federal penitentiary in Leavenworth, Kansas, for his conviction.

Perhaps Johnson's most famous bout was against James Jeffries in Reno, Nevada, on July 4, 1910. Jeffries, who had retired from boxing in 1905, was lured back into the ring against Johnson in an attempt to recapture the heavyweight championship for the white race. In a much-ballyhooed match fought under a scorching sun, Johnson defeated Jeffries in fifteen rounds. Though Johnson's description of the bout, originally part of his autobiography, is rather casual in terms and tone, his victory resulted in white violence against blacks all across the country and renewed efforts to find a white fighter to defeat Johnson.**

——— ———

The day of the fight finally arrived. It was a beautiful one—the weather, excepting for the intense heat, was superb. The atmosphere was clear as crystal, and one could see for miles. More than 25,000 people had gathered to watch the fight, and as I looked about me, and scanned that sea of white faces I felt the auspiciousness of the occasion. There were few men of my own race among the spectators. I realized that my victory in this event meant more than on any previous occasion. It wasn't just the championship that was at stake—it was my own honor, and in a degree the honor of my race. I was well aware of all these things, and I sensed that most of that great audience was hostile to me. These things, while they impressed me with the responsibilities that lay upon me, did not disturb or worry me. I was cool and perfectly at ease. I never had any doubt of the outcome. Outside of a contemplation for a moment of the auspiciousness of the gathering, I was thinking for the most part of getting home. That had been my thought when I crawled through the ropes, and as Fury was tying my gloves I saw in the audience the yardmaster who had charge of the special trains. I sent Fury to ask him to come and speak to me. When he did so, I told him I wanted to leave right after the fight and that I wished him to make arrangements for my immediate depar-

---

* The best portrayal of Johnson's life and boxing career is Roberts, *Papa Jack.* See also Gilmore, *Bad Nigger!;* Farr, *Black Champion;* W. Wiggins, "Jack Johnson as Bad Nigger."

** For responses to Johnson's victory, see Walton, "Search for a 'White Hope."

Jack Johnson and his wife (with trainers), Reno, Nevada, 1910 (Courtesy Nevada Historical Society)

ture. He said it would be impossible—that it could not be done. I said it must be done, and that if he would do it I would give him a tip that would make plenty of money for him. He stared at me for a moment, then said that he would get me out on a special.

"Do you mean that?" I asked. He said he did.

"All right, then," I told him. "Bet on me; I am going to win."

I do not know what his winnings were, but he was as good as his word, and two hours after the fight, I was on my way to Chicago on the train which he arranged for me.

I was the first to enter the ring. There was one shady corner and in this I seated my-self. Jeff followed a little later with his seconds, and proposed that we toss a coin for the shady corner. I declined to toss, but offered to relinquish the shade to him, an offer which he accepted, and I moved over into the sun. The crowd gave me a very hearty reception, but that given Jeff was twenty times greater than mine. When the fight started Jeff was a 10 to 4 favorite, but in the fourth round I was the favorite by the same odds.

Hardly had a blow been struck when I knew that I was Jeff's master. From the start the fight was mine, and, as I have just observed, the fourth round brought the crowd to a realization that Jeff had little chance to win. He fought in his usual style and I think with as much of his vigor, speed and endurance as ever. If he had not been fit, and if there had been the smallest particle of dope in him, as some have contended, he never could have stood under that hot sun for fifteen rounds withstanding the punishment I gave him. He fought his best. He brought into play some of the old swings and blows for which he had been noted. His brain was working keenly, but he found it almost impossible to get through my defense and at no time did he hurt me. He landed on me frequently but with no effect. He devoted his attention to fighting and did not take much part in the run of conversation which was going on. About all he said, was, once, when I struck him on the head:

"Say, but that's a tough old head," he remarked.

As for me, I took part in the palaver that went on, addressing myself particularly to Jim Corbett, a member of Jeff's training staff, who took occasion to send a few jeering remarks in my direction. I told Corbett to come on in the ring, that I would take him on too. At the same time I was demonstrating, that, contrary to Jim's disparaging remarks, I was putting over a good, fast fight. I hit Jeff at will. There was no place that was beyond my reach, and I landed some stiff jolts on him, but not as stiff as I might have, for I really did not have any desire to punish him unnecessarily. The cheering for Jeff never ceased. The spectators urged him on and gave him every possible encouragement, but their cheering turned to moans and groans when they saw that he was suffering as he was. There came up to me from the ringside gasps of astonishment that turned to cries of pity, and more than once I heard them shout:

"Stop it! Stop it!"

The great crowd cheered Jeffries for his grit and supreme effort and they pitied him in his suffering, but they did not for a moment lose their admiration for him. As for me, they learned that I was not a quitter; they realized that I had not entered into

Johnson-Jeffries fight, Reno, Nevada, July 4, 1910 (Courtesy Nevada Historical Society)

any crookedness, and that Little, Langford and others who had swung much of the betting against me had let them in for a good trimming. However, it was not enough that the fight should be a meritorious one and that the best man had won on his worth or that the entire mill had been clean and square; the crowd was by no means pleased. The "white hope" had failed, and as far as the championship was concerned it was just where it was before the beginning of the fight, except that I had established my rightful claim to it beyond all possible dispute. But from that minute on the hunt for the "white hope" was redoubled, and when it proceeded with so little success other methods were taken to dispose of me.

Jack Johnson, *In the Ring and Out* (Chicago: National Sports Publishing, 1927), 183–86.

15. Booker T. Washington and Jack Johnson: Race Men and Respectability

There is relatively little in the public record that suggests Booker T. Washington's interest in sport per se. Early in his autobiography, Up from Slavery, *he mentioned that it was not until he had secured his reputation as an educational leader that it had occurred to him "that there was no period of my life that was devoted to play. From the time that I can remember anything, almost every day of my life has been occupied in some kind of labour; though I think I would now be a more useful man if I had had time for sports." We know, however, that despite Washington's emphasis on industrial education and a strict regimen of discipline and work at Tuskegee Institute, the school fielded intercollegiate football teams as early as 1894, and provisions for expanding recreational facilities were made before the turn of the century. We also know that Washington approved of the genteel sport of croquet (it was a game that Frederick Douglass had played); what's more, both Washington and his wife enjoyed watching students compete at tennis on the court that stood adjacent to the president's campus residence.**

Still, what dominated Booker T. Washington's life as a spokesman for black America were his strenuous efforts to reassure the dominant culture about the steady progress being made by his race to uplift itself—to a certain point—as well as his ability to extract from the wealthiest white Americans large sums of money to endow black institutions such as Tuskegee. From the late 1890s until his death in 1915, he pursued this agenda tirelessly, which meant that he publicly distanced himself from most manifestations of an expressive black culture, just as he denounced anything that might appear to discredit the race in the eyes of white people. Thus, almost from the outset of Jack Johnson's reign as heavyweight champion, Washing-

---

* See Washington, *Up from Slavery* (the quote is from page 4); Harlan, *Booker T. Washington*. Private correspondence and other materials reveal that Washington's adoptive brother or half-brother, James, "taught and coached the baseball team" at Tuskegee after 1890, and "when football became popular, he learned that sport and served as the coach of the school's squad." A letter from Scotland after the turn of the century mentions a round of golf there with the philanthropist Andrew Carnegie. Significantly, Washington's last "Sunday Talk" to Tuskegee students before his death in 1915 was titled "On Team Work." In it, he encouraged the campus to show greater spirit in support of the athletic teams. See Harlan, *Booker T. Washington Papers*, v. 2 (1860–89), 21; v. 3 (1889–95), 456–57; v. 10 (1909–11), 382; v. 13 (1914–15), 391. The quotes in this note are from v. 2, 21.

Booker T. Washington,
1906 (Library of
Congress)

ton's personal secretary, Emmett Scott, had issued statements encouraging Johnson to "refrain from anything resembling boastfulness." And in response to the hearings surrounding Jack Johnson's indictment for violation of the Mann Act, Washington strongly asserted—in a telegram to a national wire service—that respectability in all matters should mark the behavior of racial representatives such as the boxing champ, that any taint of immorality further stigmatized African Americans everywhere.**

FROM THE UNITED PRESS ASSOCIATION

New York, October 22, 1912

We believe Nationwide agitation resulting action pugilistic Jack Johnson due primarily thoughtless of public failing recognize better element colored race condemns Johnson severely as whites we believe statement from you would do much to restore

---

** It is a telling detail, however, that during the Johnson-Jeffries fight in Reno, Washington set aside an assembly room at Tuskegee Institute to hear special telegraphic reports from the site of the bout. For this and a full account of Johnson's career, see Roberts, *Papa Jack*. On Scott's feelings see Emmett J. Scott to J. Frank Wheaton, March 23, 1909, in Harlan, *Booker T. Washington Papers*, vol. 10, 75.

sane public thought would greatly appreciate 500 words telegraphed statement to be used exactly prepared by you.

United Press Ass

A Statement on Jack Johnson for the United Press Association*

[Tuskegee, Ala.] October 23, 1912

Please Rush!

Replying to your telegram, please publish the following statement exactly as submitted:

Jack Johnson's case will be settled in due time in the courts. Until the court has spoken, I do not care to either defend or condemn him. I can only say at this time, that this is another illustration of the almost irreparable injury that a wrong action on the part of a single individual may do to a whole race. It shows the folly of those persons who think that they alone will be held responsible for the evil that they do. Especially is this true in the case of the Negro in the United States today. No one can do so much injury to the Negro race as the Negro himself. This will seem to many persons unjust, but no one can doubt that it is true.

What makes the situation seem a little worse in this case, is the fact that it was the white man, not the black man who has given Jack Johnson the kind of prominence he has enjoyed up to now and put him, in other words, in a position where he has been able to bring humiliation upon the whole race of which he is a member.

I do not believe it is necessary for me to say that the honest, sober element of the Negro people of the United States is as severe in condemnation of the kind of immorality with which Jack Johnson is at present charged as any other portion of the community.

In making this statement, I do not mean to, as I have said at the beginning, say how far Jack Johnson is or is not guilty of the charges that have been made against him. This is a question for the court to decide.

Booker T. Washington

*Prepared by E. J. Scott and Robert E. Park while BTW was away from Tuskegee. (BTW to Scott, October 24, 1912, Con 619, BTW Papers, DLC.)

Louis Harlan, ed., *The Booker T. Washington Papers* (Urbana: University of Illinois Press, 1982), vol. 12, 43–44.

16. W. E. B. Du Bois and Jack Johnson: The Scholar's Pugilist and the Heavyweight Champ as Folk Hero

"That Mr. Johnson should so lightly and carelessly punch the head off Mr. Jeffries," observed the New York World *in 1910, "must have come as a shock to every devoted believer in the supremacy of the Anglo-Saxon race." Self-conscious and competitive, black leaders such as*

W. E. B. Du Bois, ca. 1918
(Library of Congress)

the Reverend Reverdy Ransom also claimed that, like Jack Johnson, African American musicians, poets, artists, and scholars were fully capable of keeping "the white race busy for the next hundred years . . . in defending the interests of white supremacy." For his part, W. E. B. Du Bois might have felt that Johnson's marriages and affairs outside the race unduly alienated white people and hampered the efforts of civil rights reformers like himself. But in the case of Jack Johnson, Du Bois joined the ranks of the anti-Bookerites, such as Ransom, and celebrated the feats of Papa Jack.*

What stands out in the first of the following documents is that Du Bois, still insistent on highlighting his own erudition, crafted an essay that positioned the heavyweight championship squarely within the realm of Western Civilization—from Greek and Roman antiquity down to nineteenth-century British innovations, such as the Queensberry rules. At the same time, Du Bois deftly contrasts pugilism with the barbarism of American football and what many people rightly sensed would be the savagery to come during the war that had recently broken out in Europe. The tone of the piece is bitterly ironic on several fronts, for

---

* Levine, *Black Culture and Black Consciousness*, 431 (both quotes).

Du Bois also declares that it was not Johnson's personal life that has caused boxing to fall in disfavor among respectable journals of opinion; it was simply Johnson's undeniable greatness combined with his "unforgivable blackness." Written or transcribed in black vernacular phrases, the second document contrasts markedly with Du Bois's formality. This verse, a raucous boast, clearly placed Johnson within what Lawrence Levine has called "the pantheon of heroes," including the bad men and bandits widely admired by the mass of African Americans at the turn of the twentieth century and beyond for their refusal to accommodate, their willingness to resist the dominant culture—come what may. Here is an image of the mythic John Henry, now allowed to show force in the athletic arena. If some black Americans looked askance at Jack Johnson's private life, the vast majority celebrated his triumphs.*

——— ———

Boxing is an ancient sport. It is mentioned in Homer's Iliad and Vergil's Aeneid and was a recognized branch of the celebrated Olympic games. During the Middle Ages boxing went out of style among most nations, the preference being given to various sorts of encounters with weapons. In England it was revived in the seventeenth century, and fighting with bare fists became a national sport in the eighteenth century. Boxing gloves were invented late in that century, and in the beginning of the nineteenth century, John Jackson (note the prophecy!) became champion and teacher of Lord Byron and other great and titled personages.

Gradually, the more brutal features of the sport were eliminated and the eighth Marquis of Queensberry drew up a set of rules in the sixties which have since prevailed.

There is still today some brutality connected with boxing, but as compared with football and boat racing it may be seriously questioned whether boxing deserves to be put in a separate class by reason of its cruelty. Certainly it is a highly civilized pastime as compared with the international game of war which produces so many "heroes" and national monuments.

Despite all this, boxing has fallen into disfavor—into very great disfavor. To see publications like the *New York Times* roll their eyes in shivery horror at the news from Paris (to which it is compelled to give a front page) makes one realize the depths to which we have fallen.

The cause is clear: Jack Johnson, successor of the eighteenth century John Jackson, has outsparred an Irishman. He did it with little brutality, the utmost fairness and great good nature. He did not "knock" his opponent senseless. Apparently he did not even try. Neither he nor his race invented prize fighting or particularly like it. Why, then, this thrill of national disgust? Because Johnson is black. Of course, some pretend to object to Mr. Johnson's character. But we have yet to hear, in the case of white America, that marital troubles have disqualified prize fighters or ball players or even statesmen. It comes down, then, after all, to this unforgivable blackness. Wherefore we conclude that at present prize fighting is very, very immoral, and that we must rely on

---

* Ibid., 367 ("pantheon of heroes").

football and war for pastime until Mr. Johnson retires or permits himself to be "knocked out."

W. E. B. Du Bois, "The Prizefighter," *Crisis* 8 (August 1914): 181.

> Amaze an' Grace, how sweet it sounds,
> Jack Johnson knocked Jim Jeffries down.
> Jim Jeffries jumped up an' hit Jack on the chin,
> An' then Jack knocked him down agin.
> The Yankees hold the play,
> The white man pulls the trigger;
> But it make no difference what the white man say,
> The world champion's still a nigger.

Lawrence W. Levine, *Black Culture and Black Consciousness: Afro-American Folk Thought from Slavery to Freedom* (New York: Oxford University Press, 1977), 432.

3

Parallel Institutions: Black Sports between the World Wars

Introduction

For the mass of African Americans, 1915 was a shock year. The death of Booker T. Washington was widely felt to be an enormous loss to the race. When Jack Johnson fell to Jess Willard in a controversial bout staged in Havana, his defeat was seen in broadly symbolic terms as a blow to black pride. What may have been worse still, the initial screenings of D. W. Griffith's *Birth of a Nation* not only won acclaim among white audiences from Main Street to Pennsylvania Avenue; the film also set the stage for the resurgence of the Ku Klux Klan. Within the next several years, two old-stock whites—propagandists for immigration restriction and the establishment of national eugenics policies—would publish works of pseudoscience, adding the trappings of scholarly research to white supremacist fervor. By turns strident and shrill, both Madison Grant's *The Passing of the Great Race* and Lothrop Stoddard's *The Rising Tide of Color* attempted to explain "Negro inferiority" in terms of evolutionary biology and genetics, rejecting the claims by progressive reformers that equality and opportunity were the keys to the "race problem" in the United States. Finally, if some black leaders such as W. E. B. Du Bois believed that participation in the Great War would allow African Americans, once again, to display valor and patriotism on the battlefield—and thus to persuade the dominant culture of blacks' "fitness" for first-class citizenship—they were betrayed by their optimism. Of the 380,000 black men who served in World War I, only 42,000 were sent into combat, and the honors those soldiers were accorded by French military authorities were offset by the derogatory comments made by American officers. The years 1917 to 1921 witnessed a rise in the number of lynchings nationwide as well as bloody riots and massacres in East St. Louis and Chicago; Washington, D.C.; Elaine, Arkansas; and Tulsa, Oklahoma.

These events, in all their bleakness, form one of the contexts for the Great Migration, which by the second decade of the twentieth century represented a flood of black men, women, and children from the rural South to the cities of the North. Between 1910 and 1940 approximately 1,750,000 African Americans left the South, settling in communities already established by an earlier generation of migrants or creating their own. The potential for war work in the factories of the North prompted some to depart; increasingly vicious forms of racial control in the South impelled others to leave. More often, it was a combination of factors. In New York City, in Philadelphia and Pittsburgh, and in the cities bordering the Great Lakes, blacks found an increasing number of outlets for their energy and initiative. They were quick to reestablish a host of social institutions—their churches, for instance—and to develop new ones, including athletic organizations.

The South remained rigidly segregated during the interwar era. Social relations in the North, while less tightly structured, nevertheless adhered to the color line. As a consequence, many of the associations created by black Americans were "parallel institutions." Whether they flourished or foundered—depending upon the amount of capital that was available to them—the majority of them, from the YMCAs to baseball leagues, bowling associations to tennis tournaments, were confined to separate status. Significantly, though, the exciting moments on playing fields, North and South, were covered by an increasingly vital black press. So were the financial activities of sporting entrepreneurs.

In fact, newspaper editors and journalists, along with political activists and business people who strived to organize African American athletic competition, played enormously important roles in the shaping of black communities in the North. During the 1920s and 1930s, the *Chicago Defender, Pittsburgh Courier-Journal,* and *New York Amsterdam News,* among scores of other newspapers, joined the *Crisis* and *Opportunity* as the most widely circulated periodicals for news and commentary about African American achievements and race relations. Such sportswriters as Chester Washington, Wendell Smith, Sam Lacy, Frank A. Young, Edwin Bancroft Henderson, and Joe Bostic became household names in their own right. Just as critically, these writers, and many others, were not content merely to describe players and games or—beyond that—to chronicle the triumphs won by African Americans in sport. Effectively, they sought to assimilate black athletes to national pastimes, thus enlisting sports in the larger campaign for civil rights.

As they surveyed the athletic scene in the years between the two world wars, participants and observers alike underscored the vitality of the social and cultural institutions that blacks had created for themselves. The "East vs. West" baseball classic, inaugurated in the midst of the Great Depression, illustrates the enthusiasm generated by black all-star competition. At the same time, a number of documents sound appeals, articulate hopes, and urge racial solidarity in support of Negro teams and leagues. The economic survival of those parallel institutions was always of grave concern. It is worth noting,

Lincoln University baseball team, 1914 (Edwin B. Henderson Scrapbook, Moorland-Spingarn Research Center, Howard University Archives, Howard University)

ultimately, that in northern sporting venues, Negro League baseball and barnstorming basketball teams, such as the Harlem Rens, fashioned distinctive patterns of play, even as the organizers of the National Negro Bowling Association and the American Tennis Association were crafting organizational plans and operational procedures that in every way possible mirrored the efforts of their white counterparts (who nevertheless remained steadfast segregationists until the 1950s and beyond).

The situation in the South was different from what prevailed elsewhere in the nation. There, the spotlight revealed the emergence of sport in the high schools and among black women, who also desired to demonstrate their athletic prowess and revel in the intensity of sporting competition. It illuminated the popularity of baseball, basketball, and track-and-field competition. Most intensely, though, the spotlight was directed toward the football programs of black colleges and universities, and especially on such rivalries as the annual Thanksgiving Day Lincoln-Howard football match-up. This contest—like Fisk versus Tuskegee, Hampton versus Morgan—was also a tremendous social occasion, drawing what one historian has called the "aristocrats of color" from near and far. Such rituals and spectacles largely resembled the festive atmosphere surrounding the Yale-Harvard game. Yet at a certain point, both the aggressiveness with which black educational institutions pursued victories on the playing fields and the ways that athletic concerns sometimes seemed to displace more important academic considerations triggered criticisms from on campus and beyond. The image of the African American athlete and, more important, the integrity of black higher education needed to be carefully guarded, argued racial reformers like Du Bois. After all, muscular assimilationism was a strategy, just as parallel institutions were a necessity—until the day, yet to come, when black Americans could compete with whites on a level playing field.

A

LEISURE AND RECREATION:
SOME CONSIDERATIONS

1. Emmett J. Scott / "Leisure Time and the Colored Citizen"

The proper use of leisure time and adequate community recreation programs were major concerns to many leaders in the African American community during the interwar period. Black educators, ministers, social workers, and recreation leaders viewed wholesome leisure activities and recreational pursuits as essential in curbing juvenile delinquency and fostering healthful and productive lives among African American children. Although they did not always agree with one another on the most beneficial pursuits, there seemed to be a unanimity of opinion among black leaders that organized recreation programs were invaluable to the increasing number of African American children confronted by the dangers and lure of city life and by mass urbanization.*

In the following document, Emmett J. Scott, secretary-treasurer at Howard University and former private secretary to Booker T. Washington, discusses the importance of leisure time and organized recreation programs available to African American children.** Elsewhere in his article, Scott had explained the dangers that can befall children if left to choose their own amusements, arguing "that the things that the undirected Negro child first learn are how to shoot craps, how to use vile language, how to fight, how to pilfer and how to commit other misdemeanors which tend to develop him into the type which makes up the criminal class." The way to combat this behavior and contribute to the healthy development and responsible citizenship of African American children, Scott notes here, is to provide adequate recreation facilities and wholesome community-wide recreation programs. Tellingly, in another portion of his discussion of wholesome recreation, Scott suggested the importance of diverting African American children from the "lower ideal" personified by the former heavyweight champion, Jack Johnson, and emulating a "new type" of ideal represented by such scholar-athletes as Sol Butler, Ed Gourdin, and Charles West.† Scott's comments are an important early use of well-known athletes as role models for younger members of the African American community.

---

* See W. H. Jones, *Recreation and Amusement.*

** For information on Scott, see Harlan, *Booker T. Washington,* esp. 260–61.

† Scott closely resembled his mentor, Booker T. Washington, in that he was appalled by Johnson's behavior, believing the heavyweight champion had harmed the race because of his refusal to acquiesce to white society and assume the role of the grateful black. See Roberts, *Papa Jack,* 97–98.

———————

In the discussion of the subject—Leisure Time and the Colored Citizen—I have been led to inquire as to how the leisure hours of the children of the negro [*sic*] race are spent, as it is the child of today who is to be the citizen of tomorrow. . . . Community recreation facilities for young and old have proved beyond cavil, their value as a deterrent of crime and also as a factor in the development of healthy and right-thinking citizenry. Statistics show that the community playgrounds have wrought wonders in the life of young and old, both with respect to health and in the lessening of criminal tendencies. School superintendents, health commissioners, police officials—so a report prepared by one of the workers of the Playground and Recreation Association of America states—all testify to the value of community-wide recreation. It is but fair to say, however, that the statistics showing these promising results are for the most part concerned with community service work among white rather than among colored children. . . .

The negro child must have facilities for recreation to the same degree as the white child, if he is to develop into the healthy and right-thinking citizen that the country needs and the nation requires. In the interest of the community and the nation, as well as in the interest of the negro child himself, there is urgent demand that greater facilities than are at present available be provided for wholesome recreation during the leisure hours. . . . And so there has grown up in America this new attitude which finds its expression in public playgrounds, in the organization of community amusements, in the inculcation throughout the entire body of young people in the community of substantially the same form of social inducement which the American college in modern times has substituted for the earlier system of social restraint. . . .

I would like to draw attention, if I may, to an article written by Mr. Attwell, presiding here this afternoon, the director of the work of the Playground Association among colored people, in which he very wisely called attention to this need of the larger consideration of colored people in the matter of the recreation movement in America. In the course of that article of his, he proceeds to say that because of the fact that several million colored people are living and will continue to live in close proximity to the rest of the people who reside in America, any movement for the betterment of our country's civilization or citizenship, whether it be for general health, for sanitation, for education, for religion or recreation, that does not promote a program to include those colored people, will eventually discover that social ills are quite similar to physical ailments; all of the parts of the body of the community must be treated, or at least all of those affected, if we desire to be entirely healthy. Mr. Attwell states that he has found no tendency on the part of colored people to migrate into neighborhoods inhabited by white people, merely because white people live there. If they move into such neighborhoods at all, he said, it is because improvements such as pavements, street lights, fire protection, sanitary plumbing and other modern comforts are there available, and because these sections are usually the first to be provided with ample park and play space and recreation facilities. The urge is because of the modern environment and not a desire for personal contact. And the keen desire on the part of the colored people for proper recreational facilities and guidance in towns and cities is in evidence in every locality where even a feigned gesture in this direction has been made.

But, as yet, comparatively small provision has been made for the needs of this respect. Playground and recreation parks are entirely lacking in many neighborhoods, even in the north where colored people reside; and in many sections of the south, play facilities have not been widely developed for either white or colored groups. An evidence of the desire of the colored people for recreation facilities is to be found in an editorial which recently appeared in a colored newspaper in an important southern city. This editorial, entitled *A Program for Negro Citizens,* called attention to the lack of facilities during the past summer by which the colored citizens could enjoy themselves. It urged colored citizens to begin formulating a program for civic improvement and recreation activities and suggested that the colored people get together and make known to the proper officials just what was needed in that particular city to make conditions among them a little better. It suggested a swimming pool, centrally located, tennis courts for the young men and women, properly equipped playgrounds for the younger children, under proper supervision, and, above all, more paved and sanitary streets for the children to play in and for negroes to live on. . . .

If I might undertake to voice an appeal in behalf of the colored people of this country, I would ask that larger consideration be given to this group of our American citizenry in the development of community recreation programs. It is suggested that when municipalities provide parks and playgrounds, the negro child have some opportunity to avail himself of those facilities. From actual practice it is known that the negro child, through lack of encouragement and sometimes because of definite prohibition, is practically and completely left out of consideration in both city planning and municipal maintenance of recreation centers in many sections of our country. In my opinion there should be increased consideration throughout the country given to the needs of the colored people in this matter of wholesome recreation. In the planning of recreation programs and in the employment of leaders, opportunity should be given for colored people to participate in the general programs. For they, more definitely than any others, have a sympathetic knowledge of the needs and the conditions of their people.

Emmett J. Scott, "Leisure Time and the Colored Citizen," *Playground* 18 (January 1925): 593–96.

B

BASEBALL BEHIND THE VEIL OF
SEGREGATION: NEGRO TEAMS AND LEAGUES

2. Beauregard F. Moseley / "A Baseball Appeal"

During the late nineteenth and early twentieth centuries, various African American entre-
preneurs attempted to form semiprofessional baseball teams and leagues in the cities of the
Northeast and Midwest. This was an arduous process, requiring the recruitment of inves-
tors, the solicitation of funds, and the search for winning combinations of players. Addition-
ally, black businesspeople needed to negotiate contracts with city governments and the pri-
vate owners of ballparks for the use of well-situated diamonds; if they chose to assemble
touring teams or full-scale leagues, they also needed to attend to travel and housing arrange-
ments—well aware that in such matters, Jim Crow had to be reckoned with on both sides of
the Mason-Dixon line. Finally, as is demonstrated here in Beauregard F. Moseley's "appeal,"
one of the tasks of the early sports entrepreneurs was to win public support. Assertions about
the intrinsic merits of sport as well as the significance of athletic competition as a symbol of
local pride and racial uplift were necessary parts in the creation of community conscious-
ness among the newly arriving blacks in the cities of the North as well as those who were
needed to sustain teams in southern cities.

In the event, Moseley's "appeal" to blacks for support of his proposed league did not prove
successful. Moseley was one of three men—Frank Leland and Rube Foster were the oth-
ers—who strived to establish semipro baseball in Chicago, and such a rivalry undermined
any notions of economic solidarity and the prospect of financial success. But his call for self-
help in the business of sport set the stage for later efforts to establish sporting enterprise on
a solid footing.*

Let those who would serve the race assist it in holding its own back up and encourage the national movement, for with it goes the hopes of the race in more than one
direction, for be it known that there is no greater leveler of men than manly sport,
such as baseball, which is admired by black and white, appeals to their pride as athletes and to their senses as the best test of physical and mental superiority and here
on the diamond before the frenzied anxious populace the Negro has the best oppor-

---

* For background on sport and community-formation, see Lomax, "Black Entrepreneurship in the National Pastime."

tunity of his present day advantage to display ability. . . . Men of the Race this appeal is to you and for you and yours.

Beauregard F. Moseley, "A Baseball Appeal of a Worthy Undertaking by Worthy Men; Read and Respond," *Chicago Broad Ax,* January 21, 1911.

3. Andrew "Rube" Foster / "Will Colored Baseball Survive the Acid Test?"

Andrew "Rube" Foster is one of the most important figures in the history of black baseball. Born in Calvert, Texas, in 1879, Foster was an outstanding pitcher who posted multiple fifty-win seasons during the early years of the twentieth century with such clubs as the Waco Yellow Jackets, Chicago Union Giants, and Philadelphia Giants. In 1907 Foster became player-manager of the Leland Giants after a salary dispute with the management of the Philadelphia Giants. He parted ways with owner Frank Leland after three years and formed his own club, which recorded a remarkable 128-6 record during the 1910 season. In 1911 Foster entered into a partnership with John Schorling, a white businessman and the son-in-law of the Chicago White Sox owner, Charles Comiskey, to form what would become the Chicago American Giants. The American Giants, with Foster serving as player-manager until 1917, when his playing days essentially ended, dominated black baseball for over a decade. In 1920 Foster made perhaps the most important move of his professional life when he founded the Negro National League.*

In the following selection from the Kansas City Sun, Foster discusses what needs to be done if the Negro National League's second season is to prove successful. He argues, among other things, that players, owners, and managers must learn to cooperate with one another if the future of the league is to be secured. Evidently, Foster did not take his own advice, because by 1925 his autocratic management style had alienated so many in black baseball that he felt the need to resign as the league's president and treasurer. The league would continue to exist until collapsing under the weight of the depression in 1931, but Foster's life would take a quick downward spiral following his resignation. In 1926 he suffered a nervous breakdown and was committed to a mental institution. He died just four years later in Kankakee, Illinois, without ever being released from confinement. Foster's sudden departure from baseball and descent into mental illness did not obliterate his many contributions to America's national pastime and as a result, he was inducted in 1981 into the National Baseball Hall of Fame in Cooperstown, New York.

———   ———

The coming season will either permanently secure baseball among us or will destroy the good that has been accomplished. Unfortunately, the hardest job that could be

---

* For information on Foster see Riley, *The Biographical Encyclopedia of the Negro Baseball Leagues;* Holway, *Blackball Stars;* Peterson, *Only the Ball Was White;* Rogosin, *Invisible Men;* Cottrell, *The Best Pitcher in Baseball;* Lomax, *Operating by Any Means Necessary.*

Andrew "Rube" Foster, c. 1920 (Courtesy National Baseball Hall of Fame Library, Cooperstown, N.Y.)

imposed on any human, was my acceptance to again head the league. This job is a gigantic position, and will test the best that is in me. Since I have accepted it, I am going to be successful regardless of any condition that may confront me. I am not easily discouraged and will work; failure is something I do not know the meaning of.

To be successful, all owners will have to do team work; they will have to pull together. Just the same as all leading clubs of players work together, their inside stuff is what will get them and baseball somewhere. Team work with me is the first letter of the alphabet and just as proficient as all my clubs have been in team work, discipline and deportment is just what I expect to develop the other owners to that same proficiency.

The most regrettable thing of a wonderful finish, breaking all records for Colored baseball, was the short-sightedness of some of the owners of our clubs. The Bacharachs have lost prestige which will take great effort to rebuild; the sending of the name Bacharachs to Cuba, with a combination of players from six different clubs, . . . was poor judgment. The wholesale fraud to the public that the Lincoln Giants are playing ball on the Coast, when in fact, only three players are out there, is bunk that the public could afford to not have, as they want the real results and truth. When they find this out, any legitimate story in the press, they will not believe and say, it's that such and such the paper said. The name Lincoln Giants has been benefited, inasmuch as the players on the coast that they have and the players they have from other clubs have played so far superior to what the Lincoln Giants can play, that they are the benefactor.

The public who pays the toll at the gate, want the real article of baseball both from the playing standpoint and the right way it should be played. Several instances the past season have clouded their memories and they have asked me: "Why do you allow such, if it is wrong?" There are many ways to cure things, and it is not policy at all times to do the thing you know to be right; circumstances should always alter cases. The main trouble is that many of the owners are parading under false colors; their patrons think that because they own the club, they know baseball and they do many things that are wrong to substantiate that belief. It makes them sick when some fan who thinks he knows the game says, "why is he letting Foster rough that over him." "Don't stand for it." The others sitting around think that because he has seen much baseball or attended league games, or was a rubber for some league club, he knows more than Foster and demand of the owner to stop Foster, when, in fact a man can see league baseball all his life and still be dumb or a man can look at a physician operate for years and then not operate; you must study and experiment with everything you want to know.

We were playing the Bacharachs for the championship at Chicago. Up came a decision that Manager Redding of the Bacharachs objected to. The umpire told him why he made the decision. Knowing Redding, I told that the decision was right, but some of the ignorant players with him said, "You are just letting Foster rub it in, don't stand for it." Redding said, "Well I'm not going to stand for it; I will take my club off." I said to the umpire, "It's alright with me, reverse the decision." He said, "Are you saying that because you think it wrong?" I said, "No, I just don't want them to quit." After the game he brought the rule book to them to show them that they were wrong and the next time such a decision comes up and the umpire rules it correctly, all of those that saw this one will call him a robber. Such men are not efficient to lead clubs of to-day. A decision came up at Kansas City that lost one game and series for us. A man was on first, one on second and one man out. The batter hit a fair ball that struck the umpire before touching a fielder. He allowed the run to score from second. I objected, explained the rule to the umpire, but he said, "I have been umpiring for various leagues and know the rules." I asked him to ask one of the sporting writers of the daily papers who had come down and both agreed that I was wrong. I finished the game under protest. After the game, I showed them the rule, saying that unless all bases were occupied, no run could score. The fans booed me at Kansas City; said that I could do that in Chicago, but could not rough that stuff over them.

I am a believer that honesty is the best policy and will not allow anyone to lead me from this belief. My success has been that everything I do I do it knowing that I am right. Where there is a benefit of doubt, I never argue the point. The public at Chicago once thought I was taking advantage of clubs, but as they were educated up to the fine points of the game, they readily saw that I was doing the right thing and where they booed me, they applauded.

The jealousy that exists between players, manager and owners must be a thing of the past. All of our future depends on just how much cooperation each will give to the other. I have never accepted any position that in any way I could be used as a figure-head. This goes with the job I have not accepted; all must pull together, agree on a policy, right or wrong, play the team work behind whatever is accepted as the best policy. No player is greater than the game that created him, no owner more supreme than the confidence his patrons have in him. The public and fans have had 24 consecutive years to consider me; their great confidence in me has stirred me to greater things; instead of my hold diminishing with them, with understanding, they rallied tenfold for me. I would not betray this confidence to be President of the United States. Now, lest all owners, players and the public pull together, with your combined cooperation, I will, with your assistance make the National Association of Colored Professional Baseball Players the ship, all other opposition the sea. Something that when your children seek employment or want to become associated with, regardless as to their education, you can hope eternal, express your co-operated desire and feel that something great is to become of your son's future, where your mother, sister, wife and sweetheart can say: I am sorry, I have an engagement, but my son is playing ball today, and we must all go to see him.

Andrew "Rube" Foster, "Will Colored Baseball Survive the Acid Test?" *Kansas City Sun*, January 29, 1921.

4. Chester L. Washington / "Satchel's Back in Town"

Leroy "Satchel" Paige was arguably the most famous player in black baseball. Born in 1906 in Mobile, Alabama, Paige had a difficult early childhood, eventually being sent to reform school after being caught stealing costume jewelry. His stay proved beneficial because that is where he honed his pitching skills and nurtured his love for baseball. After his release, Paige pitched for several semiprofessional teams before beginning his professional career in 1926 with Chattanooga, Tennessee, of the Negro Southern League. Two years later, Paige joined the Birmingham Black Barons where he posted a 28-18 record over three seasons. He joined the Nashville Elite Giants early in 1931 and later that year signed with the Pittsburgh Crawfords, the club organized by perhaps the most prominent black sports entrepreneur of his age, Gus Greenlee.

After achieving enormous popularity with the Crawfords, Paige became involved in numerous salary disputes, which forced him to play over the next few seasons with clubs elsewhere in the United States, as well as in Santo Domingo and Mexico. In 1939, he joined the Kansas City Monarchs, leading the team to five Negro American League (NAL) pen-

Satchel Paige (Courtesy
National Baseball Hall of
Fame Library, Coopers-
town, N.Y.)

nants in some eight years. Paige got his first taste of major league baseball in 1948, when he
was signed to a contract by Bill Veeck of the Cleveland Indians. In 1965, he became, at age
fifty-nine, the oldest player ever to pitch in the major leagues when he hurled three innings
for the Kansas City A's. Paige became the first Negro League player elected to the National
Baseball Hall of Fame in 1971.*

The following document describes Paige's role as black baseball's greatest gate attraction.

---

* The extensive secondary literature on Paige includes Rogosin, *Invisible Men*; Bruce, *Kansas City Monarchs*; Peterson,
Only the Ball Was White; Holway, *Blackball Stars*. See also one of Paige's autobiographies with David Lipman, *Maybe I'll
Pitch Forever.*

Here Chester Washington correctly notes that Paige created more fan interest than any player in black baseball, a result of his superior pitching skills, individual performance style, and the fact that he was a "natural showman as spectacular as a circus and as colorful as a rainbow." Washington's comments are important because they seem to lend credence to the argument of some scholars who contend that Paige and other black athletes emphasized an improvisational style characteristic of African American culture. This improvisational style, according to some cultural commentators, drew its origins from the same roots as jazz and served several possible functions, including a device for masculine self-expression in a society that has historically limited the opportunities for such expression among black males.*

Like Lulu, Satchel's back in town!

The long, lean Leroy "Satchel" Paige, prodigal son of the Pittsburgh Crawfords, who shoots a baseball across the plate like an expert machine-gunner, is glad to be "home." The stellar Satchel must have missed his admiring "rabble" and the "boys" out in the wilds of Bismarck, North Dakota last year, so he's back to sparkle in the National Association firmament.

Like Joe Louis and Jesse Owens, Paige is another one of those stars who fell in Alabama. Little Leroy was born in a modest farm in Mobile, Alabama, not far from the Brown Bomber's birthplace, on the night of August 26, 1907 [*sic*]. He grew up like a weed in a marsh. When he came to age, he scraped the skies at 6'3". His reach is like the long arm of the law. The satchel-like shape of his feet earned him the nickname that he bears today. His first pitching assignment was with the Chattanooga Black Lookouts of the Southern League in 1925, where his speed gave him a running start toward a spectacular career. Later, he joined the Birmingham Black Barons, where his ability gained him national recognition.

Last year, we jumped on Satchel with both feet and advocated his exile from the National Association when he treated his two-year contract like a "scrap of paper" and walked out on the Crawfords. We contended that he was setting a bad precedent for the league. And we have no apologies to make for our stand. But now, he's back in the fold again, and we're going to chronicle his praises as one of the greatest speedball pitchers in the game today.

"Satch" holds the distinction of being one of the hardest players in the game to handle, but also the unique honor of being Negro League baseball's biggest gate and name attraction. He is to colored baseball what Dizzy Dean is to the majors, with many debates developing as to which player is the "dizzier" at times.

But Paige has many virtues. In addition to being a brilliant pitcher, he has "that certain thing" that the fans like. Whether it's "it" or "that" or maybe "that's it," we're not sure, but whatever he has, the pasteboard purchasers go for it in a big way. On the diamond, Satchel "outsteps" Stepin' Fetchit on the screen. He's a natural show-

---

* On the innovative style of many black athletes, see Majors, "Cool Pose." See also "The Black Myth: Basketball as Jazz," in Novak, *The Joy of Sports*, 98–114; Greenfield, "The Black and White Truth about Basketball."

man as spectacular as a circus and as colorful as a rainbow. Added to this, an amusing nonchalance marks his every move even under the most trying circumstances. It was a crucial moment in the East-West game of 1934 when two picked all-star teams were vying for national honors. There's a man on second, no outs, and no score. A signal from the East's manager and a tall, shuffling shadow moves slowly from the dugout toward the pitcher's box. He ambles along slowly, like a pallbearer in a funeral procession. "It's Satchel Paige," the crowd roars. "It won't be long now," someone in the stands echoed. And it wasn't . . . after Satchel got ready to pitch. He picked up a handful of dirt . . . rubbed the ball . . . glanced indifferently at third . . . looked sidewise at the catcher for a signal . . . shook his head up and down slowly . . . wound up like a man cranking a "Model T Ford," and then finally let one go. It shot across the middle of the plate like a bullet and the batter apparently never saw it. Three men faced Satchel in that memorable inning, and three men walked back to the dugout while the scorekeeper chalked up three "S.O.s." The crowd roared its approval . . . and Satchel's's team won the game 1-0. Pitching against the Dayton Ducks only a few days ago, the Satchel diamond circus wheeled into action again.

As if to prove that one of the overanxious Duck batters was "all wet" about his idea that he could get a hit, Satchel yelled to catcher Josh Gibson:

"What one of y'all you [calling for] now, Josh?"

Gibson dropped two fingers below his mitt.

"Well, there you are," Satch called, as he shot it across the plate.

The bewildered batter reached in vain like a man reaching for the moon and the ball whizzed by.

"How'd you like that?" the sweet Satch smiled.

Again the crowd roared and, of course, the Crawfords won.

Among Satchel's many achievements include the decisive defeat of several teams composed of major league stars, striking out 18 in one game and completely shutting out the Homestead Grays for the first time in their history.

The return of Satchel to the Crawfords will greatly enhance the drawing power of this already popular club. And Owner Gus Greenlee says Satch is worth every penny he's spent on him. Especially in the east, fans are practically Crawford crazy, and when Satch sweeps into town with them, it will be like the coming of the circus. Already, New York is waiting with keen expectancy the triumphant return of that elongated, streamlined pitching sensation who beat our Slim Jones of Philly in 1934 in the Yankee Stadium game. And Satch is also anxious to show his wares again in Gotham this Sunday when the Pittsburgh Crawfords appear there in their league opener with Alexander Pompez's New York Cubans.

With Paige back in the league, he may practically be the Moses who will help to lead Negro baseball into the promised land of economic prosperity. At any rate, when Satchel comes to town, watch the turnstiles click.

Chester L. Washington, "Satchel's Back in Town," *Pittsburgh Courier-Journal,* May 9, 1936.

5. Nat Trammell / "Baseball Classic—East vs. West"

In 1933, Gus Greenlee, the widely connected numbers king, peddler of bootlegged liquor, and owner of the Pittsburgh Crawfords, revived the Negro National League (NNL) and inaugurated the East-West All Star Game. The latter event became the centerpiece of black baseball, an extremely important social and athletic spectacle in the African American community that drew literally thousands of fans from across the country each year. Originally a game between players from only the NNL, it evolved into a contest between players representing both the NNL and Negro American League (NAL). The East-West All Star Game, which was usually played in Comiskey Park in Chicago and remained in existence until 1950, highlighted the outstanding players in Negro League baseball. In fact, the black press, most notably the Pittsburgh Courier, *utilized the game to showcase the talents of players in the Negro Leagues and convince major league owners that those players had the requisite ability to play at the highest level of competition.**

The following document, an article by Nat Trammell from the Colored Baseball and Sports Monthly, *a short-lived but nicely edited magazine that covered baseball and other sports of African Americans, discusses various aspects of the 1934 East-West All Star Game. Although he wrote this piece before the game reached its height of popularity, Trammell was obviously very enthusiastic about the early success of the sporting extravaganza. The article, combined with many other pieces written about the contest, reminds us that the East-West All Star Game was much more important to African Americans than was the Negro League World Series, which had been played sporadically since 1924. This was just the opposite in major league baseball, where the World Series took precedence, and resulted from a number of factors, including the economic reality of the African American community, the structural problems of Negro League baseball itself, and the social appeal of the all-star game. While the Negro League World Series was seriously weakened by the lack of franchise identity in black baseball and the fact that African Americans were financially incapable of supporting a series of games, the East-West All Star Game achieved success because it involved black baseball's greatest players, was held in a major league ballpark in the middle of the season, and provided an ideal setting for black fans to socialize and to mark their presence in the world of sports. Within the constraints of a segregated society, such rituals of athletic achievement—flamboyant social affairs and "classic" displays of sporting excellence—spoke emphatically to race pride.***

Whenever the word Classic is mentioned, adjusting one's mind to the proper stimuli is another problem. The East-West game at Chicago was one of those classics where you must draw upon your aesthetic appreciation to fully digest its beauty.

---

* For information on the East-West All Star Game, see Rogosin, *Invisible Men,* 25–26, 96–97, 189, 218; White, *Creating the National Pastime,* 139–43; Chadwick, *When the Game Was Black and White,* 97–99; P. Dixon, *The Negro Baseball League,* esp. 160–67.

** See White, *Creating the National Pastime,* 139–43.

Comiskey Park, Chicago, last August 26th, was the scene of the battle. It was a beautiful and suggestive day, the sky blue and the sun radiant with baseball enthusiasm. 25,000 inhabitants of Chicago, peaceful and otherwise, donned their best sport togs and planted themselves in the cool, spacious stands of the great ball area.

The necessary ceremonies had to take place as befitting all such occasions. The bands had to play Old Glory, the flag must rise, the photographers must satisfy the eyes of their camera, the ground keepers must knock away every match stem and iron out every hill one-tenth of an inch high. They sprinkle a little H_2O here and there. Then the umpires, all clad in the darkest hues of blue, confer with the opposing captains as to how those rules must be adjusted to benefit or handicap both as the case might be. After all this formality the umpires adjourn to their respective positions, and a white pill tossed out to start the melee. The Western team, acting as home club, trots onto the field, and the elongated Mr. Trent tosses five over the platter to test his accuracy. Up steps Whosis, and the game is on.

But whatta game and what a thrill. When Bell stole second base and Wilson of the Philadelphia Stars singled to break up a six pitchers duel, you should have heard the mob, they forgot themselves temporarily. They made the promoters know that they could enjoy such baseball the rest of their natural lives.

Who knows that they had not seen the greatest ball game ever played. 1-0 indicates a perfect ball game or near perfect, anyway.

The great throw by Crutchfield to nip Suttles at the plate will live in the memories of the fans for days without end. Thrilling plays and moments like these when big crowds are there naturally carry a long ways in one's mental faculties.

Baseball classics are rarer than football classics. There are football classics in every section of the country practically every Saturday in the season. But in baseball it is a treat that elevates one's anticipation beyond the average level. The fans are overexcited at classics and every play has its incentive, but did you stop to think of the ball players executing these plays. These boys are over-thrilled, over-awed and keyed up to a higher nervous pitch than the fan.

Ball players in classics and championship battles are usually nervous and excited, not to the extent they are fearful, but that they produce unusual feats at this time because of this awesomeness.

Manager Richard Lundy, premier shortstop of the Eastern Stars, acclaimed these yearly classics the greatest events in his playing career. And he is one of the type that can do seemingly impossible deeds in the shadows of great crowds. Manager Lundy, at present connected with the Newark Dodgers, was always a master showman and great performer when the gallery was packed. Most ball players are greater when the crowds are large. They rise to stardom in a split second.

The West was represented by Mr. David Malarcher as manager, a very fine, gentlemanly ball player and at one time the greatest third baseman in the business. Malarcher was a product of Rube Foster and a member of that formidable ball club. Malarcher has that winning spirit and was an aggressive star.

These two popular managers met in friendly combat to match their wares in that great game. Two greater men could not have been selected. This was indeed a great honor for any manager. The East-West classic is the greatest event that could be put over by anyone for the benefit of promoting interest in Colored baseball. This game is an incentive to young ball players as well as those who are already supposed to be made. This single adventure is causing many ball players to improve their style and ability. It gives them something in which to look forward. The average Colored player has been interested more or less in his salary and what it would be, but now they all are trying to make the East-West classic.

This great idea is the highest achievement of baseball and marks a new era in the development of the game. The Negro National League is responsible for this idea. Mr. W. A. Greenlee is president. Mr. R. A. Coles, of the Chicago American Giants, and Mr. Tom Wilson, of the Nashville Elite Giants, are co-workers of this gigantic plan. Along with the deeds of great ball players there should be some living appreciation shown these great club owners for their interest and enthusiasm in the development of the game. Today we have only two or three clubs owned and operated by our Nordic friends. The time is fast approaching when all clubs will be controlled and owned by our own people. There is something peculiar about some of our white owners. They work a ball player cheap and then offer him no publicity or chance to develop himself. That's the treatment you get for playing ball with the wrong owners. That psychology is dead. The new Colored man thinks differently now. They are too wise to be made a fool of and taken unfair advantage of by someone of a different nationality. Fans and ball players alike patronize those ball clubs that are offering opportunities for advancement and creating a new livelihood for the ball player who wants to develop himself.

It is a source of joy to us to learn of the success of the East-West game. Mr. Greenlee is a real business man and a baseball promoter. He has recently pulled a game here in New York at the Yankee Stadium between four of the greatest Colored teams in the world today. This venture was more than a financial success. It was an eye opener to those who thought baseball was on the outgo. This attraction was even greater than the East-West classic. If you missed it you missed two of the greatest games ever played at Yankee Stadium. Four of the greatest Colored teams in the world were represented. How would you enjoy a combination of any two pitted against the Giants or the Detroit Tigers. Schoolboy Rowe and Satchel Paige or Hubbell and Slim Jones would really produce a show. If you witnessed the East-West game at Chicago, and the four team doubleheader you are convinced that Colored baseball players rank on a par with any major leaguer. The East-West affair was a game of all stars from the East and West. The four team doubleheader was played with each team operating complete. Fans who have witnessed these games pledge their support to all Colored clubs in 1935.

Nat Trammell, "Baseball Classic—East vs. West," *Colored Baseball and Sports Monthly* 1 (October 1934): 6.

C

AN ARRAY OF VENUES—AND ACCOMPLISHMENTS

6. The Harlem Rens, "Incomparable Courteers"

Of the many outstanding black basketball teams in interwar America, the most famous were not affiliated with educational institutions, YMCAs, or other service organizations. Rather, they were professional barnstorming quintets who traveled the country playing against almost anyone willing to meet them on the hardwoods. The best of these teams, and certainly the one that most fully caught the imagination of the black sporting public, was the New York Renaissance Five. Taking its name from Harlem's Renaissance Ballroom, the team was founded in 1923 by Robert L. Douglas, an enormously popular and business-savvy black West Indian immigrant. The Rens played the top teams in the country, including the original Celtics, Philadelphia SPHAS (named for the South Philadelphia Hebrew Association), Harlem Globetrotters, Detroit Eagles, Akron Firestones, Savoy Big Five, and Chicago Collegians. The Rens, with an extraordinary group of players on their roster, amassed over twenty-four hundred victories during twenty-seven years of play. In 1933, the Rens beat the vaunted Celtics in seven of eight games, the following year won eighty-eight consecutive games while posting an overall record of 127-7, and in 1939 won the First World Championship Tournament for Professional Basketball. In honor of their great record and contributions to the sport, the Rens were elected, as a team, to the Naismith Memorial Basketball Hall of Fame in 1963.*

The following article provides brief descriptions of the players on the Rens team of 1929. The four most important players described are Clarence (Fats) Jenkins, James (Pappy) Ricks, Eyre (Bruiser) Saitch, and Bill Yancey, who combined with Charles T. (Tarzan) Cooper, John (Casey) Holt, and William (Wee Willie) Smith to form "The Magnificent Seven" that would lead the Rens to their greatest triumphs during the 1930s.** Although their day-to-day experiences are not mentioned in the article, the lives they led as barnstormers in early twentieth-century America is an essential part of their history. Unwelcome in the white organized leagues and not fortunate enough to have their own league like their black counterparts in baseball, the Rens were almost constantly on the road playing semipro teams in small towns

---

* For information on the Rens, see Peterson, *Cages to Jump Shots*, esp. 95–103; Rayl, "The New York Renaissance Professional Black Basketball Team"; Henderson, *The Black Athlete.*

** Several members of the Rens were outstanding all-around athletes who distinguished themselves in other sports. For example, Fats Jenkins and Bill Yancey played for several years with the New York Black Yankees and other teams in black baseball. Eyre Saitch was a champion tennis player who captured several American Tennis Association (ATA) titles, among others. See Rayl, "The New York Renaissance Professional Black Basketball Team," 518–23.

Harlem Renaissance basketball team, 1925; founder Robert L. Douglas, inset (Courtesy Basketball Hall of Fame, Springfield, Mass.)

and cities in the East and Midwest, and occasionally the deep South. These long trips, which were concentrated between the months of November and April, were arduous enough, but as black men in that era they were forced to endure the racial slights and discrimination experienced by others in their community. While on the road, the Rens players were denied access to "white only" drinking fountains and restrooms, were prohibited from frequenting restaurants and hotels that catered to whites only, and always had to be sensitive to offending white men for fear of violent retribution. Because of these circumstances, particularly on the trips south, the Rens players often had to depend on local blacks for meals, transportation, and sleeping accommodations.

A Natural Attraction

Sport chroniclers of the future must count the Celtics and Renaissance Fives among the greatest pro ensembles that ever played. The Colored team, built around the wonderful Clarence ("Fat") Jenkins, is really an all star aggregation—though it took a few patient years for Bob Douglas to round them into the formidable machine opponents throughout the United States find them to be.

No discussion of present day professional basketball stars is complete unless due credit is given one of the finest little players and gentleman the game has ever produced in the person of Clarence Jenkins—who is just plain "Fat" to his countless admirers of both groups. Not much taller in stature than "Nemo Leibold"—clever little Chicago White Sox outfielder of some years back, Jenkins is rated the second fastest man in basketball and by not a few commentators as without a peer for sheer speed, agility, and shiftiness. Only Davie Banks of the "Celtics" is considered over the mighty Colored star when the discussion of speed on the court comes up. Built along the general lines of old Joe Walcott, "Fats" can maintain the diggiest pace ever attempted by a human being for forty minutes against the best type of basketball player followers of the last quarter century have seen. His teammates fairly worship him and he is an inspiration when the fight becomes hardest. Captain Hilton Slocum, dubbed the "Boy Wonder" during the years that he jumped center for the great Spartan Braves, is a floor man par excellence. So wonderful are his muscle reflexes and coordination, that he makes hard plays appear simple and as if he were trying as hard as the rest of the crew. Slocum is never outfoxed by an opponent and as a diagnoser of plays and all around tactician—he rates high up with the game's best thinkers. Harold Mayers—a guarding demon if we know anything about the Zeppelin and that sort of thing, is a rough smashing type of player likely to demoralize the system of any club. "Hugo" gets in there and snags a pass like Sam White of Princeton was accustomed to pick up fumbles on the gridiron against Harvard and Yale. Bob Douglas grabbed Mayers from the Old St. Christopher Club when he had numerous flaws, and developed him into one of the best guards in the entire history of basketball—and we don't mean perhaps.

Yes, Mayers belongs with the best that ever did it—and is deserving of the flowers, etc. "Pappy" Ricks is the best shot in basketball. A wiry iron man type of player, he is the triple threat of basketball, being positively poisonous once inside the fifteen foot mark and from any angle position. Ricks just manoeuvers into position and with a smile that goes from ear to ear drops in those sickening whistle like baskets that must sound like the crack of doom to all and sundry opponents.

Sanders is the most improved center man in the pro ranks, and an artist at dropping markers with his arms upstretched over an opponent's head and in getting the tap. "Longy" is a whale of a floor man, and the word quit is not in his vocabulary as well as it is lacking among the rest of the upstanding greats who are feared country-wide.

Saitch at Best

If Eyre Saitch, former National Colored Tennis Champion will only play as he did against the Savoy Club of Chicago, the Celtics will imagine they are up against a mechanical man and not a genuine flesh and blood one. This powerful young giant was a host by himself in that particular game and for the past two months has been exhibiting a brand of court play on a par with the best. Monroe and Hill are smart, courageous reserves who can fill in at a moment's notice.

Bill Yancey Signed

Bill Yancey, sensational star of the Philadelphia Giants is to appear in the lineup of Renaissance against the Celtics for the series. This is a ten strike, as Yancey a player of the Jenkins type is one of the rear wizards of the court. Yancey will appear at short-stop for the Lincoln Giants Baseball Club this coming summer—Wotta man!

"Incomparable Courteers," *Inter-State Tattler*, April 5, 1929.

7. Gerald Norman / "National American Tennis Association Championships"

One of the most important things about the interwar years was the emergence of a national sporting culture in the African American community that placed great emphasis on admin-istrative oversight and bureaucracies. While sport in the white community essentially evolved from an informal, unorganized activity to a more highly structured and organized enter-prise during the latter stages of the nineteenth century, the same process did not take place in the African American community until the early decades of the twentieth century. The increasing number of blacks in large urban settings, the expansion of sport as a consumer product, and a continuing racial segregation in American society all contributed to the found-ing of more elaborate sporting organizations in the black community that codified rules, formalized playing schedules and tournaments, and provided financial support at each level of competition. These organizations, while providing important evidence of black self-reli-ance and bringing middle-class African Americans together to share in the excitement of athletic contests, were very similar in both name and administrative structure to the vari-ous white sporting organizations founded earlier. The Colored Intercollegiate Athletic As-sociation (1912), American Tennis Association (1916), Negro National League (1926), and the United Golfers Association (1926) are just a few of these organizations.*

The following document describes the results of the 1928 National American Tennis As-sociation championships. Gerald Norman makes clear that the championships at Borden-town, New Jersey, like the great football classics between historically black colleges, the Penn Relays, the East-West All Star Games, and so many other sporting events in the African American community, were seemingly as much a grand social gathering for the upper reaches of black society as an opportunity to determine tennis supremacy. He explains that the "en-tertainments provided were of the highest order, and society came in large numbers from Washington, New York, Baltimore, Philadelphia, Boston, Trenton, Newark, Chicago, and many other centers to witness the matches and enjoy the festivities." Norman also provides information on famous players from the world of black tennis largely unknown to people in the white community. There were, among others, Eyre Saitch, the great all-around athlete who became most famous as a member of the Renaissance Five basketball team; Isadora Channels, four-time winner of the American Tennis Association (ATA) women's singles ti-tle, who also starred in basketball for the Chicago Romas; Reginald Weir, the outstanding player from City College of New York who captured several different championships over a

---

* For information on the all-black sporting organizations in the early part of the twentieth century, see D. Wiggins, "Critical Events Affecting Racism in Athletics"; Ashe, *Hard Road to Glory;* Chalk, *Pioneers of Black Sport.*

Finalists, mixed doubles, National American Tennis Association, 1947. Left to right: Harold Mitchell, Oakland, California; Ora Washington, Philadelphia; R. Walter Johnson, Lynchburg, Virginia; Althea Gibson, Wilmington, North Carolina (R. S. Darnaby Collections, Tuskegee University Archives)

long and distinguished career; and Talley Holmes of Washington, D.C., who had captured the first ATA men's singles championship in 1917 at Baltimore's Druid Hill Park.

———

"See you in Bordentown," the parting words heard so often for several weeks previous to the week of August 20–25th. And why not? The National Championships of the American Tennis Association were conducted at Bordentown, New Jersey, during that week.

The Manual Training Institute is one of the few ideal places for staging an event of such wide importance, and one that commands the interest of the entire Negro population of the country. The situation on a bluff overlooking the Delaware River, its beautiful and spacious campus, its wooded lawns, attractive dormitories and well-built courts serve to make conditions as ideal as possible for accommodating players and enthusiasts from every section of the United States.

The Tournament in itself was one of the best conducted by the Association. There were two distinguishing features which stand out in a most favorable comparison, and which in a way eclipse the record of the previous year—the entrants and the playing exhibited was of a much higher caliber—the best in the history of the Association from the Juniors up to the Men's Singles event.

The lists contained many champions of their respective sections, as well as five former National Champions in Men's Singles, such as Tally [*sic*] Holmes, Sylvester Smith, and Ted Thompson of Washington, D.C.; Edgar G. Brown of Indianapolis, Ind., and Eyre Saitch of New York City. There was also Reggie Weir, New York's Junior Champion, and two former Women Champions in Miss Isadora Channels of Chicago, Ill., and Miss Lulu Ballard of Philadelphia, Pa.

The local champions included James Stocks, Champion of California, Dr. E. Downing, Southern Champion, Richard Hudlin, Southeast Champion, Mrs. L. Wade, New York's Champion, and Miss Eunice Brown, Southeast Champion, the two latter in Women's Singles.

The above players, along with many other representing the best colored talent of the country, exhibited a brand of tennis, that would command respect in any tournament, outside of the National Championships at Forest Hills.

The Finals between E. G. Brown and T. Thompson staged on Saturday afternoon before a brilliant gathering of over a thousand spectators, was halted by rain, after a few games had been played. The following morning play was continued on a wet court with Brown in top form. His strokes were deep and well placed, and to the surprise of all, he had no difficulty in returning Thompson's sliced drives on his backhand. Ted played good tennis, but Brown was once more playing a carefully planned game. He passed Thompson, if he came to the net, and repeatedly bested him in the many driving duels. Brown lost the first set 6-3, then won the next two. Thompson came back and won the fourth, but it was his last great effort, as Brown, playing craftily and with confidence, won the fifth and deciding set with little trouble. He had regained the National Championship after a lapse of four years, and with it, the valuable three-leg Trophy donated by Dr. B. M. Rhetta of Baltimore.

Junior Singles—This event proved as interesting as any other, owing to the fact that these youngsters display a brand of tennis equal to, if not better than most of the seniors as a group. They stroke exceedingly well, have splendid form, plenty of pace and speed, and exhibit creditable style in handling their rackets. They are the champions of the near future and bear watching.

Reggie Weir of New York proved the king of them all, as he went through the tournament without losing a set. He defeated A. Walker, of Baltimore, a most promising youngster of 14 years, in the finals, 6-1, 6-4.

The Tournament on the whole was a most successful one in every way. It is the only National athletic event among Negroes, and it attracts players and spectators from all parts of the country. The demand for accommodations on the campus of the school was so great, that although over four hundred people were provided for in advance, on Saturday before the Tournament every room had been reserved. The overflow was sent to Bordentown village, Trenton, Philadelphia and nearby towns.

The entertainments provided were of the highest order, and society came in large numbers from Washington, New York, Baltimore, Philadelphia, Boston, Trenton, Newark, Chicago, and many other centers to witness the matches and enjoy the festivities. The big ATA Ball on Friday night was a gala event, and served as an appetizer for the Finals on Saturday. Unfortunately, the rain spoiled a beautiful setting, and what promised to be one of the greatest in the history of Negro Tennis.

Gerald Norman, "National American Tennis Association Championships" *Opportunity* 6 (October 1928): 306–7.

8. J. Elmer Reed on the National Negro Bowling Association

Racial discrimination found its way into bowling just as it did in other sports during the first half of the twentieth century. The most visible manifestation was the inability of African Americans to become members or use the alleys under the jurisdiction of the American Bowling Congress (ABC), the reigning national organization in control of the sport. The ABC, like the Professional Golf Association (PGA) or United States Lawn Tennis Association (USLTA), excluded African Americans from its organization solely on the basis of race. As a result of these racially discriminatory practices, the National Negro Bowling Association (NNBA) was organized in 1939 to provide opportunities as well as facilities for African Americans to participate in the sport. The NNBA, which eventually changed its name to the National Bowling Association, is still in existence today. Unlike some separate sports organizations in the African American community, the NNBA survived the integration process (specifically the desegregation of the ABC in 1950) to become a thriving institution that by 2000 had some thirty thousand members.*

The following document, a letter written in March 1942 by J. Elmer Reed, the NNBA secretary, to Art Carter, the highly regarded sports editor of the Baltimore Afro-American, *was a response to a previous letter from Carter. Reed briefly provides details on the founding of the NNBA, the financial success of the organization, and membership data. It is apparent that he was extremely proud of the NNBA, undoubtedly heartened by the fact that the organization was a thriving institution that did not have to depend on white patrons for its existence. To Reed, the NNBA provided the necessary structure to promote the sport of bowling and epitomized the self-help, economic independence, and racial solidarity so important to middle-class African Americans at the time.*

——— ———

---

* For information on the NNBA see Dent, *In Search of Black America,* 357–72.

Mr. Art Carter
Sports Editor
Afro-American
Baltimore, MD

Dear Mr. Carter:

I am very sorry that I did not answer your letter before but I have been very busy conducting a Head Pin Tournament in Cleveland.

The NNBA is the father of Negro Bowling and the only organization representing our group in this sport. We formed this organization to bring all race bowling under one head, and improve upon the conditions surrounding our people that liked this game. The American Bowling Congress, better known as the ABC, will not permit Negroes to join and alleys under jurisdiction of the ABC enforce the rules. After six years of this, we formed the NNBA.

The NNBA is an organization set up to protect all Negro investors, we supply the business. In every city where Negroes have built alleys, as soon as they open their doors the business is waiting, they do not have to look for it. All we ask is for the owners to cooperate and maintain their alleys for the best interests of bowling.

In four years we have over $450,000 invested in Negro owned and operated alleys. The United Recreation, Inc. 8217 Cedar Ave. Cleveland, O., 10 Brunswick alleys, new building cost $65,000. Fun Bowl 750 N. West St., Indianapolis, Ind. 12 Brunswick alleys, new building cost $78,000. Paradise Bowl 640 Adams Ave., Detroit, Mich. 20 Brunswick alleys, new building $250,000. Play Bowl 1206 Linn St., Cincinnati, Ohio 4 complete and 8 to complete after war. These four alleys have paid salaries to employees over $100,000 in 1942. The alleys owned by white and operated by Negroes I do not have any record of salaries but they are doing a great business. But I will tell you that we leave every white alley as soon as a Negro builds one in that city.

Enclosed is the NNBA constitution and the results of our last tournament in Indianapolis, Ind. also scores of all tournaments on page following the list of officers. Mr. Oscar Harrison of Chicago has four 300 games in league play. The high score list for this season will not be available until June.

Scores to date		
Lemar Collins of Chicago	298	
Lloyd Thomas of Cleveland	277	
Teams		
Log Cabin, Cleveland, Ohio	3 games 2896	one game 1052
Douglas Club, Cleveland Ohio		one game 1053
Sheridan Williams, Chicago	3 games 2885	one game 1077

The NNBA has 1,800 members registered to date, some cities late. Over 300 teams bowling weekly in city leagues in Cleveland, Cincinnati, Columbus and Toledo, Ohio: Ann Arbor and Detroit, Mich.: Chicago, Ill: Indianapolis, Ind.: Racine, Wis.: Kansas City, Mo.: Louisville, Ky.: Harrisburg, Pa.: Wilmington, Del.: Elizabeth and Rahway, New Jersey.

I will be glad to send any further information you may desire.

Yours for better sports,

J. Elmer Reed, Sec. NNBA

Letter from J. Elmer Reed to Art Carter, March 5, 1942, Art Carter Collection, Moorland-Spingarn Research Center, Howard University.

9. Frank A. Young / Cum Posey: Athlete and Entrepreneur

Cumberland Posey made significant contributions to black sport in Pittsburgh and on the national level during the 1930s and 1940s. Born in 1891, in Homestead, Pennsylvania, Posey gained considerable recognition for his athletic accomplishments while a student at both Holy Ghost (now Duquesne University) and Pennsylvania State University. However, as Rob Ruck makes clear in his Sandlot Seasons: Sport in Black Pittsburgh, *Posey first gained a national reputation in the "crowded, steamy gymnasiums and second-floor dance halls of club basketball."* In 1911 he founded the Monticellos, a local black Pittsburgh basketball team that would eventually become well known as the Loendi Club. With Posey serving as floor general on the court and acting as both financial manager and promoter of the team, the Loendi Club became a championship basketball quintet that went four consecutive years without losing to another black team. In addition to his involvement with the Loendi Club, Posey first played for and then became owner of the Homestead Grays, one of the most powerful teams in black baseball. The Grays, with such players as Cool Papa Bell, Josh Gibson, Smokey Joe Williams, and Oscar Charleston on the roster at various times throughout its history, was a famous club that regularly defeated black baseball's greatest teams. Unfortunately, like many clubs in black baseball, the Grays had a very difficult time turning a profit. The only time the club apparently ended the season in the black was 1941, the third year it split time playing at Forbes Field in Pittsburgh and Griffith Stadium in Washington, D.C.*

Here, in the Chicago Defender, *one of the most highly regarded sports journalists of his generation, Frank A. Young, pays homage to Posey shortly after the death of the athlete and entrepreneur of black sport in 1946. Tellingly, Young's celebration of Posey's life and accomplishments highlights connections between playing fields and the African American community. Even as other sportswriters sang his praises, thousands of people of both races paid their respects as Posey's body lay in state; his funeral was attended by such luminaries as J. B. Martin, president of the Negro American League; Gus Greenlee, the Pittsburgh Crawfords owner; David L. Lawrence, mayor of Pittsburgh; and Art Rooney, owner of the Pittsburgh Steelers.***

---

* Ruck, *Sandlot Seasons*, 126.

** The best information on Posey can be found in Ruck, *Sandlot Seasons*, esp. 124–36, 170–73, 179–81, 186–88. See also Rogosin, *Invisible Men,* esp. 15, 43, 52–53, 107, 127.

Cum Posey, standing on the left, owner of the Homestead Grays, spring 1931 (Art Carter Papers, Moorland-Spingarn Research Center, Howard University Archives, Howard University)

That was Cum Posey.

And now he is no more.

He left this world like he lived . . . asking no favors. That was the way Cumberland Willis Posey, owner of the Homestead Grays, died in Homestead, Pennsylvania. On Monday, April 1, the city schools of Homestead closed in honor of Posey, who was a member of the board of education there since being elected in 1931.

To Ira F. Lewis, veteran newspaperman and president of the Pittsburgh Courier Publishing Company of which Posey was a stockholder, Posey had declared that he prided himself on never being a good loser. "Good losers are seldom winners," he told Lewis.

Posey's fame ran all the way from Canada to Mexico into Puerto Rico and South America, where various members of his team went to play ball in the winter months. From the Atlantic to the Pacific, there was but one Cum Posey—just like there was but one Rube Foster in the latter's heyday. Posey and Rube were friends sometimes and again they were unable to agree. Rube at that time was for organized baseball and Posey was a fly in the ointment. Then when they got Posey into the fold, he was wont to kick over the traces. Of course, there was trouble.

Posey was for a winning ball club—one that won all the time. We never saw him sad, except when the Grays went down to defeat.

The last football game we worked with Posey was the Morehouse versus Bluefield game back in the late 1920s, in Columbus, Ohio, on a Thanksgiving Day. He was head linesman. The line and backfield coaches of Ohio State were referee and umpire.

We've seen him when he was a wizard on the basketball floor and when he was a thorn in the side of the old St. Christophers and the Incorporators of New York City. It took the great *Chicago Defender* five of Sol Butler, Bobby Anderson, Hubbard,

Blueitt and company to worry the Loendi club of Pittsburgh. The feud was a hum-dinger. It was East against West with the West never bowing. When basketball history is written, Posey and the Leondi club that succeeded the Monticello Delaneys, will have a very important place.

Few knew Posey coached the Homestead High School teams in basketball and football. Few knew he was a letterman from Penn State, who, at one time, attended Duquesne.

True, the world has lost a man who made himself famous in three branches of sports. But it is also true that it is a sad state of affairs when both friends and enemies wait until that man dies before they will admit his true worth.

Posey and we disagreed many times. He always said we were for the Negro Ameri-can League and the West. Sometimes, he'd hop on us through his column but never with any spleen—simply a difference of opinion. Then he'd meet us and we would shake hands. His only excuse would be, "Well, that's the way I thought it at that time," and laughingly would add, "You know there ain't no way for me to rub the doggone thing out."

There won't be those familiar arguments over the merits of the East's teams in the East versus West classics—if there are any, they won't be the same as if Posey was there. He'll be missed at future Negro National League meetings. He was secretary. He will be missed at the joint meetings. He won't be there to say, "You sit down, doggone it, you haven't got a thing to do with it," and 10 minutes later would have cornered us in the hallway with, "you know, you know," etc.

But he had a way, even when he became overwrought, of never falling out with you. He had a way of making his enemies respect him and sometimes winning them over as friends. As for his friends, he could rely on their loyalty. He had a forceful way of making you agree with him.

That was Cum Posey.

And now he is no more.

Frank A. Young, "Cum Posey Is No More," *Chicago Defender,* April 13, 1946.

D

INTERSCHOLASTIC AND COLLEGIATE SPORT: MUSCULAR ASSIMILATIONISM

10. Developing a High School Basketball Tournament

Interscholastic sports became increasingly important and far more organized in the African American community during the early years of the twentieth century. The number of teams multiplied, tournaments were organized, and associations formed in a variety of sports and in different sections of the country. Although opportunities to participate in organized athletics were not as great as those in the white community, African American youth could choose among competitions in such sports as baseball, basketball, and track and field.*

One of the most important sporting events for African American youth was the West Virginia Athletic Union basketball tournament. Inaugurated in 1925 at West Virginia State College, the yearly tournament was designed to determine the best black high school basketball team in the state. The tournament, which existed until 1957, initially consisted of eleven teams who played a double elimination format. Eventually, it evolved into a single elimination format involving eight teams who qualified to participate either by capturing or being runner-up in one of the state's four regional championships. The tournament involved great players, great coaches, and great teams, including state championship clubs such as Browns Creek District High (Kimball), Kelly Miller High (Clarksburg), Garnett High (Charleston), and Douglass High (Gary).**

The following article announces the upcoming 1926 tournament. Although intended to create fan enthusiasm, the article shows a genuine interest in the tournament and a degree of racial pride so characteristic of the "New Negro" in America at the time. In fact, the article makes clear that the tournament was not merely a sporting event but already a grand cultural affair that brought together African Americans from around the state and served as an important example of black enterprise and symbol of possibility. (Note the names of several of these schools: not just Lincoln, but also Douglass, Garnett, Du Bois, Dunbar, Washington, and Kelly Miller—the last after the distinguished Howard University professor and cultural commentator.) Like other sporting events behind the walls of segregation, the "efficient running of the tournament" had important implications for African Americans in the state who—like their brethren elsewhere—were continually looking for ways of over-

---

* For information on African American involvement in interscholastic sports, see Ashe, *Hard Road to Glory,* 13–14, 62; Gems, "Blocked Shot"; Henderson and Joiner, *Official Handbook;* D. Wiggins, "Edwin Bancroft Henderson: Physical Educator."

** Specific information on the tournament can be gleaned from Barnett, "'The Finals.'"

turning stereotypes about Negro inferiority. This highly organized event stood as yet another representation of black community-building and race pride.

——— ——

The high schools of the state will meet to determine the State Basketball Championship in a tournament to be held March 19th and 20th, at the West Virginia Collegiate Institute. This tournament is held annually under the auspices of the West Virginia Colored High School Athletic Association. Last year, the first year of the tournament, there were eleven teams entered. After two days and a night of thrilling competition, Lincoln High School of Wheeling, emerged as victors, defeating in the finals a fast and plucky little team from Browns Creek District High of Kimball. Kelly Miller High, of Clarksburg, and Simmons High of Montgomery, were in the running right up until the last minute. Other teams showing up well were, Sumner of Parkersburg, Garnett of Charleston and Genoa Avenue High of Bluefield.

Since the inauguration of the basketball tournament, the number of high schools belonging to the Association has increased materially. Eleven of the sixteen high schools in the Association last year sent teams to the tournament. This year, when there are more than 22 members, it is expected that there will be about sixteen teams representing. To date, eleven high schools have signified their intention of being present. Among these are Lincoln High of Wheeling, Kelly Miller High of Clarksburg, Sumner High of Parkersburg, Dunbar High of Fairmont, Gary High of Gary, DuBois High of Williamson, DuBois High of MacDonald, Washington High of London, Garnett High of Charleston, Douglass High of Huntington and Browns Creek District High of Kimball. Other entries are expected daily, among whom will probably be Genoa Avenue High of Bluefield, a team which has been winning games with surprising regularity throughout the present season, and which has already been heralded to become a "dark horse" at this tournament. From here and there in the state come all sorts of advance messages as to the teams, their preparations for "bringing home the bacon," and the financing of the various expeditions. Lincoln High School, in spite of losing through graduation, several of her best men and even reliable substitutes, has managed to make a creditable showing in the majority of her games and believes in herself to such an extent that a corps of rooters, including "Miss Lincoln," are coming along to cheer her on to a second championship. At the same time word comes from Kimball and from a dignitary at the southern end of the state proclaiming to the world the fact that the team from Browns Creek District High has not lost a game in nine starts, and cannot be stopped by any high school team which goes about on ten legs. But, at the same time, comes further word, telling about the "wonder team" at Gary High, a team which played last year for the first time, but which has been making a very creditable showing this year. DuBois of Williamson was forced by finances to remain out of the competition last year, but has decided that this year they will not be denied a chance at the big silver basketball trophy which is being offered the winner by the Athletic Association of the West Virginia Collegiate Institute. Kelly Miller High School is the only school in years to have beaten the Lincoln team both at

Wheeling and on the Clarksburg floor and is almost confident that the year's championship will repose safely in the halls of Kelly Miller High School.

At present the athletic authorities at the Institute are busy making ready for the suitable entertaining of the competitors and for the efficient running of the tournament. They are guarding with a religious enthusiasm all information respecting the type of trophy, except that it is silver. Alumni from the various high schools who are now doing their college work at the West Virginia Collegiate Institute are preparing to take care of their friends and root for their teams. President John W. Davis has left everything in the hands of the Athletic Committee with the assurance that he will do anything in his power to make the exciting affair a success.

"Eleven Teams to Compete at Institute," *Pittsburgh Courier-Journal,* March 13, 1926.

11. African American Women Make Their Marks in Sport

During the early years of the twentieth century, the black colleges and universities of the South began to sponsor women's participation in sport. These efforts were never so thoroughly developed as they were for male undergraduates; they were always qualified by concerns about the middle-class norms of femininity and proper deportment among African American women. While the students themselves embraced many forms of physical recreation and games, their elders on campus and beyond remained ever cautious about the image projected when women trained hard and played with the same intensity as the men. The debates took place at many levels and over many years. Some physical educators advocated a highly circumscribed set of "girls' rules" for basketball, while a former player who was then a coach argued that the "girls of today are red-blooded, virile young creatures, and are no longer content to conform to the masculine ideal of feminine inferiority and frailty. The clinging vine has given way to the freely moving, sensibly clad young Amazon of today. Such fineness of physique cannot be maintained or secured through the inadequacies of girls' rules in basketball."*

It is within this context that the documents below should be read. They illuminate the tentativeness of the development of sporting programs for women and the spiritedness of the students themselves. But there is a story that lies beyond these documents. In the years following the announcement of the formation of a track team for women at Tuskegee Institute, the most outstanding women's track and field athletes in the entire nation came from historically black state universities. Joining Tuskegee, such schools as Florida A&M, Alcorn A&M, Prairie View A&M, Alabama State, Fort Valley State, and Tennessee State fielded great teams that captured various relay titles and championships at the local, regional, and national levels of competition. In contrast to the campus culture at the liberal arts colleges and black universities of the South, such as Fisk and Howard and their white counterparts, many African American communities displayed a more expansive notion of womanhood and supported athletic competition in demanding sports. In addition, African American women

---

* Liberti, "'We Were Ladies,'" 577; see entire article for information on competitive sports. On physical education generally, see Dunham, "Physical Education of Women at Hampton Institute." See also Grundy, *Learning to Win,* chaps. 5, 8.

Tuskegee women's relay team, late 1940s (Courtesy Tuskegee University Archives)

themselves did not, in the words of Susan Cahn, "tie femininity to a specific, limited set of activities and attributes defined as separate and opposite from masculinity."* In large part, African American women fashioned an ideal of womanhood out of their unique historical experiences, emphasizing multiple roles and the cultivation of emotional and physical talents publicly displayed in the political arena, black churches, the entertainment business, club life, and sports.

Ultimately, Tuskegee Institute established a breathtaking record of accomplishments in track and field. Between 1937 and 1951 the "Tigerettes," as the female athletes were called, captured fourteen National AAU outdoor championships and six indoor titles. Coached by the legendary Cleveland Abbott, among others, and including such great individual performers as Mabel Walker, Nell Jackson, and Alice Coachman (before her transfer to Albany State and becoming an Olympic gold medalist), the Tuskegee women sometimes doubled the point total of the second place teams in relay competition.** By the early 1950s, the quality of the Tuskegee women's track-and-field team had diminished significantly, but the team's place

---

* Cahn, *Coming on Strong,* 118; Cahn's work offers numerous insights into the participation of African American women in track and field.

** Welch, "Tuskegee Institute," 12.

was swiftly taken by Tennessee State, which was coached by Ed Temple and graced with such talented Olympians as Audrey Patterson, Mae Faggs, Emma Reed, and, ultimately, the great Wilma Rudolph. *

———— ————

"Girls to Have Track Team"

The Tuskegee girls will have a track team, it has been announced by Coach Amelia C. Roberts. At a recent meeting the formation of a track team was discussed. The girls voted very heartily in favor of it. Some of the young women had already been participating in the spiked shoe sport and have shown satisfactory progress in track work. Among those who have entered training for the cinder path are: Mildred Daly, Clarissa Crowley, Minnie Ingram, Irene Hill, Iva Hill, Lois Russ, Rosa Welch, Helen Steward, Nannie M. Marsh, Lillian Williams, Annie B. Finley, Roberta Pugh, Thelda Berry, Ruby Byrd, Annie Stalworth, Ruth Hart, Mary Askew, Ruth McGlocton, Wilmer Washington, Georgia Martin, Mary Williams, Doris Hooker, Myrtle King, Evelyn Burroughs, Lucinda Dunbar, LaPearl Hill, Susie Hill, Hester Kinney, Carrie Owens, Ruby Austin, Livy Thomas, Hattie Lindsay, Eloise Birch, Marie Clark, Trepoia Flowers, Myrtle Napier, Otis Clark, Reba Francis, Letha Brown, Theresa Crawford, Theresa Adams, Estella Pearson, Colotta Hayward, and Dorthea Doyle.

Fidelia Adams, guard on the basketball team, aspires to hurl the javelin and she is already able to throw the shaft for good distances. Miss Adams is also endeavoring to become proficient with the discus. Hattie Lindsay, another basketball star, who has established a record as a sprinter, will be a contender also in the high jump and shot put events.

An added feature of the Tuskegee Relays this year which will be held in the Alumni Bowl, May 4, will be a one-fourth mile Relay Race for co-eds for the National Championship of America. Trophy for this event will be offered by one of Tuskegee's successful women graduates.

"Girls to Have Track Team," *Tuskegee Messenger,* March 9, 1929.

"Campus Athletics"

In spite of rain in the earlier part of April 11th, Founders Day, the athletic meet, which always has an important place in the program of events, was an unusual feature. After the rally in Howe Memorial everyone went onto the Oval in front of Rockefeller Hall to witness the presentation of English Country Folk Dances. Each class was represented by one or two circles in either the *Newcastle,* the first dance, or *Jenny Pluck Pears,* the second. The College classes were known by the colors of their socks and ties; freshmen, blue; sophomores, yellow; juniors, red; seniors, green. After the Folk Dances everyone remained on the green until Miss Mary Louise Smith as the Goddess, Diana,

---

* For a solid analysis of both the Tuskegee and Tennessee State programs in relation to the Olympic Games see Gissendanner, "African American Women Olympians"; idem, "African-American Women and Competitive Sport."

Spelman College Founder's Day celebration, 1937 (Courtesy Spelman College Archives)

commanded the Greek athletes to appear. At this command lovely, graceful forms in purple and gold came running, leaping, jumping onto the field. Their dance served as a reminder of the many exercises of the Greeks for the development and beautifying of the body. In the group representing Greek athletes were Ruth M. Westmoreland, Fannie Allen, Carolyn Lemon, Frances Brock, Sophia Sullivan, Themla Fuller, Doris Murphy, and Annlizabeth Madison.

The dances by the class representatives and the Rythmics groups were only a part of the show. The next event was an archery tournament. Although this is something new on our campus the contestants bravely entered into the sport and made a creditable showing. The scores were as follows: Clara Haywood, 17 points (one goal, three hits); Rachel Davis, 5 points, one hit; Lottie Lyons, 5 points, one hit.

On account of the rain the baseball game was postponed until afternoon when two teams, made up of members of three college classes, played the game. Although there were few spectators for this event, the game went off very well. The teams were as follows: Players from the Freshman and Junior classes against the Sophomores. The scores amounted to 10 for the Sophomore team and 7 for the Freshman and Junior team.

The baseball game brought to a very successful close the Athletic Meet on Spelman's fifty-second anniversary. The representatives of all groups had been trained by Miss Leolya Nelson, Director of Physical Education, to whom much of our success in the athletic and aesthetic features is due.

"Campus Athletics," *Spelman Campus Mirror,* April 15, 1933, 7.

12. Women's Basketball and the Shape of Things to Come: Bennett College vs. the Philadelphia Tribunes

The women's teams at Bennett College, Greensboro, North Carolina, abided by the very strict rules set by campus officials about dress and public behavior, yet at the same time they often practiced against a group of high school boys in order to learn what one player called the "tricks of the trade." "We were ladies," she later told a historian, "we just played basketball like boys." The Bennett teams of the 1930s were the strongest quintet to play intercollegiate basketball. As Rita Liberti has shown, they needed to balance the demands of genteel femininity with their desire to play the best basketball teams around and to win. *

Bennett's triumphant 1934 season against college opponents prompted some athletic officials to set up a series of contests against the reigning professional championship team, a contingent sponsored by the Philadelphia Tribune, *a leading African American newspaper. The match-up inspired interest throughout the nation and suggests that black Americans followed women's sport with much the same fascination that they had for collegiate football and Negro League baseball. The contests are instructive for another reason, as Liberti's interviews with former Bennett players ably demonstrates. The collegiate game stood in marked contrast to the way the professionals comported themselves, starting with the uniforms. Bennett's were modest in style and color. As one former Bennett player recalls, the* Tribune *team "changed uniforms, they had red and white uniforms one half, and gold and purple the next half, and socks to match!" What is more the Bennett women clearly stood in awe of Ora Washington—a nationally recognized tennis champion as well as basketball star. Washington, as well as some of her teammates, played a particularly rugged brand of basketball, and Bennett players recall in some detail the number of elbows thrown during the series. Finally, Liberti reconstructs the off-court actions of the two teams as "important evidence of the diverse notions of womanhood and respectable behavior within the black community during this period." As one Bennett athlete remembered: "We went to the locker room [at half time] and that's when them girls pulled out little half pint jars, they had corn liquour in it. . . . Now all of them didn't have it . . . two or three of them didn't. But the rest of them would take two or three big swigs and set it down somewhere over there and go right on out and play!"* **

Apart from observations about rough versus respectable demeanors, what stands out from the episode is the widespread acknowledgment of the high level of competition. Here were displays of talent and energy that prefigured black women's contributions to sport up to the present day.

------

* Liberti, "'We Were Ladies,'" 575 (quote).
** Ibid., 574.

Bennett College basketball team (Courtesy Mrs. Ruth Glover Mullen and Rita Liberti)

"LITTLE NAPOLEON'S WARRIORS FOUGHT 'EM ALL"

That great gallant fighting 1934 North Carolina collegiate champion Bennett College girls' basketball team . . . coached by F. M. Staley, the "Little Napoleon," after conquering all foes in college circles, tackled the world's champions, the mighty Otto Briggs' Philadelphia Tribune Five, a professional aggregation.

"Little Napoleon's Warriors Fought 'Em All," *Norfolk Journal and Guide,* March 31, 1934.

"TRIBUNE GIRLS SETTLE FUSS ON COURT WITH BENNETT'S 5"

Greensboro, N.C.: The strong Bennett College girls basketball team met its Waterloo this week when thrice the Philadelphia Tribune misses swept 'em down to defeat in games that were thrill packed throughout. The first game went to the Philadelphia girls, 31 to 22; they won the second 18 to 13, and closed the series, 31 to 20, Bennett, favored because of its great forward, Vic Johnson, found Ora Washington just as good and the story is told right here.

The second was the most bitterly fought and for that reason we'll tell you how it was done. Shifting the scene from the huge sport arena to the beautiful Penn high school gymnasium, High Point, N. C., the warring Bennett team, 1934 champions, and the great Tribunes met in a thriller which resulted in an 18 to 13 victory for the world's fastest and greatest girls quintet. This game proved to be the best of the three game series. The Staley-coached collegians several times showed their superiority and it was not until the last three minutes of the game that almost supernatural shots by the Tribunes put the game on ice.

Throughout the first quarter, the world's champions were able to garner only one point. The half found the collegians leading, 4 to 3. The third quarter terminated in a 9 to 9 tie. With one team alternating taking the lead by only a point margin the game proceeded until within five minutes of the expiration of the playing time. Then Duke sank impossible shots in the basket, terminating the greatest exhibition ever staged in North Carolina.

Vic Jackson of Bennett was high scorer of the evening, making 7 of the 13 points by her team. This brought her total to 19 points for the two games. The mighty Ora Washington was held to two points. The scoring by both teams was well distributed. Features were the shooting of Jackson and Duke and the airtight guarding of Mills, Culbreath, Townsend, Lennon and Glover of Bennett.

"Tribune Girls Settle Fuss on Court with Bennett's 5," *Chicago Defender,* March 24, 1934.

13. "Nation Eyes Lincoln and Howard Game"

In the immediate post–World War I era, annual Thanksgiving Day football games between rival institutions became a significant feature of black college sport. Yearly rituals that were partly athletic spectacles and partly social events matched such historically black institutions as Fisk and Tuskegee Institute, Virginia Union and Virginia State, Wiley and Prairie View, Howard and Lincoln (Pa.), Livingston and Johnson C. Smith, and Hampton and Morgan. They attracted thousands of spectators, drew a great deal of media attention in the black press, and brought together students, faculty, and alumni to share in the excitement of football and make broader cultural statements about race pride. These Thanksgiving Day games, while similar in many ways to those held between predominantly white institutions, reflected a change in the African American community brought about by northern migration of southern blacks, the rise of a consumer culture, and the increasing popularity of sport. *

At least one rite attending football at some historically African American institutions contrasted sharply with the autumn spectacles on the campuses of northern and western colleges. This was the "Rabbles," a halftime pageant wherein the grandstands emptied and students, clad in their finest, some carrying their own musical instruments, danced around the field, perhaps self-consciously in contrast to the precision marching bands that were the pride

---

* The best sources of information for these games are black newspapers and the student newspapers and yearbooks of each institution. Details of the games can also be gleaned from W. H. Jones, *Recreation and Amusement,* 73–78; and Horace Mann Bond's unpublished essay, "The Story of Athletics at Lincoln University" (Langston Hughes Memorial Library, Lincoln University, Oxford, Pa.). Bond's essay was prepared for but not included in a book that was published posthumously under his name (*Education for Freedom: A History of Lincoln University, Pennsylvania* [Lincoln, Pa.: Lincoln University, 1976]). See also Hurd, *Black College Football.*

Football Classic of 1926 in the New Howard Stadium—Howard 32-Lincoln 0 (Courtesy Moorland-Spingarn Research Center, Howard University Archives, Howard University)

of many predominantly white universities. "The ending of the first half was the cue for 'rabble' exhibitions," reported the Howard University Record *about the game against Lincoln in 1921: "The rabbles of both schools pounced upon the field in spite of its mudsoaked condition and the continuous rain. The 'Blue and White' rabble, headed by its band, executed a wild snake dance while the Lincoln horde did its serpentine dance. The weather forbade society exhibitions . . . and kept the ladies in their seats, prohibiting the fur coat parade of last year."**

The annual encounter pitting Howard against Lincoln—two of the most prestigious historically black institutions—was one of the most famous of the Thanksgiving Day contests. Between 1919 and 1929, in particular, the yearly games between the two schools drew thousands of fans and national attention. The following selection from the Chicago Defender *previews the 1922 contest. Like the coverage given this annual match-up by other black newspapers during this period, the article provides details about the upcoming game itself and the various social events surrounding it. It gives information on individual players as well as the strengths and weaknesses of each team, and announces banquets, receptions, dinner parties, and accommodations for the media, guests, and out-of-town visitors. Perhaps most important, however, is the tenor of the article, the ceaseless promotion and hype used to attract attention to the game and assure its success.*

——— ———

Football fans have literally captured the nation's capital on the eve of the annual classic to be played Thanksgiving morning between Lincoln University of Chester, Pa., and Howard University of this city. It will be the eighteenth meeting of the two elevens. Every incoming train brings its quota. The vanguard of the hosts who will watch tomorrow's struggle are busy renewing acquaintances. The "Flapper Special" from New York City is due in early in the morning as is a special from Pittsburgh and one from Philadelphia and every morning train will bring the balance who will help to make up the gayest throng that ever witnessed a football game anywhere and the largest that has ever witnessed a struggle between any two institutions representing our people.

---

* *Howard University Record* 16 (December 1921): 126. See also Miller, "To 'Bring the Race Along Rapidly.'"

Season's Biggest Attraction

To say that this particular game is the biggest social event in the country would be to put it mildly because it is not only the biggest social event nationally, but it is the biggest game, the most important game in the country as far as we are concerned. It is on a par with the Harvard-Yale contest. Each year the crowd is larger, each year the businessman, the professional man, those of the fourth estate, the alumni of each school, the student body and the football fan in general looks forward to this one and turns out to see it. This year Howard University has added another step to make the coming to this city attractive to the visitors outdoing the elaborate social activities held at Philadelphia last year. There is a reception and dance at the Coliseum tomorrow afternoon sponsored by the department of physical education and in the evening another gala reception and ball is to be held at the same place. This also is fostered by the department of physical education. The game is to be played at 10:30 in the morning at the American league park. Tonight the visiting newspaper men who are here to cover the game are to be the guests of Howard University at a banquet. A number of other private affairs have been arranged, such as dinners, theater parties, etc.

Everybody is interested in the outcome of the game, however. The biggest topic of conversation is whether Howard can win. Both elevens have been beaten. The upset of the dope which seemed to go astray in many cases this fall was the winning of Hampton over both Lincoln and Howard. The Seasiders copped a 9 to 7 contest from the Lions and then added fuel to the fire by defeating the Wildcats in a 13 to 0 tilt which caught the Blue and White followers by surprise and cast a cloud of gloom into the local camp.

Dope Goes Astray

Lincoln started the season like Howard with a win. Lincoln turned Morgan back with a 52 to 0 score and a week later Howard won from the same school, 52 to 6. This gave the dopesters a chance to do a little figuring. Morgan could possibly improve enough in a week's time to score on Howard, which left the elevens of both Lincoln and Howard on the same footing. But Lincoln again caused the spilling of the dope when she journeyed to Charleston, W.Va., and there lost to West Virginia Collegiate Institute, 19 to 14, although, due to the unfamiliarity of the rules and the interpretation of the same, the officials caused the score to be such, when it should have been 14 to 14. The play in question was ruled as a touchdown when it should have been called a safety. Hampton's victory followed in the wake of Institute's.

On Nov. 18 Wilberforce University played Lincoln in Philadelphia, the only big intersectional game of the season. The Lions led in the first half. When the Westerners came back on the field they were full of fight and in the last quarter they opened up one of the most brilliant air attacks ever seen on any field. With tears streaming down their cheeks, their captain on the side lines painfully injured, these Western lads, led by Huff of Chicago and Willette of Cleveland, really earned a tie with Lincoln, but the inefficiency of officials again played a part and Lincoln was given a 13 to 12 win, although a flagrant violation of the football rule book was deliberately perpetrated. I have no regard for incompetency, therefore I write as such. No ruling can be both right and wrong at the same time. It is one or the other.

This brings me to the present day. Lincoln, although only having scored 129 points during the season against 40 of her opponents, has a little of the edge on Howard, who has scored 105 points to 25 of her opponents because at no time during the season has Lincoln failed to cross the opponents' goal line. Hampton held Howard scoreless. The failure of Virginia Normal and Industrial to win in Washington, being on the short end of a 7 to 6 score, gave Howard a big scare. Then came Hampton's victory. The season was nearing an end. The team was being pointed by Dr. Morrison, head coach, and his assistant, Trigg, for the Lincoln game. The work of the team was disappointing.

So much for the season's record of both elevens. "How about tomorrow, Young?" everybody asks. Well, to tell the truth, football is hard to dope out. If the field is heavy it is Lincoln in a 'walkaway. The light back field of Howard will find the going just as tough as last year in Philly. Lincoln outweighs Howard. The dope favors Lincoln, but the dope has been upset so much this fall until football experts have come to the point of stop trying to figure it out.

There are many folks close to the game and close to both schools who feel that both Lincoln and Howard having their eye on the winning of the annual classic have kept something hidden all season.

Howard Has Veterans

This year's Blue and White eleven are mostly veterans of last year's struggle. The twenty-five thousand expected to see tomorrow's fray will see "Bulldog" Williams, crack end and captain of Howard, in action. He was one of the outstanding features in the 1920, 42 to 0 slaughter of the Lions. "Cute" Carter, also a member of the 1920 winning aggregation and who was barred by a faculty ruling last year, is back at quarter. His toe is likely to spill the dope. At the other end is Long. He is good and fast. Holton at center is looked to put up a rattling good game, but Morgan of Lincoln outweighs him by forty pounds. Howard is confident of winning. With every man on the squad in tip top shape and her former captains back to help polish up plays, the Wildcats were given a light signal drill yesterday, and tonight will get a "skill practice" from the blackboard. Coach Morrison, star on Tufts College eleven of Medford, Mass., later assistant coach to Charlie Brickley of Harvard fame at Boston University, doesn't say much. You can bet one thing is assured and that is all that the boys have to give will be given for their alma mater tomorrow morning.

Lincoln's Squad Uncertain

So much for Howard. Lincoln is not banking on the services of Whirlwind Johnson who has been sick with tonsillitis. He will start the game, but there is no telling how long he will remain in it. One certainty, he will be watched closely by the Howard eleven. Johnson is a plunger of the rarest kind. In the West Virginia Institute game, it was this same lad who almost single handed tore up the mountaineers' line and gave Lincoln two touchdowns. The Lincoln head coach, Johnny Law, captain of last year's victorious eleven, has as his assistants Morgan Gardner of West Virginia, "Kid" Collins and "Piggy" Auston, both former captains of the old Gold and Blue squads. These men with Secretary Cain of the Arctic Avenue YMCA in Atlantic City have given Law much valuable help in the closing days of this year's training season.

Crudup, last year's star end, who was kicked in the head last year in the game with Virginia Union, has been out for practice only two weeks. From all appearances he has recovered from his injury and will start the game, although Johnny Law may switch at the last moment and send in Lancaster who is fast on his feet in getting down the field on punts and is a sure tackler, although lacking in experience. On the other end will be Skinker, a local lad who needs no introducing to the public after his work last year. He will wear the same number as in the last game, number 19. Physically, Skinker this year, so far, has not been the same player as last year. His condition has not been good. Lancaster hails from Bridgeport, Conn., where he played on the high school eleven for three years.

In case Johnson cannot go through Law has a youngster named Goodman, who, although being a disappointment early in the season, has found himself during the last two weeks and who is living up to the advance reputation that preceded him to Chester from Hartford, Conn. He is just 19 years old, weighs 175 pounds and is fast.

Photos of individual football players superimposed on football graphic, Tuskegee University Crimson and Gold Yearbook, 1927 (Courtesy Tuskegee University Archives)

Another good sun is "Butts" Brown of Flemington, N.J. Pollitt of Newport, R.I., is another backfield man who is sure to give the Wildcats plenty of trouble, his kicks ranging at all times from 40 to 60 yards. Wilson of Augusta, Ga., is another plunging backfield security. At quarter is the flashy McLean of Jersey City with a good understudy in "Jass" Byrd. The team follows McLean better, but he is not reliable in the pinches.

The Lincoln eleven is quartered at the YMCA which is also the quarters of the Lincoln men. The Lincoln Alumni will hold a get together meeting tonight. Tomorrow morning, headed by a 60-piece band, the alumni headed by Drs. Cannon and Alexander of New Jersey, Prof. Saunders of West Virginia, with their pet lion cub sent from Liberia by the United States minister, an alumnus of Lincoln, will head for the park from the Whitelaw hotel, bedecked in Lincoln's colors, singing their "Alma Mater" as they do. All Lincoln adherents will follow in the line.

Defender's Headquarters

The Chicago Defender headquarters will be at the Liberty hotel and at 1019 U Street Northwest. Circulars will be distributed, free of charge, by the Defender with names and the numbers of players who will take part in the game.

The offices of Dr. Emmett J. Scott, secretary-treasurer of Howard, and Dr. W. C. Alexander of Newark, N.J., graduate manager of Lincoln, are flooded with inquiries. These two men have worked diligently for the past three years to make this game the biggest in the history of our institutions and they have borne the brunt of the hard work. To them more than to any other two should go the praises that go with the success.

"Nation Eyes Lincoln and Howard Game," *Chicago Defender*, December 2, 1922.

14. Hildrus A. Poindexter Discusses the Gridiron World: Lincoln, 1922–23

The Lincoln University (Pa.) teams that competed against Howard University in the annual Thanksgiving Day football games during the 1920s were made up of an extraordinary number of true student-athletes who went on to distinguished careers in business, law, medicine, and other professional fields. One of those athletes was Hildrus Augustus Poindexter. An outstanding lineman for Lincoln in 1922 and 1923, Poindexter graduated cum laude from the university in 1924, took his medical degree from Harvard University in 1929, and earned a Ph.D. from Columbia University in 1932. He became professor of community health practice in the Department of Bacteriology, Preventive Medicine and Public Health at Howard University and medical director of the United States Public Health Service. In addition, Poindexter was a highly decorated military officer during World War II and was awarded four battle stars, two official commendations, and a Bronze Star.

In the following selection, taken from his autobiography, My World of Reality, *Poindexter provides a rare first-hand account of a black athlete's experiences at a historically black university. He describes being taught to play lineman by Paul Robeson when the former*

Rutgers all-American visited campus one day a week from his law studies at Columbia. He also details the selection process for the varsity squad at Lincoln and some of the honors he received for his football exploits. Poindexter provides, moreover, some information about Lincoln football in general, including the names that made up the great squads of the 1920s.

——— ———

Football was the major athletic event at Lincoln in the 1920's. It was played during the fall terms. To be a member of the varsity football team or a strong candidate for it put the student in a preferred category so far as getting a bid for the college fraternity and for some other social recognition. I was fresh from the steel industry of Detroit where I had worked as a laborer and molder. I was as hard as nails. I had never played football, but I reported to the coach for the purpose of joining the freshman squad.

There were sophisticated and experienced young men also reporting for the squad. Some of them had been selected as "stars" in their respective high schools and at least two had been selected as "All State Stars." I brought only brute strength and a desire to make the team.

While others were getting in shape after a long summer of easy living, I was already in shape after a long summer of hard work. My ability to give and absorb punishment was soon recognized. Those were the days of "flying wedges" and "get a mule" tactics on the gridiron, where referees saw only where the ball was declared dead and literally nothing that went on between the 21 other men on the field. So the ability to give and take punishment was an asset to the squad. The rules of limiting the varsity to only the three upper classmen were not rigidly adhered to in the Colored Intercollegiate Athletic Association (CIAA). A good player on the freshman team might, therefore, play with the school varsity and thus travel with them to play teams of other CIAA members. The struggle was on to win a place on the freshman team. I was tried as a fullback, but fumbled too much. I was tried as a halfback, but I had too many passes intercepted. In those days halfbacks as well as the quarterbacks threw forward passes. Finally, I was assigned to a lineman's position. There, as a guard, I grew in stature and soon was the left guard of choice for the freshman team. During this freshman year, I studied the football rule books, avoided eating sweets during the football season, and kept my weight to 174–176 lbs. During my four years of athletics my weight never varied more than 5 lbs. from the 174–176 level.

There was nothing startling about my first year "out for football." I grew up as a football player during the sophomore year. During that year the famous Paul Robeson and Fritz Pollard would come to Lincoln one day a week from their graduate studies in Law and Dentistry to coach the Lincoln Team. As a lineman I came under the tutelage of Paul Robeson. Me and the man. I worshiped Robeson and absorbed his every principle and tactic for playing on the line. I learned to charge fast, low, and hard. I learned to punish an opponent and to accept punishment without complaint to referee or coach. Then came an awful day; a day of victory and remorse. It was the custom of the regular coach at Lincoln University to schedule a day, after some weeks of practice and coaching, for the selection of a first string team or the main "varsity squad."

This varsity squad would eat together at a special "training table" in the refectory, train as a unit, travel first class to other CIAA member schools for games, and would even get some consideration from the teachers for absenteeism from classes whenever they conflicted with football practices, blackboard drill sessions or travel. Each of the 11 positions on the team was up for "grabs." The number one choice would have to show superiority over all other challengers for that position even vanquishing the challenger if necessary. This was carried out by pitting Team A against Team B, and the winners in this scrimmage were reorganized into a new team and tried out again on Team C. In that method a final first team was selected with alternates selected from the runner-ups. I wanted to make this first team and felt that if I could only combine my physical energy with the skills which Paul Robeson had taught me, I could make the squad.

I, being a non-sophisticated rural southern boy, was on that day going to be pitted against guards who had played on high school teams in New England, the Middle Atlantic States and other parts of the country. I was frightened but I had confidence in my physical ability.

The day before the elimination and selection contest was to take place, the grapevine got news to me that a conspiracy was being formed by other contestants for the left guard position to eliminate me by concentrated attacks designed to cripple me. I lay awake practically all of that night becoming more and more angry. I did not eat the next morning. When the afternoon came for the contest, I was overcharged with rage. Before the long shadows of the trees had stretched across the football field and the sun had gone to rest in the west, one opponent was in the hospital with three fractured ribs, another opponent (a former All State guard) had left the game and subsequently turned in his uniform, and I was firmly established as the left guard for the first string Varsity team with all the recognition which goes to a remorseful victor. From that date and for the next three college football seasons, I played nearly 60 minutes per CIAA game a week except for one session in which a dislocated knee kept me out of the game. With a hinged steel brace on my knee, I was able to play for a few minutes even in this lone game. During these three years I was given many names such as "Pigiron," "Tarzan," "Amby," etc., all associated with my action on the gridiron. There was adequate local and national recognition. I was named to the second CIAA All American Team in 1922 and was the first CIAA All American left guard in 1923. The press coverage was small, except for my name in the line-up. The names of the linesmen from tackle to tackle were rarely noticed or mentioned. When "Jazz" Byrd ran 84 yards for a touchdown against Howard University, the headlines declared "Jazz" Byrd beats Howard. No mention was made about the hole in the center of the line opened by Poindexter and All American center Morgan on the right side of the line and by right guard Walls, or Walls and All American tackle Coston, etc.

In the early 1920's Lincoln University was in its heyday in football, playing such teams as Howard, Hampton, Morgan, West Virginia State, Union, Tuskegee Institute, Wilberforce, St. Paul's Polytechnic Institute, and Shaw. Members of those winning football teams at Lincoln during the 1920–1924 seasons include such renowned names as Jason, Coston, Crudup, Skinker, Diggs, Poindexter, Walls, Morgan, Lancaster,

Goodman, Laws, Jones, Hogans, Howard, Byrd, McLean, Brown, Lee, Beldon, the Johnsons, Jackson, Wood, Parr, Trigg, etc. I played in 20 CIAA football games. The two schools that gave me the hardest time were Hampton and West Virginia State. In two of the games against Hampton, Lincoln used the Dartmouth shift as a result of Coach Shelbourne's coaching. Shelbourne was a football star at Dartmouth. The responsibility of the guard on offense was to shift, pull out, and lead the blocking for end runs or off-tackle play. When the play was to the left, the left guard led the play; when to the right, the right guard led the play. In these left end runs, I was supposed to "take out" the first man I saw as he crossed the line in front of the ball carrier. This man on the Hampton Team was the "Roving center" or "line backer," "All American center" "Red" Dabney of Hampton. I had less than 50% successes against All American Center "Red" Dabney of Hampton, and at the end of these games I was too bruised and battered to attend the receptions. As stated before the referee only saw the ball where it was blown dead. What happened to the twenty-one other players the referee rarely saw. All American center Dabney used knees, fist, thumbs, cleats, and his 230 lbs. to maim me, but in true Paul Robeson fashion, no complaint was registered. All American center Dabney was undoubtedly the greatest center and defensive linebacker in the CIAA. Even though I could not contain All American Dabney, my showing was sufficient for the critics to give me All American left guard recognition.

During a West Virginia State game played on the rocky field at Charleston, I played against a guard named Huff of about 240 lbs. Huff was tough and he used his weight and toughness to rub my head and face over the stony field. Tremendous lacerations over my eyes and face still show scars and torn ligaments about the knees, still bear witness to Huff's toughness. The last 30 minutes of the game were played on instinct because both I and the right guard Walls were just about "washed out." Lincoln had run out of replacements due to injuries so the two regulars after a short rest were compelled to re-enter and continue. I was awarded my "L" and sweater for football three years in a row.

Hildrus A. Poindexter, *My World of Reality: An Autobiography* (Detroit: Balamp Publishing, 1973), 33–36.

E

CULTURAL CRITIQUES

15. "The Colored Basketball Referee Finally Arrives"

There was a substantial debate within the African American community throughout the first half of the twentieth century concerning the dependence on white rather than black officials in all-black sporting contests. Many African Americans denounced the reliance on white umpires in Negro League baseball, white referees in football games between historically black colleges, and other whites called on to interpret the rules in sporting contests involving black participants. Such dependence on white officials indicated to some African Americans that members of their community had no faith in their own officials and, even worse, reflected feelings of racial inferiority. The concern over the dependence on white officials was part of a much broader discussion regarding the African American community's lack of patronage of its own businesses and lack of trust of its own professionals in positions requiring high levels of competence and expertise. Kenneth L. Shropshire, in his In Black and White: Race and Sports in America, *notes that this negative race consciousness has been evident among segments of the African American community for years and still exists today. He cites numerous examples, including the oft-told story, usually credited to Malcolm X, of the African Americans in a small southern town who were willing to stand in a long line under a hot, boiling sun to purchase ice from a white rather than black vendor because "everybody knows the white man's ice is colder."**

In the following article from The Competitor, *the argument is made that the few black referees allowed to officiate at basketball games were at a disadvantage because of the attitude of members of their own community. Black referees were not supported and encouraged to be successful by either players or spectators. As soon as black referees stepped on the court, they were harassed by players for fouls they had called and referred to by every name imaginable for not keeping the game under control. The implication of all of this, of course, is that black fans and spectators had little trust in black referees. White referees, regardless of their experience, expertise, and ability level, were perceived to be the only true arbiters of the rules and the only authorities capable of controlling unruly crowds. To combat stereotyping and train a new generation of athletic officials, Edwin Bancroft Henderson, the black physical educator and historian of the black athletic experience, created the Eastern Board of Officials (EBO), an organization established to improve the working conditions of black officials and secure them more assignments. He also frequently expressed his displeasure concerning the dependence on white rather than black officials in all-black sporting contests.***

---

* Shropshire, *In Black and White*, 129.

** See D. Wiggins, "Edwin Bancroft Henderson, African American Athletes, and the Writing of Sport History," in his *Glory Bound*, 225; idem, "Edwin Bancroft Henderson: Physical Educator," 96.

―――――――

The big game in New York on January 29, lent more to basketball than the honor of bringing out the largest crowd yet to witness a game in the history of the fascinating winter sport. On that winter's night a colored basketball referee arrived in the person of Mr. Chris Huiswoud, AAU official. We say arrived advisedly, because, figuratively speaking, they have been at sea for some time. This is certainly meant as no reflection upon the brave colored men who have tried the exacting role of a basketball referee; and we say brave, because we shall explain later why it has required a brave man to tackle the job.

Much has been written and wide and diversified has been the comment on this particular score. Hardly any big game has been staged that has not drawn some comment as to why the white referee? In our experience in writing sport news we have been called upon several times to give some reason for the absence of colored referees.

In the first place there is hardly a game in the annals of sport in which the official enters into the game so much as does a basketball referee. It is within his power or the scope of his ability to make a game interesting or disinteresting. He can be too technical in his application of the rules and spoil the interest by slowing up the game in calling fouls, which can be construed as having been unintentionally committed. On the other hand if he has the common sense to size up the situation as regards the temperament of the players, their ability and his audience, he can make a very pleasing and at the same time fair and lively contest. While some might contend that this feature has nothing to do with the application of the rules, it is a noteworthy fact that the successful referees are the ones who take in all these contributing phases, and conduct themselves accordingly. A referee who has the ginger to get about the floor and keep the players going at top speed eliminates the chances of "squawks" from the player who tries to make himself believe that he has not committed a foul. The official who has confidence in himself and his own interpretation of the rules and who unhesitatingly calls a foul and shows right on the spot who makes it and how, is bound to have the support of the audience, and thereby lessen the objection of the guilty player. This latter kind of a referee is sure to be a popular official, because he convinces; convinces with the evident confidence in his own work.

Now we would not be guilty of saying or even intimating that the colored men who have tried to become officials have not had these qualities; we would not think that it would be impossible for our men to learn and interpret the rules after the same manner of the other fellow. But the main trouble with our fellows who have tried their hands at acting as a basketball official is, the player and the spectator do absolutely nothing towards encouraging a colored referee to make good. The moment he comes on the court, even to referee a preliminary contest, the young players bawl at him about calling a foul on them; thinking, of course, that their protest imparts the knowledge that they know what they are talking about and that it makes them big in the eyes of the crowd. The nervous official instead of running away from the protesting player and keeping the game going, stops to argue the point with the youngster, and eventually gets the crowd on him. To get a basketball crowd on your neck is worse than shaking a red flag at a bull. The spectators will call you everything from a tree frog to a whale.

Once the young players see that the crowd is on you—then good night. The result being that before the embryo official can get ten cents worth of confidence in his own ability he is thoroughly disgusted, discouraged and throws up the game as a bad job. True, we have had some men to start who knew the game thoroughly, and were not thin skinned, but it is not so much a question of applying the rules as it is the knack of mastering the situation rather than allowing the situation to master you. Then, too, the crowd would expect more, if anything, from a colored referee who is just starting or trying to start than from a seasoned white veteran.

As an example of some of the fine points of refereeing, the writer spoke to Al Slack, undoubtedly one of the very best officials the game has ever produced. Mr. Slack refereed the Princeton-Yale game in Pittsburgh this season, when both met on a neutral floor during the holiday trip, and who generally referees most of the big college games for the University of Pittsburgh, himself, a great admirer of the present Loendi team. In speaking to Mr. Slack about a few incidents of the Harrisburg-Loendi game in which he officiated, we said casually, "Say, Al, slowing up a little old man, eh? We saw Posey and Gilmore pull a couple on you under the basket the other

Football game between black colleges, with African American officials (R. S. Darnaby Box; courtesy Tuskegee University Archives)

evening, in cleverly blocking and protecting the fellow who has received the ball for a shot at the basket."

"No, not slowing up at all," he said, "but what's the use of spoiling the fine points of basketball, those men are big time players, and I am a big time referee."

That in a nutshell shows some of the judgment and discretion a capable official must use. It's a great game and it takes a brave man to start out to become a referee. We certainly congratulate Mr. Huiswoud upon his signal success in measuring up to the required standard in this Blue Ribbon clash. He was tried and proved equal to the occasion.

And though he is an AAU official sanctioned by that august body to represent it in officiating at basketball contests, it took more than two hours of convincing one of the most advanced colored athletic clubs in America that he did not need a white official to help him handle the contest. He showed no more at Manhattan Casino that night than he was capable of showing at any time because he had the goods, and knew how to deliver them, but the folks—our folks, if you please, would not give him the chance.

The work of Mr. Huiswoud in this titular battle left nothing to be desired. His handling of the high-tensioned situation brought entire satisfaction to both player and spectator, eliciting as much comment afterwards as did the game. Throughout the contest he worked with that smoothness and precision characteristic of the workman who knows his job.

We, therefore, hope that other basketball centers will look at the refereeing situation in the proper light and let players and fans each lend a hand towards developing other such capable men.

"The Colored Basketball Referee Finally Arrives," *The Competitor*, March 20, 1920.

16. "Tuskegee and 'Force' Rapped for Tribute to Knute Rockne"

When the famed Notre Dame football coach Knute Rockne died tragically in a plane crash in March 1931, he was mourned throughout the nation. Tributes from newspaper writers as well as rival coaches were published immediately; the telegrams and letters sent by ordinary people still crowd the university archives. It would not be until the autumn of 1931, however, that many formal testimonials to Rockne were staged. During that gridiron season, African American fans of college football also honored one of the nation's most distinguished sportsmen—at least on one occasion.

Such zeal to participate in mainstream rituals and spectacles might be admirable in other circumstances; much of the rhetoric of racial reform suggested that sports provided a vehicle of assimilation for black Americans, who for so many years and in so many ways suffered the stigma of exclusion. Yet in some instances, as editorialists from both the Chicago Whip *and* Baltimore Afro-American *indicate, this enthusiasm could be misguided. Rockne had done nothing to alter the racial situation in the United States, they assert; in fact, he* *had a lengthy record of telling "darkey stories" during after-dinner speeches and radio talks. Thus it represented a kind of "false consciousness" for African Americans to lament in public the passing of someone who had been no friend to the race.**

The editorial below clearly foreshadows Wendell Smith's concerns expressed in "A Strange Tribe" that black Americans need to demonstrate greater "race pride" in their athletic loyalties. It shows that the black press often saw itself as having a critical role in shaping culture and consciousness. And it anticipates, by many years, the militancy of the black power movement—avowedly antiassimilationist. But the document might be read most profitably next to Carter G. Woodson's The Mis-Education of the Negro, *which was published in 1933 and warned that those blacks who blindly admired or emulated Western traditions, or white culture, in significant ways imperiled the advancement of the race.*

The following comment is made by the *Chicago Whip* on the tribute paid to the late Knute Rockne by teams and spectators at the Tuskegee-Wilberforce football game in Chicago two weeks ago (the game was played in Mills Stadium on October 24, 1931): "When the great football teams of Tuskegee Institute and Wilberforce University locked horns last Saturday at Mills Stadium in Chicago, ten thousand or more members of the colored race stood bare-headed as the bugle sounded taps for the late, lamented Knute Rockne, great football coach at Notre Dame University. Now Rockne was a white man, no colored boys ever played upon his teams, in fact we know of no colored students even attending Notre Dame during Mr. Rockne's regime. Then why should ten thousand of us stand uncovered in tribute to him and why should colored boys sound taps?

"The reasons offered are that the coaches of Wilberforce and Tuskegee had attended summer coaching classes conducted by Mr. Rockne. This seems to us indeed far-fetched. We can see no reason for it. We believe that it is a good policy to 'Render unto Caesar the things that are Caesar's and unto God the things that are God's.' If Mr. Rockne had shown any concrete interest in the athletic development of the colored youth, if he had shown any particular interest in lifting the status of an unfortunate people or even if he had made any positive gestures toward racial goodwill we would feel that the tribute paid to his memory by our people would be entirely in order but we know of nothing done by the departed athletic genius in this direction.

"We have listened to Rockne telling 'darkey stories' over the radio and we have sensed the fact that colored people in general terms were 'persona non grata' with him. It was stupid and silly for us to uncover and sound taps for him. We are a strange people who are not easily insulted, we are forgiving and long suffering but not withstanding these laudable virtues, we are guilty of some very asinine acts. This incident is a case in point."

"Tuskegee and 'Force' Rapped for Tribute to Knute Rockne," *Baltimore Afro-American,* November 7, 1931.

---

* The University of Notre Dame would not admit African American students until after World War II. As Charles Martin notes in his path-breaking work on the desegregation of college sports, the Fighting Irish would not put an integrated varsity basketball team on the court until the 1951–52 season; the first black football players made their appearances in the fall of 1953. See Martin, "The Color Line in Midwestern College Sports."

17. Wendell Smith /"A Strange Tribe": On the Loyalties of Black Fans

For much of the first half of the twentieth century sportswriters from leading black newspapers around the country waged a vigorous campaign against the exclusion of black players from organized baseball. Highly creative in their methods and relentless in their approach, such sportswriters as Sam Lacy, Joe Bostic, A. S. "Doc" Young, and Wendell Smith attacked organized baseball's exclusionary policies through a series of editorials, feature articles, and interviews with major league players and managers. These men, who did not have to worry about direct reprisals from the sports establishment or society at large, countered any questions about the black players' athletic skills by pointing out their superior performances in games against barnstorming major leaguers. Not only did these writers denounce baseball's power elite for their racially discriminatory practices; they also made clear to everyone the hypocrisy of asking blacks to defend their country in world conflicts while denying them access to what was purported to be the most "democratic" of all American sports and the national pastime.

Perhaps the most influential of this group was Wendell Smith, the very talented writer of the Pittsburgh Courier-Journal *who campaigned vigorously on behalf of black players and eventually recommended to Branch Rickey that Jackie Robinson was the man best suited to integrate the national game.* The following selection is from Smith's column "Smitty's Sport Spurts" and appeared in the* Courier-Journal *on May 14, 1938. This was the first time Smith publicly addressed the issue of organized baseball's exclusionary policies and he chose, interestingly enough, to direct most of his criticism toward the African American community. Smith indicted African Americans for, among other things, their continual economic support of major league baseball. He was terribly disturbed that African Americans continued to attend major league games, applauding the exploits of white players while spending their hard-earned money on segregated white business enterprises. Most troubling to Smith was the fact that African Americans were not patronizing their own ballparks and showing support for the outstanding teams and brilliant players in black baseball.***

——— ———

Why we continue to flock to major league ball parks, spending our hard earned dough, screaming and hollering, stamping our feet and clapping our hands, begging and pleading for some white batter to knock some white pitcher's ears off, almost having fits if the home team loses and crying for joy when they win, is a question that probably never will be answered satisfactorily. What in the world are we thinking about anyhow?

---

* For specific information on Smith's campaign, see D. Wiggins, "Wendell Smith." See also Simons, "Jackie Robinson." The key work on the desegregation of baseball remains Tygiel, *Baseball's Great Experiment.*

** The black leagues had realized a modicum of financial success by the time of Smith's column. They always had difficulty achieving economic stability, however, because of structural problems and the exorbitant prices charged them by major league owners for rental of ballparks and use of concessionaires. Information on the black leagues can be found in Rogosin, *Invisible Men;* Ruck, *Sandlot Seasons;* Peterson, *Only the Ball Was White.*

Wendell Smith (far left) as a student reporter, 1936. He would later become a celebrated sports-writer for the *Pittsburgh Courier-Journal* (Courtesy West Virginia College Archives)

Not Wanted

The fact that major baseball refuses to admit Negro players within its folds makes the question just that much more perplexing. Surely it's sufficient reason for us to quit spending our money and time in their ballparks. Major league baseball does not want us. It never has. Still, we continue to help support this institution that places a bold "Not Welcome" sign over its thriving portal and refuse to patronize the very place that has shown it is more than welcome to have us. We black folk are a strange tribe!

Making Progress

Negro baseball is still in its infancy. In the last ten years it has come a long, long way. Gone are the days when the players having the most knives and razors won the ball game. Gone are the days when the teams appeared before the public dressed like scarecrows and reminded us of the lost legion. Gone are the days when only one or two good players were on a team. Now their rosters are filled with brilliant, colorful, dazzling players who know the game from top to bottom. Negro teams now have everything the white clubs have. Except, of course, the million dollar ball parks to play in; parks that we helped to build with our hard earned dollars. Nevertheless, we ignore them and go to see teams play that do not give a hang whether we come or not.

Sounds silly, doesn't it? Well—it's true! Despite the fact that we have our own teams and brilliant players, the most colorful in the world, mind you, we go elsewhere and get a kick out of doing it. Suckers! You said it brother!

No Encouragement

They're real troopers, these guys who risk their money and devote their lives to Negro baseball. We black folk offer no encouragement and don't seem to care if they make a go of it or not. We literally ignore them completely. With our noses high and our hands deep in our pockets, squeezing the same dollar that we hand out to the white players, we walk past their ball parks and go to the major league game. Nuts—that's what we are. Just plain nuts!

From Dixie

Listen! If any one of us wanted to talk to one of the ball players whom we've been spending our hard earned dough on, screaming and hollering, stamping our feet and clapping our hands for, we'd probably be ignored. If he did speak to us it would probably be a disrespectful salutation such as "Hello George," or "What ya' say, Sam." Or maybe even worse than that. Oh, he wouldn't, eh! That's what you think. Don't forget that he comes from Mississippi, Georgia, Texas or any other place you can think of below the Mason-Dixon line. And he's white. He looks upon us as something the cat brought in. Even though he is playing ball in a northern city, making northern money, he still looks upon us that way. He's a leopard and you know what they say about their spots. You can't change 'em!

Tough Fight

We have been fighting for years in an effort to make owners of major league baseball teams admit Negro players. But they won't do it, probably never will. We keep on crawling, begging, and pleading for recognition just the same. We know that they don't want us, but still we keep giving them our money. Keep on going to their ball games and shouting till we are blue in the face. Oh, we're an optimistic, faithful, prideless lot—we pitiful black folk.

Yes sir—we black folk are a strange tribe.

Wendell Smith, "A Strange Tribe," *Pittsburgh Courier-Journal,* May 14, 1938.

18. W. E. B. Du Bois, Allison Davis, and Langston Hughes on the Excesses of Black College Sport

The rapid expansion of intercollegiate football throughout the nation during the first decades of the twentieth century was attended by mounting concerns about corruption in sport and what that meant for higher learning in America. Unethical recruiting practices, the disbursement of athletic "scholarships," and the use of "ringer" or "tramp" athletes on varsity teams all threatened to subvert the educational mission of institutions large and small. This was as true for black colleges and universities, located mainly in the South, as it was for other schools. However, "race men" like W. E. B. Du Bois, Allison Davis, and Langston Hughes—among a host of others—perceived a greater danger when those institutions violated the rules governing intercollegiate athletic competition. Because the status and integrity of HBCUs had long remained vulnerable to challenges by those who maintained the notion of white supremacy, the reputation of those schools needed to be protected at all costs.

Throughout the 1920s and 1930s, many cultural commentators and educational reformers *inveighed against "King Football" and the "vulgarization of the American college," and the Carnegie Foundation for the Advancement of Teaching conducted an exhaustive, thoroughly documented survey of the athletic practices of more than one hundred (white) institutions of higher education.* Despite the fact that a substantial number of dedicated students (such as Hildrus Poindexter) were participants in intercollegiate sports, the programs of numerous black colleges also came under criticism for their unfair recruiting practices and indifference to academic standards of eligibility, as well as for the subsidization of their best passers, pitchers, and runners. Accusations about violations of rules filled the mails from one campus to another. Such allegations also flowed from the pages of the* Crisis, *where W. E. B. Du Bois and his prótegé George Streator periodically railed against a long litany of abuses in sports, breaches of the spirit if not always the letter of the "laws" then defining amateurism. Claflin College admitted athletes without reviewing their transcripts, Streator reported in one lengthy article, while South Carolina State College fielded several athletes who had seen considerable action around Orangeburg during the preceding eight years and several more who had played collegiate ball elsewhere. The indictment ran to several fact-filled pages, and Streator even ranked black colleges according to the extensiveness of their athletic excesses.***

In the writings that follow, W. E. B. Du Bois expresses his hope that "New Negroes" in the sporting realm would play the same games in the same manner as the athletes at the most prestigious (and upright) institutions found in the Northeast and Midwest. Meanwhile, in lines that are at once earnest and sardonic, Allison Davis highlighted the problems of a student culture that was clearly not directed outward to larger social concerns. At the time, Davis was moving from his undergraduate career at Howard University toward advanced studies in social psychology; in 1942 he would become the first African American professor appointed to a full-time position by a predominantly white university. Finally, Langston Hughes, speaking from the viewpoint of his widely beloved character Jesse B. Semple, or Simple, offers his own wry commentary on the ways college sport was often perceived.†

W. E. B. Du Bois / "Athletics in Negro Colleges"

Now that Negro colleges are being admitted to the associations of standard colleges, and even now are debating with these colleges and universities, it is even possible that some Negro college will play games with the members of the "Big Ten" or some other Carnegie-investigated groups. I wonder if we will have the nerve to say that "Chicago exhibited great racial prejudice in refusing to play unless Fisk benched Brown, her mainstay in the backfield for the last ten years"?

W. E. B. Du Bois, "Athletics in Negro Colleges," *Crisis* 37 (June 1930): 209–10.

---

* See Savage et al., *American College Athletics.* See also Sinclair, *The Goose-Step;* Tunis, *$port$;* and R. Harris, *King Football.*
** See Streator, "Negro Football Standards"; idem, "Football in Negro Colleges." The list of the worst offenders included Lincoln (Pa.), Wilberforce, South Carolina State, Allen University, Claflin, and Morris Brown. "Medium, in need of further reform," were Fisk, West Virginia State, Knoxville, and Kentucky State. He ranked Hampton, Howard, Morehouse, Wiley, and Tuskegee as good. Streator, "Football in Negro Colleges," 129, 141.
† For more on these issues, see Miller, "To 'Bring the Race Along Rapidly.'"

W. E. B. Du Bois / "Education and Work"

The average Negro undergraduate has swallowed hook, line, and sinker, the dead bait of the white undergraduate, who, born in an industrial machine, does not have to think, and does not think. Our college man today, is, on the average, a man untouched by real culture. He deliberately surrenders to selfish and even silly ideals, swarming into semi-professional athletics and Greek letter societies, affecting to despise scholarship and the hard grind of study and research.

W. E. B. Du Bois, "Education and Work," in *The Seventh Son: The Thought and Writings of W. E. B. Du Bois,* ed. Julius Lester (New York: Random House, 1971), vol. 1, 563.

Allison Davis / "The Second Generation"

Juggling basketballs
And women
You won't work,
You won't study,
You won't marry.

But you have four "letters"
And a fraternity pin.

College education
Of a hundred like you every year
Will bring the race along rapidly.

Allison Davis, "The Second Generation: College Athlete," *Crisis* 35 (March 1928): 87.

Langston Hughes / "Simple Discusses Colleges and Color

"Delbert is going to college," said Simple, "so if I live and nothing happens—and I get straight—I am going to send him the money for his first pair of football shoes. . . ."

"Well, if Delbert is going to college, what you should think about helping him buy is not football shoes, but books. Men go to college to study, not to play football. . . ."

"Footballing is all I ever read about them doing," said Simple. "Since I do not know any college boys, I thought they went there to play. . . ."

"They do not," I said. "Of course, the ones who play good football get their names in the papers. But there are thousands of others who graduate with honors and never even see a football game."

Langston Hughes, "Simple Discusses Colleges and Color," *Phylon* 10 (December 1949): 399–400.

4

The Quest for Racial Reform: Affirmation and Protest in the Sporting Realm, 1920s and 1930s

Introduction

The "New Negro" was a term that came into vogue during the 1920s—the Jazz Age—at the same time that a cultural and artistic renaissance, identified with Harlem, captured the imagination of blacks across the nation. The notion signified a greater assertiveness and sense of pride among African Americans, an increasing willingness to highlight the achievements of black poets and scientists, musicians and philosophers—and athletes. It suggested as well that while blacks would continue to struggle for civil rights and the opportunity to participate fully in American society, they also publicly celebrated the distinctive qualities of black culture and recognized that people of African heritage had long contributed substantially to the shaping of the United States. Conceived in terms of "muscular assimilationism" as well as cultural nationalism—as a medium of social engagement and an expression of self-respect—sport offered a source of inspiration on various levels. For many New Negroes, its potential role in forging racial solidarity as well as channeling the energy and aspirations of black Americans seemed immense.

The Jazz Age was also the era when wide-ranging and regressive immigration laws were set in place and when Nicolo Sacco and Bartolomeo Vanzetti were tried for murder and executed, as much for their Italian heritage and anarchist political beliefs as for the evidence mounted against them. The twenties marked the high tide of Klanism, and the Scopes trial showed that militant religious fundamentalism possessed a powerful appeal for many Americans who feared the challenges of modernity. Whether African Americans still labored as sharecroppers or tenant farmers in the cotton fields of the South or struggled to make their way into better-paying factory jobs in the North, they remained aware that the politics of intolerance still prevailed in America.

This sad truth compelled many African Americans to focus on community formation: the maintenance of churches, the creation of business enterprises, and the establishment of social organizations predicated on self-help and uplift. Racial reformers of this era—though espousing diverse ideologies and articulating a wide range of programs for social change—also felt emboldened to fight racism, to denounce segregation and the indignities that confronted black Americans everyday, everywhere in the United States. During the interwar years, the NAACP incessantly called for federal antilynching legislation, and W. E. B. Du Bois of the *Crisis,* along with more militant activists and editors, such as A. Phillip Randolph and Chandler Owen of *The Messenger,* chronicled the daily acts of terrorism that continued to haunt black Americans. Additionally, "race men" never failed to boast of black accomplishment or to underscore the potential of African Americans to contribute further to the democratic institutions that were supposed to define the nation. Though leaders like Du Bois and Marcus Garvey fervently disliked and distrusted one another, they were kindred spirits in voicing their pride in black achievement.

Celebrating African American successes was not a simple task, however. While James Weldon Johnson might render an impressive list of boxers and jockeys—from the early nineteenth through the early twentieth centuries—who stood alongside artists and intellectuals in forging a "black Bohemia" in New York City, other commentators clearly set black triumphs and travails within broader contexts. Descriptions of African American victories in the Olympic Games might juxtapose those gold medals with the far-reaching patterns of segregation in the United States or the grim job prospects awaiting even the most accomplished black athletes. Not just in the South, but also in other regions of the nation, municipal authorities attempted to segregate recreational facilities and place restrictions on interracial athletic competition. It was a telling fact that from the time of Marshall "Major" Taylor, at the turn of the twentieth century, through the interwar years, many black athletes and entertainers were so embittered or felt so constrained that they gave up on American society and attempted to make their way in more tolerant places such as France. But for every step forward made by black Americans in sport, a formidable new obstacle seemed to be set in place.

Ultimately, what would become the most pervasive and pernicious assault on the victories won by black athletes was the assessment by racist ideologues and pseudoscientists, as well as many white sportswriters, that accounted for African American triumphs in the boxing ring or on the track oval strictly as the result of "natural ability." Since the mid-nineteenth century, the "athletic creed" had lauded success in sports as measures of character and courage—of striving to excel in national pastimes and international competition. To sustain longstanding racial hierarchies, however, numerous commentators drew on racist stereotype and lore in their endeavor to reduce black athletic achievement to crude biological terms. At this point, homegrown white supremacy made a vague but firm alliance with the ideas that had long informed European colonialism and imperialism. During the 1930s, these representations also resembled notions of Aryanism and Nazi pronouncements and policies regarding race.

African Americans mounted forceful responses to this and other challenges. While black journalists asserted that champions had always been recognized for their hard work, dedication, and drive, W. Montague Cobb, the foremost black anatomist and physical anthropologist of the era, systematically refuted the allegations made by the scientific racists. The abilities of athletes such as Jesse Owens—who would become the hero of the 1936 Berlin Olympics—did not derive from some anatomical advantage, Cobb strenuously argued. By the mid-1930s, the black response to racism would also be embodied in the figure of Joe Louis, probably the most popular African American sportsman of the twentieth century. To understand that his victory over the Italian-Argentine boxer Primo Carnera was widely beheld by black Americans as a counterpunch to Italy's invasion of Ethiopia, to read accounts by Marcus Garvey and Richard Wright concerning the importance of his beating of the German Max Schmeling, or to listen to the songs recorded in his praise is to comprehend the pride and passion that made Louis a race hero. Significantly, at the same time that black Americans created a legend in Joe Louis, they continued to denounce segregation in the sporting world and persisted in their agitation for the extension of fair play and sportsmanship throughout American society. On the eve of World War II, they acclaimed the breakthroughs in the color line—still few and far between—though they also asserted that the greatest victories for democracy needed to occur at home. Long before Pearl Harbor, the accomplishments by black athletes in sports had been fully enlisted in the broader civil rights crusade.

A

THE "NEW NEGRO" IN SPORTS

1. James Weldon Johnson on Sportsmen in *Black Manhattan*

James Weldon Johnson was a poet, songwriter, journalist, educator, and activist. His most memorable contribution to African American culture may have been "Lift Every Voice and Sing" (composed with his brother John Rosamond Johnson), which is widely known as the "Negro national hymn." But he was also a prominent voice in many of the literary debates that characterized the Harlem Renaissance, and he edited several anthologies that brought Negro spirituals and contemporary African American poetry to a wider audience than ever before. As field secretary for the NAACP, Johnson was involved in the drive for political and legal reform in the United States; at the same time, he strived to promote race pride through his depiction of the rich and diverse cultural achievements of African Americans. Among these accomplishments, he counted black success in sport.

Indeed, what distinguishes the chapter of Johnson's book Black Manhattan *(1930) devoted to sport is that Johnson firmly situates jockeys, ballplayers, and prizefighters within the larger cosmos of African American achievement. His portrayal here places many of them—at one point or another in their careers—in New York City, alongside the actors, playwrights, and other intellectuals who were creating a black bohemia. The exploits of boxers such as Bill Richmond and Tom Molineaux—who stood among the greatest pugilists of the early nineteenth century—animate this chapter. So does a description of one of the most famous bouts fought by Jack Johnson, whom he knew well.* Ultimately, James Weldon Johnson adds the story of sport to the pageant of African American culture in ways that had not been elaborated before his time. What is more, his litany of black champions in various disciplines of athletic competition would contribute to the collective memory of many "race men" and women in the years to come.*

I have indicated that during the fourth quarter of the last century there was a pause in the racial activities of the Negroes in the North. It would be more strictly true to say that there was a change in activities. In New York the Negro now began to function and express himself on a different plane, in a different sphere; and in a different way he effectively impressed himself upon the city and the country. Within this period, roughly

---

* The career of Jack Johnson is also discussed in James Weldon Johnson's autobiography, *Along This Way* (1933).

James Weldon Johnson
(Library of Congress)

speaking, the Negro in the North emerged and gained national notice in three great
professional sports: horse-racing, baseball, and prize-fighting. He also made a beginning
and headway on the theatrical stage. And New York, the New York of the upper Twenties
and lower Thirties west of Sixth Avenue, became the nucleus of these changed activities.

Horse-racing as an American sport reached development first in the South. The
Southern landowners and aristocrats had taken up from the English gentry both riding
to hounds and racing early in the last century. By the middle of the century there was
local racing on tracks at New Orleans, Mobile, Charleston, Richmond, Nashville, Lexington (Kentucky), and Louisville. . . . The Southern horse-owners, naturally—in fact,
of necessity—made use of Negro jockeys, trainers, and stable-boys; so there grew up a
class of Negro horsemen unequaled by any in the land. When the first Kentucky Derby
was run, out of the fourteen jockeys who rode in the race thirteen were coloured.
Therefore when the centre of horse-racing was shifted to the East and became, somewhat in the English sense, a national sport, Negro jockeys constituted the very first
ranks of the profession. When racing shifted to the East and became also a profitable
business venture, with the book-maker as a recognized factor, the great jockeys jumped

into national popularity. In the hey-day of racing the name of the winner of the Futurity, the Suburban, the Realization, the Brooklyn Handicap, the Metropolitan Handicap, or the Saratoga Cup was as widely heralded and almost as widely known as the
name of the winner of a present-day championship prize-fight. In the days when jockeys were popular idols, none were more popular than the best of the coloured ones. No
American jockey was ever more popular than Isaac Murphy. . . . Other famous Negro
jockeys were: Pike Barnes, Andy Hamilton, Jimmie Winkfield, Willie Simms, Johnny
Stoval, "Tiny" Williams, the two Clayton brothers, "Soup" Perkins, "Monk" Overton,
Linc Jones, Bob Isom, Emanuel Morris, Felix Carr, and Jimmie Lee. . . . Willie Simms
was one of the best jockeys of all time. In a great degree the success of the Dwyer sta-
bles was due to his horsemanship. Riding abroad under the Croker-Dwyer colours, he
was the first non-English jockey to win a race on an English track. . . .

The record of the Negro in professional baseball makes not so full a page. He did
not have so much of a chance in baseball as he had in racing and pugilism. He never
gets so fair a chance in those forms of sport or athletics where he must be a member
of a team as in those where he may stand upon his own ability as an individual. . . .

The Negro player could not front the forces against him in organized baseball; . . . .
[therefore] he was compelled to organize for himself. The first professional Negro team
to be formed was the Gorhams of New York. From the Gorhams came the famous Cuban Giants. Following the success of the Cuban Giants, coloured professional and semiprofessional clubs called Giants of some kind were organized in a dozen or more cities.
These professional clubs have become better organized and now play a regularly scheduled series of games. They play very good ball and are quite popular, especially when
they are pitted against white teams—and they are quite frequently in New York. . . .

The Negro's fairest chance in the professional sports came in the prize-ring. Here
was brought into play more fully than in any other sport the advantageous factor of
sole dependence upon his own individual skill and stamina. The prize-fighter had an
advantage over even the jockey, who might be handicapped by hopeless mounts. The
Negro prize-fighter, of course, often ran up against the hostility of the crowd, an intangible but, nevertheless, very real handicap. This very antagonism, however, according to the stout-heartedness of the fighter, might serve as a spur to victory. This is
what actually happened when George Dixon defended his title of featherweight
champion of the world and defeated Jack Skelly at New Orleans in 1892. This was
more truly the case when Jack Johnson held his title of heavyweight champion of the
world by knocking out Jim Jeffries at Reno, July 4, 1910. Johnson has said that not only
did he have to fight Jeffries, but that psychologically he also had to fight the majority
of the thousands of spectators, many of whom were howling and praying for Jeffries
to "kill the nigger." In truth, Johnson had to do more; on that day he had to fight psychologically the majority of the population of the United States. Jeffries had been
brought forth as "the hope of the white race." Indeed, during Johnson's term of
championship and up to his defeat by Willard at Havana in 1915, every white fighter
who was being groomed as a heavyweight contender was known as a "white hope." A
good part of the press and some literary fellows were industrious in fomenting the
sentiment that the security of white civilization and white supremacy depended upon

the defeat of Jack Johnson. One of these writers assumed the role of both prophet and comforter and before the Reno battle wrote in the red-blooded style of the day that Jeffries was bound to win because, while he had Runnymede and Agincourt behind him, the Negro would be licked the moment the white man looked him in the eye. This psychic manifestation of white superiority did not materialize, but that sort of thing did help to create a tenseness of feeling that constituted something real for Jack Johnson to contend with, and, furthermore, immediately after the fight, expended itself in the beating up of numerous individual Negroes in various parts of the country as a sort of vicarious obliteration of the blot of Jeffries' defeat, and in a manner not at all in accordance with the Marquis of Queensberry rules. In fact, the reaction was so great that pressure was brought which forced Congress to pass a law prohibiting the inter-state exhibition of moving pictures of prize-fights—a law which still stands to plague and limit the magnates of pugilism and of the movies. . . .

The story of the Negro in the prize-ring goes back much further than one would think; and, curiously, the beginning of the story is laid in New York City. The earliest acknowledgment of any man as champion of America was made about 1809; and that man was Thomas Molineaux (sometimes written Molyneaux). Tom Molineaux was born in 1784, a black slave belonging to a Molineaux (or Molyneaux) family of Virginia. When he was about twenty years old, he came to New York as a freeman and got a job as porter in the old Catherine Street market. The precise manner in which he procured his freedom does not seem to be known, but it appears that it was not by running away. Catherine market was headquarters for Negro boxers, and the newcomer soon proved himself the best of them all. . . .

Molineaux, after he had beaten every worthwhile fighter in America, both Negroes and the whites belonging to the crews of British vessels in port—white Americans had not yet taken up pugilism as a profession—was persuaded by the captain of one of the foreign vessels in port to go to England and seek a fight with the famed Tom Cribb, champion of England and of the world. He did go and, through the assistance of Bill Richmond, got the match. The fight between Cribb and Molineaux, which took place on December 18, 1810, at Capthall Common, Sussex, is one of the greatest prize-ring battles of England. Compared with the theatrical performances and business-like transactions of today, it takes on titanic proportions. A reading of the contemporary accounts of the fight gives the impression of an ancient gladiatorial struggle to the death. The records of the time and later English authorities on boxing admit that, technically, Molineaux won the fight and consequently the championship of the world. He lost the decision through a bit of trickery on the part of Cribb's seconds. . . . In that age, even as today, there were excuses or "alibis"; and it was asserted that Molineaux lost because up to the time of the fight he had to go barnstorming about the country in order to make a living, while Cribb underwent the best of training at Captain Barclay's estate in Scotland and was in the finest condition. It is to Molineaux's credit that this excuse was not offered by him. Molineaux fought and won a great many fights in England, Scotland, and Ireland. He lost two to Cribb, but the courage and stamina he displayed in both fights with the champion won for him the admiration of the fancy and the British public. He remains today one of the great figures in the history of the English prize-ring. . . .

Within the United States the Negro has made a high record of pugilism. In every important division of the sport since its organized establishment a Negro has held the championship of the world. In the bantamweight, George Dixon; featherweight, George Dixon; lightweight, Joe Gans; welterweight, Joe Walcott; middleweight, Tiger Flowers; light heavyweight, Battling Siki (won in France); heavyweight, Jack Johnson. In addition to these champions, there is a long list of noble Negro pugilists. . . . Peter Jackson was the first example in the United States of a man acting upon the assumption that he could be a prize-fighter and at the same time a cultured gentleman. His chivalry in the ring was so great that sportswriters down to today apply to him the doubtful compliment, "a white coloured man." He was very popular in New York. If Jack Johnson had been in demeanor a Peter Jackson, the subsequent story of the Negro in the prize-ring would have been somewhat different. Nevertheless, it should be said for Johnson that, whatever he may have lacked in behavior and good sense, he was a first-class fighting man, rated, in fact, the best defensive fighter the American ring has ever seen. During the first decade of the century there was a trio of formidable Negro heavyweights: Sam Langford, Sam McVey, and Joe Jeanette. One of the most sensational fighters in the ring today is Kid Chocolate (Eligio Sardinas), the black Cuban bantamweight.

New York, the New York of the upper Twenties and the lower Thirties, was the business and social centre of most of the coloured men engaged in these professional sports, as it was also of the genuine black-face minstrels, the forerunners of the later coloured performers; wherever their work might take them, they homed to New York. And because these men earned and spent large sums of money, there grew up in New York a flourishing black Bohemia.

James Weldon Johnson, *Black Manhattan* (New York: Knopf, 1930), 58–73.

2. Robert Hayden / "Free Fantasia: Tiger Flowers"

Theodore "Tiger" Flowers was one of the fighters mentioned by James Weldon Johnson in Black Manhattan. *He won 115 of his 157 bouts between 1918 and 1927 and held the world middleweight title for roughly ten months in 1926—the first black champ in any weight division since Jack Johnson. Known as the "Georgia Deacon" because of his Bible reading and clean living, Flowers captured a wide following among black Americans. Robert Hayden's fame as a poet would arrive much later, though he published richly textured and technically impressive work from the end of the 1940s through the 1970s. In 1976 he became the first African American to be appointed consultant in poetry to the Library of Congress. But as this "symbolic portrait" shows, it was in his youth that Hayden was drawn to Flowers, during the height of the cultural and literary renaissance of the 1920s.**

Though written perhaps fifty years later, the poem seems to draw inspiration from such Harlem Renaissance writers as Langston Hughes; it is filled with affirmation and irony, the

---

* For more on Robert Hayden, see N. Jones, "Robert Hayden," who uses the phrase "symbolic portrait," p. 86; Turco, "Angle of Ascent"; Andrews, Foster, and Harris, *Oxford Companion to African American Literature,* 347–48.

hopes (and wagers) of everyday people bustling through Hayden's native Detroit. "Free Fantasia" suggests that reports of Flowers's "bluesteel prowess" charged conversations among the men and women whom Hayden remembers fondly as hanging around a local brothel. In its clear, clipped phrases, the poem also delivers image after image linking such passion for the ring to religion. This symbolism sets up the concluding lines, which for those who know the story, are all the more poignant. In 1927, less than a year after he gave up the middle-weight crown, the "Georgia Deacon" died suddenly during surgery to remove scar tissue from around his eyes. He was thirty-two years old. *

——————

The sporting people
along St. Antoine
that scufflers'
paradise of ironies
    bet salty money
on his righteous
    hook and jab.

I was a boy then, running
(unbeknownst to Pa)
errands for Miss Jackie
and Stack-o-Diamonds' Eula Mae.
. . . Their perfumes,
rouged Egyptian faces.
Their pianolas jazzing.

O Creole babies,
Dixie odalisques,
speeding through cutglass
dark to see the macho angel
    trick you'd never
    turn, in his bluesteel prowess
    In the ring.

Hardshell believers
amen'd the wreck
as God A'mighty's
will. I'd thought
    such gaiety could not
die. Nor could our
    elegant avenger.

Frederick Glaysher, ed., *Robert Hayden: Collected Poems* (New York: Liveright/Norton, 1985), 130. Poem originally published in *Angle of Ascent: New and Selected Poems* (New York: Liveright, 1975).

---

* See Crawford, "Tiger Flowers." See also Chalk, *Pioneers of Black Sport,* 168–69; Sammons, *Beyond the Ring,* 56. For the story of another charismatic fighter of the 1920s, see Gerald Early, "Battling Siki: The Boxer as Natural Man," in his *Culture of Bruising,* 66–85.

3. *Paris Noir:* Eugene Bullard on the Expatriate Experience

For writers like James Weldon Johnson, who helped promote the Harlem Renaissance, there was much to celebrate during the Jazz Age. For others who surveyed the African American cultural landscape, the 1920s stood out as an era when the masses of black Americans who participated in the "Great Migration" reinforced African American communities already established in the North and when the "New Negro" made ever-bolder claims to full participation in the social, economic, and political life of the nation. It was a time when an increasing number of blacks spoke more openly and assertively about racial reform and the shape of things to come. At the same historical moment, however, the persistence of racism and discrimination, North and South and in so many forms, persuaded other black Americans to leave the United States and to seek their way in life in what they hoped would be a more tolerant Europe.

Eugene Bullard's expatriate experiences actually began before the Roaring Twenties. While his story stands on its own as a tale of heroism—in two world wars—and numerous hardships in making a life as an athlete and entrepreneur on the other side of the Atlantic, it is also representative of the careers of other alienated black Americans: the champion cyclist Marshall "Major" Taylor at the turn of the century, the jockey Jimmy Winkfield during

Eugene J. Bullard in advertising photo for his Paris gymnasium, 1920s (Courtesy Richard K. Reid)

the 1910s, and the flamboyant "Panama" Al Brown, among scores of prizefighters during the interwar years. Bullard's life also intersected with the literary world of Paris, where black artists, intellectuals, and entertainers created a lively colony for themselves, one element of its vitality measured in the shared sense of the distance between the openness of Montmartre and the prevailing laws and customs of Jim Crow America.

Here the fragments from Bullard's unpublished autobiography, "All Blood Runs Red," only begin to reveal the richness of his life. Born in Columbus, Georgia, in 1895, Bullard worked his way out of the South until by 1912 he arrived in Great Britain, where he set himself up as a vaudeville performer and a prizefighter—under the tutelage of Aaron Lester Brown, the fabled "Dixie Kid." He spent the next several years as a vagabond, "on the stage and in the ring," his biographer tells us, "from Liverpool and London to Paris, Berlin, and Moscow." During World War I he served with the French Foreign Legion, then as a combat aviator, ultimately becoming a war hero for France. After the war Bullard owned and managed nightclubs and a gymnasium in Paris, while continuing to take good offers—in Alexandria, Egypt, for instance—to display his boxing skills. But Bullard never counted on his athletic prowess alone. Rather, he employed his skills as a boxer and trainer, along with his considerable managerial talents, in the creation of his own business enterprises, such as the club Le Grand Duc. This helped remake the cultural centers of Europe, although—as the second of these passages suggests—even in the City of Light, provocations often impelled proud black men to defend their honor in the street. A central figure in the Parisian black community during the interwar years, Eugene Bullard became friends with the jazz immortal Sidney Bechet and was in constant contact with Ada Louise Smith, better known as "Bricktop," who was perhaps the consummate entertainer-entrepreneur during this period. His acquaintances included Josephine Baker and Louis Armstrong, Charles Chaplin, Gloria Swanson, the Prince of Wales, and Ernest Hemingway. All these encounters contributed substantially to the celebrated jazz scene, cabaret culture, and sense of community that inflects the black presence in Paris to this very day.*

——— ———

The boxers in Paris then were all equally nice to each other and to me. I loved them all. There never was any name-calling like "Nigger." It seemed to me that the French democracy influenced the minds of both black and white Americans there and helped us all to act like brothers as nearly as possible. This made me feel that France was what my dear loving and great father had told me she was. It convinced me, too, that God really did create all men equal, and it was easy to live that way. . . .

I treat everybody with respect and I do not allow anyone to treat me rudely. It was to find equal treatment, to find freedom that I struggled so long and hard to get across the ocean to France. It was to defend the freedom of our Allies that I fought in two

---

* The key sources on Bullard's life start with Carisela and Ryan, *Black Swallow of Death*, although this book derives largely from the autobiography. Far more expansive in its documentation and sense of context is Lloyd, *Eugene Bullard*. See also Stovall, *Paris Noir*, and Arroyo, *"Panama" Al Brown*. One should also note that large numbers of African American baseball players found more economic opportunity and considerably less racism when they played in Mexico and the Caribbean. See Tygiel, *Baseball's Great Experiment*.

bloody wars. Never have I gone against my principles about freedom for each decent person and freedom for democratic nations.

Defending my self-respect and that of others who were unjustly abused or insulted is the reason I have had many fights outside the ring. Any contempt shown to a fellow human being just because of his race, creed, or color I consider a sickness. Even animals fight back when they are attacked, and I have no respect for a man who is too cowardly to stand up for himself. Everybody admires a man who defends his honor. By doing that, by demanding that people treat me with as much respect as I treat them, I have made many friends.

Eugene Bullard, "All Blood Runs Red," quoted in P. J. Carisella and James W. Ryan, *The Black Swallow of Death: The Incredible Story of Eugene Jacques Bullard, the World's First Black Combat Aviator* (Boston: Marlborough House, 1972), 70–71, 207.

B

NEGOTIATING THE TERMS OF
BLACK ATHLETIC ACHIEVEMENT

4. Harry Levette and Herbert Henegan:
Two Considerations of the 1932 Olympic Games

Not until the Los Angeles Olympic Games of 1932, when Eddie Tolan won gold medals for both the 100-meter and 200-meter dash—with Ralph Metcalfe taking silver and bronze for the two events and Edward Gordon claiming the gold for the long jump—were black athletes recognized as a significant presence in international competition. African Americans had participated in previous Olympics: George Poage won two bronze medals for hurdles races in 1904 and DeHart Hubbard, the gold, and Edward Gourdin, the silver, for the long jump in 1924. Subverting the notion that black athletes possessed "great speed but little stamina," Earl Johnson, one of the best American distance runners, captured a bronze medal for the 10,000-meter cross-country race in the 1924 games. But it was the elaborate ritual and spectacle staged in the Los Angeles Memorial Coliseum during the summer of 1932 that substantially reinforced the significance of the achievements by the black trackmen.

The particular importance of the victories by Eddie Tolan was not lost on the African American press. As the following verses show, black commentators cast their appraisals of the Olympics in far different terms than those customarily employed by their white counterparts. One poem celebrates the outcome of the 100-meter dash, as an emblem not of patriotism but of race pride. The other clearly rejects any notion that an Olympic victory was a triumph of "the American way" by juxtaposing Tolan's distinction as the "world's fastest human" with his status as a black man in a racist society. Written in different styles, the poems are complementary in yet another way. Harry Levette renders in the most explicit terms the indignities and outrages of American segregation, and just as emphatically his anger at the prevailing racial situation in the United States. Though it ends with an allusion to the mannered verse of Countee Cullen, this newspaper poem is suggestive of a black vernacular that would achieve greater currency during the 1930s. In contrast, Herbert Henegan's classical imagery and his use of indirection and irony speaks to a different strand of the "New Negro" movement, its elevated tone doubtless a calculated appeal to the readership of such journals of uplift and assimilation as the Crisis. *The references in the verse to Viking ships and Nordic gods cleverly engage the dominant racial theories of the day concerning the alleged superiority of the white race. For black Americans, weary of the claims to world mastery of the Teuton, Saxon, and Aryan, the understated humor of Henegan's poem offered a telling counterpoint to the provocative lines written by Levette.*

Finally, it is important to note that racial reformers worked beyond the immediate instances of African American excellence in sport to craft a strategy of "muscular assimilationism." Victories in sport, they asserted, were emblematic of blacks' enormous potential to contribute to the social, economic, and political life of the nation. Thus, when congratulating the black victors of the 1932 Olympic Games, Arthur Howe, president of Hampton Institute, would declare that the accomplishments of those athletes bespoke "many less advertised victories . . . in more significant realms." Triumphs on the athletic field called attention to the fact that in every decade since the Civil War, African Americans had "improved their lot in literacy, health, home ownership and property holdings" and had actively participated in important educational, literary, and intellectual developments. The successes of blacks in sports "should be a source of pride and inspiration," Howe concluded. Ultimately, they also challenged "everyone to give the Negro his due in justice and opportunity."*

————————

Harry Levette / "Eddie Tolan Is the Fastest Human—But"

He's a "nigger" right on
He can't run against white runners in Georgia
He can't eat with white runners in Alabama
He can't go to school with white runners in South Carolina
He can't ride the train with white runners in Texas
He can't sit beside a white runner in a street car in Florida
He can't pray in a church with white runners in Tennessee
He can't pose with white runners in Arkansas
Because he's just a "nigger."
Eddie's the "fastest human"—but
Mistreatment shall be his portion as long as life shall last
He's a "coon."
Who cares if he ain't got nothin' to eat?
He wants to be a doctor but money is scarce
Who cares?
Who'll give him a chance?
Filipino, Japanese, Chinese, Mexican, Indian—Opportunity for All—
But Eddie's a "nigger"
Dirty, different.
He can run like hell, but—he's a nigger right on.
He wins honors for American, but nothing for himself
He must plot right on, passing up eating places while he's hungry
Begging for somebody to take his part so he can inch along.

---

* Howe, "Two Races and What They Symbolize," 387. Bearing witness to that declaration, Ralph Metcalfe went on to become an instructor at Xavier University (New Orleans), then a member of the Chicago City Council. In 1972 he was elected to the U.S. House of Representatives and served until his death in 1978.

The better he does the worse it hurts.
Like Cullen, he can exclaim, "I who have burned my hands upon a star."

Harry Levette, "Eddie Tolan's the Fastest Human—But," *Minneapolis Twin Cities Herald,* August 27, 1932.

HERBERT HENEGAN / "THE 100 METERS FINALS AT THE OLYMPICS"

Two swarthy ships
Sailing in the breeze
Like mighty Thors
Astride a blast of thunder
On they come, annihilating time
And space.
Upon a sable sea of cinders
See them fly—
Cutting calm waves of wind
Wind their sharp black prows
Leaving a helpless, trailing spray
Of Nordic foam.

Herbert Henegan, "The 100 Meters Finals at the Olympics," *Crisis,* November 1933, 262.

5. "Black Mercuries": The Meaning of Black Athletic Achievement

The poems about the meaning of the 1932 Olympic Games for African Americans only hint at the commentary revolving around the increasing number of black triumphs in international sport. Since the turn of the twentieth century, black Americans had been forced to confront a new twist on the arguments made by white supremacists or those who invoked "science" to protect the interest of the Nordic races. Theretofore, scientific racism was largely devoted to proving the inequality of the races by referring to weird diagrams of facial angles and measurements of cranial capacity. Swiftly, though, even as the first modern generation of black champions was emerging in such sports as boxing, bicycle racing, and track and field, white racial theorists began to allege that certain anatomical differences such as an elongated heel bone accounted for, and qualified, black success in athletic competition. *

What began as a campaign to "prove equality" on the playing field thus required additional research and interpretation for those black editors and commentators who linked sports to civil rights. One part of their task was becoming easier year by year. Blacks were winning championships and setting records in a variety of events. From Marcus Garvey's Negro World *to the* Norfolk Journal and Guide, *the black press took considerable pride (and pleasure) in noting that the victor of the 1928 Olympic marathon was a North African runner,*

---

* For more on the 1932 Games, see C. Williams, "Negro Athletes in the Tenth Olympiad." Regarding shifting racial theories and sport, see D. Wiggins, "'Great Speed but Little Stamina,'" and Miller, "Anatomy of Scientific Racism."

Ralph Metcalfe and
Jesse Owens, mid-1930s
(Art Carter Papers,
Moorland-Spingarn Col-
lection, Howard Univer-
sity Archives, Howard
University)

Boughera El Ouafi. The marathon, remarked the Pittsburgh Courier-Journal, *requires "an
amount of stamina and endurance sometimes regarded as a distinctively Nordic attribute."
Defenders of Nordic superiority now had to come to terms with the fact that the 26-mile,
385-yard race "had been won by a brown-skinned Algerian Arab, with a dark-skinned Chil-
ean second, and two yellow-skinned Japanese fourth and sixth, while the white race had to
be content with third and fifth places." By the era of Tolan and Metcalfe, in the 1932 games,
and in the years leading up to the Jesse Owens Olympics, African American journalists enu-
merated black triumphs in sport and echoed Arthur Howe's refrain that this measure of
success obliged white America to expand opportunities for blacks, both on and beyond the
playing field.**

*Opportunity and striving became the watchwords for those who then took on the task
of explaining why black runners and jumpers and boxers excelled. As the following article
suggests, the achievements of black Americans in sports were not the result of some inherent*

---

* "El Ouafi," *Negro World*, August 18, 1928, 4; "Olympic Results Hurt Nordic Pride, Scientist Declares," *Pittsburgh Courier-Journal*, August 11, 1928 (quotes). See also Dyreson, "American Ideas about Race and Olympic Races."

biological advantages but rather of blacks' chance to participate in open competition and to prove themselves in venues where the starting line was the same for all. This piece from the Peoria Transcript *is a modest but eloquent argument that anatomy was not destiny in the realm of athletics. Black Americans simply wanted to believe that the rhetoric of "equality" and "opportunity" had some meaning in constitutional and cultural terms. Whenever they could, they accepted the challenge to compete. But a more formidable obstacle has remained. For scholars and intellectuals who have long dealt with assertions about "great speed" and the "bell curve"—along with a host of anthropologists and biologists who have shown how Aryan racial theory and eugenics contributed to the Holocaust—the specter of scientific racism has simply not gone away.**

———————

A call may be going out one of these days for new "white hopes" to regain Caucasian supremacy in athletics. A Negro high school boy has recently equaled the fastest time ever recorded for anyone in the 100-yard dash, beating all white high school boys, present and past, in that and other events of speed and agility. Much of America's hopes in the last Olympic Games were based on the speed of two Negro runners. At a recent national high school and college meet the three leaders in the 100 and 200 meter sprints were Metcalfe, Johnson and Owens, all colored.

Black feet have often been regarded as funny. They are inclined to be large, flat and to have projecting heels. Yet there is certainly something in the combination of those feet with black legs and powerful lungs that have placed Negro boys at the top of the list of American sprinters.

There is something more than physical development in the achievement of the Negro. It is a moral urge that of late has been revealing itself in many fields of endeavor. Americans have been discovering unsuspected gifts lately in their black people, notably in the fields of music and drama. Recognition of the Negro as a valuable member of society may bring out other gifts.

"Black Mercuries," *Peoria Transcript*, July 9, 1933.

6. W. Montague Cobb / "Race and Runners"

For many years W. Montague Cobb was one of the leading physical anthropologists in the nation. Since the medical profession and allied associations were formally segregated during most of his career, Cobb's prominence in the field would find expression in his editorship of the Journal of the National Medical Association *and as longtime chair of the Department of Anatomy at Howard University. From those platforms, though, Cobb made distinguished contributions to medical training and the improvement of health care nationally.*

It was relatively early in his scientific career that Cobb entered the debate over the size

———————

* See Graves, *The Emperor's New Clothes*.

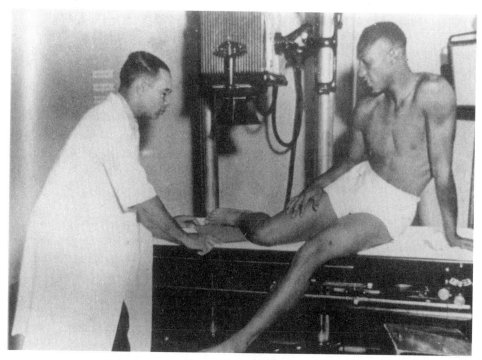

W. Montague Cobb, left, in medical lab with Jesse Owens, 1935 (Courtesy *Chicago Defender*)

of the calf muscles of athletes or the length of the heel bones of blacks and whites. During the nineteenth and early twentieth centuries, racial scientists were devoted to the measurement of cranial capacity and the length of limbs, and then to various IQ tests, largely with the objective of proving the inequality of the human races. When black athletes started gaining an increasing number of successes in the athletic arena after the turn of the century, defenders of white supremacy turned to anthropometry—the measurement of bones and muscles—to account for the excellent performances turned in by runners and jumpers such as Jesse Owens, which they then attributed to some kind of natural endowment. Cobb, for his part, was among the first of a younger generation of biologists who emphasized not only that there was more variability within the so-called human "races" than between them. He also subscribed to Franz Boas's notions of cultural difference, that is, a social theory that was not bound to heredity or hierarchy.*

Cobb's investigations of elite performance in track and field yielded significant results. Simply stated, shotputters and distance runners did vary substantially in build; whites and blacks competing in the same events did not. Examining the anatomy of the sprint champion Jesse Owens, for instance, Cobb found that in some of the categories/dimensions then used by the anthropometrists, Owens came closest to the "Caucasoid" type; in others, Owens resembled the "Negroid" type. This was one element in a broader argument against rigid for-

---

* On Cobb, see Rankin-Hill and Blakey, "W. Montague Cobb"; Scarupa, "W. Montague Cobb." For a discussion of anthropometry, see Gould, *The Mismeasure of Man.*

mulations of racial difference. Another required only clear vision and good sense: record holders such as Howard Drew and Ned Gourdin were light skinned with straight hair. Cobb asserted that they might well be taken for white men "by those not in the know." Ultimately, it was—and remains—pernicious folly to measure for distinctly or purely racial types. As Cobb later wrote: "Science has not revealed a single trait peculiar to the Negro alone, to which his athletic achievement could be attributed."*

Cobb was writing against the backdrop of centuries of racial discrimination in the United States. Though in 1936 he could not have known the outcome of the quest for racial purity in Europe, he knew well the purposes to which scientific racism had long been applied.

———————

As the physical anthropologist scans the fascinating panorama of contests in simultaneous progress at a great track meet like the Penn Relay Carnival, he becomes aware of an association between certain types of bodily build and special events. Conspicuous contrasts are the large, heavily muscled, occasionally paunchy athletes who put the shot and throw the hammer farthest, and the tall, lean young men who jump highest. The leading high hurdlers are tall and the stellar distance men of medium to slender build. In the other running and field events distinctive types of bodily build are less apparent. Almost every variety of human form and style of performance competes successfully in the relay races which endlessly circle the track.

Since athletic accomplishment is jointly dependent upon physical constitution, technique, and the will to achieve, it is obvious that in a few specialized events a particular bodily build may confer advantages which cannot be overbalanced by any amount of training and determination on the part of the less gifted. In the shot put, great bodily weight is an advantage, increasing the impetus imparted to the shot; in the high jump it is a handicap, adding to the load which the muscles must lift from the ground. Similarly, it can be shown that tallness is of advantage to both weight man and high jumper.

Among the sprinters and broad jumpers a diversity of physical types is seen. It is apparent that here determination of the influence of bodily build on performance will be more difficult.

As the anthropologist surveys the striving field in the stadium, he sees nothing to suggest an association between race and competition in any particular event. He notices Negro youths in nearly every phase of competition. Their bodily build varies like that of other athletes. The weight men are big fellows, while those topping the bar are more sparely built. However, a number of recent comments in the press upon the current success of American Negro sprinters and broad jumpers have either directly ascribed this success to a longer heel bone or stronger tendon of Achilles than those of their white competitors, or implied that in some way it has been due to racial characteristics. The wide circulation which these suggestions have received warrants a careful appraisal of the facts.

---

* See Cobb, "Does Science Favor Negro Athletes?" 74–77 (quote on 77). See also D. Wiggins, "'Great Speed but Little Stamina'"; Miller, "The Anatomy of Scientific Racism."

In the 1932 Olympics two American Negroes, Eddie Tolan and Ralph Metcalfe, carried off top places in both the 100- and 200-meter dashes, Tolan setting new Olympic records in each event; and another Negro, Ed Gordon, won the broad jump. Since the tenth Olympiad, Negroes have continued to dominate the national field in the sprints and broad jump in the persons of Metcalfe, Jesse Owens, Eulace Peacock, and Ben Johnson. . . .

. . . Jesse Owens, like Metcalfe a persistent performer, won the national AAU broad-jump championship in 1933 and 1934. He has made and equalled various intermediate sprint records. In one afternoon at Ann Arbor, Michigan, in May, 1935, he performed the greatest track feats ever wrought by a single man, breaking three world's records and equalling a fourth. He leaped 26 feet 8¼ inches in the broad jump, ran the 220-yard dash in 20.3 seconds, and won the 220-yard low hurdles in 22.6 seconds for new records, besides equalling the world mark of Frank Wykoff of 9.4 seconds for the 100-yard dash. . . .

Wide attention has thus come to be focussed on the fact that in the past champion sprinters and broad jumpers have often been Negroes. The first was Howard P. Drew who became national AAU champion at 100 yards in 1912 and 1913 while at Springfield (Mass.) High School. He 1913 he also won the 220-yard title. In 1914 Drew went to the University of Southern California where he became co-holder with Arthur Duffey of Georgetown of the world's record of 9.6 seconds for the 100-yard dash, a mark which stood for many years. Drew also equalled the world's record for the 220-yard sprint, which at that time was 21.2 seconds. His action photographs are displayed today as models of perfect form. . . .

There is . . . no running event and few field events to which Negroes have not contributed some outstanding performer and there is no indication of ineptitude in any event in which no champion has yet appeared. It is to be noted, however, that the sprint and broad jump champions have appeared in a rapid succession, culminating in the present group of contemporaneous performers. For this reason they have been especially conspicuous in the public eye. It is this prominence which has probably stimulated the notion that these stars might owe their success to some physical attributes peculiar to their race.

The Old, Old Story

This sort of suggestion is by no means new. In the days when peerless Paavo Nurmi daily fired every youngster's imagination with new world's records broken in Olympic competition, in the months afterward when more records fell during the memorable duels of Nurmi and his doughty Finnish team-mate, Willie Ritola, while the two toured America, there were reams written on why the Finns seemed to have a permanent corner on supremacy in the distance runs. The historians extolled the conquests of the mighty Hans Kolehmainen in 1913. Geographers showed how Finland's rugged climate bred endurance such that the rest of the world might as well turn in its spikes. Moralizing editors completely effervesced on the subject. But still the ancient records (1904) of England's immortal Al Shrubb for the 6-, 7-, 8-, and 9-mile runs are the world's best. Along have come Kansas' Cunningham, Princeton's Bonthron, and New

Zealand's Lovelock to run the mile with "impossible speed." Who can say whence the next athletic "trust busters" will come, or what records they will attack? . . .

But to pursue seriously our original inquiry about the relation of the Negro's anatomy to his feats on cinders and pit, track coach and anthropologist must pool their knowledge.

Coach and Anthropologist

To detect and develop athletic talent is the prime function of our track coaches. The track coach is professionally interested only in those qualities of an athlete which make for excellence in performance. He has no concern with the measure in which those qualities may also be characteristic of men of particular occupations or races. These are the business of the physical anthropologist.

Let the track coach set down the factors that make a great sprinter and the anthropologist the distinguishing features of the American Negro. If on comparison the two lists have much in common, race may be important; if little, race is of no significance.

Almost at once, however, we are beset with vagaries. The track coach cannot categorically describe the physique and character of the sprint champion, nor can the anthropologist define with useful accuracy the physique and character of the American Negro. . . .

The personal histories and constitutions of our sprinters have not yet been sufficiently analyzed for the formula for the perfect sprinter or jumper to be given. We are not able to say what measure of natural capacity is due to physical proportions, or to physiological efficiency or to forceful personality. Nor can we weight capacity and training scientifically. This does not mean that strongly biased opinions on the subject are non-existent. For instance, it has been said that superior sprinting and jumping ability must be a matter of nine-tenths capacity and one-tenth jumping because the Negro is not disposed to subject himself to rigorous training.

Despite the fact that adequate data are not available for scientific analysis of sprinting and jumping ability, many useful conclusions may be drawn from a common sense approach to the problem. We know first of all that the physique, style of performance, and character of our champions have been highly variable. . . .

When the track coach arrays before his mind's eye the galaxy of stars who have done the hundred in 9.6 seconds or better, he notes no uniformity of physique, style, or temperament. . . . For fine distinctions, data of desirable precision are not available but we can say from general inspection that there have been long-legged champions and short-legged ones; some with large calves and some with small. Record-breaking legs have had long Caucasoid calves like those of Paddock and short Negroid ones such as Tolan has. . . . In the matter of style, there have been fast starters like Hubbard and Simpson and slow ones like Paddock and Metcalfe. We have had "powerhouse" sprinters such as Metcalfe and smooth graceful flashes like Owens whose performances see without effort. In respect to temperament again we find no homogeneity. . . . There have been champions of great courage who were undaunted by defeat or misfortune and others who reacted very severely to "bad breaks." . . .

We have seen that the variability of the physical, physiological, and personality traits of great sprinters and jumpers, and inadequate scientific data prevent a satisfactory statement as to just what traits are responsible for their success. . . . Let us now go to the anthropologist. He has to deal with men categorically designated as American Negroes, but they do not look alike. Genetically we know they are not constituted alike. There is not one single physical feature, including skin color, which all of our Negro champions have in common which would identify them as Negroes. . . .

From his photographs Howard Drew is usually taken for a white man by those not in the know. Gourdin had dark straight hair, no distinctly Negroid features, and a light brown complexion. In a great metropolis he would undoubtedly be often considered a foreigner. . . . [E]xtending his view, the anthropologist fails to find racial homogeneity even among the white sprinters. We find blond Nordic and swarthy Mediterranean types and various mixtures. In fact if all our Negro and white champions were lined up indiscriminately for inspection, no one except those conditioned to American attitudes would suspect that race had anything whatever to do with the athlete's ability.

W. Montague Cobb, "Race and Runners," *Journal of Health and Physical Education* 7 (January 1936): 3–7, 52–53, 54, 56.

7. Walter White to Jesse Owens on Race Pride and the Nazi Olympics

From almost the moment Adolph Hitler assumed power in Germany, a worldwide debate ensued among sport leaders as to whether the Olympic Games should be held in Berlin in 1936. Perhaps nowhere was the debate more intense than in the United States. Between July and December 1935, in particular, various individuals and groups argued for either participation or nonparticipation of America's athletes in the Berlin games. Those who advocated participation, including, most notably, Avery Brundage—at that time president of the United States Olympic Committee—argued that politics should not interfere with something as sacred as the Olympic Games. Those who advocated nonparticipation, including Jeremiah T. Mahoney, president of the Amateur Athletic Union, argued that allowing American athletes to compete in Berlin would be giving at least implicit approval to Hitler's regime and Nazi atrocities. *

Among those brought into the debate over the 1936 Berlin Olympics were some of the outstanding African American athletes who had qualified to compete in the games. Jesse Owens, Ralph Metcalfe, Cornelius Johnson, and other black Olympians were frequently asked their opinion on the debate and, in some cases, strongly urged to boycott Hitler's Olympics. In the following telegraph addressed to Owens on December 6, 1935, Walter White, execu-

---

* The secondary literature is replete with studies of the 1936 Olympics. See, for example, Mandell, *The Nazi Olympics*; Hart-Davis, *Hitler's Games*; Krüger, "Fair Play for American Athletes"; Gottlieb, "The American Controversy over the Olympic Games"; D. Wiggins, "The 1936 Olympic Games in Berlin." See also Miller, "The Nazi Olympics, Berlin, 1936," a review essay about the exhibition at the U.S. Holocaust Memorial Museum, Washington, D.C.

tive secretary of the National Association for the Advancement of Colored People, provides the text of an address he had made at the Mecca Temple in New York City. White expressed the hope that black athletes would decline the invitation to compete in Berlin. Although confessing he would find pleasure in the triumphs of African American athletes over Nazi youth, White argued that Owens and others selected to the Olympic team would live to regret their decision to participate; they would look foolish competing in an Olympiad hosted by a man who violated every principle of decency and fair play. Tellingly, White was also quick to point out that efforts should continue to rid the United States of the racial discrimination that existed in the sporting world and beyond. He was not alone in linking the fascism practiced by Hitler to the situation faced at home by millions of African Americans.

——— ——

December 4, 1935

My dear Mr. Owens:

Will you permit me to say that it was with deep regret that I read in the New York press today a statement attributed to you saying that you would participate in the 1936 Olympic games even if they are held in Germany under the Hitler regime. I trust that you will not think me unduly officious in expressing the hope that this report is erroneous.

I fully realize how great a sacrifice it will be for you to give up the trip to Europe and to forgo the acclaim, which your athletic prowess will unquestionably bring you. I realize equally well how hypocritical it is for certain Americans to point the finger of scorn at any other country for racial or any other kind of bigotry.

On the other hand, it is my first conviction that the issue of participation in the 1936 Olympics, if held in Germany under the present regime, transcends all other issues. Participation by American athletes, and especially those of our own race, which has suffered more than any other from American race hatred, would, I firmly believe, do irreparable harm. I take the liberty of sending you a copy of the remarks, which I made at a meeting here in New York, at Mecca Temple, last evening. This sorry world of ours is apparently coming in a fumbling way to realize what prejudice against any minority group does not only to other minorities but to the group which is in power. The very preeminence of American Negro athletes gives them an unparalleled opportunity to strike a blow at racial bigotry and to make other minority groups conscious of the sameness of their problems with ours and puts them under the moral obligation to think more clearly and to fight more vigorously against the wrongs from which we Negroes suffer.

But the moral issue involved is, in my opinion, far greater than the immediate or future benefit to the Negro as a race. If the Hitlers and Mussolinis of the world are successful it is inevitable that dictatorships based upon prejudice will spread throughout the world, as indeed they are now spreading. Defeat of dictators before they become too firmly entrenched would, on the other hand, deter nations, which through fear or other unworthy emotions are tending towards dictatorships. Let me make this quite concrete. Anti-Semitic, anti-Catholic and anti-Negro prejudices are growing alarmingly throughout the United States. Should efforts towards recovery fail, there is no telling where America will go. There are some people who believe that a proletarian dictatorship will come. I do not believe this will happen and the course of history clearly indicates that it is not likely to happen. Instead, it is more probable that we would have a fascist dictatorship.

It is also historically true that such reactionary dictatorships pick out the most vulnerable group as its first victims. In the United States it would be the Negro who would be the chief and first suffered, just as the Jews have been made the scapegoats of Hitlerism in Nazi Germany. Sinclair Lewis, in his last novel, IT CAN'T HAPPEN HERE, has written what seems to me to be a very sound picture of what may happen. I have written at greater length than I had intended at the outset. I hope, however, that you will not take offense at my writing you thus frankly with the hope that you will take the high stand that we should rise above personal benefit and help strike a blow at intolerance. I am sure that your stand will be applauded by many people in all parts of the world, as your participation under the present situation in Germany would alienate many high-minded people who are awakening to the dangers of intolerance wherever it raises its head.

Very sincerely
Walter White
Secretary
NAACP

Mr. Jesse Owens
Ohio State University
Columbus, Ohio

Letter from Walter White to Jesse Owens, December 4, 1935, NAACP Papers, Library of Congress.

C

RECKONING WITH JOE LOUIS

8. Marcus Garvey / "The American Negro in Sport"

Marcus Garvey was a black nationalist who organized the largest and most powerful mass movement of blacks in American history. Referred to by one of his biographers as the black Moses, the Jamaican-born Garvey founded the Universal Negro Improvement Association (UNIA) in 1914 to help foster racial pride, economic independence, and worldwide unity among "all people of Negro or African heritage."* To espouse his personal philosophy and publicize UNIA's various initiatives, including the promotion of the Black Star Shipping Line, in 1918 Garvey founded the Negro World, *which became an enormously popular weekly that had a circulation between 50,000 and 200,000 at the height of its popularity. In 1933,* Negro World *ceased publication and was succeeded by the* Black Man. *Published from London after November 1934 and appearing irregularly throughout the second half of the 1930s, the* Black Man *always had a Garvey poem on the front cover, an editorial section dealing with current events, columns discussing the lives of prominent black figures, and, perhaps most important, letters from Garvey detailing his views on racial issues and UNIA programs. The* Black Man *ceased publication sometime in 1939; Garvey was ultimately unable to keep the magazine afloat any longer because of the lack of financial support.*

In the following account from an issue of the Black Man *in 1937, Garvey provides one of his occasional exposés of sport. His comments, plus additional remarks he makes in other issues of the journal, substantiate much of what we know about Garvey from the secondary literature. First, Garvey was a close follower of boxing, especially the life and career of Joe Louis.** He took pride in the "Brown Bomber's" ring triumphs, even disrupting the 1935 UNIA convention so that participants could listen to Louis's fight with Primo Carnera.† Second, it is clear that Garvey viewed the success of African Americans in boxing specifically and sport more generally as important ammunition in the battle against racial stereotypes and discrimination. Although claiming that there was a "more serious side of life," Garvey believed that the extraordinary amount of attention paid to sport in the black press was necessary because the public announcements of the triumphs of individual African American athletes—especially in competitions with white athletes—helped break down notions of racial inferiority and had an uplifting effect on people of African ancestry everywhere. To Garvey, as for many of his followers, victories by black athletes resonated with symbolic significance far beyond the realm of sport.*

---

* See Cronon, *Black Moses,* 16–17.

** Other writings by Garvey on Joe Louis appeared in *Black Man* 2 (July–August 1936): 19; 3 (July 1938): 1; 4 (February 1939): 20.

† Sammons relays this information from James Spady in Sammons, "'Race' and Sport," 220.

In sports, general athletics and on the stage the American Negro is making history for the Negro race. As a fact no one can raise any objection to the positive statement that the American Negro is leading the world as far as Negroes are concerned. By virtue of his environment he has raised himself to an eminence that keeps him continuously before the spotlight of things. He is the best all-round sportsman that we know. Although he has been used unfortunately against himself on the stage he has raised the status of the race as artists. When we write this way we are thinking of those Negro artists who have consistently upheld the best traditions of the group. We are not so much thinking of men like Paul Robeson who allow themselves to be used damagingly. Joe Louis, Jack Johnson, Harry Wills and other great Negro pugilists have brought to us undying honour and given us recognition that we probably would not have had so easily otherwise. If in nothing else, in the realm of boxing, the Negro has raised the status of the black man. As a fact the black man is considered the only dangerous competitor of the white man in the ring and he has knocked him out so often as to

Marcus Garvey (Library of Congress)

Poster for Joe Louis
movie, *The Fight Never
Ends,* 1949 (Library of
Congress)

leave the impression that he is safely the world's champion. All this is due to the wonderful initiative of the American Negro in launching out competitively and not being
afraid to challenge all comers. The American Negro newspapers indulge in sports to a
great extent. Sometimes more than fifty percent of their issues are devoted to sports
news and activities. This may not be very constructive but it is very helpful. Sooner or
later the more serious side of life will be advocated but until the Negro finds his level
in that, he ought not to be discouraged from indulging in the sport that is characteristic of him.

Marcus Garvey, "The American Negro in Sport," *Black Man,* March–April 1937, 17.

9. Richard Wright / "High Tide in Harlem: Joe Louis as a Symbol of Freedom"

The second bout between Joe Louis and Max Schmeling lasted all of 124 seconds. That's less time than it would have taken fans on that night of June 22, 1938, to pass through the turnstiles in Yankee Stadium and find their seats. Two years earlier, Schmeling had won a highly controversial contest with a twelfth-round KO. As Richard Wright describes it here, the rematch was not so much a fight as a demolition. It would be celebrated by African Americans—and other black people around the globe—not just for hours and days, but for half a century and more.

For his part, Wright was fascinated by the ring, but he was even more caught up in the symbolic significance of Louis's victories. His first piece of journalism, "Joe Louis Uncovers Dynamite," described the 1935 Louis triumph over Max Baer, black over white. During the next several years, while writing the short stories that would be collected in the volume Uncle Tom's Children, *Wright moved from Chicago to New York City. But his politics remained leftist, and he was widely recognized as one of the most militant contributors to the Federal Writers Project.*

Sport was politics, of course, and Wright perceived the ideological significance of black triumph in the athletic domain. Two days after the second Louis-Schmeling bout, Wright contributed a special report to the Communist Party Daily Worker *titled "How He Did It—And Oh!—Where Were Hitler's Pagan Gods?" "High Tide in Harlem" followed. This latter article echoes the first piece he wrote for the* New Masses; *at the outset the prose may seem overwrought. Wright is setting the scene for an epic struggle. Then the prevailing metaphor quickly shifts to puppetry—anticipating one of the central motifs in Ralph Ellison's* Invisible Man *(1952). During the mid-1930s it would have been difficult to exaggerate the symbolic significance of the bout. Louis and Schmeling squared off as representatives of democracy and fascism, respectively, and to many black Americans each punch that Louis landed was a blow struck for racial equality and against the theories of Aryan superiority. Ultimately, Wright's article matches up intriguingly to what Malcolm X, Lena Horne, Maya Angelou, Lofton Mitchell, and other black Americans later remembered about "the Brown Bomber." But it is his assessment of the victory celebration that distinguishes "High Tide." In Harlem on the night after the fight, black people declared a symbolic holiday from segregation, discrimination, and the preachments of white supremacy. Simply stated, Joe Louis's boxing career made such holidays possible time and again at midcentury.**

_____

The colossal bowl of seventy thousand hazy faces, an oval-shaped tableau compounded of criss-crossed beams of light and shadow, waited almost in silence for the gong to

---

* "Joe Louis Uncovers Dynamite," appeared in the *New Masses* on October 8, 1935. For more on the reception of Louis's athletic triumphs, see Mead, *Champion;* Edmonds, "Second Louis-Schmeling Fight." Concerning Wright's career, see Fabre, *Unfinished Quest,* See also Rowley, *Richard Wright.*

Richard Wright
(National Archives)

sound that would start the Louis-Schmeling million-dollar fight. The gaze of the seventy thousand eyes was centered on the "squared circle," a single diadem-like spot of canvas lit to blinding whiteness under the intense glare of overhead floodlights. So dwarfed was the ring by the mammoth stadium that it seemed that each man and woman was straining forward to peer at a colorful puppet show.

The Louis-Schmeling fight for the heavyweight championship of the world at the Yankee Stadium was one of the greatest dramas of make-believe ever witnessed in America, a drama which manipulated the common symbols and impulses in the minds and bodies of millions of people so effectively as to put to shame our professional playwrights, our O'Neills, our Lawsons, and our Caldwells. . . .

Each of the seventy thousand who had so eagerly jammed his way into the bowl's steel tiers under the open sky had come already emotionally conditioned as to the values that would triumph if his puppet won. Attached to each puppet, a white puppet and a black puppet, was a configuration of social images whose intensity and clarity had been heightened through weeks of skillful and constant agitation; social images whose emotional appeal could evoke attitudes tantamount to two distinct ways of life in the world today. Whichever puppet went down the Greek route to defeat that night would leave the path clear for the imperious sway of the balked impulses of one side or the other. The puppet emerging victorious would be the symbol of a fond wish gratified, would feed the starved faith of men caught in the mesh of circumstances.

Joe Louis, the black puppet who wore black trunks, was the betting favorite; but that was no indication as to how much actual sentiment there was for him among the seventy thousand spectators, for men like to bet on winners. And, too, just how much sentiment there was for Max Schmeling, the white puppet who wore purple trunks, no one, perhaps, will ever know; for now that the violent drama is ended the backers of the loser do not want to parade their disappointment for the scorn of others. But the two puppets were dissimilar enough in "race, creed, and previous condition of servitude" as to make their partisans wax militantly hopeful.

But out beyond the walls of the stadium were twelve million Negroes to whom the black puppet symbolized the living refutation of the hatred spewed forth daily over radios, in newspapers, in movies, and in books about their lives. Day by day, since their alleged emancipation, they have watched a picture of themselves being painted as lazy, stupid, and diseased. In helpless horror they have suffered the attacks and exploitation which followed in the wake of their being branded as "inferiors." True, hundreds of thousands of these Negroes would have preferred that that refutation could have been made in some form other than pugilism; but so effectively and completely have they been isolated and restricted in vocation that they rarely have had the opportunity to participate in the meaningful processes of America's national life. Jim Crowed in the army and navy, barred from many trades and professions, excluded from commerce and finance, relegated to menial positions in government, segregated residentially, denied the right of franchise for the most part; in short, forced to live a separate and impoverished life, they were glad for even the meager acceptance of their humanity implied in the championship of Joe Louis.

Visits to Joe Louis' training camp revealed throngs of Negroes standing around in a state of deep awe, waiting for just one glimpse of their champion. They were good, simple-hearted people, longing deeply for something of their own to be loyal to. When Joe appeared, a hush fell upon them and they stared. They took Joe into their hearts because he was a public idol and was respectfully enshrined in the public's imagination in a way they knew they would never be.

But because Joe's a Negro, even though he has to his credit a most enviable list of victories, there have been constant warnings issued by the Bilbos and Ellenders from south of the Mason-Dixon Line as to the wisdom of allowing a Negro to defeat a white man in public. The reactionary argument ran that such spectacles tended to create in Negroes too much pride and made them "intractable."

Naturally, Max Schmeling's victory over Louis two years ago was greeted with elation in reactionary quarters. A close study of Louis' stance, which revealed that he could be hit, together with a foul blow delivered after the bell, enabled the German boxer to win. Louis' defeat came as a shock to the boxing world and provided material for countless conversations and speculations. It was taken for granted that the second-rate Schmeling's defeat of the then reigning champion, the aging Braddock, was but a matter of time. But due to squabbles among promoters, Louis, not Schmeling, fought Braddock for the championship and won the title by a knockout in a thrilling bout in Chicago. Immediately the Nazi press, in America and in Germany, launched a campaign of slurs against Louis, dubbing him the "so-called champion," and declaring that Schmeling's prior victory over Louis was proof of "Negro inferiority." Schmeling boasted to the press that it would be easy for him to defeat the Negro again because (1) Negroes never forgot beatings, (2) his mere "white" presence would be enough to throw fear into Louis' heart, and (3) he would enter the ring with a "psychological edge" over the Negro. An open friend of Hitler and an avowed supporter of Nazis, Schmeling caught the fancy of many reactionary Americans, plus the leaders of Nazi Germany, fascist Italy, Japan, and even certain circles in England. To bolster the aims of the forces of fascism, Schmeling's victory was interpreted to mean the ability of the "Aryan race to out-think inferior races." The logical implication of such a line of reasoning was that all Negroes, colonial people, and small nations were inherently backward, physically cowardly, a drag upon the rest of civilization, and should be conquered and subjected for the benefit of mankind.

But when faced with this specious proposition, the common people instinctively revolted. They knew that the majority of all prizefighters came from the so-called "backward people," that is, the working class; their capacity to fight stemming from an early life of toil in steel and iron foundries, coal mines, factories, and fields. Consequently, in his fight against Schmeling, Louis carried the good wishes of even the poor whites of the Deep South, something unparalleled in the history of America.

The appearance of the white puppet sent the crowd into a frenzy. The black puppet's ovation seemed incidental. The ring was cleared and the fight was on. The entire seventy thousand rose as one man. At the beginning of the fight there was a wild shriek which gradually died as the seconds flew. What was happening was so stunning that even cheering was out of place. The black puppet, contrary to all Nazi racial laws, was punching the white puppet so rapidly that the eye could not follow the blows. It was not really a fight, it was an act of revenge, of dominance, of complete mastery. The black puppet glided from his corner and simply wiped his feet on the white puppet's face. The black puppet was contemptuous, swift; his victory was complete, unquestionable, decisive; his blows must have jarred the marrow not only in the white puppet's but in Hitler's own bones.

In Harlem, that area of a few square blocks in upper Manhattan where a quarter of a million Negroes are forced to live through an elaborate connivance among landlords, merchants, and politicians, a hundred thousand black people surged out of taprooms, flats, restaurants, and filled the streets and sidewalks like the Mississippi River overflowing in flood time. With their faces to the night sky, they filled their lungs with air and let out a scream of joy that seemed would never end, and a scream that seemed to come from untold reserves of strength. They wanted to make a noise comparable to the happiness bubbling in their hearts, but they were poor and had nothing. So they went to the garbage pails and got tin cans; they went to their kitchens and got tin pots, pans, washboards, wooden boxes, and took possession of the streets. They shouted, sang, laughed, yelled, blew paper horns, clasped hands, and formed weaving snake-lines, whistled, sounded sirens, and honked auto horns. From the windows of the tall, dreary tenements torn scraps of newspaper floated down. With the reiteration that evoked a hypnotic atmosphere, they chanted with eyes half-closed, heads lilting in unison, legs and shoulders moving and touching:

"Ain't you glad? Ain't you glad?"

Knowing full well the political effect of Louis' victory on the popular mind the world over, thousands yelled:

"Heil Louis!"

It was Harlem's mocking taunt to fascist Hitler's boast of the superiority of "Aryans" over other races. And they ridiculed the Nazi salute of the outstretched palm by throwing up their own dark ones to show how little they feared and thought of the humbug of fascist ritual. With no less than a hundred thousand participating, it was the largest and most spontaneous political demonstration ever seen in Harlem and marked the highest tide of popular political enthusiasm ever witnessed among American Negroes.

Negro voices called fraternally to Jewish-looking faces in passing autos:

"I bet all the Jews are happy tonight!"

Men, women, and children gathered in thick knots and did the Big Apple, the Lindy Hop, the Truck—Harlem's gesture of defiance to the high cost of food, high rent, and misery. These ghetto-dwellers, under the stress of the joy of one of their own kind having wiped out the stain of defeat and having thrown the lie of "inferiority" into the teeth of the fascist, threw off restraint and fear. Each time a downtown auto slowed, it became covered with Joe Louis rooters, and the autos looked like clusters of black ripe grapes. A bus stopped and at once became filled with laughing throngs who "forgot" to pay their fares; children clambered up its tall sides and crawled over the hoods and fenders.

It was the celebration of Louis' victory over Carnera, Baer, Pastor, Farr, and Braddock all rolled into one. Ethiopian and American flags fluttered. Effigies of Schmeling chalked with the swastika were dragged through the streets.

Then, nobody knows from where and nobody bothered to ask, there appeared on the surface of the sea of people white placards hurling slogans of defiance at fascist pretensions and calling upon native lovers of democracy to be true to democratic ideals. Oust Hitler's Spies and Agents; Pass the Anti-Lynching Bill; Down with Hitler and Mussolini; Alabama Produced Joe Louis; Free the Scottsboro Boys; Democracies Must Fight Fascism Everywhere. Carry the dream on for yourself; lift it out of the trifling guise of a prizefight celebration and supply the social and economic details and you have the secret dynamics of proletarian aspiration. The eyes of these people were bold that night. Their fear of property, of the armed police fell away. There was in their chant a hunger deeper than that for bread as they marched along. In their joy they were feeling an impulse which only the oppressed can feel to the full. They wanted to fling the heavy burden out of their hearts and embrace the world. They wanted to feel that their expanding feelings were not limited; that the earth was theirs as much as anybody else's; that they did not have to live by proscription in one corner of it; that they could go where they wanted to and do what they wanted to, eat and live where they wanted to, like others. They wanted to own things in common and do things in common. They wanted a holiday.

Richard Wright, "High Tide in Harlem: Joe Louis as a Symbol of Freedom," *New Masses*, July 5, 1938, 18–20.

10. Willis P. Armstrong / "A Toast to Joe Louis"

The inspiration that blacks derived from the victories of Joe Louis cannot be overstated. In contrast to Jack Johnson, who earlier provoked considerable controversy within Afro-America, Louis had become a universal icon of race pride during the late 1930s. What is more, his ascendancy in the ring over such opponents as Carnera and Schmeling had made him a national hero—especially during the years when an increasing number of Americans wanted to project their own sense of might against the forces of fascism. Until U.S. troops actually entered combat, such elemental assertions were mounted on the athletic front—and Joe Louis stood as a standard-bearer for both his race and nation. Black Americans took pride in the image of Louis pounding with patriotism.

Often they did so in verse and song. Black children created rhymes about Louis that would accompany their jumping rope. A host of musicians created songs in jazz, ballad, gospel, Tin Pan Alley, and the blues, by one recent count forty-three compositions in all. According to Paul Oliver:

> There are no blues devoted to the achievements of Paul Robeson, George Washington Carver (the Black scientist) or Ralph Bunche (Black politician and diplomat), though those figures would probably have been known to the more literate and especially the city-dwelling singers. . . . Not even Jesse Owens was commemorated in a blues, at any rate on record. . . . For the blues singer, Joe Louis was the singular inspiration of a man who had within his achievements all the drama, the appeal and the invincibility of the traditional ballad hero.[*]

For his part, Richard Wright wrote "King Joe," thirteen stanzas long. In it he drew on the animal characters of black folklore such as Brer Rabbit and thus created a link between figures from the lore of antebellum slavery and those from the modern sporting arena. He referred to Louis's upbringing in Detroit and fashioned a compelling analogy between the boxer and the heroic figure of John Henry, avatar of black industrial labor: "Old Joe wrestled Ford engines, Lord, it was a shame; / Say Old Joe wrestled Ford engines, Lord, it was a shame; / And he turned engine himself and went to the fighting game." At another point, he tells us that Louis's boxing prowess expresses not only race pride but also a means of veiling resentment: "Wonder what Joe Louis thinks when he's fighting a white man / Bet he thinks what I'm thinking, cause he wears a deadpan." No less a personage than Count Basie set the lyrics to music, and Paul Robeson, singing blues for the first time—though by all accounts

---

[*] Oliver, *Aspects of the Blues Tradition*, 146, 149. Lawrence Levine offers the cultural context for such celebrations in *Black Culture*, 420–40.

not very ably—recorded the song. Other musicians traced the champ's life from his rural origins in Alabama, to Detroit, then the early years of his career in the ring. Some of these songs were recorded within a day or so of a particular Louis triumph, helping to sum up the meanings of those victories for countless black Americans.*

In the following document, a letter to a prominent black newspaperman, and then in the "toast" that he offered, Willis Armstrong made no claims for his artistry. His poem falls into the genre of newspaper verse, which was excruciatingly well rhymed and widely popular through the interwar years. This was a slice of a vernacular culture, compelling in how simply and earnestly it expressed itself. Then again, at a critical point the verse shifts from third-person praise of the hero and his accomplishments to direct address: Louis becomes "old Chappie" and the toast ("here's to . . .") becomes a personal note to the champion from an ardent fan and fellow "race man." Significantly, then, the verse is for Joe Louis, not just about him.

Armstrong hoped to provide a testimonial to the enormous impact that Louis exerted on the consciousness of many African Americans, who saw the fighter as a kind of savior. Just as Louis redeemed for black Americans a strong sense of their place in the making of the nation as a world power, he also stood as a symbol for the ideals and institutions that would fight against fascism. Writing even before the formal declaration of war, Armstrong asserts that black Americans would be willing to lend their courage to the international conflict. Yet at the same time, emboldened by the triumphs of Joe Louis, Armstrong reveals the hopes embodied in such sacrifice. The key word "respect" toward the end of this verse implies something more expansive. During World War II, African Americans also wanted to fight for freedom and democracy on the home front.**

———— ————

October 5, 1941
Washington, D.C.

Mr. Arthur Carter

Dear Sir:

I am submitting a copy of a poem I composed of Joe Louis. I am hoping you will insert it in the *Afro-American* newspaper at your earliest convenience. . . . I am one of a million or more Joe Louis admirers and one of many *Afro* readers. I appreciate your hospitality and remain respectfully yours

Willis P. Armstrong

---

* W. Wiggins, "Reflections on the Joe Louis Recordings"; the verses quoted are from "King Joe" on the *Joe Louis* CD. See also Margolick, "Music"; Mead, *Champion.*

** The "Double V" campaign mounted by black activists encouraged African Americans to consider the war a fight against discrimination and segregation within the United States as well as a crusade against totalitarianism abroad. For insights into this movement, see *The Black Press,* videorecording produced and directed by Stanley Nelson. For a survey of black participation in the armed services, see Nalty, *Strength for the Fight.*

Here's to Joe Louis, the world's greatest fighter,
    As famous a guy as any first nighter.
He's fought them all, with that expression of stone,
    He's beat the best, he's in a class alone.

He's as loyal a fighter, as ever donned a glove,
    And the power in his punches seems to come from above.
He's as clean as they come, and you can rely on that,
    Irrespective of rumors, you can't deny facts.

He's brought the art of boxing up from the shady side,
    And he's a man the whole world now looks on with pride.
He beat "Tony Galento," who called him a bum,
    And he likes them the bigger and tougher they come.

He's a shuffling, shifting, punching machine,
    He's as near super human as the ring ever seen.
Though we sometimes demand and over rate him by far,
    He's emerged from each battle, without even a scar. . . .

He's going to hang up his glove for a much better right,
    And we all must pitch in and help in this fight.
He could lick all the Germans, as he did Schmeling that night,
    If it were decent and fair, but it's not that kind of fight.

Hitler has bullied all Europe, and don't think he's through,
    For he's already endangered the Red, White, and Blue.
But we're not like the others unprepared and sitting tight,
    We've got red blooded Negroes that will do their bit and fight.

So old Chappie though the going sometimes is a bit unfair,
    The U.S.A. knows that we're true blue, and of fight we do not scare.
It took the Negroes in the last war, and it will take them this time too,
    And all we ask is the same respect that we demand for you.

And though you've come a long way down the road of fisticuff to fame,
    You've left a goal to shoot at, that no Negro is ashamed.
And I wish you all the happiness that good luck does imply,
    And may your good name live forever and your good deeds never die.

And in the end, good luck Joe, and may all things go well,
    For to reach the place in life you have, you had to fight like hell.
And I'm sure I'm not mistaken that when you go to camp,
    You'll go in Uncle Sam's Army, the world's Heavyweight Champ.

Letter from Willis P. Armstrong to Arthur Carter, October 5, 1941, Art Carter Papers, Moorland-Spingarn
Library, Howard University.

D

DENOUNCING RACIAL PREJUDICE

11. Concerning the Snubbing of Paul Robeson

Long before he became world famous as an actor and concert singer, long before he played on the international stage as an advocate of the liberation of people of color everywhere, Paul Robeson was widely recognized as one of the best athletes of his generation. Born in 1898 in Princeton, New Jersey, Robeson was raised by his father—who had escaped slavery to fight for the Union army, then became a minister in the American Methodist Episcopal Church—to aim high in the matter of education. Robeson was inspired by one of his older brothers to compete athletically as well. By the time he entered Rutgers University—only the third African American student to attend since its founding in 1766—he not only ranked as one of the outstanding high school scholars in the state of New Jersey; he had also amassed an impressive record in football, basketball, baseball, and track and field (he was also sports editor of his high school newspaper). Robeson would translate both his imposing size and his enormous energy into headline news. From 1916 through 1919, he led the Rutgers football team to a succession of victories over more highly ranked teams; during the war years Walter Camp twice selected Robeson for his prestigious All-Service and All-America squads.

*In all, Robeson gathered twelve varsity letters while at Rutgers. A member of the college literary society, he also joined the Cap and Skull Club, a senior honor society. By the time of his graduation in 1919, he had won the most significant prizes in declamation and oratory that the university could bestow and he had been elected to Phi Beta Kappa. He would continue to participate in sports while attending law school, and then after 1922 he shifted his career toward the theater, film, and the concert stage. Robeson's college days were not idyllic, however, and the rest of his life would be marked by numerous controversies. Though the following document does not elaborate all the occasions when Robeson confronted bigotry on the playing field, it does suggest the ordeal of integration even for the most outstanding African American athletes. In fact, on the first days of practice, Robeson was forced to battle his own teammates in order to make his case for inclusion on the Rutgers varsity. Thereafter, as James D. Carr demonstrates in his letter of protest to the president of Rutgers, the school played games of expediency when it came to benching its black champion against southern schools such as Washington and Lee University. What stands out in this document—written by the first black graduate of Rutgers—is that African Americans were prepared to denounce racial prejudice whenever and wherever it appeared. Carr's formal language bespeaks a commitment to traditional notions of honor; these were standards and ideals that he fully expected his alma mater to meet. Here is an elegant statement about the pursuit of "equality of opportunity" in the sporting realm, in higher education, and throughout American society.**

---

* See the impressive biography by Duberman, *Paul Robeson*, esp. 19–30; F. Harris, "Paul Robeson."

Paul Robeson (Courtesy Rutgers
University Libraries)

Robeson was not always so well defended during his long and varied career as a racial activist. For nearly thirty years, he was frequently vilified by white Americans, though they were not always clear what it was about Robeson that intimidated them most: his linkage of race and class, which resembled at times the line taken by the Communist Party, or his participation in an international movement for black liberation. Sadly, too, Robeson encountered enormous criticism from many other racial reformers, who sought to place some distance between their organizations and Robeson's more militant and universalist agendas. Yet his contributions to the cultural front against all forms of oppression made Robeson a folk hero for the masses of black Americans. His career crossed those of Joe Louis and Jackie Robinson—at very sharp angles—and transcended sport in very different ways. But his activism enabled a later generation, perhaps most forcefully embodied by Muhammad Ali, to explore new means to "speak truth to power."

———————

City of New York Law Department
June 6, 1919

President William H. S. Demarest, LL.D.
Rutgers College
New Brunswick, New Jersey

Dear Sir:

During the celebration of the one hundred and fiftieth anniversary of Rutgers College, a statement appeared in the public press that Washington and Lee University, scheduled for a football game with Rutgers, had protested the playing of Paul Robeson, a regular member of the Rutgers team, because of his color. In reading an account of the game, I saw that Robeson's name was not among the players. My suspicions were immediately aroused. After a considerable lapse of time, I learned that Washington and Lee's protest had been honored and that Robeson, either by covert suggestion, or official athletic authority, had been excluded from the game.

You may imagine my deep chagrin and bitterness at the thought that my Alma Mater, ever proud of her glorious traditions, her unsullied honor, her high ideals, and her spiritual mission prostituted her sacred principles, when they were brazenly challenged and laid her convictions upon the altar of compromise.

Is it possible that the honor of Rutgers is virile only when untested and unchallenged? Shall men, whose progenitors tried to destroy this Union, be permitted to make a mockery of our democratic ideals by robbing a youth, whose progenitors helped to save the Union, of that equality of opportunity and privilege that should be the crowning glory of our institution of learning?

I am deeply moved at the injustice done to a student of Rutgers in good and regular standing of good moral character and splendid mental equipment—one of the best athletes ever developed at Rutgers—who, because guilty of a skin not colored as their own, was excluded from the honorable field of athletic encounter, as one inferior. . . . Not only he, but his race as well was deprived of the opportunity of showing its athletic ability, and, perhaps, its athletic superiority. . . . Can you imagine his thoughts and feelings when, in contemplative mood, he reflects in the years to come that his Alma Mater faltered and quailed when the test came, and that she preferred the holding of an athletic game to the maintenance of her honor and principle? I am provoked to this protest by a similar action of the University of Pennsylvania, heralded in the public press less than two weeks ago when Annapolis protested the playing of the Captain of one of the athletic teams of the University of Pennsylvania, a colored man. Almost unanimously his fellow athletes decided to withdraw from the field and cancel the contest. In this, however, they were overruled by the athletic manager. . . . Such prostitution of principle must cease, or the hypocrisy must be exposed.

The Trustees and Faculty of Rutgers College should disavow the action of an athletic manager who dishonored her ancient traditions by denying to one of her students, solely on account of his color, equality of opportunity and privilege. If they consider an athletic contest more than the maintenance of a principle, then they should disavow the ideals, the spiritual mission and the lofty purpose which the sons of Rutgers have ever believed that they cherished.

> Very respectfully yours,
> James D. Carr
> Rutgers '92

Letter from James D. Carr to William H. S. Demarest, June 16, 1919, Rutgers University Archives; reprinted in *Freedomways* (Summer 1969): 221–29.

12. The Economics of Bigotry: New Orleans Bars Blacks, Loses a Track Meet

The Amateur Athletic Union (AAU), like other national organizations both within and outside of sport, had to deal with southern racial prejudices throughout the first half of the twentieth century. Although a national association with rules established to ensure open access and equality of opportunity, the AAU was confronted by the refusal of its local chapters in the South—as well as other groups in the region—to permit African American athletes to compete against white athletes in highly organized sport. The AAU seemed to establish no uniform approach to these racial incidents. On most occasions, the organization acquiesced to southern racial mores, declining to intercede on behalf of African American athletes or make any efforts to abolish segregated sport in the region. Less frequently, the AAU took a more progressive stance and fought to guarantee that African American athletes could compete at all levels of sport and in any region of the country.

One occasion on which the AAU stood up for African Americans was its national track meet in 1927. As noted in the following editorial from the Pittsburgh Courier-Journal, *the meet had been awarded that year to the city of New Orleans. Almost immediately, however,* *trouble began brewing there when city officials insisted that the AAU bar the several African American athletes expected to participate in the meet. The AAU secretary, Fred Rubien, denied the request, resulting in New Orleans's decision not to host the meet. This would not be the last time New Orleans would be mired in controversy concerning African American athletes. In another instance, occurring in 1965, the twenty-two African American players on the East-West squads forced Commissioner Joe Goss to move the American Football Conference all-star game to Houston from New Orleans because of the city's racial policies.* The struggles of nearly forty years between the national AAU track meet and the AFC all-star game had obviously not brought about racial equality in the Crescent City.*

———

In the midst of all the talk about the New South, little incidents arise to demonstrate the fact that much of the spirit of the old South still remains below the celebrated line of Messrs. Mason and Dixon. The Southern gentlemen of Nordic extraction remain obdurate on the question of color discrimination. Receptive to the inroads of the mechanical age and modern business methods, they continue to nourish the prejudices and narrow views in regard to people of color. And they continue to do this, even to the extent of losing much money and prestige. When it comes to deciding between coin and color, the latter is usually awarded the palm. The recent decision of the civic body of New Orleans not to accept the annual track meet of the Amateur Athletic Union is considered a great credit and advantage. Cities in all parts of the country vie for it. New Orleans was among the number who strove for the 1927 national track meet. It strove so mightily that it won the meet. But there was a fly in the ointment. About a half dozen noted Negro athletes were scheduled to take part in the contests. Naturally they were to compete against white athletes. It was probable that some of these black athletes would win first and second places. Was New Orleans to run the risk of having Negroes competing on terms of equality with whites? Were the old traditions of the South to be disregarded and ignored? Were members of the superior race to be vanquished by inferior Negroes in the plain sight of thousands of descendants of Confederates who had fought for four bloody years to keep the blacks in bondage? A thousand times No, said the good fathers of the Crescent City. Send us floods, plagues, tornadoes, earthquakes, or what have you, said they, but spare us this black invasion.

In accordance with the celebrated Southern spirit of chivalry and fair play, pressure was brought to bear upon the Amateur Athletic Union to bar Negroes from the national track meet, lest the Civil War have to be fought over again. The spirits of "Stonewall" Jackson, Robert E. Lee and Jeff Davis were invoked and the Stars and Bars were unfurled and flung to the breeze. The Daughters of the Confederacy were shaken by shivers and gentlemen who winked at social intimacy with the blacks at night, frowned upon the prospect of athletic intimacy to Mr. Fred W. Rubien, secretary of

———

* See Mix, "Was This Their Freedom Ride?"

the Amateur Athletic Union, beseeching him to spare them from the black invasion on terms of equality. Mr. Rubien could not see the point. An irresistible force had met an immovable object. The result: the Paris of America loses the track meet; the metropolis of the world gets it. Reluctant tears in New Orleans: resounding cheers in New York. It may be perfectly all right to cut off one's nose to spite one's face, but the loss hardly adds to one's attractiveness. Some day even New Orleans will learn that.

"Cutting Off Its Nose," *Pittsburgh Courier-Journal,* May 7, 1927.

13. Integrationism in Public Recreation: Denver as a Case Study

During the late 1920s and 1930s black communities in both the North and South became increasingly vocal about the need for public recreational facilities, desiring to put into practice the arguments earlier made by W. E. B. Du Bois and Emmett Scott about the importance of leisure development. The situation varied according to region, and African American activists dealt with the politics of Jim Crow in diverse ways. In the South, segregation prevailed. There, according to a 1928 survey of the urban scene, when municipal authorities spent money on parks, recreation centers, bathing beaches, or swimming pools, those venues were restricted to whites only. During the depression era, when public works and development projects were being federally funded—largely as reemployment measures— black leaders insisted that some of the new parks as well as places along lakeshores and ocean fronts be set aside for the African American community.*

Circumstances were different in the North (and West) and so was the thrust of black activism. As the following article demonstrates, black citizens in Denver protested the creation of new recreational facilities that were being hastily constructed and explicitly dedicated as "Negro recreational centers." Denver's blacks had certainly suffered from discrimination, but they knew that formal segregation had been prohibited in the state constitution and that the city had never before imposed such a rigid plan of racial separation. Their civic campaign thus differed strikingly from the activism of their counterparts in the Deep South. Critically, the scenario outlined in the Chicago Defender *article was being enacted in other parts of "the North" as well. In midwestern cities such as Indianapolis, for instance, once the black population had risen past a certain percentage of the total population—the "tipping point," as sociologists sometimes call it, was roughly 15 percent—city officials would propose to build new high schools or recreational facilities in the very center of the emerging black communities. The protest in Denver concerned something more than de facto segregation; it spoke to the ways American apartheid was tried and tested, not just in the South, but throughout the nation.*

---

* See Henderson, *The Negro in Sports,* 766; Miller, "Sport as 'Interracial Education.'"

Denver, Colo, Nov. 13, 1931

The grim specter of segregation hovered lower over Denver and Colorado last week when two daily papers carried articles with the bland announcement that a "Negro recreational center" had been proposed and that a swimming pool and tennis courts were about to be provided, with the work to be started "as soon as possible" in preparation for the coming summer.

No sooner had the morning paper reached the homes of prominent people in the political and social life of the city than telephones began to ring among the various individuals and groups, and a conference was planned to lay before the city planning commission, Mayor George Begole, Walter B. Lowry, manager of improvements and parts, and City Engineer A. K. Vickery, the unanimous objection of citizens to such a procedure. Effective follow-up measures have been planned and will be met to defeat this effort to carry out the policy of a segregated recreational center. At the present time, while certain facilities are taboo, all elements of the city's population use the parks and playgrounds with which the city is rather plentifully supplied.

The school situation in Denver has also been the cause of considerable dissatisfaction on the part of the Race. While no separation has been attempted except in the matter of easy transfers of pupils of the white race from schools largely attended by our Race because of locations, still some measure of mixing is the rule.

The legal safeguards against discriminations and segregation in the state of Colorado are among the strongest in the entire country, and will be invoked in this case if the citizen's protest is ignored.

More than 50 years ago Congress, in giving the territory the right to form a state, passed an act embodying among other things the following provisions: "Provided, That the Constitution be republican in form, and make no distinction in civil or political rights on account of color or race."

"Citizens Suspect Segregation Move in Recreation Center," *Chicago Defender,* November 13, 1931.

14. Next Bout—The NAACP vs. Jim Crow: Charles Hamilton Houston on the Politics of Sport in Washington, D.C.

In small towns and big cities—in political jurisdictions of all sizes—the pace of racial integration in sport occurred at an uneven rate during the first half of the twentieth century. While the black press was clamoring for the desegregation of professional football and baseball, efforts were being made to combat racial discrimination at all levels of competition in a variety of sports across the country. One of the most interesting, and symbolically important, struggles to integrate sport took place in Washington, D.C. The seat of government of what purported to be the model of democracy for the world of nations, Washington remained for the most part a southern city in its racial mores and attitudes. The city perpetuated rigid *racial segregation on its playgrounds, in both interscholastic and intercollegiate athletics. African Americans had access to "black-only" playgrounds, were unable to attend certain sporting events at the city's Uline Arena, were barred from local boxing matches and track meets sponsored by the AAU, and had to endure the racist policies of George Marshall and his Washington Redskins football team. Tellingly, these various forms of discrimination did not go unchallenged as black activists and socially conscious white liberals, in cooperation with local civil rights organizations, consistently fought to have them overturned.* *

In the following letter, Charles H. Houston, noted civil rights lawyer and educator, appeals to Eleanor Patterson to permit black fighters to participate in the Golden Gloves boxing tournament promoted and financially supported by her newspaper, the Times-Herald. *Houston argues that the citizens of Washington, D.C., would be willing to witness interracial boxing matches, claiming further that continued exclusion of black boxers from the tournament was hypocritical, especially "in these days when America is complaining about the proscription of the Jew." Unfortunately for Houston and others involved in the cause, black boxers were not able to participate in the tournament until 1947. In that year the tournament opened its doors to black boxers for the first time after Patterson and her paper's archrival, the* Washington Post—*finally succumbing to the arguments of racial reformers—threatened to withhold their support of the event if it was not integrated.*

N.A.A.C.P. Papers, D.C. Branch #1153
Time-Herald Golden Gloves Boxing Tournament

November 28, 1938

Mrs. Eleanor Patterson
Publisher of the Patterson Papers
Washington, D.C.

My dear Mrs. Patterson:

October 21, 1937, I had occasion to write you concerning the Washington, D.C. Golden Gloves Tournament of 1937. I appealed to you to open the tournament to Negro amateur boxers.

Another tournament is now beginning but I am advised that the color line is drawn against Negro boxers and they will not be permitted to participate.

I fully appreciate the responsibilities which you have to the Washington public in having this tournament conducted under the auspices of the Washington Herald and the Washington Times, but I appeal to you to take the forward step of opening the tournament to Negro boxers confident that the public, which cordially accepts Negro professional boxers' supremacy in four classes, would be willing to see mixed bouts in the District of Columbia.

---

* See D. Wiggins, "Edwin Bancroft Henderson: Physical Educator."

You may recall the concern which many persons in New York felt when Joe Louis was first exhibited in mixed bouts. The announcer always took the pains to state that the bout was merely a sporting event, did not settle any question of race supremacy, and he appealed to the sportsmanship of the crowd. So far as I know, no disorder occurred at any of Joe Louis' bouts. Certain street crowds staged noisy, good-natured demonstrations but there was no malice; and even the street crowds understood that they were merely celebrating a sporting victory in their own fashion, just as college students celebrate football victories with bonfires, dances and parades.

I feel sure that the Washington public which attends the Golden Glove Tournament bouts would show just as good sportsmanship as the New York public and the tournament would then be a real elimination contest and the Washington boxers would not be subject to the criticism of having two teams in the national finals.

In these days when America is complaining about the proscription of the Jew, it is inconsistent to countenance such unnecessary proscription against the native-born citizens of this land of "equal opportunity."

Yours very truly,

CHARLES H. HOUSTON

Letter from Charles H. Houston to Eleanor Patterson, November 28, 1938, NAACP Papers, Moorland-Spingarn Research Center, Howard University.

E

STRATEGIES OF APPEAL

15. Edwin Bancroft Henderson / "The Negro Athlete and Race Prejudice"

Civil rights activist, physical educator, historian of sport: Edwin Bancroft Henderson was probably the person most responsible for enlisting black athletic accomplishments in the broader campaign for racial justice. His long career as a chronicler of African Americans in athletic competition began in 1911 with an article in the Crisis. *It extended to six and a half decades. In* The Negro in Sports *(1939), Henderson brought together much of the information he had compiled during the previous years, rendering black achievement in heroic terms. In fact, the concluding chapter of the book, "The Meaning of Athletics," explicitly drew a line from Greek and Roman antiquity—and the significance of sport in the building of Western civilization—to the efforts by modern-day African Americans to make success in sport a touchstone for more expansive arguments about equal opportunity.**

Here Henderson makes the case that blacks provided significant contributions to American sport, that the distinctions won by Joe Louis and Jesse Owens against foreign opponents or in the Olympic Games rendered those athletes "national" heroes. At the same time, Henderson introduces the work of the anatomist Montague Cobb, which disproved the claims by pseudoscientific racists that the laurels won by African Americans in sport derived from some natural ability or some vestige of a primitive past. The campaign against such crude representations of blacks as Arthur Brisbane's in the Hearst press, like the evidence marshaled against the anthropometrists, was an important element in Henderson's efforts to characterize black athletic success in terms of mainstream values and ideals. It was hard work and adherence to the athletic creed that explained the making of African American champions, Henderson maintained. Henderson represented a generation of muscular assimilationists who believed that what black athletes accomplished on the athletic field testified to the potential contributions of other African Americans in all fields of endeavor.

———————

Will history record the Negro athlete a significant factor in the moderation of racial prejudice in America? Is our Negro athlete contributing much to an all-round New Deal for the Negro group?

---

* On Henderson's career, see D. Wiggins, "Edwin Bancroft Henderson, African American Athletes, and the Writing of Sport History," in his *Glory Bound*, 221–42.

Edwin Bancroft Hender-
son, "Founder of Black
Sport History" (E. B.
Henderson Collection,
Moorland-Spingarn Re-
search Center, Howard
University Archives,
Howard University)

On one Sunday morning three years ago, the names of two black boys made great headlines on the first page of many of America's great conservative newspapers,— including the *New York Times*. Their pictures glared from millions of front page copies of the world's press. Since then, news columns, sporting sections, and editorial comments have referred to Negro athletic achievement more than to any other artistic, political or educational phase of Negro life.

Sociologists are questioning the extent that this interest in the Negro athlete is affecting race prejudices. Another interesting question is, how have Negro boys made progress against the tide of race prejudice to reach the goals they have attained?

Athletics, in the main, begin with school life. In the South, after we leave the border states, are found the poorest of schools, and in a sampling survey made by the writer, there was found to be practically no physical education programs or athletics in schools for Negroes below the college level. The separate school systems provide little beyond the tool subjects, not much progressive curriculum material, but frequently a lot of worn out traditional educational content largely discarded by contemporary school systems. Time allotment and provision for play, games and other socializing educational media are absent in the great mass of Negro schools. However, the great trek of Negroes northward put a generation of colored boys in the schools of the more liberal states. There, the physical education programs gave them their chance. That they make the teams is due to rugged abilities, social adaptiveness, and the desire of the coach or school to gain prestige through athletics with its accompanying personal or institutional appraisal.

To make a success in team athletics, the colored boy must be definitely superior. Sometimes color aids him by marking him conspicuously in the course of the activity but frequently it identifies him as the bull's eye for the shafts of the opposition. He must make adjustments in realization of the prejudices of teammates, and must learn to "take plenty" from opponents. Often he must find separate lodgement when on tour. He must survive the humiliation of being left behind when his team plays the "Service" schools or the gentlemen of the South. In most such cases, he will receive a compensatory good will gesture as an effort of the coach to offset the humiliation. . . .

Without superior blockers to get him away from the maelstrom of the opposing line and backs, Red Grange would have been just another ice-man. To dim the lustre of a star Negro back, it is only necessary for a blocker to conveniently fail at his job occasionally. That Ossie Simmons would get his team's support during the past season became an item of publicity and that he performed so well was due to the support he did get despite being behind a line not up to the charging strength of some opposing teams. It is also a fact not generally known that where "scholarships" are the means by which many a poor boy gets to and stays in college for athletics, some of the bigger scouting colleges make it a policy not to subsidize college life for more than one good colored athlete per team.

Our professional or money-seeking athletes in the profit making game are up against different problems. Backers and promoters are openly in the game for money. If the color of an athlete is a financial factor of importance, or if he is an exceptional athlete, despite his color, he will be sought and used wherever the mores of the community are not taboo to colored athletes. . . . Although all contact games have the capacity to stimulate the fiercer emotions, the present-day rules of the boxing game and short bouts have put a premium on skill, strength, timing and endurance and probably limits the express of instinctive responses of rage and prejudiced hate. In this as in some other sports, promoters frequently find color an asset, and are inclined to depend a great deal upon the growing sense of American spectator sportsmanship. In some southern cities, the local fight promoters have begun to use colored fighters in non-mixed bouts on the same card with white fighters. In Missouri, the boxing ban against mixed bouts has been lifted. . . .

During the past year there has hardly been a sports commentator or columnist who has not advanced some reason for the unprecedented rise of Negro track and field athletes. For the last ten to twenty years, Negro broad jumpers have practically dominated the records in this event. Only two white athletes and one Japanese have excelled in this event. Theorists, many of them honest, have attempted to prove that Negro athletes were endowed with some peculiar anatomical structure of foot, leg or thigh that enables them to run or jump better than white athletes. Dr. Montague Cobb, associate professor of Anatomy at Howard University, in studies undertaken at the laboratory of Ohio State University, has shown with painstaking research, tests, and x-rays of the body of Jesse Owens that the measurements of Owens fall within the accepted measurements of white men.

Prejudiced thinking as to race and athletic success has served to stimulate further poisoned-pen comments from men like Brisbane of the Hearst press. Brisbane has a wont to compare athletes with "Grizzlies" or gorillas whenever an outstanding Negro athlete looms on the horizon. Recently, a story of Louis' great grandparent overcoming a baboon in a wrestling match on a slave farm in Alabama became a current press fable to account for the descent of strength to Louis. Several generations ago when the dark continent was invaded by explorers, the hunt was on for the "Missing Link," or the man-monkey. If slave-traders and exploiters could have satisfied the world that the Negro was on the border line between man and beast, this would have been justification for his classification as a beast of burden to be worked, enslaved or starved with only the compunction that Christians have been inspired with by the principles of the Society for the Prevention of Cruelty to Animals. The implications of the hunt for the missing link of the 18th century have their counterpart in those of the Brisbanalities of the present day "Negro-phobiacs."

General Hugh Johnson dismisses the question as to Negro supremacy in his brusque language by saying, "They're just too physical for us." Dr. Cobb has scientifically disproved the one and twenty theories that Negro athletes have peculiar anatomical structures. Therefore, the writers' guess is as good as some others. When one recalls that it is estimated that only one Negro slave in five was able to live through the rigors of the "Middle Passage," and that the horrible conditions of slavery took a toll of many slaves who could not make biological adjustments in a hostile environment, one finds the Darwinian theory of the survival of the fit operating among Negroes as rigorously as any selective process ever operated among human beings. There is just a likelihood that some very vital elements persist in the histological tissues of the glands or muscles of Negro athletes.

It is the belief of many students of race phenomena that the Negro athlete is making a considerable contribution to the spread of tolerance and improved race relations. Negro artisans and some intellectuals have risen to high planes of social relationships with individuals of other races through the recognition of values that transcend the physical. But the mass of humanity still is motivated by feelings and emotions. The main springs of action are still located in the glands. Fear, love and hate determine attitudes towards neighbors of foreigners. Our keenest pleasures and most poignant pains are born of feelings rather than of intellect. . . .

Even the most intellectual, no matter how far we strive to appreciate sophisticated music, non-understandable art symbols, or high values in literature, we still respond readily to the call of the chase, the fight, the race or the hunt and live over something of our early ancestral experiences when we thrill or despair with the runner, boxer or other athlete. The world still loves a fighter, whether he be the winner or loser.

Joe Louis has thus captivated the fancy of millions. He is to some a symbolic Sphinx of Egypt or a human replica of Rodin's "Thinker." In the ring he associates ideas and responds with lightning-like rapier thrusts about as rapidly through the medium of mind and muscle as an Einstein calculates cause and effect in cosmic theory. Jesse Owens, Metcalf, Tolan, and a host of others have likewise provided a feeling of pride and joyful relationship for many. These athletes are American athletes. They claim the loyalty of the thousands of students at this or that university. They are emulated by thousands of growing youth of all races, and above all they gain for themselves and the Negro the respect of millions whose superiority feelings have sprung solely from identity with the white race.

If Negro athletes do contribute to racial respect, and despite its nature, it is conceded by many that they do, then it behooves educators and racial agencies for uplift to make greater social use of athletics. Every opportunity for extending the games and plays of the physical education program of schools should be a part of education for Negroes. School teachers of little one-room school houses can encourage practice in a variety of activities by which the qualities known collectively as good sportsmanship as well as the skills can be learned by Negro youth. More happiness may be brought into the lives of the less-privileged, and at the same time we will be developing future good-will ambassadors through athletics.

Edwin Bancroft Henderson, "The Negro Athlete and Race Prejudice," *Opportunity* 14 (March 1936): 77–79.

16. Roy Wilkins / "That Old Southern Accent"

By the mid-1930s, commentators like Edwin Bancroft Henderson could note substantial breakthroughs in the realm of sport; those editors and journalists who wrote expansively about the meanings of athletic success could claim with some pride that African American athletes were contributing to racial reform. Beyond the boxing ring, where Joe Louis and increasing numbers of talented black fighters were making their mark, there was the Olympic stadium. The 1936 Berlin Games was every bit as much the Jesse Owens Olympics, in the minds of many sport fans, as it was the Nazi Olympics. Like Louis in bouts against contenders from other nations, Owens stood out as a "national" hero.

College sports also offered opportunities for the best black athletes to impress white spectators and reporters. The increasing popularity of intersectional football competition—especially match-ups between schools from the South and those of the Northeast or Midwest—posed an enormous problem, however. Since the turn of the twentieth century, southern institutions had insisted that their northern opponents withdraw black athletes from any competition, no matter where the game was played. For many years this arrangement between athletic officials was characterized as a "gentlemen's agreement." In 1929, when University of Georgia officials prevailed upon NYU to bench one of its leading athletes, Dave Myers, because he was black, the northern university did so—concocting a bizarre injury for Myers during the days immediately preceding the game. This cynicism and hypocrisy was roundly denounced by black and white sportswriters alike. One prominent editorialist inveighed against "the gutless coach" of a "gutless school." In the aftermath of several protests, rival schools began to draw up contracts with carefully worded "forfeiture clauses." But if intersectional athletic competition had long been a source of frustration for muscular assimilationists, by the mid-1930s there appeared some reasons to believe that segregation in sport could be further challenged.

The first crossings of the color line in college sport were subtle but significant events. Here Roy Wilkins, who was editor of the Crisis *before he became executive director of the NAACP, provides an account of the first contest where a southern squad traveled north and faced a northern opponent without questioning the right of a black athlete to participate. The article surveys some of the background of the NYU–University of North Carolina contest of 1936. What is more intriguing about the piece is Wilkins's wry commentary on the subject of mixed-race athletic competition: there was no "rehash of the War of 1860–65," he avers, and once the southern school agreed to play against a Negro, there was "no record of anyone asking that famous question: 'Would you want your daughter to marry one?'" But as Wilkins was aware, this game had the makings of a momentous development. If other southern schools followed the precedent set by UNC—and if other northern institutions insisted on it—then the color line could be erased in intercollegiate athletics. The path toward that goal was not a broad or certain one, however. In the years leading up to World War II, the benching of black athletes, both in northern and southern sporting venues, was still a regular occurrence—although it continued to draw the ire of racial reformers. Meanwhile those reformers worked strenuously behind the scenes to orchestrate the desegregation of sport. When the breakthroughs did occur, the black press celebrated them like knockout punches and Olympic gold medals.* *

——— ———

The air at the Polo Grounds and the Yankee Stadium was heavy last Saturday afternoon with a Southern accent that could be cut with a knife. Tulane from New Orleans was playing Colgate, and North Carolina from Chapel Hill, was playing New York University. North Carolina brought along a band and about 700 rooters, including Governor J. C. B. Ehringhaus.

At the Polo Grounds there was just a football game, but at the Stadium history was being made. For North Carolina was playing without protest against a Negro member of the New York University team. Ed Williams, 210-pound Violet halfback, played practically the entire game, being taken out in the fourth period.

One can never see everything in a football game from the stands or even from the sidelines, but I watched intently for three periods, hardly taking my eyes off Williams, and it did not seem to me that Williams received any unusually rough treatment. He carried the ball again and again on direct line smashes and was stopped as any other back would be stopped, by hard sure tackling. He ran back one kick-off about fifteen yards before being smothered by Carolina tacklers. On the defense it was Williams who batted down a North Carolina forward pass right on the Violet goal line which if caught, would have resulted in another touchdown. Time and again it was his tackling which finally brought down a southern ball carrier who had crashed through to the secondary defense.

There were no boos and in my section of the stand I heard none of the familiar cries of "Kill the Negro!" So far, the University of North Carolina is still standing and

---

* For more on the NYU-UNC contest and the breakthroughs of the 1930s, see Miller, "Slouching toward a New Expediency." See also Martin, "The Rise and Fall of Jim Crow."

none of the young men representing it on the gridiron appears to be any worse off for having spent an afternoon competing against a Negro player.

It is a fairly safe prediction that no white North Carolinian's daughter will marry a Negro as a result of Saturday's play, much to the chagrin of the peddlers of the bugaboo of social equality.

Perhaps Williams, out there in the mud, did not realize he was making history. Perhaps the North Carolina boys did not know it either. The chances are none of the players thought about it after the first whistle. But, as I watched the teams shuttling up and down the field, the parade of other intersectional clashes came to mind. It was this same New York University which withdrew its star Negro lineman, Dave Meyers, some years ago when the team of the University of Georgia came here for a game. Meyers developed a convenient "bad ankle" and had to sit on the bench.

More recently there was the Willis Ward incident at Michigan. Georgia Tech came up to Ann Arbor to play the Maize and Blue. Ward was the star end of the Michigan team and the day of the game he saw it from the grandstand. Georgia Tech claimed it did not demand Ward's withdrawal, but that a "gentleman's agreement" had been reached.

It was not so many years ago that Ohio State had a giant star tackle in the person of William Bell. But when Ohio State went to Baltimore to play Navy, Bell was sent away to scout another team which Ohio State was to play later. Navy didn't want to be defeated by a Negro.

The theory behind all these shenanigans has been that the prestige of a southern school suffers in some way if its sons compete in games with Negroes. Not only that, but the South and the white race generally were supposed to suffer something or other. Honor allegedly was involved. Sociology, anthropology and political science were dragged into the argument, the whole thing topped off by a rehash of the war of 1860–65.

There is no logic in this position, but prejudices are never logical. There is no sportsmanship in it either, but prejudices come first and sports second. Two schools agree to have their teams meet in a game. Each school will have on its team the very best football talent on its campus. But when one school finds a valuable Negro player (and he has to be good to make these teams), the other says it will not play against him. It is thus taking an unfair and unsportsmanlike advantage of its rival, forcing him to enter the contest at less than his full strength. Like a spoiled child, the South has insisted on having its way, on forcing its home town rules and traditions on its northern hosts.

North Carolina would have none of this. Just as that state and its great university have broken away from other traditions of the deep South, it broke at last this silly rule. Chapel Hill is known far and wide for its leadership in educational circles. It is head and shoulders above the other southern institutions of learning. The story is that when the New York game was arranged, North Carolina was told there would probably be a Negro player on the Violet team. It is said the athletic board of control at Chapel Hill did not faint or grow purple with anger. It did not pound the table and rant of white supremacy. There is no record of anyone asking that famous question:

"Would you want your daughter to marry one?" The North Carolinians merely said they would not object and would not protest.

Now this does not mean that North Carolina is entirely emancipated on the color question. No doubt there are plenty of people on and off the campus who still think it was wrong to play against Ed Williams. It does mean, however, that North Carolina has made another step forward and has set an example for other southern schools. Its action indicates that the younger generation of white southerners want to approach the difficult business of race relations on a different basis than that used by their fathers and grandfathers.

Three southerners with pronounced drawls sat next to me in the Stadium and when Williams came off the field, one of them who apparently had not known of the colored boy, said, "Do you mean HE has been playing against North Carolina?

To which another one said, "Yes, and it's about time. That's old stuff. If our southern schools are going to play in the North, they ought to play against them."

Yes, it's about time. Princeton will have its chance soon in its game with Cornell. Princeton, which does not admit Negroes and doesn't like to play against them, will face Cornell's Negro player, Brud Holland. But North Carolina has made it hard for Princeton to be anything but sporting about Holland. Which may or may not be another indication that this race problem is going to be settled eventually by southern whites and southern Negroes.

Roy Wilkins, "That Old Southern Accent," *New York Amsterdam News,* October 23, 1936.

17. Paul D. Davis / "Students, Teachers Blast Ban against Lacrosse Player": Harvard University and the Color Line

African Americans have participated in intercollegiate athletics on predominantly white university campuses since the latter half of the nineteenth century. In that time, they have experienced unparalleled success and garnered many of the most prestigious awards college sport could bestow. In their efforts both as individuals and as "race men," however, those same athletes suffered untold indignities and numerous outrages both within and outside the domain of sport. "Good sportsmanship" and "fair play" stood—and still stand—as the cornerstones of the athletic ideal; yet with respect to the participation of blacks in college sport from the turn of the century to the era of the civil rights movement and beyond, the litany of abuses of those hallowed notions has run long.

If not the most blatant form of discrimination, perhaps the most frustrating for black Americans occurred when northern institutions acquiesced to southern racial practices by agreeing to keep black players out of games against the colleges and universities of the white South. From Jim Crow contracts to "gentlemen's agreements" between numerous intersectional rivals, a widespread and deeply rooted pattern of exclusion characterized college sport for more than half a century. Such administrative calculations, weighing the outcome of an athletic contest against prevailing racial ideologies and practices, kept prominent black ath-

letes such as Paul Robeson of Rutgers, Dave Myers and Leonard Bates of NYU, Lou Montgomery of Boston College, Willis Ward of Michigan, and Wilmeth Sidat-Singh of Syracuse out of games against southern schools at different times during their careers. Who wasn't in the lineup thus constitutes a significant chapter in the history of college sport during the era of segregation, South and North. *

One of the more publicized and noteworthy of these episodes of exclusion involved two of America's leading institutions, Harvard University and the United States Naval Academy. In the spring of 1941 Harvard's athletic director, William J. Bingham, withdrew Lucien Alexis Jr. from a lacrosse match against the Naval Academy at the request of the latter institution's superintendent, Rear Admiral Russell Willson. The withdrawal of Alexis drew an angry response from students on the Harvard campus, a reaction perhaps best articulated by Paul Daniel Davis in the following selection from the Pittsburgh Courier-Journal *of April 19, 1941. Davis, a Harvard graduate and law student who was among the leaders of the protest, makes clear that students at Harvard were no longer going to tolerate the racially discriminatory practices of southern institutions. Tellingly, the response of the students, combined with action from the school's faculty and other groups, would eventually lead to a public statement by Harvard condemning any further acts of discrimination and announcing that the school would no longer compete against institutions that violated the standards of fair play.* **

———————

All the past week the Harvard campus has been in an uproar following the disclosure that a Negro undergraduate was barred from participation in a Harvard-Navy lacrosse game at Annapolis on April 5. The central figure in the controversy is Lucien Victor Alexis, Jr., Harvard College Junior of New Orleans, Louisiana, of Adams House, a graduate of Exeter Prep School, Exeter, New Hampshire, and a midfield player on the lacrosse team. His father is a Harvard man class of 1918 and principal of a New Orleans high school.

In the first game against the University of Pennsylvania in Philadelphia, Alexis played without causing so much as a murmur. In the second game, against the University of Maryland, the student was at first not allowed to play. Administration officials hemmed and hawed and thought up every possible excuse, but Alexis finally competed.

Upon the team's arrival at the Naval Academy they ate in the dining room, but as soon as it was discovered that Alexis was on the team the coach, Richard Snibbe, former St. John's College of Annapolis All-American lacrosse player and the manager, Robert B. Seidman, a senior, were called in by Commander Davis, director of athletics, and were told that it would be impossible to play Alexis against the Navy. One reason being fear of race riots in the town—an assertion dropped when informed of Alexis playing at College Park. The same was reiterated by Commander Perry, the

---

* For a description of Paul Robeson's experiences on the Rutgers football team, see Duberman, *Paul Robeson*, 19–24, 76–77, 760. On the Bates case, see Spivey, "'End Jim Crow in Sports'"; on Lou Montgomery, see Stout, "Jim Crow Halfback."

** For more on this episode, see Miller, "Harvard and the Color Line."

graduate manager of athletics. Finally, they were taken to see Admiral Willson, the superintendent of the Naval Academy.

By this time the manager and coach had become accustomed to this type of red tape because they had to eventually see the President of the University of Maryland before Alexis was allowed to play there. And then the President left it to the discretion of the coach, who in turn left it with the men on his Maryland squad as to whether they would play Harvard with a Negro on the team—they did with none of the men objecting. The Admiral gave the coach and manager three choices: (1) to bench Alexis for the game and Navy would bench a player of similar ability; (2) to take the game from Navy on forfeit; (3) to permit the Admiral to phone the authorities of Harvard and settle the issue. The last of the three was chosen and then ensued a series of agitated telephone calls and telegrams and finally the Harvard director of athletics, William J. Bingham was reached at Brattleboro, Vermont. Bingham was surprised to hear from the Admiral who began a long curt harangue on the fact that the Academy had never participated against a team with a Negro on it for 96 years and did not intend to do so now; that Harvard should have informed him of such; that he was not prejudiced because he was a northerner, New York, but it was just Navy policy and must be followed.

Bingham stood his ground and continued to state to the Admiral that Navy was the host and that Harvard was the guest and expected decent treatment, since Alexis was a member of the team he had to be allowed to play. However, later in the evening a wire came from Bingham to the coach saying that Alexis was not to dress or play against the Academy. What took place between the time of the Admiral's conversation with Bingham and the wire telling Alexis not to play no one seems to know, however, Alexis took the evening train, 24 hours ahead of the team, and returned to Boston.

The Crimson Begins the Crusade

As soon as Harvard reopened from the spring vacation on Tuesday, the Crimson took to task the Harvard officials who asked Alexis to return and accused them of "Kowtowing to the intolerable jim crowism of Navy bigwigs" and accused the Navy of practicing undemocratic principles. "It was not the students at Annapolis who wanted Alexis to go, for they told the Harvard players just the contrary."

Harvard Students Protest Navy Ban

Following the disclosure by the Crimson, students were incensed by the Annapolis incident and prominent student leaders met and drew up a petition which was circulated asking the director of athletics Bingham for a clarification of Harvard's policy in the matter and for a guarantee that such action will not take place again in the future. The petition was as follows: "We believe that almost unanimously the undergraduate body is of the opinion that racial consideration should not be allowed to determine the fit or unfitness of a student to compete on an athletic team. In view of this belief, we, the students of Harvard University, wish to disapprove heartily of the course of action taken by the college authorities when under pressure from the United States Naval Academy, they agreed to bar a student because of racial consideration from participating in an athletic contest."

"By yielding to the Naval Academy's demands, Harvard has taken an indefensible position in the eyes of a democratic nation. In the belief that the University's action was the result of an over-hasty decision rather than a sanction of jim crowism we request from the Harvard authorities a clarification of the University's athletic policy with regard to colored athletes. We believe that Mr. Bingham will make it clear that in the future Harvard will not tolerate athletic relationships with institutions which discriminate on the basis of race or creed, and that such discrimination has never had, and never will have, any place in Harvard."

Among those who drew up and signed the petition were John C. Robbins, Jr., of Cleveland, president of the Crimson; Bruce Barton, Jr., of New York City; Paul D. Davis, of Columbia, Georgia, Negro Law School student; President Franklin D. Roosevelt's godson, Langdon P. Marvin, Jr., of New York City, President of the Student Council.

The same evening the petition was circulated throughout the houses of the college and over half of the freshman class spontaneously signed a petition in fifteen minutes. On Wednesday morning a committee composed of the various groups and student leaders on the campus presented the petition to Bingham. The committee which waited on Bingham included Paul D. Davis, Negro Law School student, who was spokesman for the committee; John C. Robbins, president of the Crimson; David Bennett, president of the Harvard Student Union; Robert Stange, of the National Council on Democracy and Education.

Paul D. Davis, "Students, Teachers Blast Ban against Lacrosse Player," *Pittsburgh Courier-Journal*, April 19, 1941.

18. William A. Brower / "Has Professional Football Closed the Door?"

The story of the African American experience in professional football varies considerably from that in major league baseball. While African Americans were excluded from the national pastime from the 1880s and 1890s until 1945, they were able to participate in professional football through much of the first half of the twentieth century. High-caliber players such as Charles Follis, Henry McDonald, Fritz Pollard, and Paul Robeson participated in the early days of professional football in Ohio and other midwestern states where the game was initially so popular. African Americans also participated in the fledgling National Football League (NFL) until 1933 when the color line was drawn. The league would not be integrated again until 1946 when Kenny Washington and Woody Strode, two former UCLA stars, were signed to contracts by the Los Angeles Rams (two other African Americans, Marion Motley and Bill Willis, were signed the same year by the Cleveland Browns of the rival All-America Football Conference). *

In the following selection from Opportunity *of December 1940, William A. Brower pon-*

---

* For the integration process in professional football, see T. Smith, "Civil Rights on the Gridiron"; idem, "Outside the Pale"; Gems, "Shooting Stars"; Ross, *Outside the Lines*.

ders the possible explanations for the exclusion of African Americans from the NFL. He first discounts any claims that there were no African Americans talented enough to play in the league, citing the outstanding performances of Cornell's Brud Holland, Iowa's Homer Harris, and other great black players at the highest levels of collegiate competition. He also discounts any claims that black and white players could not play together without racial incident, citing the success of African Americans in the league prior to the drawing of the color line in 1933, and the fact that white players had not shown any resentment when competing with or against their black counterparts in college football. Brower concludes by placing blame on NFL owners for the exclusion of African American players from the league. Although praising the owners for raising the status of the game and acknowledging their contributions to the league, Brower points out that they had shown no commitment to erasing the color line. He hoped that they would soon welcome the return of black players both to strengthen the league and to remove the tarnish of racial discrimination from its reputation.

——— ———

In a recent issue of the magazine *Golf,* Bob Considine, young sport sage of the *New York Daily Mirror,* made this pertinent observation: "One of the great success stories in the history of sport is the rise of pro football. It has advanced from the gutters of the gridiron to a position where it is the darling of rich young backers and the alma mater of John Doe. A little more than a decade ago the New York Giants gave away 5,000 passes a week to a reluctant public and estimated that only half of them were used. This coming season (the current campaign) the Giants will draw in the neighborhood of a quarter of a million customers, all of whom will lay their dough on the barrel head."

Last December, shortly after the championship contest between the Green Bay Packers and the Giants, Sam Balter, eminently fair and forthright sports commentator, struck a different note. On one of his daily broadcasts, heard on a major network, he read an open letter to the magnates of the National Professional Football League, inquiring if it were malice aforethought that each of the ten clubs neglected to select Kenny Washington, great Negro half-back of the University of California, Los Angeles branch, during their draft session at Milwaukee the day preceding the titular game. If so, he asked them to make a public announcement, stating unequivocally whether such a practice, which inferentially debars Negro football players from active engagement in major league pro football, be a permanent policy of their organization. For this purpose he volunteered the facilities of his program and the network which carried it.

What is the kindred of these two sport items, with the obvious exception that they pertain to professional football? To the naked eye any other affinity may appear lacking. But if you explore the nether regions you will find them linked closely—rather closely—together. This relationship may be explained simply and in a few words: Easy money and prejudice tend to gravitate toward each other.

The most assailable fault of a Democracy is that whenever symptoms of prejudice are manifested, somebody's feelings are hurt. In this instance, if the magnates have by concerted accord definitely decided to close the door to Negro gridiron stars in big-time post graduate football, the feelings of (in round numbers) thirteen million Negro citizens, augmented by an undetermined number of sportsmanlike white spectators, are going to be seriously impaired.

But Negro pigskin performers do not have to lean too heavily on sentiments. They have made a cogent case for themselves solely on the basis of merit. Each year several turn in notable, sometimes extraordinary, performances for their alma maters in white collegiate circles. In fact, in recent years a noticeable number have achieved All-American recognition. Cornell's Brud Holland twice attained this distinction, in consecutive years. On conference and sectional teams, they have also gained impressive representation. At the conclusion of the 1937 season, members of the University of Iowa team chose Homer Harris, versatile linesman, as their captain. Negro participants in College All-Stars-Professional Champions games have likewise acquitted themselves admirably.

In the Negro collegiate realm, there lies a fertile field still fallow as far as the cognizance of the cash-and-carry magnates are concerned. Here, because of limited numerical strength, a premium is placed on durability. Sixty-minute men, a rarity in white colleges, are not uncommon. Competition among high-ranking teams is taut and stern, the players having to absorb terrific punishment. Despite the recent increase in player-limits, one still must be able to take it to survive in the pro game.

Are the professional football bigwigs cheating Negro players out of the opportunity to participate in their league? One look at the workings of their "draft system" is enough to answer that question.

This system has been in operation for three years in the National Professional Football League. It works very simply. At the close of the regular college and professional schedules, representatives of the ten teams comprising the circuit assemble at a designated site, usually the scene of the championship game, where a prepared list of top college players whose eligibilities have expired is handed around for inspection. These men have been carefully scouted during their careers and the gridiron wheat has been detached from the chaff. Each team is allowed to select a quota of ten men. Inversely, according to the standing of his team at the conclusion of the regulation campaign, each representative picks an individual. (The aggregation lowest in rating having the choice prerogatives, though there are invariably more than enough good men to go around.) This procedure is repeated until the prescribed share has been reached by all.

Coincident with the institution of the draft system came an era in which white colleges produced a bumper crop of Negro players, both qualitatively and quantitatively. The array has been artistically attractive; yet none has been chosen in the brief annals of the selective process. Hearken to this catalogue and you will better get the point: In 1937, the first year of the draft, eligibles included Dwight Reed, Minnesota's fine flankman. In 1938, the contingent contained Holland and Harris; Bernie Jefferson, star halfback of Northwestern; Horace Bell, sterling guard and place-kicking specialist from Minnesota; Ed Williams, better-than-average fullback of New York University; Fritz Pollard, Jr., South Dakota's backfield flash; Roland Bernard, able linesman of Boston University, and Wilmeth Sidat-Singh, accomplished passer from Syracuse. Last season, aside from the illustrious Washington, there was Woody Strode, talented end, whose reputation exceeded just being Washington's teammate. All these admirable performers were blandly ignored in the voluntary conscription of college stars!

In trying to find the logical reason for the apparent prevailing discrimination against the ebony athlete in professional football, one is inclined to wonder if its bigwigs are not tracing the footsteps of the warmer-weather neighbor—baseball. The game that is generally recognized as our national pastime has been kept lily-white since it became an organized sport. The ostracism of the Negro from professional baseball is predicated on untested premises and, thus far, inexorable traditions. Some contend that because the majority of major league teams train in the south during spring conditioning exercises, matters of delicate nature might arise if an attempt to use a Negro were made. Others cite the preponderance of white southern athletes in the big leagues and express the opinion that the infiltration of Negro players might mean the sacrifice of technical efficiency and harmony.

There are no arresting or rational excuses for professional football to follow the dubious precedent set by professional baseball. Before pro football was elevated to its present position of prominence and affluence on the national sporting panorama, Negroes were identified with it in playing capacity without displeasure. Joe Lillard, the old Oregon star, contributed excellent backfield work to the cause of the Chicago Cardinals as late as 1932; Duke Slater, former Iowa All-American, performed superbly at tackle for the same team earlier; and Ray Kemp, who did his collegiate chores on the gridiron at Duquesne, distinguished himself in the employ of the Pittsburgh Pirates at guard. It is a plausible deduction that if players of color were used then with satisfactory and beneficial consequences, they could be used with similar results now.

But that is only a portion of the story. The playing personnel of professional football is by and large constituted of college players from all sections of the country—no single section predominates. All are intelligent young men with a sound sense of human values. Many of them either played alongside of, or face Negro stars, without resentment. It is inconceivable that they would renege when goaded by the additional incentive of receiving cash emoluments for their gridiron labors. In fact, if a survey were conducted it is reliably believed that you would discover a minute percentage of conscientious objectors.

Any fear that if Negro athletes shared in the cash-and-carry sport it would create mental rifts and technical discord is sort of a delusion and should be summarily dismissed. It has already been inferred that they play on college squads without embarrassing the mechanical coordination or undermining the morale of the units. There is nothing to indicate that team function and spirit would suffer in the professional phase of the sport. Truthfully such a contingency in the play-for-pay game is diminished because playing football is a job, the primary source of income, for many of the players. They can ill afford to let internecine strife and private predilections interfere with team unity and welfare.

Oze Simmons, another former Iowa luminary, recently wrote a letter to Chester L. Washington, sports editor of the *Pittsburgh Courier* leading Negro weekly, concerning this very point. Simmons wrote: "I know whereof I speak. The owners contend that the reason colored stars are not playing in the National Football League is because there are too many southern players in the league. I had the pleasure of playing with the Paterson (N.J.) team in the American Association for two years. And not only did the southern boys block for me, they even fought for me. The players have a job to do—WIN GAMES—and they are out to do their best, because that's what they are getting paid for. And if they can't produce they are fired."

Jimmy Powers, sports editor of the *New York Daily News,* had this to say on the heels of the All-Star–Green Bay Packers game in Chicago: "If I were Tim Mara or Dan Topping, I'd sign Kenny Washington. He played on the same field with boys who are going to be scattered through the league. And he played against the champion Packers. There wasn't a bit of trouble anywhere. Kenny was tackled hard once or twice, especially after he ran a kick-off 43 yards right through the entire Packer lineup. But that's routine treatment for jack-rabbits. You slam your opposing speed merchants about, hoping to wear them down. Kenny took it all with a grin."

Another element in favor of the argument for Negro participation is that every franchise is located in a city where athletic miscegenation is not prohibited. Fans in Detroit, Chicago, New York, Cleveland, etc., are not allergic to one set of players because their skin pigmentation, by whims of birth, is darker than another group, but are largely interested in the skill and capability of their exploits on the playing terrain. A considerable segment of professional patronage is drawn from the college clientele. They demonstrate the same cosmopolitan reaction at a professional contest that they exhibit at a college combat. The same emotional currents circulate. They exude the same instinctive flair for sportsmanship. They emit exhortative yells when the battle conforms to their preference; they sit in frustrated silence when a change of complexion adversely affects them. They show accolades for a deserving deed, no matter who executes it, with the same spontaneity and sincere enthusiasm.

When you simmer everything down there is only one direction in which to look when you go to attach the blame—categorically in the faces of the National Professional Football magnates. There is no record of any authenticated commitment by them on the issue. Professional football is to a large extent autocratic, but it is hard to think that it will continue, premeditatively or differently, to flout fair-minded fans whose cash provides the ways and means for the game's existence. It is hard to think, too, that it can further injudiciously disregard the professional and commercial value of such Negro players of excellence as Kenny Washington, Brud Holland and Oze Simmons.

You realize it is difficult to entertain any particular grievance against Tim Mara, George Halas, George Preston Marshall, Art Rooney and others of the NPFL officialdom. These are gentlemen of estimable character. They purged their game of all the poison with which it was formerly rife. It was their promotional ingenuity, generous and patient investment, courageous perseverance and commendable foresight which proved to be the optimum for the prevalent salutary status of the game. Their combined efforts lifted pro football from a floundering business in the ruck into an aura of respectability as an established enterprise of sports.

But the evidence of double-jointed action towards the Negro somewhere along the line is transparent. The professional game of football has flourished with amazing celerity. One hopes that its guardians will not let its prestige continue to be retarded and tarnished by discrimination because of color—the most truculent tentacle of Prejudice.

William A. Brower, "Has Professional Football Closed the Door?" *Opportunity* 18 (December 1940): 375–77.

5

African American Athletes and Democratic Principles: Interpreting the Desegregation of Sport, 1940s and 1950s

Introduction

If there was a single moment in American history when sports unambiguously signaled a new age in race relations, it occurred on October 23, 1945. On that day, Branch Rickey signed Jackie Robinson to a contract with the Brooklyn Dodgers baseball organization, thus ending—at least in symbolic terms—the sixty-year reign of Jim Crow policies and practices in major league baseball. Critically, it was only a matter of months later that professional football readmitted African Americans to participation. Without fanfare or controversy, a few years after the desegregation of the national pastime, the fledgling National Basketball Association would follow suit. What one historian has called "baseball's great experiment" constituted a landmark in racial reform, setting a precedent for other institutions and organizations in which social justice had long been denied. Apart from Harry Truman's executive order to desegregate the military, no other instance until the *Brown v. Board of Education* decision of 1954 would speak so forcefully to the momentum being gathered by the civil rights crusade.*

The signing of Robinson was an epochal event, but in fact the seemingly sudden breakthrough in baseball derived from years of activism by black editors and journalists who had long argued that the stars of the Negro Leagues could more than hold their own against white players in the majors. Athletes such as Satchel Paige and Josh Gibson, "Cool Papa" Bell and Oscar Charleston had actually done so in hundreds of off-season or barnstorming contests. Just as significant, the desegregation of baseball followed closely upon World War II, where black Americans had distinguished themselves in combat and demonstrated their patriotism in countless other ways. The 1948 presidential order that formally initiated the desegregation of the armed services, like Robinson's rookie season for the Dodgers, also stood against the backdrop of the cold war. How could the United States make its case for democracy and opportunity in the "free world" if the expansive newsreel and print coverage that fueled the propaganda wars against the Soviet Union continued to show American men in uniform—not just soldiers and sailors, but also baseball players—thoroughly segregated by race? The time had come for substantial changes in race relations throughout the nation.

Yet those changes did not occur swiftly or without considerable anguish. One consequence of the move to desegregate sport was the devastating economic effect of such efforts on African American enterprises, such as Negro League baseball. Another was that black athletes would encounter enormous hostility from competitors and spectators. Moreover, wherever they traveled they continued to be subjected to discriminatory treatment—in lodging arrangements, for instance, and restaurants. The burden could take a heavy toll: "I am pleased that God made my skin black," Curt Flood would later declare. [B]ut I wish He had made it thicker." Still, many athletes, in a variety of sports, were anxious to become pioneers. Contemporary commentators on the significance of Jackie Robinson emphasized that the heroism and sacrifice of a new generation of athletes endeavoring to breach the color line in sport represented the yearnings of countless other

---

* See Tygiel, *Baseball's Great Experiment.*

African Americans, who were poised to make *their* contributions once the political, economic, and social systems in the United States opened up.[*]

During much of the time Jackie Robinson held center stage in the midcentury drama of African American hopes and strivings, Martin Luther King Jr. was still an undergraduate at Morehouse College in Atlanta and then a seminarian in schools farther north. Ella Baker, for her part, having cofounded an organization that supported school desegregation efforts in the wake of the *Brown* decision, then helped to coordinate the Montgomery bus boycott. The steps being taken to desegregate the national pastime had counterparts at the local level—in southern towns in the Mississippi Delta and within black communities in the urban North. But it was clear to the mass of African Americans that the walls of segregation were not tumbling down simply because of baseball; that edifice would need to be dismantled brick by brick by many activists. The massive resistance mounted by white authorities in the South to every civil rights initiative suggested the problems yet to be confronted; so too did the escalation of violence and intimidation. For many black Americans the most memorable occurrence of 1955 was not the World Series, won by Brooklyn, led by Robinson. It was the lynching of Emmett Till.

Sport ultimately played into the civil rights movement in richly symbolic terms. Black heroes on the baseball diamond, football gridiron, or track oval and in the basketball arena or boxing ring reinforced race pride and established role models for African Americans who believed that the time had come to assert their claims to *full* participation in the life of the nation. Sports offered one source of spiritual strength. There were, however, a few dissenting voices, such as that of E. Franklin Frazier, who warned that the excessive attention devoted to sports diverted black people from the larger prize. Controversies over the purported "whiteness" or "blackness" of the Louisiana boxer Ralph Dupas called attention to the warped logic of the "one-drop rule" of hypodescent. Battles over the desegregation of golf courses and tennis courts would be fought long after the time when many Americans believed that the civil rights era had officially concluded.

What emerged, though, from the early phase of the movement in the late 1940s and 1950s was a sense that black Americans—well-represented by black athletes such as Jackie Robinson in the national pastime, as well as Althea Gibson and Wilma Rudolph in international competition—also contributed to America's democratic experiment. The black women who won at Wimbledon or held aloft their Olympic gold medals not only displayed individual athletic talents and embodied the aspirations of many other African Americans; they also stood for the nation at large. Such, at least, was the ideal.

---

[*] Flood, quoted in Tygiel, *Baseball's Great Experiment,* 303.

A

THE MEANINGS OF JACKIE ROBINSON

1. Walter White / "Jackie Robinson on Trial"

Jackie Robinson's entry into the major leagues was received with unabated enthusiasm by members of the African American community. The front-page, eyewitness accounts of Robinson's early career written by Wendell Smith, for instance, drew 100,000 additional subscribers to the Pittsburgh Courier-Journal. *That an athlete such as Robinson finally won the opportunity to display his talents represented the culmination of a long campaign waged by black sportswriters like Smith and Sam Lacy (as well as by their white allies) to integrate baseball. The broader acknowledgment of Robinson's achievements, increasing week by week, season by season, also appeared as evidence that the national pastime was, symbolically at least, a great leveler within the American social system. This initial move toward a truly democratic ideal was perhaps best expressed—with regard to many of the ambiguities that now confronted white fans—by the baseball chronicler Roger Kahn: "By applauding Robinson, a man did not feel that he was taking a stand on school integration, or on open housing. . . . But . . . to disregard color even for an instant is to step away from old prejudices."**

Attending such observations and impulses, however, was the fear on the part of many whites and some African Americans that the "great experiment" would fail if Robinson did not play well, if black fans acted inappropriately, or both.

For his part, Branch Rickey, worried that his plan would be undermined if it antagonized whites, called a meeting of some thirty influential black New Yorkers in February 1947 to tell them that the greatest risk to Robinson's success—"the one enemy most likely to ruin that success—is the Negro people themselves." In extremely negative terms, Rickey admonished his black audience with a stern lecture. "You'll hold Jackie Robinson days . . . and Jackie Robinson nights. You'll get drunk. You'll fight. You'll be arrested. You'll wine and dine the player until he is fat and futile. You'll symbolize his importance into a national comedy . . . and an ultimate tragedy—yes, tragedy."**

In the following document, Walter White, executive secretary of the NAACP and a recipient of the Spingarn Medal, echoed many of Rickey's comments from just two months earlier by imploring African Americans to exercise patience and restraint as Robinson traveled the major league circuit. To avoid jeopardizing the former UCLA star's chances for success and the subsequent struggles on behalf of black players, black fans must not interpret every action on the field against Robinson or any verbal sparring as being racially motivated, White contended. Black fans must act "like civilized human beings" and realize that many of those

---

* Kahn, quoted in Tygiel, *Baseball's Great Experiment*, 343–44.
** Both quotes are from Rampersad, *Jackie Robinson*, 160.

Jackie Robinson (National Baseball Hall of Fame Library, Cooperstown, N.Y.)

things that take place on the playing field, such as "base runners with sharpened spikes rising high to break up double plays or lunging back to the bag to avoid being picked off are a normal part of professional baseball." In addition, noted White—perhaps too enthusiastically—the majority of major league players, even those from the southern states, would treat Robinson fairly and avoid hurting him "for fear they may be accused wrongly." In large part, White clung to Rickey's view that it was important to deemphasize the racial component of an experiment that was, in fact, largely racial in nature. Ironically, as this document reveals, it was supposed to be the responsibility of black Americans to accomplish this.

———— ——

It is profoundly to be hoped that baseball fans, especially colored ones, will respect Jackie Robinson's request that he be allowed to pioneer as the first known Negro ball player in the big leagues without too much ill-advised interference from the stands. There will be enough pressure on him from prejudiced fellow players and white fans to test the mettle of any human being.

Base runners with sharpened spikes rising high to break up double plays or lunging back to the bag to avoid being picked off are a normal part of professional baseball. A man's livelihood causes him to do lots of things he wouldn't ordinarily do, especially when players remember that the next season's contract and salary depend on batting averages, runs scored and batted in, bases stolen and all-around aggressiveness.

Jackie Robinson may during the coming season be spiked or otherwise injured just as he was during the late days of the training season when Bruce Edwards of the Brooklyn Dodgers ran into him on the base paths and shook him up. A lot of white ballplayers will also be injured between the opening and closing of the season in similar fashion. Let's be careful about charging that Jackie was deliberately hurt unless it can be clearly proved. Most of the big league players will treat him like any other player and in fact, probably go out of their way to avoid hurting Robinson for fear they may be accused wrongly.

And just because a lot of the white players are Southerners most certainly does not mean that every last one of them will be anti-Robinson. Clay Hooper, Jackie's manager at Montreal, did everything he possibly could to help him make the big leagues. Hooper is from Mississippi. A number of Southerners like Carl Hubbel, the great screw-ball pitcher of the Giants of a few years ago and many other Dixie players have expressed themselves as favoring the admission of Negro ball players to the big leagues during recent years solely on the basis of their ability. And some Northern players have publicly or privately taken just the opposite stand. We should be intelligent enough to refrain from going off half-cocked on this score.

Harm of Misguided Enthusiasm

An example of how misguided enthusiasm for Jackie can do him and the cause of breaking the color line in baseball much more harm than good occurred at Ebbets Field in Brooklyn the day of the first exhibition game of the season. A large number of colored fans turned out. Jackie was cheered as lustily when he slapped into a double play as though he had hit a homer with the bases loaded. That was bad enough but not the worst example of bad manners. Whenever Dixie Walker came to bat he was lustily and even profanely booed for allegedly having said he would not play on the same team with a Negro. PM [the liberal New York daily], ardently pro-Robinson, quotes Walker and asserts its belief he is telling the truth in denying he made any such statement. Whatever the circumstances, Walker and Robinson ARE playing on the same team. Let's wait and see what happens.

Finally, may I plead with that minority of Negroes who appear to believe a baseball game can be seen only through a haze of alcohol to postpone their drinking until after the games in which they go to see Jackie (or any other player or team) play. I used to take my family and friends to the Yankee Stadium or Polo Grounds to see colored professional teams play. But for the past few years I have not done so because the drinking and loud-mouthed profanity, vulgarity and fighting of some colored fans, female as well as male, so disgusted us. The overwhelming majority of the crowds were as well-behaved as any other patrons. But the few were so obnoxious that that gave all Negroes a bad name. To cap the climax one such character who was arrested when he beat up another man (which is precisely what should have happened) had the gall to appeal to the NAACP on the alleged grounds that he "had been discriminated against because of his color."

"Let's Do Our Part"

Jackie Robinson has demonstrated his ability as a ball player and his level-headedness and courage as a man. The best help we can give him to smash for all time the color line in highly lucrative professional baseball for himself and for others is to act like civilized human beings.

Branch Rickey has done his part. Whether any other major league managers will give opportunity to other Negroes will depend in part on us, almost as much as on the players themselves. Let's do our part.

Walter White, "Jackie Robinson on Trial," *Chicago Defender*, April 26, 1947.

2. Sam Lacy / "Campy, Jackie as Dodgers"

The reentry of African Americans into major league baseball did not put an immediate halt to racial discrimination and segregationist practices off the playing field at southern spring training sites. Jackie Robinson, Roy Campanella, Don Newcombe, Hank Aaron, and the other early black entrants into the modern game continued to suffer racial slights and experience segregation while preparing for the regular season. They were forced to live in private homes or boardinghouses rather than appointed team hotels. What is more, they were also frequently prevented from dining, traveling in buses and taxis, patronizing stores, and attending theaters, nightclubs, and other public facilities with their white teammates. Tellingly, some of these same forms of discrimination, while usually less frequent and overt, continued to be inflicted on these black players after they moved north to begin the regular season. In some of the southernmost major league cities, Cincinnati and St. Louis in particular, black players were often taunted by white fans; bigotry beyond the base paths was a fact of life for the first generation of black major leaguers.*

In the following selection from the Baltimore Afro-American *of April 1, 1950, Sam Lacy describes the racial discrimination experienced by Jackie Robinson and his black teammates in spring training in Vero Beach, Florida, as well as during the regular season. Lacy, the former Negro League infielder who became one of the most well known and influential black sportswriters in the country, explains that while the new black members of the Brooklyn Dodgers were realizing their dream of being in the major leagues and seemingly proving that*

---

* For an impressive discussion of the desegregation process at southern spring training sites, see J. E. Davis, "Baseball's Reluctant Challenge." See also Lamb, "I Never Want to Take Another Trip Like This One"; Tygiel, *Baseball's Great Experiment,* esp. 265–69.

baseball's experiment in integration was a success, off the field the players confronted the most hideous forms of racism. *

——— ———

VERO BEACH, FLA.—If the reports emanating from this quarter are so glowing as to give the impression everything in baseball's integration experiment is now honey and whipped cream, let me assure you that is far from the truth.

The blame for such a misconception—if one be alive—perhaps rests with me. It is very probably due to the rose-colored glasses I so frequently don when this type of assignment comes my way.

Regardless of any impressions you may have gotten to the contrary, the South has not accepted inter-racialism in baseball. It is merely tolerating it.

Jackie Robinson, Roy Campanella, Don Newcombe and Dan Bankhead are recognized in Dixie as Brooklyn Dodger baseball players, sure. But they are also recognized as colored men.

South Still the "South"

And to "Mr. and Mrs. Southerner," the latter fact takes precedence over the former. The monkey-suits of Ebbets Field don't give them first-class citizenship any more than do their gray or blue civilian clothes and brown faces.

To them, and to me, the South is still the South.

Once we leave Dodgertown, the city within the city of Vero Beach, Fla., we are on our own. White members of the organization go in one direction; we cross the railroad tracks and go the other way.

Whenever and wherever possible, Dixie whites waste no time reminding us what has been the status quo for more than 84 years.

Some Improvement Noted

In fairness, however, it should be pointed out here that there are some white southerners whose attitudes have improved considerably. These greatly outnumbered few have disclosed a friendship that is gratifying.

But for the most part, the traditional animosity prevails. Not always vocal, but always present.

Two weeks ago, three of the players—Robinson, Campy and Newcombe—as well as your reporter, used a car for the trip to Miami for the game with the Boston Braves. The machine was a rental obtained by the Dodgers' road secretary, Harold Parrott, from a Vero Beach drive-yourself company, for his own use around the base.

Car Rental Bias

In order to circumvent any likely embarrassment evolving from roadside eating, etc., we were given use of the car for transportation to and from Miami, and, once we were in town, to and from the ballpark.

———

* For information on Lacy, see his autobiography, *Fighting for Fairness.*

Somehow, the car rental company learned we had used the machine, and the next day, Parrott was requested to return it immediately. Officials of the agency made no effort to conceal the reason for its sudden decision. "No niggers" can drive their cars, they fumed.

A few days later, Campanella was named as the lone colored player on a squad to play in West Palm Beach. En route back to Vero Beach, the team stopped for dinner at a roadside inn.

Forced to Eat in Bus

Several players who are on the squad for no more than tryouts and who will end up in Class A or B ball, went in, sat at the tables and ordered what they wished. Campanella, generally recognized as the best catcher in baseball, was forced to sit alone in the bus and eat what was brought out to him on a tray.

Again, a few days later, Campy bore the brunt of responsibility of showing at least one colored player in a game at West Palm Beach. This time, to play it safe, he ate dinner in West Palm Beach and then took a late train to Vero Beach.

When he arrived at 2 A.M., he discovered that there had been a mix-up of instructions at the base and there was no one on hand to meet him. White taxicabs refused to take him as a fare, and the result was the star catcher has to walk the estimated 2.5 miles to the base.

The southern treatment has played no favorites. Each of us, at one time or another, has been confronted with indignities and inconveniences that Dixie reactionaries seem to save especially for colored persons.

Reporter Stopped Twice

The other day, en route to Vero Beach, your reporter had a small case of the poison administered. Twice in the five-mile round-trip, I was stopped by city cops and made to show my operator's license and car credentials for no apparent reason other than I was a colored man driving a Lincoln Cosmopolitan (belonging to Dan Bankhead).

Perhaps, I should make it clear that it isn't only during the Spring that the Brown Bums meet up with this sort of thing.

It happens in the regular season too.

Dodger brass was forced to change its Philadelphia hotel because the management frowned at the thought of housing colored ballplayers with the whites. Since 1948, the Brooks have been lodging at the Warwick.

Room Service Only

In Cincinnati, while the Netherlands-Plaza accepts the whole group, it is "suggested" that the colored members of the party stay out of the dining room. A special arrangement is made whereby their meals are served in their rooms.

The Dodgers' hotel in St. Louis is the Chase. On arrival in that city, the white players take cabs in one direction and the colored in another.

Last September when the Brooks went into St. Louis for their final crucial series with the Cardinals, the party split up as usual.

Poor Accommodations

Inferior ballplayers, some just up from the minors as low as Class B, packed away to exquisite Chase. Many of them couldn't carry Jackie's bat or Campanella's glove or Newk's rosin bag. But, they went to their first class accommodation.

The four of us squeezed into a third-class hotel in the colored section, Jackie and Campy having to put up together. Newcombe, who was slated to pitch the next day, spent the night trying to sleep in a room located directly over a constantly screeching jukebox. I fitted myself into a basement room the size of an overfed telephone booth.

For an inconsequential sportswriter, that was a pardonable sin. But, think what irony Southern prejudice was dealing out in the case of the others.

Only Colored Counted

While Class B squirts were lounging in luxury at the town's best hostelry, Robbie, the National League's Most Valuable Player; Newcombe, the 1949 Rookie of the Year; and Campy, the greatest catcher in the game, were trying to find rest in a Jim Crow house in what many cities in Dixie call "Colored Town."

Uptown, in air-conditioned splendor, were three players on whom the Dodgers had asked waivers, meaning they could be had by any other club that wanted them for $10,000 each.

Downtown, in heat and noise and all-around discomfort, were three players whose combined value could conservatively be estimated at $1 million.

Sam Lacy, "Campy, Jackie as Dodgers: Integration in Dixie Halts When Players Leave the Field," *Baltimore Afro-American*, April 1, 1950.

3. Effa Manley / "Negro Baseball Is at the Crossroads"

It has been said that "no figure cast a larger shadow in Negro baseball in its late period than the amazing Effa Manley." Such an assessment would be hard to dispute. Manley, co-owner with her husband, Abe, of the famous Newark Eagles, was an enormously talented and charismatic person, a genuine power broker in the Negro National League and a symbolic figure in the history of entrepreneurship within Afro-America. She was widely recognized by black fans of the national pastime, but also exerted substantial influence beyond the playing fields—as treasurer of the New Jersey NAACP, sponsor of highly publicized "anti-lynching days," and as a founding member of the Citizens League for Fair Play, a group responsible for the desegregation of department stores in Harlem in the 1930s. Manley's remarkable career was paradoxical in many ways: here was a white woman who commanded enormous respect in an enterprise largely dominated by black men; here was an entrepreneur who also championed the movement that would ultimately put her out of business.*

In the following article Manley warns that the future of black baseball was in serious jeopardy because black fans were flocking to see Jackie Robinson and other African American play-

---

* Rosogin, *Invisible Men*, 108–10, 186–87, 212–13 (quote on 108).

ers who had integrated major league baseball. She called on "newspapers, fans, owners, and everyone interested in the welfare of our people" to come together and preserve black baseball. While never mentioning it in the article, Manley knew first hand the difficulty in luring fans to black baseball now that the best black players were finding their way into the major leagues. In 1946, a year after Robinson signed with the Dodgers, the Newark Eagles attendance had dropped from 120,000 to 57,000, and by 1948 was down to a low of 35,000. It is important to note that for much of her career, Manley campaigned for the integration of major league baseball. She even negotiated the sale of Larry Doby from her own Eagles to the Cleveland Indians in 1947. This apparent inconsistency on Manley's part was a result of the dilemma faced by all the owners in black baseball. While they recognized the need to voice their support for racial integration in baseball so as not to appear to be inhibiting racial advancement, the owners in black baseball also realized that the entry of blacks into the major leagues would eventually lead to the demise of their own league. Manley herself probably expressed the situation best years later when noting the owners' position as "being squeezed between intransigent racial considerations on one hand and cold business reasoning on the other."*

——— ———

(Editors Note—Mrs. Effa Manley, former owner of the Newark Eagles, gave the following statement to the Negro Newspaper Publishers Association during its meeting in Washington, D.C., June 16–18.)

Organized baseball today, stands at the crossroads. The success or failure of the teams to draw this year may determine the future of our Negro leagues. The past two seasons have seen our Negro fans desert our ballparks to follow the exploits of Jackie Robinson and Roy Campanella of Brooklyn and Larry Doby of the Cleveland Indians.

This season the trend of our fans still is toward the major league parks, and unless a real campaign is launched to retain their interest in Negro baseball, our Negro leagues may be unable to continue operating. It is this situation which impels me to release to the Negro publishers this statement as an individual who has owned a team in organized Negro baseball for the past 15 years. I am firmly convinced that if organized Negro baseball is to be saved, the Negro press will have to save it. This poses the question: "Is Negro baseball worth saving?"

Develop Players

The answer to that question can be found in a number of players who were developed in our leagues and are now making good in the majors. It is hardly necessary for me to remind you that Robinson, Campanella, Doby, Paige and Newcombe are all products of organized Negro baseball. If Negro fans want to see our boys in the majors after the present group have ended their career, then it is necessary that they support our Negro leagues which discover and develop players capable of playing in the majors.

If we fail to support our Negro leagues in this crucial period we may be hastening the day when no Negroes will be playing in the majors. The boys cannot make the

---

* Quoted in White, *Creating the National Pastime*, 153; see also Overmyer, *Queen of the Negro Leagues*.

jump from sandlot baseball into the big leagues without going through a period of development such as they are given in the Negro leagues. It is also evident that there will not be a sufficient number of our boys scattered throughout the minor league chains to meet the situation. At present we have ten clubs in the Negro American League, and eight in the American Association that employ about 350 ball players, all being paid substantial salaries, receiving training and competition that inspires them to give their best. This is the only practical source for future Robinsons and Dobys.

I believe that some affirmative steps must be taken by those of us who want Negro baseball to survive.

Something Must Be Done

My point is this: some steps must be taken to establish a firm relationship between the major leagues and the present Negro baseball leagues.

Unless something is done we are now seeing the last crop of Negro players in the big leagues. They have killed themselves off, because at the same time, Negro professional baseball is being killed.

We must never lose sight of the fact that the origin of Negro baseball as it is presently constituted was born of discrimination. We would never have had all-Negro teams, or even all-Negro audiences if it had not been for the Jim Crow practices all of us have sought to eliminate.

If the signing of Negro baseball players means a step in that direction, we must not let its very accomplishment be the factor which will defeat us for all time. We are at the crossroads. The future of Negro baseball is at stake.

The Negro press has a very definite responsibility in helping to preserve the leagues. If the sports writers on your publications will evidence the same enthusiasm toward our Negro baseball leagues and our colored boys playing in these organizations as they do about the feats of the Negro players in the white major leagues, the future of Negro baseball will not be in jeopardy. If they will give us the space, coverage, and buildup, the fans will give us the support necessary to make the Negro teams financially successful.

Newspaper fans, owners, and everyone interested in the welfare of our people must get together on a common basis. We must do something and do it immediately. Otherwise, Negro baseball is in great danger of folding . . . and that must never happen.

Effa Manley, "Negro Baseball Is at the Crossroads," *Norfolk Journal and Guide,* June 25, 1949.

4. Gerald Early / "American Integration, Black Heroism, and the Meaning of Jackie Robinson"

Writing in a collection of essays published in 1951, the eminent poet, essayist, and educator Sterling A. Brown argued that after so many years of dealing with dreams deferred, African American athletes and artists had finally begun to glimpse the ideal of integration. By inte-

gration, Brown meant "a parallel in sports and the arts to what the political spokesmen call 'first-class citizenship.' The integration of the Negro athlete or artist means his acceptance as an individual to be judged on his own merits, with no favor granted, and no fault found, because of his race. It means that, whether second-baseman or pugilist, jazz trumpeter or concert singer, poet, or painter, the Negro will be judged evenly, neither over-rigorously nor over-gently, according to the standards of his calling." Brown went on to assert that "the integrated man is a whole man, not a fractional"; the ideal did not mean the loss of distinctive qualities of black culture "derived from the folk, such as jazz and popular dance." Still, so much had occurred so rapidly that there had not really been sufficient time to discuss the many implications of the breaking of the color line in sport. *

This topic lies at the center of Gerald Early's essay on integration, black heroism, and the meanings of Jackie Robinson. In it, Early—a cultural commentator and prizewinning essayist—moves back in time to lay out the arguments made by Robinson and Effa Manley concerning the impact of integration on Negro League baseball and black community solidarity. (Following the Brown decision and the desegregation of the medical and legal professions, similar discussions animated black educators, physicians, and lawyers, who watched the organizations they had been forced to create under Jim Crow recede in influence, then crumble.) Here, though, Early's examination of the desegregation of major league baseball places the Robinson-Manley debate in a deeper context. Clearly, many of the "parallel institutions" created behind the veil of segregation possessed enormous vitality and reinforced race pride in countless ways, but "the prize" long envisioned by most black Americans was ultimately full participation in the social, economic, and political life of the nation. Writing at a distance from the original fray, Early emphasizes further that Robinson's bold moves on the field and off may have assimilated one element of race pride to organized baseball, but he also suggests that this particular breakthrough would occur on terms of assertive black masculinity, within a tradition of heroic resistance and protest. What African American scholars, engineers, and other professionals would later achieve in far more meaningful numbers, Early concludes, still could not match the breathtaking episodes on the playing fields that helped launch the civil rights crusade.

——— ——

By the end of the semicentennial celebration of Jackie Robinson's breaking the color line in professional baseball, the sheer volume of repetitious, melodramatic acclaim for his valor is likely to make him seem more trite than titanic. But there is something vital to be learned about the nature of American society and American race relations by trying to understand just what the heroism of this man is supposed to mean, especially to blacks today. For Robinson's achievement was fraught from the beginning with ambivalence, both his own and that of the blacks for whom he was a hero. And that ambivalence is characteristic of black assimilation into many arenas of American life.

Robinson arguably was the person who launched the American era of racial integration after World War II. This rush and flood of people and events—the *Brown* de-

---

* See S. Brown, "Athletics and the Arts," 117–24; all quotes, 117.

cision, the Montgomery bus boycott, the sit-ins, Martin Luther King, Jr., the Watts riot, Malcolm X, affirmative action, multiculturalism, the Million Man March—provoked unprecedented historical change in how Americans perceived pluralism and race, but shockingly, in the end, did not at all lessen the abiding sense of alienation that African Americans feel toward their native land.

A famous passage in Richard Wright's *Black Boy* discusses this alienation: Wright describes "the essential bleakness of black life in America" and says that blacks have "never been allowed to catch the full spirit of Western civilization." Agreeing with Wright, Ralph Ellison later said that, "Western culture must be won, confronted like the animal in a Spanish bullfight, dominated by the red shawl of codified experience and brought heaving to its knees." The sports metaphor, or, perhaps more precisely, the metaphor of spectacle, is crucial in explaining the complexity of Jackie Robinson's significance as a race hero. The metaphor suggests a kind of black masculine spin on the Hemingwayesque moral code of grace under pressure: a combination of stoicism and élan, of the tragic and triumphant confrontation with an adversarial, savage universe.

What Ellison values here is a style of action, a principle of engagement, that evoked what his disciple, Albert Murray, was to call "the blues hero." Ellison's metaphor suggests that African Americans must claim Western culture through an act not of submission, but of domination; through the power of ordering their experience, sculpting it out of both the chaos of life and the dominant, inimical white culture. Western culture is, thus, a complex set of brute impulses and vested interests represented in various institutions, a force that one must make one's own by courageously making demands of it.

Jackie Robinson was, most profoundly, an Ellisonian blues hero. He confronted Western experience publicly and alone, yet within the democratic context of a team. He confronted both absurdity and injustice, taking his chances within the sunlit arena (baseball was still . . . performed most often in the afternoon), armed solely with a set of highly specialized, elite skills. Robinson became a public spectacle in a way that no other African American had quite been before, and he subdued Western culture through his sheer will to win.

It is telling that we did not celebrate with anything near the same intensity the semicentennial of Joe Louis's 1938 defeat of the German Max Schmeling, in its time an athletic event of at least as much potential importance as Robinson's integration of baseball, nor was the anniversary of Jesse Owens' track victories at the 1936 Berlin Olympics —also considered a momentous event in race relations—met with as much fanfare. Both earlier events were public spectacles in which blacks seized an Ellisonian moment of domination. Indeed, both events might be said to be even more important than Robinson's entry into the big leagues because of their international significance. Yet it is probably, in some measure, their international significance that contributes to our valuing them less than we should, our American provincialism being what it is.

Robinson's greater resonance as a hero has to do with the very local meaning of baseball, not merely as a sport but as a well-ordered ritual of American life associated with contradictory impulses that grew out of its industrial-age origins: an obsession with quantification and statistics and nostalgic quest for pastoralism.

Gunnar Myrdal's *An American Dilemma*, published just three years before Robinson's ascension to the major leagues, presented a mountain of numbers and graphs demonstrating the disorder of black American life, as did, of course, any number of sociological studies done over the years, by both black and white scholars. And the dominant portrayals of black Americans then were such degrading pastoral images as Sambo, the comic darky, Old Black Joe, and other variations of minstrelsy. What more vivid, extraordinary way for blacks to reinvent and regenerate themselves than through the very cultural means that had been used to deny their humanity, through the pastoralism and statistics of baseball?

Baseball is also tied to our mystical, sentimental idea of democracy as teamwork and fair play. This is why Robinson's act of assimilation-as-heroism has such a powerful impact on the American imagination; it is also what makes it so tangled and, for many blacks, so paradoxical. For blacks always approached professional baseball, from the time they were denied the opportunity to play it alongside whites in the 1880s, as a vehicle for assimilation.

Arising out of the insult and stigma of segregation, the Negro leagues were never meant to be an end in themselves. But because, through the leagues, blacks developed a more elaborate and enduring institutional relationship with baseball than with any other sport, baseball became not only a means to assimilate but also a black cultural and commercial venture. Black baseball demonstrated black independence as much as it showed whites that blacks were able, competitive, and desired very much to play baseball with them.

By expressing the desire for freedom and respect, even esteem, through entrepreneurship and enterprise, as well as demonstrating the nationalistic urge of blacks to act independently of whites, the leagues—like black colleges, black churches, and other "shadow" institutions that blacks developed—became an end in themselves, took on a compelling racial mission. Robinson's heroism, as a contradictory form of liberation, cannot be understood outside this conundrum, one that explains a great deal about the ambivalence that African Americans feel about integration as a political and social goal.

This ambivalence among blacks is evident in a debate that took place in the press between Robinson and Effa Manley, co-owner with her husband, Abe, of the premier Negro-league team, the Newark Eagles. In June 1948, one year after Robinson's major-league debut and amidst the general sense among both blacks and whites that integrated professional baseball was here to stay, Robinson published an article in *Ebony* titled "What's Wrong with Negro Baseball."

In it, he described Negro-league baseball as chaotic and mediocre. He never had a contract with the Kansas City Monarchs, the Negro-league team he played for in 1945. The umpiring was sloppy and often biased, he said. There was virtually no spring training or conditioning for the players. The pay was too low. The bus travel was interminable and uncomfortable. There was too much barnstorming and road accommodations were awful.

Robinson wrote that when he first joined a Brooklyn Dodger farm club, "I was convinced that my leaving Negro baseball would stimulate interest in the colored leagues. Later it was my earnest desire to do all I could to make good with the Dodgers because I felt it would make the fellows in the [Negro] league I just left play harder, train harder, and give the fans much better baseball."

Two months later, the sharp-tongued Manley answered Robinson in an article titled "Negro Baseball Isn't Dead!" in *Our World,* another black publication. She argued that Negro-league pay was on a par with that in the white leagues, especially when one considered that the Negro teams drew fewer fans than white teams and thus generated less revenue for their owners. Indeed, she argued, it was Robinson, the gate attraction for the Brooklyn Dodgers, who was being underpaid in the major leagues. She maintained that bus travel was comfortable, better than going by train, and that road accommodations were bad because of Jim Crow, not because of the venality of Negro-league owners.

She reminded Robinson that at least her Newark Eagles, if not other Negro-league teams, did have contractual arrangements with their players, which major-league owners refused to honor, and that the barnstorming was necessary largely because Negro leagues lacked their own playing facilities. "Wittingly or unwittingly," she wrote, "Jackie Robinson has lent his powerful name to the destruction of Negro baseball."

Here, in miniature, is the black debate over integration as both a tactic and a principle—or, more precisely, the black debate over the meaning of pluralism in American life. Robinson's description of Negro-league baseball is accurate but also self-serving; it justifies major-league owners' use of black baseball as a virtual labor pool, a practice that gutted the Negro leagues.

What Robinson described was so chaotic that Negro baseball could hardly deserve respect as a business or even as something organized. (White professional baseball, both major and minor leagues, always called itself "organized," suggesting that all other professional baseball was unorganized.) Robinson was under no obligation to say anything at all about his Negro-league experience to explain his desire to play in the major leagues. He must have denounced it in such harsh terms to justify, to himself and to other blacks, his own decision to abandon black baseball.

Effa Manley's view was also accurate, and also self-serving. Although many of the problems in the Negro leagues were a direct result of racism, Manley here, as well as in other pieces she wrote and press interviews she gave, said the Negro-league owners' lack of unity greatly exacerbated their disorganization. She seemed to be making a pitch for racial loyalty, virtually admitting that her team and Negro baseball existed because whites refused to use black players.

The owners of many black businesses, in fact, opposed integration on the grounds that it would break up the virtual monopoly they enjoyed. Black professionals—doctors, lawyers, architects, and the like—could hardly expect to have clients and patients, especially in a culture that so promoted white supremacy, without appealing to racial loyalty. In short, for Manley, what made racism so difficult for blacks was their inability to generate an organized, unified response to it. But baseball commerce on racial loyalty suggests that blacks have no basis for community beyond the forces of segregation and racism that have made them a "community" in the first place.

Both Robinson and Manley were responding from their positions as members of other "communities" as well: Robinson endorsed a kind of individualism because he was, after all, a worker for hire. Manley, on the other hand, supported group organization and group integrity because she was an employer who was losing her workers to a competitor. Both, however, represented the rise of a highly driven, urban black middle class, essential to the development of a truly democratic black community and true democratic participation by blacks in the larger society.

For blacks, was pluralism in America to mean the redemption of the group through the actions of the individual, or the redemption of the group through the group itself? Was power in America diffused in a muddled middle, where remarkable individuals therefore made a difference, or was power largely the function and expression of a group dynamic and cohesion? In this instance, in 1948, Robinson was the radical who challenged the system; Manley was the reactionary who wanted things to remain the same. But also in this instance, a powerful public drama was being enacted and a powerful public debate was taking place about the nature and meaning of the African-American social contract.

What did integration cost? I have never heard a black person mention Jackie Robinson without noting that he died a physical wreck, at the age of 52—a fact attributed to the stress of his years as a major-league player. And it is undeniable that once the Negro leagues died, once baseball ceased to have an institutional presence in black life, blacks generally lost interest in professional baseball as spectators and fans.

What makes Robinson such a fascinating figure is how—as a symbol of integration—he combined militance with a sense of martyrdom and combined defiance with deference. We have the 1944 Robinson, who was court-martialed for insubordination to his white officers. We have the 1949 Robinson, who testified before the House Un-American Activities Committee, at its request, to reassure whites of black patriotism after Paul Robeson said that blacks ought not to fight for the United States against the Soviet Union. (The irony of asking a man who couldn't stand being in a Jim Crow army to testify as an example of blacks' loyalty and willingness to serve their country seems to have escaped the members of the HUAC.) We have the Robinson who endured three years of abuse as a major leaguer, took umbrage at even the smallest slight and argued about anything he didn't like on the field of play.

Robinson was both Mr. Inside and Mr. Outside, reassuring white authority while his very presence seemed to undermine it, espousing belief in democratic ideals while the singularity of his presence and the reaction to it revealed how far Americans were from achieving those ideals. In this way, he was much like Martin Luther King, Jr., who also was Mr. Inside and Mr. Outside, reassuring whites that he supported their values while, both intentionally and inadvertently, subverting them.

The ambiguity of Jackie Robinson's heroism takes on another dimension today, given the cultural significance of black athletes in contemporary America. . . . It seems true that the harsh oppression that blacks have endured, which often created an intense need to conform to the group to achieve unity and gain protection—coupled with the rampant anti-intellectualism in American life generally—has made blacks overvalue their physical accomplishments. But athletes often best represent the heroism and achievement of an oppressed group, because their accomplishments are not seen as compromised by the fact that the athletes may be paid for their efforts. This is especially true among blacks, because of their continuing concern that black masculinity be seen as an uncompromised, assertive political and cultural force. In our patriarchal culture, black freedom has historically been the quest for black manhood.

Intellectual achievement, on the other hand, long has been suspect; African Americans historically have not been able to reward their best intellectuals and thus could never fully trust those who were largely supported by whites.

Moreover, as male intellectuals seem compromised, they appear decidedly less manly, especially to an oppressed group that devoutly wishes to see the arrogance of its oppressors challenged. And even as blacks may prize their engineers, scientists, and researchers, intellectuals do not operate in a framework where their besting of white competitors is the public spectacle that it is for the professional or highly placed amateur athlete. Although blacks have never been able consistently to support or reward their best athletes, either, the athletes' excellence and the political and cultural significance of that excellence for the group as a whole is largely unaffected by that fact. Robinson was an outstanding ballplayer in the Negro leagues, and he was an outstanding player in the major leagues. . . .

Is it possible that there can be, in the sunlit arena where one confronts the animal of Western culture, a man without a shadow? Can a black hero be without the shadow of race, the shadow of ambivalence about assimilation? Is the African American condemned, as the lyrics of the old song "Me and My Shadow" suggest, to provide his or her humanity simply by imitating whites?

This is what we are forced to ask about the achievement of every great and important black athlete, and every black person whose achievements require the compromise of assimilation. In remembering Jackie Robinson, what we have is a poignant rendering of a glorious fanfare of uncertain trumpets.

Gerald Early, "American Integration, Black Heroism, and the Meaning of Jackie Robinson," *Chronicle of Higher Education,* May 23, 1997, B4–B5.

B

SPORT, CULTURE, AND COMMUNITY
IN BLACK AMERICA

5. E. Franklin Frazier / "*Society:* Status without Substance"

One man's fan is another's fetishist. Many of the people who most exasperated the Howard University sociologist E. Franklin Frazier came from the black middle class. Their fascination with sport, he claimed, contributed to white hegemony. Such passions, he believed, detracted substantially from the larger cause of civil rights activism.

To a significant extent, African Americans have followed sport and been drawn to participation in the athletic arena for many of the same reasons that animated other ethnic groups to appreciate an individual's physical performance, to see the significance of ritual and spectacle in terms of community formation, or to understand that the realm of athletics could be integrative in social, cultural, and even political terms. The sports pages have long informed notions of the ladder of success and assimilation. For the chroniclers of both immigrant and African American history, moreover, athletic accomplishments also represented significant contributions to the national experience.

According to these sociological formulae, the transit from margins to mainstream and the maintenance of black consciousness within a larger framework of acculturation were not especially complicated processes. Frazier saw race relations in more complex terms. In writings dating from the mid-1920s, he raised critical questions about the meanings of enterprise, uplift, and assimilation. In numerous articles and books, especially the controversial volume Black Bourgeoisie, *he perceived the increasing distance that the African American middle class put between itself and the black masses as a measure of "false consciousness."*

Here, Frazier—an expert on the black family and black culture more generally—describes what he believes was the black middle-class obsession with sport. Effectively, Black Bourgeoisie *is an indictment of many members of Du Bois's Talented Tenth for having been co-opted by mainstream cultural ideals. Like many of their other social activities, their fandom, Frazier believed, largely estranged black "society" from the black masses; this was a problematic development, detrimental to the ideal of racial solidarity and the advancement of the ideal of civil rights.**

———

* See Platt, *E. Franklin Frazier Reconsidered;* Gaines, *Uplifting the Race.* For a reading of black working-class culture that offers an expansive definition of politics and resistance to oppression, see Kelley, *Race Rebels,* esp. 35–54.

As a consequence of the prestige of "society" many Negro professional men and women take more seriously their recreation than their professions. Once the writer heard a Negro doctor who was prominent "socially" say that he would rather lose a patient than have his favorite baseball team lose a game. This was an extreme expression of the relative value of professional work and recreation among the black bourgeoisie. At the same time, it is indicative of the value which many Negro professional men and women, including college professors, place upon sports. Except when they are talking within the narrow field of their professions, their conversations are generally limited to sports—baseball and football. They follow religiously the scores of the various teams and the achievements of all the players. For hours they listen to the radio accounts of sports and watch baseball and football games on television. They become learned in the comments of sportswriters. Often they make long journeys in order to see their favorite teams—white or Negro—play baseball and football games. Although they may pretend to appreciate cultural things, this class as a whole has no real appreciation of art, literature, or music. One reads, for example, under what "People Are Talking About," in the September 2, 1954, issue of *Jet,* that a "wealthy" Negro doctor in Detroit is planning to install a "Hammond organ" on his "luxurious yacht." The decor of their homes reveals the most atrocious and childish tastes. Expensive editions of books are bought for decoration and left unread. The black bourgeoisie, especially the section which forms Negro "society," scarcely ever read books for recreation. Consequently, their conversation is trivial and exhibits a childish view of the world.

The prominent role of sports in the "serious playing" of Negro "society" stems partly from certain traditions in the Negro community. It reflects to some extent the traditions of the "gentleman" who engaged in no serious work. But in addition, the preoccupation of Negro "society" with sports is related to its preoccupation with gambling, especially poker. This latter preoccupation is especially significant because it is related to the religious outlook of the black bourgeoisie, especially Negro "society."

E. Franklin Frazier, *Black Bourgeoisie* (New York: Free Press, 1957), 207–8.

6. Dan Burley / "The Top Ten of the First Fifty Years"

Dan Burley had a distinguished career as musician, lexicographer, and newspaper editor and reporter. Born in Lexington, Kentucky, raised primarily in Fort Worth, Texas, and a graduate of Chicago's Wendell Phillips High School, Burley worked as a journalist for such well-known black publications as the Chicago Defender, New York Age, Amsterdam News, Jet, *and* Ebony. *Although many of his writings dealt with popular entertainment, he also became notable for his publications on sport. His columns, always eloquently written and forthright, covered everything from golf to baseball to racial discrimination in sport; he was perceptive in his assessments of individuals and teams both in predominantly white competition and within the African American community.**

---

* For biographical information on Burley see Reisler *Black Writers/Black Baseball,* 127–29.

In the following column, published in New York Age *in 1950, Burley ranked the ten African American athletes he viewed as most significant during the first half of the twentieth century. Burley did not delineate the specific criteria for his selections, but at the time it might have been difficult to argue with his picks. Today, we would note that he omitted women athletes and included just one individual (Rube Foster) from an all-black sporting organization. Such a list might be accounted for by the fact that Burley, like many other African Americans, attached enormous symbolic importance to the victories garnered by black athletes against their white counterparts in national and international competitions. The triumphs of Jack Johnson, Joe Louis, Jesse Owens, and the others on Burley's list served as examples of achievement and symbols of possibility for an African American community intent on both proving its worth and gaining recognition in a rigidly segregated society.*

A study of the past 50 years in sports projects a few athletes and teams as candidates for immortality in the sports world. My selections of who was who in sports from 1900 to Jan. 1, 1950, numbers only ten since I tried to confine it to "Firsts" and to champions. Some of the selections are deceased, but their performances in the period, 1900–1950, are still on the books. What they meant to sports at the time they were active on the scene was also weighted in the selections made. In order of their importance, my nominees are as follows:

No. 1—Jack Johnson. The first Negro to win the world heavyweight boxing championship, knocking out Tommy Burns at Sydney, Australia, in 1908, to acquire the title after the usual runaround. He defended it at Reno, Nevada, July 4, 1910, against James J. Jeffries, in what has since been considered the actual title fight. . . . Johnson was the first "Man's Man" produced by the race in sports. . . . He stood on his own two feet at a time when race prejudice was riding high and wide. . . . Afraid of no man, Johnson drew biting criticism from those of his own race who were timid about making their recent "masters" mad at the conduct of one of them; he was roundly hated and feared by those whom he taunted with sneers and jeers as he knocked them out right and left and walked among them alone, undaunted. He had no help in the hostile world in which he ruled as king. . . . Jack Johnson was a "Man's Man" every step of the way.

No. 2—Joe Louis. The Brown Bomber achieved what no other heavyweight fighter was permitted to achieve in this spectacular rise to the world championship. . . . That throne was supposed to be verboten forever to Negroes because of what Jack Johnson had supposedly done. . . . Louis was guided into the title joust by the smart men who handled him—Johnny Roxborough, Julian Black and Mike Jacobs. . . . Once on the throne, Louis proceeded to demonstrate his ability as a champion of champions whose name must go on all selections of the greatest of the great. . . . I am not making an issue of personal conduct in this piece, a bracket in which Louis would lead the list among prizefighters. . . . Instead, it is merit and in that phase, Louis was and is still head and shoulders above all contemporaries. . . . In addition to his ability between the ropes, the Brown Bomber gets credit for reviving interest in and forcing a general cleanup in a sport that had fallen into disrepute before he hove onto the scene.

No. 3—Jesse Owens. Although he followed in the sprint steps of such predecessors as Howard P. Drew, U. of Southern California, will o' the wisp, DeHart Hubbard of Michigan, Ned Gourdin of Harvard, Eddie Tolan of Michigan and Ralph Metcalfe of Marquette, Jesse Owens must go down in the books as the greatest track and field personality of 'em all. On May 25, 1935, the lithe, honey-colored Alabama-born speed demon broke three world records and tied a fourth in the most amazing performances in the history of sports. He clipped the tape in 9.4 to equal the 100 yard dash record; he broad jumped 26 feet 3¼ inches for a new world mark; he set a new record for the 200 yard dash of 20.3, and topped the timbers in the 200 yard low hurdles in 22.6, a new world mark. What Owens did in the 1936 Olympics forms further proof that this amazing person deserves all-time recognition and especially for the first half of the century.

No. 4—Fritz Pollard, Sr. He took the spotlight shortly after Johnson was railroaded to prison in disgrace, shorn of the heavyweight title, and finally emerged as the nation's No. 1 collegiate athlete at Brown University in the days when all Negro athletes had to share the cloud that was cast over Johnson. . . . Single-handedly, he defeated Harvard and Yale in games in which he scored three touchdowns each. . . . He battled prejudice in its early forms as did Johnson, but had a school behind him that swore by him and helped clear the path to the top. . . . Relatively small, he developed into one of the all-time greats of the gridiron, immortalized by Walter Camp as one of the three original Negro All-Americas—William H. Lewis, Pollard and Paul Robeson. . . . The spell he cast on collegiate football still lasts even today, when critics persist in including his name in their comparisons, estimates, and Hall of Fame selections. He was the first Negro pro in football.

No. 5—Rube Foster. The "Father of Negro Baseball," this Texas-born pioneer in the national pastime carved his own niche in the Hall of Fame and suffers mainly because of a common failing his people have in according honor where it is due and deserved. . . . John J. McGraw said his were the "greatest brains in baseball," conceding an honor commonly handed to himself to the big ex-pitcher, who in 1920 formed the first organized Negro pro baseball league. . . . It was Rube Foster, who in pitching duels bested such major league aces as Rube Waddell, outfoxed Jeff Tesrau, barnstormed his Chicago Schorlings and later his Chicago American Giants against Chicago Cubs, White Sox, Phillies, and the best teams the big league could produce. . . . It was Rube Foster who served under McGraw as a coach of pitchers for the New York Giants. . . . It was Rube Foster who first called the attention of the sports world to the fact that Negroes could play baseball as well if not better than the white stars.

No. 6—Jackie Robinson. Like Joe Louis, Robinson has been a child of destiny in baseball. . . . Where others like Josh Gibson, Buck Leonard, Bruce Petway, Frank Duncan, Chappie Gardner, Bullet Joe Rogan, Chacon, Terris McDuffie, Willie Wells and other Negro stars were denied entry, Robinson was selected as the Noble Experiment by Branch Rickey who put him through the mill at Montreal and brought him to the Brooklyn Dodgers as a polished, seasoned performer who was to win the Rookie of the Year Award his first season in the big time and later to gain the Most Valuable Player title as well as the National League batting championship as evidence of his ability. . . . Starting at a time when most ball players are considered through, Robinson's progress has been all the more remarkable.

No. 7—Henry Armstrong. No fighter since the days of the immortal Joe Gans brought to the lightweight division the class, color and excitement that did little Hammering Hank. The only fighter in history to simultaneously hold three world championship—the featherweight, light and welterweight crowns—he will always rank as one of the greatest ring performers of all time. . . . His shuffling style will be imitated by coming generations of leather pushers and his exploits told at the fireside by graybeards who will recall with glee that they saw him when he was at his peak.

No. 8—Binga Dismond. Where John Taylor at the University of Pennsylvania became nationally known as a quartermiler, this Richmond-born wonder-runner in 1915 raced the 440 to equal the world record set by the immortal Ted Meredith, a 47.4 effort, which remained until after 1939 as the Big Ten record. . . . He ran for the University of Chicago at a time when epithets like "coon," "darky," "blackamoor," and the like were common in the written prose of the sports writers and on the tongues of the fans, but all had to bow at the altar of achievement as the speeding Dismond swept so far ahead of the field that he looked around twice to see how close was his nearest competitor.

No. 9—Harrison Dillard. This Baldwin-Wallace College, Ohio, hurdling demon, set new world records or tied his own almost every time out in his specialty. . . . He beat every hurdler in the nation as well as in the world until it came time for the 1948 Olympics when he suffered his first major defeat. . . . He went to London, however, and proved the greatness of his undaunted heart by entering the 100 meter run, "just for kicks" as most observers thought, but a race in which he stunned the world by an unprecedented, unthought-of-triumph. . . . He's now on the public relations staff of the Cleveland Indians baseball team.

No. 10—John Davis. World and Olympic weight-lifting champion, he stands supreme in the No. 1 sport of Europe and at least half the world which still worships at the primitive shrine of the Strong Man. . . . In the world weight-lifting championships at Vienna in 1938, Davis, who hails from Brooklyn, won in the light heavyweight class, and a New Yorker, John Terry, was fourth in the featherweight class and the maker of anew world snatch record for his weight. . . . This is a form of sports rarely indulged in by Negro athletes. . . . Davis is king in Europe and his ability is regarded with awe by his tremendous following across the waters.

Dan Burley, "The Top Ten of the First Fifty Years," *New York Age,* January 14, 1950.

7. Fritz Pollard "Explains Reasons for Having a Negro Hall of Fame"

Fritz Pollard was born in 1894 in Chicago, Illinois. In spite of his small stature, the five-foot-seven inch, 150-pound Pollard became an outstanding high school football, baseball, and track-and-field performer. After graduating from high school, Pollard briefly attended several schools before enrolling at Brown University, where in 1916 he became the first African

American to play in the Rose Bowl and won a place on Walter Camp's prestigious All-America football team. He played professional football for some seven years, leading the Akron Pros to a championship in 1920. He was the head football coach at Lincoln University in 1918, became the first African American head coach in NFL history when he took over the Akron Pros in 1921, and was head coach of two other NFL teams as well as the all-black Chicago Black Hawks and New York Brown Bombers. Besides his outstanding career in football, Pollard had a number of successful business ventures. He operated an investment firm in Chicago until the stock market crash forced him to declare bankruptcy, then established and operated the first African American tabloid newspaper, the Independent News, *in New York. Later he served as a booking agent for African American nightclub entertainers and operated a rehearsal studio in Harlem. The producer of a motion picture,* Rockin' the Blues, *and writer of a nationally syndicated sports column, Fritz Pollard was as energetic as an entrepreneur as he had been as athlete and coach.* *

Here, in an article that first appeared in the Kansas City Call *in 1953, Pollard provides a rationale for his founding of the Negro Athletic Hall of Fame, explaining that his desire was to honor outstanding African American athletes and those whites who had supported them. Tellingly, Pollard's Hall of Fame never became a reality. As he suggests here and made explicit years later to the black sports writer Carl Nesfield, Pollard encountered substantial resistance from members of the black community, including athletes, to the creation of another segregated institution. Although parallel institutions had served the community well and provided an untold number of opportunities for African Americans in a variety of fields during the first half of the century, there was no enthusiasm for a segregated Hall of Fame at a time when black athletes were gradually finding their way into predominantly white organized sport. Only in 1974, during the latter stages of the civil rights movement, did an institution of this type become a reality when Charles (Charlie) A. Mays, a sprinter and long jumper in the Mexico City Olympic Games, founded the Black Athletes Hall of Fame.* **

——— ———

There is so much controversy at the present time about the various Halls of Fame. I thought it might be a good idea to explain why I founded the Negro Athlete Hall of Fame.

In the past two years there have been no elections to the Football Hall of Fame. They can make the Sullivan Awards, Helms' Awards and others, but there is always going to be a controversy about who should have been awarded, who should have been elected, and who should not have been elected.

Not Segregation

For some reason people are inclined to believe that the newly organized "Negro Athlete Hall of Fame," is a segregated institution. It is not. Perhaps a little understanding of my background will explain my reasons for wanting to establish such an institution.

---

* See Carroll, *Fritz Pollard.*

** Nesfield, "Pride against Prejudice," 81. See program, First Annual Black Athletes Hall of Fame Banquet, March 14, 1974, Edwin B. Henderson Papers, Moorland-Spingarn Research Center, Howard University.

Fritz Pollard as an
undergraduate, 1915
(Courtesy Brown Uni-
versity Library)

I knew nothing about segregation until after I had entered college. I was born in
an all-white community—attended grade school and high school with my brothers
and sisters, and we were the only colored students who attended. My father was a barber and my mother was a seamstress. We became an integral part of the community.
The question of segregation was never allowed to enter our minds. We attended the
churches in the community; we engaged in all athletic activities in the community
and were a part of the social life of the community.

Whenever we were not invited to a party or social gathering, we never took it
upon ourselves to think that an invitation was not extended to us because of our
color—we merely felt that these particular people did not want us.

Above Humiliation

I grew up with this philosophy until, after my collegiate days, I went to a hotel with a professional football team. They told me the last room was gone. Instead of feeling humiliated, my attitude was that "I was too good for the hotel." If I went into a restaurant and they appeared not to want to serve me, my attitude was the same.

When I went to the coal region of Pennsylvania to play professional football, I was threatened. A police escort took me to the game, stayed on the field at half-time to give me protection and took me from the field after I had played 60 grueling minutes of football.

A week later I was invited to the grade and high schools to lecture. However, I learned later that the real reason they invited me was to let the children in the coal region see what a modern Negro looked like. I took no offense, but felt proud I was a Negro and that I had "equalized" myself to such an extent that I was accepted.

With these things in mind and with the experiences I had, I felt it necessary to establish such an organization and name it the "Negro Athlete Hall of Fame" so that the people of this country could realize that Negroes are capable of doing many things for themselves and to encourage the Negro, not with the idea of segregation, but with the idea that a Negro organization does not have to be a segregated organization.

To Include Whites

Our Negro Athlete Hall of Fame could take in such men as Coach Brown of the Cleveland Browns (Indians), Bill Veeck, Branch Rickey, Herman Hickman of Yale, Otto Graham of the Cleveland Browns, Bob Waterfield of the L.A. Rams and other outstanding heroes who have stood by and helped the Negro athlete become famous.

It appears that the majority of our complaints have come from people who themselves have attended Negro grade and high schools, and Negro colleges. Some have become doctors and have been forced to go to Negro hospitals for their internship. These people, of course, are sensitive and react unfavorably to any project or organization that is labeled Negro. I hope they will remember that our designated Negro Hall Fame has been done with the desire to extol those Negroes who have achieved, and all others who have helped to make it possible so that future generations may be aware of the fine work of our Negro athletes.

Fritz Pollard, "Fritz Pollard Explains Reasons for Having a Negro Hall of Fame," *Kansas City Call*, January 30, 1953.

8. Nelson George on the Harlem Globetrotters

The Harlem Globetrotters are perhaps the most popular basketball team in the world. Founded by Abe Saperstein and originally known as the Savoy Big Five, the Globetrotters resembled many other all-black sports teams; they gained fame as barnstormers who toured the country playing hundreds of games each year against both black and white quintets. Always a crowd-pleasing team exhibiting a wide range of talents, the Globetrotters were initially a very *serious and competitive club that captured important titles and championships. In 1940, for instance, the team won the prestigious world tournament in Chicago, defeating such outstanding teams as the Chicago Bruins of the National Basketball League, and the Renaissance Five.**

By the early 1950s, the Globetrotters had been transformed from a serious basketball team into one that emphasized trick ball-handling and shooting, comedy routines, and clownish behavior. The change in format was the work of Saperstein, who no longer had the market on the best African American players because of the racial desegregation of professional basketball. The transformation in playing style only seemed to heighten interest in the Globetrotters as thousands of fans of all ages—in venues around the world—witnessed the basketball talents and slapstick routines of such legendary performers as Meadowlark Lemon, Reece "Goose" Tatum, Curly Neal, and Marquis Haynes. It is significant that the highly engaging black players unfailingly humiliated their all-white opponents in athletic "contests" staged in Berlin as well as in Madison Square Garden during the era of the cold war. Such facts add a twist to the broader meanings of the Globetrotter appeal.

Still, athleticism shared the court with minstrelsy at Globetrotter appearances. In the following document, Nelson George looks back on one dimension of the Globetrotter phenomenon—the antics of the team and the ways its repertory reflected the racial stereotypes so deeply embedded in American culture. The clowning, argues George, was both good business on Saperstein's part and a visual representation of white America's racialist thinking about black males. Performing their warm-up drills to the sounds of "Sweet Georgia Brown," donning hula skirts, raising the pitch of their voices, and uttering wild screeching sounds, the players embodied the stereotypical notion of black men as lazy and comedic fools.** Minstrelsy of this nature held up a fractured mirror to the American dream of success through dignified labor. In many ways it suggested the depth and range of racism in the United States.

The Harlem Globetrotters' story perfectly captures the hypocrisy and brilliance that are emblematic of America's tortured history of race relations. The financial and cultural promotion (and exploitation) of African-American artistry, a staple of U.S. (and European) business, is one key element in the Globetrotters' story. So is the formal inventiveness of Blacks in taking Naismith's game and laying the groundwork for the kind of athletic aesthetic that would come to dominate the game after World War II. In the nineties the Trotters are merely inconsequential, even embarrassing showmen; once they were arguably the most talent-laden, finest basketball organization in the country. From World War I to the late fifties the Trotters had first pick of every Black player who wanted to make a career in roundball. If you were a Black kid with b-ball talent, the Trotters were basically your only shot at making money playing. One team. Twelve spots on the main squad. All sought by a nation of gifted, excluded men. That desire

----

* For information on the Globetrotters, see Peterson, *Cages to Jump Shots*, esp. 95–96, 105–7; Lemon, *Meadowlark*; Zinkoff, *Go Man Go!*

** See Lombardo, "The Harlem Globetrotters and the Perpetuation of the Black Stereotype"; Vecsey, "Retro Globetrotters Triumph by Losing." See also Boskin, *Sambo*; Lott, *Love and Theft*. For an expansive study—cast in terms both of cold-war ideology and race relations—see Hill, "The Harlem Globetrotters' Cold War."

Harlem Globetrotters in action against the SPHAs (Courtesy of Basketball Hall of Fame, Springfield, Massachusetts)

drove some to greatness, making them not merely "legends of the game" but artists who reshaped the sport to their taste. But by virtue of the man who owned them and the way comedy was used to reinforce prejudice, the Trotters were a definitive example of white paternalism and Black male submission. The Trotters represent innovative Black basketball and the compromise of dignity to acquire a few scarce quarters. . . .

How Blacks who knew Saperstein viewed him says as much about them as it does about the Trotter founder. In 1947, one-year-old Chicago-based *Ebony* magazine, the vehicle of enrichment for a bright, Black businessman named John Johnson, praised Saperstein for "scurrying around the country digging up obscure Negro athletes and building them into top bracket stars" and promoting match races that pitted Jesse Owens against horses, heavyweight champion Joe Louis, and baseball speedster George Case. *Ebony*'s description was the kind of fawning adulation that saw almost any white use of Black talent, no matter how condescending, as a step toward integration. Meadowlark Lemon, who would become one of the Trotters' most famous clowns, felt affection and resentment toward Saperstein, usually at the same time. Lemon, who twice attempted to form his own barnstorming teams, admired Saperstein's ability to keep the Trotters fully employed and paid on time. At the same time he admits, "We never knew what was going on with the finances. There were a lot of people around the team making more money than the ball players ever were." Saperstein was at the top of that list. Wilt Chamberlain, a political conservative with a survival-of-the-fittest business philosophy, thought Saperstein was a "dear friend" and called his time with him in 1958 and 1959 the "most fun of his career." Appropriately, perhaps, his archrival Bill Russell disliked Saperstein, noting in his first autobiography, *Go Up for Glory,* that the Trotter chief told the press he'd pay Russell $50,000 to go to the Olympics and then join his fiefdom. But when they met, Saperstein spoke to Russell only of the "social advantages" of being a Trotter, while he talked business with University of San Francisco coach Phil Woolpert. Russell, a man with pride and intellect, decided, "If I'm not smart enough to talk to, then I'm too smart to play for him."

It was Saperstein's instincts for the prejudices of the white working class, in many regions largely immigrants, and their stereotypical attitudes toward Blacks that led him to make comedy the centerpiece of the Trotters, turning the team from players into performers. In the official Trotter video history narrator Lou Gossett says the genesis of Trotter clowning was a winter game in Iowa. The gym was ice-cold, so the locals circled the court with several potbellied stoves. Inadvertently, Willis "Kid" Oliver leaned his backside on one and his shorts caught fire. Oliver's butt burn sent him screaming across the court, stopping play and making the predominantly white audience guffaw.

Clowning, according to Trotter lore, subsequently became an integral part of Trotterdom as a way to rest tired players. As one player dribbled around befuddled opponents, the others relaxed and even slid over to the bench for a drink. In addition, because the Trotters were so much better than the competition the clowning kept scores down and fan interest in games up. In his 1987 autobiography Meadowlark Lemon says the ball-handling technique became institutionalized during a game the Trotters were up, 112-5. All of this makes sense and is, no doubt, technically factually true.

But all official discussions of Trotter jokes or "reams," as the players called them, are viewed within the narrow confines of Trotter games. We have to remember that Saperstein's Trotters played and were hired in a world where the lynching of Black males for "reckless eyeballing" of white women was still commonplace in the South and more prevalent in the North than is generally acknowledged. The idea of five Black men rolling into a Midwestern town, kicking ass, and getting paid could not have been the easiest sell ever (nor, as the NBA found in the seventies, would it ever be). Clowning Black men have always been more popular in this country than stern no-nonsense brothers. It's no accident that the Trotters' antics found favor with white fans at a time America's favorite Black movie star was Lincoln Theodore Monroe Andrew Perry, also known as Stepin Fetchit. This Florida-born actor embodied every vicious stereotype of Black man—cowardly, comic, and lazy with a capital L. Not coincidentally, his performances were brilliant. As a comic actor Perry's timing, intonation, and the physicality of his character were truly superb. When you watched Fetchit move on-screen, you suddenly felt lazy yourself. As Joseph Boskin wrote in *Sambo,* his study of racist Black comic images, "[he was] the most prominent practitioner of the Black fool in films. It is more than an act; it becomes an art form." Fetchit, along with Willie Best, Mantan Moreland, Eddie "Rochester" Anderson, and Hollywood's other sambos, coons, and fools, was clearly an inspiration for Saperstein's cooning brand of ball, though the owner was smart enough never to say so.

It's impossible today not to view the way the Trotters adopted comedy as good business and an affirmation, no matter how skillfully done, of racist attitudes toward Black males. And the Trotters were not alone. Louis Armstrong, the greatest jazz innovator of the pre–World War I period, often wore the coon's mask in films and lived with this duality of artistry overlaid with crap. As a national star during this era—he regularly appeared at Chicago's Savoy in the late twenties—Armstrong made an eloquent defense of musical clowning, one that could also be applied to the Trotters: "The best band in the world is the clown's band in the circus. You gotta be a good musician to hit a bad note at the right time." Amplifying Armstrong's view, Wilt Chamberlain wrote in his autobiography: "They [the Trotters] had—and have—highly developed skill for comedy, for making people laugh at them. It's the same skill that guys like Jerry Lewis, Charlie Chaplin and Jackie Gleason have. They're clowns, actors playing a role Jews would call the 'shlemiel' or a 'shlimazl.'" Without the Trotters' existence, Wilt argues, many players might have "become janitors or gone on welfare." Whether you agree or disagree with Wilt's view, Saperstein's commercial judgment was sound. Playing against the primarily white semipro clubs around the country, the Trotters, much like many Black entertainers and Negro League baseball teams, utilized comedy laced with racial stereotypes to please white fans and spread their fame. In 1940, the Trotters defeated the Harlem Rens, taking the world championship title from the first great all-Black team to start a decade of clowning professional b-ball supremacy.

During the forties the Trotters set up housekeeping at the Evans Hotel, a seven-story Black-owned establishment at Evans and 61st Street on the South Side. Players received a room, a bath shared with an adjoining room, a telephone, a dresser, but no radio. During the tryout periods no one beefed because the players' only concerns were basketball and sleep. Tryouts consisted of two separate four-hour practices with over 100 prospects bidding for spots on the "A" or Eastern Unit, the secondary Western or Southern units, or, barring that, a place on one of the traveling opposition outfits. "I saw all those young guys flying, and I mean flying, through the air, slam dunking, rebounding, dribbling, shooting long jump shots, doing everything spectacular," wrote Meadowlark of his first camp. "It looked like a waterfall of balls going through baskets."

Survivors were instructed in "the Trotter way," a style that had developed two important structural quirks. As in basketball strategy since the center jump era, the pivot man was key. Only in Trotter ball he didn't simply rebound and score. The center position, a spot held by Inman Jackson for fourteen years, was designated court jester. From a position in the high post area near the top of the key the center told jokes, made funny faces and sounds, and starred in most of the reams, from shifting suddenly into baseball to throwing water on the referees. Opposing players were allowed to guard the Trotters closely except during the breaks for the Trotters' more elaborate skits. As part of the ground rules for playing then, the Trotters were also allowed uncontested passes into the post area since most of their reams were designed around the center position.

Another Trotter signature was their lack of traditional guards as such. Both guards and the small forward all had ball-handling responsibilities. With the center at the high post and the other big man in one corner, the three other players went into a weave of dribbles, behind-the-back passes, and clever ball exchanges. This flash-and-dash, done with more rapidity than almost any other team of the day, pro or college, was showcased in the Magic Circle routine before every game.

Nelson George, *Elevating the Game: The History and Aesthetics of Black Men in Basketball* (New York: Simon and Schuster, 1992), 41–42, 47–51.

C

THE FIRST ROUNDS OF THE
SECOND RECONSTRUCTION

9. "New Faces in Pro Football"

The reintegration of professional football in 1946 did not result in the immediate and whole-sale raid on black players by the owners in the sport's two major conferences. Throughout the 1950s, however, teams from both the National Football League (NFL) and the All-America Football Conference gradually added black players to their rosters. Influenced by the enormous success of the racially integrated Cleveland Browns, owners increasingly realized that the future fortunes of their own clubs could be enhanced by the addition of physically gifted black players. By 1961, there were eighty-three blacks on NFL teams. In that same year the Washington Redskins became the last team in professional football to desegregate when they signed Bobby Mitchell, John Nisby, Leroy Jackson, and Ron Hatcher.*

The following document from a 1952 issue of Our World *provides details about black players then participating in professional football. Perhaps most notable is the data furnished on the number of black players on each team, and that nearly six years after the initial entry of blacks into professional football, there were still two clubs that were all white. This is further indication that the desegregation process in professional football, like that in professional baseball, took place gradually and at an uneven pace. The owners in professional football in the post–World War II era proceeded cautiously as they weighed the advantages of integrating their teams in a sport that was soon to become a national obsession.*

This season, football fans will thrill at seeing more new Negro football stars in action in professional ranks than ever before. There are no less than a dozen new men on clubs and they have already had their pro baptism in the world's roughest game.

Joining the parade of teams with Negro players in their line-ups this year are the Pittsburgh Steelers, the Chicago Bears, the Chicago Cardinals and the Philadelphia Eagles. Two new men are added to the world champion Los Angeles Rams and the Green Bay Packers also added other Negro players to their roster which had included that fancy end, Bob Mann. All of the new players have excellent records and are highly regarded as prospects.

Out of step are the star-studded Detroit Lions and the fading Washington Red-

---

* See T. Smith, "Civil Rights on the Gridiron"; idem, "Outside the Pale"; Gems, "Shooting Stars."

skins, neither team having Negro players. The Lions at one time had good Negro stars, but the recent trend has been to sign only "name players" from big white colleges.

Of the new men in pro football, most of the players are flashy ends, dazzling, speedy backs or heavy duty line rippers. With the accent on the two-platoon system, most of the new men are "defensive players." Unless one turns out to be an Emlen Tunnell, few will make headlines or become publicized heroes.

Highly touted Negro stars had chances with the Packers, the Bears and the old Yanks, but when the time came for cutting the squads, first to go were the Negroes. Those good enough went to Canada where they still are playing. But this year, most of the rookies came with the "Stonewall Jackson" idea. When Stoney came to the New York Giants for a tryout, he brought four trunks to training camp, something unheard of for a rookie. Fresh out of North Carolina A&T College, "Stoney" was a regular fashion plate. And when the other players kidded "Stoney" for bringing so many trunks, the big fellow straight-facedly told everybody, "When I go some place, I usually go to stay." And "Stoney" stayed.

Several old players will be sporting new uniforms this year. Buddy Young and George Taliaferro are "way down in Texas" with the Dallas "Texans." They were formerly with the Yanks. And their team mate, Sherman Howard, one of the best halfbacks in the business, has transferred to the Cleveland Browns where he will have an opportunity to really shine. Howard always was a highly rated back, good runner and an excellent pass receiver. Under Paul Brown, Sherman should be one of the league's most brilliant football players.

Bad luck overtook two prized recruits, if it can be called bad luck. Donald "Mike" Riley, counted on by the Packers to bolster that backfield was called for Army service. The same fate overtook terrific Don Coleman, the pint-sized Michigan State tackle, who made every All-American last year. Riley had been signed by the Packers and Coleman had been picked by the Chicago Cardinals. Both are playing football in the Army now on camp teams.

Los Angeles Rams lead the league with seven Negro players. Cleveland Browns have six, Giants two, 49ers two, Dallas Texans two, Philadelphia Eagles, three, Chicago Cardinals two, Chicago Bears one. That totals twenty-seven Negro players in the professional league. Next year, with rebuilding now under way with several teams featuring older Negro stars like Motley and Bell at Cleveland, replacements from other schools will be coming up and it is not too fanciful to expect some of the new players will be Negro players from Negro colleges.

Added to that is the increased number of Negroes enrolling in white schools and going out for football. Now, young Negroes know there is a future in following the pigskin and they are out to make good.

"New Faces in Pro Football," *Our World,* December 7, 1952, 62–64.

10. "Are There Too Many Negroes in Baseball?"

By 1954, the pace of integration in major league baseball had accelerated. In that year twelve of the sixteen major league clubs had black players on their rosters, including such newcomers as future hall of famers Ernie Banks of the Chicago Cubs and Henry Aaron of the Milwaukee Braves. These two men, along with Willie Mays, Roy Campanella, and other great black athletes who entered the league earlier in the decade, formed a cadre of black players that would achieve enormous success in the game and lay the foundation for further integration.*

The increasing number of black players entering the league, however, caused major concern for owners. Although recognizing that the continued recruitment of black players was necessary if they were to stay competitive with other clubs, the owners in major league baseball were fearful that if there were too many of these players, it would alienate white fans and result in a drop in attendance and in profit margin. This concern was so acute that most clubs, if not all, according to Benjamin Rader in his Baseball: A History of America's Game, *"had unwritten understandings to restrict the total number of blacks."** The logical extension of all this, of course, is that black players had to be decidedly superior to their white counterparts if they expected to make a team and play.*

The following document speculates as to whether the color line was again being drawn in major league baseball and asks specifically if Sandy Amoros's recent benching by the Brooklyn Dodger manager, Walter Alston, was racially motivated. While never answering that question in a definitive manner, the article makes clear that some white fans were terribly disturbed by the larger number of blacks entering major league baseball. This was in direct contrast, interestingly enough, to fans of previous years who never voiced their complaints about the preponderance of white ethnic groups in the sport.

————

Is the color line being drawn on Negroes in baseball? Has the "saturation point" of hiring Negro players been reached? These leading questions startled New York last April when they came up in an unusual manner. One day when Don Newcombe was scheduled to pitch, suddenly, Dodger manager Walter "Smokey" Alston benched Sandy Amoros, one of the six Negro players on the team. If Sandy played, Brooklyn would have had five Negro players on the field, with another on the bench.

The sports world buzzed with speculation. Embarrassing questions were hurled at Manager Alston. Emphatically he denied that Amoros' color had anything to do with his benching. Alston said the speedy left fielder was benched because he wasn't hitting. However, Manager Alston never played five Negroes at one time although they represented the best players available. Such managerial strategy kept the entire baseball world wondering.

However, Dick Walsh, assistant farm director for the Dodgers, strongly denies

---

* See Tygiel, *Baseball's Great Experiment*, 294; Rader, *Baseball*, 152.

** Rader, *Baseball*, 153. On the correlation between Robinson's signing, the integration process, and fan attendance, see Fetter, "Robinson in 1947."

"color" ever is a consideration concerning Brooklyn players. And according to Walsh, color had nothing to do with Alston's benching Amoros. Walsh affirmed the fact that Amoros was not hitting at the time. Nor was he living up to the promise he showed in spring training. Then Amoros was banging the ball like mad and fielding like a hawk. In the big leagues, where every game counted, Amoros slumped badly. "So," added Walsh, "Amoros was sent back to the minors, but not because of his color. It was for two other reasons. First, he was the only outfielder on the Dodgers who could be optioned out again. Second, Alston couldn't afford to experiment any longer; Amoros was given every opportunity to show what he could do in left field, the only spot he can play. Color? That's the last consideration here at Brooklyn."

What Walsh says may be true, but does it reflect the feeling of the fans? Let's face it. How would Brooklyn fans, or any others for that matter, react to a team preponderantly Negro, even if the players represented the very best team that could be fielded? While that may be true democratically, it does not necessarily represent the interests of the fans who pay the freight.

Yet young Negroes are not to be blamed for trying to make the majors. For many, who also love to play ball, it is a livelihood. Ever since Jackie Robinson opened the gates, there has been a general rush to sign them.

Many of them are showing up better than white youths. The reason? They know baseball pays well. As a result, leagues all over the country, except one, are studded with Negroes. Only exception is the 54-year old Southern Association. This year, Atlanta tried to break the bar and hired Nat Peebles. They released him after the first game. However, the nearby Sally League, operating eight teams, has Negro players on five of them.

Baseball players seem to come in cycles. Time was when most were Irish like the Delahantys, Murphys, Dugans, McInnis'. Then came the Germans with the Schaefers, Schultz', Gehrigs, Koenigs. The Italians followed with Bodies, Crossettis, Lazzerris and DiMaggios. Then Italians filled the left field bleachers at Yankee Stadium, lifting huge banners every time a countryman came to bat. Yet nobody dared say there were too many Italians in baseball. Today, with the trend toward Negro players, some people are howling murder.

So tough is the competition among major league teams for Negro players, five teams have Negro scouts. Bill Yancey, former Black Yankee star, is with Milwaukee; Judy Johnson, another old-timer, is with the Athletics; Quincy Troupe, former catcher, is with the St. Louis Cards; Donaldson, former pitcher, is with the Chicago White Sox and the New York Giants have Frank Forbes and Alex Pompez.

They scour the country, following Negro League teams (who still play good baseball and draw good crowds in the South), semi-pro teams, Negro high schools and colleges. They have discovered some excellent players, but all of them will tell you that fellows like Willie Mays don't grow on every bush in Dixie.

In spite of the criticism and embarrassment Negro players still face, they have come far since 1946. That year, the Baseball Writers annual dinner presented a skit caricaturing Robinson and Commissioner Chandler. Here's how Art Daley of the New York Times reported the affair. "The curtain opened showing a 'darky' in satin breeches . . . disclosing the upper part of a uniform as a Montreal shirt." In the dialogue, Chandler called out, "Jackie, you wooly-headed old rascal," and in reply, Jackie, the butler, spoke tenderly of "Massa Rickey."

Recently Warren Brown of the Chicago American blasted baseball's bigots who still refuse to hire Negro players. He was encouraged, no doubt, by Baker and Banks who have made the Chicago Cubs come alive. And the Cubs once were as allergic to Negroes as are the present day Yankees, Tigers and Boston Red Sox. The complaint that there are too many Negroes in the leagues is phony. Although there may be a concentration of Negroes on clubs that had the foresight to grab the good ones, a look at the figures shows something else. In both big leagues today, there are 26 Negroes out of a total of 400 players. And these are scattered among 11 teams. The truth is there aren't enough Negro players.

For every player who gets to the big leagues and sticks, 99 fail. "Out of every 100 who start," says Dick Walsh, "only four will reach the majors, three of them for no more than a cup of coffee."

That's not too encouraging, but year after year promising rookies are dug up by scouts. These kids start at the bottom. The way to the top is so rough, many youngsters fail in their first year.

The best prospects baseball men say, are kids of high school age. They are right for teaching. Usually a prospect is sent to a "Class D" league to learn the ABCs of organized baseball. And it takes only one year to discover whether the prospect "has it" or not. If he has it, promotions follow rapidly with the fellow often "skipping" leagues. By the time the rookie reaches Class AAA, he is almost ready for the big league. However, of the starting 100, only ten get as high as this. Half of them lose out the first year and are busted out like Robert Cole. Last year, Cole was a sensation. He was the MVP in all New York's high schools. Five teams were after Cole but the Dodgers landed him. They sent him to a Class D team, but Cole failed to improve.

On the other hand, the Giants took a chance on Andre Rodgers, a native of the Bahamas. Andre never played baseball, he played softball. When he wrote the Giants for a trial, he was told he could come—but at his own expense. "Andre had trouble with the Immigration Authorities," Giant farm director Jack Schwarts told OUR WORLD. "He paid his expenses in our camp only one week. By then, we learned Andre was a natural curve ball hitter. Now he is with Olean, N.Y. and is one of our better prospects."

Today the American Association, International League, Pacific Coast League have many Negro players, some are ex–big leaguers who flopped. Others are youngsters on the way up.

The picture is the same all over. John Davis, 33, is an outfielder at Montgomery in the Sally League where he is knocking down fences. He will hardly go higher, but he's happy and helping others who will.

In this game, which gobbles up talent, hundreds of new players are needed every year. The question where will they come from: The answer is Negro players.

Baseball means money to owners. All they are interested in is will a player make dough for them. If he is a drawing card, they are prepared to dispense with whatever prejudices they may have. As it now stands, Negro players are filling the demand. There aren't too many Negroes in the leagues, they are just taking advantage of their opportunities.

"Are There Too Many Negroes in Baseball?" *Our World,* August 1954, 42–46.

11. To Desegregate the Golf Courses of America

The post–World War II period witnessed an increasing number of legal battles against golf's racially discriminatory policies. Calvin Sinnette, in his book Forbidden Fairways, *argues that these increased legal battles resulted in part from the growing popularity of the sport in the African American community, the rising militancy among African Americans, and the limited number of privately owned and public golf courses available to African Americans.* *

One of the more heavily publicized legal battles fought against golf's racially discriminatory practices was waged by William "Bill" Spiller, Ted Rhodes, and the lesser-known Madison Gunter. In January 1948, Spiller and Rhodes finished in the top sixty at the Los Angeles Open, significant accomplishments for the two players, which automatically qualified them for the upcoming Richmond Open near Oakland, California. Unfortunately, Spiller and Rhodes never played in the tournament. After traveling to Oakland and playing two practice rounds, the golfers were told by the tournament chairman, George Schneiter, that they would not be able to compete since they were not PGA members. (The PGA had at the time a "Caucasian race" clause in its constitution.) Spiller, Rhodes, and Gunter (who also had qualified for the tournament) decided to file suit against both the PGA and the Richmond Country Club. The case was eventually settled out of court when Jonathan Rowell, a San Francisco lawyer representing the three plaintiffs, worked out an agreement to drop the suit in exchange for the PGA's promise to stop excluding African American golfers from its tournaments.

The following letter to Thurgood Marshall was written by Jonathan Rowell three days after the suit was filed. Requesting support and financial assistance from the NAACP, the letter points out the amount of damages sought on behalf of the three plaintiffs and the circumstances surrounding the suit. The evidence does not indicate if Marshall responded to Rowell or if the NAACP ever provided support of any kind.

——— ———

January 20, 1948

Thurgood Marshall, Esq.
100 Massachusetts Avenue
Washington 1, D.C.

RE: Spiller, Rhodes, Gunter v. Professional Golfers Association

---

* Sinnette, *Forbidden Fairways*, 124–25.

Dear Mr. Marshall:

I am writing to you at the request of Mr. Henry Johnson, Jr., Executive Secretary of the N.A.A.C.P. in Oakland, California. He advised me that he received a telegram from the national office of the N.A.A.C.P. offering cooperation and help in the case being brought by the above-named three negro golfers against the Professional Golfers Association and Richmond Golf Club. Your offer was received with gratitude and appreciation on the part of the plaintiffs and myself.

First off, to further identify the writer, may I state that I have for many years been active in fighting discrimination against minority groups; that before the war I was associated with the N.A.A.C.P. in San Francisco in their attempts to prevent discrimination by industrial concerns against negroes, and that I am, at the present time, president of the Redwood City Chapter of the Council for Civic Unity, which chapter was formed as the direct result of the burning of a negro's house in this territory. I also represent the negro whose house was burned, John Walker, in this civil action against those we believe did the burning.

Returning now to the matter of the golf discrimination case, I filed a complaint on January 17, 1948, in the Superior Court for the County of Contra Costa, in which county the Richmond Golf Club is located and in which county the discrimination took place. The complaint in substance states causes of action on behalf of the three plaintiffs, first against the Richmond Golf Club and the Professional Golfers Association, seeking recovery of damages for the actual discrimination which took place at Richmond. This recovery is sought under the provisions of Sections 51 and 52 of the California Civil Code, which sections provide in part: "All citizens within the jurisdiction of this state are entitled to the full and equal accommodations, advantages, facilities, and privileges of . . . places of public accommodation or amusement."

It is further provided that any person who denies such full accommodations, etc., and any person who aids or incites "is liable in damages in an amount not less than $100.00, which may be recovered in an action at law brought for that purpose."

Of course the sections referred to were intended to apply to patrons of the establishments or places referred to. I believe this case of professional golfers seeking to enter a professional golf tournament can be brought within the terms of the statute. The complaint seeks $5,000 damages for each of the plaintiffs on the theory that they suffered actual damages of possibly $2,000 by not being allowed to compete, and on the further theory that they are entitled to damages for their humiliation, anguish, and distress. The basis of the cause of action against the golf club itself is that by signing the tournament contract with the Professional Golfers Association, an association which they knew discriminated against negroes, the club thereby aided and incited the discrimination. If this point can be made to stick, it may well have the result of causing many golf clubs to think twice before they ever put on another P.G.A. sponsored tournament.

The complaint then goes on to state the causes of action on behalf of the three plaintiffs against the Professional Golfers Association and seeks damages in their behalf of $100,000 each on the basis that the Professional Golfers Association has a substantial monoply [sic] of employment opportunities for professional golfers, and that the plaintiffs, by reason of their exclusion from the association, have been and will be denied an opportunity to earn the sums prayed for. This aspect of the complaint is based on the case of James v. Marinship, 25 Cal. 2d 721 in which our State Supreme Court ruled that a union which had a closed shop contract and thus a monoply [*sic*] of the employment opportunities at the employers' plants could not lawfully exclude negroes from membership.

It is apparent that the case filed on behalf of these three men presents novel and important legal points. Likewise, it is highly probable that the case will be contested through every possible court. I have advised the plaintiffs and the N.A.A.C.P. representatives in Oakland that I do not expect to charge a normal fee in this case, but they understand, and I am sure you will, that there will be substantial expenses to meet. The Oakland N.A.A.C.P. has expressed its desire to help, and as I said at the beginning of this letter, have conveyed to me your offer to help. I believe that the expenses of the preliminary phases of the proceeding, the taking of depositions (some of which may have to be taken in Chicago), and with investigation work might not run too much more than approximately $250. It would greatly aid my ability to carry on with this case if your organization could contribute this amount toward the payment of preliminary expenses. Of course, no one can estimate at this time the total expenses involved, as this depends upon future developments and upon the extent to which the case is contested.

I would appreciate your taking this matter up with the proper persons and advising.

Yours very truly,
McCarthy & Rowell

By Jonathan H. Rowell
JHR:eb

Letter from Jonathan Rowell to Thurgood Marshall on Behalf of William "Bill" Spiller and Others Regarding the PGA, NAACP Legal File, January 20, 1948, Library of Congress.

12. Rufus Clement / "Racial Integration in the Field of Sports"

Jackie Robinson's entry into major league baseball in 1947 and the integration of other sports throughout the following decade resulted in a spate of writings about African American athletes. Buoyed by the integration process and the apparent fact that American sport was finally living up to its professed principles of fair play and equality, an increasing number of black writers proudly recounted the road to stardom for African American athletes. These writings focused primarily on the exploits of African American athletes in predominantly white organized sport so as to engender racial pride and serve as symbols of possibility. *

---

* See for example, Henderson, *The Negro in Sports*. This was the second edition of Henderson's book and included new material on the shattering of the color line in American sport. It preceded by two years a special issue he edited on "The Negro in Sports," *Negro History Bulletin* 15 (December 1951). Some other writings in this genre are S. Brown, "Athletics and the Arts"; "Sports: They Set the Pace in 1947," *Opportunity* 26 (Spring 1948): 83; "Sports," *Negro History Bulletin* 28 (February 1955): 120–22.

Here, Rufus E. Clement, president of Atlanta University, civil rights activist, and former college coach, charts the progress of racial integration in American sport. Clement's narrative is remarkably detailed, containing important analysis of significant players and events pertaining to African American involvement in both intercollegiate and professional athletics. It is also insightful, long on interpretation, and full of Clement's personal opinions on the significance of individual African American athletes. Subsequent events in American sport would confirm Clement's hope for the future, but equal opportunities for African American athletes would not come easily and would certainly not be realized without significant agitation and protest.

――――――

Acceptance of Negroes as fully qualified to participate in sports right along with their white competitors has not been thrust upon us nor has it come with any great degree of suddenness. The social historian would probably have a difficult time if he attempted to pin down with any degree of exactitude the date, the place, the event in which for the first time an American Negro competed as an individual in an organized or amateur sport against white athletes or played as a member of an interracially mixed team. . . .

The first achievement in the field of interracial sports was to have Negroes accepted as members of the competing teams or accepted as individuals to compete against other individuals in athletic events. By the 1930s this situation was not only firmly established, but met with general approval in all those sections of the country where there were no laws dealing with segregation of the races on the statute books of the states in which the events took place.

The second step in integration in the field of sports now had to be made. It had been established that Negro athletes could be good and they could be gentlemen. What would happen when they, either as individuals or as team members, might be expected to compete with teams coming from below the Mason-Dixon Line where Negroes had not been accepted in the same manner or where the Northern teams moved South across the Line in intersectional contests? On a number of occasions Southern teams went north and played against local teams which had Negro members. This was particularly true in the field of college football and in track and field events. In truth, in these latter events individual white boys from the South had for many years been competing against Negroes in the national AAU championships, the Penn Relays, and at other times when regional and national champions were being chosen. There were a few memorable clashes. Washington and Jefferson College in Washington, Pennsylvania, had to cancel a football game with a Southern opponent rather than bench a regular half back who happened to be a Negro. On another occasion, Harvard refused to send a team into the South when it was requested that it leave behind one of the team members, a Negro. (Be it here stated to the credit of the University of Virginia that at a subsequent date Harvard brought a Negro lineman down to Charlottesville, where he played in the football game against the University of Virginia and from all accounts was treated as just another member of the Harvard team.)

Gradually Southern teams which scheduled events with Northern opponents recognized the right of the opponent to place on the field as its representative any man who met the athletic and scholastic standards of the institution. Today there is probably not a single Southern college team in the country which, having scheduled a game with a Northern opponent on the latter's home grounds, would raise a question of race with respect to the men who would represent the host team.

As I have indicated above, the third step is now being taken, though it is as yet not a very big step: some Southern colleges and universities will permit Northern colleges to bring into the south whomever they desire as qualified representatives of their institutions when they engage in athletic events. The colleges in Texas have been particularly noteworthy in this respect. But it is also true that institutions located in the upper-tier of the Southern states—Maryland, Virginia, Kentucky, Missouri, Oklahoma—have without bitterness and without undue publicity—engaged in athletic contests at home against racially-mixed teams. If memory and the records do not fail me, the University of North Carolina should be placed with this liberal group of institutions located in the South.

It is a bit too early to know what the attitude of the Southern colleges will be toward permitting Negro athletes to represent them, since at the present time most of the Negro students who are enrolled in Southern institutions generally recognized as institutions for white persons are registered in the graduate and professional schools and are therefore not eligible for intercollegiate athletic competition. However, it has recently come to my attention that one Southern institution which has enrolled Negroes in its undergraduate college of liberal arts is interested in bringing Negro athletes to its campus and is expecting to have these men represent the institution. In this connection I cannot forego [sic] relating an account of a conversation this writer recently had with an alumnus of the University of South Carolina. We were discussing the prodigious feats of J. C. Caroline, Negro star half back on the 1953 University of Illinois football team. Caroline's home town is Columbia, South Carolina; he was graduated from a Negro high school in that city, but he wound up as a star performer on a great football team hundreds and hundreds of miles away. This alumnus was bemoaning the fact that the University of Illinois was receiving the acclaim and the publicity which resulted from Caroline's great performances on the gridiron, when his Alma Mater might well have benefited from a hometown boy's activities.

The last great citadel of lily-whiteism in American sports was organized baseball. This was also probably the hardest to conquer....

Once many years ago when I was coaching the baseball team at Livingstone College, we played the team from Johnson C. Smith University at Wearn Field, Charlotte, North Carolina, on an Easter Monday. One of the big league teams was playing the local Charlotte white baseball team the next afternoon. Players and officials of the big league team were in the stands during part of the Livingstone-Smith game. The Negro short stop of the Livingstone team was approached by an assistant manager with the proposition that if he would decide to change his name and claim Cuban ancestry and nationality, his team would be glad to give the youngster a tryout.

The young man, William Evans of Louisville, Kentucky, refused the offer—for the simple reason that he preferred to get an education.

For a number of years before Negroes were openly admitted into organized baseball there were barn-storming, end-of-the-season tours with scheduled games between groups of star white baseball players on one team and outstanding Negro players on the other. Lyman Yokeley, star Negro pitcher of Winston-Salem, North Carolina, one-time student at Livingstone College and later mainstay of the Baltimore Black Sox baseball team, was for several years a member of the Negro team recruited to play against the big leaguers. Competition between the two groups was keen. In one season in the late 1920s Yokeley pitched against and shut out the white All-Stars in three games. On one occasion he struck out the National League home run king, Hack Wilson of the Chicago Cubs, four times in succession. At the end of the game Wilson good-naturedly gave his bat to Yokeley—who promptly painted it black and blue, the colors of his school team, Livingstone, and sent it back to the campus as a trophy.

In such ways as this did the American public first begin to notice the calibre of some Negro baseball players and at the same time accept the idea of seeing them compete against white Americans. Meanwhile the color-bar persisted.

When Jack Roosevelt (better known as Jackie) Robinson was signed to play with the Montreal, Brooklyn Dodger Farm team in 1946, the first open, actual dropping of the racial barrier in professional baseball occurred. The rest of Robinson's phenomenal career in organized baseball to date is well known to almost every baseball fan, white or Negro, South or North, in America. After the first year at Montreal, in which he led the International League in batting with an average of .348, stole forty bases, led the second basemen of the League in fielding with a .985 percentage, and tied for League-leading scoring honors with 113 runs, Jackie was signed in 1947 with the present Brooklyn Dodgers team. He soon became not only the first Negro in the major Leagues, but he was named Rookie of the Year in the National League for 1947. From there he went on to win many other well-deserved honors. . . .

His contribution to race relations cannot be praised too highly. . . . His bearing, culture, intelligence, deportment and demeanor, and his pleasant personality buttressed his great athletic ability and made of him an individual who could be accepted by people of all racial groups. To Branch Rickey, General Manager of the Brooklyn Dodger baseball empire, must always go the credit for his courage, intelligence and foresight in picking a man like Robinson to spearhead the effort to get Negro players accepted in the Great American Sport. Mr. Robinson himself must always receive the credit for making good as a pioneer in a very difficult situation.

Rufus Clement, "Racial Integration in the Field of Sports," *Journal of Negro Education* 23 (1954): 222–30.

13. "And They Call This a Democracy": Little League Baseball and the Struggle for Equality

Little League baseball is one of the most important youth sport programs in the world. Founded in 1939 by Carl Stotz, Little League baseball has become so popular that its annual World Series in Williamsport, Pennsylvania, is nationally televised. Unfortunately, Little League baseball, in spite of its enormous success, was extraordinarily slow to accept girls and African Americans into its program. The league actually fought to maintain its gender exclusivity, arguing in several court cases that girls were both emotionally and physically incapable of participating in highly competitive sport. It was not until Congress amended the National Little League charter in December 1974 that girls were officially allowed to participate with boys on league-sponsored teams.*

African American youths in the South fared little better in their efforts to participate fully in Little League baseball. For approximately the first sixteen years after the founding of Little League baseball, they were segregated into their own teams and leagues without any chance to advance to the World Series championship. Like many other national organizations in America at the time, Little League baseball was unwilling to overturn the decisions of its local chapters in the South and thus insist on equality of opportunity for the region's young African American players.

The following document describes the fate suffered by Charleston's Cannon Street YMCA Little League team in 1955. With its sights set on making it to the world series in Williamsport, the all-black Cannon Street YMCA team entered the South Carolina tournament against other clubs in the state. The Cannon Street team, however, never had the opportunity to participate since the fifty-five white teams from South Carolina refused to compete against it and withdrew from the tournament. This action should have resulted in the Cannon's automatic berth in the regional tournament in Rome, Georgia, but Little League baseball denied them that chance along with the opportunity to participate in the world series. Ironically, within two weeks of the Cannon Street affair, national Little League officials actually disqualified eleven white teams from the northwest district tournament in Florida for their refusal to play the black Pensacola Junior Chamber of Commerce team. The JC's, as they were called, went on to play in the state tournament in Orlando, the first black Little League team to do so in the South.**

A mean bunch of little men got together and shut out all of South Carolina's Little League teams from participation in the playoffs for the national title last week, and they did it because of the color of some little boys' skins.

---

* See D. Wiggins, "A History of Highly Competitive Sport for American Children"; Jennings, "As American as Hot Dogs."

** For details on both the Cannon and Pensacola teams, see Lacy, *Fighting for Fairness*, 179–82. For a postscript on the Connor Street All-Stars and the recollections of former players see "The Team That Never Played," San Luis Obispo *Tribune*, August 16, 2002.

Rather than see one Negro team compete against fifty-five white teams in the state playoffs, South Carolina Little League officials withdrew the white teams from play, thus giving the Cannon YMCA team of Charleston the state title by default.

National officials announced later that the Cannon team could not compete in the Rome, Ga. tourney which leads to the national finals in Williamsport.

Danny Jones, Little League Regional Director of South Carolina who had quit the movement because of its ruling in favor of Negro teams, commented sourly "to use 8 to 12-year-old boys in an attempt to undermine the laws and customs of our people is a dastardly act."

Robert F. Morrison, president of the Cannon "Y" replied, "If anyone was guilty of undermining the laws and customs it was Danny Jones, himself, when he became connected with a national organization such as the Little League which demands that every boy between 9 and 12 should have an equal chance to play in their program."

Jones has set out to organize a "little boys league" for the fifty-five white secessionist teams but has been told by National Little League officials that the present South Carolina Little League setup would be out of a franchise if it does so.

"And They Call This a Democracy," *Pittsburgh Courier-Journal,* August 6, 1955.

14. "Weekend at the Penn Relays"

The University of Pennsylvania Relays is one of this country's most famous track meets. It has long been especially significant for the African American sporting community. Sometimes referred to as the "Negro Olympics," the Penn Relays allowed individual black athletes to participate from almost the moment it was founded in 1895. Many great black track-and-field performers from predominantly white institutions such as John B. Taylor of the University of Pennsylvania, Charlie West of Washington and Jefferson College, and John Shelbourne of Dartmouth College, exhibited their athletic talents in front of thousands of fans of both races, who regularly packed Philadelphia's Franklin Field during the spring festivities. Beginning with Howard University's participation in 1920, entire teams from historically black colleges entered the Penn Relays, competing against Syracuse University, Penn State, and the University of Pittsburgh, among others. This is an indication that the Penn Relays, like games between the Renaissance Five and white quintets, or contests between barnstorming major leaguers and black baseball teams, provided occasions for interracial athletic competitions despite the rigid racial segregation and discriminatory practices of the period.* Such integrated forums, as scarce as they were, paved the way for more expansive developments linking sports to the civil rights movement.

The following document discusses the enormous popularity of the "Penn Relays Weekend" to the African American community during the 1950s. Claiming that the event out-ranked the Howard-Lincoln football game, the Kentucky Derby, the Cotton Festival in Mem-

---

* For information on black athletes in the Penn Relays, see "Colored Athletes in the Famous Penn Relays"; Chalk, *Black College Sport,* esp. 314, 321–22, 327–28.

phis, and New Orleans's Mardi Gras, the article notes that race pride initially attracted African Americans to the Penn Relays to watch great track athletes. The Penn Relays evolved, however, into a social event as much as an athletic one. This apparent transformation is not surprising nor an unusual occurrence in American sport. Sporting events, whether held in predominantly white or in African American communities, have always been occasions to test athletic prowess and to reinforce social ties among race men and women. In later years, such prominent Philadelphians as Bill Cosby would help publicize the inclusive nature of the competition that has for many years been a hallmark of the Penn Relays.

———— ————

New Orleans can have its Mardi Gras. Memphis can have its Cotton Festival. Louisville can have Derby Week. Philadelphia has its Penn Relays Weekend. All along the Atlantic seaboard, "The Weekend" has become an important fixture in the Spring social season. Many social butterflies think it is the biggest event, out-ranking the Howard-Lincoln Game or Derby Week. In recent years the P.R. Week-end has attracted more and more Negroes to Philly. Like many sports dates of its kind, its interest was at first limited only to track-minded people. Race pride brought them from everywhere to see guys like Dewey Rogers, famous Penn quarterman, and Eddie Tolan burn up Franklin Field's cinder-path. That fierce pride became a blazing fire when the Jesse Owens–Ralph Metcalfe, Eulace Peacock–Johnny Borican crowd took over. The fire has never gone out. Now there is a new crop of athletes and spectators. But many of the hundreds to flock in from Boston, New York, Baltimore, Miami, and Chicago wouldn't know an anchor-leg from a sprint-medley. Some never see the relays at all. For many of society's ladies, the East stands are just an advantageous setting for showing off the new mink scarf or new frock.

Philly may be dull—but not during "The Week-end." This is one time it lives up to its name as the "city of brotherly love." Hospitality hits a new high. And in fact Philly jumps. From early Friday until late Sunday the balling stays in high gear. The formals are hectic. The private parties are spirited. Famous Pyramid Club throws out the mat.

For many of Philly's quiet livers this is splurge week. Some of the city's best known names have helped to make Penn Relays Weekend "the thing." Names like Dr. Lawrence Christmas, Dr. Woodley Wells, Raymond Pace Alexander, Dr. William Hamilton, Carleton and Kay Richards. For years now the Alpha formal has been a tradition of "The Weekend," and more recently the Guardsmen and the Lincolnettes have followed the lead. Wilbur and Charlotte Stickland's party has long been a feature. Evelyn Reynolds' affair used to be a must, when she entertained. Last year, the Jim Ramsays threw a $4,000 "bombshell" which stood Philly on its head.

This year's Penn Relays Weekend was no different from others, generally. The relay carnival itself had its good points. Ever since Charlie Drew took them to the Relays in 1926, Morgan teams have been trying to get into national track lime-light. This year people came away from the relays talking about four lightning-fast Morgan boys who zoomed their way to the Mile Relay College Championship and cracked an 11-year-old record hung up by Pittsburgh University. The Morgan Bears also took the Freshman College Relay, establishing themselves as a force soon to be reckoned with.

In the two days, one college record, and three track marks were cracked; one meet mark was equaled. A gaily dressed crowd with a majority of dark faces numb with cold, saw Seton Hall triple threat Andy Stanfield win the broad jump; saw Wilber Lancaster (Former CIAA Champion) lose the 100-yard dash by a step and saw schoolboy Vern Dixon do a 47.7 quarter leg.

By Monday, Philly was again a Blue Law town.

"Weekend at the Penn Relays," *Our World,* August 1950, 38–42.

D

UP CLOSE AND PERSONAL

15. Adam Buckley Cohen / The Mugging of Johnny Bright

For those Americans in 1951 who followed sport with an eye to race relations and popular culture, the year would have been remarkable mainly because some new figures entered the athletic fray, further challenging the old order in some of the national pastimes. Willie Mays joined the New York Giants that year and bore witness, as Jackie Robinson had done before him, to the combination of speed, power, and poise that black athletes brought to the highest levels of sport. The naming of Roy Campanella as the National League's most valuable player and, in a distant venue, Althea Gibson's first appearance at Wimbledon added to the impression that in matters of race relations, the second half of the twentieth century would not resemble the first.

Then again, in that same year, one of the most brutal and highly publicized racial episodes occurred in intercollegiate football. Johnny Bright of Drake University, one of college football's best African American players, was physically attacked and seriously injured. The assault was captured on film and made headline news throughout the nation. In Drake's October 20 game against Oklahoma A&M, Bright, while handing off to his teammate and far removed from the action as well as the eyes of the officials, took vicious blows to the head from A&M lineman Wilbanks Smith on three separate occasions. Bright suffered a broken jaw as a result of the blows and eventually had to be removed from the game.* In combat sports such as football, violence is not extraordinary. For five hundred years white violence against blacks had not been considered extraordinary either. Written fifty years after the assault on Bright, the following document offers a moving human interest story—and closure—but it also suggests that "race" was beginning to matter in different ways during the early years of the civil rights crusade, even on the sports pages of the mainstream press. That a black man had been attacked without provocation would have been mere "history" to the majority of African Americans. But this assault provoked some outrage, as well as some Pulitzer prize–winning photographs, and that was news.

Without the pictures, Johnny Bright's broken jaw probably would have been considered just another football injury.

With fewer than eight minutes gone in the first quarter, and with the nation's

---

* For information on the Bright incident, see Lucas and Smith, *Saga of American Sport*, 392–93; Sperber, *Onward to Victory*, 480–81; "Caught by the Camera" *Life*, November 5, 1951, 121–24; McMahon, "Pride to All."

The mugging of Johnny Bright (Photo by photographers John Robinson and Don Ultang, copyright 1951, *Des Moines Register and Tribune Company.* Reprinted with permission.)

leading ground gainer out of the Oct. 20, 1951 game, A&M—later to become Oklahoma State—erased an early deficit and rolled to victory over previously unbeaten Drake University.

It was not until the next day that Bright's injury took on a more sinister cast. The *Des Moines Register* had devoted an entire page of the Sunday paper to a sequence of photos from the game. The pictures, which would earn a Pulitzer Prize for photographers Don Ultang and John Robinson, showed A&M defensive tackle Wilbanks Smith pummeling Bright on two separate plays.

Bright was nowhere near the action on either play.

He was simply standing in the backfield, watching the ballcarrier, when Smith delivered a forearm—or perhaps a fist—to his unprotected jaw (helmets did not yet have face masks).

While the photos were shocking for their depiction of savage, unsportsmanlike play, they might have faded on the pages of the *Register* had it not been for one thing: Smith is white, and Bright was African American.

When Bright went to Drake in 1948, he was one of only a few African Americans at the small private university in Des Moines.

"There was a distinct line between us and the rest of the student body," says Jim Ford, an African American who attended Drake in the late '40s and early '50s and shared an apartment with Bright. "We were not permitted to live on campus."

If Bright was troubled by Drake's housing policy, he kept it to himself.

"When you tried to talk to Johnny about segregation, he'd make a joke out of it," says Ford. "He'd tell you, 'Don't bring this garbage to me. . . . If you want to prove something to me, prove it out there on the football field.'"

Bright's desire to view life through the prism of football was understandable.

Off the field, he might have been a second-class citizen.

On the field, he was the biggest star Drake had seen.

In 1949, he became the first sophomore to lead the nation in total offense, running and passing for nearly 2,000 yards as a halfback in the old single-wing formation. The next year, he gained a record-setting 2,400 yards in total offense and became the first player to both rush and pass for 1,000 yards in the same season.

"He epitomized what I thought was the ideal running back—the splatter type," recalls Jim Trimble, who coached against Bright at Wichita State. "When he got rolling, he just splattered people."

Bright could also take a hit.

"Against Abilene Christian, I saw him get hit so hard," recalled Bill Coldiron, a Drake offensive lineman at the time. "He just bounced back and got in the huddle and said, 'OK, guys, we're all veterans now. Let's go get 'em.'"

Bright kept up a constant patter on and off the field. "I can see him now, running his mouth continuously," says Ford, laughing. Still, Ford believes his friend's playfulness masked a lonely, alienated side. "Because of his athletic skills, he could run around in the white community," Ford says. "But he realized he was not accepted." Adds Arvil Stille, another former Drake teammate, "I can remember once on a train trip coming back, he sat on the edge of my bunk. He got real serious, and he told me, 'You know, as a black man, I've got only two things. I've either got to make it in sports or entertainment.'"

In his sophomore season, Bright, an Indiana native, got his first taste of the Jim Crow South when Drake played Missouri Valley Conference rival Oklahoma A&M in Stillwater.

"Oklahoma was totally segregated," says Hannah Atkins, the first African American woman to serve in the state's legislature. "Transportation, water fountains, everything."

Still, the 1949 game between Drake and the all-white A&M squad went off without incident, thanks perhaps to a pregame admonition from A&M Coach Jim Lookabaugh, who, according to the *Des Moines Register,* said "that Bright was the first Negro ever to play at A&M . . . [and] should be treated fairly."

Despite Bright's efforts—the *Tulsa Daily World* reported that "the flashy Negro scooter . . . was the only bright light for the Bulldogs"—A&M dispatched Drake, 28-0.

In 1951, Drake returned to Stillwater with high hopes. Boasting a 5-0 record, the Drake players thought they had a good shot at knocking off A&M, which had struggled to a 1-3 start.

Gene Aldridge, who played defensive back for A&M, remembers that A&M Coach J. B. Whitworth, who had replaced Lookabaugh, stressed that the key to beating Drake was stopping Bright, who was leading the nation in rushing and total offense.

According to Aldridge, Whitworth had noted a weakness in Bright's game while studying films: When Bright was not carrying or throwing the ball, he stood in the backfield and rested. During practice, Whitworth emphasized that the defensive linemen should keep Bright "moving around."

"That meant he didn't want Bright resting," says Aldridge. "So if you don't want somebody resting, you're going to go back there and put a hit on him."

When Drake fullback Gene Macomber visited a Stillwater barbershop for a trim the day before the game, he remembers that the barber "told me words to the effect that the black guy would not finish the game."

Life magazine wrote later that there were "even supposed to be betting pools on when the Aggies would get Bright."

"I didn't hear any rumors," says Joe Sotelo, who played cornerback for Drake. "But the coaching staff told Johnny to protect himself. . . . The only time I can recall that being brought up was at the Oklahoma A&M game."

Nevertheless, on the first play from scrimmage, Bright ignored his coaches' warning.

After handing the ball to Macomber, he stood in the backfield watching the play develop. A&M's Smith leveled Bright with a shot to the face. "There he was, out cold," remembers *Register* photographer Ultang. "No one who was at the game saw what happened. . . . Everyone's eyes were on the ballcarrier." After regaining consciousness, Bright threw a wobbly pass that went for 61 yards and a touchdown. But on Drake's next offensive series, Smith again KO'd Bright as he stood watching a teammate carry the ball. Once more, no whistles were blown.

When Smith knocked Bright cold a third time, the play again escaped the attention of the officials. But others had seen it. "The third time, we saw clearly," says Bob Spiegel, a reporter who was working as a spotter for photographers Ultang and Robinson. "We saw him cold-cock John. He just drew back his fist and smacked the guy." A few plays later, Bright was taken to the locker room where doctors discovered a broken jaw, and the Drake star's game was over. "After Johnny got his jaw broken and was taken out of the game, our safety, Chuck Lanphere from Arkansas—he was a rebel all the way—he just broke down crying. In fact, he cried in Johnny's chest at halftime," remembers Drake's Sotelo.

For the rest of the game, Bright's teammates did their best to get revenge for the injury to their star. "It was a rough, dirty day," Sotelo recalls. "Physically, we gave as much as we took." Drake sidelined three A&M running backs and, adds Sotelo, "just murdered their quarterback—absolutely demolished him—in retaliation." Still, without Bright, Drake's offense foundered, and A&M won, 27-14. After the game, doctors wired Bright's jaw shut. He walked up to us, and he had these wire cutters around his neck—actual wire cutters," recalls Coldiron. "They were there so if he got sick, he could cut the wires."

As the Drake team waited in an Oklahoma station for its train back to Iowa, a station worker saw Bright sitting in a section reserved for whites." This little guy came out from behind the cage where the ticket window was and said to John, 'Sir, you can't sit there,'" remembers teammate John Jennett. "And John, of course, had his jaws wired. And he said, 'Mister, if you think you're man enough to move me, you just try it.' The guy turned around and walked behind the gate." When Ultang and Robinson's photos hit the newsstands, a furor ensued. *Time* magazine called the episode "the year's most glaring example of dirty football," and *Life,* after running the photos, received nearly 300 letters condemning Smith and A&M. The *New York Times* called it "one of the ugliest racial incidents in college sports history."

When contacted for this story, Smith would say only: "Race had nothing to do with what happened that day." Smith's former teammate Aldridge agrees: "I just don't think anyone went after Bright because he was black." Targeting an opposing team's star player—black or white—was common, he says. "That kind of stuff happened." Of the three African Americans who played for Drake that day, only Bright was injured. Although Whitworth eventually admitted that Smith had twice hit Bright in violation of the rules, the coach took no disciplinary action against the lineman. Drake withdrew from the Missouri Valley Conference in protest after the conference declined to act on its appeal.

With his jaw wired shut, wearing a helmet equipped with a protective face mask, and taking oxygen on the sidelines, Bright was able to play only a portion of one more game. Still, he finished fifth in Heisman Trophy balloting and much later was voted into the College Football Hall of Fame. When the Philadelphia Eagles selected him with the seventh overall pick in the 1952 NFL draft, he became only the second African American ever chosen in the first round. But in 1951, NFL salaries were not what they are today. "I think the Eagles had offered him maybe a $300 bonus," remembers Ford. "Then here comes Canada, offering greenbacks. . . . His bonus was, I think, $2,000, which he'd never seen before. And friends like myself, who had never seen any money like that either, said, 'Go. Take that. Go. In a hurry!'"

Bright became a superstar in the Canadian Football League, amassing five consecutive 1,000-yard seasons and four rushing titles. He retired in 1964 as the league's all-time leading rusher—two players have since surpassed him—and was inducted into the Canadian Football Hall of Fame. "John was a super player," remembers NFL Hall of Fame coach Bud Grant, who played and coached against Bright in Canada. "Going into the line at 220 or something like that, he was a terror. He caught the ball exceptionally well, very durable—I don't ever remember him missing a game."

In 1983, Bright, then a junior high school principal in Edmonton, Canada, died of a heart attack. He was 53. A friend of Bright remembers that one of those who sent a floral arrangement to the funeral was Wilbanks Smith.

Adam Buckley Cohen, "Photos Taught a Lesson," *Los Angeles Times,* October 20, 2001.

16. Andrew W. Ramsey / "The Skies Refused to Fall": Crispus Attucks High School and Indiana Basketball

Crispus Attucks, an all-black Indianapolis high school named after the Revolutionary War hero, opened in 1927. Located in a racially segregated city in a state well known for its Ku Klux Klan activity, Crispus Attucks was similar to other black high schools in Indiana in that it was underfunded and lacked proper facilities. The school would eventually estab-

Indianapolis Crispus Attucks High School basketball team, 1956 (Courtesy Indiana Basketball Hall of Fame)

lish a reputation for its outstanding basketball teams, however, capturing back-to-back state titles in 1955 and 1956. Led by coach Ray Crowe and the star player Oscar Robertson, Crispus Attucks's first state title was garnered at the expense of Roosevelt High of Gary, which was led by Dick Barnett, while its second championship came against Jefferson-Lafayette. These victories, which were televised throughout Indiana, had special resonance in a state that had both a poor history of race relations and a passion for basketball. The Indianapolis Recorder, one of the most prominent black newspapers in the country, filled its columns with details of the triumphs of Crispus Attucks while the city's African American community held postgame celebrations reminiscent of those following a Joe Louis championship victory. Nelson George notes in his Elevating the Game: The History and Aesthetics of Black Men in Basketball *that historians have suggested that Crispus Attucks's state titles accelerated the integration of the city's educational institutions since "whites feared, with some justification, that the flow of all of Indianapolis's Black students to one school could make them perennial champions."**

The following article by Andrew Ramsey discusses fan reaction to Crispus Attucks's victory over Gary's Roosevelt High in the 1955 state title game and the ramifications of that

---

* George, *Elevating the Game*, 121. See also Gildea, *Where the Game Matters Most*, 149–50. The two most expansive and detailed studies of the significance of Crispus Attucks in regard to race relations are Pierce, "More Than a Game," and Roberts, *But They Can't Beat Us.*

victory for race relations. Although failing to mention that the racial component of the game was greatly diminished because both teams were black, Ramsey explains that in spite of "dire predictions" no race riots took place during or following the contest. Even the mayor of the city was supportive, helping lead cheers for the team and ensuring the safety of fans by providing police protection. Perhaps most important, Ramsey argues that the victory by Crispus Attucks undermined the belief in African American inferiority, disproved the theory that black athletes could not succeed without a white coach, and even held out hope that racial equity was gradually becoming a reality.

——— ———

Despite the dire predictions of the racist prognosticators of gloom and despair, the skies did not fall when Attucks lowered the boom on hapless Gary Roosevelt in the final game of the 1955 basketball derby.

True, there were expressions of frustration from the disciples of white supremacy in the interval between the singing of the Star Spangled Banner in the afternoon session and the Crazy Song as the Tigers delivered the "coup de grace" to their sepia opponent.

Sullen and hostile looks on the faces of many white spectators pouring from the Feldhouse [sic] relieved now and then by a racial epithet lent credence to the theory held by the columnist of a rival weekly that Indianapolis was anti-Attucks.

And minor incidents reported from here and there gave impetus to this theory.

In one such incident William Radmer, a student at Butler University and part-time clerk at a large chain super market, personified the otherwise decent white people who just could not take it.

Noticing Attucks buttons on some of the customers in the store, Radmer blurted out to a fellow clerk, "The Ink Spots will be out at the Fieldhouse tonight!"

Then finding himself looking into the face of this writer, he looked very embarrassed and hurried into the back of the store.

The manager apologized for the clerk, explaining that he was a very good Christian.

(Radmer was dismissed by the store official the following day for this breech [sic] of good breeding and lack of respect due the feelings of all respectable peoples.)

A white Attucks fan reported that in the Sullivan Grocery at Fortieth and Boulevard Place, the cashier hoped that Attucks would gets its block knocked off because she explained there would be no getting along with the local Negroes in case they won.

And most of the trade at her store is with Negroes!

Contrasted with the above-mentioned attitudes was the fine spirit exhibited by His Honor Mayor Clark.

He not only supported Attucks by his words, he personally led the Attucks cheering section to the Fieldhouse and gave them the full protection and courtesy of the police department.

An [sic] after the game many white persons lined Meridian Street and wildly cheered Indianapolis' first basketball champions and many true white sports fans, who were not jaundiced by prejudice, joined in the victory celebrations on the Circle and at Northwestern Park.

The victory as well as the appearance of two Negro teams in the final game struck at the vitals of the myth of the inherent inferiority of the Negro and belied the calamity howlers who in 1941 predicted that if Negro schools were admitted to the then lily-white Indiana High School Athletic Association, race riots would follow.

It also undermined the myth that explained the stellar performance of Negro athletes on integrated school teams, but denied the possibility of a Negro-coached team ever excelling—the myth that Negroes need the guidance of a white man in order to accomplish anything great.

The victory also called to mind an article in *Esquire* magazine a dozen or so years ago under the title "May the Best White Man Win."

The article called attention to the exclusion of Negroes from certain sports like baseball and golf in which champions were chosen yearly.

Within a few years after the penning of this article Negroes had been admitted to the baseball monopoly and had made an enviable name for themselves and had made some headway in tennis.

The admission of the three Negro high schools and the Catholic high schools by the Indiana High School Athletic Association came also in the period after an NAACP-sponsored bill to put high school athletics under the state without racial or religious restrictions was introduced in the General Assembly by Senator Robert Lee Brokenburr.

As a compromise the barred schools were admitted despite the misgivings of many of the big guns in the association and among local school officials.

Finally, Attucks' winning the crown served as a barometer of America's progress toward the realization of her most beautiful dream.

There was in the victory an odd mixture of the new and the old. The very existence of three all-Negro schools in Indiana is a denial of the democracy that Attucks and Roosevelt's appearance in the final game affirmed.

The masterful manner in which the Tigers won the victory and the gentlemanly conduct of the members of the quintet and their supporters allayed some fears and perhaps won some converts to racial equity but it raised the unanswered question of what next and when.

As for the skies that were supposed to fall, they are unshakeable for they are the very same skies that we sing about in America the Beautiful, "O Beautiful for spacious skies."

They are the skies of an America becoming conscious of her potential greatness.

Andrew W. Ramsey, "The Skies Refused to Fall," *Indianapolis Recorder*, March 26, 1955.

17. Is Ralph Dupas Negro or White?

The story of Ralph Dupas is doubly revealing, for it not only illustrates the lengths to which southern whites would go to impede the civil rights movement; it also illuminates the bizarre "biologic" of race—the one-drop rule of descent—that has long prevailed in the thinking of many Americans. As a response to the landmark Supreme Court rulings of the mid-1950s bar-

ring segregation in education, the state legislature of Louisiana endeavored to tighten restrictions on interracial contact. In 1956 it passed a law prohibiting "dancing, social functions, entertainment, athletic training, games, sports, or contests and other such activities involving personal and social contact in which participants or contestants are members of the white and negro race." Though condemnation of the law came from the New Orleans NAACP and boxing interests throughout the nation, the legislature and governor stood firm.

In the midst of this controversy, Dupas, a relatively light-skinned boxer hoping to move up in the lightweight division rankings, was confronted with the accusation that he was, in fact, Ralph DuPlessis, born of black parents. Here, the two articles carried in the Baltimore Afro-American *offer brief sketches of the imbroglio that threatened Dupas's athletic career. In April 1957, after hearing testimony from former acquaintances of Dupas, the Louisiana State Athletic Commission found in his favor. He proceeded to win his match against Vince Martinez to become the fourth-ranked lightweight in the nation. But then the Louisiana State Boxing Commission, bowing to pressure from the state attorney general's office, insisted that Dupas produce his birth certificate before it would sanction any future matches for him. In the ensuing hearings, the Bureau of Vital Statistics held that Dupas was black under Louisiana state law, although it became apparent that the bureau had not originally issued a birth certificate to him and, indeed, had altered subsequent documentation in order to classify him as a member of the "Negro race."*

The following year, the Louisiana State Supreme Court resolved the issue of the tainted "birth certificate," ruling that there was a lack of evidence that Dupas was black. As the historian Jeffrey Sammons observes, however, "the victory was a mixed one, because as a white man he could not fight blacks in Louisiana; hence a proposed bout with Joe Brown for the lightweight championship would await a change in the law." But the significance of the Dupas affair—and the issue of racial mixing—extended beyond the sports realm. Louisiana had a long history of creolization, the mingling of people with diverse backgrounds. Not just there but throughout the South, the question of the color line remained a vexing issue for those who strived to maintain white supremacy and racial segregation. Who was white? Who was black? If examining the color of one's skin or the texture of one's hair didn't answer these questions, how far back in the past must marriage and birth records be examined? In several respects, the Dupas case exposed the essential absurdity of defining race in biological terms. What is more, as the second piece in the Afro-American *suggests, the biggest victory in the Dupas case was to come not in the boxing arena but in the courts, when Louisiana's discriminatory legislation was finally "wiped off the books." Ultimately, in the years following the civil rights revolution, such autobiographical accounts as Gregory Howard Williams's* Life on the Color Line, *as well as the golfer Tiger Woods's self-identification as "Cablinasian"—Caucasian, Black, Native American, and Asian—have further revealed the paradoxes still bound to thinking about "race" simply in terms of black and white.* *

———

* For details on the Dupas episode, see Sammons, *Beyond the Ring,* 188–90 (quote, 189–90). See also Fairclough, *Race and Democracy.* On racial mixing, see G. Reginald Daniel, "Either Black or White: Race, Modernity, and the Law of the Excluded Middle," and Paul Spickard, "The Power of Blackness: Mixed-Race Leaders and the Monoracial Ideal," in Spickard and Daniel, *Uncompleted Independence;* Malcomson, *One Drop of Blood.*

"Boxer Must Prove He's Not Colored"

NEW ORLEANS—With $50,000 "riding" on proof of his racial identity, Ralph Dupas, lightweight boxing contender, declared last week "I'm white and don't know why I have to prove it."

The previous night, the Louisiana State Athletic Commission held a three-hour executive session on charges by some persons that the 21-year old, sixth ranked challenger from this city was born of colored parents. . . .

The hearing fell like a pall between Dupas and the biggest payday in his long career. He is scheduled to meet fourth ranked welterweight contender Vince Martinez in a 10 round go on April 8, with Promoter Heard Ragas predicting a $50,000 gate. . . .

The Louisiana Legislature passed a law last year banning athletic contests between colored and white persons. Martinez, 27, stiff punching defensive stylist from Paterson, N.J., is recognized as white. . . .

"You are a N—o. I know you are a N—o. Now put me in jail if you don't like it," one of his accusers shouted at Dupas as he waited with members of the fight crowd, reporters and witnesses outside the hearing room.

She was Mrs. Lucretia Gravolet, an aged school teacher from Placquemines Parish, La., where, she said, Dupas was born of colored parents.

Miss Rose Nell Tomeny, an English teacher at Nichols High School, one of Dupas' former teachers, came to his aid. She contended that "This is nothing but cruel sadism. It only takes a little mud to ruin a masterpiece."

Dupas said he was born in New Orleans Oct. 14, 1935, while hostile witnesses contend he was born at Pointe a La Heche on Oct. 15 of the same year. He says he was baptized in St. Peter and Paul Roman Catholic Church here. . . .

"This whole thing's a farce," [Dupas's attorney, Sam A.] Zelden asserted, adding "And I'll tell you one thing . . . if this commission says Dupas is colored—and I know I can prove different—there's going to be more damn libel suits than you ever hear of."

"Boxer Must Prove He's Not Colored," *Baltimore Afro-American,* April 6, 1957.

"A Much Easier Way"

Ralph Dupas, the fourth ranking lightweight boxing contender, has filed suit in the U.S. District Court demanding that the city of New Orleans issue him a birth certificate listing him as white.

Louisiana law forbids bouts between colored and white contestants.

Dupas apparently has no birth certificate but points out that his brothers and sisters have certificates identifying them as white.

The Louisiana Athletic Commission, however, has heard testimony from a woman who says she knew Dupas' family and swears he is colored.

In a situation like this, it appears to us that Dupas would find it much easier and cheaper to challenge the constitutionality of Louisiana's slavery time law. Moreover, he would most surely win, and benefit the whole community by getting discriminatory legislation like this wiped off the books.

"A Much Easier Way," *Baltimore Afro-American,* August 31, 1957.

18. Althea Gibson / "What Now?"

Althea Gibson's life and career in tennis are well known to those with a knowledge of the history of African Americans in sport. She was a forerunner to Zina Garrison, then to Venus and Serena Williams, later champions who have explicitly acknowledged Gibson as a role model. Born in 1927 in Silver, South Carolina, Gibson spent most of her early years in Harlem where she first honed her tennis skills under the direction of the noted musician Buddy Walker and then later with Fred Johnson, the head professional at the Cosmopolitan Club, the most prestigious African American tennis club in New York City. In 1946, Gibson moved to Wilmington, North Carolina, where she lived with Dr. Hubert A. Eaton, continued refining her tennis skills, and finished her three remaining years of high school. A year later Gibson won her first of ten straight American Tennis Association (ATA) national championships. In 1956, just three years after graduating from Florida A&M University, Gibson became the first African American to capture a grand-slam tennis championship when she won the French Open. The following year she won both the Wimbeldon and U.S. Lawn Tennis Association (USLTA) championships. In 1958, Gibson captured her second consecutive Wimbeldon and USLTA championships and then retired shortly thereafter from tournament tennis.

Gibson spent the next few years on assorted projects, including promoting her autobiography; releasing a record album, Althea Gibson Sings; *appearing in a film,* The Horse Soldiers; *and touring with the Harlem Globetrotters. In 1960, Gibson turned her attention to golf, eventually winning two North-South Women's Amateur Tournaments and becoming the first African American on the Ladies Professional Golf Association (LPGA) tour. For her many accomplishments, Gibson was elected to both the International Tennis Hall of Fame and the International Women's Sports Hall of Fame.**

In the following selection from her first and most notable autobiography,** Gibson explains that she is a "tennis player, not a Negro tennis player" and that she was decidedly different from Jackie Robinson in that she was "not a racially conscious person." While Robinson relished his role as an African American struggling for equal rights, Gibson claimed she was not a militant who consciously fought to overcome injustice and racial discrimination. Importantly, however, Gibson also noted that she wanted her "success to speak for itself as an advertisement for my race." In large measure, then, Gibson was clearly aware that members of the African American community viewed her as a much-needed example of achievement and a symbol of future success. Like Robinson and other well-known African American athletes who integrated predominantly white organized sport, Gibson found herself cast as a role model with the hopes and dreams of her race riding on each of her tennis wins. It is apparent from her comments, moreover, that Gibson took the position of many African

---

* For information on Gibson, see Henderson, *The Black Athlete,* 268–71; Festle, *Playing Nice,* esp. 53–54, 59–64, 67–68.
** Her other autobiography is the less well known *So Much to Live For* (New York: Putnam, 1968).

Althea Gibson (Library of Congress)

Americans, particularly during the late 1950s and early 1960s, who believed success on the athletic field—and not active protest—was the best weapon against racial prejudice in sport and the larger American society.

——— ———

As far as the color question is concerned, I have no feeling of exclusion any more. At least, I don't feel I'm being excluded from anything that matters. Maybe I can't stay overnight at a good hotel in Columbia, South Carolina, or play a tennis match against a white opponent in the sovereign state of Louisiana, which has a law against such a social outrage, but I can get along without sleeping at the Wade Hampton and I don't care if I never set foot in Louisiana. There is, I have found out, a whole lot of world outside Louisiana—and that goes for South Carolina, Mississippi, Georgia, Alabama, and all the other places where they haven't got the message yet. Actually, I think there has been a lot of good will shown on both sides lately, and I think we're making progress.

I am not a racially conscious person. I don't want to be. I see myself as just an individual. I can't help or change my color in any way, so why should I make a big deal out of it? I don't like to exploit it or make it the big thing. I'm a tennis player, not a Negro tennis player. I have never set myself up as a champion of the Negro race. Someone once wrote that the difference between me and Jackie Robinson is that he thrived on his role as a Negro battling for equality whereas I shy away from it. That man read me correctly. I shy away from it because it would be dishonest of me to pretend to a feeling I don't possess. There doesn't seem to be much question that Jackie always saw his baseball success as a step forward for Negro people, and he aggressively fought to make his ability pay off in social advances as well as fat paychecks. I'm not insensitive to the great value to our people of what Jackie did. If he hadn't paved the way, I probably never would have got my chance. But I have to do it my way. I try not to flaunt my success as a Negro success. It's all right for others to make a fuss over my role as a trail blazer, and, of course, I realize its importance to others as well as to myself, but I can't do it.

It's important, I think, to point out in this connection that there are those among my people who don't agree with my reasoning. A lot of those who disagree with me are members of the Negro press, and they beat my brains out regularly. I have always enjoyed a good press among the regular American newspapers and magazines, but I am uncomfortably close to being Public Enemy No. 1 to some sections of the Negro press. I have, they have said, an unbecoming attitude; they say I'm bigheaded, uppity, ungrateful, and a few other uncomplimentary things. I don't think any white writer ever has said anything like that about me, but quite a few Negro writers have, and I think the down-deep reason for it is that they resent my refusal to turn my tennis achievements into a rousing crusade for racial equality, brass band, seventy-six trombones, and all. I won't do it. I feel strongly that I can do more good my way than I could by militant crusading. I want my success to speak for itself as an advertisement for my race.

Althea Gibson, *I Always Wanted to Be Somebody* (New York: Harper, 1958), 157–59.

19. Alex Haley on Wilma Rudolph / "The Queen Who Earned Her Crown"

Wilma Rudolph was one of this country's greatest track-and-field performers. Born in 1940 in Bethlehem, Tennessee, Rudolph contracted scarlet fever and double pneumonia at a very early age and was forced to wear a cumbersome leg brace and special high-top shoes for much of her childhood. Eventually, through hard work and perseverance, she overcame her physical disabilities to become a star in both basketball and track and field at Burt High School in Clarksville, Tennessee. Rudolph's talents were so prodigious that she was all-state in basketball three times, and during her junior year she qualified for the 1956 United States Olympic team. In the 400-meter relay in Melbourne, Australia, she helped her quartet to a bronze medal. Over the next four years, while competing for the Tennessee State University Tigerbelles, Rudolph captured several individual titles in track and field, including the 1957 national junior championships in the 75- and 100-yard dashes and the 1959 Amateur Athletic Union championship in the 100 meters.

Rudolph realized her greatest triumphs when she captured gold medals in the 100 meters, 200 meters, and 4 × 100-meter relay in the 1960 Rome Olympics. These victories brought her international acclaim from fans around the world, who were enthralled with her combination of beauty, grace, and speed. Following her track career, Rudolph worked in a number of capacities, including teaching and coaching, cohosting a network radio show, serving as U.S. goodwill ambassador to French West Africa, and giving motivational speeches for American children. She was honored for her athletic accomplishments by being elected to the National Track and Field Hall of Fame, International Women's Sports Hall of Fame, and the U.S. Olympic Hall of Fame. She died in 1994 at her home in Brentwood, Tennessee, following a battle with brain cancer.*

Alex Haley here discusses the tribulations faced by Rudolph as she rose to stardom in track and field. Haley, who became most famous for Roots *and for his part in writing* The Autobiography of Malcolm X, *recounts with admiration how Rudolph overcame debilitating childhood diseases to become one of the world's most widely recognized and esteemed track stars. He also provides some details about the relationship Rudolph forged with her college coach, Ed Temple, and her Tennessee State Tigerbelles teammates. It is apparent from Haley's account that the Tigerbelles, under Temple's tutelage, were an extremely close-knit group of athletes who represented themselves and their school with great pride. For many of those athletes, their hard work and camaraderie would earn them prominent places on the international athletic stage.*

——— ———

Spectators packing Rome's huge white Stadio Olimpico on an overcast day last September suddenly hushed as the six Olympic teams competing in the woman's 400-

---

* For more information on Rudolph, see Rudolph, *Wilma;* "Wilma's Home Town Win," *Life,* October 17, 1960, 114; "Girl on the Run," *Newsweek,* February 6, 1961, 54; "The Fastest Female," *Time,* September 19, 1960, 74–75.

Wilma Rudolph (National Archives)

meter relay final took their positions on the track. All eyes were on a light brown 20-year-old who was to run the anchor leg for the U.S. team. Wilma Rudolph, a 5-foot-11 coed from Tennessee State University, had already won two Gold Medals, for the 100- and 200-meter sprints, and in the semifinals on the relay she had played a large part in setting a new Olympic and world record. If the United States team won this final, Wilma would make Olympic history as the first American woman ever to win three Gold Medals in track.

The starting pistol cracked. The first runners shot from their starting block, raced the baton to the second. The second to the third. And now Lucinda Williams, of the U.S. team, was in the lead, flashing toward Wilma, who had already started her forward motion. Then, somehow, the baton pass was bobbled. Wilma had to stop to grasp it and a gasp went up from the crowd. Germany's Jutta Heine was flying two strides ahead.

But now Wilma's great, scissoring, incredible strides began to burn up the track. She came abreast of Jutta Heine . . . pulled slightly ahead . . . and burst the tape in first place. A roar went up from 60,000 throats. In the din, a confused spectator asked a French photographer standing near the finish line who had won. He replied, "La Gazelle, naturellement. La 'Chattanooga Choo-Choo.'"

Wilma Rudolph's spectacular triumphs at the Olympics were to bring her many honors in the United States and abroad. Last December, European sports writers in the annual United Press International poll named her Sportsman of the Year, the first woman ever voted this award. In the U.S. she was voted Woman Athlete of the year by the Associated Press. But more remarkable than all the honors is the triumph which she achieved over a staggering handicap: for one-third of her life she was a cripple unable to walk. Two great personal influences aided her in her struggle: a mother who practiced and counseled the personal philosophy of never giving up, and a coach who taught that notable success demands that one usually prepare himself.

A tiny 4½ pounds at birth, Wilma was the 17th child in the poor home of a Negro store clerk and a domestic in Clarksville, Tennessee. Always sickly, she was 4 when she began to toddle. Then she was stricken with scarlet fever. Soon double pneumonia set in, and her tonsils inflamed dangerously with her condition too desperate for the doctor to chance taking them out. The child lay near death for weeks. Finally she rallied and pulled through, but her left leg had suffered a form of paralysis.

Her mother, a resolute woman, decided that this pitiful child was as deserving of good health as the rest of her youngsters. Wrapping Wilma in a blanket, Mrs. Rudolph took her by bus the 45 miles to the Negro Meharry Medical College in Nashville. Meharry specialists exhaustively tested the baby. They said that years of daily therapeutic massage might restore the use of the leg. "I can't bring her here every day—can you teach me?" the mother asked. The doctors could, under the circumstances, but there had to be scheduled clinic whirlpool and heat therapy, also, with special apparatus. For the next two years, Mrs. Rudolph, on her weekly day off, made the 90-mile round trip to the Meharry clinic. The six other days, after arriving home tired from work, she prepared the family supper and afterward she carefully massaged the wasted small leg until long after the child had fallen asleep.

When a year after the doctors could detect only slight improvement in the muscular reflexes, passionately determined Mrs. Rudolph taught three older children to massage, and there began four daily shifts of "rubbing Wilma."

"She's going to walk," Mrs. Rudolph declared.

By 1946 Wilma could manage a sort of hop for short distances, and then the leg would buckle. By the time she was 8 she was sufficiently improved to walk with a leg brace. That summer the Meharry clinic substituted a specially reinforced high-top left shoe for the brace, and Wilma limped the eight blocks to school happily.

A brother, Westley, had a basketball, and he mounted a peach basket on a pole in the wide, dirt back yard. To the family's surprise and delight, Wilma began playing with Westley. Catching on from watching him, she was soon on the court, and played almost fanatically. Ignoring the heavy orthopedic shoe, she swivelled and pivoted away from Westley, dribbled in a weaving crouch toward the peach basket, and suddenly sprang up to make her shots. "Not one of all my boys ever played hard as that child making up all the playing she'd missed. I would watch her nearly about to cry," recalls Mrs. Rudolph.

Competing brother-sister teams formed around Westley and Wilma. When the rest tired and dispersed after hot contests she continued with phantom opponents. One day the mother did cry. Returning home from work, she stood slack-jawed with astonishment—Wilma was bounding around under the peach basket barefoot! She no longer needed the shoe. "It went on clear through her grammar school. She was basketballing when I left for work, and when I came back. I've had to start out in the yard with a switch to make her come and eat."

Upon entering Burt High School in 1953, 13-year-old Wilma went out for basketball. She played with such fervor that during one game she collided with Coach-referee Clinton C. Gray. "You're buzzing around like a 'skeeter' whenever I turn!" Gray exclaimed, exasperated. "Skeeter," as Wilma promptly was nicknamed, did make the team, and not long afterward Coach Gray inaugurated girls' track. Burt High had been invited to a state high-school meet to be held at Nashville's Tennessee State University. When Coach Gray saw "Skeeter" run, he timed her—and stared at his stop watch in disbelief. The gangling, unknown "Skeeter" proved the sensation of the state meet, winning the girls' 50-, 75-, and 100-yard dashes. Watching her like a hawk was Tennessee State University's coach of woman's track, Edward Stanley Temple. Temple badly wanted his young co-ed team of "Tigerbelles" to gain wider recognition for the Negro University through winning some of the important national competitions. He was sponsoring this high-school meet and attending others about the country in search of new talent. In "Skeeter" he saw tremendous natural speed hamstrung by grievous flaws in style—correctable flaws if she would work. And she had the perfect sprinter's body, the legs long and powerful, the height—unusual for a woman. He recognized in her a potential champion.

Temple explained that he was developing a "farm system," trying out ten high-school girl stars each summer, and those proving of Tigerbelle caliber could receive a work-aid scholarship for four years at Tennessee State. "Be glad to try you out," Temple said casually. Wilma gulped that she would do her best. The news elated the Rudolph household. After several days the mother drew Wilma aside. "You're the first one in this house that ever had the chance to go to college. If running's going to do that, I just want you to set your mind to be the best! You can if you never give up."

The high-school year finally ended, and Wilma arrived at Tennessee State along with nine other bobby-soxed speed stars from Negro high schools about the United States. Welcoming them in the field house, Temple said, "You're going to find it tougher to get invited back." He showed movies of his Tigerbelles winning breathtaking races. Suddenly, he was curt: "O.K. Get togs from the manager, tomorrow be at the track." The girls had come expecting to display speed, but Temple's initial order was cross-country jogging for about five miles over rough farm pastures. About halfway, Wilma was gasping for breath. She had passed other girls sagged down exhausted, some even retching. But she somehow kept going until she stumbled and fell. When all had dragged back to the track after the ordeal, Temple was blunt: "If you want to run here, when you leave this campus for a meet you have to be in condition."

After a night to recover physically, the prep stars were routed from dormitory beds at 5 A.M. the next day. The college Tigerbelles were on the field. Pairing each with a prep girl, Temple ordered 50-yard sprints. Each crack high-school runner finished a humiliating five to ten yards behind. Even most of the other high-schoolers outran Wilma. Back in the dormitory, sick with shame, she anguished that she had ever come. Never could she be as fast as the Tigerbelles.

But she thought of her mother's admonition to "never give up."

Temple knew precisely that he was planning fierce incentives and competitiveness. By week-end, Wilma's starting humility had become fury at him. Relentlessly, Temple criticized the flaws in her style. "Stop digging postholes! Stretch out those long legs—stride! . . . Your elbows look like a windmill! The arms are pumped straight, like this—" Angrily she worked at effecting the changes in style, just to get Temple off her back. "No clenched fists! With open palms, you're running more relaxed! . . . Don't grab that baton, grasp it!" One day when Wilma was ready to explode, he knew. "Look, Skeeter," he said, calming kindness in his voice, "right now, I'd call you a fair runner. Most teams have good runners. But I want great runners. You're hot under the collar because my Tigerbelles make you look bad. You know the reason? They're better prepared than you are. Always remember, on this track, anywhere else, the one who is the best prepared you find at the top. Now I'll tell you, you can go home tonight if you want to. Or you stay and I'll teach you these things that will help you to win races." Pausing, Temple added, "I think you can be a champion if you want to."

Standing there with sweat running down into her eyes, Wilma was speechless. Three days later she was again staggered when Temple quietly read her name among the four Junior Tigerbelles he was taking with his college stars to Ponca City, Oklahoma, to participate in National A.A.U. competition. The junior division 440-yard relay was won by Temple's four prep trainees, including Wilma. With breath-stopping suspense, their big sister Tigerbelles swept all senior-division sprints and the relay. Tennessee State had its first A.A.U. championship!

Wilma returned to her family and schoolmates a heroine—to everyone but herself. Deeply she was convinced that she could never run so brilliantly as Temple's college girls. Her mother figured the trouble; finally she picked it out of Wilma. "It looks like you can't," she said, "but you can't think you can't! You just got to forget everything but trying!

Through remaining high-school summers, Wilma drilled in the countless details of Tigerbelle style. By the time she enrolled as a freshman at the University, Temple was admonishing his summer trainees, "Watch how Rudolph does it." Training herself, countless times she raced 100 yards, walked back to the starting line, then raced again. She had heard so many starter pistols, and counted her early strides so often, that by now instinct triggered her catapulting takeoffs, then next told her the exact instant to begin straightening up and "floating," and, seconds later, when to start leaning to meet the tape. In the relay, she, Martha Hudson, Barbara Jones, and Lucinda Williams learned to fuse their very reflexes in top-speed exchange of the baton. Temple approached the fanatic about this: "Sloppy baton-passing loses relays!"

Everywhere they raced, the Tigerbelles demolished the opposition. Wilma's permanence on the relay team ranked her among the four fastest Tigerbelles. Yet the other three inevitably beat her in the hotly jealous vendettas of intrasquad racing. "You've got the physical equipment and style—you're supposed to be winning; what's wrong, Skeeter?" Temple asked often. In truthful embarrassment she would say, "I don't know, Coach," for she was trying with all she had to win.

Then in early November, 1959, Wilma began suffering from a sore throat. Gradually her tonsils flared into a swelling agony. Temple hustled her to a Nashville doctor. Immediate surgery was performed. "Those tonsils were terribly infected, Coach," the doctor commented. "They've sapped the girl's strength for years, draining poison into her system." A strange light came into Temple's brown eyes. After three weeks in the University infirmary, Wilma returned to the track—for the first time in her life in full health. In a few days, in the Chicago 1960 Indoor A.A.U. Nationals, she blazed to victory in three races! "I can't believe it! I feel so wonderful!" she exclaimed to flabbergasted sister Tigerbelles.

In Corpus Christi, Florida, she shaved three-tenths of a second off the Olympic and world 200-meter record! In the Olympic tryouts in Abilene, Texas, she took the 100 and 200 meters, and anchored the winning Tigerbelle relay team that would represent the United States. "Somebody'll have to set a new world record to beat her in Rome," the jubilant Temple crowed to Earl Clanton, his assistant. And now he dared to dream of the greatest triumph that a coach and athletes can have—a "clean sweep" of every event entered, against Olympic world competition!

Seven Tigerbelles were among the 310 U.S. athletes who in August flew from New York City to Rome. In the first 100-meter women's sprint, Wilma scorched to a new Olympic record of 11 seconds flat. In the 200-meter trials the following day, Wilma cracked the Olympic time! Then in the finals she blazed to breath-stopping victory over Germany's great 200-meter star, Jutta Heine! Deafening ovation exploded in Stadio Olimpico. Not since the immortal "Babe" Didrikson's phenomenal performance 28 years before had the United States boasted a woman double–Gold Medalist.

No woman ever had won three Gold Medals in track, the Italian morning press reported: "La Gazzelle Nera" (The Black Gazelle) would make that Olympic history if the Tigerbelles won the women's relay. This they did—despite the bobbled pass.

A new Olympic women's relay record! An unprecedented triple–Gold Medalist! "Gazzelle Nera!" "Perle Noire!" "Wilma!" "Skeeter!" A hundred thousand throats fed the reverberating din of merged accents, and hats, newspapers, programs, and autograph books rained down on the emerald-green field as the lean, brown girl half-circled, slowed, and jogged toward the sidelines. "Coach Temple! Coach Temple!" Wilma was crying as sister Tigerbelles, other athletes, and photographers mobbed her. She was the World's Queen of Track, flooding out tears of gratefulness for Coach Temple's long, persevering training, and for her mother's determination that a puny, crippled daughter must walk.

Back in the United States Wilma was so lionized that it was ten days before she could return to a clamorous home town. Clarksville's "Welcome Wilma Day" saw every school and business closed, and the entire population lined up to cheer the champion. But Wilma takes all such adulation in her graceful stride. She has settled quickly again into life at the University. She is winning races, indoors and out, wherever she runs. At school she is majoring in elementary education, preparing for a career of grammar-school teaching and coaching high-school girls' track. In the roles of teacher and coach she will pass on to other youngsters the important lesson she learned: that those who really want to can win.

Alex Haley, "The Queen Who Earned Her Crown," *The Rotarian,* May 1961, 38–39, 57–61.

6

Sport, the Civil Rights Movement, and Black Power, 1960s and 1970s

Introduction

If the first years of the civil rights movement largely reflected widespread hopes among blacks that equality and opportunity would prevail in all American institutions—not just on the playing fields—the 1960s and 1970s revealed the enormous obstacles that needed to be surmounted in order to reach that ideal. The most formidable challenge was, of course, to overcome the resistance by much of white America to opening up the political and economic system in the name of social justice. Critically, too, there was no one plan of action that could be pursued in order to put civil rights ideals into practice, to deal with patterns of discrimination in different places, or to take on the problem of widespread poverty in the United States. No unitary voice spoke for Afro-America; the movement had many leaders. Martin Luther King Jr. and Malcolm X—each in his own way—mastered the media; so did Stokely Carmichael. Yet those who have studied the civil rights era in close detail have been compelled to examine the everyday actions of "local people," who ultimately created an awe-inspiring organizational and administrative complex at the grassroots level and orchestrated lunch counter sit-ins, freedom rides, and voter registration drives. Ultimately, we know a lot about the members of the Southern Christian Leadership Council (SCLC) and the Student Non-Violent Coordinating Committee (SNCC). The history of the march from Selma to Montgomery, moreover, has been recounted in the most dramatic and inspirational terms, both in memoir and on film. Many of the other heroes of the civil rights crusade, though, worked with a telephone, cranked a mimeograph machine, or walked onto the wooden porch of an isolated farmhouse, then managed to direct the ensuing conversation toward the U.S. Constitution. This is how, in part, the most significant social transformation in twentieth-century America took place.

There were many other dimensions to black liberation in America, however, and sports would play a substantial role in the larger debates concerning the changing political, economic, and social order. The image of the African American athlete was among the most powerful—and controversial—representations of the desire by civil rights crusaders and black power activists to alter the racial landscape for good. Should black athletes simply play the role of model citizens, go about their business, and represent the race through their abilities in sporting competition, or could the platform of sports be transformed to make more expansive statements about race relations and social justice in America? What forms should protest take? Could, in fact, black athletes exert a lasting influence on the dominant culture, or was the sports page too far removed from the headline news for African American athletes to make a difference? Ultimately, if muscular assimilation represented part of a broader set of ideals, what was its relationship to a strenuous cultural nationalism—captured in the phrase "Black Power" and embodied in the protests by an increasing number of black activists, athletes included?

These questions emerged against a backdrop of enormous dedication and courage displayed by civil rights marchers and freedom riders during the middle years of the 1960s. What was occurring in the White House and on Capitol Hill would have a huge impact on race relations in the years to come; the Civil Rights Act (1964) and the Voting Rights Act (1965) marked the high tide of the "Second Reconstruction." Indeed, the conscience of the nation was being tested in the corridors of power in Washington, D.C. But the flashpoints for social change were places like Birmingham, Alabama. There, news agencies from around the world recorded on film the powerful fire hoses and snarling police dogs unleashed on black protesters. From around the nation, many people—including some black athletes—spoke out against the violence then sweeping through the Deep South, as well as the history of racism in America.

Many African Americans in the sports world, however, remained notably silent, and this was a constant source of tension during the civil rights years. The debate took shape in several ways. One concerned the backgrounds and personalities—as well as the political stances—of black boxing champions. The Patterson-Liston fight of 1963 and the ring career of Muhammad Ali from the early 1960s through the mid-1970s focused attention on the image projected by athletes who represented the race. For his part, Ali spent much of the 1960s and 1970s challenging the mainstream social order. Later, such sports heroes as Jesse Owens and Arthur Ashe would comment on the burdens placed on them by the African American community to speak out and would then join the protest against discrimination in sport and the world beyond. The best strategies, they would assert, are only perceived in retrospect. Another issue, probably the most explosive one of the 1960s, linked African American sportsmen to black power when a boycott of the 1968 Olympics was proposed. That initiative failed, yet the photo of the black-gloved fists raised in protest by Tommie Smith and John Carlos while they stood on the medals podium after the 200-meter finals in Mexico City was probably the most widely circulated sports image of the decade.

What black athletes could accomplish by means of overt political protest has remained a controversial issue. But activism can occur in different registers. In demonstrations of skill, strength, and speed as well as the acumen needed to succeed at the top levels of sport, black athletes subverted longstanding stereotypes. Their excellence, as well as their increasing numbers in baseball, football, basketball, and boxing, made compelling statements about the need to change the culture and consciousness of the nation at large. It is here that the civil rights movement in the United States coincided with efforts for political liberation by peoples of color around the globe. American foreign policy during these years was a fiasco. Between the quagmire of Vietnam and covert actions elsewhere, the United States government gained a reputation for arrogance and extreme brutality. So it should not come as a surprise that in many emerging nations—in Africa especially—the most widely recognized and highly regarded figure emanating from America during the 1970s was not a political official but rather Muhammad Ali.

A

SPEAKING OUT AND HANGING IN

1. "Negro Athletes and Civil Rights"

The civil rights movement of the 1960s posed a serious dilemma for many African American athletes. Pressured by more militant blacks to become involved in the struggle, athletes could either actively take part in the black protest movement and jeopardize their careers or acquiesce to the white power structure and risk being labeled "Uncle Toms." Black athletes, faced with these complex alternatives, had to negotiate their lives very carefully in order to maintain their careers and exhibit the racial pride and sense of dignity so crucial in the African American community's crusade for equality and opportunity. Black athletes as a group during this period confronted their numerous constraints with varying amounts of commitment, ingenuity, and sophistication. At times they actively protested racial discrimination, while on other occasions they expressed a somewhat distant solidarity with those involved in the protest movement. Sometimes, too, they remained silent on racial issues. In large measure, black athletes during the civil rights era had to balance individual ambition and collective action, a difficult proposition for a group who knew full well that conformity and a certain deference to authority were the typical behaviors essential for survival in sport.*

Ultimately, conscience and social commitment are individual as much as collective matters. The following article from Sepia *lodges a complaint against those African Americans who were attacking black athletes for not becoming more involved in the civil rights movement. Referring to the pressure being exerted by various black activists and civil rights organizations, including Mal Whitfield's proposed boycott of the 1964 Olympic Games, the article argues that it was unfair to insist that black athletes become more militant and involve themselves in picket lines, boycotts, and other racial demonstrations.** First, not every black athlete was suited to be an active participant in the civil rights movement. Second, black athletes had already done a great deal for civil rights through their outstanding performances on the athletic field. Although militancy was one approach to rectifying racial problems, triumphs by black athletes had actually "reached more anti-Negro people" and "changed more anti-Negro hearts." Last, and perhaps most important, the piece in* Sepia *maintains that any suggestion that black athletes withhold their services in international sport as a show of protest would be counterproductive since boycotting would deny them "singular moments of glory" and would have a negative effect on both their race and American society.*

———— ————

---

* See D. Wiggins, "The Notion of Double-Consciousness"; Spivey, "Black Consciousness."
** Mal Whitfield suggested a boycott of the 1964 Olympic Games in his article "Let's Boycott the Olympics."

In the past year, a scatter-gun attack has been leveled at Negro athletes by people who believed that they should take a more active part in various civil rights movements. When the going was roughest for a great Negro major league baseball player in 1963, a Negro attorney, once head of a local civil rights organization, wrote him a blistering letter, charging that the player's failure was due to a feeling of guilt over his failure to go home to Birmingham and join the picket lines. From the safety of his office, a writer claimed that then-world's heavyweight champion Sonny Liston was "gutless" because he didn't participate in the same fray.

More recently, an ex-Olympian has suggested that Negro athletes boycott the 1964 Olympic Games in Tokyo in protest over racial inequities here.

This scatter-gun attack has created controversy of a serious nature in one of the two substantial areas of American life where, generally speaking, democracy functions quite effectively on the performance level. This area is sports. The other is show business. The three examples mentioned here are, perhaps, the notable ones; but there have been many others. The letter to the baseball player was vicious and insulting. The charge against Liston was, at best, curious, since many Negro leaders had openly expressed their shame and disappointment when Sonny first won the title from Floyd Patterson because in their opinion, Sonny wasn't "a proper" representative of the race (whether he was or not seemed pointless, when these same people never protested the presence of others with similar, or near-similar, histories in boxing, a sport never noted for its Sunday School aspects). The advisor of prospective 1964 Olympians was, at the time, promoting public tours to the Olympic Games!

The basic question—should Negro athletes be civil rights fighters?—goes deeper than selected incidents or personalities. It now involves, in many cases, the situation or problem or case of "Black Nationalism" and the widespread intolerance, on the part of publicized civil rights demonstrators, of all Negroes who aren't walking picket lines or laying their bodies down in front of trucks, or sitting in or wading in or getting "in" in some other way. This form of intolerance, no better than any other form of intolerance, hits certain Negroes over the head with the bag of guilt complex, regardless of whether they are suited for the picketing role just as the "you did it to us" line flays Caucasian Americans as a group, regardless of how constructively liberal they may be, or actually have been. It is the scatter-gun aspect of this form of attack which is tragic. The people firing the guns are, in most cases, operating on one-track minds; in some cases they are snobs; in others, they are faddists. The latter statement may sound harsh, but the obvious fact is, the mass demonstrations of 1963, so highly publicized in the public press, amounted to no more than a fad, like the Twist, for a considerable number of follow-the-crowd participants.

Among the hoi-polloi of Negroes, the self-proclaimed intellectuals among the teachers, preachers, and other professionals, athletes often have been persona non grata. The mere idea that Jackie Robinson, the all-time great Brooklyn Dodger, might make a fine NAACP executive secretary elicited nothing but guffaws from representatives of this branch of the Negro race.

Then there was the time when a Negro athlete, head of a professional basketball team, tried with all his might to obtain non-obligatory consent from a major civil rights organization for a series of twelve benefit games on its behalf, guaranteeing net proceeds in the vicinity of $50,000. The top functional executive of the civil rights organization, though crying poverty all over the nation, apparently couldn't find the time to 1) meet with the athlete; 2) answer letters from him; 3) or give serious consideration to the idea.

The suggestion that Negroes boycott the 1964 Olympic Games may carry the suggestion of important weight, since it was made by an ex-Olympian. On the other hand, this idea, coupled with the charge that Negro athletes should be more militant generally, points up a gross fault committed by many Negroes today, which is: lack of interest in the national welfare as well as racial welfare. No one who thinks can say that things in America are racially perfect; but, on the other hand, Negroes are members of the American family. If Negroes boycott the Olympic Games, meaning primarily, the male athletes, then it is an almost-certain fact that the Russians will win and the resulting Communist propaganda will embarrass our country.

Members of a family don't do things like this to each other. Instead, they close ranks in times of adversity or threatened adversity. They may fight like dogs among themselves, but they don't raise the shutters for the world to show their fights in their homes. While Negroes fight on the home front, as members of the American family, for full-fledged equality, fully deserved and no mistake about it, they, like all other Americans, have obligations to the United States too. Sitting home, depriving America of its best shot against other nations in the Olympics, personally depriving themselves of singular moments of glory, is hardly to be construed as a constructive idea. Why? Because, competing on equal terms in the East and West, in the North and South of the United States, these athletes (track and field) have proven that the races can pull together for the greater good of all; they have changed some important Caucasian thinking from negative to positive. They have wrought repeated good on the international level. Hitler's Aryan superiority theories were made a worldwide joke in 1936 when Jesse Owens and Company flashed to victory after victory in the Olympic Games at Berlin.

Now, the suggestion is, Negro athletes should desert the United States, embarrass their country before the world, on the theory that this will do some good at home. Will sheer folly accomplish any more good than active participation?

The whole thing boils down to this: Not every Negro is suited for the boycott or the picket line. This approach to the solution of the Negro's problems here is only one prong, one prong only, in what should be a diversified attack on the conditions that plague us. Full equality will not be achieved solely by boycotts. Nor will it be achieved solely by demonstrations. There are many more, perhaps even greater, obligations on both sides. Negro athletes already have done more than most to "make things better" in this country. They deserve far more credit than they receive; they don't deserve the scatter-gun attack leveled against them; they shouldn't be asked to play "unnatural" roles.

Long before protest demonstrations became a national entity, Joe Louis was changing anti-Negro attitudes to pro-Negro attitudes. No American civil rights fighter has yet reached the 300 million (or more) people as Willie Mays does, around the world, in a World Series. Two years prior to the Supreme Court's momentous school integration decision, Negroes starred in Southern baseball and three years prior to the Supreme Court's decision, Southern baseball was integrated. Integrated baseball was seen and accepted in such states as Louisiana, Tennessee, Georgia, Florida, and Virginia long before local authorities got around to serious consideration of overall democracy. Baseball fought segregated housing, eating facilities, segregation in other areas in the South.

Major league clubs have invested heavily in Dixie hotels and motels because they didn't want their Negro players embarrassed at spring training camps.

All pro sports, and many representatives of amateur sports, have brought democracy to bear on otherwise segregationist areas in the last few years. Whether the pro-Negro action has come voluntarily or because of pressure, the Negro athletes rarely have failed to hold up their end of the "bargain" on the field. In most cases, they've suffered in silence the "behind-the-scenes" insults and frustrations because they wanted to make the more important public impression.

So called "militant" Negroes who don't know the score come forth with rash suggestions, suggestions which, in most cases, would do the Negro race more harm than good. Where is the gain if Willie Mays quits the Giants for a time to walk picket lines in Birmingham and, because of his absence, the San Francisco Giants, to which he also has an obligation, loses a pennant in the National League? Where is the gain if Sonny Liston, bowing to his critics, goes into Dixie on a civil rights mission, is water-hosed, and decides, in a natural reaction, to fight back? Where is the gain if Negro track stars rebel in force this year and leave their own country in the lurch while the Russians, who don't give a hang about Negroes except in exploitation terms, run away with the gold medals?

All this isn't to say that Negro athletes should shun the militant role. Not at all. Where a Negro athlete feels that he should participate in militant actions, then he should. Bill Russell, the great center of the pro-basketball Boston Celtics, had something he wanted to get off his chest in a militant way last winter and he did so. His article, published in a major, general-circulation magazine, created a controversy; but it wreaked no havoc on his career and, by its very nature, it set many people to thinking.

Jackie Robinson has never bitten his tongue, not since he achieved stardom in pro sports and release from the temporary commitment to "keep the peace" he made with Branch Rickey, about civil rights subjects. But it should be remembered that, first, Bill Russell and Jackie Robinson are genuinely sensitive to racial problems, and second, they are well-educated, well-spoken, brilliant-minded men. They are equipped, personally and professionally, for the roles they play.

Not every athlete, just as not every Negro, is suited for the obviously militant role. Not every athlete is a public speaker, or a picket-line walker; but then, not all Negro businessmen, teachers, lawyers, dishwashers are members of the clan.

A Willie Mays who makes a fine, clutch catch or hits a pennant-winning home run does a great deal of good. Every time Jimmy Brown scores a touchdown, a pure segment of America cheers. Every time Wilt Chamberlain dunks a shot for the San Francisco Warriors or Oscar Robertson makes an assist for the Cincinnati Royals or a Negro scores a point for a Dixie team, a little bit of good is done for the race, the nation and the world. Collectively, Negro athletes have reached more anti-Negro people, changed more anti-Negro hearts, than any other professional group now in existence. The sheer weight of their public suggests this. Negroes who look down their noses on Negro athletes from the grandiose heights of certain race relations theories are merely whistling Dixie.

"Negro Athletes and Civil Rights," *Sepia*, June 1964, 35–39.

2. Chet Walker / "On the Road in the South, 1960"

Chet Walker was one of the outstanding basketball players of his era. Born in 1940, Walker was a high school basketball star in his hometown of Benton Harbor, Michigan. He continued his basketball career at Bradley University in Illinois, where he scored 1,975 points and collected 1,036 rebounds during his four years of play. These accomplishments, combined with his great all-around skills and team play, helped him garner second-team honors his junior year and first-team honors his senior year on the Sporting News *all-American teams. In 1962, Walker was a second round NBA draft choice by the Syracuse Nationals (later the Philadelphia 76ers) and went on to an outstanding thirteen seasons in the league. He averaged in double figures, played in seven all-star games, and scored a total of 18,831 points during his NBA career. Alongside Hal Greer, Luke Jackson, and Wilt Chamberlain, in 1967, Walker helped lead the 76ers to the NBA championship.** *

Here, Walker details the racial discrimination that he and his African American teammates confronted during the Bradley basketball team's 1960 road trip in the South. He describes being denied hotel accommodations and restaurant service as well as facing the ever-present racial slurs and Confederate flag waving. Walker explains that he became so despondent over his treatment in the South that he came close to leaving school or flunking out intentionally. Ultimately, Walker recognized that he was only a "commodity" to Bradley, "valuable as a sports hero, but not as a young black man."

–––––– ––––––

In my sophomore year (1959–60) at Bradley, I scored 111 points in my first three games. I was elevated from being a former high school basketball hero in Benton Harbor to a campus hero at Bradley, and the national press began to spread the news. We were ranked fourth in the nation behind the University of California, Cincinnati with Oscar Robertson, and West Virginia with Jerry West. I felt that I was about to join the basketball elite. Such was the high point of my optimism about equality through sports.

With all this attention, I began to feel pretty good about myself. Maybe my celebrity meant I no longer had to feel inferior. Maybe we were all equal. Basketball really could take me a long way in American society. But I lost that notion on my first road trip in the Deep South, where I had been born.

As we prepared to take our first extended trip of the season to St. Louis, Houston,

––––––––––––––

* For details on Walker's career, in addition to his autobiography, see Porter, *Biographical Dictionary*, 315–16.

Chet Walker above the rim (Special Collections Center, Bradley University Library)

and Denton, Texas, Coach Chuck Orsborn called in the black players on the team—Al Saunders, Bobby Joe Mason, Mack Herndon, and me—to remind us that we had to expect racism and offensive treatment, that it was just the way things were and there was nothing he or we could do about it. Implicit was the idea that we better not cause any incident that would reflect badly on the team or on Bradley. The message was that the South was going to be different because we were different: this is your lot, accept it, don't make waves if you want to play.

Orsborn was in fact warning us about what was to come. I heard him but didn't really believe it. The warnings sort of went in one ear and out the other. I thought I was on my way to being an All-American. I was bigger than all this race business. Orsborn had been through this sort of discrimination against some of his black players in previous years. But this was a kind of blackmail I didn't yet understand. Our white teammates gave us little sympathy; if they gave it a thought, they seemed just to accept Orsborn's views because they never said anything about it.

Bradley's first road trip in 1960 began in St. Louis. Before the game that night, the St. Louis University band marched out playing "Dixie," and we came out on the court surrounded by a sea of waving Confederate flags, which almost made me sick to my stomach; to me, going onto that court was like running headlong into a military rally. But we had a great strategy to counter the fan's attention to the band. We would commence to dunk everything in sight during lay-up drills. We would throw stuff down off spins and swoops, and jam balls up to our elbows. That would make the people stop listening to and wailing "Dixie." They would start oohing and aahing at our moves. When we'd totally distracted the Confederate singalong, we would stop just like that and make sedate little lay-ups, and everyone would say, "Awwhh . . ." Once the game began, however, it was business as usual. With racial taunts and slurs stinging our ears, our 81-71 victory was doubly sweet.

After the game, Al, Bobby Joe, and I went for dinner at a Chinese restaurant near the hotel. We went in and sat down, amidst all the lanterns and little miniature pagodas. I felt like a real man of the world. The smells coming from the kitchen were delicious. Through the swinging doors to the kitchen we could see the skinned ducks hanging feet first just ready for the pot. But I became aware that other customers were giving us strange looks. Before we could warm the seats of the booth, the cook, who I assumed was the owner, came out of the kitchen screaming and yelling. He didn't speak English very well, but we all understood what he was saying: "No serve color, no serve colored." Some white customers seemed to take great delight in seeing this tiny Chinese man run big colored boys out the door. To them it was entertainment.

Bobby Joe Mason and Al Saunders didn't have the same intense reaction to the Deep South that I did. Bobby Joe was from Centralia, a town in southern Illinois, and Al was from Chicago. They certainly knew racism. But for me, going back to the South was a nightmare. Everything from my early years in Mississippi came back as if I'd been returned to jail. What was another slight for them was deeply painful to me. I was naive to think I'd left it all behind.

The three of us went back to the hotel and stayed hungry because there was nowhere we could eat. We were not allowed in the hotel restaurant, and it was too late for room service. I tossed and turned with my stomach growling. It didn't help to know that our white teammates probably had a good meal and a good night while we were hungry and depressed. Yet we were supposed to carry on as if nothing had happened and, not incidentally, carry the team. Why didn't we protest? We knew if we did that Bradley University might accuse us of being troublemakers. We would get the blame. We felt our only choice was to let the incident pass and wait for breakfast.

The road trip moved to Houston, Texas, where the team was refused hotel accommodations because of our black players. So we were all moved to the student dormitories at the University of Houston. The only reason the black players got to stay with the white players was that because it was Christmas vacation time at the university, the administrators made an exception for us "under the circumstances." So we stayed in the girls dorm at Houston, but we still had to get our meals across town at Texas Southern University, a black school.

Such endless maneuvering just to eat and sleep somewhere took its toll on us. During warm-ups for the Houston game, fans threw lit cigarette butts on the floor at us and screamed, "Nigger!" I was in a state of great confusion and frustration, and scored only one point in the first half, wondering why I was subjecting myself to such abuse. At halftime, Coach Orsborn had a different take on the game. He was all over me in the dressing room. He berated me, yelling, "Don't quit on me, Chet. Just don't quit on me!" With a final sneer he concluded more softly, "All-American, my ass!"

Well, there it was, the accusation that I didn't have what it took when the going got rough. He didn't care about the trauma of this trip to a nineteen-year-old kid. He just wanted to win, and I was supposed to help him. To Orsborn, I could see I was basically a black kid who played basketball well. I wanted to put all the blame on him, but I knew it was my shock at my new life coming apart. My fleeting sense of equality was gone. Heaven help me if I permanently lost the ability to play basketball. I came out and scored more than 20 points in the second half, but we lost a close game.

Our last stop on the trip was North Texas State in Denton, Texas, a real pit. By that time our anger had reached the boiling point. The night before the game, Al, Bobby Joe, and I left the hotel (where, of course, we couldn't eat) to get some burgers at the White Castle down the street. As we walked back and stood on the corner waiting for the light to change, a car full of white guys slowed to a crawl, and a low voice growled out the car window, "Nigger, I don't want to catch you on the street after dark."

Without saying anything, we all knew that someone would have to pay for this whole road trip, but we also knew we could exact this punishment only on the court. At the arena in Denton, we faced the usual screaming, hostile crowd. The Missouri Valley Conference crowds were almost always all-white, but in Denton, we could see a few black fans huddled in a high corner. A black player notices things like that when he's on the road.

Two minutes into the game, a big redneck on the North Texas State team jammed Saunders in the throat with an elbow. It was just the incident to set things off. Al threw one of the prettiest right hands I've ever seen in my life and laid him out. A free-for-all began, and both benches emptied. Police came on court to break it up, and our team was escorted back to the locker room. After a fifteen-minute delay, the game continued with police holding hands and ringing the court. Stowell and Orsborn were scared to go back out on the court, but I never felt so good in my life. It was a small vindication. We went back out and played a great game, and I scored 40 points. We always had a mission to get after teams in these racist strongholds on the road.

I vividly remember my white teammate Ed Wodka, a great big Polish guy from Fenger High School in Chicago, fighting beside us in the Denton melee as if he felt our pain. He fought for us, and with us, as if it were the last moment of his life. Somehow he was with us. We never talked about that moment. Al, Bobby Joe, and I never discussed race with our white teammates. We didn't know if they wanted to talk about it, and we all would have been uncomfortable if they had.

I will never forget those games, those fans, those towns, and the way I felt. After we returned to school, I called my mother and told her I wasn't sure that I could keep going. Everything had turned so ugly. I said I couldn't stay at Bradley.

When she was able to get a word in, she said, "Let me ask you a question. If you leave school, is that gonna change racism? If you leave school is that gonna change the coach's opinion?" I said, "Nope." "So why are you going to leave?" she asked. "Chester, it's not a perfect world. You have to find the good and enjoy it, make the most of it. Chester, we survived living in Mississippi. We survived living in the projects. Chester, you mean to tell me that you can't survive three years in Peoria?"

Despite my mother's attempt to brace me, I was so upset that my mind raced through various scenarios—all of which revolved around my getting away from Bradley, from Peoria, and from the specter of more southern trips. I thought of transferring, especially to Michigan State, which would have put me closer to home in Benton Harbor. One day, Orsborn called me into his office and told me Fordy Anderson, the Michigan State coach, was on the line. Anderson said it would be in my best interest to stay at Bradley and that he wouldn't accept me as a transfer student. The two coaches had rigged the deal, and I could see that Orsborn was not about to lose me to some other team.

I became desperate enough to consider flunking out. If I couldn't play for another school, I would just fail and go home. Of course, my lack of self-confidence had taken over. Like countless black kids before and after me, I'd been placed in a white society that seemed unnavigable. I had no support systems. I was lonely. My options were zero. I remember taking a music appreciation course that spring. For the final exam we listened to recorded selections and then identified the composer, such as Mozart or Bach. I scrawled across the top of my exam, "The only music I can appreciate is the Blues," and then left the rest of the paper blank. The professor gave me a C and wrote on the exam that I showed "great vision." So I was caught. Bradley would never let me flunk out! It sounds ridiculous today, but that's how I felt. Bradley had me as its employee; they had me as a commodity for as long as I was of use. If I publicly expressed my anger or desire to leave, they would destroy me.

Of course, once I found the resolve to stay and get everything I could from the experience, I was glad in a strange sort of way that I was so important. I was valuable as a sports hero. But not as a young black man. Not as a man. I knew that.

My time in the public eye lasted for roughly two decades, from the mid 1950s to the mid-1970s. During that time I experienced a constant ebb and flow of confidence and fear of failure, of shyness and suspicion coupled with a need to be liked and to trust people. One minute I was an All-American basketball player as full of myself as a powerful young man could be. But the next minute, I was reduced to the nigger in the doorway. No amount of sports heroism in America could change that. Early on I understood this doubleness and that it would never truly change for me. . . .

In St. Louis, after we were chased out of the Chinese restaurant, I thought of Jackie

Robinson and his legacy to black men and black athletes. He was a hard man to follow for all of us. Jackie had to hold all his pain and anger inside himself for so long. People praised Branch Rickey for combing the minor leagues to find just the right combination of brains, heart, talent, and character. He then told Jackie that he wanted a fighter but one "who had enough guts not to fight," who would turn the other cheek at all times when events and hatred become unbearable. Jackie was college-educated and militant enough to have been court-martialed for leading a bus boycott in the army. But Rickey knew Jackie was well spoken and mentally tough.

Sometimes I feel Rickey should have given Jackie permission to punch somebody's lights out. The incident might have resulted in a race riot, the end of the "great experiment." But suppose not? Suppose that Robinson's courage had validated an outward expression of just anger? Suppose it was acknowledged that Jackie had a right to express that anger instead of being lionized for withholding it? Because Jackie had the great strength to endure, he set a precedent. All black athletes since have had to live up to his powerful dignity and forbearance. But my soul died a little each time a nightmare like that southern trip had to be lived through.

Chet Walker, with Chris Messenger, *Long Time Coming: A Black Athlete's Coming of Age in America* (New York: Grove, 1995), 77–82.

3. A. S. "Doc" Young / "Rebellion at Cal"

African American athletes played a significant role in the many racial protests that took place on predominantly white university campuses between 1968 and 1972. Shedding what seemed their customary conservative approach to racial matters, African American athletes became involved in the civil rights struggle and spearheaded what the political activist Jack Scott terms the "athletic revolution." They insisted on the hiring of African American coaches and other support personnel; they lodged complaints about everything from unfair dress codes to inadequate treatment by prejudiced athletic trainers; and they staged sit-ins and boycotts in response to what they believed were the racist policies of athletic departments and university administration.

The immediate consequences of these protests could be dramatic. On some campuses the disturbances were so intense that black athletes lost their scholarships, coaches resigned or were fired, athletic directors had their power curbed, special groups were established on campus to deal with the problems of racial discrimination, and national organizations such as the NAACP became involved in the campus uprisings. *

One of the most highly publicized racial disturbances involving African American athletes took place on the campus of the University of California, Berkeley. A center for the counterculture, the antiwar movement, and the civil rights struggle, the Berkeley campus was rocked at the beginning of 1968 by a dispute pitting the school's head basketball coach, Rene Herre-

---

* For information on African American athletes and racial disturbances on predominantly white university campuses, see Edwards, *Revolt of the Black Athlete;* Scott, *Athletic Revolution;* D. Wiggins, "The Year of Awakening"; idem, "The Future of College Athletics."

rias, against his African American players. This fray is the focus of the following document by A. S. "Doc" Young, the longtime sportswriter of the Chicago Defender. *Young, who would be an outspoken opponent of Harry Edwards and the proposed boycott of the Mexico City Olympic Games later in the year, was generally correct in his analysis of the dispute at Berkeley (although Bob Presley was initially dismissed from the team by Herrerias for missing a practice rather than for the length of his hair) and obviously sympathetic to the plight of African American athletes on campus. Young would also prove to be prophetic when he wrote that "the crisis isn't over at Cal." In fact, within the two months following the grievance, Pete Newell resigned his position as athletic director and Herrerias stepped down as basketball coach. In addition, Berkeley, like so many of the institutions involved in racial confrontations with African American athletes, put together a fact-finding committee that recommended, among other things, that the athletic department make a more serious effort to recruit minority coaches and administrators, develop a recruitment program that was consistent with the university's policy of nondiscrimination, and establish an in-service program that would enable its members to become more sensitive about minority issues and concerns. These reforms were among the broader legacies of campus protests in the 1960s, although it was not the creation of special committees alone that eased racial tension at many predominantly white institutions of higher learning. That process would begin only when white administrators, professors, and students more fully accommodated themselves to the notion of integration.*

––––– –––––

At the University of California the other day, Caucasian basketball coach Rene Herrerias suspended Negro star Bob Presley for "undisclosed reasons," and, thereby, opened up a barrel of rotten apples. Or, to be more precise, rotten racial relations. It was the sort of thing that is popping up ever more frequently in the sports page, the sort of thing which just might replace box-scores and sports stories, per se, if certain people don't get smart, quick.

Briefly, this is what happened at Cal: Presley was suspended indefinitely under a nebulous charge. Presley was to claim that he was suspended because he wouldn't cut his "natural hair" (a rather handsome lad, Presley wears an extreme natural which, according to a UPI photo, could indeed stand both a cutting and a combing). A short time later, Presley was reinstated, whereupon the white players on Cal's team rebelled, claiming that Presley had lied about the hair incident and racial overtones, that he had been guilty of violating "basketball ethics" numerous times, and that Coach Herrerias had been pressured by the school administration into reinstating him. The white guys said they wouldn't play on the team under the circumstances.

The black players—about 35 Negro athletes on the campus—then organized a protest, demanding that three coaches, including Herrerias, be dismissed on the grounds of "general incompetence," lodging various charges of racial discrimination and demanding that the school administration hire "five or six" Negro coaches. Herrerias vacillated, issued nebulous statements. But, he announced a practice session and the broad hint was this: Whoever showed up for practice would play out the rest of the season. Meanwhile, he talked to the white guys, one of whom had been called

B

THE POLITICS OF PROTEST: THE 1968 OLYMPIC GAMES

4. Harry Edwards / "Mounting the Revolt"

Harry Edwards has been one of the most outspoken critics of racism in sport and the larger American society. Raised in East St. Louis and a basketball and track standout at both the interscholastic and intercollegiate levels of competition, Edwards first came to national attention in the fall of 1967 when he led a protest movement of black students at San Jose State that resulted in the cancellation of the season-opening football game between that institution and the University of Texas at El Paso. Shortly after the racial confrontation at San Jose State, Edwards assembled a group of well-known black athletes who participated in a boycott of the New York Athletic Club's one-hundredth-anniversary track meet in February 1968 and threatened not to compete that year in the Mexico City Olympic Games. Calling the venture the Olympic Project for Human Rights (OPHR), the black athletes ultimately elected to compete in the games, choosing instead other forms of protest against racial discrimination in America and around the world.*

The following selection provides details and background information about some of the events preceding the proposed boycott of the 1968 Olympic Games. Edwards makes clear that the black athletic revolt was inevitable and a legitimate aspect of the larger black liberation movement then taking place in America. He contends that black athletes were beginning to shed their more conservative approach to racial issues by speaking out against various forms of racism. Two examples Edwards provides to illustrate the newfound outspokenness of black athletes were Bill Russell's book Go Up for Glory *and the refusal of black players to participate in the 1965 American Football League's East-West all-star game in New Orleans. This latter event has attracted little scholarly attention, though it was important in the civil rights struggle.** As Edwards notes, the black athletes involved in the East-West all-star game displayed remarkable unity, a difficult task considering the number of players involved and the risks they took in confronting the sports establishment.*

---

* For information on Edwards, including his involvement in the 1968 Olympic protest movement, see Edwards, *The Struggle That Must Be*; idem, "The Olympic Project for Human Rights"; Spivey, "Black Consciousness and Olympic Protest Movements"; D. Wiggins, "The Year of Awakening."

** For details on the racial strife surrounding the 1965 American Football League's East-West all-star game, see Mix, "Was This Their Freedom Ride?"; Baker, *Sports in the Western World*, 290.

Poster for Olympic Project for Human Rights (OPHR) (from Harry Edwards, *The Revolt of the Black Athlete* [New York: Free Press, 1969])

RATHER THAN RUN AND JUMP FOR MEDALS
WE ARE STANDING UP FOR HUMANITY
WON'T YOU JOIN US?

The revolt of the black athlete in America as a phase of the overall black liberation movement is as legitimate as the sit-ins, the freedom rides, or any other manifestation of Afro-American efforts to gain freedom. The goals of the revolt likewise are the same as those of any other legitimate phase of the movement: equality, justice, the regaining of black dignity lost during three hundred years of abject slavery, and the attainment of the basic human and civil rights guaranteed by the United States Constitution and the concept of American democracy. It was inevitable that this revolt should develop. With struggles being waged by black people in the areas of education, housing, employment, and many others, it was only a matter of time before Afro-American athletes, too, shed their fantasies and delusions and asserted their manhood, faced the facts of their existence. The revolt was as inevitable as the rising of the sun. Within the context of the overall black liberation struggle, the revolt of the black athlete has its roots and draws its impetus from the resistance of black people in the dim and distant past to brutal oppression and callous exploitation. The movement for black liberation dates from the first moment that a black captive chose suicide rather than slavery. More recently, lynchings, murders, and beatings have served only to heighten their resistance and to give the movement new force and direction. And now, at long last, the black athlete has entered the arena as a warrior in the struggle for black dignity and freedom.

The Undercurrent of Revolt

The first publicly acknowledged indications that a revolt by black athletes was imminent came with the publication of Bill Russell's book *Go Up for Glory*. Unwilling to communicate the same old tired clichés, glittering generalities, and distortions, Russell in the book attempted to put the real sacrifices a famous black athlete endures and the rewards he receives in proper perspective. The consequences for Russell were severe. He was lambasted by the nation's leading Negro and white sport reporters; he was accused of being ungrateful and egotistical; and, of course, he was charged with the old ungrateful bit— "But look what sports, and coaches in particular, have done for you. Why, if it were not for basketball, you wouldn't be what you are today." But at least part of Russell's theme was that perhaps if it were not for him, basketball would not be all that it is today. His concern was not only for what basketball had done for him, but what white coaches and white-controlled amateur and professional basketball had done to him. This approach represented a radical departure from the fun-and-games, win-some-lose-some style of autobiography typically ghost-written for Negro and white sports stars.

Other early rumblings of revolt revolved around the issues of segregation and social discrimination. For instance, in the late fifties and middle sixties, there were numerous cases where black athletes refused to participate due to discrimination in spectator seating at athletic events or because of discriminatory practices encountered by athletes themselves. A firm indication that the revolt was brewing appeared in 1965 when the black athletes chosen to play in the American Football League's East-West All-Star game banded together and refused to play in New Orleans, Louisiana, because several of the Afro-American stars had been refused entrance to some of the city's social clubs. As a result of the athletes' threat to boycott the event, Joe Foss, then commissioner of the league, had the game moved to another city. This incident marked the first time in modern athletic history that a sporting event had actually been changed to another site because of discrimination against Afro-American participants. And the threat succeeded largely because of the unity among the black athletes involved, a unity forged from their firm conviction that they were men and that they in fact were going to be treated as such. From that time on, the days when black athletes would play the role of unthinking machines on the field and submissive sub-humans off the field were definitely numbered.

In the realm of amateur athletics there had been rumblings too. In 1960, someone suggested to Rafer Johnson that he boycott the Olympic games of that year in order to protest the treatment of black people by the police during the civil rights protests in the South. Johnson laughed the whole notion off and walked away. But the incident reached the press and was, from that day on, irrevocably planted in the minds of black people as perhaps yet another tool to use in dramatizing the gravity of the plight of Afro-Americans in racist white America.

In 1963, Dick Gregory, black human-rights activist, politician, and comedian, attempted to organize a boycott of the Russian-American Track and Field meet by black athletes. The boycott itself failed, but the brief movement gave impetus to the whole idea of utilizing amateur athletics as a means of dramatizing racial injustice. In 1964, Gregory once again found little support among the athletes, but Gregory did manage to get about a dozen people to picket the United States Olympic trials.

Once the black athletes who competed in the 1964 Olympic games arrived at Tokyo, there were new indications of the rising tide. There were rumblings in the American Olympic quarters centering around the treatment of the black Olympians on the U.S. team, treatment involving social activities, athletic assignments, and housing accommodations. The incidents were quickly settled, however, and the whole affair was hushed up by the press. But after the 1964 games, what hitherto had been merely rumblings turned into full-throated roars. The American press went to great ends to quiet the furor, but to no avail. At every major track meet that followed the games black athletes got together and talked about the possibility of a black boycott of the 1968 Olympics to be held in Mexico. They discussed the justifications for the move and also the possible ramifications.

Then, in the fall of 1967, two events occurred that brought all the talk and discussion to a head. First, Tommie Smith, in Tokyo for the University Games, casually commented that some black athletes would perhaps boycott the 1968 Olympics. He merely gave a simple answer to an equally simple inquiry. A Japanese sports reporter had asked, "Do I understand correctly that there is talk in America about the possibility that black American athletes may boycott the 1968 Olympic games at Mexico?" Smith answered, "Yes, this is true. Some black athletes have been discussing the possibility of boycotting the games to protest racial injustice in America." The effect of Smith's brief and noncommittal statement was immediate and its repercussions were enormous. The major American wire services and most of the country's sports pages carried the story, proclaiming that Tommie Smith had stated that there was considerable sentiment among black athletes favoring a boycott of the Olympic games in order to protest racial injustice. Of course, Smith at that time had made no such statement.

The second event was a revolt of black students and athletes at San Jose State College in California, which just happened to be the institution at which Tommie Smith and a number of other "world-class" athletes were matriculating. The significance of this event was that sixty of the seventy-two Afro American students on campus (out of a college enrollment of 24,000) had banded together and for the first time in history utilized collegiate athletics as a lever to bring about social, academic, and political changes at an educational institution. The whole plan for the revolt originated from a discussion between me and Kenneth Noel, then a master's degree candidate at San Jose State. He, like most of the black males on campus, was a former athlete. Most of the Afro-American males on San Jose State College's campus were former athletes who no longer had any college athletic eligibility left but who had not yet graduated for precisely the reasons discussed earlier. Ken was one of the three who had graduated after a six-year term as an undergraduate and then continued on for a Master of Arts degree. Our rather casual conversation centered around the old and the new aspects of life at San Jose for black students. After talking for about an hour, it suddenly dawned on us that the same social and racial injustices and discrimination that had dogged our footsteps as freshmen at San Jose were still rampant on campus—racism in the fraternities and sororities, racism in housing, racism and out-and-out mistreatment in athletics, and a general lack of understanding of the problems of Afro-Americans by the college administration.

Harry Edwards, *The Revolt of the Black Athlete* (New York: Free Press, 1969), 38–43.

5. The Boycott Debate: Tommie Smith on "Why Negroes Should Boycott" the Olympics, and Ralph Boston on "Why They Should Not"

It is clear that Harry Edwards and his Olympic Project for Human Rights (OPHR) never had unanimous support from the black athletes expected to participate in the 1968 Mexico City Olympics. From the very beginning of discussions about a possible boycott of the games that year, some black athletes supported the idea while others adamantly opposed it. Those who apparently supported a boycott, including most notably such athletes as John Carlos and Tommie Smith, argued that refusing to participate in the games would make the problems of racial inequality more visible to the American public and ultimately lead to increasing freedoms for blacks around the world. Those opposed to a boycott, including such athletes as Charles Greene and Ralph Boston, argued that participating in the games, and all sports for that matter, was one of the best ways to combat racial discrimination and improve the lives of all blacks. As it turned out, the large majority of black athletes—with the important exception of Lew Alcindor (now Kareem Abdul-Jabbar)—chose to participate in the games and demonstrate in other ways their dissatisfaction with the racial caste system in America. The most famous of these protests was the black-gloved power salutes of Smith and Carlos while on the Olympic victory stand following their first- and third-place finishes in the 200-meter dash.*

In the following documents, Tommie Smith explains his reasons for supporting a boycott while Ralph Boston details why he favored participation. Smith, the great sprinter from San Jose State, notes that he was not a militant but claims he would willingly participate in a boycott of the Olympics to further the cause of racial equality in America. Smith also makes it clear that the boycott was closely tied to his sense of self-worth and manhood, indicating he "would be less than a man" if he did not follow his conscience and fight for what he believed. Boston, the stellar long-jumper from Tennessee State who competed on three Olympic teams, explains that he was strongly opposed to an Olympic boycott. Although agreeing with the resolutions passed by the OPHR,** Boston argues that black athletes "can do more good for themselves and their race by going to the Olympics and doing well than they can by staying home."

---

* Abdul-Jabbar was heavily criticized for his refusal to participate in the 1968 Olympic Games. See Abdul-Jabbar and Knobler, *Giant Steps*, 170–72. Smith and Carlos were immediately suspended from the team and told to leave Mexico City within forty-eight hours following their victory-stand demonstration. For details, see D. Wiggins, "The Year of Awakening": idem, "The Notion of Double-Consciousness"; Matthews, *My Race Be Won*, esp. 191.

** The OPHR threatened a boycott unless several demands were met, including restoration of Muhammad Ali's heavyweight title; appointment of at least two blacks to the U.S. Olympic Committee; addition of at least two blacks to the Olympic track-and-field coaching staff; exclusion of both Southern Rhodesia and South Africa from Olympic competition; elimination of racial segregation in the New York Athletic Club; and removal of Avery Brundage as president of the International Olympic Committee. See Edwards, *Revolt of the Black Athlete*, esp. 38–69.

——— ———

Tommie Smith / "Why Negroes Should Boycott"

The Black Youth Conference, held in Los Angeles, Dec. 23–25, 1967, produced the accompanying resolution, with which I agree and for which I voted.

I have deep convictions that the proposed resolution, if upheld, would be beneficial to all Black men. I believe that total agreement, or something close to total agreement, is necessary for success in this. If my brothers and the majority of the outstanding Negro Olympic prospects cannot concur in this resolution and are not prepared to accept such action, then I will go on to fulfill my ambition to become an Olympian.

I act on my own, not on behalf of my family or any other individuals or groups. I believe my family had a harder life when I was growing up than the average family. My father, as Negro, did not have the opportunities to secure an education and to advance in life as are afforded many others in this country. I believe that when I was young I was not as aware of what was denied me as I am now.

We learn through observation and education. I know more now than I did when I was a boy. I know now, for instance, that Negroes do not have equality in the United States and do not have all of the rights supposedly granted them by the Constitution of the United States. What is right is right. What is wrong is wrong. I recognize wrongs and I am willing to fight for right.

I know politics enter into Civil Rights issues, but I am not a politician and I do not belong to any so-called "Black Power" organizations. Many persons apparently do not realize that there are many different such organizations and they have many different philosophies. I do not agree with everything every one of these groups does or believes. But they are my people and they are helping to fight my fight and I am sympathetic to them. If we are being kicked, we must begin to fight back.

I know Harry Edwards, the San Jose State College professor, and I respect him. He was one of the spokesmen of the Black Youth Conference and is in sympathy with the five-point resolution which emerged from it. I am not concerned with who was behind that conference or with who is behind the presently proposed Negro boycott of the Olympics or the other points on the proposal. I am only concerned with the fact that I sympathize with these and am prepared to join in the boycott. I am not helping to organize such a boycott. I am not seeking to talk anyone else into joining it. I am, however, lending my support to it.

I agree that segregation should be eliminated from the New York Athletic Club. I agree that if black athletes are not allowed to participate in South Africa, then white athletes from South Africa should be barred from participation in the Olympics and in the U.S. I agree that Negroes should be properly represented on the U.S. Olympic Committee and the U.S. Olympic team coaching staff. And I believe that Cassius Clay, who has asked that he be called Muhammad Ali, should be reinstated as heavyweight boxing champion of the world. Whatever the merits of his stand, he was lawfully convicted of refusing induction into the service, but he also is lawfully free on appeal, and so he has unlawfully and unfairly been stripped of his title. What is right is right.

I am not a militant. I am an extremist only where a fight for my rights as a human being are concerned. I recognize that Negroes have had greater opportunities in sports in general and the Olympics in particular than they have had in other field. But I am an athlete, I have stature only in the field of athletics, and any action I take can only be effective in the field of athletics. And I do not feel that Negroes have had fully equal opportunity in sports and in the Olympics. If a thing is not entirely right, one should fight to make it entirely right.

I believe a Negro boycott would hurt the U.S. cause in the Olympics. I believe it would cost the U.S. many medals and much world prestige. But I am not out to embarrass the U.S. or take revenge on my country. I wish to dramatize a cause in which I believe and to act in the only area I can act effectively. To emphasize my point, I have said I would give up my right arm to win a gold medal in the Olympics, but I would not give up my personal dignity.

I have trained and worked hard to achieve success in athletics. I have been prepared to train and work harder, to make many sacrifices, to attain the greatest goal any amateur athlete can have—participation in and success in the Olympic Games. I have dreamed of it most of my life. If I give it up, it will be painful to me, and probably will cost me prestige that will affect me the rest of my life.

But I am prepared to do just that if it will help my people gain full equality in their country. Just as a soldier is willing to die for his country, I am a member of the ROTC. I do not know what I would do if I were ordered to fight in Vietnam. I will cross that bridge when I get to it, if I do. It does seem, however, that I am standing at the bridge to the Olympics right now.

I have been asked why I did not and do not boycott athletics in college, at San Jose State, if I am willing to boycott the Olympics. Through athletics, I got a scholarship to San Jose State. Through my scholarship, I am getting an education. That is what I want for myself and what I want for all Negroes—a chance for an education. I am one of the lucky ones. I have athletics. I believe I am fighting for those who are not as lucky as I am.

I had no scholarship offers from Negro colleges. If I had, I would have considered them along with offers from white colleges. Negroes and Whites both attend San Jose State College. I would like to think the time is not far off when there are no "Negro" and no "White" colleges, but just colleges, open equally to all men. In choosing a college, I chose the one that I thought would be best for me, from among those I had a chance to attend.

I do not know if a Black boycott of the Olympics actually will take place. I do believe we have attracted attention to our cause by the stand we have taken and I do believe that a boycott is very possible. I believe the possibility of a successful boycott depends on Negroes acting as a group for their own good.

I believe some Negroes disagree with our stand. I believe they should stand up and be counted, as we are standing up to be counted. It is not an easy thing to do, you know. Since I made my stand public, I have been ridiculed. The press has not come to me asking my opinions, but has used me to present their own opinions. I have been misquoted a great deal.

My real friends remain my real friends. Those who speak to me and welcome me only because I am a "name" athlete are not so kind to me now. I don't mind this. I want to be treated as a person, with a wife and a life outside of sports, not only as a man who can run fast. I don't care about those people who are my friends only when I win a race.

I am not entirely sure of my actions. No one could be. But I have searched my conscience and I am acting as I believe I should act. I am concerned that I may have harmed my "image" and thus damaged the future I hope to make for my family. I would be a fool not to be concerned. But I would be less than a man if I did not act for what I believe.

Everything I do is to the very best of my ability, whether it is striving to attain my human rights or striving to win a gold medal in the Olympics. But Black comes first. I say it flatly and simply, if there is a Negro boycott of the Olympics, I will participate in it willingly. If there is not, I will go to the Olympics and I will go to win.

Tommie Smith, "Why Negroes Should Boycott," *Sport,* March 1968, 40–41, 68.

RALPH BOSTON / "WHY THEY SHOULD NOT"

I know of the Black Youth Conference which was held in Los Angeles and of the resolutions which emerged from it. I am sympathetic to the motives of the conference and to some part of the resolutions, but not to all. I am very definitely not in favor of a Negro boycott of the Olympic Games. I know Tommie Smith. I like him and I admire him. I have gone over the statement he has made for Sport Magazine regarding his support of the Black Youth Conference resolutions and I agree with him on some points and I disagree with him on others.

Tommie Smith is standing up to be counted. He is taking a stand and voicing his opinions openly. This takes great courage, and I admire him for it. He says he believes some Negroes disagree with the stand he and others are taking and says he believes they should stand up and be counted, too. I agree and so I am going to do just that. I do not believe it is fair to call Negroes names such as "Uncle Tom" simply because they disagree with some of the stands taken by other Negroes.

I am a Negro and I want to make it very clear that I am proud I am a Negro and I would not want to be anything else. I do not believe Negroes have had equal rights or have enjoyed equal status in this country and I believe that it is good and right that we fight for our people and for what we should have, but there are different ways of fighting and one man's way is not necessarily the right way, nor does it necessarily have to be my way. I believe it is my duty as a Negro and as an athlete and as an American citizen to speak up for what I believe, and I do not believe I should be called names or shunned for it.

I also want to make it quite clear that I speak only for myself. I have been referred to as a spokesman for some Negro athletes, but I have no official appointment to that effect. If some Negro athletes wish to point to my statement and say they go along with it, as I believe many would, that is fine with me, but I do speak only for myself, a Negro, an athlete and an American.

As for the Black Youth Conference resolutions:

Ralph Boston in long-jump competition (*Sport Magazine*)

I competed in the New York Athletic Club indoor track meet in Madison Square Garden, New York, before I was aware the club practiced any segregation. And I have competed in it since I was aware of the charges. Frankly, I have always enjoyed competing in the NYAC meets. I understand they are planning to have the Russians in the next meet. If I am in shape, I would like the chance to compete against the Russians. I look forward to the meet. But I must say that I am totally opposed to any discrimination practiced by the NYAC and if this cannot be corrected and if there is a Negro boycott of NYAC events in the future, I'd support it. This is different from a Negro boycott of the Olympics. In general, the Olympics have treated Negroes equally and fairly.

I might point out in passing that I do not like the term "Jew" in connection with those who, along with Negroes, have reportedly been discriminated against by the NYAC. I prefer to say "people of Jewish faith" or something like that. The term "Jew" as applied to Jewish people reminds me of the term "Jap" when applied to Japanese people, and seems like something of a slur to me. I do not like "name-calling" in any form. I do not like discrimination in any form. I do not believe Negroes are the only people who have been discriminated against in this country or any other, and I think Negroes should be aware of this.

Jewish people have had to deal with discrimination. So have the American Indians. They were here first, this was their country, and we took it away from them, shoved them onto reservations and have generally treated them like dirt. I think Negroes should work to make conditions better for Indians, too. There is a term "poor White trash," which refers to a certain segment of our society, people who have been discriminated against, too. It has been said that "even poor White trash" can get jobs and so forth before Negroes, and this may be true, but people should work to help these people, too. As Tommie Smith says, right is right and wrong is wrong.

I have read of the problems Negroes face in South Africa and Rhodesia, though I have no personal knowledge of these. If true, they are totally unfair and I would like to see them corrected. Perhaps our country should insist that Negroes such as Tommie Smith and I be permitted to compete in South Africa and Rhodesia, but I do not believe two wrongs make a right. If we barred their athletes, we would be as wrong as they are in barring ours.

I have met Paul Nash and have been treated as a normal human being by him. I do not believe Paul Nash and Gary Player should be held totally responsible for the policies of their governments, no more than many Americans want to feel totally responsible for our government's policies in Vietnam.

I know Stanley Wright, a Negro and one of our Olympic coaches, and I think he is a great guy and a great coach and a fair man. I believe he is fair to all athletes, including Negroes, and I would like to see him continue as an Olympic coach. I do not believe it is right or serves any useful purpose simply to label Mr. Wright or Jesse Owens as "Uncle Toms" because they do not agree with some Negroes on some issues. I do not believe we Negroes have been as well represented on the Olympic committee or coaching staff as we should be and I believe we should fight for the right men to represent us, white or black, but I do not pretend to know who all the right men or wrong men are. These are very deep issues and I don't think we should pass hasty judgment on any man.

I do agree that Muhammad Ali should not have been stripped of his title. I think, as Tommie has pointed out, he remains lawfully free on appeal, and so has this time been hastily deprived of his title. In this country a man is supposed to be innocent until proven guilty. I do not know if the actions taken against him were taken because he is a Negro, but if so, this is racial discrimination at its worst. Whatever the reason, he has been discriminated against, and, as Tommie says, wrong is wrong.

But I do totally disagree with a Negro boycott of the Olympics. I believe sports has generally afforded Negroes more opportunity to do good for themselves and for their people than any other area of our life, so I do not believe we should punish these for wrongs committed by others. I agree with Tommie that Negroes have not been treated entirely fairly in sports; and, like him, I believe we should work to correct this, to make something which is not entirely right as right as it can be. But I do not believe a boycott will help this. I believe Negroes can do more good for themselves and their race by going to the Olympics and doing well than they can by staying home.

I might point out that the Olympics stand for competition among individuals, not among nations. American Negroes who stay home will not be denying our country any official points or medals, they will only be denying themselves.

I have gone to the Olympics. I have won there and I have lost there. I have never been prouder than when I stood highest on a platform with a gold medal draped around my neck and heard The Star Spangled Banner being played in recognition of my accomplishment.

I personally grew up poor. My father worked on a farm. I worked on a farm. Of course I have not had it as bad as some Negroes. And, I must admit sadly, I feel some prejudice against Whites for the way Negroes have generally been treated. But I do feel that there have been very definite improvements for the Negroes in the U.S. in recent years. There just haven't been enough and they haven't come swiftly enough.

So I can understand the deep bitterness many Negroes feel and the desperate desire to make their bitterness heard. I understand Tommie Smith when he says that since he is an athlete he feels athletics is the area in which he must act, but I do not agree with the particular action he has chosen to take.

These are deep, complex problems. I do not pretend to have all the answers. I do not know what is right or wrong. I only know what I feel is right and wrong, and how I think we should act. I don't believe rioting, looting, destroying, is the way to show we deserve fair treatment. I don't believe a boycott of the Olympics is the way to show we deserve fair treatment. But I must admit that I understand and have sympathy for those Negroes who feel drastic action is necessary.

I am not for a boycott of the Olympics and I hope it never comes off. I think it is wrong, but let me say this: if there is a boycott and it is strongly supported by the great majority of Negro athletes, I would have to go along with it. I say this because I am a Negro, because I believe in Democratic principles, and because I would not want to do anything that the majority felt would be harmful to the cause of my people.

I believe the best thing Negroes can do is to help all Negroes get a first-rate education. I believe all progress must stem from education. I am grateful to athletics for helping me to get an excellent education. I have my bachelor's degree from college and I am currently doing my post-graduate work at Tennessee A&I in Nashville in quest of my Master's degree. I like to feel that I have earned respect, not just as an athlete or a Negro, but as an educated person, and I would like to think people look up to me in that regard. I hope to use whatever name I have from track, plus my education, to help all people who are discriminated against whenever and wherever I can.

I believe we should use athletics and the Olympics to further our cause. So I disagree with Tommie Smith and some others in this and in some other matters. But I admire him for standing up and speaking out and being prepared to act for what he and others believe is right. And I hope it will not impair my standing with him and the others if I stand up and speak out and act for what I believe is right.

Ralph Boston, "Why They Should Not," *Sport*, March 1968, 42–43, 68–69.

C

CULTURE AND DISSENT: BOXING

6. James Baldwin / "The Fight: Patterson vs. Liston" (1963)

Since the time when Jack Johnson first wore the belt of the heavyweight boxing champion, black intellectuals have highlighted the significance of that most elemental of sports. With Johnson (especially in the bout against Jim Jeffries) and then Joe Louis (especially in his contests against Max Schmeling), their fascination centered on the images of African American fighters as racial representatives battling numerous "white hopes." The 1963 match between Floyd Patterson and Sonny Liston, however, drew on different impulses and evoked a new set of considerations among black Americans—and numerous white commentators as well. Because of the contrasting backgrounds and demeanor of the titleholder and challenger, the Patterson-Liston bout prompted wide-ranging discussions about the measures of toughness and respectability that the heavyweight champ should embody.

Enter James Baldwin, who, in the brief time between the death of Richard Wright and the advent of the black arts movement, stood out as the most widely recognized African American intellectual on the scene. The year 1963 also marked the continuing controversy over his novel Another Country, *published the year before, and the first debates over his recently released essay* The Fire Next Time, *though the essay offered here seems to offer little insight into his more famous work. It is noteworthy that Baldwin's foray into "new journalism" and the world of sports contrasts enormously with the way Richard Wright celebrated the victories of Joe Louis and the ways artists of a later generation, such as Amiri Baraka and Ishmael Reed, would celebrate themselves as street-fighting poets. What Baldwin does with the buildup to the bout and then, only briefly, with the contest itself, is to deflate all the hype. He portrays two complex individuals, both troubled with the images of themselves that had been hacked together by the press. He shows them to be two athletes who seemed to him very different from one another in size and strength, though more similar than anyone else granted in terms of soul. Although he does not use the latter term, it seems to describe the basis for both fighters' tug on his sympathies. Before the contest even begins, Baldwin's view of the contrasting training camps reveals the ways black athletes were treated by the attendant contingent of journalists, who were overwhelmingly white. Within what Gerald Early has called the "culture of bruising," James Baldwin found two men whom he admits he did not fully understand. There was more to these boxers than most commentators would ever want to explore—and much less to the spectacle, the circus, surrounding the contest. It is that substance which makes Baldwin respect both of* *them, if only vaguely, not for what they were supposed to represent but for who they were as human beings.* *

———

We, the writers—a word I am using in its most primitive sense—arrived in Chicago about ten days before the baffling, bruising, and unbelievable two minutes and six seconds at Comiskey Park. We will get to all that later. I know nothing whatever about the Sweet Science or the Cruel Profession or the Poor Boy's Game. But I know a lot about pride, the poor boy's pride, since that's my story and will, in some way, probably, be my end.

There was something vastly unreal about the entire bit, as though we had all come to Chicago to make various movies and then spent all our time visiting the other fellow's set—on which no cameras were rolling. Dispatches of journalists invaded the Patterson or Liston camps, hung around until Patterson or Liston appeared; asked lame, inane questions, always the same questions, went away again, back to those telephones and typewriters; and informed a waiting, anxious world, or at least a waiting, anxious editor, what Patterson and Liston had said or done that day. It was insane and desperate, since neither of them ever really did anything. There wasn't anything for them to do, except training for the fight. But there aren't many ways to describe a fighter in training—it's muscle and sweat and grace, it's the same thing over and over—and since neither Patterson nor Liston were doing much boxing, there couldn't be any interesting thumbnail sketches of their sparring partners. The "feud" between Patterson and Liston was as limp and tasteless as British roast lamb. Patterson is really far too much of a gentleman to descend to feuding with anyone, and I simply never believed, especially after talking with Liston, that he had the remotest grudge against Patterson. So there we were, hanging around, twiddling our thumbs, drinking Scotch, and telling stories, and trying to make copy out of nothing. And waiting, of course, for the Big Event, which would justify the monumental amounts of time, money, and energy which were being expended in Chicago.

Neither Patterson nor Liston have the *color,* or the instinct for drama which is possessed to such a superlative degree by the marvelous Archie Moore, and the perhaps less marvelous, but certainly vocal, and rather charming Cassius Clay. In the matter of color, a word which I am not now using in its racial sense, the Press Room far outdid the training camps. There were not only the sports writers, who had come, as I say, from all over the world: there were also the boxing greats, scrubbed and sharp and easygoing, Rocky Marciano, Barney Ross, Ezzard Charles, and the King, Joe Louis, and

---

* See Gerald Early, "James Baldwin's Neglected Essay: Prizefighting, the White Intellectual and the Racial Symbols of American Culture," in *Tuxedo Junction,* 183–95, where he assesses Baldwin's relative indifference to sport in light of his homosexuality (that, indeed, Baldwin perceived the ring as homophobic ritual and spectacle) and contrasts Baldwin's essay with those of writers like Norman Mailer and Ben Hecht, who emphasize the (hetero)sexual dimension to the violence in the ring. See also Early, "The Black Intellectual and the Sport of Prizefighting" and "The Unquiet Kingdom of Providence," in *Culture of Bruising,* 5–65.

Ingemar Johansson, who arrived just a little before the fight and did not impress me as being easygoing at all. Archie Moore's word for him is "desperate," and he did not say this with any affection. There were the ruined boxers, stopped by an unlucky glove too early in their careers, who seemed to be treated with the tense and embarrassed affection reserved for faintly unsavory relatives, who were being used, some of them, as sparring partners. There were the managers and trainers, who, in public anyway, and with the exception of Cus D'Amato, seemed to have taken, many years ago, the vow of silence. There were people whose functions were mysterious indeed, certainly unnamed, possibly unnameable, and, one felt, probably, if undefinably, criminal. There were hangers-on and protégés, a singer somewhere around, whom I didn't meet, owned by Patterson, and another singer owned by someone else—who couldn't sing, everyone agreed, but who didn't have to, being so loaded with personality—and there was some improbable-looking women, turned out, it would seem, by a machine shop, who didn't seem, really, to walk or talk, but rather to gleam, click, and glide, with an almost soundless meshing of gears. There were some pretty incredible girls, too, at the parties, impeccably blank and beautiful and rather incredibly vulnerable. There were the parties and the post mortems and the gossip and speculations and recollections and the liquor and the anecdotes, and dawn coming up to find you leaving somebody else's house or somebody else's room or the Playboy Club; and Jimmy Cannon, Red Smith, Milton Gross, Sandy Grady, and A. J. Liebling; and Norman Mailer, Gerald Kersh, Budd Schulberg, and Ben Hecht—who arrived, however, only for the fight and must have been left with a great deal of time on his hands—and Gay Talese (of the *Times*), and myself. Hanging around in Chicago, hanging on the slightest word, or action of Floyd Patterson and Sonny Liston.

I am not an *aficionado* of the ring, and haven't been since Joe Louis lost his crown—he was the last great fighter for me—and so I can't really make comparisons with previous events of this kind. But neither, it soon struck me, could anybody else. Patterson was, in effect, the *moral* favorite—people *wanted* him to win, either because they liked him, though many people didn't, or because they felt that this victory would be salutary for boxing and that Liston's victory would be a disaster. But no one could be said to be enthusiastic about either man's record in the ring. The general feeling seemed to be that Patterson had never been tested, that he was the champion, in effect, by default; though, on the other hand, everyone attempted to avoid the conclusion that boxing had fallen on evil days and that Patterson had fought no worthy fighters because there were none. The desire to avoid speculating too deeply on the present state and the probable future of boxing was responsible, I think, for some very odd and stammering talk about Patterson's personality. (This led Red Smith to declare that he didn't feel that sports writers had any business trying to be psychiatrists, and that he was just going to write down who hit whom how hard, and where, and the hell with why.) And there was very sharp disapproval of the way he has handled his career, since he has taken over most of D'Amato's functions as a manager, and is clearly under no one's orders but his own. "In the old days," someone complained, "the manager told the fighter what to do, and he did it. You didn't have to futz around with the guy's *temperament,* for Christ's sake." Never before had any of the sports writers been compelled to deal directly with the fighter instead of with his manager, and all of them seemed baffled by this necessity and many were resentful. I don't know how they got along with D'Amato when he was running the entire show—D'Amato can certainly not be described as either simple or direct—but at least the figure of D'Amato was familiar and operated to protect them from the oddly compelling and touching figure of Floyd Patterson, who is quite probably the least likely fighter in the history of the sport. And I think that part of the resentment he arouses is due to the fact that he brings to what is thought of—quite erroneously—as a simple activity a terrible note of complexity. This is his personal style, a style which strongly suggests that most un-American of attributes, privacy, the will to privacy; and my own guess is that he is still relentlessly, painfully shy—he lives gallantly with his scars, but not all of them have healed—and while he has found a way to master this, he has found no way to hide it; as, for example, another miraculously tough and tender man, Miles Davis, has managed to do. Miles's disguise would certainly never fool anybody with sense, but it keeps a lot of people away, and that's the point. But Patterson, tough and proud and beautiful, is also terribly vulnerable, and looks it. . . .

Presently, here he came across the grass, loping, rather, head down, with a small, tight smile on his lips. This smile seems always to be there when he is facing people and disappears only when he begins to be comfortable. Then he can laugh, as I never heard him laugh at a press conference, and the face which he watches so carefully in public is then, as it were, permitted to be its boyish and rather surprisingly zestful self. He greeted Gay, and took sharp, covert notice of me, seeming to decide that if I were with Gay, I was probably all right. We followed him into the gym, in which a large sign faced us, saying *So we being many are one body in Christ.* He went through his workout, methodically, rigorously, pausing every now and again to disagree with his trainer, Dan Florio, about the time—he insisted that Dan's stopwatch was unreliable—or to tell Buster that there weren't enough towels, to ask that the windows be closed. "You threw a good right hand that time," Dan Florio said; and, later, "Keep the right hand *up. Up!*" "We got a floor scale that's no good," Floyd said, cheerfully. "Sometimes I weigh two hundred, sometimes I weigh 'eighty-eight." And we watched him jump rope, which he must do according to some music in his head, very beautiful and gleaming and far away, like a boy saint helplessly dancing and seen through the steaming windows of a storefront church. . . .

We followed him into the house when the workout was over, and sat in the kitchen and drank tea; he drank chocolate. Gay knew that I was somewhat tense as to how to make contact with Patterson—my own feeling was that he had a tough enough row to hoe, and that everybody should just leave him alone; how would I like it if I were forced to answer inane questions every day concerning the progress of my work?—and told Patterson about some of the things I'd written. But Patterson hadn't heard of me, or read anything of mine. Gay's explanation, though, caused him to look directly at me, and he said, "I've seen you someplace before. I don't know where, but I know I've seen you." I hadn't seen him before, except once, with Liston, in the Commissioner's office, when there had been a spirited fight concerning the construction of Liston's boxing gloves, which were "just about as flat as the back of my hand," according to a sports writer, "just like wearing no gloves at all." I felt certain, considering the number of people and the tension in that room, that he could not have seen me *then*—but we do know some of the same people, and have walked very often on the same streets. Gay suggested that he had seen me on TV. I had hoped that the contact would have turned out to be more personal, like a mutual friend or some activity connected with the Wiltwyck School, but Floyd now remembered the subject of the TV debate he had seen—the race problem, of course—and his face lit up. "I *knew* I'd seen you somewhere!" he said, triumphantly, and looked at me for a moment with the same brotherly pride I felt—and feel—in him.

By now he was, with good grace but a certain tense resignation, preparing himself for the press conference. I gather that there are many people who enjoy meeting the press—and most of them, in fact, were presently in Chicago—but Floyd Patterson is not one of them. I think he hates being put on exhibition, he doesn't believe it is real; while he is terribly conscious of the responsibility imposed on him by the title which he held, he is also afflicted with enough imagination to be baffled by his position. And he is far from having acquired the stony and ruthless perception which will allow him to stand at once within and without his fearful notoriety. Anyway, we trailed over to the building in which the press waited, and Floyd's small tight, shy smile was back.

But he has learned, though it must have cost him a great deal, how to handle himself. He was asked about his weight, his food, his measurements, his morale. He had been in training for nearly six months ("Is that necessary?" "I just like to do it that way"), had boxed, at this point, about 162 rounds. This was compared to his condition at the time of the first fight with Ingemar Johansson. "Do you believe that you were overtrained for that fight?" "Anything I say now would sound like an excuse." But, later, "I was careless—not overconfident, but careless." He had allowed himself to be surprised in Ingemar's aggressiveness. "Did you and D'Amato fight over your decision to fight Liston?" The weary smile played at the corner of Floyd's mouth, and though he was looking directly at his interlocutors, his eyes were veiled. "No." Long pause. "Cus knows that I do what I want to do—ultimately, he accepted it." Was he surprised by Liston's hostility? No. Perhaps it had made him a bit more determined. Had he anything against Liston personally? "No. I'm the champion and I want to remain the champion." Had he and D'Amato every disagreed before? "Not in relation to my opponents." Had he heard it said that, as a fighter, he lacked viciousness? "Whoever said that should see the fights I've won without being vicious." And why was he fighting Liston? "Well," said Patterson, "it was my decision to take the fight. You gentlemen disagreed, but you were the ones who placed him in the Number One position, so I felt that it was only right. Liston's criminal record is behind him, not before him." "Do you feel that you've been accepted as a champion?" Floyd smiled more tightly than ever and turned toward the questioner. "No," he said. Then, "Well, I have to be accepted as the champion—but maybe not a good one." "Why do you say," someone else asked, "that the opportunity to become a great champion will never arise?" "Because," said Floyd, patiently, "you gentlemen will never let it arise." Someone asked him about his experiences when boxing in Europe—what kind of reception had he enjoyed? Much greater and much warmer than here, he finally admitted, but added, with a weary and humorous caution, "I don't want to say anything derogatory about the United States. I am satisfied." The press seemed rather to flinch from the purport of this grim and vivid little joke, and switched to the subject of Liston again. Who was most in awe of whom? Floyd had no idea, he said, but "Liston's confidence is on the surface. Mine is within. . . ."

. . . I mainly remember Floyd's voice, going cheerfully on and on, and the way his face kept changing, and the way he laughed; I remember the glimpse I got of him then, a man more complex than he was yet equipped to know, a hero for many children who were still trapped where he had been, who might not have survived without the ring, and who yet, oddly, did not really seem to belong there. I dismissed my dim speculations, that afternoon, as sentimental inaccuracies rooted in my lack of knowledge of the boxing world, and corrupted with a guilty chauvinism. But now I wonder. He told us that his wife was coming in for the fight, against his will "in order," he said indescribably, "to console me if—" and he made, at last, a gesture with his hand, downward. . . .

. . . Liston's camp was far more outspoken concerning Liston's attitude toward the press than Patterson's. Liston didn't like most of the press and most of them didn't like him. But I didn't, myself, see any reason why he *should* like them, or pretend to—they had certainly never been very nice to him, and I was sure that he saw in them merely some more ignorant, uncaring white people who, no matter how fine we cut it, had helped to cause him so much grief. . . . Again, I was not particularly appalled by his criminal background, believing, rightly or wrongly, that I probably knew more about the motives and even the necessity of this career than most of the white press could. The only relevance Liston's—presumably previous—associations should have been allowed to have, it seemed to me, concerned the possible effect of these on the future of boxing. Well, while the air was thick with rumor and gospel on the subject, I really cannot go into it without risking, at the very least, being sued for libel; and so, one of the most fascinating aspects of the Chicago story will have to be left in the dark. But the Sweet Science is not, in any case, really so low on shady types as to be forced to depend on Liston. The question is to what extent Liston is prepared to cooperate with whatever powers of darkness there are in boxing; and the extent of his cooperation, we must suppose, must depend, at least partly, on the extent of his awareness. So that there is nothing unique about the position in which he now finds himself and nothing unique about the speculation which now surrounds him. . . .

Liston, as we all know, is an enormous man, but surprisingly trim. I had already seen him work out, skipping rope to a record of "Night Train," and, while he wasn't nearly, for me, as moving as Patterson skipping rope in silence, it was still a wonderful sight to see. The press has really maligned Liston very cruelly, I think. He is far from stupid; is not, in fact, stupid at all. And, while there is a great deal of violence in him, I sensed no cruelty at all. On the contrary, he reminded me of big, black men I have known who acquired the reputation of being tough in order to conceal the fact that they weren't hard. Anyone who cared to could turn them into taffy.

Anyway, I liked him, liked him very much. He sat opposite me at the table, sideways, head down, waiting for the blow: for Liston knows, as only the inarticulately suffering can, just how inarticulate he is. But let me clarify that: I say suffering because it seems to me that he has suffered a great deal. It is in his face, in the silence of that face, and in the curiously distant light in the eyes—a light which rarely signals because there have been so few answering signals. And when I say inarticulate, I really do not mean to suggest that he does not know how to talk. He is inarticulate in the way we all are when more has happened to us than we know how to express; and inarticulate in a particularly Negro way—he has a long tale to tell which no one wants to hear. I said, "I can't ask you any questions because everything's been asked. Perhaps I'm only here, really, to say that I wish you well." And this was true, even though I wanted Patterson to win. Anyway, I'm glad I said it because he looked at me then, really for the first time, and he talked to me for a little while.

And what had hurt him most, somewhat to my surprise, was not the general press reaction to him, but the Negro reaction. "Colored people," he said, with great sorrow, "say they don't want their children to look up to me. Well, they ain't teaching their children to look up to Martin Luther King, either." There was a pause. "I wouldn't be no bad example if I was up there. I could tell a lot of those children what they need to know—because—I passed that way. I could make them *listen*." And he spoke a little of what he would like to do for young Negro boys and girls, trapped in those circumstances which so nearly defeated himself and Floyd, and from which neither can yet be said to have recovered. "I tell you one thing, though," he said, "if I was up there, I wouldn't bite my tongue." I could certainly believe that. And we discussed the segregation issue, and the role, in it, of those prominent Negroes who find him so distasteful. "I would never," he said, "go against my brother—we got to learn to stop fighting among our own." He lapsed into silence again. "They said they didn't want to have the title. They didn't say that about Johansson." "They" were the Negroes. "They ought to know why I got some of the bum raps I got." But he was not suggesting that they were all bum raps. His wife came over, a very pretty woman, seemed to gather in a glance how things were going, and sat down. We talked for a little while of matters entirely unrelated to the fight, and then it was time for his workout, and I left. I felt terribly ambivalent, as many Negroes do these days, since we are all trying to decide, in one way or another, which attitude, in our terrible American dilemma, is the most effective: the disciplined sweetness of Floyd, or the outspoken intransigence of Liston. *If I was up there, I wouldn't bite my tongue.* And Liston is a man aching for respect and responsibility. Sometimes we grow into our responsibilities and sometimes, of course, we fail them. . . .

From my notes: Liston entered the ring to an almost complete silence. Someone called his name, he looked over, smiled and winked. Floyd entered, and got a hand. But he looked terribly small next to Liston, and my depression deepened. My notes again: Archie Moore entered the ring, wearing an opera cape. Cassius Clay, in black tie, and as insolent as ever. Mickey Allen sang "The Star-Spangled Banner." When Liston was introduced, some people boo'd—they cheered for Floyd, and I think I know how this made Liston feel. It promised, really, to be one of the worst fights in history.

Well, I was wrong, it was scarcely a fight at all, and I can't but wonder who on earth would come to see the rematch, if there is one. Floyd seemed all right to me at first. He had planned for a long fight, and seemed to be feeling out his man. But Liston got him with a few bad body blows, and a few bad blows to the head. And no one agrees with me on this, but, at one moment, when Floyd lunged for Liston's belly— looking, it must be said, like an amateur, wildly flailing—it seemed to me that some unbearable tension in him broke, that he lost his head. And, in fact, I nearly screamed, "Keep your head, baby!" but it was really too late. Liston got him with a left, and Floyd went down. I could not believe it. I couldn't hear the count and though Hecht said, "It's over," and picked up his coat, and left, I remained standing, staring at the ring, and only conceded that the fight was really over when two other boxers entered the ring. Then I wandered out of the ball park, almost in tears. I met an old colored man at one of the exits, who said to me, cheerfully, "I've been robbed," and we talked about it for a while. We started walking through the crowds and A. J. Liebling, behind us, tapped me on the shoulder and we went off to a bar, to mourn the very possible death of boxing, and to have drink, with love, for Floyd.

James Baldwin, "The Fight: Patterson vs. Liston," *The Nugget,* February 1963.

7. Eldridge Cleaver / "The Muhammad Ali– Patterson Fight"

Muhammad Ali gained hero status among large segments of the black community because of his great ring triumphs. But it was also because he upheld his religious beliefs and refused to acquiesce either to the sport establishment or to the expectations of a repressive society. Even those African Americans who were appalled by the Nation of Islam's extremism and segregationist policies often expressed their racial pride concerning Ali's boldness in confronting the United States government and exposing some of the hypocrisies that characterized racism in America. The heavyweight champion helped subvert stereotypes about blacks and inspired members of his race whose daily lives were often filled with despair and frustration. African Americans of every age group, economic class, political affiliation, and religious denomination were emboldened by Ali's refusal to sacrifice his principles when the clash came between individual success in sport and the imperatives of group action. In essence, Ali was much more than an athlete or celebrity or entertainer to African Americans. He was a proud black man of moral courage who symbolized for African Americans unlimited possibilities of achievement and encouraged opposition to racial and social oppression.

In the following selection, Eldridge Cleaver, a former inmate at San Quentin and Soledad prisons and minister of information of the Black Panther Party, discusses, as have Gerald Early and other cultural commentators, the inherent symbolism of boxing.* Utilizing the first Ali–Floyd Patterson fight as a point of departure, Cleaver claims that Ali was the "first 'free' black champion ever to confront white America." Unlike black champions of the past who had been manipulated by whites, Ali was an independent black man, a "genuine rev-

---

* See Gerald Early, "Hot Spicks Versus Cool Spades: Three Notes toward a Cultural Definition of Prizefighting," in *Tuxedo Junction,* 115–29.

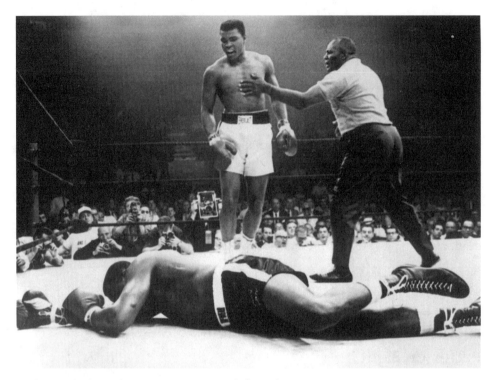

Muhammad Ali standing over Sonny Liston (Allsport)

olutionary" who served the important psychological needs of black Americans who, at the time, were hungry for change and disillusioned with the racial realities of this country. On the other hand, Ali's refusal to be manipulated and his insistence on living his life on his own terms were crushing blows to many whites who sought to maintain their feelings of superiority by controlling the private lives of black champions.

——— ———

The broad support for Muhammad Ali among Negroes had nothing to do with the black Muslims' racist ideology. Even the followers of the late beloved Malcolm X, many of whom despise Muhammad Ali for the scurvy remarks he made about the fallen Malcolm, nevertheless favored him over Patterson as the lesser of two evils— because Ali was more in harmony with the furious psychic stance of the Negro today, while Patterson was an anachronism light years behind. In time of war, in the very center of the battle, the man of peace cannot command the ear of his people and he loses ground to the man of war. The revolutionary rage in the black man's soul today, which boiled over and burned Watts to the ground, means nothing if it doesn't mean business, and it was focused in cold, deadly hatred and contempt upon Floyd Patterson and the bootlicking art of the puppet in the style of his image.

There is no doubt that white America will accept a black champion, applaud and reward him, as long as there is no "white hope" in sight. But what white America demands in her black champions is a brilliant, powerful body and a dull, bestial mind—a tiger in the ring and pussycat outside the ring. It is a hollow, cruel mockery to crown a man king in the boxing ring and then shove him about outside, going so far as to burn a cross on his front doorstep, as whites did when Floyd Patterson tried to integrate a neighborhood. "A man's home is his castle" is a saying not meant for Negroes; a Negro's castle exists only in his mind. And for a black king of boxing the boundaries of his kingdom are sharply circumscribed by the ropes around the ring. A slave in private life, a king in public—that is the life that every black champion has had to lead—until the coming of Muhammad Ali.

Muhammad Ali is the first "free" black champion ever to confront white America. In the context of boxing, he is a genuine revolutionary, the black Fidel Castro of boxing. To the mind of "white" white America, and "white" black America, the heavyweight crown has fallen into enemy hands, usurped by a pretender to the throne. Muhammad Ali is conceived as "occupying" the heavyweight kingdom in the name of a dark, alien power, in much the same way as Castro was conceived as a temporary interloper, "occupying" Cuba. It made no difference that, when Patterson announced that he would beat Ali and return the crown to America, Ali protested vigorously, asking "What does he mean? I'm an American too!" Floyd Patterson was the symbolic spearhead of a counterrevolutionary host, leader of the mythical legions of faithful darkies who inhabit the white imagination, whose assigned task it was to liberate the crown and restore it to its proper "place" in the Free World. Muhammad Ali, in crushing the Rabbit in twelve—after punishing him at will so there could be no doubt, so that the sports writers could not rob him of his victory on paper—inflicted a psychological chastisement on "white" white America similar in shock value to Fidel Castro's at the Bay of Pigs. If the Bay of Pigs can be seen as a straight right hand to the psychological jaw of white America, then Las Vegas was a perfect left hook to the gut.

Essentially, every black champion until Muhammad Ali has been a puppet, manipulated by whites in his private life to control his public image. His role was to conceal the strings from which he was suspended, so as to appear autonomous and self-motivated before the public. But with the coming of Muhammad Ali, the puppet-master was left with a handful of strings to which his dancing doll was no longer attached. For every white man, feeling himself superior to every black man, it was a serious blow to his self-image; because Muhammad Ali, by the very fact that he leads an autonomous private life, cannot fulfill the psychological needs of whites.

The heavyweight champion is a symbol of masculinity to the American male. And a black champion, as long as he is firmly fettered in his private life, is a fallen lion at every white man's feet. Through a curious psychic mechanism, the puniest white man experiences himself as a giant-killer, as a superman, a great white hunter leading a gigantic ape, the black champion tamed by the white man, around on a leash. But when the ape breaks away from the leash, beats with deadly fists upon his massive chest and starts talking to boot, proclaiming himself to be the greatest, spouting poetry, and annihilating every gunbearer the white hunter sics on him (the white hunter not being disposed to crawl into the ring himself), a very serious slippage takes place in the white man's self-image—because that by which he defined himself no longer has a recognizable identity. "If that black ape is a man," the white hunter asks himself, "then what am I?"

It was really Sonny Liston who marked the coming of the autonomous Negro to boxing. But he was nonideological and so the scandal he caused could be handled, albeit with difficulty and pain. The mystique he exuded was that of a lone wolf who did not belong to his people or speak for them. He was for Liston and spoke only for Liston, and this was not out of harmony with the competitive ethic undergirding American culture. If every man is for himself, it was rational for Liston to be for himself. Although even this degree of autonomy in a Negro was bitterly resented, white America could tolerate it with less hysteria, with less of a sense of being threatened. But when the ideological Negro seized the heavyweight crown, no front of cool could conceal the ferocious emotional eruption in white America and among the embarrassed Uncle Toms, who were also experiencing an identity crisis. Yes, even old faithful Uncle Tom has a self-image. All men must have one or they start seeing themselves as women, women start seeing them as women, then women lose their own self-image, and soon nobody knows what they are themselves or what anyone else is—that is to say, the world starts looking precisely as it looks today. For there to be so deep an uproar over Muhammad Ali should indicate that there is something much more serious than a boxing title at stake, something cutting right to the center of the madness of our time.

Eldridge Cleaver, *Soul on Ice* (New York: McGraw-Hill, 1968), 91–94.

8. Elijah Muhammad Disciplines Muhammad Ali

The relationship between Muhammad Ali and Elijah Muhammad, the self-professed Messenger of Allah and leader of the Nation of Islam, was a mutually beneficial one, though from the outset it seemed to be predicated on the needs of the respective individuals rather than genuine friendship. In Elijah Muhammad, Ali apparently found a surrogate father, a powerful man who taught him the ways of the world and nurtured his emerging sense of social and political responsibility. Inspired by Muhammad's talk of a separate black nation and glorious African heritage, Ali took increasing pride in his own negritude and fought valiantly to dispel the notion of black inferiority and white superiority. Elijah Muhammad, for his part, realized the symbolic importance of Ali's membership in the Nation of Islam; he therefore helped transform the heavyweight champion into the movement's leading example of black pride. In Ali, he perceived an individual who could spread word of the Nation of Islam and serve as a model of righteousness for blacks who had been instilled with a false sense of racial inferiority by white America and the Christian religion. In many respects, Ali became a replacement for the defrocked Malcolm X, who had been dead for five years by the time Muhammad Speaks *ran the "clarification of actions" taken by "The Messenger" in the case of Ali.**

---

* Information on Ali, including his involvement with Elijah Muhammad and the Nation of Islam, can be gleaned from Gorn, *Muhammad Ali: The People's Champ;* Hauser, *Muhammad Ali: His Life and Times;* Early, *The Muhammad Ali Reader;* Sammons, *Beyond the Ring.*

Muhammad Ali (dark suit), with Elijah Muhammad at the podium (Library of Congress)

As with Malcolm, so ultimately with Ali: their independence of thought and action chal-
lenged the authority of "The Messenger" and thus the framework upon which the Nation
of Islam was constructed. The always tenuous relationship between Elijah Muhammad and
Ali deteriorated toward the latter part of the 1960s and eventually resulted in Ali's one-year
suspension from the Nation of Islam. In the following selection, taken from Muhammad
Speaks *of April 11, 1969, Muhammad explains why he suspended Ali. It is clear from Mu-*
hammad's comments that he took action against Ali because of the fighter's refusal to ad-
here to the Nation's exacting code of behavior. By expressing a desire to resume his fighting
career and his need to recoup money lost through forced retirement, according to the arti-
cle, Ali had mistakenly shown a dependence on white society for affirmation and material
goods, "a leetle money." This, in turn, revealed an absorbing self-interest and lack of com-
plete trust in the Nation of Islam and its doctrines. To Muhammad, such behavior earned
Ali a loss of privileges, ostracism from the "Brotherhood of the Followers of Islam," and even
the erasure of his good name.

––––– –––––

Mr. Muhammad Ali (Cassius Clay) has been preaching to the Black Man here in America that Allah would give him money, good homes and friendship in all Walks of Life.

Mr. Muhammad Ali (Cassius Clay) did not seem to care anything about what Allah (God) promised nor that Allah (God) has the power to back up His Word.

Mr. Muhammad Ali (Cassius Clay) decided to go with the white man as soon as he found that they had deferred him from going to the Army. This act only shows that the world of sport and play was in the heart of Mr. Muhammad Ali (Cassius Clay) all the time and that he wanted to make money real fast. Holy Quran Chapter 29:64.

Ever since he was a little boy he enjoyed fighting his Black brother and sometimes white people, in the ring for the joy of the white man. He knew that they were gambling on his skill as a fighter.

Mr. Muhammad Ali (Cassius Clay), when he crossed over the rope to fight his opponent, knew that he had many people sitting down on the sidelines and all over the country and the world, betting on him to whip his opponent.

An accidental blow could be fatal to his opponent. People are being killed in the ring. How would Mr. Muhammad Ali (Cassius Clay) feel if he should kill his own brother for the sake of a "leetle money" to show for his years of fighting in the ring.

Mr. Muhammad Ali (Cassius Clay) has boasted that the government should let him go free because he was making millions of dollars for them. It does look like he was making millions of dollars for them as he, himself, does not seem to have a "leetle money." He is asking them to let him come back for the sake of a "leetle money" . . . going, as though to say that "I was over here and couldn't get a leetle money, so let me come over there." He was trying to make the teachings a lie, when Allah (God) cannot lie. He has the power to make that which He says come to pass.

Mr. Muhammad Ali (Cassius Clay) is such a foolish thing, by going back into the ring and wants me to keep him in the pulpit too. Bible Lu. 9:62 tells us that no man who deserts the pulpit for the sake of the world is fit for the Kingdom of God. Bible Mt. 6:24 means that he wants to serve Allah (God) and Mammon. Allah (God) says in His Holy Quran that you cannot serve two gods and be honest with both for you do not have two years. Since you have only one heart, then you can only serve one God.

I gave him the Muslim name Muhammad Ali and removed the slave name, Cassius Clay. This made him famous all over the world. Asia, the Muslim world recognized him to the highest, but no more when they find that he is still Cassius Clay, everywhere.

Why would Asia respect Muhammad Ali (Cassius Clay): They have respected him because of his name, Muhammad Ali. They did not respect him for the sake of the sport, boxing. They do not have prize fighting in the Muslim world. They respected Muhammad Ali (Cassius Clay) because he was a Muslim and was whipping the white man and the Black man out of the honor of being the Champion man of the fistical world of sport.

Do you still think that they will still respect Muhammad Ali (Cassius Clay). No! If they did they would not be good Muslims. If I take Muhammad Ali (Cassius Clay) down as being worthy of the respect of the Islamic World, do you think they would still respect him. No! If the Muslims did not continue to respect him, they would be unfit themselves to be called Muslims. . . .

I have proved to you, that the Black Man owns both the heavens and the earth. Allah (God) came for the express purpose, as it is written, to give the kingdom to us, this means also Muhammad Ali (Cassius Clay). It is written in the Bible, that Allah

(God) would give the Lost-Found the treasures of the heathens. Peoples would even come from afar to bring treasures. . . .

Mr. Muhammad Ali (Cassius Clay) said and did enough in this action of stepping down from the pulpit, to return to the world of sport, to deceive millions of our people who are hungry to do anything for the devil for a little money. The devil tries to tempt us with a promise of wealth that he will never be able to fulfill. To you who are seeking clarification of my actions, this is it.

You must remember, that Revelations of the Bible teaches you that those who worship the enemy was deceived by the enemy. He deceived the world. They were deceived by what he promised them. That is why they went into a Lake of Fire. Maybe that is what Mr. Muhammad Ali (Cassius Clay) decided that he wanted to do, but not Elijah Muhammad.

It does not detract one atom from the truth of the Promise of Allah (God) by them going around being the enemy of Allah (God).

Those of you who desire to follow Mr. Muhammad Ali (Cassius Clay) for the sake of a little money from the devil, I say help yourself, but I, Elijah Muhammad, will wait on Allah (God).

Muhammad Ali, is out of the circle of the Brotherhood of the followers of Islam under the Leadership and the Teachings of Elijah Muhammad for one (1) year in Class, "F."

This means, that Mr. Muhammad Ali (Cassius Clay) is not respected in the society and circle of Islam for the next year, from the date of this statement and issue of *Muhammad Speaks* newspaper.

This is the law which Allah (God) gave to me with which to punish my followers.

Mr. Muhammad Ali shall not be recognized with us even under the Holy Name, Muhammad Ali. We will call him Cassius Clay, with us. We take away the Name of Allah (God) from him, until he proves himself worthy of that name. This is the law of Allah (God), to me. . . .

The Islamic Prayer, in such case is, "O Allah, We cast off and forsake him who disobeys Thee and we are quick. We hope for Thy mercy!"

To those of you who are calling and asking for a clarification . . . you are not the judge of this matter. This is for Allah (God) and myself to judge and not the world. Followers of mine, my actions taken in this matter, are taken under the demand of Allah (God).

I hope this clarifies the actions taken against Mr. Cassius Clay. I hope this answers your questions.

Let this be a lesson to you who are weak in the faith.

Elijah Muhammad, "Classification of Actions Taken by Messenger Muhammad against Muhammad Ali's Action," *Muhammad Speaks*, April 11, 1969, 2–3.

9. "Muhammad Ali Faces the Nation"

By the mid-1970s, Muhammad Ali had won the hearts of a broad segment of American society. The transformation of the Nation of Islam after the death of Elijah Muhammad—combined with the winding down of the Vietnam War, the lessening of racial turmoil, and other social developments—would all contribute to greater admiration of Ali by members of both races. Although still proud and outspoken, Ali found increasing acceptance from an American public preoccupied with economic issues, women's rights, and Richard Nixon and Watergate. The newfound appreciation and respect for Ali became visible in a number of different ways, including the naming of a street after him by his hometown of Louisville, his selection as "Fighter of the Year" by the Boxing Writers Association, and his appearance on the television show Face the Nation.*

The following selection is the Congressional Record *transcript of Ali's interview on CBS's well-known program. The interview, which covered a wide range of topics, illustrates Ali's adroitness in handling reporters' questions and reflects the American public's continuing fascination with his private life and membership in the Nation of Islam. In one intriguing exchange, Fred Graham, one of the two CBS correspondents on the show, asks Ali about changes in the Nation of Islam following the death of Elijah Muhammad. Ali responded by telling Graham that Wallace Muhammad, the son of Elijah and the new leader of the once vilified group, was now teaching his followers that skin color was no basis for determining the worth and goodness of people. With racial discrimination apparently diminishing in American society, Wallace Muhammad was teaching his followers that devils were not determined by skin color. "So we have white Muslims, brown Muslims, red Muslims, yellow Muslims, all colors," Ali noted. This was not the first of Ali's forays into the realm of racial reconciliation; it also would not be his last.*

———

Mr. Mansfield, Mr. President, on Sunday last, I had the pleasure of watching and listening to Mr. Muhammad Ali on the CBS program, "Face the Nation." The reporters on that occasion were George Herman of CBS News, Peter Bonventre of Newsweek and Fred Graham of CBS News. I found the interview fascinating. I found it very much worthwhile. I had never seen Mr. Muhammad Ali except in pictures in the public prints before. I was impressed with his performance. I ask unanimous consent that the transcript of the Face the Nation broadcast, which starred Muhammad Ali, be printed at this point in the Record.

There being no objection, the transcript was ordered to be printed in the record as follows:

Face the Nation

Herman: Mr. Ali, you have said that you like to lecture better than you like to box.

You've become certainly a very well-known world figure; people know about you

---

* See Sammons, *Beyond the Ring*, 226.

in every corner of the earth. You say you want to be a sort of a black Henry Kissinger. What is it you want to do after you stop fighting?

Mr. Ali: Well, I figure that we only have so many hours a day to do whatever we have to do, so many years to live, and in those years we sleep, about eight hours a day, we travel, we watch television; if a man is 50 years old he's lucky to have had 20 years to actually live. So I would like to do the best that I can for humanity. I'm blessed by God to be recognized as the most famous face on the earth today, and I cannot think of nothing no better than helping God's creatures or helping poverty, or working for good causes where I can use my name to do so, to help this country, and other countries where we're having various problems where my influence might help.

Bonventre: Muhammad, what do you think you would have become if you didn't get into boxing?

Mr. Ali: I really don't know. I started boxing when I was 12 years old. I was not that educated in school, and I don't know what I would have done—probably a factory worker, or could have been somewheres dead, wound up in the wrong game, or the wrong life, but if I had heard the Islamic teachings, and if I'd heard the Muslim teachings, which I've accepted, I would probably have been a minister or doing something else good for mankind, but not in a larger way.

Graham: . . . I want to ask you a sort of Walter Mittyish question. Is there ever going to be another great white hope, a white heavyweight that's going to come in and whip all of you black heavyweights?

Mr. Ali: Well, there's a great possibility. We can't foresee him now, like—they come up—we might have one now, might come out of the next Olympics. One might be in some gymnasium now, and he'll knock out somebody next week—we never know until it happens.

Graham: Why are there so few American white fighters? You're going to fight a white man in Germany, but why so few American white heavyweights?

Mr. Ali: I really don't know. One time we had Jack Dempsey, Gene Tunney, John L. Sullivan, Rocky Marciano, Max Baer, Tony Galento, we had good fighters—-Carmen Basilio, Gene Foreman, and they're just not here now.

Graham: Well, let me ask you about this Japanese wrestler. Isn't that denigrating your position as a champion to go over and take part in a gimmick like fighting a wrestler?

Mr. Ali: I would say for an ordinary champion, yes, but people expect these things of me, I have a great imagination, I'm always doing something. I don't think you've ever had a boxer on this show, because the things that I've done calls attention, so this is going to be—we're going into the oriental world—these things I want to do for people over the world, and I can get through them through sports, where when I'm out of boxing, they'll all know me. Now we're working on the oriental part of the world for some things we'd like to do there, and we get to meet them through sports, plus I have a family, I'm looking to take care of my family, it's a nice payday and it's interesting. Many people want to know what would a boxer do with a wrestler. Then they'll have a chance to see.

Herman: Now let me ask you about that nice payday. It seems to me that in February of 1975, you said all your fights from now on were going to be free, that you were going to give all the money to various black charities and to help small businesses and so forth.

Mr. Ali: Not just black charities. We have all type charities, all type people, so I want to get that straight now. Yes, the monies that I make after all taxes, I say I like to do all I can to help people and work for charity groups, and I want to say this on the show now—I get millions of phone calls from people thinking I'm the First National Bank. We don't give away monies. I have lawyers, I have attorneys who check the organizations, the movements, and we don't have no individuals in business that have propositions. It's only for groups of people who need, and this is what I want to do.

Herman: Is it lawyers and attorneys who went to that Jewish old people's home in New York, where there are just about 50 people, or was it Muhammad Ali himself?

Mr. Ali: That was me, this was me, but things such as this, I almost don't have to get permission to help, because we know this is right, and there's no greed involved on no part of no individuals.

Bonventre: Muhammad, what would you say to your son if he came to you and expressed a desire to box?

Mr. Ali: Well, I would—I think I'm going to control him, or help my wife to control him, and let him get educated first and get his mind together, and I wouldn't encourage him to box. I'd let him do it as a game, a sport, for health, but not as a livelihood because it's too dangerous, but teach him foreign language and get him— see, we are all born for a purpose, every tree, the moon, rain, snow, everything God created has a purpose, and man has a purpose, and the wise man is he who finds his life purpose and we want to help him find his purpose in life, which I'm sure is not boxing.

Bonventre: Are you worried about the burden he'll have to bear, being the son of Muhammad Ali? You're a tough act to follow.

Mr. Ali: Well, if my act is not a good act, and if I'm not doing nothing right for people, and if my image is bad, it'll be bad. But if I can do the things that I'd like to do for God and the service of mankind, then I'm sure he'll be honored to be known as my son, and he would like to follow in my footsteps and people will admire him for that, but if my image is bad, then it's bad for him.

Graham: Can I go back to the question of money we were talking about before. By a rough estimate you've made almost $25 million in purses since you came back to fight. Now we've had the spectacle of some former champs who end up in the gutter. What are you doing to avoid that? Are you going to avoid that?

Mr. Ali: Yes, sir. I pray to Almighty God Allah I do. I think the best thing that I can do, or anybody can do, is to save their money—

Graham: What's you're money in?

Mr. Ali: Government tax-free bonds is the best thing, I think a man can put his money in. Investments are bad, there are no real good investments, all of them are gambles. And we pay the government all its taxes before I get mine, but this is why we fight so regular, because I think two halfs is better than just one, so we plan to save as much as we can, and—

Graham: You are a conservative, aren't you, champ? Government tax-free bonds— you're a pretty conservative man with your money.

Mr. Ali: Well, I have a lot of conservative fellows advising me.

Herman: Let me ask you about something you said just a moment ago in reply to a question by Pete. You said, advising your son, you would say boxing was too dangerous. Has it been dangerous for you? Have you been hurt, have you been injured, have you been damaged in any way?

Mr. Ali: Oh yes, my jaw's been broke, and one nerve is just coming back from under here where I couldn't feel for about a year or two, and right now my eardrum in Manila with Joe Frazier—training for Frazier—and I just had it rebusted, the same one again in Italy—healed itself in about two weeks, but this is about all. I've had a few sore ribs.

Herman: I asked because there's been some belief in some quarters that boxing was a dying sport in the United States. I noticed it dropped out of a lot of schools and a lot of colleges. I'm told that now it's coming back in some colleges. What do you think of boxing as a sport for amateurs?

Mr. Ali: I think boxing is dangerous. Any man been hit in the head and the brain's a delicate thing—I think you should be well protected. If a fellow is not qualified, he shouldn't be allowed to fight, but football is proven to have more deaths, baseball, ice hockey, horse racing—car racing is much more dangerous, but I would advise nobody to box if they get hit too much and it's too dangerous. . . .

Graham: . . . I know you have more of an interest in religion, and you've said that's one of the things you want to devote a lot of time to later, but now, Mr. Ali, what about this image also as a womanizer that you also have. Is that—you're looking at me a little incredulously here, I don't know why, but—

Mr. Ali: I'm trying to figure out what you mean by womanizer.

Graham: Well, you have a reputation as—you're separated from your wife, and you have a reputation as a man who has a sharp eye for the ladies. Now, how is that going to be consistent with your role as a religious leader in the years ahead?

Mr. Ali: Well, as far as my personal beliefs are concerned, I don't talk about them in public, as far as my personal problems with family, these are things I don't discuss in public especially on high-class shows like I was told yours would be so, I don't even expected to talk about that here.

Herman: You said from time to time that a wise man can play the fool but a fool can't act like a wise man, and then you've said, "I've always got to talk. People expect it of me." Is that a role that you play? Are you trying to be an actor?

Mr. Ali: What I was talking about, I used to watch a wrestler named Gorgeous George, and he would always talk about how he would do this and do that, and people came to see him get beat. And this is where I got the idea. So the talking and the gimmicks and the predicting, which I don't do nowadays like I used to, was only to promote the fights which has now elevated me over all athletes in the history of the world as far as drawing power and world attractions in a sense. This is just a purpose of publicity, all the talking. That's why I did that. I don't have to do it.

Herman: You kind of disappoint me, I have to admit. I sort of thought this poetry, this float like a butterfly, sting like a bee, was the real Ali, not some kind of a commercial gimmick.

Mr. Ali: No, that's all. It wasn't a commercial gimmick, but it was promotion, and it was the real Ali. I do float like a butterfly, sting like a bee. But the little poems and the gimmicks were just to promote the fights. Newspapers, gave them something to write about.

Graham: If I can go back just for a minute, and this is obviously meant in a spirit of friendliness. The question of the Islamic religion and your future in that—do you, the impression one gets is perhaps it is loosening up a bit after the death of Elijah Muhammad. Do you think it's changing now, and that your role in it can change?

Mr. Ali: Well, what the honorable Elijah Muhammad taught was good for the time, during the thirties when black people were being castrated, lynched, deprived of freedom, justice, equality, raped. He had to teach that the white man is the Devil, his actions towards us is that of the Devil. Now that we're no longer being lynched, raped, castrated, we're given equal justice, we can go anywhere to live, even the North fights the South to have, so we can have certain rights. People are not acting this way today. So honorable Wallace Muhammad is on time. He's teaching us it's not the color of the physical body that makes a man a Devil. God don't look at our colors. Minds, hearts have no color. God look at our minds and our actions and our deeds. So we have white Muslims, brown Muslims, red Muslims, yellow Muslims, all colors. So it's the color. So the big thing in the change now, we have white people who have accepted our faith and we now recognize all men as brothers and we look at them according to their works. Some blacks can do evil, and whites. So it's not the color now, we look at the actions. . . .

Herman: Okay, thank you very much, Muhammad Ali, for being with us today on Face the Nation.

Congressional Record, 94th Congress, 122, May 4, 1976, 12372–75.

7

Progress, Protest, and Alienation in the Sports Factory, 1970s and Beyond

Introduction

It was after the 1960s that the first black man was hired as a manager of a major league baseball team or became a television network commentator for NBA basketball games. During the 1980s and 1990s, African Americans could claim part-ownership in big-time sporting franchises. The success of the civil rights crusade could be measured in many other ways as well. Beyond the major pieces of legislation and the appointment of African Americans to positions of power in Washington, D.C., during the last third of the century, and beyond the creation of African American studies programs at many institutions of higher education throughout the nation, many developments suggested that racial reform would advance at a steady pace. Significant changes in politics at the municipal level were certainly promising. In 1971 there were eight African American mayors in the United States; in 1975 that number stood at 135 and included Coleman Young of Detroit and Thomas Bradley of Los Angeles. Less than ten years later, Chicago inaugurated Harold Washington as its first black mayor, and even in the Deep South, cities such as Atlanta and Birmingham would be led by African American politicians in the 1980s and 1990s. As one textbook declares, "the era of the black elected official had arrived."*

Programs such as affirmative action were part of a process devised to redress a long history of racial inequality and to encourage changes in the structure of government institutions, the professions, and academia. Such changes, ideally, would make the faces in the boardroom, the law firm, and the lecture hall look a little more like those in the American population at large. A consequence of these plans of inclusion was, ultimately, the expansion of the black middle class in America, though many African American leaders and policy analysts found that the programs did not go very far toward alleviating the distress of many other black people. Even a more honest distribution of jobs and scholarships did not engage the fact that so many children were born and raised in poverty. The most successful initiatives still flowed from the top down and thus would not relieve the everyday turmoil of inner-city life. That was but one qualification on the claims of accomplishment by the movement.

What was even worse, from the vantage point of progressive thinkers, black and white, was the enormous backlash against the modest but meaningful achievements of civil rights activism. Mainstream white resentment came to the fore before the "Reagan revolution" of 1980. The antibusing violence in northern cities such as Boston suggested the breadth and depth of racism. The Supreme Court's *Bakke* decision of 1978, while ambiguous in many respects, nevertheless lent code words to conservatives for the next two decades; affirmative action would thus be characterized as "reverse discrimination," and the term "quotas" would be widely circulated whenever the ways of expanding minority participation in business and higher education were being debated. First under William Bell, then under Clarence Thomas, the Equal Employment Opportunity Commission (EEOC) was drastically cut back during the Reagan administration. Tellingly, both the president and his appointees opposed the commission's reason for existence in the first place.

---

* Hine et al., *African-American Odyssey,* 547.

Such reactionary impulses did not prevail on the playing fields. But it is within this frame of reference that protest and alienation did extend to the sporting realm. The statistics concerning the number of black athletes competing at the highest levels of sport—especially in major league baseball, the NBA, the NFL, and international track and field—conveyed an image of unalloyed success in the struggle by blacks to gain a level playing field. The desegregation of intercollegiate athletics, even in the Deep South, was another reason for celebration, and the stories describing that process were often inspirational. More gratifying still were the many instances when African American athletes assumed leadership roles on their teams and in their sports—and even in the world beyond the athletic arena. To analyze the careers of Frank Robinson, Bill Russell, Walter Payton, Magic Johnson, and Arthur Ashe, for instance, would be to discern a growing awareness—across the color line—that black athletes brought diverse exemplary talents as well as enormous dignity to sport, that they possessed the expertise as well as the experience to become leaders in the profession.

Yet several issues shadowed such tales of success. For many African American athletes, the ordeal of integration took a substantial toll because advances were so late in coming and were so often begrudged by white America. Understandably, many blacks would look back on their athletic careers with bitterness. They noted, for instance, that once the teams departed the stadium or arena, white athletes went their separate ways. African Americans had never been treated with the same respect as their white counterparts, others contended, and they were not able to reap the same financial rewards for their talent. The sports industry did not treat all of its employees equally; the prospects for promotion to managerial and administrative jobs were limited. Moreover, whites in authority and many who commented on sport, such as Al Campanis and Jimmy "the Greek" Snyder, publicly articulated longstanding beliefs that black athletes did not have "the necessities" to move up to front-office jobs in the athletic world. The prevailing image of African American athletes accentuated brawn not brains; it was a troubling truth that within the dominant culture the allegations of the "scientific" racists—going all the way back to the late nineteenth century—seemed to remain largely in place.

Ultimately, one other issue focused the concerns of many African American educators and cultural commentators. That was the continued exploitation of black athletes by institutions of higher education. When the National Collegiate Athletic Association (NCAA) created admissions requirements (including minimum SAT or ACT scores) for incoming athletes, a storm of controversy swirled around the differential impact these standards would have on black and white athletes. The details were, and remain, complex. But in their most expansive arguments, black leaders such as Jesse Jackson, Harry Edwards, and Arthur Ashe—often echoing the words of educators like Lloyd Hackley—emphasized that American colleges and universities had a responsibility to educate "student athletes." They needed to establish legitimate admissions standards—yes—but they also must monitor the quality of courses and graduation rates. Intercollegiate athletic competition had finally been desegregated, but if the classroom and library were abandoned—if incoming black athletes were simply handed over to coaches for a few seasons of labor on the gridiron or basketball court—then the playing fields would never be integrated into the broader world beyond.

A

CHALLENGING THE COLOR LINE

1. Jesse Jackson on Blacks and the Sports $$$

Jesse Jackson has always been interested in the role of black athletes in American sport. The eloquent and outspoken civil rights leader, perhaps best known for serving as field director for the Congress of Racial Equality (CORE), coordinating Operation Breadbasket for the Southern Christian Leadership Conference (SCLC), and founding People United to Serve Humanity (PUSH), has fought through the years on behalf of racial justice in American sport and campaigned to include more African Americans in coaching and upper-level adminis-trative positions and to guard again their exploitation. Jackson's latest, and in many ways most significant, effort on behalf of racial justice in American sport was his formation in 1994 of the Rainbow Coalition for Fairness in Athletics (RCFA). Working in conjunction with the Center for the Study of Sport in Society (CSSS), the RCFA has pressured the leaders in both amateur and professional sport to increase the number of ethnic minorities in staff and administrative positions. ***

The following interview from Black Sports *touches on a number of issues related to Af-rican American participation in sport. An overriding theme of the document, however, is Jackson's characterization of American sport as a white-dominated industry that exploits black athletes for pecuniary gain. He contends that the plantation-style trafficking of black bodies of more than one hundred years ago is being duplicated in contemporary sport. Like the black cotton-picker from yesteryear, African American athletes perform all the work while whites control all the resources and all the money.*

——— ———

BS: Jesse, you made a reference to athletics being "an industry." In what way is it that?

Jackson: It's an industry because of the number of people who work in it and be-cause of the money made and because of the products it takes to keep it going. Some-body makes footballs and basketballs and baseballs and bats and somebody builds arenas and makes basketball rims and football goalposts and somebody makes athlet-ic uniforms and shoes. It is an industry. Absolutely.

BS: The essence of that industry being the trafficking in human bodies.

Jackson: The trafficking in human bodies. And, as I said earlier, 100 years ago we were in the boxing ring but we were not in the box office. Black boys in the boxing

---

* For information on the Rainbow Coalition for Fairness in Athletics, see Shropshire, *In Black and White*, esp. 72–73, 85–86, 153. For an intriguing study of activism after the civil rights movement, see A. Reed, *The Jesse Jackson Phenomenon*.

319

ring, fighting with bare knuckles and white people were up on the box office counting the money.

One hundred years ago we brought the cotton bales to the storehouse and we got a pat on the back and they told us we were the strongest Blacks in all of the county. We made all-county cotton-picker and went back down to our little shack. We pick the cotton, white people pick the money.

One hundred years later, we take the basketball to the hoop or the football to the goal line and we get a pat on the back and we are all-county, all-state, All-American, all-pro and we get a trophy and a percentage of the money but the little white people upstairs get the bulk of the money. They choose who can play, who can't play. They determine who will be blackballed.

BS: It was a surprise to many, to say the least, when Jesse Jackson and Operation PUSH announced a threatened boycott of the National Invitational Basketball Tournament (NIT) in New York. How did you become involved?

Jackson: Well, I became involved, number one, because I have a relationship with many of the Black coaches and athletic directors in the Middle Eastern Athletic Conference and the Southwest Athletic Conference. And I keep up with sports. Beyond this, I'm sensitive to discrimination wherever I see it. I observed the NIT's list of teams selected and they had Manhattan College with a 13-11 record, St. Peter's was 15-11 and Providence was 17-10 and North Carolina A&T had just won the MEAC tournament which is a very significant tournament to Black people. Out of that tournament had come Al Attles, Earl Monroe and countless others. So the quality of the ball there is very good. Then we looked at Bishop with a 25-3 record and there are other Black schools with phenomenal records. Kentucky State was No. 1 in the country. Yet all of these schools were ignored. We simply raised a question. The fact is these teams have far superior records. In the 38-year history of the NIT only one Black school had ever participated and that was last year when they allowed Maryland–Eastern Shore to participate. Of course, they made a good showing. As a matter of fact, they won one game and lost in the semi-final round by a couple of points.

BS: What was the response to your questioning the "integrity" of the NIT?

Jackson: We received the impression that we were out of place raising that kind of question. So we raised it again. We wanted to find out who was the NIT. Come to find out, the selection committee was all white. When we challenged them, they responded by saying that 94 percent of the players in the tournament are Black. We countered by pointing that all the coaches are white, the commissioners are white, and all the money is going to white schools. That's not really progressive, is it? . . .

So we raised the question and threatened to boycott Madison Square Garden at which time Mike Burke (president of the Garden) called a meeting which involved all those people from the NIT as well as the commissioners from the MEAC and SWAC and we resolved the issue. They committed themselves to putting a Black athletic director on the selecting committee. Next year they will choose at least one Black college team for that tournament. So it was a successful negotiation.

BS: Who was it that gave you the initial impression that you had no right questioning the prestigious NIT?

Jackson: Well, when we initially talked with the chairman of the committee of the NIT, a cat named Pete Carlesimo, we received that impression. Many white sportswriter types have a very paternalistic attitude toward protecting their trained animals from the outside world of Blacks. In other words, they (Black people) all march and fight politically but these Black athletes, they're our property. We're the ones who describe them and put images upon them. This is not something for y'all. They almost try to make the Black athlete superior to the rest of the Black thrust in this country or different from it. And I think that's in part because they resent a Black getting as much influence as many Black athletes do, and then being able to impart that influence or imprint it on a broader audience since they have so much access to a broader media. That is why they resented for so long calling Muhammad Ali his name as opposed to Cassius Clay. They resented for white kids to have to begin to deal with his Islamic religion. At any level. That's why many of them still refer to Kareem Abdul-Jabbar as Lew Alcindor, so called Kareem-Jabbar. That kind of thing. They resent it; they are a very conservative bunch and they've done a very good job locking out Black sportswriters. There is no Black syndicated columnist in the country except Doc Young and he's basically in Black papers. Most people know Black athletes by the image projected by white writers of them. Which is a cruel situation. For white people to control the money, to control the management and to control the image apparatus is to really have us in slavery and limit us to the status of gladiators. . . .

BS: This brings up the matter of the increasing involvement of policies in sports, such instances as using the Olympics as a forum for social or political protest. And now your recent efforts using pressure outside of sports to have some bearing on sports. How should we view this marriage?

Jackson: Well, sports have always been very political except that white people have never had to protest to gain application of their political decisions about sports. It was political to have all-white baseball players, basketball players, football players, track members. It was political at one time to have all whites to represent America in the Olympics. And, of course, there's the choice of who is going to head up the Olympic committee. They're usually chosen by governors and chosen by mayors. It's always been political. Who will get a license to be a boxing commissioner or to be a boxing promoter in a state? Who will get the license to have a franchise in a given city? So it's always been very political except that now that Black folks are beginning to protest our being exploited by the political arrangement, it's seen as a forward force. It's not forward at all . . . and it's not very new. . . .

There's [also] the . . . notion about the Vietnam War. There were a whole lot of white athletes who protested against the Vietnam war but it was Muhammad Ali whose belt they took because the notion of a guy of his prominence not supporting that war had to have political ramifications. It was politicians who made the move to take his belt and not athletic commissioners per se. The commissioners wanted Ali and needed him. But the politicians prevailed upon the athletic bodies not to renew Ali's boxing license. So it's mess when they come running to me asking, "Are you going to [bring] politics into sports?" No, we're going to [bring] justice for Black people into the sports arena!

BS: What you're saying then is that the struggle in sports for Black athletes is just a part of the larger struggle within the American mainstream?

Jackson: Absolutely. Black athletes are not off limits to the struggle; they have an obligation to participate in it. If they think that because somebody is screaming for them tonight and their picture is in the paper that they have it made, you wait until the day when there's a choice between a white boy with equal or less ability and see what happens. . . .

BS: What can the Black community do to get a greater share of the dollars in athletics since primarily Blacks are the performers, not the managers?

Jackson: First of all, understand that it is an industry and money is involved and that we do have leverage. And we ought to use it. Our consciousness has to precede our conduct. Then Black athletes who have arrived at a measure of prominence must use that platform to protect their future. Not only to analyze how many points they made tonight but it is the points they made tonight that they must use to declare that they want to engage in the types of endorsements that will allow them to survive beyond their point-making days.

In those situations, when we are blatantly being ignored we have to be willing to picket, to boycott, to disrupt, to write, to raise the right issues at the right time. You see we have too many Blacks in the athletic and entertainment industry, who represent the legitimate work of the Black community, to allow them to be taken advantage of and Black people not benefit in their success.

BS: It seems, however, that Black people aren't often aware of the efforts of Black athletes who do work in that direction. And partly that's the fault of the media. For example, recently when Muhammad Ali announced that he would donate part of the purse from the Chuck Wepner fight to charity and Dick Young, a nationally recognized writer, said it was a "meaningless gesture."

Jackson: I think the gesture was good. Ali was identifying closely with his religion and with the Black business community and with the conduct of Black people. I think that is commendable. Dick Young may not be in a position to appreciate the impact of what Ali has done on the Black community. But then again Dick Young is a white man trying to project himself into that situation. What Black writers have to say about Ali is more important to me than what Dick Young has to say.

BS: It seems that increasingly what Jesse Jackson has to say on sports is having sizable impact, too. With what ability that you had to restructure your career after the disappointments in football and baseball, how can young Black athletes be helped to develop that same skill?

Jackson: I think that most of them have that ability. What they need is the principles to go along with that athletic ability now. In order to be successful on the court and beyond it, it's not so much your aptitude but your attitude that determines your altitude, plus a little intestinal fortitude, and you'll always be a man.

"RAP on Blacks and Sports $$$," interview with Jesse Jackson, *Black Sports*, May 1975, 22–25, 61–62.

2. Phil Petrie / "The NFL Sacks the Black Quarterback"

African American athletes have traditionally been overrepresented in certain playing positions and underrepresented in others. For instance, they have been most heavily concentrated in outfield positions in major league baseball; found most often at safety, cornerback, and end on defense, and pass receiver and running back in both college and professional football; and most likely to be spiker in women's intercollegiate volleyball. Academicians, particularly sport sociologists who have investigated this topic since the early 1970s, have referred to the overrepresentation of African Americans and other racial groups at certain playing positions in team sports as stacking, and they have argued that its existence corresponds with a certain "racial logic" in American society.* In short, stacking is closely tied with popular beliefs about skin color and a combination of such traits as intelligence and leadership, motivation, dependability, and jumping and running skills.

In the following selection, Phil Petrie asks why there were so few black quarterbacks in the National Football League during the 1960s and 1970s. Petrie provides no definitive answers but presents the various arguments given for the dearth of black quarterbacks in professional football. The most common, and perhaps even most viable, argument cited by Petrie is that blacks were not permitted to be quarterbacks because whites did not believe they have the qualities necessary to play the position. More specifically, whites, imbued with the racist thinking so prevalent in American society, believed blacks did not have the intelligence and leadership abilities requisite to directing a team to victory. Interestingly enough, now that there are more black quarterbacks in both college and professional football, the description of the position has apparently changed. It is now more common to hear sportscasters and other observers of the game describe quarterbacks as great athletes rather than intelligent leaders of men, a subtle twist in semantics that fits neatly into the dangerous racial logic that permeates sport and the larger American society.**

When the National Football League (NFL) opened its 1976 season last month, all of its 28 teams were well integrated. In 1975, 437 NFL players were Black (38 percent of the total), and although team rosters are not firm at this writing, it is expected that there will certainly be as many, and probably more, Black players as there were a year ago.

The truly observant is aware, however, that almost all of those Blacks playing on faked turf in NFL member stadiums are, so to speak, in the trenches and only one—James Harris of the LA Rams—is directing a team as quarterback. One other Black player, Parnell Dickinson of the Tampa Bay Buccaneers, is a backup quarterback.

Last year, when the now defunct World Football League (WFL) was in existence,

---

* There has been a plethora of research studies conducted in sport sociology that focus on stacking patterns. See for example: Eitzen and Sanford, "The Segregation of Blacks"; Yetman, "Positional Segregation"; Leonard, "Stacking in College Basketball"; Lavoie, "The Economic Hypothesis of Positional Segregation."
** See Bolland and Walter, "The Black Quarterback."

there were six Black quarterbacks in U.S. professional football. Five of the six are now either out of the game or playing in a position other than quarterback.

With so many Black players in the game, why are there so few Black quarterbacks? The answer, of course, depends on whom you ask and ranges from insufficient training of Black college quarterbacks—they can't read defense zones—to racism—White management and players don't want Blacks in leadership positions. In between these arguments are heard others: The Black college quarterback is spoiled and undisciplined. Joe Gilliam, a starter for the Pittsburgh Steelers, missed practices and ran afoul of the law, and one Black quarterback allegedly committed the most cardinal of sins: he "fooled around" with White women.

Another argument advanced is that the Black quarterback is multitalented, a "super" athlete. This enables him to play positions other than that of quarterback. So, rather than have this expensive property sit on the bench (as do White rookie quarterbacks for three and four years), he is used to earn money—pay his way—in other positions such as wide receiver, free safety, and running back. This puts the Black quarterback in a Catch-22 situation. He must be superior in order to make the team and this very superiority is used as the reason to keep him from playing quarterback.

Whatever the argument, the fact is that there is only one Black starting quarterback in the NFL—and there are persistent rumors that he is on his way out. Why is there all this fuss over one position out of 11?

Is it that this position is actually more important than any of the other ones? This is unlikely to be so in a team sport. That old saying about a chain and its weakest link is true in this case—ask any quarterback without a good offensive line. Joe Namath, all will agree, is a fine quarterback. This year the Jets have a weak and inexperienced line. In a preseason game against the Pittsburgh Steelers, Namath completed 12 of 23 passes for 109 yards but was sacked six times. His replacement, not the Black third-year quarterback who was cut the next day but a White rookie quarterback, was sacked four times in one quarter.

Is it the fact that this position is the highest paid one on the team? Economics is a strong motivator in a capitalist society, but the quarterback is not necessarily the highest paid on the team. O.J. Simpson earned more than Buffalo quarterback Joe Furguson but it could be argued that O.J. did more than Furguson. On the other hand, Fran Tarkenton, quarterback of the Minnesota Vikings, earned a whopping $240,000 last year while Chuck Foreman, voted the most valuable player on the team, earned only $40,000.

It is the concept of quarterback as team leader, the head of the organization—sometimes translated as the brains—for which Blacks would like to be recognized. Leadership ability and intelligence are presumed to be the prerequisites of a quarterback and these are precisely the qualities in which many Whites consider Blacks to be deficient. The success of Blacks in other areas of football is attributed to their "natural" ability. This "naturalness" eliminates training and intelligent choice as factors in their achievement. It is interesting to note that Archie Manning, White quarterback of the New Orleans Saints, was said to be "clever" while Joe Gilliam, a Black quarterback waivered by the Saints for missing practice, was said to have good "instincts."

Such semantic quibbling would go unnoticed except that Blacks have been weighted down and held back by such labeling and feel that the difference is conceptual rather than semantical. Noted American scholars have been saying for two centuries, as did James Schouler, that Blacks are "a servile race, sensuous, stupid, brutish, obedient . . . and childish." Such attitudes are still prevalent and crop up in such guises as an "exciting" player (sensuous); a player with "natural instincts" (though it's not the same as stupid, it's not synonymous with intelligence); a "spoiled" and "undisciplined" player (childish).

When pressed or pushed to change, the NFL points out that over a third of its players are Black and that even one Black starting quarterback is an advancement. But many would ask, an advancement to what? Certainly not to equality. Equality is indivisible. You either have it or you don't. Leonard A. Rapping and Anthony Pascal made a study of professional baseball for the Rand Corporation and, among other things, concluded that baseball appears to restrict major league opportunities to those Blacks who are demonstrably superior to their White counterparts. In other words, there is "unequal opportunity for equal ability." A study of professional football would bring, it is believed, the same conclusion.

The continued denial of Blacks as quarterbacks in the NFL and the battle to get them into that position take on the appearance of a war. The armor of battle is hip and shoulder pads; the place of battle a hundred yards of dirt; the winner (or loser) humanity. Expressed in such broad and rhetorical terms, it is easy to see why the individual, the lone Black player, is lost. The Black quarterback has become a symbol, a cause. The fact that a person is involved is sometimes forgotten.

Some of these individuals cannot adjust to the treatment meted out to them by the NFL. These potential quarterbacks become problem players. The first shock that faces them is that they are not going to be quarterbacks. No matter their achievement in college, the NFL has already made a pre-judgment about them. It appears to be a blatant form of racism on the part of the NFL.

Cornelius Greene was Ohio State's starting quarterback for three years. He played no other position and his team was ranked no lower than third in the country throughout his college career. In the NFL draft he was picked by the Dallas Cowboys as a wide receiver and has since been cut from the team. Why did Dallas think that he could play in that position, or, more importantly, why didn't they draft him at the position (quarterback) which he played so well so long? Dallas' move effectively removed Greene from professional football and has severely limited his income potential and deferred a dream.

Greene's case is not a singular one. It is a norm for the treatment of Black college quarterbacks. Wilburn Hollis was an All-American quarterback at Iowa, a team that finished number one in the nation his senior year, 1958. Hollis was not drafted at all.

Rather than accepting such demeaning gestures, some players choose to play in the Canadian Football League (CFL). In effect, they're driven from home to seek their fortune and complete their dreams. Chuck Ealey was one of these. Ealey was a Black quarterback for the University of Toledo for three seasons (1967–71). During his college career he never lost a game, but in the NFL draft, incredibly, he was passed up. Ealey went to the CFL and led Hamilton, his team there, to a CFL championship. Jimmy Jones, a quarterback at the University of Southern California, like Ealey also chose the CFL.

Marlin Briscoe, called "The Magician" because he could do so much with the ball, was the first Black quarterback in the NFL. Although he had an impressive college record, his arrival at the position of NFL quarterback was due to circumstance and accident. Briscoe had attended the University of Omaha and was the greatest quarterback in the school's history. He piled up 1,318 yards rushing; 4,935 yards passing; and completed 333 of 609 passes for 52 touchdowns with an accuracy average of 54 percent. In spite of this sensational record he was drafted as a defensive back by the Denver Broncos. But a misfortune became his good fortune. On the first day of practice he pulled a muscle and this limited his running ability. Denver's two backup quarterbacks didn't make the grade and so when Steve Tensi, Denver's regular quarterback, broke his collarbone, Marlin Briscoe—5'11" and 170 lbs.—had a job as quarterback. He was astounding. On his first play he completed a 22-yard pass. He threw 14 touchdown passes and ran for three the remainder of the season. Louis Saban, then coach of Denver, said that Briscoe had "a lot to learn, but he's receptive and he knows he's got a lot to learn and that's the most important thing." Evidently Briscoe didn't learn fast enough or wanted money Denver felt was excessive in the learning process. He was cut from the team. Miami picked him up but not as a quarterback. He became a wide receiver, quenched his pride, cooled his blood.

James Harris, presently the only Black starting quarterback in the NFL, picked up the torch Briscoe carried so fatefully. Harris attended Grambling College, one of the most formidable schools in Black college sports. Grambling has sent more players to the NFL than any small college and is second only to Notre Dame in total number of players drafted by the NFL. Harris was drafted by the Buffalo Bills and made his debut as quarterback in 1969. He went to Buffalo somewhat at a disadvantage for he didn't get a playbook during the off-season. "They told me that books weren't out yet, but when I went to Buffalo I found out that (Dennis) Shaw had had one for a month." Harris was cut by Louis Saban, the same coach who had let Briscoe go, when Saban became Buffalo's coach. Eventually, the Los Angeles Rams picked him up. He earned the position of starting quarterback. It is interesting to note that Harris is not agile enough to play any position other than quarterback. It's either quarterback or nothing. And many would like for it to be nothing. Dave Anderson, a *New York Times* columnist, called for Harris' ouster not because he wasn't winning but because the team didn't win a championship. If Anderson were honestly motivated, several NFL quarterbacks should be on the way out, especially Fran Tarkenton. Harris must play under enormous pressure each game amid speculation of his worth. There were even rumors during the summer that Joe Namath was going to replace him. Still he is the quarterback, although working under great odds. Experience indicates that if he has one or two bad games he's out. Fans all over the country wish him well. He's the lone Black hope.

In 1975 there were five other Black quarterbacks in professional football in the U.S. giving comfort and competition to Harris. Three of these players were in the WFL: Reggie Oliver and Eddie McAshan of Jacksonville and Mat Reed of Birmingham.

Oliver attended Marshall University and was passed over by both the NFL and the

WFL. He came to Jacksonville as a free agent and won his position over another Black aspirant, Eddie McAshan. McAshan had been premier quarterback at Georgia Tech but was suspended during a bowl game. He was picked up on the final round of the draft.

Mat Reed, like Harris, is from Grambling College, and he says that Black quarterbacks are told that they "can't read or recognize defenses fast enough." Reed obviously is the exceptional reader for he led the Birmingham Americans to a WFL championship.

When the WFL folded, none of these players were picked up as quarterbacks.

J. J. Jones from Fisk University, a small liberal arts college in Tennessee, was picked up by the N.Y. Jets and was the number two quarterback behind Joe Namath. This was his third year. When Richard Todd, a highly rated quarterback from Alabama, Namath's alma mater, was drafted by the Jets, the cognoscenti knew that it was all over for Jones. He was cut from the team before the first game of the regular season. Another dream deferred.

Of the six Black quarterbacks in 1975, many believed that Joe Gilliam was the most talented of the lot. He came out of Tennessee State with an impressive record (not quite as impressive as his predecessor, Eldredge Dickey, who didn't make it as a quarterback in the NFL although many feel that he was the best quarterback Black college football has produced). Gilliam led his college team to a 21-1 record. When the Pittsburgh Steelers drafted Gilliam the prognosis for his career was not promising. After all, the Steelers had blond Terry Bradshaw and an ex-Notre Damer, Terry Hanratty. Gilliam waited patiently and got his chance when Hanratty sustained an injury. He responded with a 7 for 11 performance. In 1974 he led the Steelers to a 6-0 record in preseason play, completing 75 of 124 passes for 1,175 yards and 11 touchdowns. Gilliam opened the season. With Franco Harris, Pittsburgh's all-pro runner, out of action, Gilliam guided the Steelers to a 4-1-1 mark. At that time a poll was taken by the local newspaper for the fans to decide who they wanted as quarterback for their team. Bradshaw won; Hanratty, who didn't even play, was second. Gilliam was benched because the team "was not winning by a big enough margin." That was the beginning of the end. Gilliam could not cause his heart to do double talk or quench his pride. He became a troubled player, missed practices, and was put on waivers. New Orleans picked him up but let him go. "A brilliant career" said the St. Louis American "has gone from bad, to promising, to hopeful, to frustrating, and to utter futility." Another man done gone.

This leaves James Harris and Parnell Dickinson. Dickinson, a rookie from Mississippi Vocational College, has gone through the preseason cuts and is now a regular member of the Tampa Bay Buccaneers, playing behind Steve Spurrier as the number two quarterback. During the preseason he attempted 27 passes and completed 9 for 130 yards. Dickinson is a "scrambler" and had 88 yards rushing from 14 attempts giving him a six-yard rushing average.

Football, whether professional or collegiate, is only a game but for the Black quarterback it has been a deadly one. Since 1968 there have been only eight. Now there are two. Patience wavers lest some Sunday we see the grief of six more men slipping past our view while we sit feet propped up, beer in hand, with eyes glued to the unfolding spectacle.

Phil Petrie, "The NFL Sacks the Black Quarterback," *Encore American and Worldwide News,* October 18, 1976, 46–47.

3. Eddie Robinson on Grambling's First White Player

Historians have spent a great deal of time examining the racial integration of predominantly white organized sport during the post-1945 period. Scholars have chronicled important events such as Jackie Robinson's entry into major league baseball, the shattering of the color barrier in other professional sports, and the elimination of racial segregation in college athletics in the South. Tellingly, very little attention has been given to those white athletes who participated in black college sport, black baseball, or other parallel institutions that were initially founded, ironically enough, in response to the rigid racial segregation practiced in both sport and the larger American society. One exception to this general rule is Larry Gerlach's study of Eddie Klep, the hard-drinking and emotionally troubled white ballplayer who had a brief stint with the Cleveland Buckeyes of the Negro American League. Another story is that of James Gregory, the white quarterback from California who played for the legendary Eddie Robinson at Grambling State University during the 1960s. The Gregory story was memorialized in a 1981 made-for-television movie, Grambling's White Tiger, *and recounted in Robinson's recent autobiography with Richard Lapchick,* Never Before, Never Again, *from which the following passages are taken.**

The excerpt describes how Gregory found his way to Grambling, the manner in which he was treated by his black teammates, and what he ultimately meant to the university. Robinson explains that he talked to his players about the proper way to treat Gregory, recalling how appreciative he was of the help he received from a legendary physical educator, Dr. Charles McCloy, during the years he spent as one of the few African American students at the University of Iowa. Robinson also points out, in a forthright manner characteristic of his entire autobiography, that he insisted Gregory play quarterback rather than wide receiver because he [Robinson] did not want people to think he was "trying to pay back the NFL" for years of neglecting the black quarterback.**

With everything going on in our nation, it was inevitable that I would decide that we needed to integrate our own team. I didn't need a star player like James Harris, but I did need a guy the other student-athletes would respect and someone who could take being a very real minority both on the team and on the campus. James Gregory was the person who filled the bill.

The way James Gregory got here is an interesting story. Ed Stevens, his coach at Corcoran High School, had "Convincer" Calloway as his assistant. Convincer had played for me at Grambling. Eventually, Ed Stevens came to work for me at Grambling as linebacker coach and as the women's track coach.

I went out to speak at a Corcoran awards banquet for coaches Stevens and Calloway. It was there that I met their player, James Gregory. He was talking to me about going to

---

* See Gerlach, "Baseball's Other 'Great Experiment'"; *Grambling's White Tiger*, Philadelphia Movies Unlimited, 1981.
** For a strikingly different response to a white football player representing a historically black institution, see Berkow, "The Minority Quarterback."

Eddie Robinson (right)
and James Gregory
(Courtesy O. K. Davis,
*Rushton (La.) Daily
Leader*)

college and I asked him about Grambling. Then he said, "Mr. Robinson, are you telling
me that I could come to your school?" I said, "Yeah, you can come to our school." His
coach said James didn't have that much experience but was sure he could help us.

Greg knew how to mix, how to get along with people, and the players liked him. The
players put a protective ring around him so certain things never happened to him. The
media came to me and told me, "Eddie, we understand that before Greg came you
talked with the team about how you wanted them to treat him." I said, "Yes, I did that."

I learned that in graduate school. The chairman of physical education at Iowa, Dr.
Charles McCloy, paid special attention to the black students who had come to Iowa.
He knew it could be lonely for people who were in a small minority. He was the advisor to all of the blacks who had been at Iowa and paid close attention to all our schedules. "I want to work with you and your schedule. I want you to graduate." And then
he said, "When you want somebody to talk to, when you get lonesome, come on over
to the office and talk to me. We can take time and talk." He was always that kind of
person, and I wanted to be like that.

So I told my players they had to see that nothing happened to Greg. I said, "We're
an American university and a lot of you'll probably end up going to a white school
someday. You're going to have to get along there. Since James is a football player here,
this is what you really need to do."

I remember a game with Wiley when they hurt James Harris. Then they hurt his backup. I went over and got Greg up to get ready to play. Henry Davis, our captain, called time-out. Davis was nicknamed "hatchet man." Gregory was snapping to get in this game. But it looked like Wiley thought they couldn't win, so they were playing the game real rough. Henry Davis came over to me and said, "Coach, do you know what you're doing?" I said, "Do I know what I'm doing? Yes, I know what I'm doing. I'm getting ready to send Greg into the game."

He said, "Coach, you can't put him in now." When I asked why, he responded, "You know how the game is being played. Wiley is trying to hurt us. If Greg comes in the ball game, I don't know if we're going to be able to protect him. But we will try, even if it causes a war." He asked me to talk to the Wiley coach. Our guys said it simply, "He's the Tiger, and we are not going to let them deliberately take shots at him."

So I told the official, "Tell the Wiley coach right now or when we have another time-out that we need to talk." After two more players got hurt, I called the ref and said I was coming out on the field to talk to the Wiley coach. "I want to talk to you. Our players are not pleased with the rough way you all are playing now. I'm putting in a new quarterback and he's white. If we have any problems, my team will aggressively protect him. They want you to know that it will be a war, and they're going to do what anybody should do to help protect people on the team. They want me to tell you to talk to your players. I'm going to tell the remainder of the guys on our bench that we don't want anything to happen." I went back and got my bench together and Wiley got its bench together. We finished that game without any trouble.

When Greg first came, the guys carried him around. He only ate at the table with the football players. We didn't have any incident. We talked about it among ourselves. We talked to him. He was the right person. I don't know anyone who could have handled it the way that he did. And Gregory came through between two of the greatest quarterbacks that we had had; James Harris was on his first team and Matt Reed was on his last team.

Gregory didn't get a chance to play as much as he would like to have played. And he didn't play as much as I had wanted him to play. He wanted me to let him be a receiver. For one thing, Greg didn't have great speed. But even if he did, imagine changing a white QB into a receiver. This was at a time when most of the black coaches were upset because so many coaches in the NFL were taking the black quarterbacks and making them receivers.

I told Greg, "Look, I know you want to play receiver, but I'm not going to let you. I'm going to work with you as quarterback. Many of us are criticizing the people in the NFL for taking every black player who played quarterback, bringing him in, and making a receiver out of him." Therefore, I told him he was going to have to really be satisfied playing quarterback because I was not going to put him in as a receiver. It probably was selfish on my part. He might have played more if he changed, but I just couldn't move him to a receiver because I thought some people might say, "Eddie is trying to pay back the NFL for what they've been doing to us." I didn't want to be like that.

James Gregory was a fine young man. He worked hard on the football field and to get along on a campus where he could have been ostracized. Greg also did well in the classroom. Nonetheless, after four years he hadn't graduated. Then he went home for vacation in the summer after the spring semester of his senior year. He called me to say he wasn't coming back to Grambling. I told him to put his Daddy and his Momma on the phone. I told them all that he had to come back. Mrs. Gregory asked, "What do you mean? He's used up his eligibility. I don't think we really can afford the costs at Grambling." I told Mrs. Gregory, "He's used up his eligibility, but we can help him until he has completed his education. He can stay here, complete his courses, and work with us in athletics. He can help us coach." Like with all our student-athletes, I said, "When James leaves here I want Grambling stamped on his back: that he has his degree from here and he's played here." They were thinking that he could finish for free or nearly free at a California state college. That would have been easy, but it wouldn't have finished the job we'd started at Grambling.

James Gregory came back to Grambling and stayed here until he had those things stamped on his back. It was a proud moment for his folks and for me when he marched in the graduation ceremony.

James Gregory became a high school football coach in California, where he had some real good teams. Some of his players came to Grambling. I have seen him at the AFCA conventions. I sold him on the conventions, so he went whenever he could. And I love to see him there. He will always have a special place for us at Grambling. Of course, I took some heat for bringing a white player to Grambling. I got a lot of letters saying that Grambling should not have done so, that we didn't need a white quarterback. But on our campus, things were quiet because everyone got to know Greg. He made that part easy.

Ironically, I had another white quarterback, Mike Kornblau, as my career came to an end in 1997. In fact, in the 1996 Bayou Classic, Grambling and Southern both had white quarterbacks. That got a great deal of national media attention and a storm of criticism. I couldn't understand that. Heck, this was near the new millennium. I guess some people have not moved as far down the racial equality path as we had hoped.

By the end of the 1960s, we had a new Civil Rights Act, a Voting Rights Act, and black officials were being elected even in the Deep South. In sports, Althea Gibson had won at Wimbledon a decade earlier and Arthur Ashe had won the 1968 U.S. Open. Charlie Sifford had won the Long Beach Open in 1957 and the Alameda Open in 1960. Bill Russell had gotten the coaching job with the Celtics in 1966. The all-black Texas Western basketball team beat Adolph Rupp's all-white team at the University of Kentucky for the national championship in 1965. Muhammad Ali had won a victory in the Supreme Court in spite of raising a storm of protest by becoming a Black Muslim and, later, challenging the Vietnam War. He seemed to be on the move toward equality.

However, the waters were hardly still. Malcolm X, Martin Luther King, Jr., and Robert Kennedy were all assassinated between 1965 and 1968. City after city, including Watts, Detroit, and Newark, burned during riots. Many blacks, especially our youth, were leaving Martin Luther King, Jr.'s message of nonviolence behind in favor of Stokely Carmichael's message of Black Power and the emerging Black Panther Party under Huey Newton and Eldridge Cleaver.

The world of sports had its own dramatic racial trauma at the Mexico City Olympics as our black athletes protested in unprecedented ways, drawing global attention to their anger as it reflected the anger of many young blacks.

But I tend to look at such complicated issues like race relations in basic terms. I had just seen my team of all black men embrace an outsider as a teammate and treat him like a brother. I knew that we had learned something from Greg and he from us. We all taught others some things in the process. It was important enough that a movie, *The White Tiger*, was made about it. Now I wish more of our nation had seen us or the movie then so that more of our citizens could have absorbed what happened at Grambling State in those troubled times.

Eddie Robinson, with Richard Lapchick, "James Gregory: Grambling's First White Player," from Robinson, *Never Before, Never Again: The Stirring Autobiography of Eddie Robinson* (New York: St. Martin's, 1999), 134–39.

4. Lloyd V. Hackley / "We Need to Educate Our Athletes": Higher Education and Sports

In 1983, the National Collegiate Athletic Association (NCAA) attempted to improve the poor academic performance and low graduation rate of college athletes by passing a rule known as Proposition 48. Following on the heels of Professor Jan Kemp's lawsuit against the University of Georgia for preferential treatment given to academically unqualified athletes, and largely in response to the pressure placed on the NCAA by the American Council of Education, Proposition 48 ruled that all freshmen athletes would be ineligible to participate on varsity sports teams if they did not achieve at least a score of 15 on the American College Test (ACT) or a combined score of 700 on the Scholastic Aptitude Test (SAT). The proposition, which would not be implemented until 1986, caused a deep philosophical split within the African American community. Some blacks were highly critical of the NCAA's guidelines while others showed just as much support. Those opposed to the proposition, including such well-known African American civil rights leaders as Jesse Jackson and Benjamin Hooks and noted basketball coaches such as John Chaney of Temple and John Thompson of Georgetown, believed the criteria used to determine athletic eligibility were culturally biased in favor of whites. Those in favor of the proposition, including the tennis great Arthur Ashe and the sports activist Harry Edwards, claimed that it was not racially discriminatory and would prove beneficial to black athletes.

In the following selection, Lloyd V. Hackley, chancellor of the University of Arkansas at Pine Bluff, argued that critics of Proposition 48 were unintentionally "retarding the progress of deprived peoples" by claiming racism and arguing against higher academic standards. He believed that the only way to improve the academic performance of African American athletes was to support the eligibility requirement included in Proposition 48 rather than denounce the unfairness of testing procedures. Anything else was exploitation and the worst kind of treatment of African American athletes. As eligibility standards and measures of academic attainment, Proposition 48 as well as the subsequent and even more stringent Propositions 42 and 16 have remained controversial among African Americans. Many are

still troubled by the guidelines' disproportionate effect on black athletes and remain uncon-
vinced that the propositions have served as an incentive for students to take school more
*seriously or have led to improved academic performance.**

———— ————

The assertions some have stated about Proposition 48 simply are not true. In essence, the ruling states that for a student athlete to participate in intercollegiate athletics during his or her freshman year, the athlete will have to have scored at least fifteen on the American College Test (or 700 on the Scholastic Aptitude Test), and more importantly, will have to have amassed eleven units in high school in a core of courses consisting of English, mathematics, science and social studies. Critics have stated flatly that this action is designed to prevent Blacks from engaging in college sports. The public needs to understand that only those major universities categorized NCAA Division I are covered. There are more than 3,000 colleges and universities in the United States; less than ten percent are in NCAA Division I. If an athlete who is accepted by one of the few schools covered by this ruling does not have the academic qualifications, which indicate that he or she can both participate in intercollegiate athletics and adjust successfully to college level academics, then that individual cannot participate in sports in the first year. (All colleges and universities should follow suit.) The truth then, without emotion, is this: Students, who are outstanding enough to be selected by the Division I schools for their athletic ability, who have experienced a meaningful education and who show by a score on an examination that they can "handle" a college curriculum, in a major, large university, will be allowed to "play ball" from their sophomore year on. If basketball players clear up their deficiencies the first semester, they can "play ball" their first year.

To those who don't understand why it might be appropriate for a closer control to be exercised with regard to academic qualifications of college athletes as opposed to non-athletes, I offer some points for consideration: First, the exploitation of athletes through academic deprivation is well documented. Second, the sooner a youngster exhibits superior athletic talent, the sooner it is likely that the world will treat that youngster differently, including academically. Third, I invite the skeptical to explain how a college student, with a set amount of academic ability, who is a football player, for example, can put in three or four hours of intense physically and mentally demanding practice daily and equal the academic attainment initially projected, or acquired, by a non–football player with the same starting academic potential. As a former intercollegiate coach, I submit that the athlete is at a distinct disadvantage. That disadvantage too often is minimized for athletic eligibility by sop courses, meaningless academic programs, and questionable summer school enrollments. Such special treatment, unfortunately, begins as early as junior high school.

What some critics of the ruling don't seem to understand (if they do understand,

---

* Perhaps the most enlightening discussion of Propositions 48, 42, and 16 is Zimbalist, *Unpaid Professionals,* 26–36. See also Coakley, *Sport in Society,* esp. 455–56; Leonard, *Sociological Perspective of Sport,* 18, 315; T. Davis, "Race, Law and College Athletics"; Shropshire, *In Black and White,* esp. 108–21, 125–27.

then they don't care) is that they have linked higher academic standards to racism. Moreover, they have said to Black youngsters that even if Blacks are educated in an enriched core of courses, and even if they are motivated to work hard in that core, they still cannot be expected to do very well. Not only does such an inference fly in the face of acknowledged educational facts, it also finds no acceptance among current educational policymakers. This group of new educators, among whom I count myself, understand the concept of intelligence and all the factors which determine the development of the abilities and motives that underlie competence and social responsibility.

After critical analysis and experience, more of us know that the intelligence of an individual is not a fixed quantity. A child's mind can be equated to a barren field for which an expert farmer (teacher) can devise a new method of cultivation, so that in place of a desert, we could have a harvest. Relating the analogy more to the issue, one can increase real intelligence—the capacity to improve—with instruction.

Well-meaning individuals, and some not so well-meaning, who have linked educational standards to racism in this athletic issue, will do more harm than they can imagine. Many Black educators have come to understand that students who are exposed to a solid curricular experience and who really put in a meaningful effort in their studies, not only score higher on "standardized" tests, but also increase their likelihood for graduating from college.

It is this particular aspect of the issue where I have my greatest problem with the critics of the ruling. Many non-educators now also understand the importance of enriched classroom experiences in overcoming educational problems that stem from economic, social, and cultural deprivation. Those who have expressed opposition are saying to our children, that even with the core curriculum and hard work, they still would be unable to make even forty-one percent of the maximum score on a general achievement examination.

If anyone takes the time to evaluate this inference, he will understand that it states inherent inferiority. However, the most devastating aspect of inferring that certain classes of people, or segments (athletes) within classes of people, are inherently inferior is that the young people come to believe that they are in fact incompetent, and they give up even trying. And the earlier they accept this false assumption, the earlier they understand that America has lower expectations for them, the more difficult it is to improve their capacity for learning (when they enroll in colleges and universities). What we expect of them, they will expect of themselves and each other.

One of the most effective means of retarding the progress of deprived peoples is to get them to become instruments of their own oppression. Getting them to fight the wrong battles is a perfect example of the implementation of this method. By focusing on the athletic aspect of this issue, we have missed the most important point. We have been drawn into an effort to make certain that Blacks can participate in sports in their first year, as if that is their main reason for getting into one of those 277 premier institutions in the first place.

Even the Educational Testing Service is emphasizing the athletic aspect of the matter. That organization has stated that if the new ruling had been in effect in 1981, fifty-one percent of the Black freshmen would not have been qualified to participate in athletics in their first year if they had enrolled in one of the 277 institutions. But the fact of the matter is that the ruling was not in effect and will not be until 1986, after the student athletes will have been required to complete the college relevant core curriculum in high school. ETS officials admit they do not have the answer. Our concern should not be directed primarily toward first-year participation in athletics, but rather toward first-year improvement in the ability of freshmen to do college level work, to gain an education and to earn a degree. Keep in mind that the overwhelming majority of Blacks who participate in athletics fail to graduate.

The answer to poor performance in primary and secondary schools by our children is not continuing exploitation in college, just the opposite. If counselors, teachers and parents realize that student athletes will have to go through the meaningful education track in public school, they will insist that this occur.

Even colleges will pay attention to what is happening to children academically at an earlier stage. Remember that if our children are taught the core courses, their scores will go up on all standardized tests. Coaches become aware of the prowess of outstanding athletes even before high school and they track them. Now they must really mean it when they tell parents they stress academics in their programs. If we as Black people don't teach our children the difference between athletics and academics, and explain to them the difference between preparing for life and entertaining fans on Saturday afternoon, then it is not cultural identity they will need, but mental maturity.

My position on this issue has put me at the opposite pole from some of my colleagues, many of whom are very significant to the Black community and to me. It is lonely to be in my posture; it would have been easier to ride along with the prevalent view. But the majority has been wrong before. The exploitation of Black athletes is a national tragedy bordering on the criminal; it should be embarrassing to the institutions that are guilty, and it should spur Blacks to greater effort in secondary schools so that we can excel in academics and athletics.

This new proposal may prevent some of our Black children from playing football in some schools the first year; some may have to forgo "big time" college ball altogether; but if we as Black people struggled in the fifties and sixties to get Blacks into mainstream colleges only to see them as low-paid entertainers who leave those schools with little or no education, then I have found the basis for our lack of progress, it is us. It is time that Black people understand what is really happening to us and what our objectives ought to be. If I have to stand alone in rejection of the exploitation of so many of our youngsters, then I will.

Lloyd Hackley, "We Need to Educate Our Athletes," *Black Collegian* 13 (April/May 1983): 35–37.

B

THE LIMITS OF INTEGRATION

5. Marian E. Washington / "Black Women in Sports: Can We Get off the Track?"

Throughout the 1960s and 1970s African American athletes won championships and set records in a wide range of sports, though as Phil Petrie (and others) suggested, those successes were qualified by the persistence of stereotyping and racial discrimination. But at the most basic level, commentators could note clear signs of progress in the realm of sports. This, argued Marian Washington, was emphatically not *the case for African American women. Their presence at the highest echelons of competition had been severely limited, and the principal image of the victorious black female athlete was as a track star. Indeed, the triumphs by black women in Olympic competition—from Wilma Rudolph and Wyomia Tyus onward—had been a source of considerable pride among African Americans, especially within the highly charged medal contest with the Soviet Union during the height of the cold war. Nevertheless, as Washington argued, the narrow thinking that confined black women to the Olympic pedestal was also responsible for circumscribing their opportunities to make their marks in other sports.*

Washington's remarks in a 1974 speech came at a time when the implementation of Title IX, which forbids discrimination on the basis of gender at schools receiving federal funding, was just beginning to alter sporting competition at the college and university levels. Investment in the cultivation of athletics among women would be partial, at best, until a decade later, but the opening up of the playing fields would not include African American women in significant numbers. One could point to Cheryl Miller and Lynette Woodard in basketball, Flo Hyman in volleyball, Debi Thomas in figure skating, and Zina Garrison in tennis during the 1980s (and of course a host of track-and-field standouts such Alice Brown, Evelyn Ashford, Florence Griffith Joyner, and Jackie Joyner-Kersee) and one could discern the significance of a new generation of coaches, such as Vivian Stringer and Marian Washington herself. But Washington's concerns were sadly prophetic. Title IX went a long way toward establishing substantial programs in women's soccer and crew—among a variety of other sports—but African American women were not full beneficiaries of these developments. As the personal account by Anita DeFrantz and a survey of athletic programs and expert commentary by the Chronicle of Higher Education *demonstrate (see documents 2 and 3 in the final part of this book), black women have often been left behind in the quest for gender equity in sport.**

---

* See Y. R. Smith, "Sociohistorical Influences on African American Elite Sportswomen"; Corbett and Johnson, "The African American Female in Collegiate Sport."

——— ———

If I were to have appeared before this group in the informal outfit of a black female athlete—and you knew nothing about me at all—chances are you'd be expecting a track outfit. And you'd be close to correct—for the major portion of my athletic career has been in relationship to track.

Consider if you will, any black female athlete whose name is of more than local fame. What event is her specialty—riding? golf? swimming? Maybe a gymnast or tennis player? All of these are doubtful, right?

In mid-January, one of the major TV companies—caught up with the emergence of women's rights—focused on women in athletics. The black representative, Cheryl Toussaint, is—of course—a runner.

For those of you that are either coaching or familiar with the situation at the intercollegiate level, you are well aware that black female participation is limited. In the 1969 National Intercollegiate Basketball Tournament for Women there were 16 teams from throughout the United States—totaling about 180 players. Of these, only three were black and two of us were from the same school. And, quite coincidentally of course, we won!

This year, in personal exposure to nine midwestern college teams, I have seen only two black players on women's basketball teams.

In field hockey, lacrosse, swimming, volleyball, and gymnastics the story is virtually the same: Black females do not compete in collegiate athletics, for track is essentially an AAU activity.

The next question could be Why[,] but that is secondary, I feel, to a more important issue: What difference does it make?

If our answer is None, then my whole presentation—though a pleasant opportunity—is of little value. Obviously, my response to What difference does it make? is a determined A Great Difference, both in terms of self-growth and accomplishment and in terms of social values and objectives.

Mention the phrase "black youth"—be they male or female—and immediately we classify them as poor and ghetto residents. Unfortunately, for too many of my people this is and will continue to be true. Millions of dollars [are] directed into youth programs in the city, but, in a narrow approach, most of it is directed toward boys' programs. Of course, we do then develop the Nate Archibalds, the Franco Harrises, the John Mayberrys, an occasional Arthur Ashe, the Muhammad Alis and the Joe Fraziers and a multitude of other stars of varying magnitudes. This is fine, for the success of today's neighborhood athlete encourages numerous other youngsters to think of high school, of college, of success.

But still narrow, because what happens to or with the black female? Is she to go through life with the boundaries of the ghetto the full extent of her world? What are her avenues to success? Who are the women she wants to imitate? There are the Robin Campbells, the Cheryl Toussaints, and the Willye Whites and some scholarships at Tennessee State and Alcorn A. & M. But beyond them, what?

Can the black female youngster identify with a Billie Jean King, a Mickie Wright, a

Peggy Fleming, or a Kathy Whitcomb? Unlikely. Not only are they white and from a world apart, but, more important, tennis, swimming, ice skating, and golf are not a part of their school curriculum or included in public recreational facilities.

Two situations come to mind. Several years ago when I was working in an inner city agency, my supervisor called me in to discuss a group meeting I had just had with some teenage girls. Frankly I was feeling quite satisfied because something went well, with the girls having played records and then having watched the boys' basketball team practice. These were their choices of things to do. Imagine my surprise and resentment when my supervisor challenged the appropriateness of the group's involvement. My explanation that "this was democratic—to let the girls choose" was met with "Why?" "Why?" Finally, the supervisor's message was put forth in this fashion: For those of you from the East, you will particularly remember that Howard Johnson's was first known for its ice cream—more specifically its 28 flavors. Exotic flavors like burgundy bravo, raspberry swirl, banana, creme de menthe. But what are their biggest sellers? You're right if you guessed vanilla, chocolate, and strawberry. And now the question Why takes meaning—people tend to choose those things which are familiar. Thus, if you want to expand horizons, to give new perspectives, and to modify value systems, you must introduce individuals to change. Slowly maybe, but surely absolutely. In short, giving youngsters their choice of activities is a limited choice at best, for their own reservoir of experience is so limited.

The second experience also came from this inner city agency. Its summer camp for disadvantaged girls featured sailboats and an intensive swimming program. Its winter program took youngsters to nearby ski slopes—the first black skiers the area had had! And this in 1968. Tennis was introduced and despite their grubby uniforms of black high-tops and jeans and multicolored shirts, a tournament was held. For the first time, a girls' basketball team was developed; its admission to what had become a suburban-oriented league was resented. And immediately its presence was felt; they were well outfitted, their discipline was controlled, and their play was surprisingly good. In fact, they made it to the city finals before they floundered and failed.

The important and essential element in all of these activities is that they were exposed to and became experienced in activities common to the so-called mainstream of society. And about time if we truly wish to avoid two separate societies and the social tensions that go with them.

With today's current awareness and emphasis upon equal rights, particularly—for our interest—in more equitable athletic programs, this leads us to new developments. While a few colleges have given scholarships to women, i.e., JFK, Midwestern, Parsons, Ouachita, Wayland, and, of course, Tennessee State and Alcorn A. & M., these have been limited. More seriously, however, these colleges have been excluded from participation in the DGWS intercollegiate competitions. This now has been changed because of several recent court decisions.

Universities and colleges are being forced to look at their expenditures and to justify one-sided treatment. And emerging is the prospect of scholarships for women. Stanford—a truly great university—will offer forty in 1974–75. As these developments are multiplied, opportunities shall expand.

From what may be viewed as a selfish point of view, I say, "Great and let's get black females thoroughly coached and skilled to be in a position to compete for them." Think a minute, though. Is it really selfish; who pays for the underachievement, underemployment, and undermotivation of any of our citizens? We all do—one way or the other.

The Why to the exclusion of black females from athletics other than track is relatively simple. It is a mixture of stereotyping (blacks run faster, blacks are not as bright, and blacks are too "antsy" to play basketball—according to a noted woman basketball coach) and the limitation of choices available to inner city residents. You should note that few public recreational facilities are being built in our cities. Rather, suburbia and the private apartment complex are developing a monopoly on pools, tennis courts, open areas, and such.

We should, I suggest, stop and look at the total picture. You, as men and women of the profession, do not need an introductory lecture on the values of athletics and sports—your very integrity is built on its meaning. In closing, what I would ask is, Broaden your perspective and commitment. Do not be so color-blind that you ignore the absence of a very significant part of our population in your programs—the black female. She too must be liberated!

Marian E. Washington, "Black Women in Sports: Can We Get off the Track?" *Proceedings of the Seventy-seventh Annual Meeting of the National Collegiate Physical Education Association for Men* (Chicago: University of Illinois at Chicago, 1974), 42–44.

6. Frank Robinson / "In America's National Pastime . . . White Is the Color of the Game off the Field"

In 1987, Al Campanis, a top executive with the Los Angeles Dodgers, suggested to Ted Koppel on ABC's Nightline *that the scarcity of African Americans in baseball management positions resulted from their lack of abilities. "I truly believe," Campanis told Koppel, "they [African Americans] may not have the necessities to be, let's say, a field manager or perhaps a general manager."[*]*

Campanis's comments caused an extensive public outcry. Journalists, politicians, civil rights leaders, academicians, businesspeople, ministers, coaches, and athletes attacked Campanis for his insensitive and disparaging remarks about African Americans. The most prominent African American and white magazines and newspapers were filled with a plethora of articles condemning Campanis and, in some cases, asking for his resignation. The Dodgers ultimately fired Campanis while baseball commissioner Peter Ueberroth, faced with a public relations nightmare, hired Harry Edwards to study the problem of racism in major league baseball and increase the number of African Americans in management positions.[**]

In the following selection, Frank Robinson, the former great Cincinnati Reds and Balti-

---

[*] Quoted in Chass, "Campanis Is Out," B13–B14.
[**] For other responses to the Campanis statement, see Hoose, *Necessities.*

Frank Robinson (Courtesy National Baseball Hall of Fame Library, Cooperstown, N.Y)

more Orioles outfielder and the first African American to manage in the major leagues, responds in an interview to Campanis's remarks and touches on the question of the lack of blacks in management positions in baseball. Robinson, like many other African Americans, claimed that he welcomed Campanis's remarks because it made public the racism that still existed in the national game. Although regretting the fact that Campanis "had to take the heat for something for which baseball is responsible," Robinson argues that the former Dodger executive's "statements are the most significant thing that has happened for blacks in baseball for a long, long time" because it "made people finally understand what goes on behind closed doors."

———————

Were you surprised by Al Campanis' comments about blacks in baseball?
No. Baseball has been hiding this ugly prejudice for years—that blacks aren't

smart enough to be managers or third-base coaches or part of the front office. There's a belief that they're fine when it comes to the physical part of the game, but if it involves brains they just can't handle it. Al Campanis made people finally understand what goes on behind closed doors—that there is racism in baseball.

Is there racial tension on the field?

Not among the players. We couldn't function on the diamond or live together eight months out of the year if there was. But that doesn't mean there is equality. As a black, you find you have to be two or three times better than a white even to play. And when it comes to front-office jobs, management believes you'll never be as good.

Why haven't blacks been able to break the management color barrier?

Because we haven't been in the position either to do the hiring or to say, "Hire me or else." Blacks haven't put pressure on baseball. So baseball says, "If we don't have to give you a job, we won't." Part of this is our fault. You talk to some black players and then say, "I'm a happy man, I'm making a good living. Why should I stick my neck out?" You talk to people outside the game, and they say, "I don't want to be bothered."

Why don't more black players speak out?

Speaking up could be damaging. Someone will get buried. The ownership might think, "He's mouthing off. Who needs him?" I won't say that today they could blackball a great player. But they could make it tough for him. At the end of his career, he might not get to play those extra years if they feel he's a troublemaker.

How have you gotten as far as you have?

By being an outstanding player over a number of years for one thing. But also by being vocal about the fact that I wanted to manage when I was through playing. Then I tried to eliminate some of the excuses baseball offers. The biggest excuse you hear is that blacks aren't willing to go to the minor leagues and prepare themselves to manage in the majors. So during the years I was still playing I would go to Puerto Rico in the winter and manage. When the day came, I had the experience without having to go to the minor leagues for four or five years and then wait for an opportunity. Still there's a double standard. Some whites like Pete Rose, Joe Torre and Ted Williams never had to go to the minors. They've gone right into big league jobs.

What are some of the other excuses you've heard?

One of my favorites is that blacks just aren't applying for management positions. I've never seen baseball advertise for a job, and I've never heard of whites applying for a job. I mean there's an old boy network, and it's lily white. The people upstairs also say white players won't play for a black manager and fans won't come to the ballpark. If the players are on a good team, they don't care who they're playing for. And if a team is playing well, the fans don't care who's managing. If the team plays poorly, they're going to holler for his scalp, whether it's black or white.

Are some baseball teams more progressive than others?

I don't see any. On the 26 Major League ball clubs, there isn't one black third-base coach. There's one Latino, Ozzie Virgil, in Seattle, but no blacks. And that's because the third-base coach is the manager's first lieutenant. If they put a black at third base, the next step is manager. Owners say, "No way." The ball clubs are dragging their feet.

How does that make you feel?

Not good. Young people say sports figures are their idols, and we have to conduct ourselves in such a manner that young people really can look up to us and model themselves after us. If we continue to allow this sort of racism to exist, we don't deserve to be idolized.

Who are the outstanding black candidates for managerial and front-office jobs?

I think former second baseman Joe Morgan, now a businessman and part time baseball commentator, would make an excellent manager or general manager. Bill White, who broadcasts for the Yankees, would make an excellent general manager and coaches like Willie Stargell of the Braves, Bill Robinson of the Mets and Elrod Hendricks of the Orioles would all be excellent managers. Still you don't really know who'll be good until they're given the opportunity.

Do you hope to manage again?

Yes, one day I'd like to manage again, but that's not my burning desire. I had two opportunities with the Cleveland Indians and the San Francisco Giants. I've been there, and there are other people who deserve a chance. If I did manage again, I'd be more selective in the ball club I work with. I don't want to get into a losing situation as I did with Cleveland and San Francisco. People ask, "Why did he take those ball clubs?" Well, somebody had to break down the barrier and keep a black man visible.

Will Campanis' remarks speed progress toward racial equality?

First, I should say that Campanis is a decent man. I'm sorry he's had to take the heat for something for which baseball is responsible. But his statements are the most significant thing that has happened for blacks in baseball for a long, long time. People are shocked. They ask, "Is that the way it really is?" You bet.

If Jackie Robinson were alive and willing today, would the lords of baseball be likely to admit him to their ranks?

No. He was too controversial—too honest. He'd create too many problems by speaking up and speaking out. White management doesn't like black people to speak their minds. They like you to be seen but not heard. And Jackie Robinson wouldn't put himself in that position.

"In America's National Pastime, Says Frank Robinson, White Is the Color of the Game off the Field," *People Weekly*, April 27, 1987, 46, 51.

7. Jim Brown / Racism in Context

Jim Brown is considered by many to be the greatest running back in the history of football. Born in 1936 on St. Simons Island, Georgia, Brown first became known for his prodigious athletic talents while a student at Manhasset High School in Manhasset, New York. He garnered thirteen varsity letters at Manhasset, exhibiting enough baseball talent to be offered a minor league contract by the New York Yankees, averaging eighteen points a game in basketball, and starring as a running back in football. After graduating from Manhasset, Brown went on to Syracuse University where he enhanced his reputation as a great all-around athlete by averaging 13.1 points per game in basketball, placing fifth in the national decathlon championship in track and field, and being selected as all-American in both lacrosse and football. In 1957, Brown was selected in the first round of the National Football League (NFL) draft by the Cleveland Browns. In just nine seasons with the team, Brown rushed for 12,312 yards, an NFL record that would not be broken until many years later by Walter Payton.

Brown retired from football following the 1965 season to pursue a career in motion pictures and participate in a variety of economic causes and political activities. He costarred with Lee Marvin, Telly Savalas, and other well-known actors in The Dirty Dozen, *and in subsequent years he assumed roles in such movies as* Ice Station Zebra, The Split, One Hundred Rifles, *and* Three the Hard Way. *He was an outspoken supporter of the black athletic revolt of the late 1960s, was involved in prison reform, and established an organization that counsels street gang members in Los Angeles. Brown has also written two autobiographies.**

In the following selection from Out of Bounds, *Brown discusses racism in sport. In his typically straightforward and bold fashion, Brown discusses such subjects as Jimmy "the Greek" Snyder, race relations in the NFL, and the lack of involvement of African American athletes in the civil rights struggle. Specifically, Brown claims, in words that now seem especially prophetic, that O. J. Simpson "can't tell the truth to America." Like other African American athletes, Simpson exhibited no social consciousness or concern for the black community. He was unwilling to speak out against racial injustices for fear that he would lose money, risk his popularity, and suffer the wrath of white America.*

–––––– –––––

Unfortunately, the civil rights movement wasn't yet in full bloom when I first played pro football. I wanted mine, made no bones about it, people called me militant. On the football field they wanted me to be brave. Wanted me to take the ball when we were all backed up, our own one-yard-line, carry us out of there, where we could be safe. Away from football, they wanted me to be another guy. They wanted me to be docile. How could I have the courage to run that hard, then be so weak off the field that I'd succumb to inequity?

I'll tell you the biggest problem when people talk about racial issues: they're so damn confusing. If there's one thing I've learned in fifty-three years, it's that life is contradictory. In sitcoms and bad movies everything is tidy and simple. Life's not that absolute, neither is human behavior, and the subject of racism is really tricky. I remember when I was in my teens, I met all those loving white people at Manhasset. Then I went to Syracuse, ran chin first into overt racism. Someone had changed all the rules, forgotten to tell me.

I was lucky, or maybe smart: I never got so confused that I became a racist. I never thought every white man was the devil. Even before I understood it intellectually, I knew instinctively that categorizing people by skin color, then hating them in groups, was not what God intended for us.

When racism is overt, it can be terribly elusive, as hard to define as it is to prove in

* See J. Brown, *Off My Chest* and *Out of Bounds.* For more information see Brown, "How I Play Fullback"; P. King, "Jim Brown."

court. It's a cliché, and a cliché even to call a is cliché, but I'll bring it up anyway because I hear it a lot. White people say, "I'm not a racist, I have two black friends." Then I hear the black refrain: "That guy's a racist. He said he has two black friends." Now the white guy doesn't know what to think. Gee, maybe I am a racist.

Not so fast. Society has isolated him in such a way, brainwashed him really, that for a white guy to have two black friends, I think he's doing pretty well. Most white folks have no education when it comes to black folks, no meaningful exposure. What they have is TV. What they see there about blacks is ninety-five percent negative. Even when the rare exception, "The Cosby Show," debuted, some critics said "Hey, that's not a real black family. Black families aren't that way." Man, there are millions of black families like the Huxtables. And there are white folks in Appalachia who don't dress like "Dynasty."

But the brainwashing continues, and not just on TV. Maybe a person gets sick of TV, opens an encyclopedia. He reads about a guy named Shockley, an American physicist, who won a Pulitzer Prize for his study on blacks—why the structure of their brain makes them mentally inferior. Next the person finds a dictionary, looks up the word Negro. I did that several times. In various references, it was said that a Negro was distinguished by a broad nose, large lips, arms that are unusually long, especially from the forearm, long legs, small calves, protruding heels, and hair that grows in an irregular manner.

No Kentucky Colonel? I love dat fried food.

It's not funny. TV, films, reference books, authority figures still spew derogatory, stereotypical misinformation. That is powerful medicine. No wonder people get mixed up.

I think Jimmy the Greek got mixed up. A close friend of mine, a white insider who knows the Greek well, says Jimmy is basically a bigot. Put that aside, because it's only one man's opinion. My opinion is that the Greek simply got mixed up. I think he was high on booze. Anyone who knows booze knows it gets you talking some dumb, convoluted shit—and believing it. I think Jimmy was high, tried to combine some stuff he'd read in Webster's, few other sources, came out with some screwy hybrid.

I thought the Greek affair was insignificant. Having garbage in reference books, on the tube, is a million times more damaging than an oddsmaker getting buzzed and getting mixed up. I felt the same way about the deal with Al Campanis, another guy I thought was talking through his scotch. I know, they said Campanis hadn't been boozing. I think he was. Either way, the episode had no real meaning. Briefly it got people talking, even emotional, but after a week, maybe two, it was off the evening news, back to the old order. What happened with Campanis altered nothing, in society or even in baseball. Baseball has two black managers. In Bill White, its National League President, baseball has one top-level executive.

As meager as that sounds, and is, the NFL is even more exclusive. They asked former commissioner Pete Rozelle a few years ago why there were no black head coaches in the NFL. Essentially, Rozelle implied that none were qualified; they had to go through the system. Pete has retired now, but you still hear similar rationalizations. We could theorize on this one for weeks, but I'll use an actual example. At the time

Rozelle made his statement, there were four NFL coaches who I used to play with on the Browns: Walt Michaels, Paul Wiggin, Monte Clark and Chuck Noll. Walt Michaels was a hell of a linebacker, with an ordinary mind. Paul Wiggin was bashful, good mind for academics, ordinary mind for football. Monte Clark, also shy, great guy, very dedicated. Ordinary mind. Out of my four teammates, the only exceptional mind in that group is Chuck Noll. Chuck knows the game as few men ever have.

I also played on the Browns with John Wooten and Paul Warfield and Bobby Mitchell. All black, all respected, all bright. I think Wooten, a Dallas Cowboys scout, is more suited to coach than at least three of those guys I mentioned before. Bobby Mitchell, the assistant GM at Washington, definitely has the skills and everything else to be a head coach. Over the years, we had a lot of black Browns who could match intellect and football smarts with the other guys I mentioned. Had they gotten just a little encouragement, maybe they'd be head coaches today. Guys who have tried anyway haven't gotten any jobs. So please don't tell me the black guys today lack the experience. How can they obtain it if they can't get coaching jobs? That Catch-22 is getting old.

The issue here is power and leadership—a head coach has them both. In America and the NFL, that's a position that is still off-limits to blacks. Meaning you can have forty Jim Browns on your team, as long as Paul Brown is white. You can have ten blacks on offense, and as long as the quarterback is white, America still feels semi-comfortable. It used to be black guys couldn't play center, quarterback, and safety. Today the black guy can't be The Man.

However, I don't run all over the NFL screaming "Racist!" every two seconds. I never called Pete Rozelle a racist, or any of the NFL owners, because I don't know that any of them are. In America, it doesn't always come down to how an individual feels about blackness. In America, actions often hinge on economics. That a white owner doesn't hire a black coach does not mean he's a racist. He may adore black people, but if ninety percent of the franchise's fans are white, he doesn't know how those ticket buyers would react to a black coach. A white coach might be better business. I can sit here and say, "Hey, hire a black coach," and you know I hope that someone does. But it's easy for me: I don't have millions of my own capital invested. You can't say to every businessman in America, "Protect your investment as you see fit," and not allow that right to the NFL owners.

I also believe if black folks are going to scream at white owners, they should first take a look at their own. Check out the black superstars who largely ignore the black community. How different are the choices they make than those of the white owners? Both are more concerned with generating income, by projecting a certain image, than they are with effecting change.

I basically like O.J. Simpson. I do like Marcus Allen. And I like Michael Jackson and Lionel Ritchie. If they don't care about black folks, that's one thing. If they do, then their contribution is lacking. I don't like saying that; I'm not saying it to try and hurt people. I'm saying it to try and help. Because if we don't help our own, who will? Until black folks take a stand, how can we expect white people to?

That's why I came out with this several years ago, began discussing the social consciousness, which I find negligible, of the modern-day athlete. That includes the modern black athlete. For years I never heard any black athletes complain that there was not one black head coach in the NFL. Where was everyone?

I can't tell anyone how to live their life. Every man has the right to look out for his own career, make a whole bunch of money. No one does that better than the Juice. He's popular, he's intelligent, he's commercial. On the other hand, O.J. can't tell the truth to America. In order to stay popular, make the money, he can't say his black brothers are getting mistreated. That's why, among hardcore blacks, the Juice gets tremendous admiration as an athlete, and very little as a man. And that's why I never call O.J. if there's black event that might be controversial, or I need guys to come down to South Central L.A. Even if he wanted to come and showed up, if someone took a photograph, and it went over the wire, the people at Hertz would be pissed. That's not the image they want Juice to represent to their consumers. I know it, Juice knows it, so I don't even put him in the position. I just don't ask. Here's the thing: white America will never accept the Juice, wholesome image or not, as fully as it will a white guy.

When I look at the black stars today, I wonder if they ever study history. How do they think they got in the position they're in? Blacks who came before them paved the way, blacks who had to do more than just play good football, who had to endure some bitter cruelties. A lot of them did more than endure. They spoke out, provoked some thought, took some damn chances, instead of saying, "Hey, I've got mine. Everything is cool." If we had done that, the guys today would be starting from scratch.

And that is my crucial point: it's thirty years later, but everything is not cool. If blacks start taking their gains for granted, future generations will have serious trouble. I don't want the guys today to give me their damn time and money. I want them to wake up. To look around, realize the struggle is only beginning.

I look at athletes today, black and white, wonder if they watch anything but MTV. They're Very Nice, Very Rote, everyone says they're Wonderful. Maybe so. But I can't help thinking. They're not that wonderful. They won't say one word about South Africa. It's the worst country there is. They have apartheid. They're terrorists, killing people in the name of white superiority. These Wonderful Guys, particularly when they're at the peak of their visibility, are the ones who can get people's attention. Why don't they speak up?

All of that said, I want to be fair here. It is not easy making choices when you're a black American. Every black man isn't a revolutionary, and it's a tough decision: do I become active in black rights, risk losing jobs, or do I protect my own career? Is it possible for me, a black man in America, to find a compromise? To help a black man make some kind of choice, he can't even draw on his own tradition. He can't say, "Well, this is how we've been doing it for five hundred years. This is my culture, this is my tradition, this is what I must fight to maintain." The black American came from many different tribes. Families were broken, sold into slavery, not only by whites, but by blacks selling other blacks. Masters were sleeping with slaves, having babies, bloodlines got mixed like crazy. Coming from so many tribes, after all of that fragmentation, the black American has no firm tradition. His only tradition is that of an American. Naturally he wants to move up. Become affluent, ride in limos, get on

"Entertainment Tonight." Nothing's more American than that. And it's tempting, when your kids are in private school, your life is full, to get a little soft. That's not black. That's human.

And I still think we have to resist complacency. We're still black, too many black guys are still getting their asses kicked. We have to help to get that foot out of the other guy's butt. Any prominent black man who doesn't make some genuine attempt, and I really believe this, will someday wake up and feel remorse.

Me? I'll talk about racism with anyone, and I'll talk about racism in sports. But I get bored when that's all people want to talk about. By the time a guy arrives in the NFL, he's eating. He doesn't have to sleep on the sidewalk. Doesn't have to sell crack. The principle of equal opportunity should be applied to every man and woman, not just guys who drive Porsches. I wish them well, I'm glad they're playing quarterback, but I can't dwell too long on poor Warren Moon and Randall Cunningham. If that were my priority I'd be a fool.

Sometimes, all this talk about black quarterbacks makes me feel I've stepped into a time warp, landed in 1958. It's almost the 1990s, people still discuss a few black quarterbacks as if they represent some meaningful breakthrough for blacks. Doug Williams, played in the Super Bowl, I kept reading that the moment was proud and historical for blacks. Is that right? To me, it sounded more like the white media working out its own hangups. The story of that game wasn't Doug Williams' blackness. It was that Doug's career was nearly expired, he had the heart to keep coming back, to stay prepared, then excelled in the most pressure-filled game of his life. That had nothing to do with his blackness, and I don't buy its profundity for other black people. Blacks in the 1990s don't need any more symbols. They need equal rights. What Doug Williams did in the Super Bowl won't do shit for a cat who can't throw a football.

Jim Brown, with Steve Delsohn, *Out of Bounds* (New York: Kensington, 1989), 47–52.

8. Rafer Johnson / The Decathlete as Community-Builder

Rafer Johnson has been in the public eye for some fifty years. Born in Hillsboro, Texas, in 1935, Johnson was a great all-around high school athlete in Kingsburg, California. He lettered in four sports, averaging nine yards a carry as a football halfback, hitting .400 in baseball, scoring seventeen points in basketball, and capturing the state championship in the 120-yard high hurdles as well as placing third in the Amateur Athletic Unions (AAU) national decathlon finals. Offered athletic scholarships by several prestigious universities, Johnson elected to attend the University of California at Los Angeles where he developed into an internationally known decathlete. In 1955, Johnson captured the decathlon championships at the Pan-American Games and set a world record in the event at a meet in his hometown of Kingsburg.

In 1960 at the Olympic Games in Rome, Johnson pulled off his greatest triumph by capturing the gold medal in the decathlon in a dramatic test of skill, strength, and speed with C. K. Yang, his good friend and former UCLA teammate. He won the Sullivan Award as a result *of his Olympic victory and then retired from competitive athletics, despite being offered a chance to play for the Los Angeles Rams in the National Football League. Johnson's retirement from competitive sports gave him time to pursue lifelong ambitions and various professional opportunities. He assumed a highly publicized role in the 1968 presidential campaign of Senator Robert Kennedy and was present when the senator was assassinated in Los Angeles. Among his public service endeavors has been a long and dedicated involvement in the Special Olympics program. For his many achievements, Johnson was honored with induction into the National Track and Field Hall of Fame in 1974 and the U.S. Olympic Hall of Fame in 1982, and he was asked to light the Olympic flame at the 1984 Olympic Games in Los Angeles.**

In his wide-ranging autobiography—structured along the lines of the events of the decathlon—Johnson discusses his upbringing as well as his career in athletics. He pauses from time to time to indict racism or to comment on current events, such as the O. J. Simpson trial. But what stands out from the passages that follow are his broader political passions and his commitment to fostering community organizations that engage everyday needs as well as longstanding ideals.

Vaulting High, Falling Far

> *Some men see things as they are and ask, "Why?" I dream of things that never were and ask, "Why not?"*
> —Robert F. Kennedy

In the years that I competed in the decathlon, pole-vault poles were made of bamboo, and later of steel. Because they did not have the recoil of today's fiberglass poles, the technique for using them was different from what it now is. You ran down the runway with the pole at your side, planted it in the take-off box, and pushed your hands out in front of you. Lifted off the ground by the speed of your run, you swung your feet up over your head and pulled on the pole to force your legs still higher. Then you pushed off, letting your momentum carry you over the bar.

At that time, before there were huge air bags to land on, you also had to be concerned about your landing. Your vaulting technique had to include a balancing system so that when you cleared the bar you were in a position to land feet-first in the sand-and-sawdust pit. If you landed awkwardly you could injure yourself, perhaps severely.

The higher you soar, the harder you fall, if you're not prepared. In 1968 my life attained heights I had never dreamed possible. I was at the side of a close friend who seemed about to become president of the United States. Then, with the speed of a pistol shot, the world around me exploded in turmoil, and I plummeted and crashed. . . .

As attorney general and later as a U.S. senator, Robert Kennedy was often criticized for not being militant enough on social issues. I took heart in that because I found myself in a similar position. Like him, I thought I was having an impact for

---

* See Phillips, "Still Carrying the Torch"; Gusky, "Two Friends, 10 Events"; Wallechinsky, *Complete Book of the Olympics*; Quercetani, *World History of Track and Field*.

Rafer Johnson (Amateur
Athletic Foundation,
AAF/LPI 1984)

good in the world, yet I was sometimes told I wasn't doing enough, or not going
about it the right way.

I was sickened by the injustices that proliferated in response to the civil rights
movement. Televised images of Southern sheriffs unleashing police dogs and fire
hoses on protesters; and the church bombings, the murders of Freedom Riders, the
cross-burnings—all of it filled me with rage. Activist friends and well-intentioned
strangers urged me to march, demonstrate, join radical organizations and lend my
name to various causes. As the atmosphere grew more and more charged, militancy
became a badge of honor and, in some circles, a measure of status. But my politics
remained moderate. I believed very strongly in Martin Luther King's vision of a color-
blind, integrated world where people are judged by the content of their character, and
I supported his strategies. The militant tactics of Stokely Carmichael, H. Rap Brown,
Angela Davis, and Malcolm X seemed divisive and sometimes destructive. Still, I was
glad they were around. They dared to utter truths that others could not, and their fer-

vor accelerated the process of social change. The larger society might never have awakened if those fierce, threatening voices had not been raised.

But I had to be true to myself and my nature. Confrontation was simply not my style. For this I was often accused of not being black enough, a charge that not only made no sense to me but was deeply repulsive.

There were reasons for my moderation. Responsibilities to loved ones who depended on me were my primary concern. For their sake if not my own, it would have been foolish to do anything that could jeopardize my ability to earn a living. Second, I was angry, but my anger was directed at ignorance, bigotry, and selfishness wherever I saw it, not at American society or white people as a whole. I understood how everyday frustration could lead to a generalized rage, and I might have felt that rage myself had my family remained in Texas. But after my experiences in Kingsburg and at UCLA, how could I possibly hate all white people or believe that they were out to bring me down?

Nor could I hate "the system." In my travels I had met enough people from other countries to know that, despite everything, America was still the best place to live, even for people of color. I don't think any of the black Americans I competed with in Russia, Hungary, Poland, Mexico, Pakistan, or Africa wanted to live in any of those places. None of this made me any less angry about what was going on in our country, but it mitigated my rage and tempered my sense of what strategies for change were appropriate and effective.

I felt that, as a public figure, I could do the most good by maintaining a positive image. For change to be lasting and meaningful it had to take root in individual hearts and minds. I seemed to be in a position to accelerate that process, since I was frequently the first or only black person in various situations. By doing whatever I did well, and doing it with integrity, I felt I could help break down stereotypes, chip away at ignorance, and shed light on our common humanity. For me it made tactical sense to stress cooperation between the races, not separatism. I had read that when the Brooklyn Dodgers arrived at a hotel dining room, Jackie Robinson would tell his black teammates, "Spread out." He meant, go and mingle with the white players. Like Jackie, I felt I could do more good by spreading out.

It was for similar reasons that I did not support the proposed boycott of the 1968 Olympics. Led by sociologist Harry Edwards, a number of black athletes had voted to stay away from the Mexico City Games as a form of protest. I was among those who were asked for a reaction. I said, "What you have to ask yourself is, 'What good is it going to do? Is it going to help housing? Is it going to help education? Is it going to help job opportunities?' I don't see where a boycott of the Olympics is relevant at all to these problems." I pointed out that the Olympics was one of the rare institutions in which blacks and whites were treated exactly the same. The Games ought to be embraced as an opportunity to build bridges and educate people. At the same time, I noted that there were no black members on the United States Olympic Committee (USOC) despite their prominence as athletes. I advocated that Jesse Owens be appointed. He never was.

Of course, the threatened boycott never took place. The enduring image of the 1968 Games is of Tommie Smith and John Carlos on the medal stand raising their fists in the Black Power salute. While it would not have been my style, I felt they were on solid ground in making the gesture, and I criticized the USOC for expelling them from the Olympic Village. Punishing two medalists made the United States look worse than anything the athletes did.

For the most part, my activism centered on issues that were close to home, and to causes that were worthy even if they were not hot-button items. As a union representative I pushed for equal opportunity in the entertainment industry. I gave time and energy to the Fair Housing Congress and to projects organized by the NAACP and the Urban League, especially in the aftermath of the 1965 Watts riot. I worked for Tom Bradley the first time he campaigned for mayor of Los Angeles, and for John Tunney and Alan Cranston when they ran for the Senate. In addition to my job with People to People, I volunteered for causes I believed in, such as the Fellowship of Christian Athletes, the Campus Crusade, the Peace Corps, various youth groups and other organizations that helped people in need regardless of ethnicity—for example, the Committee on Mental Retardation of the Department of Health, Education, and Welfare.

The one time I attended a national demonstration was in June 1966, when James Meredith organized a twenty-one-day march to mobilize black voters in Mississippi. For one reason or another, I had been unable to be in Washington in 1963 when Martin Luther King, Jr., delivered his "I Have a Dream" speech, or at the march in Selma, Alabama, in 1965. But in 1966 a labor strike freed me from my job at KNBC, and I signed on for a chartered flight to Mississippi with a contingent from Hollywood. That plan was dropped when the Ku Klux Klan threatened to blow up the plane. Since James Meredith had already been wounded by a sniper earlier in the march, the threat was taken seriously and the charter was cancelled.

Some of us still wanted to go, however, and Frank Sinatra offered to lend us his private plane. I flew down with Sammy Davis, Jr., Marlon Brando, and Anthony Franciosa. We joined about 10,000 people at a rally at Tougaloo College. Sammy, James Brown, and Dick Gregory performed, and Marlon gave a moving speech in which he called civil rights workers "the real heroes of America." Afterward we drove to a small airport in the middle of a sugar cane field; we were inspired by the rally but concerned that we might be marked men, driving in a conspicuous limousine in the dark Mississippi night. We took off safely, feeling good that we had lent support to those who had bravely stood up for justice. . . .

Going the Distance

Let us lay aside every weight, and the sin which doth so easily beset us, and let us run with patience the race that is set before us.

   —Epistle to the Hebrews, 12:1

Most of my outside commitments have been in the nonprofit sector. For example, I joined the board of directors of the Close-Up Foundation, which brings high school students to the nation's capital to learn how government works. (I've watched the program grow to include 25,000 youngsters of all ethnic and economic groups who participate each year.) At one time or another, I have served charities like the March of Dimes, the Muscular Dystrophy Association, and the American Red Cross; sports-related organizations such as the National Amateur Sports Development Foundation, the National Recreation and Park Association, the United States Athletic Foundation, and the Athletic Advisory Panel of the U.S. State Department; and community groups such as the San Fernando Valley Fair Housing Counsel and the Voter Registration Program. Speaking of voting, I campaigned for George McGovern in the 1972 presidential race. He was the closest thing to Bobby Kennedy that we had at the time, and his running mate, Sargent Shriver, was Bobby's brother-in-law, my good friend, and a major force behind Special Olympics.

I became devoted to Special Olympics quickly, and it has kept me busy ever since 1969 when I helped establish the California chapter with a competition for 900 athletes at the L.A. Coliseum. Over the years I've done my best to help administer the program, raise funds, and mobilize individual and corporate volunteers. (I'm currently national head coach and chairman of the board of governors for Southern California.) It's been enormously satisfying to watch the organization grow from humble beginnings to a year-round program of high-quality training and regular competitions in twenty sports. Over 25,000 athletes participate in California alone.

I've always considered the time and energy I've given to Special Olympics a gift from me to the athletes and to the Kennedy family. In truth, I've gotten more out of it than I've given. As I always tell volunteers, it's impossible to come away from the Special Olympics Games without feeling better about yourself. Each year I preside over the opening ceremonies at UCLA, in the track stadium named for my late coach, Ducky Drake. I never fail to be inspired when I lead the ringing chorus of voices in the athlete's oath: "Let me win, but if I cannot win, let me be brave in the attempt." . . .

Compared to earlier years, I enjoyed relative anonymity during the seventies. Then, unexpectedly and gloriously, I was thrust back into the spotlight.

Earlier, when Los Angeles was awarded the 1984 Olympic Games, the Olympic movement had been in trouble. The 1972 Games in Munich had been marred by the tragic slaying of Israeli athletes by terrorists; the 1976 Games in Montreal had been a fiscal disaster that cost Canadian taxpayers a billion dollars. As a result, Los Angeles was able to negotiate an unprecedented deal with the International Olympic Committee (IOC): The city would not be held liable for the cost of the Games; the city would not build new stadiums or an Olympic Village, but use existing facilities instead; funds would not come from the government but would be raised from the private sector.

I was asked by Mayor Tom Bradley to join the board of directors of the Los Angeles Olympic Organizing Committee (LAOOC) and was later named to the executive committee. It was an honor I accepted eagerly. I had participated in the Olympics as a competitor, a journalist, and a spectator. Now I would be behind the scenes in the planning and organizing stage of something that meant the world to me. . . .

To mastermind the opening ceremonies, Peter [Ueberroth] turned to David L. Wolper, the renowned producer of theater, movies, and television programs ranging from *Roots* to a documentary about me. David set out to create a "twenty-goose-bump" show that would be emotional without being corny. . . .

Historically, the centerpiece of the opening ceremonies is the lighting of the Olympic torch that burns for the duration of the Games. In 1984 a new twist was added to the journey of the flame from Greece to the host city. This time, when it arrived in the United States, the torch would zigzag through all fifty states in a relay involving thousands of citizens and covering more than 9,000 miles. Relay legs were sold to sponsors at $3,000 per leg, with the proceeds going to finance sports programs for youth. . . . Traditionally, the identity of the person who is to light the torch at the opening ceremonies is kept secret until the last minute. In 1984 the choice was Peter Ueberroth's to make. Speculation ran rampant, not only within the LAOOC family but the media as well. Who would be given the honor? Would it be Bruce Jenner, who had set a new world record while winning the Olympic decathlon at Montreal? Bruce lived in Los Angeles and had been a popular figure ever since he took his memorable victory lap with the American flag. Would it be Mark Spitz, another Californian and the winner of an amazing nine gold medals in Olympic swimming competition? Would it be Wilma Rudolph, whose spectacular performance in Rome opened the doors to greater participation in sports by women? Or would it be Nadia Comaneci, the gymnast who, at age fourteen, had captivated the world with perfect tens in Montreal? More speculation surrounded Nadia than any other possible choice because the Soviet Union had retaliated for the U.S. boycott of the 1980 Olympics in Moscow with a boycott of its own. All the Soviet satellites were staying home, with the notable exception of Yugoslavia and Romania, Nadia's homeland, and Nadia was coming to Los Angeles at Peter's invitation. . . .

I did not know why Peter chose me. He joked that it was payback for my casting the deciding vote that gave him his job. In his own book, *Made in America,* he said it was because I represented "what the Olympics are all about" and because I "brought all of those ideals to our organizational efforts." It was his way, perhaps, of thanking me for being there whenever I was needed during the five years of preparation. I simply wanted to give something back to the Olympics; now the Olympics were once again giving me something, only this was an honor I had never dreamed of. . . .

. . . Trumpets and timpanis blared the opening theme. Skywriting planes formed the Olympic rings and scrawled "Welcome" across the heavens. Girls passed out flowers with "Welcome" written in several languages on ribbons attached to the stems. Powered by a jet pack, a man flew into the stadium and landed on the infield. "Welcome" was written on his back. Over a thousand marchers performed a drill with five-foot balloons while the huge video screen showed Angelinos waving to their guests and an animated film of the word "Welcome" spelled out in 23 languages. The drill team formed the Olympic symbol, then marched into the letters of "Welcome."

A marching band, an orchestra, a choir of a thousand voices, and hundreds of dancers depicted the nation's history through the music of American composers. Eighty-five grand pianos rolled through the Coliseum arches and played George Gershwin's "Rhapsody in Blue." The entertainment ended with the drill team forming a map of the United States. Then came a moment I wish I'd seen in person. Colored plastic cards had been placed on every seat in the Coliseum. On cue, 92,655 spectators held up their cards, forming a gorgeous mosaic of the flags of all 140 nations present.

The parade of nearly 8,000 athletes took about an hour and a half. . . . When I heard that all the athletes had been assembled, I walked up close to the tunnel exit and looked out onto the field. The U.S. team was right in front of me, decked out in red, white, and blue uniforms. I saw Edwin Moses, the great hurdler, with tears in his eyes. I ducked back into the tunnel so my emotions wouldn't get the best of me. I paced back and forth and shook my arms and legs to release some of the adrenaline. . . .

A familiar feeling swept over me—nerve endings tingling and muscles aching to be used. I had been nervous before every speech I ever gave, on the set of every movie I acted in, and in every television studio while waiting for the red light on the camera to go on. This was a feeling I'd had only when competing. And now I was, in a sense, an Olympian again, preparing to will my body to do something exceptional. Was I concerned about making it to the top of the stairs? Yes. Was I thinking about whether I might trip or fall? Yes. Did I have any doubt that I would come through? No. I was going to be the best torchbearer that I could be. . . .

As I jogged up the steps, the grand arch of the Coliseum peristyle looked golden in the light of the setting sun. On either side of me, splendidly bedecked in white, the thousand members of the Olympic choir applauded. Atop the permanent steps, the metal stairway built for this moment rose like an ancient monolith on hydraulic lifts. It glistened like solid silver as it filled the archway. But it was as rickety as an old ladder and, with its 50-degree angle, just as steep. As I climbed it I touched each of the twenty-five steps to make sure I didn't miss one. . . .

I raised the torch in the direction of the presidential box. I was saluting Peter Ueberroth as well as President Reagan. Then I turned toward the athletes and held up the torch as a tribute to them. The gestures had not been rehearsed, they just seemed to be the right thing to do. After a brief salute to the other side, I returned to the center and lifted the torch to the gas jet attached to the bottom of the arch. I heard a whoosh. The flame took hold, rose up to outline the five intertwined circles of the Olympic symbol, then followed a pipeline to the top of the peristyle. A moment later, the cauldron burst into flame. The torch had reached its destination.

In a sense, so had I. Standing at the pinnacle of the Coliseum, having been afforded this singular honor, with my face being beamed to a billion homes around the world as ABC's Jim McKay called me "a great American"—well, it was a long way from the cotton fields of Hillsboro, Texas. It was all I could do to keep from weeping. . . .

The L.A. Games revitalized the Olympic movement. For one thing, it created a legacy of corporate sponsorship for amateur sports that has made a huge difference to American athletes. . . . Thanks to Peter Ueberroth, whose success with the Olympics led to a stint as commissioner of baseball, the Games piled up a $200 million surplus. With those funds the Amateur Athletic Foundation was created. Housed in a handsome facility in Los Angeles and run by the capable Anita DeFrantz, a former Olympic rower, the AAF provides programs and training grants for young athletes. I've been proud to sit on the board of directors ever since AAF was established, and even more proud to have been given its Lifetime Achievement Award in a dual presentation with C. K. Yang. (At that event I said that without C. K.'s help I would not have beaten him in 1960; he said that without my help he would not have come as close to beating me.). . . .

The years since the 1984 Games have been surprising and satisfying. I'll mention some of the most important highlights.

When Kingsburg decided to build a new junior high school, someone proposed that it be named after me. Of the five-member school board, only one was in favor. Two wished to name the school for Thomas Jefferson and two wanted to call it Kingsburg Junior High. My old friend Karl Finley sampled public opinion and found a lot of support for naming the school after me. The board didn't budge. Some citizens were apparently concerned that something scandalous might be revealed about me and embarrass the town. Finally the townspeople were asked to decide the issue at the ballot box. With Karl and his wife Julie leading the charge, my supporters won 81 percent of the votes. . . . Rafer Johnson Junior High School was dedicated in 1993. . . .

I sometimes imagine Martin Luther King, Jr., and Bobby Kennedy looking down at us. I know they'd be dismayed, and I know they'd be angry, but I also know they would tell us to roll up our sleeves and do something constructive. They would tell us to stop being so divisive and not lose sight of the common ground. They would tell us to stop wasting time on ideological arguments and get practical; that families, charities, businesses, schools, churches, civic groups, and government all have a role to play in making things better. They would surely encourage self-reliance among the poor and disadvantaged, but they would not give up on social programs just because some haven't worked as well as planned and because "liberal" has been turned into a dirty word. . . .

Writing this book has been, in part, an attempt to encourage bridge-building. I've tried to show what hard work and focus can accomplish when people of goodwill look beyond their own self-interest and embrace their fellow citizens with compassion. I've had a good life, thanks to people with a generous spirit. I'd like to see every child given the kind of breaks I received. Perhaps my story will bring hope to young people and inspire their elders to build communities like the one I knew in Kingsburg.

Rafer Johnson and Philip Goldberg, *The Best That I Can Be: An Autobiography* (New York: Doubleday, 1998), 182–83, 188–91, 238, 241, 243–52.

9. David Aldridge / "A Team's True Colors": Washington Redskins on and off the Field

The shattering of the color line in American sport during the mid-twentieth century was extremely difficult for African American athletes. Jackie Robinson and other African American athletes involved in the early days of racial desegregation confronted racial taunts from players and fans almost daily and maintained little contact with white teammates off the playing field. In his well-known autobiography, I Never Had It Made, *Robinson mentioned that some of his white teammates on the Dodgers only tolerated him because he "could help fill their wallets."**

Racial taunts and other overt forms of discrimination experienced by the first African Americans to integrate sport have slowly diminished. It is still true, however, that African

---

* Robinson, *I Never Had It Made,* 10.

American and white athletes seemingly confine their closest relationships to teammates of their own race. Although cooperative and friendly to one another during practices, games, and other team functions, African American and white athletes typically have limited contact off the field. One explanation put forward is that African American athletes, because of their heightened awareness of racial issues, are reluctant to interact with whites who embrace America's dominant racial ideology. This ideology may also explain a reluctance by white athletes to nurture social relationships with their black teammates outside the sport setting.*

In the following selection, David Aldridge discusses the relationships between African American and white athletes on the Washington Redskins. Aldridge makes clear that interracial social contact on the Redskins is the exception rather than the rule. Although together for long periods of time during training camp, at practices and team meetings, on the plane, and at team parties, African American and white players established few close relationships outside of sport. Aldridge suggests, among other things, that the lack of interracial social contacts on the Redskins was due in part to cultural differences and to a clash of taste and style. Closer to the truth may be the fact that while African Americans represented the majority of players on the team, they still remained a minority in a society that holds fast to structures of social relations based on race.

———————

In the inner sanctum of Redskin Park, next to the whirlpool and across from the showers, Washington Redskins tight end Scott Galbraith is getting a haircut. The subject isn't cut blocking, or which young quarterback is doing better. The subject isn't football at all. It's race relations.

"I admit that this is not the real world," Galbraith says. "Why is it not the real world? Because if a guy 300 pounds is rushing at you, I don't care whether you're pro-choice or pro-life. Block that [guy]. And when you block him, I'm going to love you for it. And once I love you for what you did in a working relationship, it can't help but open up the door to my inquisitive nature to find out more about you."

Gailbraith continues, hypothetically:

"What is the origin of this person who just laid it on the line for me in a pressure, high-stress situation? Who is this person? Well, I found out he was a redneck from Idaho, who went to the University of Wyoming, and all people from Wyoming ain't prejudiced like I thought. You tell me—how else would I have found that out? How else would I have wanted to have found that out?"

If the American church at 11 A.M. on Sunday mornings is one of the nation's more segregated places, a National Football League locker room that fills up an hour later could be one of the more integrated. In that room, black men and white men put aside their racial differences for three hours for a common cause: in this case, winning football games. They are asked to do what many others struggle to do on a daily basis: make race in the workplace irrelevant.

Each week's game is the end product of a nearly year-long training regimen in

———————

* See Coakley, *Sport in Society,* esp. 266–67.

which black and white players live in their own mini-society. They spend most of their time with one another. They lift weights together, take part in spring mini-camp together, endure summer training camp together in the blistering July and August heat, and live together during camp in college dormitories.

Then the regular season begins and the relationship intensifies, with players spending the next six months in one another's company, at least eight hours a day, five days a week. They practice all week, and then for sixteen Sundays (and the occasional Monday night), they sacrifice muscle, bones and blood together, some of them veterans, some of them just out of college, but all of them scrutinized daily—by coaches, by media and by fans.

At its best, a football team is a meritocracy, the quintessential level playing field, where excellence is measured objectively and then richly rewarded. At its worst, a sports team can be as troubled a workplace as any in America. Camaraderies forged on the field can be shattered by other kinds of competition: who gets paid the most, who plays and who doesn't, who's the boss, on or off the field, who's a star and who's not.

The Redskins locker room offers another way of looking at how well we all get along—and whether a functional, if not utopian, relationship between the races is possible.

"It is, relatively, two teams," said Terry Crews, 27, a reserve linebacker. "On every team I've been on, it's always at this table, it's all black, and at one table there's all white, and when the workday's done, black guys go one place, or party at one place, and white guys go to another. I think it's always going to be that way, as long as there are differences."

Culture Clash

Of the fifty-three players on the Redskins' active roster as of November 1, 42 (79 percent) were black and 11 (21 percent) were white. That's a little higher than the average team racial makeup of 68 percent black, 32 percent white, according to figures from 1994 in the annual Racial Report Card of professional sports by the National Rainbow Coalition. So if there is an adjustment to be made in this world, it frequently is by the white player.

Redskins quarterback Heath Shuler, 23, grew up in Bryson City, North Carolina. One black student attended his high school. So when he went to the University of Tennessee, and to a football team with lots of black players, Shuler had to adjust.

"A lot of it, I was shocked about," he said. "Just little things. One time, a guy asked me, 'You going to your crib this weekend?' I'm like 'Uh, no.' I didn't understand what he was talking about. Cliff Dutton was a black guy on the team and I told him 'Cliff, you've got to help me out. These guys are saying stuff and I have no idea what they're talking about. They want me to go to the crib this weekend. What kind of place is that?' It was hilarious. Then he told me that means going home."

Many Redskins told less humorous stories about their college days. Kicker Eddie Murray, 39, who like Shuler is white, recalled driving from New Orleans to a beach an hour or so away near Biloxi, Mississippi, while a freshman at Tulane University in 1976, and seeing Klansmen on the side of the road handing out pamphlets. And running back Reggie Brooks, 24, said that at Notre Dame, some white players "just came right out and called you nigger in your face."

In the NFL, that sort of thing is rare. But there are occasional clashes of taste and style. In the weight room, more often than not, the deep bass beat of rap music, or other black popular music euphemistically called "urban contemporary" by radio stations, provides the background for arm curls and dead lifts by the black players. Only when most of the black players are out of the weight room—and there are as many white players as black—is the station changed to a country music station.

A Subtle Segregation

The pro player's daily life is filled with dozens of team-mandated interactions—meetings and practices, on the plane and on the trainer's table, at team parties during training camp and voluntary Bible study sessions on Monday nights. But when players are in less structured situations, blacks and whites often don't seem to integrate. Like in a cafeteria.

"I'm not going to say 'I'm not sitting there because there are three black guys over there, and there are three white guys sitting over here,'" Murray said. "Although that does happen. Is that a conscious thing? I don't know if it is or isn't."

In one corner of the Redskins locker room sits the "Dog Pound," an informal area where, every day, players get together to trade gossip, insults and jokes. All of the players in the Pound are black. Yet the players who populate the Pound insist that the division is along economic lines.

"It's a lot of guys that came off the waiver wire [players released by other teams and claimed by the Redskins], a lot of guys that are free agent rookies," defense tackle Marc Boutte, 26, said. "It's a time to get away from football, have a little fun, joke and have a good time. We call it the 'hood, the ghetto. You go across the locker room and you see the Rod Stephens and the James Washingtons, all those guys [with big contracts]. It's totally economic."

But players of both races acknowledged that their workplace is like many others: When the day is done, many go their separate ways. They cited numerous reasons: differing backgrounds and interests, length of service, marital status.

"Most of the people here have families, or are married," said guard Tré Johnson, 24, who is black and single and a Redskin only two years. "They're all old."

Linebacker Crews, who played in Germany this past spring for the Rhein Fire of the World League, pointed out that many black players with the Redskins now live in neighborhoods in Loudoun and Fairfax counties near Redskin Park in Ashburn, where they may be the only black person on the street, and may bond with black players in the locker room to be around people like themselves again. Other players are self-described loners, who don't pursue any football friendships.

James Washington, 30, and linebacker Marvcus Patton, 28, are both black and were fraternity brothers at UCLA. They both came to the Redskins this season. Yet when the day is over, they frequently go their separate ways.

"It all depends on what you have going," said Washington, who counts players of both races among his closest friends on the team. "Personally, I don't hang out with the defensive backs [all of whom, like him, are black]. They like to golf, and I don't know how to golf that well."

One for All

The main concern of the team, however, is for its players to work together in the meeting room and on the field, not necessarily to be fast friends.

"I talk to our team about it," says Coach Norv Turner. "You can look at it from a racial deal, black and white, but . . . my feeling was the one thing we know we have in common is that we want to win. That's the one thing that's going to bring us together."

Yet outside influences can still split teammates. Money is one. Sixteen-year veteran Murray recalled his rookie year of 1980: "I got $10,000 in a signing bonus, so when I see guys getting $13 million, or $6 million just to put their name on a piece of paper, it can create some animosity because of the unproven factor. I never saw the reasoning behind that, and sometimes, that creates tension."

Shuler got a $5 million signing bonus last year. He said he was encouraged by teammates during his contract negotiations to get as much from the Redskins as he could. But there were, and are, occasional grumblings about the financial commitment the Redskins made to Shuler that aren't necessarily good-natured.

But friendships between black and white players are not unusual. Linebackers Matt Vanderbeek, 28, who is white, and Darrick Brownlow, 26, who is black, are close. Centers John Gesek, 32, and Vernice Smith, 30, became closer during training camp. Both were married but their wives were back home. And both of them started to get closer with Trevor Matich, 34, the team's special teams center. Gesek and Matich are white; Smith is black.

"Vern and I, we'd be friends off the field if we'd have met working for A&P," Matich says.

The three of them would eat together, and sit together in the whirlpool, working out their numerous aches and pains. And they'd talk. They still do.

"We talk about politics, we'll talk about the welfare system in politics, we'll talk about Republicans and Democrats," Smith said. "A lot of times, we'll find that we want to end up in the same place, the same area. We just have different ways of getting there, different opinions of how to get to that end."

Gesek, who grew up in San Francisco, is baffled by the notion that there could be something special in his relationship with Smith because they are of a different race. And Matich takes great pains to discuss the irrelevancy of race in football.

"You'd have to make a concerted effort to be a racist in this kind of a setting," Matich said. "When you look at what we go through together, starting with the off-season and working hard and going into training camp and sweating and bleeding and playing hurt next to one another, and then getting into the season and playing games when your teammates are all you've got, and you're all they've got . . . it's hard to look at anything except character and performance, and that's it."

But various forces work against the creation of longtime friendships of any color. The Redskins of the 1980s spent nearly a decade together, establishing ties in the community. Now, with the advent of greater free agency—the ability of a player to sign with another team once his contract expires—players come and go from year to year. There are sixty-five new Redskins on the roster from just two years ago, and that constant movement impedes friendships.

Harsh Reminders

And while black players constitute the racial majority on their teams, they are still a minority in the real world—and very much reminded of it.

Defense tackle William Gaines, 24, a six-foot-five, 294-pound defensive tackle, has been stopped by police more than once driving home in suburban Virginia from Redskin Park.

"Being a black American, you see [race] everywhere," Gaines said. "You're more [likely] to see it than a white American would. Because I've been pulled over here a couple times in my truck, doing the speed limit. Just riding on 66 or whatever. Once they pulled me over, though, they didn't give me any trouble. They checked to make sure it was my truck. . . . I guess because I had my truck fixed up, they thought it maybe was a drug thing or whatnot." Linebacker Ken Harvey, 30, an African American who played in Phoenix for six years (the godfather of his children is Italian) before signing with Washington in 1994, felt a double standard for athletes there—and here—as well.

"If you're an athlete, you're O.K.," Harvey said. "Whereas if you weren't an athlete, you might experience [racism] a little more. Because I'm big, and I look like a player, people automatically assume you're a player, so you get treated a bit differently. But I've had people follow me in the stores, and get nervous when you come on the elevator with them. It's there, no doubt about it." Athletes could be the wealthiest collection of black men on the planet. But when it comes to speaking out on issues in sports and outside the field, where their words could have as big an impact as their play on the field, most are usually silent.

The Struggle Continues

One rare exception was the recent Million Man March on the Mall in October. More than a dozen Redskins attended, despite criticism of the march and the participants in it because it was organized by Nation of Islam leader Louis Farrakhan, the controversial minister who many feel is anti-Semitic and homophobic.

Turner let them attend the march—and miss scheduled meetings and film study that Monday—as long as they came in early on Tuesday to make up for the missed time.

"I think in any situation, if people are going to be given something, they have to give something back," Turner said.

Most white players said they didn't have any problem with the black players going, though some didn't understand the need for it.

Said quarterback Gus Frerotte, 24: "It's hard for a person like me to understand that, because I haven't been put through that, or my heritage hasn't been put through something like that. . . . But I didn't have a problem with it. It's something they believe in."

Another American racial controversy made its way into the locker room this season—the O.J. Simpson trial. During the months of testimony, little was said about the trial. But as the verdict neared, tensions increased.

On one memorable day during closing arguments, a debate about Simpson's guilt or innocence started in one corner of the locker room between Matich and Galbraith, bounced to the Dog Pound, continued toward Brian Mitchell's locker, came out of the locker room and up the stairs and wound up back in the locker room.

The verdict did not polarize the locker room, though Turner said a few players had to "stand up for themselves" and explain their views to others who disagreed with them. Some white players, like Shuler, thought enough reasonable doubt had been established for acquittal. But there were differences that fell along racial lines.

"It got heated up in here at times. It did," fullback Marc Logan, 30, said. "There were some arguments going on. I thought it was good to hear people's viewpoints, and some of them, I thought they were crazy."

Mitchell, Leslie Shepherd, and Terry Allen had frequent talks with Matich about the trial. In most cases, they agreed to disagree.

On occasion, the strange world of pro football produces relationships that would be welcomed outside the locker room doors: a connection between black and white in which there is mutual respect for one another, some moments of closeness, and few of racial rancor.

"Vanderbeek is a country western rocker that drives a hyped-up Chevy and fits every qualification that you have, sterotypically, as a white boy," Galbraith said. "And I would go to war with Vanderbeek, and I would spend my time with Vanderbeek . . . because he's a person of integrity, he's a person of character, a person of honesty. I respect him because he's a tough guy, and I've seen him run around here and knock the hell out of people. We're in an occupation that—beautifully or tragically—allows us to see people as people."

Galbraith said, "beautifully or tragically," as if there was something wrong with seeing a person as a person. But why make that qualification?

"Because of the experiences that I've had, and the kindred [*sic*] I've had with [Cowboys tight end] Jay Novacek, and other people I've been with, it leaves me vulnerable," Galbraith said. "Because I kind of go into the world with a false sense, thinking that everybody . . . is nice and kind. It's not true. . . . When I go over to the mall, those aren't my teammates, those are white people. And I'm black."

David Aldridge, "A Team's True Colors," *Washington Post,* December 16, 1995.

10. David Zang / An Interview with Calvin Hill

Calvin Hill garners far less attention these days than his son Grant, the former Duke Blue Devils and now Orlando Magic basketball star. The elder Hill, however, carved out a highly successful professional career both within and outside of sport. Born in 1947 and raised in Turner's Station, a steel-mill area just outside of Baltimore, Hill was selected to Parade *magazine's all-American football team while at Riverdale Preparatory School. He continued his education at Yale University where he won national acclaim as a football and track star. A first-round draft pick of the Dallas Cowboys in 1969, Hill fashioned a distinguished professional career as a running back with the Cowboys, Washington Redskins, and Cleveland Browns. Since his retirement from football, Hill has performed valuable community service and pursued a number of professional opportunities, including working as an advisor to the Cleveland Browns and serving as a board member of both the Baltimore Orioles and San Diego Padres baseball teams. Most recently, Hill and his wife, Janet—a noted Washington, D.C., lawyer and a former classmate of Hillary Clinton at Wellesley College—have worked as consultants to the Dallas Cowboys on such issues as family assistance, career counseling, and prevention of drug and alcohol abuse.*

In addition to his many accomplishments, Hill is an enormously sensitive and thoughtful man, a fact that became quite clear when he sat down for an interview with David Zang during the late 1980s. Hill provides detailed information about being a black student at a predominantly white preparatory school and at Yale, his admiration for Martin Luther King Jr. and William Sloan Coffin, and his career as a professional football player. Perhaps most important, Hill offers his opinions on why there have been a disproportionate number of African Americans in football and an apparent overemphasis on sport in the black community. Hill claims, among other things, that the triumphs gained by African American athletes have largely been the result of the "many black success stories" portrayed in the media and the expectation of achievement by African American athletes themselves. This "visualization process," as Hill calls it, can be instructive, not just for the playing fields but for other fields of endeavor, once opportunities have been opened up and the framework for black achievement has been constructed.

——— ———

Zang: I'm interested in what sort of vision you had then as a child in Turner's Station.

Hill: Until my father sort of insisted upon it, my vision was one where you went to high school, you graduated, and you went to work with Bethlehem Steel. My father was not a steelworker, but that's what most of the men in my community did. That was what my father had to battle against: the idea that I might limit myself. He felt there was more for me. His big thing was to use your mind to make a living instead of your back. He was always trying to reinforce that message. . . .

The other thing I saw growing up was a perception of a family that was nuclear, that was together, so, I had very strong feelings about the importance of a family. What I had in terms of my father should be the norm, and it isn't. And that's frightening because I know I derive a lot of my sense of self, my esteem, from my father. My father made me feel like being a Hill was important. There were certain standards that you had to meet. You had to take care of your family, you had to be a decent human being.

Zang: Did he encourage your participation in athletics?

Hill: Yeah, he did. It was something that I wanted to do, and my participation initially was not very successful, at least it wasn't in joining a Little League. Even (at) six or seven, a lot of it was political, and I wasn't playing very much early on. So my father started coming to a lot of the games to make sure the manager of the team (who was another father) was equitable in giving us playing time. And he'd go out and

Calvin Hill (*Journal of Sport History*)

catch the ball with me and I can think how many times I came here [Memorial Stadium] to see games. So I always felt good about myself and that was encouraged. . . .

Zang: Sounds as though he was an enormous influence—it must have been difficult to leave him behind when you went to Riverdale. How did that whole situation come about, with the Schenley scholarship and your decision to leave?

Hill: There was a man (in Baltimore) who was on the Board of Riverdale, and at the time he was president of Schenley [Distillery]. My family doctor wanted to get his son out of the public schools in Baltimore (there were remnants of segregation still). They sent (him) to Riverdale, and it was a positive experience for him. Evidently, in talking with the headmaster one day, he mentioned that he knew other kids who could really benefit from that kind of experience. He (the headmaster) told Dr. Wade:

If there are some good kids in Baltimore, we'd like to have more blacks obviously, because there weren't very many blacks, and I think if you can find the right people, we can get money for them. So, Dr. Wade told my father and mother about Riverdale and about the scholarship. They had, in talking with Dr. Wade, echoed some of the same feelings he had about the school system and whether or not I was going to be able to tap my full potential. And so—I'll never forget—I came home one night, and it came time to ask me if I were interested. I wasn't really interested in leaving a comfortable sort of existence, but they made the decision for me, and once they made it, it became a challenge. I realized that, although it wasn't something I necessarily wanted to do, it probably was the best thing—there was no reason otherwise for them to send me away to ninth grade. So it became a challenge to try to pass these tests and to do good.

Zang: What was it like?

Hill: Well, it was a culture shock because I had gone from an all black area with very limited exposure to white people to a white environment. I don't think I had any exposure with the exception of playing some baseball games—I doubt very seriously if I'd ever even talked to or met anybody white, with the possible exception of the ice cream man who came through our neighborhood and the guy who owned the drugstore. . . .

I got there [to Riverdale] and I suddenly became aware that—in my little world in Turner's there were black people and there were white people, and although I knew there were Jews and Italians and other ethnic groups, I didn't realize it was as big a thing. I became aware that white people tended to discriminate among themselves. I suddenly became aware that the Jewish people suffered some discrimination because they were Jewish. I remember one day an Italian kid and a Jewish kid were having an argument, and the Italian kid told the Jewish kid: "You guys killed Christ." And it was shocking to me. I became aware that Jews did not recognize the divinity of Christ. All the things that I hadn't been exposed to, I was exposed to them at Riverdale. I think the one thing that Riverdale taught me was, although there are a lot of superficial differences among people, and a lot of it manifests itself in cultural or ethnic food or traditions, that people are people. Essentially they all have the same insecurities and hopes and dreams. So my four years at Riverdale were a period where I really felt a kinship with a lot of the people who were totally different from me. . . .

Zang: Why did you pick Yale, then?

Hill: My senior year in high school I made *Parade* magazine's All-America team as a football player. Suddenly I was a pretty hot commodity as a football player to be recruited. And really I was thinking about going to bigger schools—someplace where they had a big stadium—where football was—

Zang: Where they filled the big stadium.

Hill: Yeah. . . . I hadn't really thought about Yale, (but) [one of the coaches at Riverdale] arranged a visit, and when I got up there I absolutely loved the place. They were playing Dartmouth that weekend and the Yale Bowl had about 63,000 people. I had a beautiful weekend, and the next day the Director of Admissions was visiting Riverdale, conducting interviews for prospective applicants. My class was about a hundred guys, and I was about number twelve or thirteen, but it seemed like everybody ahead of me was applying. And I knew Yale only took three or four guys from Riverdale. But I said what the heck, I might as well see this whole thing through, and I signed up. And I got an A rating, which meant that all I had to do was apply and I was in. . . . I remember I called my father and told him I'd gotten into Yale, and I think he had vaguely heard of Yale, but his question was: "Is that a good school?" And I said "Yeah, it's gotta be one of the tops." And he said: "Well if it is," he said, "you gotta go for it."

Zang: How were you treated at Yale?

Hill: Well, Yale was a shock too, although I was prepared for it having gone to Riverdale. I guess the big shock at Yale was that everybody is number 1 or 2 in the class, everybody has something that highly recommends them. It was like going from the Chesapeake Bay to the Atlantic. I was used to sailing in a big ocean, but the ocean just got bigger, and there were more good sailors out there with me.

You know I was a quarterback in high school and fully expected to be a Yale quarterback, and I was shifted from quarterback to linebacker on the freshman team. And I was working as hard as I'd ever worked in my life, (but) I felt like a piece of plankton—I was just going with the drift. The B's and A's that I'd gotten were C's initially, and that was very traumatic. It was like nothing was balancing anything else the first month or so. . . .

Zang: There were some big movements that were taking place both in athletics and within black culture during the years you were at Yale: separation into black studies, etc. Were you drawn into that?

Hill: Well, my class was one of the first big classes of black students. We had eighteen or nineteen students, and prior to that classes had always been two or three or four. We started a group my freshman year. The initial thrust was social. A lot of guys were not meeting women. There were women in the town of New Haven, but you couldn't meet women at any of the other Eastern schools or the "Seven Sisters" or the other Ivy League schools. So we initially planned a social weekend where there would be some cultural activities, but the big thing was social my freshman year. Now a change occurred between my freshman year and sophomore year: the thrust became more cultural. In my sophomore year (1966–67), guys came back with Afros and dashikis and those kinds of things. When I was shifted from quarterback there were some black students on campus who approached me and asked me if I wanted to make an issue of the fact that as a black I had been shifted. I remember meeting an upperclassman, had lunch with him, I guess my second week there, and he asked me: "How would you feel about us picketing the offices because they shifted you from quarterback?" I'd been there four or five days. The last thing I wanted to do was to cause any controversy, you know? I mean I was trying to figure out what the hell was happening at Yale.

But, in terms of our seeking as a group of black students things that were relevant to us, I really think that Yale aided us. The lines of communication were open between the black students and the administration. Yale was the first school to offer an Afro-American studies [program]. I went from an American history major with a minor in Russian history to a guy specializing almost in Afro-American history. Eugene Genovese taught me in courses. We didn't feel the sense of alienation from the administration. They were there, they listened, and while they didn't always agree, the lines of communication were open. . . .

Zang: Did you get any sense of white Yale students being physically afraid of the whole Panther movement and militancy?

Hill: I don't think so. Perhaps there was a fear of outsiders. But in terms of the students at Yale, there were enough of us who were members of the Black Students at Yale who were also members of white fraternities and white societies and lived in the colleges where we didn't necessarily segregate ourselves. I think a lot of times you have fear because you don't know what the other guy is thinking. It's the unknown that causes the fear. In my mind, Yale was like one constant dialogue. I think in some respects Yale may have been a bad place for me (before) going down to Texas because at least some of my teammates didn't understand that I'd come from a place where you were encouraged to speak your mind. I had teammates at Dallas from southern schools who might view me as a militant because I objected or I stood up for certain things, but Yale was an interesting place in that sense. I think in some respects when I get out and I see people in the real world, I realize how things could be if people would be willing to communicate, to put aside their petty differences and get to the substance because it is an integrated sort of world that works in which people are given their dignity—not have it taken away from them.

Zang: When you got to Dallas, how were your pro football experiences different from the athletic involvement at Yale?

Hill: Well, very obviously it was more intense. I went from an environment where football was important to an environment where football was extremely important, not only because it was professional in nature, but also Texas football was much more important. It was part of the ethos, I thought. I figured out in that initial training camp I was spending almost 20 hours a week in the classroom in addition to the six hours a day the first two or three weeks on the field. On a weekly basis, I was spending more time in the classroom looking at films and talking over strategy than I had spent in the classroom my last year at Yale. (At) Yale, the fact that you were a football player meant that people might know your name because football had some importance on the campus, but it didn't differentiate you, it didn't entitle you to anything other than a banquet or a letter. As a professional football player, I realized there were entitlements. That was kind of shocking.

Zang: How did you deal with that?

Hill: Well, I got swept up by it. It was very seductive. There were kids from time to time at Yale who might have asked me for my autograph, but suddenly grownups were asking me and it was amazing. People would give you things because of who you were, because you'd had a good game—you'd get a prize, you might get a car for a week or a car for a month. My first contract I was making $22,000 a year which is a game check for a lot of these guys now. To me, it was all the money in the world. That was amazing that somebody would pay me that kind of money to play—something I'd done for free in college. To see how people defer to you, it was incredible. . . .

Zang: At what point in your life did you begin to develop your sense of the difference between the black and the white athlete?

Hill: Probably it's occurred more as a fan. I can be more objective, I suppose, and see certain trends. As an athlete, I knew lots of blacks who were terrible athletes. At Riverdale the best basketball players were not the black players. There were a couple guys who were good, but there were more guys who were bad. The fastest guy at Yale when I was there was not a black guy. Probably it's been more recent. There seem to be more blacks playing sports now than when I was coming through high school and college and even for the first part of my professional career, there weren't as many blacks playing professional sports. I guess I'd been around enough white players to know that there were good white athletes.

Zang: Well, your ideas with the middle passage (in slave ships), were they things you became aware of at Yale or more recently as a fan?

Hill: That's something that I've been aware of for awhile. When you think about the harshness of slavery and the fact that so many who died, if in fact forty million died, then why didn't these people die? It had to be natural selection—what you have remaining are the hardiest physically or mentally or whatever. You add to that this whole visualization thing. When you expect to achieve or to be somewhere, come hell or high water that's what you're going to do—because you can visualize it.

Zang: You had mentioned the first time that we met that there were some black cornerbacks that you had played with in professional football who would remark that they wouldn't let a white beat them, and there was certainly a disproportionate number of blacks who were successful in the NFL compared to the distribution of blacks in the population. What were the reasons that you felt as a pro football player explained that disproportionate number?

Hill: I think a lot of it has to do with where the energies are. One finds in the athletic programs of any inner city high school a prioritizing of the sports. Usually it's basketball, football, and then baseball. And if you look at the major sports and the participation of minorities, basketball is the highest, football is second. What happens—and certainly Nike realized this when they signed Michael Jordan—is it's very easy for a kid to buy a $50 pair of sneakers and suddenly he feels like he's transformed. Kids want to be like Michael Jordan, Magic Johnson, and Dr. J. I think the visualization process is much slower or not as intense when it comes to baseball. They don't identify with baseball players like they do football players and most certainly like they do with basketball players.

Zang: Okay, so there's a hierarchy in the visualization process within sports? What explains the visualization of athletics as having a higher priority than that of doctor or lawyer?

Hill: I think it's because they see, via the media, success stories in sports, and they don't see that many black success stories in law and medicine. Consequently, to a lot of young black kids, it's not going against the odds to think in terms of becoming an NBA player or an NFL player because they see a lot of blacks doing it. They lose sight of the fact that for every one you see, there are maybe a thousand who don't make it. But they don't see the down side, they see the up side. And these sports do a good job of using their athletes to market the sport, especially basketball. They see the black stars and they can identify with the fact that that person is from the ghetto or he's from an environment a lot like theirs. And the problem is that they put too much energy into trying to emulate those people, not understanding the odds. In Baltimore, for example, one of the medical doctors who helped perform the separation of the German Siamese twins was a black guy, and yet I doubt very seriously if you went down into that black area right around Johns Hopkins Hospital that you would find very many young black kids cognizant of that. But they all know that James Worthy was the MVP in the NBA finals. So it's a question of what they see around them and what they perceive as the logical ways to achieve success. They all know that Moses Malone makes two million dollars and Magic Johnson makes three million dollars, and the various periodicals—*Ebony* and *Life* and all the others—will take you to their homes and show you the lifestyle of the rich and famous. They concentrate solely on athletes and entertainers, and you don't see a lot of the other success stories in our society. Jesse (Jackson) is trying to tell people that they can achieve, but he's battling a mindset. Hopefully, the visualization process for politics will now be more intense as people see what he has accomplished. He's there in living color, and television plays a very big role, I think, in formulating the hopes and desires of a lot of black people.

Zang: Well, the visualization process has been narrowly limited to athletics. The flip side is that it has maybe resulted in what you have termed a positive "enabling" attitude, at least within sports. Is that balanced or is it too far out of whack?

Hill: I think it's too far out of whack because you have too many young kids putting all their energies (into) trying to emulate the stars. A lot of them have nothing to fall back on. They don't use the sport to get an education, they use the sport to get them closer to their dream of becoming a professional sport player. The visualization allows them to get in a position where they are exploited and they don't have anything to show for it. And so, what Harry Edwards says is true—we have too many kids trying to be Dr. J. or Magic J. or Kareem Abdul J. or Reggie J. and probably are going to end up uneducated and unemployable and faced with a lifetime of having no J., and that's so true, that's so true. I'd like to see kids visualize themselves as doctors or lawyers or teachers. And that's not happening. You find a lot of energy going toward trying to do the things that are long shots. Or you sometimes see them going into the drug culture which has been glamorized and romanticized. And that's unfortunate, too, because it may be more attainable than becoming an NFL player, but it's a very short life. What I'd like to see are situations where blacks can visualize themselves as politicians and the kinds of things that the black community really needs if it's going to succeed.

Zang: Is there a sense that it's easier to get a fair shot in sports than in other places in society?

Hill: Probably. There's a feeling that things in sports are more empirical, are more concrete. The methods of measuring achievement are black and white in most things. You can measure speed, jumping ability, accuracy, and quickness. Even things like quickness and lateral quickness, they've created methods of measuring. Perhaps that creates a sense that this is an avenue that I should go to. There are some politics obviously, but I think there's a feeling that you can minimize the impact of the effect of politics just by what you do wherever you're performing. The other thing is the instant gratification. Willie Mays is on a farm, poor, and then suddenly he's in New York riding around in Cadillacs. To a kid who's on a farm or a kid who's poor, he can visualize that. The psychological power of a Willie Mays or a Magic Johnson is almost like the psychology of a casino where lots of people are playing the slot machines and suddenly one person wins. The other people realize: "Hey, I'm that close, that could be me." And so there's always: "That could be me," and in sports, kids are saying that. Even when the odds are great, they feel they have as good a shot as anybody else. Growing up in Turner's, I only saw two black doctors so I didn't see that as "that could be me." Now I had other things in my life that made me feel good about Calvin Hill and so, although I spent a lot of time playing baseball, the energies that I may have put in sports was counterbalanced by other things. And I think maybe that's what we need: somebody to create balance, somebody to tell them that in fact, the odds of becoming a doctor are much more in your favor than the odds of becoming a professional basketball player.

Zang: Where does the prescription for getting balance get started though? Is it going to have to take political pressure?

Hill: It's funny. I find myself sometimes thinking "is it hopeless?" I spoke at an all-star football banquet last week, and I feel so sorry for some of these coaches because they're outmanned. The streets are an opponent. To a certain extent, the school system is an opponent. But I think somehow black people are going to have to go back to basics, and it starts with the family. We have to create some sort of pressure to keep the family intact. The subscription in the black community to the lifestyle of divorce and out-of-wedlock babies is devastating to us. We've gotten into a vicious cycle: both male and female babies having babies, and it's devastating—the psychological damage, the economic damage, the social damage. We have to figure out some way to restore the nuclear family. And until we can do that, we're really going to be behind the eight ball. It's not a question of being smart, it's a question of where the priorities are. And education is the key.

Zang: Well, all of American culture seems to be getting away from the nuclear family. Is it particularly devastating though in the classes that are already disenfranchised?

Hill: Yeah, because you're trying to get from being underprivileged to privileged. To look at it in the broader perspective, I'm one who believes the dissolution of the American family is a tremendous problem. When you add the transient nature of society and the changing economic scene in American society, this is why drugs have become a problem not just in the ghetto but in society at large. When you look at it from a black perspective, we're never going to participate in the dream as equal partners until we get ourselves together. So, it exacerbates an already bad situation. And every other group has looked at education as the key, the most recent of which are the Vietnamese and the Southeast Asians who have come here.

Zang: In that sense, then, if in fact the whole process of slavery and selection of the hardiest has some validity, it's almost like a double-edged sword, creating an area in which there's enormous pride in success—athletics—but also making it difficult to stress that other side to get the balance.

Hill: The problem is there's no balance. The equal opportunity in education, what we saw after *Brown v. The Board of Education,* that momentum has been lost. My father, who didn't have an education when he migrated up from South Carolina, saw education as the key. But a generation later, education is no longer seen to be that important. It could be a reflection on people thinking things were going to move a lot faster. It could be a function of the general hopelessness that occurred after the sixties when there was so much expectation and the dream sort of died (with) King's death, and the Kennedys (being) killed. Somehow we're going to have to get that hope back and we're going to have to start emphasizing the importance of the family. . . .

Zang: As you look back over all the circumstances that took you to Yale and had you gain a successful career in athletics, what are the changes that you have seen that have brought things to the point that they are now?

Hill: I was thinking this in terms of my own son, because economically at least he has advantages that I didn't enjoy. On the one hand, it looks like he has—a generation later—a greater chance to succeed. But I wonder if society is better now than it was when I was in Turner's Station in terms of people caring for one another. I wonder sometimes if, as we have leapfrogged in terms of knowledge and technological innovations, we haven't lost some of the basics. So I wonder who's better off—me growing up poor in Turner's Station or my son growing up upper middle class in Reston, Virginia. The world's gotten so small and so transient and people are here today and gone someplace else tomorrow. I honestly feel that society with all of its incessant activity is not necessarily all that nurturing and all that good. I don't think there are a lot of people who feel as grounded as I felt growing up. People (now) can't establish roots. And that's bad, I think. The family is not there. People are transient, so your community is not there. Your values are not there. . . .

Zang: If you were raising your son now in Turner's Station, would you consider there to be more opportunities available to a working class black in 1988 or fewer than there would have been in your childhood?

Hill: Probably there are more opportunities. The atmosphere is different now. One of the things that I certainly felt when I was growing up in Turner's Station is that people cared about one another. Maybe it was just growing up in Turner's Station in the fifties and then (going through) the sixties—that whole period of civil rights and brotherhood. I don't see that atmosphere anymore. Somehow that bubble burst and so, to answer your question, there may be more opportunities in terms of quantity of life; I don't think there are more opportunities in terms of quality of life. There used to be that quality of life in Turner's Station. In some ways it's better the way it is now, but in some ways it may have been even better then because everybody needs to feel that they are a part of something. That's part of feeling good about oneself, knowing that you have come from something.

Zang: It's not surprising, then, I guess that as it's so tough to find an identity, that if you can find one anywhere, even on the playground—

Hill: Sure. People want to feel good about themselves. I'm sure that's what you see with these drug dealers—suddenly they have some money in their pockets and they can go downtown with their girlfriends and buy them something. I remember when my father and I would go out to dinner. They'd ask us what we wanted and they always said "mister." He said they always call you mister when you have got some money in your pocket. Money is a symbol of a person's worth in our society. So a lot of those kids who either are getting money or dreaming of making money, they are putting their energies toward something that's going to give them more doing what it takes to feel good about oneself.

David Zang, "Calvin Hill Interview," *Journal of Sport History* 15 (Winter 1988): 334–55.

11. Margo Jefferson on Arthur Ashe: "On the Court, in the World"

Arthur Ashe Jr. was first, but not merely, a champion tennis player. His life—his saga—was cut short after he had won all his athletic laurels. Yet for those who follow the history of sport as a means of transforming society, Ashe offered patient inspiration. Ashe's journey began on public athletic facilities in the segregated South; by the time he had spoken and written his last words, he had become a statesman. His social activism and humanitarian efforts had transcended sport. In fact, Ashe hoped to achieve a means to get past the sports page, to address issues such as education and black liberation on a global stage.

Born in 1943 in Richmond, Virginia, Ashe learned the game of tennis from Ron Charity, a local player, and later from Dr. Walter Johnson, a highly regarded instructor of black players who had tutored the great Althea Gibson, among others. Ashe's prodigious talents became evident during the latter half of the 1950s and early 1960s when he captured several boys' and men's national singles titles sponsored by the segregated American Tennis Association (ATA). He won the NCAA singles title (while at UCLA) in 1965, the U.S. Open in 1968, the Australian Open in 1970, and in 1975 the All-England (Wimbeldon) title. He was an outstanding Davis Cup player for a number of years and served as the nonplaying captain of the team from 1981 to 1985.

Beyond his career in tennis, Ashe engaged a range of social issues from the 1960s until his death in 1993. At first, he was tentative about political advocacy and thought deeply about his role as a celebrity and activist. Navigating the racial divide as a well-known black athlete in American society was in many ways perilous, he asserted, and in diverse public forums he offered sympathy for his forerunner, Jesse Owens, who, during the 1960s and 1970s was being pushed and tugged from many constituencies to take political positions that ultimately appeared contradictory and confused.* For his part, Ashe often seemed to evoke W. E. B. Du Bois's classic notion of double-consciousness, the constant struggle of African Americans to reconcile being both black and American. Ashe was one of those athletes in the public eye who had been pressured to adhere to differing forms of behavior—or to espouse various causes—by the black and white communities. But he made it perfectly clear he wanted to be free to act according to his own principles regardless of what others expect-

---

* See Owens, "How I Learned"; Ashe, "Don't Tell Me How to Think."

ed of him. Ironically, Ashe's insistence on such freedom was most severely tested when he was forced years later to announce he had AIDS after it became clear that USA Today would publicly disclose his illness. In customary fashion, however, Ashe overcame his initial anger at having his privacy violated and set about to help find a cure for the disease by establishing the Arthur Ashe Foundation for the Defeat of AIDS.

By that time, he had already established himself as a significant public figure. He had spoken out against the inadequate education of young black athletes, actively opposed South Africa's apartheid policies, and forcefully deplored the treatment of Haitians seeking asylum in the United States. He had also written three thoughtful works of memoir and autobiography as well as a general survey on the history of African Americans in sport.*

Here, Margo Jefferson reviews Days of Grace, *the eloquent product of Ashe's collaboration with the scholar and biographer Arnold Rampersad. Jefferson, who taught American studies and writing at Columbia University before becoming a highly influential cultural critic for the* New York Times, *appraises the life as well as the book, capturing the versatility and tenacity that characterized Ashe both on and off the court. Like Arthur Ashe's career, this piece helps form a bridge between the documents assessing "progress, protest, and alienation" for black athletes and the texts in the final portion of this book, which often recapitulate the arguments of the civil rights generation even as they endeavor to come to terms with African American identity and race relations in sport at the end of the twentieth century.*

–––– ––––

Arthur Ashe died on Feb. 6 at the age of 49. We had been watching him die—or trying not to watch him die, or hoping that we were not watching him die—for nine months, and, as it turns out, he was watching himself and recording his progress, his thoughts, his feelings: about sports, politics, religion; about being an "aging jock" who wanted to be taken seriously; about the parts he had played (sportsman, race man, spokesman, icon, "Negro tennis star," protester against apartheid, person with AIDS). *Days of Grace* is a memoir, a manifesto and a message from the grave. It starts with the day in April 1992 when, knowing that *USA Today* was about to break the news of his illness, Ashe went on television to announce that he had AIDS. It ends with a letter to his 7-year-old daughter, Camera, filled with parental pedagogy and grief.

Of course we can all remember the Arthur Ashe who first made his way onto the culture's center stage. It was 1968, and he had just won the United States Open at Forest Hills, ending a 13-year drought when no American had won there, and ending a 100-year blight when to dream of a male African-American tennis champion was to dream, in the words of the 19th-century debate about free soil and slavery, of "an imaginary Negro in an improbable place."

He was a stylistic enigma. He had the restrained manners developed when tennis was the avocation of gentleman jocks, and he had the restrained manners developed when a Negro was taught that every action one took would reflect well or badly on the Race as a whole. He had cool, and he was also something of a dweeb. The combi-

---

* See Ashe, *Off the Court;* idem, *Portrait in Motion;* idem, *A Hard Road to Glory;* Ashe and Rampersad, *Days of Grace.*

Arthur Ashe (Allsport)

nation worked well for tennis, I thought, where manners are a mask for a strategic one-on-one brutality otherwise only found in boxing. (With her prom-queen manners and hit-man nerves, Chris Evert had a similar effect.)

Arthur Ashe became a star—a leading man of mass culture. *Life Magazine* put him on its cover and said he had "icy elegance." His opponents said he had a game that could be stoical, quicksilver or swashbuckling. John McPhee captured this wonderfully in his 1969 book, *Levels of the Game,* a docu-drama of the semifinal match at Forest Hills that led to Ashe's United States Open Championship. Cross-cutting between Ashe and his opponent, Clark Graebner, Mr. McPhee exposed two men, one sport and a nation under pressure. (Ashe on Graebner's game: "He plays stiff, compact, Republican tennis. He's a damned smart player, a good thinker, but he's not a limber and flexible thinker." Graebner on Ashe's game: "He plays the game with the lackadaisical, haphazard mannerisms of a liberal. . . . In a way, 'liberal' is a synonym for 'loose.' And that's exactly the way Arthur plays.")

Eleven years later, Ashe had his first heart attack. The quadruple bypass operation meant to prolong his life did no such thing, and he found himself forced to retire at 37, touring the museums of Europe and staring gloomily at Rembrandt's "Prophet Jeremiah Lamenting the Destruction of Jerusalem." ("Oh my," said his wife Jeanne. "Are we Jeremiah now?") He embarked on psychotherapy (generally disdained by male athletes and distrusted by blacks, he notes). He had a five-year stint as captain of the Davis Cup team, he lectured, he went into business, he organized an anti-apartheid sports boycott and he wrote *A Hard Road to Glory,* a three-volume reference book on the history of black athletes in America.

And yes, *Days of Grace* could easily have become a well-meant and plodding "highlights from the life of a celebrity who did good things" book. And yes, the fact of his illness and his death gives weight to moments that might otherwise be as ordinary as home movies. But this is a truly gripping book. It's gripping, it's moving, it's admirable; and what makes it so is Ashe's capacity for evaluating himself and the world with intelligence and honor.

He was wise to choose Arnold Rampersad as his collaborator. I like to think he did so not only because Mr. Rampersad has written meticulously fine books on Langston Hughes and W. E. B. Du Bois, but also because of what he has said about biography in general and black biography in particular: "One cannot trim his sails, mince his words or hide his thoughts to protect the race—a natural sense, given our history, but that should be overcome. . . . The black biographer can hardly allow himself or herself to imagine that the reputation of the race can be affected by what he or she writes about a particular subject . . . whether that topic is sexuality, politics, or racial apostasy."

Sexuality, politics, and iconoclasm are all Ashe's subjects, and his will to think them through honestly is visible on every page. The Ashean style is to begin with a calming observation, something between a generality and a platitude, then proceed, quietly but implacably, to an astute, cutting, or thoughtful end. "The problem with you, Arthur," Jesse Jackson once told him, "is that you're not arrogant enough." "You're right, Jesse," Ashe answered. "But I don't think my lack of arrogance lessens my effectiveness one bit." It's an earnest but innocuous answer: advantage Jackson. And then, Ashe goes on. "The trouble, however, is that once empowered and turned loose, egotism and arrogance are hard to control. I am not sure that Jesse, in his own life, has ever understood this lesson fully, despite the good work that he has done." Deuce, and possibly advantage, Ashe. . . .

In the end, though, the matches with himself are what count most—the struggles and collaborations between two Arthur Ashes: one cool, aloof, detached, conservative; one vehement and radical. Why did he become an anti-apartheid spokesman after a discreet silence on racial issues during the early and middle 60s? The memory of growing up in the segregated South is the cleanest, prettiest answer, but Ashe attaches a less clean, less pretty question to it: "To what extent was I trying to make up . . . for my relative inaction a decade or more earlier during the civil rights struggle?" "I was undoubtedly timid away from the court," he says of his upbringing. "Blacks did not publicly protest much in Virginia when I was growing up; and they protested even less in my father's household." (Young Arthur once tried to throw his racquet down in a fit of pique: before it hit the ground he heard his father, who was watching from the house, slam the screen door and head for the court.)

His first arrest for protesting apartheid, in 1985, was a choreographed event with no real danger involved, yet it rattled him, simply because "I had spent my life making sure no one would ever have cause to arrest me for anything." When he declares, "I want no stain on my character, no blemish on my reputation," it can send a chill through you—it suggests the conformist prig he might have become. (The dark side of a cool, mannerly dweeb is a stiff-necked prig.)

Ashe's political versatility can make a reader dizzy: he organizes Athletes for Jesse Jackson in 1984, votes for George Bush in 1988 and proudly hails Nelson Mandela in 1991. But I find his political opinions coherently diverse—rather like the 16 variations on a backhand that he once had in his tennis repertory. He dislikes great athletes who grow suddenly demure when politics, not trophies, are at issue. (Names named include the white South African Gary Player and the black American Michael Jordan.) He detests the environmental imbalance between sports and academics that young black athletes face; likewise the greedy self-absorption that can so readily unite athletes of all colors. He derides the florid cult of the Black Leader as Race Savior—"the very fact that we speak of 'leaders' and 'role models' as much as we do tells of our lack of power and organization"—and the discreetly lethal habit of racial "tipping" whereby blacks are deemed "acceptable in a token amount, toxic beyond it." He believes that the morality once at the heart of African-American culture has yielded to an "amoral quest for naked and vengeful power," and the question he most wants to answer is, what happened to black America? But he will not let any reader forget that this question calls for and responds to another of equal depth and greater breadth—namely, what happened to America as a whole?

By now you must have noticed a certain symmetry (black-white, progressive-conservative and so on) in his choice of targets. It is insistent; some would even say compulsive. But read on. Ashe is not after rhetorically glib symmetries—his view of the world is fearfully complicated. You can dissect, amend and refine his theories to your heart's content; you are being dealt with fairly, and you are meant to talk and think back.

Ashe spends the final chapters of his book as he spent the final months of his life, while taking 30 pills a day—discussing AIDS and civil rights, putting his beliefs on health care, gay rights and bigotry in all its infinite variety on record. He describes getting through mornings that were "an ordeal of listlessness and diarrhea" and fighting not to make his illness a metaphor for every lurking form of despair and self-hatred.

The approach of death can give an aura of omniscience to every word one utters. This can be impressive, but I value far more Ashe's willingness to admit to the mixed feelings that always inflect one's principles. So he can be anxious and rueful about his 7-year-old's going to sex education classes, and also conclude that in the midst of an epidemic, there is "no time for moral evasions and euphemisms or other genteel discretion in teaching young people who are either sexually active or on the brink of becoming so." So, too, he can discuss homosexuality, homophobia, racism, anti-Semitism, feminism and the elaborate social and behavioral distinctions between the men's and women's tennis tours without sounding smug, sappy or ostentatiously (hence unconvincingly) enlightened.

There is a fraught and fascinating moment in the chapter entitled "The Burden of Race." "I do not mean to appear fatalistic, self-pitying, cynical or maudlin," he writes. "A long time ago, I made peace with the state of Virginia and the South. . . . But segregation had achieved by that time what it was intended to achieve: it left me a marked man, forever aware of a shadow of contempt that lay across my identity and my sense of self esteem. . . . I don't want to overstate the case. I think of myself and others think of me, as supremely self-confident. . . . Still, I also know that the shadow is always there; only death will free me, and blacks like me, from its pall."

This is followed by a brisk account of a televised 1992 tennis benefit for the Arthur Ashe Foundation for the Defeat of AIDS. A white friend had brought Ashe's daughter a doll with blond hair, and Ashe suddenly realized that she might be seen on national television playing with it. That day in 1954, when black lawyers had argued in *Brown v. Board of Education* that black children's preference for white dolls revealed the psychic damage wrought by segregation, loomed large. So did a more pedestrian fear of public opinion. He turned to his wife: "'Jeanne,'" I whisper, 'we have to do something.'

"'About what?' she whispers back.

"That doll. We have to get Camera to put that doll down.'

"Jeanne takes one look at Camera and the doll and she understands immediately. Quietly, cleverly, she makes the doll disappear. . . .

"I feel myself becoming more and more angry. I am angry at the force that made me act, the force of racism in all its complexity. . . . I am angry with myself because I have just acted out of pure practicality, not out of morality. . . . Racism ultimately created the state in which defensiveness and hypocrisy are our almost instinctive responses, and innocence and generosity are invitations to trouble."

Having told this tale, I feel compelled, as Ashe did, to assure you that his daughter has dolls of every color and plays happily with them. Death does free one from this sort of thing. In the meantime, his book gives us a little more elbow room as we make our way through our American muddle of the small-minded and the heart-wrenching.

Margo Jefferson, "On the Court, In the World," review of Arthur Ashe and Arnold Rampersad, *Days of Grace, New York Times,* June 13, 1993.

8

Black Cultural Commentary: Race Relations and Sport at the Turn of the Twenty-first Century

Introduction

When surveying the highlights of athletic competition over the course of a season, a decade, or a century, even the most conscientious sportswriters and television journalists tend to focus on championship games or the records of athletic heroes: rushing yards, points per game, home runs. The stories offered in sports page history can be compelling—though for some readers, such appraisals are often offset by the numbing repetitiveness of the genre. For commentators on the meanings of black contributions in sport, the legends in sepia offer a significant starting point for discussions of broader developments in society and culture, economics and politics. Critically, the analyses provided by African American journalists and scholars during the last decade of the twentieth century have not only recapitulated the hopes and concerns of many intellectuals who came before; they have also raised important questions for the future. Thirty and forty years ago, much of the black commentary on sport first surfaced at historically black colleges and universities or found enthusiastic editors solely in the African American press or periodicals like the *Crisis* and *Opportunity.* In recent years, however, many of those dispatches have emanated from departments of African American studies such as the one at Harvard University, made their way into mainstream periodicals like the *New Yorker* and *The Nation,* or originated as columns published in major metropolitan newspapers. University and trade presses, which for many years denied a voice to black Americans, now track down and sign up authors who speak both personally and professionally to the legacies of slavery and more than a century of discrimination thereafter—who address stereotypical racial representations in popular culture as well as problems in the workplaces of America. Other scholars and commentators, meanwhile, engage in discussions of mixed racial heritage and, at ever-deeper levels, the many meanings of the larger "projects" of imperialism, colonialism, and the categorization of peoples by race and ethnicity—then, too, about the re-conquest of identity by those who have been historically subjugated. An expanding scholarship and commentary about the grim record of American race relations carries multiple messages. The stories and analyses themselves are as depressing as they are liberating; yet that so many people are involved in revealing oppression and recovering the lives of those who have struggled against it might also suggest a substantial measure of social change in the recent past.

Among the myriad images of sports from the 1990s, however, some are troubling ones, reflecting deeply rooted and persistent problems. From the first half of the decade one might recollect the figure of Michael Jordan, hovering above a basket and twisting in midair, seeming to defy gravity, then somehow twisting again to score a winning goal. Jordan ultimately gained an enormous following throughout the world—and a raft of lucrative endorsements. And one of the great questions of the era became, in MJ's case, could he soar above race? Next to that vision one can juxtapose the promotional hype for the 1995 film documentary *Hoop Dreams.* The ironies and ambiguities in the portrayal of two high school basketball players and their quest for athletic scholarships, then fame and fortune in the NBA, were betrayed by the build-up. These were talented young black men, like thousands of others in the United States, prodded by family and friends, exploited by coaches, struggling in the classroom while enjoying local success on the court. Just how far from the NBA their futures lay it would have been difficult to discern at the moment, but there was pathos as much as inspiration in their project.

Skip ahead several years and one could picture once again the dominant figure of Michael Jordan, now joined by Tiger Woods and Venus and Serena Williams as household names and darlings of the advertising industry. Significantly, though, by 2000 Jordan was wearing a business suit and was part owner and general manager of his own franchise. Here was the fulfillment of a vision once elaborated by black commentators like Edwin Bancroft Henderson that success in athletic competition would fully translate into notable achievements beyond the arena itself. The image of Anita DeFrantz, one of the highest ranking officials on the International Olympic Committee, carried the same message about progress. Then again, what the daily news and year-end sociological surveys show us is that a significant segment of black male youth is not involved in athletic pursuits or educational programs but, rather, is bound to the criminal justice system, either in jail or on probation.

These contrasting images have formed the context for much of the debate about sport and society at the end of the twentieth century and into the twenty-first. The issue of the role of education in transforming college sport into a platform for more expansive patterns of achievement for black Americans has been a concern for more than a century. But in the 1990s and early 2000s the problem of athletic exploitation has seemed particularly acute. Likewise when "hoop dreams" run up against the laws of athletic supply and demand at the collegiate and professional levels, African American commentators have been emphatic about the need for more broad-based community programs to direct black youth from the ball courts and into the classroom. The starkness of Harry Edwards's comments below about the use of sports as a "hook and handle" to help relieve the distress and alienation of inner-city youth suggests that it is far too early to celebrate the millennium of black athletic achievement.

Recent African American commentators, while discussing sport, culture, and community, often recall the celebrations and admonitions made by W. E. B. Du Bois, Richard Wright, and E. Franklin Frazier in earlier years. More critically still, black intellectuals have not hesitated to direct their arguments against prevailing inequalities within American society at large or to juxtapose success in the sports realm to problems in the workplace and marketplace. Race relations in the United States remain a troubling issue largely because mainstream public opinion has not shifted as dramatically as was once hoped and government policies have not addressed a radically skewed social and economic structure. While some black intellectuals may lament the lack of protest emanating from an increasingly influential black sporting community, others also recognize that real power, or most of it, still lies outside the fields of athletic competition. Ultimately, many of those who have assessed the meaning of sports for African Americans around the turn of the twenty-first century have largely refined the arguments made by earlier generations of racial reformers. Sport may be a necessary part of transforming American society and culture, but by itself it is not sufficient.

A

SCHOOL AND SOCIETY:
ATHLETICS AND ACADEMICS

1. Henry Louis Gates Jr. / "Delusions of Grandeur"

The success of African American athletes has long been enormously symbolic for much of the black community in the United States. Decidedly image conscious, members of the black community have seen the triumphs of individual black athletes as crucially important because these achievements presumably helped break down the prevailing opinions of black people's inferiority, had an uplifting effect on blacks themselves, and could possibly hasten progress in race relations generally. Important, too, many members of the black community have long emphasized that African Americans should strive for success in other fields and develop their "brains" as well as their "brawn."* While they believed sport was a worthy activity and proudly pointed to the achievements of individual black athletes, the African American intelligentsia continually cautioned against an overemphasis on sport and stressed the importance of preparing for life after baseball or basketball. A balance was needed. Rather than slavishly aspiring to careers in sport, which were extremely limited in opportunity, young African Americans would be better served by honing those skills necessary to achieve success in other professional fields. **

In the following document, Henry Louis Gates Jr., W. E. B. Du Bois Professor of the Humanities at Harvard University, echoes the concerns about athletic competition expressed by many of the black thinkers who preceded him. Here he does so—at least in part—in a conversational way. Gates goes on, moreover, to provide some somber statistics about African American participation in sport, accurately noting that there are far more black doctors, dentists, and lawyers in the United States than black athletes. In spite of these statistics, Gates writes, many African Americans continue to pursue careers in sport as if it were the surest means to achieve fame and fortune. An Ivy League professor making bar bets in rural West Virginia represents an enormous cultural provocation; the point that Gates is trying to make, however—another provocation—is that black athletic success in recent years has served a hegemonic *function. It has distracted many African Americans from more practical professional opportunities and careers.*

---

* See, for example, Ashe, "Send Your Children to the Libraries"; Fisher, "The Best Way Out of the Ghetto"; R. Brown, "The 'Jock-Trap'"; Edwards, "Sport within the Veil"; idem, "Educating Black Athletes"; E. Graves, "The Right Kind of Excellence," 4, 9.

** The breadth and depth of this discourse on black success was almost entirely ignored by Hoberman in his *Darwin's Athletes.*

——— ———

Standing at the bar of an all-black VFW Post in my hometown of Piedmont, W.Va., I offered five dollars to anyone who could tell me how many African-American professional athletes were at work today. There are 35 million African Americans, I said.

"Ten million!" yelled one intrepid soul, too far into his cups.

"No way . . . more like 500,000," said another.

"You mean all professional sports," someone interjected, "including golf and tennis, but not counting the brothers from Puerto Rico?" Everyone laughed.

"Fifty thousand, minimum," was another guess.

Here are the facts:

There are 1,200 black professional athletes in the U.S.
There are 12 times more black lawyers than black athletes.
There are 2½ times more black dentists than black athletes.
There are 15 times more black doctors than black athletes.

Nobody in my local VFW believed these statistics; in fact, few people would believe them if they weren't reading them in the pages of *Sports Illustrated.* In spite of these statistics, too many African-American youngsters still believe that they have a much better chance of becoming another Magic Johnson or Michael Jordan than they do of matching the achievements of Baltimore Mayor Kurt Schmoke or neurosurgeon Dr. Benjamin Carson, both of whom, like Johnson and Jordan, are black.

In reality, an African-American youngster has about as much chance of becoming a professional athlete as he or she does of winning the lottery. The tragedy for our people, however, is that few of us accept that truth.

Let me confess that I love sports. Like most black people of my generation—I'm 40—I was raised to revere the great black athlete heroes, and I never tired of listening to the stories of triumph and defeat that, for blacks, amount to a collective epic much like those of the ancient Greeks; Joe Louis's demolition of Max Schmeling; Satchel Paige's dazzling repertoire of pitches; Jesse Owens's in-your-face performance in Hitler's 1936 Olympics; Willie Mays's over-the-shoulder basket catch; Jackie Robinson's quiet strength when assaulted by racist taunts and a thousand other grand tales.

Nevertheless, the blind pursuit of attainment in sports is having a devastating effect on our people. Imbued with a belief that our principal avenue to fame and profit is through sport and seduced by a win-at-any-cost system that corrupts even elementary school students, far too many black kids treat basketball courts and football fields as if they were classrooms in an alternative school system. "O.K., I flunked English," a young athlete will say. "But I got an A plus in slam-dunking."

The failure of our public schools to educate athletes is part and parcel of the schools' failure to educate almost everyone. A recent survey of the Philadelphia school system, for example, stated that "more than half of all students in the third, fifth and eighth grades cannot perform minimum math and language tasks." One in four middle school students in that city fails to pass to the next grade each year. It is a sad truth that such statistics are repeated in cities throughout the nation. Young athletes—particularly young black athletes—are especially ill-served. Many of them are functionally illiterate, yet they are passed along from year to year for the greater glory of good old Hometown High. We should not be surprised to learn, then, that only 26.6% of black athletes at the collegiate level earn their degrees. For every successful educated black professional athlete, there are thousands of dead and wounded. Yet young blacks continue to aspire to careers as athletes and it's no wonder why; when the University of North Carolina recently commissioned a sculptor to create archetypes of its student body, guess which ethnic group was selected to represent athletes?

Those relatively few black athletes who do make it in the professional ranks must be prevailed upon to play a significant role in the education of all our young people, athlete and non-athlete alike. While some have done so, many others have shirked their social obligations: to earmark small percentages of their incomes for the United Negro College Fund; to appear on television for educational purposes rather than merely to sell sneakers; to let children know the message that becoming a lawyer, a teacher or a doctor does more good for our people than winning the Super Bowl; and to form productive liaisons with educators to help forge solutions to the many ills that beset the black community. These are merely a few modest proposals.

A similar burden falls upon successful blacks in all walks of life. Each of us must strive to make our young people understand the realities. Tell them to cheer Bo Jackson but to emulate novelist Toni Morrison or businessman Reginald Lewis or historian John Hope Franklin or Spelman College president Johnetta Cole—the list is long.

Of course, society as a whole bears responsibility as well. Until colleges stop using young blacks as cannon fodder in the big-business wars of so-called nonprofessional sports, until training a young black's mind becomes as important as training his or her body, we will continue to perpetuate a system akin to that of the Roman gladiators, sacrificing a class of people for the entertainment of the mob.

Henry Louis Gates Jr., "Delusions of Grandeur," *Sports Illustrated,* August 19, 1991, 78.

2. Anita DeFrantz / Overcoming Obstacles

The last two decades have seen a significant increase in the number of women actively participating in various sports at all levels of competition. Title IX, the women's movement, increased emphasis on fitness, and a host of other factors have all combined to provide more opportunities for women of every age group and socioeconomic class to compete in both amateur and professional sport. Unfortunately, while women have found increasing opportunities to compete on the playing field, they have not had comparable chances in coaching and upper-level administrative positions within sport. This is particularly true for African American women, who have found even fewer opportunities than their white counterparts. Dana Brooks and Ronald Althouse note that in the late 1990s just 1.5 percent of the 6,881 women's teams in the NCAA were coached by African American women, and as of January

Anita DeFrantz (Courtesy Amateur Athletic Foundation)

1999, only one Division I institution had an African American woman athletic director.* The reasons for the limited number of African American women in these positions are many and complex but certainly have been influenced by the unwillingness of those in leadership roles to take minority candidates seriously and overcome their deep-seated stereotyping concerning both race and gender.

In the following selection, Anita DeFrantz, an Olympic bronze medalist in rowing and until recently the only female member of the International Olympic Committee, briefly describes her own challenges as a participant in highly organized sport and the continued difficulties African American women encounter in assuming coaching and administrative positions. She contends that the intersection of racism and sexism is responsible for the dearth of African American women in these positions. The reality of the situation, notes DeFrantz in words that echo those of both male and female black athletes throughout the years, is that African American women had to be "twice as good" as their white counterparts if they expected to be offered coaching and upper-level administrative positions. The article written

---

* For information on the lack of African Americans in coaching and upper-level administrative positions in sport, see Brooks and Althouse, "African American Head Coaches and Administrators."

by Anita DeFrantz for Sports Illustrated *in 1991 acknowledges the efforts of black women forerunners, such as Marian Washington; tellingly, though, her somber assessment also foreshadows the verdict of many experts made ten years later for the* Chronicle of Higher Education, *found in the next selection: in the quest for equality and opportunity on the playing fields, black women have too often been left behind.*

——— ———

In 1976, I rowed seven seat in the U.S. eight-oared shell that won a bronze medal at the Montreal Games. Since 1986, I have been a member of the International Olympic Committee. My term of office lasts until I turn 75 in the year 2027. Only 10 years passed between my becoming an Olympian and my election to the IOC. But for me, an African-American woman, reaching the top of international sport seemed like the accomplishment of 10 generations.

Even in those sports that are largely sustained by black athletes, the guiding decisions are still made by white males. As a consequence, any African-American woman who finds herself in a position of influence in U.S. sport is a magnificent overachiever. And the number of such women, always small, is dwindling. A remarkable resource is in danger.

When I was growing up in Indianapolis, I became curious about the energy and endurance of my great-grandmother, Laura Ethel Lucas. She was in her mid 70's, yet she carried sacks of groceries that I—at nine—could not lift. When I asked her how she got so strong, she said, "I wanted to be a nurse. But because I was a colored girl, they wouldn't let me go to school and get the necessary training. So I worked in white people's homes, cleaning, washing their clothes and preparing their meals. It was hard work, so I had to be strong. But things are changing. You can get an education. You can be whatever you want to be."

I knew right then that I wanted to be strong, strong as Grandma Lucas was, strong enough to take on a world I knew would be hostile to me simply because of the color of my skin.

I saw other black females who were not able to sustain that strength. As a child, I swam during the summers for the Frederick Douglass Park team. All of us were black. A teammate of mine won almost every race, even against the white kids who trained year-round at the Riviera Club. The mostly white crowds on such occasions received this gifted girl in silence. Eventually she quit the team.

At Connecticut College, I discovered rowing, a discipline that would take all the strength I could muster. My skin color made me conspicuous in the sport. As a result, I never pulled at half pressure. I knew that I had to be better than my teammates. Today, that is the creed of every black female coach or administrator. "Twice as good?" says former USOC vice-president Evie Dennis. "Try five times as good."

I know from experience that it is painful to acknowledge that you are the target of racism or sexism, but I believe it is essential to call people on it. So here are some hard facts:

A survey of 106 Division I schools that field women's basketball teams found that only 11 are coached by black women.

In those 106 schools, there is only one athletic director who is an African American woman.

There are no black women among the executive directors who lead the 50 governing bodies for U.S. Olympic sports.

There has never been a black woman on any U.S. Olympic basketball coaching staff.

Even worse, in U.S. amateur sport, there are fewer female coaches today, black or white, than there were only 10 years ago. Decisions on women's staff and spending used to be the province of the female administrators who were responsible for women's athletics. Now decisions are usually made by white male athletic directors, whose imperatives are football and the bottom line. Cost-cutting has led to a shrinkage of non-revenue sports and the coaching jobs that go with them. In response, black female student-athletes are turning their backs on programs that would prepare them for jobs in those fields. The obstacles are too formidable.

Marian Washington, a black woman who is in her 19th season as the women's basketball coach at Kansas, says, "You constantly believe people will judge you by your work. It's such an unhappy surprise when they don't."

And, ultimately, it's enormously debilitating. After many years of watching other coaches receive opportunities to coach in international competitions, Washington finally decided to stop caring about it. "When I started to question myself and my capability because I wasn't being chosen, I decided not to allow myself to remain in that environment," she says.

Two American traditions collide here: Black women's belief in our own strength slams head-on into society's refusal to let us choose where to employ that strength. Sport doesn't lead society, it reflects it. To bring African-American women fully into American sport, attitudes must be changed. Sports executives must search their souls to see whether they are judging black women coaches and administrators fairly on their work, not dismissing them on the basis of their sex and the color of their skin.

Read about the obstacles faced by men—the stacking, stereotyping, discouraging and dumping—described in this magazine's series on the black athletes, then take my word for this: It's worse if you're female. And those who would deny all women their rights will oppose black women even more.

The strength and leadership ability of African-American women has been tested for centuries, and we have never failed to perform. Harriet Tubman escaped enslavement, led others to freedom and became a scout for the Union Army. Today's African-American women are ready and able to contribute to this nation through sports. But only if given the opportunity, only if given the chance.

Anita DeFrantz, "We've Got to Be Strong: The Obstacles Facing Black Women in Sports Have Scarcely Diminished with Time," *Sports Illustrated,* August 12, 1991, 77.

3. Welch Suggs / "Left Behind": Title IX and Black Women Athletes

Ten years after Anita DeFrantz penned her lament about the limited opportunities available for African American women in sport, indeed more than a quarter-century after Marian Washington's call for action, the Chronicle of Higher Education *made the most expansive assessment to date regarding the effects of Title IX on black female athletes. The results, as Welch Suggs indicates, were depressing. Where college sports had expanded rapidly, in both the number of women competing and the number of sports in which to participate, statistics also show that black women have not found as many opportunities as their white counterparts.*

Economics plays a significant role in the disparity. The athletic programs at Historically Black Colleges and Universities, for instance, are not nearly as well funded as those of the major football- and basketball-playing schools, and women's sports programs suffer as a consequence. Another factor is that the high level of competition today means that women like Anita DeFrantz, who came to her rowing career as a "walk-on," compete in far fewer numbers; most varsity athletes of the present era have been practicing their sports for years before they entered college. Finally, Suggs calls attention to the findings by Tina Sloan Green that the problem centers on access. Sports such as soccer have become well developed in suburban America, much less so in the urban centers where many African Americans live. Beyond that, the equipment and coaching resources necessary for young women to become accomplished at golf, tennis, and rowing—to highlight the Chronicle's *prime example— are not equally distributed throughout the social landscape. All of this amounts to a continuing problem of equity and opportunity in the sporting realm, so it will be interesting to track the good intentions of the NCAA and various sporting federations to see where, in the next decade, such efforts will lead.*

——— ———

Black women don't row. Or play soccer or lacrosse. Or compete in equestrian sports. They play basketball, or they run track. Or they don't do sports at all. That's the stereotype, and even though she breaks it herself, Brannon Johnson says there's more than a little truth to it.

"We had family basketball games growing up," Ms. Johnson, who is African-American, says of her childhood in Philadelphia. And in the neighborhood, "the height of competition was to see who could beat each other down to the corner store."

That makes Ms. Johnson, a freshman on the varsity crew at the University of Texas at Austin, the exception that proves the rule: Black women have been bypassed in the tremendous expansion of female sports under Title IX of the Education Amendments of 1972.

Nearly a third of the women shooting hoops in Division I of the National Collegiate Athletic Association are black, as are nearly a quarter of female track athletes.

But only 2.7 percent of the women receiving scholarships to play all other sports at predominantly white colleges in Division I are black. Yet those are precisely the

Female Athletes, in Black and White

Among female athletes, African-Americans represent the largest nonwhite racial group ...

All female athletes, 1999-2000

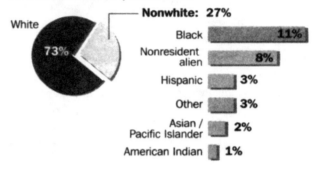

White 73%

Nonwhite: 27%

Black	11%
Nonresident alien	8%
Hispanic	3%
Other	3%
Asian / Pacific Islander	2%
American Indian	1%

... but in the newer categories of sports, black females' share is diminished:

Female athletes, excluding basketball and track, 1999-2000

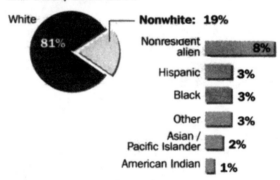

White 81%

Nonwhite: 19%

Nonresident alien	8%
Hispanic	3%
Black	3%
Other	3%
Asian / Pacific Islander	2%
American Indian	1%

Among women in each group, here are the proportion who are black:

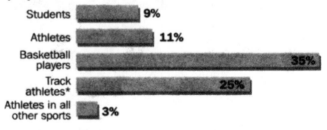

Students	9%
Athletes	11%
Basketball players	35%
Track athletes*	25%
Athletes in all other sports	3%

* Outdoor track and field

Note: Includes all Division I colleges except historically black colleges and universities. Numbers of athletes include only recipients of athletics scholarships.

Figures are rounded.

SOURCE: NCAA

Female Athletes, in Black and White: Graphs from *Chronicle of Higher Education,* November 30, 2001 (Source: NCAA) sports—golf, lacrosse, and soccer, as well as rowing—that colleges have been adding to comply with Title IX, the federal law that forbids sex discrimination at institutions receiving federal funds.

All the women's sports that colleges have added over the past 14 years attract masses of white suburban girls, but very few others. Participation rates for Hispanic, Asian, and American Indian female athletes are even tinier. Even so, colleges recruit quite a few foreign women for soccer, rowing, and other sports.

Some experts blame the NCAA and the (white) women's-sports establishment for promoting sports in which minority athletes are unlikely to participate. But the problem lies deeper than that: Coaches can't be blamed for failing to recruit women of color, when so few of them show up in the clubs and tournaments that help top athletes develop. Colleges can't really be lambasted for their choices of sports, when those sports simply don't draw minority women the way track and basketball do.

Yet black women and women from other minority groups clearly are not participating in most sports as much as men and white women are. And that troubles coaches, administrators, and advocates for minority issues.

Progress . . . for Some

Title IX has been around for nearly 30 years, but only in the past 14 have colleges demonstrated measurable progress in adding opportunities for women. Since 1987, when Congress passed a law that strengthened the enforcement of Title IX, the fastest-growing sports in the NCAA have been women's soccer, rowing, golf, and lacrosse. The numbers of teams and of athletes have doubled and in some cases tripled in all four sports.

However, the number of women's basketball and track teams has risen only about 26 percent, despite the scores of colleges that have migrated into the NCAA from the National Association of Intercollegiate Athletics over that time. (Of course, black women in basketball and track have benefited from Title IX in other ways, as colleges have spent money on those programs to improve their facilities, their coaching, and their visibility.)

College fields, courts, and rivers are now teeming with equestriennes, female soccer players, rowers, and other athletes, but almost all of them—70 percent—are white. Women from other minority groups are similarly underrepresented in college sports: Only 1.8 percent of all female athletes are Asian, and only 3 percent are Hispanic. Coaches are happy to look further afield, though: More than 7 percent of female athletes are from other countries. And members of all minority groups except black women have been going out for Division I sports in increased numbers since 1990–91, according to NCAA statistics. The proportions of American Indian, Asian, Hispanic, and foreign athletes on women's teams have skyrocketed, while the proportion of black women has remained steady between 13.9 and 15.6 percent over the past decade. Even so, black women continue to outnumber women of all other races except white.

A Lack of Exposure

Researchers, coaches, and athletes themselves offer a number of reasons for the dearth of black women in sports, including economics, culture, and psychology. For Tina

Sloan Green, though, they all revolve around access. Ms. Green, the director of the Black Women in Sport Foundation and a professor of physical education at Temple University, points out that most urban high schools don't have the green space need-ed for sports such as soccer, lacrosse, and especially golf. They don't have coaches for those sports. There is nothing to suggest to a girl that she might be successful at them. "When you have access to a sport, either you have success, or someone else sees that they might be successful," says Ms. Green. "But the cities are so jammed up."

Ms. Green, who is African-American, has some experience in this area. As a stu-dent at Philadelphia's Girls' High School, for gifted students, she found herself with a variety of sports to play, and excelled at field hockey. At West Chester University, the lacrosse coach persuaded her to add that sport to her repertoire. Ms. Green then coached both those sports at Temple, winning three national lacrosse titles in the 1980s with the Owls before leaving coaching in 1991 to concentrate on teaching and foundation work. Her daughter, Traci, played tennis at the University of Florida. The Greens had access to good coaching and the junior tennis circuit, the costs of which are far out of reach for many families. Having a top-ranked junior tennis player can cost up to $30,000 a year, Ms. Green estimates. The private-club system dominates most sports like soccer and softball as well, and—unlike sports like basketball, where shoe and apparel companies cover most costs for athletes—participation is nearly as expensive as tennis. Because virtually all of the good players go through the club sys-tem, all the coaches offering college scholarships do, too.

Access to the rich talent on the playing fields of Dallas and Houston was part of what prompted Chris Petrucelli to leave a job as coach of the University of Notre Dame's women's soccer team for the same job at Texas in 1999. "Soccer in the U.S. is a suburban sport with a lot of little white girls running around," says Mr. Petrucelli. "There are [African-American] kids out there, but the pool we look at is very selective and relatively small. There are usually one or two minorities in it. We recruit them, but we haven't gotten them yet."

Beyond the economic hurdles, black women who do find their way into sports such as soccer or crew often have a hard time being such a small minority on their teams, according to Teresa P. Stratta, a sociologist at the University of Tennessee at Knoxville. "There's a high correlation between the number of African-Americans on a team and their cultural expression," says Ms. Stratta, who is white. She recently con-ducted a two-year ethnographic study of women's teams at Temple. "A low represen-tation of black athletes leads to more cultural inhibitions, having to put up with lis-tening to country [music] and things like that." If two or fewer players on a squad are black or from another minority group, they find that coaches stereotype them into certain positions, and teammates won't bond with them. It's an isolating experience, Ms. Stratta says.

"Even if you get just three or four black athletes on a team, there's a dramatic dif-ference," she argues. "And if it gets to 30 percent to 40 percent, you have the really dy-namic environment where there's an interchange, a very healthy model."

Problems at Black Colleges

Many historically black colleges and universities offer the sports that women of color shun at predominantly white institutions. But those colleges don't necessarily give students the best chances to compete. Colleges in the Mid-Eastern and in the Southwestern Athletic Conferences—which together include all but one of the historically black colleges in Division I—tend to allocate less money for women's sports than other comparably sized predominantly white institutions in their regions. They also offer fewer playing opportunities for women, especially given that there are far more women than men at those colleges. Most colleges in the Mid-Eastern conference, for example, average about 60-percent female, while only 40.5 percent of the athletes at those institutions are women, for a difference of nearly 20 percentage points. In the Southern Conference, which consists of colleges in roughly the same region as the Mid-Eastern league, the difference in proportions is only 12.7 points.

Colleges in the Southwestern Athletic Conference each spend an average of $607,452 on women's sports, or 29 percent of their total operating budgets for sports. Colleges in the Southland Conference, by comparison, spent just over $1-million apiece on women's sports, or 40 percent of their overall operating budgets. Part of the reason has to do with economics: Most historically black institutions sponsor football teams, which require many male athletes and a lot of money, but don't make any profits that athletics departments could use for women's sports. However, the same is true of many predominantly white colleges at the lower levels of Division I, yet more of them do a better job of accommodating female athletes than do most historically black colleges.

In the MEAC and the SWAC, the main concession athletics directors have made to women is adding bowling teams, which are cheap to support and don't require much training or any new facilities. The NCAA has named bowling an "emerging sport" for women, and by 1999–2000 there were 21 teams in Division I, more than any other added sport except water polo. "Part of what we have found is that the sports at major institutions don't necessarily have strong support from our constituents at the high-school level, so there is no natural feeder system," says Charles S. Harris, commissioner of the MEAC and chairman of the NCAA's Division I Management Council.

Mr. Harris adds that the population of elementary- and high-school students is growing increasingly diverse, and that the association might face a problem if non-white children continue to avoid the sports that are popular right now.

No More Walk-Ons

In the past, college coaches often would introduce themselves to women on campus who might make good athletes. Anita L. DeFrantz remembers walking to class at Connecticut College and seeing a long, skinny boat in front of a classroom building. "I went over to inquire, and there was a man standing there," recalls Ms. DeFrantz, who is African-American. "I didn't know he was the coach, but he said, 'This is rowing, and you'd be perfect for it.' Since I'd never been perfect at anything, I thought I'd give it a go."

That encounter led her to an outstanding career in rowing, and she was named to the U.S. Olympic teams in 1976 and 1980, winning a bronze medal in the former. She is now president of the Amateur Athletic Foundation of Los Angeles and a member of the International Olympic Committee.

But her story is a little outdated, for most sports. Athletes specialize at ever-earlier ages, and college coaches recruit players with years of experience at high levels of play. The chances of someone "walking on" to a Division I soccer team today, without being recruited or having years of experience, the way Ms. DeFrantz picked up rowing in the early 1970s, are somewhere between slim and none.

Is the largely white sports establishment to blame for the lack of black women in those sports? No and yes, according to administrators and advocates. Coaches can't be blamed for recruiting only the most skilled athletes they can find, or at least that they can get into their institutions. They're paid to win, not to provide growth opportunities for athletes who can't contribute.

Some advocates for female athletes blame the women's movement. According to Ms. Green of Temple, feminists, and particularly advocates for women's sports, have overlooked the needs of minority women. "When you increase scholarships in these sports, you're not going to help people of color," she says. "But that's not in their line of interest. Title IX was for white women. I'm not going to say black women haven't benefited, but they have been left out."

Donna A. Lopiano, president of the Women's Sports Foundation, says Ms. Green has a point. "The women's movement is so focused on so many gender issues that the plight of women of color, who are in double jeopardy, is oftentimes on the back burner," Ms. Lopiano, the former women's athletics director at Texas, said in an e-mail message.

Encouraging Signs

Ms. Lopiano says it has been difficult to get sports-participation statistics for college and high-school sports broken down by race, while it is relatively easy to get those numbers for the sexes. The *Chronicle* used the NCAA's 2001 graduation-rates statistics, which include demographic data for scholarship athletes but not for college athletes over all. Moreover, the NCAA's rules requiring athletes to meet minimum standards for standardized-test scores to be eligible to play college sports have further restricted opportunities for black women, Ms. Green says.

Ms. Johnson is adjusting to college life and college rowing. Classes are tough, she says, but she's enjoying them as well as the rest of her two-months-and-growing adventure. She is the first in her family to attend college. "People may look at you twice" at regattas, she says, because a black woman in a boat is still a rarity. But her teammates have made her welcome.

She got into rowing through a program for inner-city kids run by Vespers, one of the oldest rowing clubs on Philadelphia's Schuylkill River. By the time she finished high school, she was among the area's top rowers, and people along the banks of the river would yell, "Go, black girl!" as she raced by, much to her embarrassment.

Similar programs to encourage kids in urban areas to play nontraditional sports have been started by most of the national governing bodies of various sports, including the U.S. Tennis Association, the U.S. Soccer Federation, and others. They haven't borne much fruit yet, but college coaches are hoping for a parallel to the "Tiger Woods effect"—kids from unusual backgrounds getting interested in their sports, much like they did in golf when Mr. Woods emerged as a star in the late 1990s.

The NCAA and its member colleges also have encouraged these kinds of efforts through the National Youth Sports Program, a college-based effort that involves coaches and athletes in putting on clinics and organizing games for children throughout the country.

Ms. Green says that the program, which she administers at Temple, has reached children who never would have been attracted to sports before. Eventually, black women will not have to be "firsts" anymore. But at least some of those who are firsts now are proud of it.

"I'm the first black scholarship rower at Texas," says Ms. Johnson with a smile on her face. "That makes me feel pretty good." But she hopes that one day, they won't have to yell "Go, black girl!" at anyone in Philadelphia. Because there will be too many.

Welch Suggs, "Left Behind," *Chronicle of Higher Education*, November 30, 2001, A35–A37.

4. bell hooks / "Dreams of Conquest"

*Historically, films depicting the athletic experience have dwelled on the surmounting of obstacles and triumph over tribulation; the concluding scenes play out in the football end zone after a winning touchdown or on the medal stand at the Olympics. There are notable exceptions to this generalization—*Love and Basketball *is one; the restaging of Shakespeare's* Othello, *at least in part, as a rivalry between white and black teammates, in* O *represents another. Still, most Hollywood movies have followed the formula. The documentary* Hoop Dreams *played it both ways. Although it tracked the progress of two Chicago-area black athletes, Arthur Agee and William Gates, as they pursued excellence on the hard court, the film also examined their family relations and explored elements of the African American community, especially the hopes for financial rewards both family and friends projected onto the young athletes.* Hoop Dreams *went further still, through a series of interviews with high school coaches and counselors, to illuminate the ways Agee and Gates were exploited, then abandoned by the educational authorities upon whom they depended. Ultimately, the documentary was widely considered an inspirational film, even as it illuminated how the two athletes remained oblivious to the realities of high-level sport. They gloried in their successes at the local level in basketball, though this meant that they stood among thousands of other talented athletes seeking scholarships to institutions known for big-time athletic programs. At the same time they understood only vaguely that certain NCAA academic standards needed to be met in order for them to qualify for admission to those universities.* [*]*

The critique of Hoop Dreams *offered here by bell hooks, Distinguished Professor of En-*

---

[*] See Frey, *The Last Shot*; Joravsky, *Hoop Dreams*.

glish at the Graduate Center of the City University of New York, echoes the challenges posed by educators and commentators such as Henry Louis Gates Jr. and Harry Edwards. Hooks also explores the ways the filmmakers both subvert and perpetuate stereotypes about black family and community relations, and she argues that university-based cultural critics, like herself, are able to see a far broader horizon of opportunity and far more channels for hard work, discipline, and unbounded ambition than do most inner-city blacks. The dreams held by the subjects of this film are constrained by the values and ideals that a white-dominated, educationally and technologically expansive society have left over, as it were, to many African American youth—just as the schoolbooks they used were the ones most recently replaced in nearby white elementary and high schools. Finally, hooks engages the "ethic of competition" that has long served as the foundation of sexism and racism in the United States. For hooks the thrill of victory, revealed in the games Gates and Agee helped win, is isolated, ultimately hollow. The careers of the talented athletes would follow very narrow paths or run into quick and demoralizing dead ends. Where others might see sad irony in Hoop Dreams, *"subsumed by the spectacle" of sport, hooks perceives something more tragic in the direct link between "the nature of the game in a culture of domination" in the United States and "the terrible loneliness" that "shrouds" one of the protagonists throughout the film—and as she assumes—in the years beyond.**

–––– ––––

Entering a movie theater packed tight with bodies of white folks waiting to see *Hoop Dreams,* the documentary about two African-American teenagers striving to become professional basketball players, I wanted to leave when it seemed that we (the two black folks I had come with—one of my five sisters and my ex-boyfriend) would not be able to sit together. Somehow I felt that I could not watch this film in a sea of whiteness without there being some body of blackness to anchor me, to see with me, to be a witness to the way black life was portrayed.

Now I have no problems with white filmmakers making films that focus on black life: the issue is only one of victim perspective. When you're living in a white-supremacist culture the politics of location matters, no matter who is making a film about people of color. In the United States, when white folks want to see and enjoy images of black folks on the screen, it is often in no way related to a desire to know real black people.

Sitting together in the packed crowd, every seat in the house taken, we joked about the atmosphere in the theater. It was charged with a sense of excitement and tension, the anticipation normally present at sports events. The focus on basketball playing may have allowed the audience to loosen up some, but without knowing much about the content and direction of the film, and whether it was serious or not, folks were clearly

---

* A 1999 follow-up on the protagonists in *Hoop Dreams* referred to Gates as "working with a company that is redeveloping the area around his old Cabrini-Green neighborhood." Agee had pursued an acting career. He gained a small part in Spike Lee's *He Got Game* and at age twenty-six portrayed a high school hoopster in a television movie, *Passing Glory.* For stories of recent high school basketball players who passed up college as they waited to be drafted by the NBA, see Berkow, "They're Still Waiting."

there to have fun. As it began, a voyeuristic pleasure at being able to observe from a distance the lives of two black boys from working-class and poor inner-city backgrounds overcame the crowd. The lurid fascination involved in the "watching" of this documentary was itself profound documentation of the extent to which blackness has become commodified in this society—the degree to which black life, particularly the lives of poor and working-class black people, can become cheap entertainment even when the filmmakers don't intend anything like this. Filmmakers Peter Gilbert, Fred Marx and Steve James make it clear in interviews that they want audiences to see the exploitative aspects of the sports systems in America even as they also wish to show the positives. Gilbert declares: "We would like to see these families going through some very rough times, overcoming a lot of obstacles, and rising above some of the typical media stereotypes that people have about inner-city families." Note the way in which Gilbert does not identify the race of these families. Yet it is precisely the fact of blackness that gives this documentary popular cultural appeal. The lure of *Hoop Dreams* is that it affirms that those on the bottom can ascend this society, even as it is critical of the manner in which they rise. This film tells the world how the American dream works. As the exploitative white coach at St. Joseph's high school puts it while he verbally whips these black boys into shape: "This is America. You can make something of your life."

White Standpoint

In the United States, reviewers, an overwhelming majority of whom are white, praised *Hoop Dreams,* making it the first documentary to be deemed worthy of an Academy Award for best picture, by critics and moviegoers alike. Contrary to the rave reviews it has received, though, there is nothing spectacular or technically outstanding about the film. It is not an inventive piece of work. Indeed, it must take its place within the continuum of traditional anthropological and/or ethnographic documentary works that show us the "dark other" from the standpoint of whiteness. Inner-city, poor, black communities, seen as "jungles" by many Americans, become in this film a zone white film makers have crossed boundaries to enter, to document (over a period of five years) their subjects. To many progressive viewers, myself included, this film is moving because it acknowledges the positive aspects of black life. It also encouraged us to look at it critically. . . .

By comparison with many films examining the experience of black Americans which have overtly political content and speak directly about issues of racism (such as documentaries on Malcolm X, or the Civil Rights series *Eyes on the Prize*), the focus of this film was seen by reviewers as more welcoming. It highlights an issue Americans of all races, but particularly white Americans, can easily identify with: the longing of young black males to become great basketball players, and to play for the National Basketball Association. No doubt it is this standpoint that leads a review like David Denby's in *New York* magazine to proclaim it "an extraordinarily detailed and emotionally satisfying piece of work about American inner-city life, American hopes, American defeat." Such a comment seems highly ironic given the reality: that it is precisely the institutionalized racism and white-supremacist attitudes in everyday American life that actively prohibit black male participation in more diverse cultural arenas and spheres of employment, while presenting sports as the one location where recognition, success and material reward can be attained. The desperate feeling of not making it in American culture is what drives the two young black males, Arthur Agee and William Gates, to dream of making a career as professional ballplayers. They, their family and friends never imagine that they can be successful in any other way. Black and poor, they have no belief that they can attain wealth and power on any playing field other than sports. Yet this spirit of defeat and hopelessness, that informs their options in life and their choices, is not stressed. Their longing to succeed as ballplayers is presented as though it is no more than a positive American dream. The film suggests that it is only the possibility of being exploited by adults hoping to benefit from their success (coaches, parents, siblings, lovers) that makes their dream a potential nightmare.

The film's most powerful moments are those that subversively document the way in which these young, strong, black male bodies are callously objectified and dehumanized by the white-male dominated world of sports administration in America. *Hoop Dreams* shows audiences how coaches and scouts, searching to find the best ball players for their high-school and college teams, adopt an "auction block" mentality that has to call to the mind of any aware viewer the history of slavery and the plantation economy, which was also built on the exploitation of young, strong, black male bodies. Just as the bodies of African-American slaves were expendable, the bodies of black male ballplayers cease to matter if they cannot deliver the desired product. In the film, the filmmakers expose the ruthless agendas of grown-ups, particularly those paternalistic, patriarchal white and black males, who are so over-invested, emotionally or otherwise, in the two teenagers.

While the trials and tribulations Agee and Gates encountered on the playing field give *Hoop Dreams* momentum, it is their engagement with family and friends, as well as their longing to be great ball players, that provide the emotional pathos. In particular, *Hoop Dreams* offers a different—in fact unique—portrayal of black mothers. Contrary to the popular myth of matriarchal "hard" black women controlling their sons and emasculating them, the two mothers in this film offer their children all necessary support and care. Agee's mother Sheila is clearly exemplary in her efforts to be a loving parent, providing vital discipline, encouragement and affection. Less charismatic (indeed she often appears to be trapped in a passive and depressive stoicism), Gates' mother is kept in the background, the single mother raising her children. The film does not throw light on how she provides economically. . . .

Even though one of the saddest moments occurs as we witness Agee's loss of faith in his father, and his mounting hostility and rage, he is never interrogated by the filmmakers about the significance of this loss, as he is about his attitudes toward basketball, education and so on. And there is even less exploration of Gates' problematic relationship to his son. Without any critical examination, these images of black father-and-son dynamics simply confirm negative stereotypes, then compound them by suggesting that even when black fathers are present in their children's lives they are such losers that they have no positive impact. In this way, a cinematic portrait is created that in no way illuminates the emotional complexity of black male life. Indeed, via a process of oversimplification the film makes it appear that a longing to play ball is the all-consuming desire in the lives of these young black males. That other longings they may have go unacknowledged and unfulfilled is not addressed. Hence, the standpoint of the film-makers is no way to see how these states of deprivation and dissatisfaction might intensify the obsession with succeeding in sports. Audiences are surprised when we see Gates with a pregnant girlfriend, since until this scene the narrative has suggested basketball consumes all his energies.

Competition Rules

This suggestion was obviously a strategic decision on the part of the filmmakers. For much of the dramatic momentum of *Hoop Dreams* is rooted in its evocation of competition, through the documentary footage of basketball games where audiences are able to cheer on the stars of the film, empathically identifying with their success or failure, or via the rivalry the film constructs between Agee and Gates. Even though we see glimpses of camaraderie between the two black males, the film, constantly comparing and contrasting their fate, creates a symbolic competition.

On one hand, there's the logic of racial assimilation, which suggests that those black folks will be most successful who assume the values and attitudes of privileged whites; opposing this, there's the logic of narrow nationalism, which suggests that staying within one's own group is better because that is the only place where you can be safe, where you can survive. This latter vision, of narrow nationalism, is the one that "wins" in the film. And it is perfectly in synch with the xenophobic nationalism that is gaining momentum among all groups in American culture.

Ultimately, *Hoop Dreams* offers a conservative vision of the conditions for "making it" in the United States. It clearly argues that the context in which one "makes it" is within a nuclear family that prays together, works hard and completely and uncritically believes in the American dream. An almost religious belief in the power of competition to bring success permeates American life. The ethic of competition is so passionately upheld and valued in Agee's family that it intensifies the schism between him and his dad. William Gates learns to critique the ethic of competition that he has been socialized to accept passively within white-supremacist, capitalist patriarchy, but is portrayed as a victim. His longing to be a good parent, to not be obsessed with basketball, is not represented as a positive shift in his thinking. After his health deteriorates he is most often represented as hopeless and defeated. The triumphant individual in the film is (the young) Arthur Agee, who remains obsessed with the game. He continues to believe that he can win, that he can make it to the top. . . .

. . . To be always in constant competition, hounded by the fear of failure, is the nature of the game in a culture of domination. A terrible loneliness shrouds Agee throughout *Hoop Dreams.* There is no escape. He has to keep playing the game. To escape is to fail. The subversive content in this film, its tragic messages, so akin to those conveyed in other hot movies on the American scene (*Interview with the Vampire, Pulp Fiction, Natural Born Killers*), are subsumed by the spectacle of playing the game—by the thrill of victory. Despite the costs, the American dream of conquest prevails and nothing changes.

bell hooks, "Dreams of Conquest," *Sight and Sound* 5 (April 1995): 22–23.

B

THE PROS

5. Jackie Joyner-Kersee, a Woman of Substance

The outspokenness of some black athletes who came to prominence during the civil rights movement, then retired to become community spokesmen and activists, has not—for the most part—been matched by a later generation of African American stars. Michael Jordan once remarked in response to a question about his political (dis)affiliation that "Republicans buy Nikes too." Indeed, the economics of athletic celebrity—the endorsements especially—demands a certain reserve on the part of individuals whose incomes rise and fall with corporate marketing strategies. This assertion may help explain the banality of recent autobiographies by black athletes (and of course other athletes too), which run the gamut from coffee table and souvenir books, to inspirational guides, to juvenilia. The Michael Jordan industry and Tiger Woods phenomenon stand out, but Jackie Joyner-Kersee's account of her life in sports also speaks rarely, and softly, about issues of politics and race.*

So, when Jackie Joyner-Kersee mentions role models that include Rosa Parks and Martin Luther King Jr. as well as stellar athletes in the document here—an interview conducted by Women's Sports and Fitness *in 1995—she places herself, albeit with a characteristic modesty, within a significant political tradition. Likewise, she carefully but clearly talks about community activism and the ways a high-profile athlete can exert influence at the local level—in this case her hometown of East St. Louis, Illinois. Finally, Joyner-Kersee here articulates the notion that she and Michael Jordan may appear side-by-side to promote a Nike-sponsored community action program, but that she wants to represent the particular aspirations and accomplishments of women in sports. Perhaps what the last portion of the document represents best is a brand of feminism that desires to hold up a corporate logo for a greater cause.*

Whenever heptathlete Jackie Joyner-Kersee steps onto the track or field, she's not just out there to defend her Olympic honors (three gold medals, a silver and a bronze). She's out there to make strides for young women, too. At a time when more and more athletes are shrugging off the mantle of role model, the 33-year-old Joyner-Kersee never wavers. Committed to furthering the ideals of young people, she provides scholarships through the Jackie Joyner-Kersee Community Foundation and, more important still, puts in time working with kids in her hometown of East St. Louis, Illinois, whenever she can. This isn't to say that the greatest female athlete in the world is

---

* See Joyner-Kersee and Steptoe, *A Kind of Grace*.

Jackie Joyner-Kersee
(Amateur Athletic Foun-
dation, AAF/LPI 1984)

all business. When WS&F sat down to chat with her, for instance, she revealed that
she's a soap-opera addict (who knew?). Here's what else Joyner-Kersee had to say.

WS&F: As a spokesperson for Nike's PLAY (Participate in the Lives of America's
Youth), you've been helping wage war on the forces that are rapidly gobbling up
recreational opportunities for kids. Is it true that a recent victim of those forces is
the community center where you used to go as a child?
JJK: Yes. When I was coming up, we went to a place that was strictly for boys, but this
guy used to open it and let us come in and play. Then the big Mayor Brown Center
opened, but now that's closed, too. Hopefully within a year and a half, with our
fund-raising efforts, we'll reopen it.
WS&F: When you were growing up, who were your role models?

JJK: I've always admired Wilma Rudolph, Rosa Parks, Dr. Martin Luther King, Babe Didrikson. Also Flo Hyman. I remember watching her play the Japanese team in volleyball. And we thought we played volleyball! It was so neat, for once, to see a woman that tall. I didn't get to shake her hand. I got close, but not close enough. At one of the Women's Sports Foundation dinners, I met Wilma Rudolph and Rosa Parks. I never thought I'd get to meet them, but because of my athletics I've been fortunate.

WS&F: Do you think about those role models when you meet kids who look up to you in the same way?

JJK: No. I've never really thought about it like that, even though it might be. I find it touching, in a sense, that people want my autograph and they're in tears. I think, my God! I'm just happy that I'm in the position I'm in and that people would even take the time to talk to me.

WS&F: You haven't gotten used to the fact that people are in awe of you and so honored to meet you?

JJK: I appreciate the kindness; I just find it funny, particularly when people I grew up with say, "Let me have your autograph." "Get out of here! I know you're joking." But they're serious! I understand the position I'm in, but I also know that tomorrow there's going to be someone else. So I try to keep things in perspective.

WS&F: *Sports Illustrated* recently came out with a list of the 40 most influential athletes of the last 40 years. Does it make you angry that your name wasn't on it?

JJK: When someone told me there were no black women on the list, I said, "Oh, really. I guess I'll have to work a little harder" (laughs). I just can't believe Chris Evert wasn't on it. I'm not happy that I wasn't, when I can make their cover three times, once with my sister-in-law. But I can't let that change me.

WS&F: You do, however, seem to be getting more recognition lately. For instance, in Nike's PLAY commercials you're represented as an equal of Michael Jordan's.

JJK: When I came on board with Nike, it was agreed that Michael Jordan and I would be co-ambassadors of the program. I love Michael Jordan, but I also feel that our mind-set has to change. Women are striving toward greatness, but society is not striving with us. Society is trying to keep us a step behind, but we're moving five steps ahead. Our performances are great. They're equal to our male counterparts'. It's not that we're trying to be superior to men; it's just that we'd like what we're doing to be showcased, so that young girls who want to do this can see that this is something they can do. If we can be role models and set a positive example, then that shouldn't be suppressed.

WS&F: Is it that much harder for a female athlete who's African-American to get endorsements and commercial backing?

JJK: It's not so much that it's harder; it's that, at times, you have to prove yourself over and over. One shot is not good enough. I don't think one shot is good enough, either. One thing I have in my favor is consistency. I've always asked that of myself, not from a commercial standpoint, but just from the standpoint of performing well. Don't be a flash in the pan. Eventually you realize that what they decide in the boardroom you have no control over. I feel that as an African-American woman the only thing I can do is continue to better myself, continue to perform well, continue to make sure that I'm a good commodity. If doors aren't opened for me, then maybe it will happen for someone else. I hope that someone who's watching me is also educating herself about what she can do to be consistent, what she can do to provide a message, what she can do to deliver a commodity as I've tried to do.

Interview with Jackie Joyner-Kersee, *Women's Sports and Fitness* 17 (January/February 1995): 21–22.

6. Michael Eric Dyson / "Be Like Mike? Michael Jordan and the Pedagogy of Desire"

Michael Jordan is one of the greatest basketball players and most popular athletes of all time. Born in Brooklyn, New York, in 1963, Jordan grew up in Wilmington, North Carolina, where he participated in a variety of sports. Although not immediately successful in basketball, Jordan would become a high school all-American in the sport and accept a scholarship to play for the legendary Dean Smith at the University of North Carolina. He enjoyed a remarkable career at North Carolina, leading the Tar Heels to the NCAA championship in 1982. He was, moreover, selected first-team all-American in 1983, and chosen first-team all-American, Atlantic Coast Conference (ACC) Player of the Year, and Consensus National Player of the Year in 1984. Jordan left North Carolina after his junior year and signed with the Chicago Bulls, who had picked him in the first round of the National Basketball Association (NBA) draft. He led the Bulls to six NBA championships, garnered the NBA Most Valuable Player award five times, and captured ten scoring titles. His successes, which included starring roles on the United States gold medal–winning Olympic basketball teams in Los Angeles in 1984 and Barcelona in 1992, resulted in multimillion-dollar contracts, an unprecedented endorsement deal with Nike, and eventually part ownership of both the Washington Wizards and the Washington Capitals.*

In the following document, Michael Eric Dyson, author of many works on African American history and culture, analyzes Jordan as a cultural icon, placing him within the context of black youth culture specifically and American mass culture more generally. Dyson contends that Jordan's remarkable achievements contributed to the cultural acceptance of the athletic black body as a transracial icon in a society still marred by prejudice. In addition, the African American elements of Jordan's game linked black cultural creativity to the dominant culture of comsumption. He had become, because of his mastery of basketball, cleancut image, and unrelenting quest of the American dream, the "quintessential American pitchman."**

Dyson's is but one of several competing visions of the meaning of celebrity and crossover appeal in the realm of sports. When Public Enemy raps about "Sneaker Pimps," the group offers an alternative rendering of the "Pedagogy of Desire." When Spike Lee names the basketball hero of He Got Game *"Jesus," he is not trying to be subtle but rather is expressing ambivalence about the culture of corporate basketball.*

Michael Jordan is perhaps the best, and best-known, athlete in the world today. He has attained unparalleled cultural status because of his extraordinary physical gifts, his marketing as an icon of race-transcending American athletic and moral excellence,

---

* For information on Jordan, see Halberstam, *Playing for Keeps;* Greene, *Hang Time;* Krugel, *Jordan;* S. Smith, *The Jordan Rules;* McCallum, "Alone on the Mountaintop"; Kirkpatrick, "The Unlikeliest Homeboy."

** Dyson, "Crossing over Jordan," 57.

Michael Jordan, midair
(*Sporting News*)

and his mastery of a sport that has become the metaphoric center of black cultural imagination. But the Olympian sum of Jordan's cultural meaning is greater than the fluent parts of his persona as athlete, family man, and marketing creation. There is hardly cultural precedence for the character of his unique fame, which has blurred the line between private and public, between personality and celebrity, and between substance and symbol. . . .

Jordan has been called "the new DiMaggio" and "Elvis in high-tops," indications of the herculean cultural heroism he has come to embody. There is even a religious element to the near worship of Jordan as a cultural icon of invincibility, as he has been called a "savior of sorts," "basketball's high priest," and "more popular than Jesus," except with "better endorsement deals." But the quickly developing cultural canonization of Michael Jordan provokes reflection about the contradictory uses to which Jordan's body is put as a seminal cultural text and ambiguous symbol of fantasy, and the avenues of agency and resistance available especially to black youth who make symbolic investment in Jordan's body as a means of cultural and personal possibility, creativity, and desire.

I understand Jordan in the broadest sense of the term to be a public pedagogue, a figure of estimable public moral authority whose career educates us about productive and disenabling forms of knowledge, desire, interest, consumption, and culture in three spheres: the culture of athletics that thrives on skill and performance, the specific expression of elements of African-American culture, and the market forces and processes of commodification expressed by, and produced in, advanced capitalism. By probing these dimensions of Jordan's cultural importance, we may gain a clearer understanding of his function in American society. . . .

Black participation in sports in mainstream society . . . is a relatively recent phenomenon. Of course, there have existed venerable traditions of black sports, such as the Negro (baseball) Leagues, which countered the exclusion of black bodies from white sports. The prohibition of athletic activity by black men in mainstream society severely limited publicly acceptable forms of displaying black physical prowess, an issue that had been politicized during slavery and whose legacy extended into the middle of the twentieth century. Hence, the potentially superior physical prowess of black men, validated for many by the long tradition of slave labor that built American society, helped reinforce racist arguments about the racial regimentation of social space and the denigration of the black body as an inappropriate presence in traditions of American sport.

Coupled with this fear of superior black physical prowess was the notion that inferior black intelligence limited the ability of blacks to perform excellently in those sports activities that required mental concentration and agility. These two forces—the presumed lack of sophisticated black cognitive skills and the fear of superior black physical prowess—restricted black sports participation to thriving but financially handicapped subcultures of black athletic activity. Later, of course, the physical prowess of the black body would be acknowledged and exploited as a supremely fertile zone of profit as mainstream athletic society literally cashed in on the symbolic danger of black sports excellence.

Because of its marginalized status within the regime of American sports, black athletic activity often acquired a social significance that transcended the internal dimensions of game, sport, and skill. Black sport became an arena not only for testing the limits of physical endurance and forms of athletic excellence—while reproducing or repudiating ideals of American justice, goodness, truth, and beauty—but it also became a way of ritualizing racial achievement against socially imposed barriers to cultural performance.

In short, black sport activity often acquired a heroic dimension, as viewed in the careers of figures such as Joe Louis, Jackie Robinson, Althea Gibson, Wilma Rudolph, Muhammad Ali, and Arthur Ashe. Black sports heroes transcended the narrow boundaries of specific sports activities and garnered importance as icons of cultural excellence, symbolic figures who embodied social possibilities of success denied to other people of color. But they also captured and catalyzed the black cultural fetishization of sport as a means of expressing black cultural style, as a means of valorizing craft as a marker of racial and self-expression, and as a means of pursuing social and economic mobility.

It is this culture of black athletics, created against the background of social and historical forces that shaped American athletic activity, that helped produce Jordan and help explain the craft that he practices. . . . Michael Jordan's skills within basketball are clearly phenomenal, but his game can only be sufficiently explained by understanding its link to the fusion of African-American cultural norms and practices, and the idealization of skill and performance that characterize important aspects of American sport. . . .

Jordan's style of basketball reflects the *will to spontaneity.* I mean here the way in which historical accidence is transformed into cultural advantage, and the way acts of apparently random occurrence are spontaneously and imaginatively employed by Africans and African-Americans in a variety of forms of cultural expression. When examining Jordan's game, this feature of African-American culture clearly functions in his unpredictable eruptions of basketball creativity. It was apparent, for instance, during game two of the National Basketball Association 1991 championship series between Jordan's Chicago Bulls and the Los Angeles Lakers, in a shot that even Jordan ranked in his all-time top ten. Jordan made a drive toward the lane, gesturing with his hands and body that he was about to complete a patent Jordan dunk shot with his right hand. But when he spied defender Sam Perkins slipping over to oppose his shot, he switched the ball in midair to his left hand to make an underhanded scoop shot instead, which immediately became known as the "levitation" shot. Such improvisation, a staple of the will to spontaneity, allows Jordan to expand his vocabulary of athletic spectacle, which is the stimulation of a desire to bear witness to the revelation of truth and beauty compressed into acts of athletic creativity.

Jordan's game reflects the *stylization of the performed self.* This is the creation and projection of a sport persona that is an identifying mark of diverse African-American creative enterprises, from the complexly layered jazz experimentation of John Coltrane, the trickstering and signifying comedic routines of Richard Pryor, and the rhetorical ripostes and oral significations of rapper Kool Moe Dee. Jordan's whole game persona is a graphic depiction of the performed self as flying acrobat, resulting in his famous moniker "Air Jordan." Jordan's performed self is rife with the language of physical expressiveness: head moving, arms extending, hands waving, tongue wagging, and legs spreading. . . .

Finally, there is the subversion of perceived limits through the use of *edifying deception,* which in Jordan's case centers around the space/time continuum. This moment in African-American cultural practice is the ability to flout widely understood boundaries through mesmerization and alchemy, a subversion of common perceptions of the culturally or physically possible through the creative and deceptive manipulation of appearance. Jordan is perhaps most famous for his alleged "hang time," the uncanny ability to remain suspended in midair longer than other basketball players while executing his stunning array of improvised moves. But Jordan's "hang time" is technically a misnomer and can be more accurately attributed to Jordan's skillful athletic deception, his acrobatic leaping ability, and his intellectual toughness in projecting an aura of uniqueness around his craft than to his defiance of gravity and the laws of physics. . . .

But the African-American aspects of Jordan's game are indissolubly linked to the culture of consumption and the commodification of black culture. Because of Jordan's supreme mastery of basketball, his squeaky-clean image, and his youthful vigor in pursuit of the American Dream, he has become, along with Bill Cosby, the quintessential pitchman in American society. Even his highly publicized troubles with gambling, his refusal to visit the White House after the Bulls' championship season, and a book that purports to expose the underside of his heroic myth have barely tarnished his All-American image. Jordan eats Wheaties, drives Chevrolets, wears Hanes, drinks Coca-Cola, consumes McDonald's, guzzles Gatorade, and, of course, wears Nikes. He and his shrewd handlers have successfully produced, packaged, marketed, and distributed his image and commodified his symbolic worth, transforming cultural capital into cash, influence, prestige, status, and wealth. To that degree, at least, Jordan repudiates the sorry tradition of the black athlete as the naif who loses his money to piranha-like financial wizards, investors, and hangers-on. He represents the new-age athletic entrepreneur who understands that American sport is ensconced in the cultural practices associated with business, and that it demands particular forms of intelligence, perception, and representation to prevent abuse and maximize profit. . . .

But Jordan is also the symbol of the spectacle-laden black athletic body as the site of commodified black cultural imagination. Ironically, the black male body, which has been historically viewed as threatening and inappropriate in American society (and remains so outside of sports and entertainment), is made an object of white desires to domesticate and dilute its more ominous and subversive uses, even symbolically reducing Jordan's body to dead meat (McDonald's McJordan hamburger), which can be consumed and expelled as waste.

Jordan's body is also the screen upon which is projected black desires to emulate his athletic excellence and replicate his entry into reaches of unimaginable wealth and fame. But there is more than vicarious substitution and the projection of fantasy onto Jordan's body that is occurring in the circulation and reproduction of black cultural desire. There is also the creative use of desire and fantasy by young blacks to counter, and capitulate to, the forces of cultural dominance that attempt to reduce the black body to a commodity and text that is employed for entertainment, titillation, or financial gain. Simply said, there is no easy correlation between the commodification of black youth culture and the evidences of a completely dominated consciousness.

Even within the dominant cultural practices that seek to turn the black body into pure profit, disruptions of capital are embodied, for instance, in messages circulated in black communities by public moralists who criticize the exploitation of black cultural creativity by casual footwear companies. In short, there are instances of both black complicity and resistance in the commodification of black cultural imagination, and the ideological criticism of exploitative cultural practices must always be linked to the language of possibility and agency in rendering a complex picture of the black cultural situation. . . . The ominous specificity of the black body creates anxieties for Jordan. His encounters with the limits of culturally mediated symbols of race and racial identity have occasionally mocked his desire to live beyond race, to be "neither black nor white," to be "viewed as a person." While Jordan chafes under indictment by black critics who claim that he is not "black enough," he has perhaps not clearly understood the differences between enabling versions of human experience that transcend the exclusive gaze of race and disenabling visions of human community that seek race neutrality.

The former is the attempt to expand the perimeters of human experience beyond racial determinism, to nuance and deepen our understanding of the constituent elements of racial identity, and to understand how race, along with class, gender, geography, and sexual preference, shape and constrain human experience. The latter is the belief in an intangible, amorphous, nonhistorical, and raceless category of "person," existing in a zone beyond the specific patterns of cultural and racial identity that constitute and help shape human experience. Jordan's unclarity is consequential, weighing heavily on his apolitical bearing and his refusal to acknowledge the public character of his private beliefs about American society and the responsibility of his role as a public pedagogue. . . .

Michael Jordan has helped seize upon the commercial consequences of black cultural preoccupation with style and the commodification of the black juvenile imagination at the site of the sneaker. At the juncture of the sneaker, a host of cultural, political, and economic forces and meanings meet, collide, shatter, and are reassembled to symbolize the situation of contemporary black culture.

The sneaker reflects at once the projection and stylization of black urban realities linked in our contemporary historical moment to rap culture and the underground political economy of crack, and reigns as the universal icon for the culture of consumption. The sneaker symbolizes the ingenious manner in which black cultural nuances of cool, hip, and chic have influenced the broader American cultural landscape. It was black street culture that influenced sneaker companies' aggressive invasion of the black juvenile market in taking advantage of the increasing amounts of disposable income of young black men as a result of legitimate and illegitimate forms of work. . . .

Basketball is the metaphoric center of black juvenile culture, a major means by which even temporary forms of cultural and personal transcendence of personal limits are experienced. Michael Jordan is at the center of this black athletic culture, the supreme symbol of black cultural creativity in a society of diminishing tolerance for the black youth whose fascination with Jordan has helped sustain him. But Jordan is also the iconic fixture of broader segments of American society, who see in him the ideal figure: a black man of extraordinary genius on the court and before the cameras, who by virtue of his magical skills and godlike talents symbolizes the meaning of human possibility, while refusing to root it in the specific forms of culture and race in which it must inevitably make sense or fade to ultimate irrelevance.

Jordan also represents the contradictory impulses of the contemporary culture of consumption, where the black athletic body is deified, reified, and rearticulated within the narrow meanings of capital and commodity. But there is both resistance and consent to the exploitation of black bodies in Jordan's explicit cultural symbolism, as he provides brilliant glimpses of black culture's ingenuity of improvisation as a means of cultural expression and survival. It is also partially this element of black culture that has created in American society a desire to dream Jordan, to "be like Mike."

This pedagogy of desire that Jordan embodies, although at points immobilized by its depoliticized cultural contexts, is nevertheless a remarkable achievement in contemporary American culture: a six-foot-six American man of obvious African descent is the dominant presence and central cause of athletic fantasy in a sport that twenty years ago was denigrated as a black man's game and hence deemed unworthy of wide attention or support. Jordan is therefore the bearer of meanings about black culture larger than his individual life, the symbol of a pedagogy of style, presence, and desire that is immediately communicated by the sight of his black body before it can be contravened by reflection.

In the final analysis, his big black body—graceful and powerful, elegant and dark—symbolizes the possibilities of other black bodies to remain safe long enough to survive within the limited but significant sphere of sport, since Jordan's achievements have furthered the cultural acceptance of at least the athletic black body. In that sense, Jordan's powerful cultural capital has not been exhausted by narrow understandings of his symbolic absorption by the demands of capital and consumption. His body is still the symbolic carrier of racial and cultural desires to fly beyond limits and obstacles, a fluid metaphor of mobility and ascent to heights of excellence secured by genius and industry. It is this power to embody the often conflicting desires of so many that makes Michael Jordan a supremely instructive figure for our times.

Michael Eric Dyson, "Be Like Mike? Michael Jordan and the Pedagogy of Desire," *Cultural Studies 7* (January 1993): 64–72.

7. John Edgar Wideman / "Playing Dennis Rodman"

Few athletes in modern times have been as controversial as Dennis Rodman. The 6'10" Rodman, known to players and fans alike as "The Worm," was one of the most devastating rebounders in basketball and helped lead the Detroit Pistons to National Basketball Association (NBA) titles in 1989 and 1990. Lightning quick with great jumping ability and unparalleled instincts, Rodman played defense with aplomb and a tenacity that intimidated opponents and directly affected the outcomes of games.

Rodman's defensive prowess was accompanied by nonconformist behavior on and off the court. He endeared himself to hometown fans and angered many opponents by stripping to the waist and jumping on the scorer's table to lead the crowd in victory celebrations. He garnered much notoriety for his brief affair with Madonna, his marriage to the actress Carmen Electra, and his wild all-night parties. He elicited perhaps even more public attention for his many tattoos, multicolored hair, body piercings, and a fondness for makeup and cross-dressing. Rodman, for his part, has explained his behavior by noting that he was not just a basketball player but an entertainer concerned with flair, style, and varying performances. *

In the following document, John Edgar Wideman, former basketball star at the Univer-

---

* On Rodman see Rodman, *Bad as I Wanna Be;* George, *Elevating the Game,* 230–31; Coakley, *Sport in Society,* esp. 237, 337, 360; Hoberman, *Darwin's Athletes,* esp. 39, 94.

John Edgar Wideman
during his college days
(From the Collections of
the University of Penn-
sylvania Archives)

sity of Pennsylvania and eminent author of novels such as The Cattle Killing *and the memoirs and meditations* Fatheralong *and* My Brother's Keeper, *contends that Rodman's sense of identity was not completely tied to the sport of basketball. Unclassifiable, or embodying what Wideman refers to as* "'tain't," *Rodman was a creative black force who resisted the white power structure. Although the NBA, and more specifically the league commissioner, David Stern, attempted to make Rodman conform to mainstream (white) values and expectations, the athlete refused to make his performances (on and off the court) meet the demands of those who govern basketball. Rodman's story, in Wideman's rendering, suggests that basketball is merely a game and not a lot more. Wideman's own relationship to the game, in many ways more complex and compelling, is the subject of a recent book-length reminiscence. It was on the asphalt court, during fifty years of pickup games, that Wideman found his portal to a keen understanding of kinship beyond family and to a set of rites, if not rules, that has bonded black males over several generations. In these scenes the game encourages a kind of outlawry. And that, Wideman suggests, is not necessarily a bad thing.*

---

* See Wideman's reminiscence, *Hoop Roots.*

. . . an attraction that has all the characteristics of breaking and entering and of the violation of a sanctuary.
  —"Simulacra and Simulation" by Jean Baudrillard

I knew the word *'tain't*. Old people used it, mainly; it was their way of contracting "it ain't" to one emphatic beat, a sound for saying "it is not" in African-American vernacular, but also for saying much more, depending on tone, timing, and inflection. But I'd never heard *'tain't* used to refer to female anatomy—not the front door or the back door but a mysteriously alluring, unclassifiable, scary region between a woman's legs ("'Tain't pussy and 'tain't asshole, it just the *'tain't*," to quote Walter Bentley)—until a bunch of us were sitting on somebody's stoop listening to Big Walt, a.k.a. Porky, discuss with his cousin Donald some finer points of lovemaking.

I didn't understand then how part of the power of *'tain't* is that you never see it exactly. Even if your eyes gaze on that little bit of in-between skin, it's the idea that stuns, that transports to a realm where desire slips its mooring from a specific object and creates new rules, new priorities that disrupt the known and familiar. Porky's crude connoisseur's riff on *'tain't* returns when I think about Dennis Rodman, the professional basketball player, and his gotta-have-it rebound jones.

Rodman embodies *'tain't*. Unclassifiable—"the most unique player in the history of the N.B.A.," according to Chuck Daly, who coached Rodman's first pro team, the Detroit Pistons, to two consecutive N.B.A. championships. Not exactly a forward, guard, or center, Rodman invented a role for himself which subverts the logic of traditional positions. His helter-skelter, full-court, full-time intensity blurs the line between defense and offense. He "scores" without scoring, keeping the ball in play until one of his teammates drops it through the hoop.

If you want to win basketball games, rebounding is crucial. The battle for domination of the boards is a fascinating game within the game. Rodman's relentless, no-holds-barred, kamikaze pursuit of missed shots foregrounds rebounding and frees it from subordinate status. The game's too easy, he says. What he does on the court is not about contributing his share to a team effort—not even about rebounding, when you get right down to it. "Snay" (hell, no), Rodman would say. *'Tain't* basketball and *'tain't* rebounding. It's just *'tain't*. Irreducible to anything else—a perpetual work in progress, compelling, outrageously amoral. Rodman immerses himself in what he does, defines himself by it, stakes out new territory: percussive behavior so edgy it threatens to wreck the game that's supposed to contain it.

I didn't much care for Rodman during his early seasons in the N.B.A.

On the playgrounds of Pittsburgh, where I learned the game, we had a word for gawkish, all elbows and knees, one-dimensional-game, rawboned hurry-with-no-finesse chumps who must be somebody's country cousin wetbacked into our sleek city run. The best we could say about a guy like that was "cockstrong": "the brother's cockstrong." Which meant all of the above plus the insinuation that he wasn't getting much love action, so all the energy he should be using up in some sweeter place got dropped on you. "Cockstrong" meant a guy was a load. And loaded. A pain in the butt to play against. You respected him, in a way—the strength, endurance, earnestness, hustle—but even when he was on your side he could be a liability, since he was minimally skilled, unpredictable, liable to hurt the team in a do-or-die situation, hurt you with his unsophisticated, indiscriminate flailing. Worse, sometimes a cockstrong player possessed real bad attitude. So much displaced, pent-up energy threatened to blow up, turn mean and ugly.

Playground basketball is the most democratic of games: when a court's crowded, all comers can call winners and play next. Everybody has to police himself (or herself, now that more women show up on the outdoor courts), so that each game contains ten referees or no referees, depending on how you look at it. In no other game is your just-about-naked body so constantly, helplessly, acutely vulnerable to a cheap shot. One push in the back when you're airborne and a whole season or a whole career could be lost. One ignorant, unreflective, selfish player endangers everybody. When Dennis Rodman broke into the league as the Detroit Pistons' primal piston, he worried me. No doubt about it, the boy was cockstrong, quite capable of hurting people—some of my favorite people, Michael Jordan and Scottie Pippen, for instance—and on occasion Rodman turned foolish enough, evil enough, to try.

But people change. Cocksure's not always pretty, but it's a much more benign way of being a jerk than cockstrong. And Dennis Rodman is nothing if not cocksure.

Cross-dressing, cross-naming himself (Denise), frequenting gay night clubs, going AWOL from his team, head-butting a referee, winning four rebounding titles in a row, painting his hair, dating Madonna, challenging the N.B.A. commissioner to suspend him, bad-mouthing the men in suits who pay his salary, Dennis Rodman, though not voted onto this season's All-Star team, verges on media superstardom. Whether or not he acts out his fantasy of performing naked in an N.B.A. game, his tale is on high-definition display each time he kangaroos down the court. I'm in this game, his body English says—in it, but not of it. "Show business is what I do on the court," he says.

In an age of hype, a world where simulation and appearance count as much as substance and authenticity, where appropriation and replication are viable substitutes for creativity, where show biz is the only business, the storm of publicity Rodman's bad-boy act generates is worth a fortune. He's large, large, and soon to be larger if his new autobiography lives up to its pre-release teases. Into this "Tempest" enter David Stern, politic lawyer, urbane huckster, commissioner of the N.B.A.: Prospero to Rodman's Caliban. In our end-of-the-century remake of Shakespeare's play, the names of the characters are too corny to be true: Stern, Apollonion administrator/accountant; Rod Man Dionysian up-and-down, in-and-out pogo stick. Follow the bouncing balls, the ones inside the scrotum with the silver loop attached.

Shakespeare's drama predicts the dynamic of colonialism. The play also births Caliban, the archetypal victim-product of colonial intercourse, part man, part fish, part devil, whose island Prospero steals and rules. Prospero despises and fears Caliban—"this thing of darkness I / Acknowledge mine." He's plagued by images of Caliban raping his daughter. But Prospero needs Caliban's labor, his skills, his knowledge of the island, so he enslaves him and enlists Ariel and other invisible spirits of the air to keep him in line.

Like Prospero, the contemporary sports czar rules by illusion, deploys spirits of the air (the media) to police his domain. Caliban, Frankenstein's monster, the Rogue Cyborg, and the Rod Man are kin, *'tain't*, tainted, neither one thing or another; hybrids, mutants, half-breeds, crossbreeds, hyperreal mulattoes, bad seeds, the worst nightmare of rulers whose greed and fantasies of control drive them to forge Faustian bargains with the Devil. The czar and his minions can make these syncretic outlaw creatures, but can't break them. Somewhere just out of sight, Dennis the Menace, the Worm, the Gangsta Rappa, the Rebel Robot plot their revenge.

I'm thinking about hoop; about my own playing days; about time; about my first language, the African-American vernacular that will always be the language of my feelings; about my daughter playing in the regional finals of the N.C.A.A. women's tournament. I'm thinking about the purity that's fading fast but still enhances and distinguishes the women's game. And I'm thinking about Dennis Rodman, wondering what's at stake.

Why couldn't people laugh at the TV ad in which Rodman bullies Santa Claus? Why does Rodman's refusal to allow his identity to be totally subsumed by a game offend people? Is our sense of who we are so fragile, our defense against chaos so easily breached, that we can't bear to look when a sports celebrity reminds us that the games we play and worship are only games? The Santa game. The gender game. The race game. The Mom, apple-pie, take-me-out-to-the-ballgame game. Maybe that's what really scares, outrages, and entertains us about Dennis Rodman. He dons the uniform, takes the paycheck, but doesn't exactly go to work. He enters a zone where play is not reducible to anything else. The game we've taken for real disappears, and we're left to deal with the reality of Dennis Rodman in our faces.

John Edgar Wideman, "Playing Dennis Rodman," *New Yorker,* April 29–May 6, 1996, 94–95.

8. Nikki Giovanni / "Iverson's Posse"

The differences between the play and the personae of Allen Iverson and Dennis Rodman are surely more significant than the similarities. Yet both basketball stars have been admired for their relentlessness—also their resilience—on the court; and both have drawn an enormous amount of attention for their resistance to the structures of authority and the image that the NBA has long been trying to project. The topic of John Edgar Wideman's article opens out to the questions, What are the boundaries of sporting culture in America? or Who sets the rules? Next to the commissioner and the coaches, who endure—merely buying more expensive, and larger, suits, or donning thicker eyeglasses as the years go by—the players are like comets. Their brightness dazzles us for a time, but it tends to pass rather quickly.

Nikki Giovanni's contribution to the discussion of culture and career directly engages Allen Iverson's early fame as a struggle between living large and living long. In both terms and tone (especially in its sexual imagery), her "letter" to the young athlete stands in marked contrast to Wideman's meditation on the "bad man" as hero. As one of the most prominent young poets of the black arts movement during the late 1960s and early 1970s, Giovanni was *initially likened to other militant black intellectuals from that era, though in the ensuing years she has written in different forms and voices about the African American experience. In poems, essays, and widely read "conversations" about race relations—often as personal as they are provocative—she seems to place herself outside conventional critical categories— perhaps a little like Rodman and Iverson. "The spirituals," she says, "teach us that the problem of the twentieth century is not the problem of the color line. The problem of the twentieth century is the problem of civilizing white people."* Here, though, she writes as an elder— maternal and wise—offering ways to keep some hoop dreams well and alive. Significantly, she wrote this note of counsel before the 2000–2001 season, when Allen Iverson established a different set of relations with his coach and the athletic community, after which he was vot- ed the most valuable player in the NBA.** *

—————

Here is a free piece of advice which you know what it is worth because you know what you paid for it: Send your posse to school

They say they love you and are your friend but what have they done for you lately

It's not that you need the car you can buy another car and another and another until your knees give out or your back gives out or you land on the wrong side of your foot and your ankle gives out but none of these things will happen Allen because you are young and talented and beautiful so if they love you they should show it isn't that what you tell the girls but baby how do I know unless you show me

So let them show you

OK OK you say they are not all that smart and what good will school do them and frankly son I don't know . . . maybe they are dumb and maybe school cannot do any- thing for them but school can do something for you because you don't seem to trust anyone but them and maybe you're scared of them maybe you think if you find new friends they will just shoot you down or rape your mother or whatever it is that men do to each other when they are afraid of being left behind I know what they do to women so maybe it's the same thing but they say you are their friend and you have proven you are their friend but what have they proven to you

Send your posse to school

If they are out of high school send them to college and please don't tell me they can't go to college because even I know many colleges who will take anyone even your posse and the money you will save sending the three of them to school will be imme- diately realized and what is more you will get a posse who can offer you some real protection

Have one of them major in pre-law so that you can get the proper representation you need when the other folks start coming at you and when your team tries to trade

* Giovanni, "Black Is the Noun," 125.

** For a sketch of Giovanni's career, see Andrews, Foster, and Harris, *Oxford Companion to African American Literature*, 316–18. For more on Iverson see Longman and Jones, "Iverson."

you and they don't want to honor your contact and they find some crazy Black woman or crazier white one to say you have raped her or looked at her like you wanted to and you have embarrassed our team for the last time and things of that nature you will have your own friend to represent your best interest and not be like poor Mike Tyson who gets screwed by everyone because he didn't have a posse to help him out though he did have Tupac but they murdered him

Have one of them major in accounting or finance or business and please don't tell me they can't major in mathematical based studies because anyone who can measure milligrams of things and anyone who can figure out how much water with how much powder and anyone who can flip a wad of bills and tell if it's short or not can do the math and they need to do the math for you instead of against themselves and certainly you need to Have one

Major in religion so that one will be able to go anywhere at anytime park anywhere and hear everything and still be able to testify to your good nature and how much you are beloved by the Beings who look after us

And someone will say How silly those boys don't need to go to school but they do Iverson because right now they are little more than domesticated dogs who sit around waiting for you to bring your light and no one should be in the dark because someone else is out working so send your posse to school

It's the right thing to do

Nikki Giovanni, *Blues: For All the Changes* (New York: Morrow, 1999), 82–84.

9. Michael Wilbon on Tiger Woods: "History in Black and White"

Perhaps no athlete in recent times has caught the imagination of the American public more than Eldrick "Tiger" Woods. Born in 1975 to Earl Woods, a retired lieutenant colonel in the U.S. Army, and his wife, Kultida, a native of Thailand, Woods has golf talents so prodigious that he was putting with Bob Hope on the Mike Douglas Show by age two, could shoot forty-eight for nine holes by age three, and by age five was featured in Golf Digest. *He won the Optimist International Junior Tournament six times, captured six USGA amateur titles, and won the NCAA title his final year at Stanford University. Woods turned professional in 1996, and in only his fifth start on the tour won the Las Vegas Invitational by defeating Davis Love III in a playoff. He captured his first major title by winning the 1997 Masters Tournament and enhanced his already legendary status by garnering victories in the 1999 and 2000 PGA championships, 2000 U.S. Open championship, and 2000 British Open championship. He has earned nearly $22,000,000 in prize money and won almost every conceivable award, including twice being named* Sports Illustrated *Sportsman of the Year (1996 and 2000). In addition, Woods's many victories, combined with his charming public persona, youthful good looks, and transcendence of golf's traditional racial and ethnic divisions, have made him a popular spokesman for many of the world's largest and most successful corporations. He is probably best known*

Tiger Woods (Allsport)

for his endorsement deals with Nike, a business arrangement that has earned him millions of dollars while at once contributing to the increased popularity of golf. *

In the following document, Michael Wilbon, a popular sportswriter for the Washington Post, *explains how he and other people of color were overcome with emotion by Woods's victory in the 1997 Masters Tournament. The triumph was historically significant and elicited the most poignant feelings because it was accomplished by a great athlete of mixed racial heritage, occurred two days prior to the fiftieth anniversary of Jackie Robinson's breaking the color barrier in baseball, and took place in one of the world's great golf tournaments— long renowned for its rigid caste system as well as racial and gender discrimination. In essence, the tournament was the occasion for a symbolic passing of the torch from Robinson to Woods, a link between two outstanding athletes who, because of their enormous physical talents, intelligence, and sense of dignity, were capable of setting positive examples for athletes of all colors and opening doors for those who have been constrained by bigotry and racial prejudice.*

–––––– ––––––

The image that I cannot shake, a full two days later, doesn't include Tiger Woods. He wasn't in the frame that's going to stay with me forever. He and his father Earl, not long past bypass surgery, had just concluded a long and loving embrace which given the state of fatherhood in black America was emotional enough. Tiger had walked in one direction, toward Butler Cabin, to be awarded his green jacket for winning The Masters. But the camera for some reason stayed on Earl Woods, who walked off in another direction.

And in the picture, pretty much all you could see was Earl Woods being royally escorted off Augusta National by a legion of what appeared to be Georgia state troopers. At that point, nothing else mattered. A brown-skinned father of a brown-skinned golfer was being guarded by southern state troopers at a country club where some members only 10 years ago would rather have died and gone to hell than see that man even walk the course, much less play it.

Words cannot adequately describe the emotions felt at that moment by millions of people in the country, most of them people of color. The southern state trooper, second only to the Klan, is the real face of the violent white south, of club-swinging, water-spraying days of the 1960s. Part of me wanted to sit there dispassionately and watch life as it ought to be and should have been. Part of me wanted to go to church and shout.

I was fortunate enough to be watching the final moments of The Masters on television with a passionate golfer, my father-in-law-to-be, an accomplished professional black man in his sixties and a Southerner who undoubtedly felt emotions that someone 30 years younger can't feel. After six people in the room had fallen totally silent, he said, "Can you believe all of this?"

It is a bit much to take in all at once. Tiger Woods winning The Masters on Sunday, and 48 hours later, the 50th anniversary of Jackie Robinson breaking baseball's

---

* For information on Woods, see Woods, *Playing Through;* Rosaforte, *Raising the Bar.*

color line being celebrated tonight at Shea Stadium. Nothing like this just happens willy-nilly, this bridge from Robinson to Woods, from Brooklyn to Augusta, Ga., from one ballplayer who endured unspeakable hatred in the name of progress to this young golfer who now has to negotiate unimaginable adulation. It certainly seems the baton has been passed once again, from Jesse Owens to Joe Louis, to Jack Robinson to Muhammad Ali to Arthur Ashe and now to Tiger Woods.

Those of us looking for a sign that young Tiger can handle this, that he indeed understands his burden and is willing to carry it, got a clear one even before he received his green jacket Sunday. Talking to CBS's Jim Nantz, who asked him about being the first African American and Asian American to win golf's most prestigious tournament, Woods demonstrated a sense of history, of indebtedness and common sense beyond his years when he said, "I may be the first, but I'm not a pioneer." And then he went on to thank, by name, Charlie Sifford, Lee Elder and Ted Rhodes, black golfers—all pioneers—who had not a prayer until recently of walking through the front door at Augusta National.

Sifford, Elder and Rhodes are to Woods as Cool Papa Bell, Satchel Paige and Josh Gibson were to Jackie Robinson, the men who took all the earliest hits, who had doors slammed in their faces and roads blocked. It is only through Woods's light that people now will begin to learn more of Sifford, Elder and Rhodes. It's not difficult to find the similarities between them. Both became educated men, Robinson at UCLA and Woods at Stanford. I'm not talking about college degrees, I mean educated, learned, scholarly.

It was easy to see in both a great deal of dignity and humility. And it was easy to see in both a sincere sense of family, Woods with his parents and Robinson with his beautiful and tough-minded wife Rachel, who was with him in the trenches and responsible for her husband's endurance in ways most of us will never know. Just as Robinson once did, Woods speaks the King's English, not some mush-mouth, excuse-making quasi-language that can't do our people any good outside of our own environs, but clear and to the point without hemming and hawing and certainly without struggle. My mother and mother-in-law-to-be, two former schoolteachers, were happier with the way Woods spoke and carried himself Sunday than they were with any drive he hit off the tee.

I should say at this point that I am not a golfer. I've had two lessons and have only recently started watching televised golf, but it seems clear that Woods and the golf explosion will in a short time dramatically change the order of sports in America. This isn't just about sports, however; the venue is sports, and, as is often the case, sports is the earliest setting for significant social change. Jesse Owens and Hitler had their silent confrontation in Berlin three years before the start of World War II. Robinson, remember, came along eight years before Rosa Parks, and before *Brown v. Board of Education*. Title IX preceded by years and years certain mainstream battles for gender equity.

This isn't about more black youngsters playing golf, though that will happen automatically and happily. It's about people, particularly people who have been stereotyped and pigeonholed and systematically eliminated from some pursuit or another, to feel free to explore whatever passions are stirring within. It's about letting people explore those passions without restrictions, without having to face bigotry and ignorance.

That, not his baseball exploits, is why I think we should honor Jackie Robinson now and forever. Those too young or too far removed to identify with Robinson's struggle can now see the identifiable bridge that has been built across the past 50 years, one that has carried us to a time when a kid of African and Asian descent can be mobbed adoringly by a predominantly white audience in Georgia on land that used to be a slave plantation, and when the uniformed sons of the Confederate are offering a handshake instead of a billy club. Shut your eyes real tight and imagine Jackie Robinson on one side of that bridge, young Tiger Woods on the other, and all the goodwill in between that can be so wonderful to explore.

Michael Wilbon, "History in Black and White," *Washington Post,* April 15, 1997.

10. William C. Rhoden / "NFL's Silent Majority Afraid to Force Change"

African American athletes have always been the subjects of unique and sometimes conflicting expectations held by their own community and society at large. Although receiving their share of plaudits from America's sporting public, earning large sums of money from their athletic exploits, and realizing personal satisfaction from participating at the highest levels of competition, African American athletes have also been expected to serve as role models and become involved in the racial issues pertinent to their own communities while at the same time feeling obligated to adhere to the dictates of the sports establishment. With the notable exceptions of such great performers as Jack Johnson, Bill Russell, and Muhammad Ali, African American athletes have generally been reluctant—and unprepared, for that matter—to speak out on larger social issues and the racial inequities existing in highly organized sport. Their reticence was largely a result of their dependence on white employers and customers. *

The unwillingness of African American athletes to voice their complaints about the racial inequities in sport is the focus of William Rhoden's article on the National Football League (NFL). Having conducted several interviews with well-known NFL players, Rhoden makes clear that many African American athletes remained silent about the lack of black head coaches and administrators out of concern that they would be jeopardizing their own careers and future earnings if they did otherwise. The close ties and necessary alliances that black NFL players established with white benefactors, while not necessarily increasing the distance they felt between themselves and other members of the black community, mitigated any outpouring of complaints about the dearth of African American coaches and upper-level administrators in the league. In essence, regardless of the success they enjoyed and the material possessions they garnered, African American athletes in the NFL have never fully

---

* See D. Wiggins, *Glory Bound,* esp. 200–204.

escaped the dictates of a powerful sports establishment that has remained largely white and impervious to any serious discussion about racial equality and freedom of opportunity.

————————

As the National Football League prepares for its final championship game of the 1900's, the league celebrates a boom that has transformed pro football from a game played on muddy fields before sparse crowds into the national signature. As it prepares for the next millennium, the NFL is entangled by the same nagging issue that has plagued the nation for the last 100 years: race, racism and an African-American presence in a white power structure.

Today the NFL offers a striking example of uncontested merit. While ownership has remained overwhelmingly white, 72 percent of the NFL's players are African American. Black athletes have played a significant role in making the league a billion-dollar enterprise and the Super Bowl the highest-rated televised sporting event of the year, a billion-dollar bonanza.

Among an increasing number of black players, however, there is growing resentment and anger over a granite ceiling that has effectively prevented the NFL's black presence on the field from becoming equally pronounced in head coaching and front-office positions. The NFL has come under increased criticism over the haphazard manner in which teams select head coaches and front-office personnel.

How can someone with impeccable credentials be passed over in favor of a candidate with a questionable track record but strong front-office ties? African Americans have been the most prominent casualties of a process that often combines the most exclusionary elements of the old boy network, a plantation and the country club. There are only three black head coaches in the NFL—Tony Dungy in Tampa Bay, Dennis Green in Minnesota and Ray Rhodes, who just went from Philadelphia to Green Bay. In 1997, there were 100 black assistant coaches.

But while the debate over hiring black head coaches escalates, the league's black players have remained the silent majority. In an industry without guaranteed contracts, where one misspoken word can result in removal without explanation, players think long and hard before saying something management may construe as impudent. Ray Buchanan, the Falcons' highly regarded cornerback, showed up at Super Bowl media day wearing a dog collar, signifying Atlanta's status as an underdog. Buchanan quickly became a favorite of the news media and predicted a Falcon victory.

One evening I reached Buchanan in his hotel, and when the subject about the absence of black head coaches came up, the outspoken Buchanan was not so quotable. "I don't want to talk about that now," he said. "It's too controversial. I don't need that right now. Talk after the Super Bowl."

He wears a spiked dog collar to media day, predicts an Atlanta victory and yet says discussing blacks and coaching is too controversial.

Art Shell, the Falcons' offensive line coach and a former head coach of the Raiders, said high-profile players like Buchanan must help raise the issue or there will be no progress. "The voice that has to be heard in the NFL is the voice of the players," Shell said today. "The players have to stand up and let it be known that they are dissatisfied with what is going on. Until they start getting involved in this thing, things just might remain the same."

John Mobley, a Broncos starting linebacker, said the silence is a combination of apathy, selfishness and intimidation. "No one wants to stir up something that really isn't affecting them directly," he said. "It's a shame, but at the same time, what can you do about it if you don't have the forces behind you?"

Asked what might happen if he called a meeting to discuss the subject and invited Terrell Davis and Shannon Sharpe, the team's high-profile stars, Mobley said: "They probably wouldn't even want to sit down and discuss it if they knew what the topic was about. They'd think it was really something silly. It probably wouldn't even get touched."

Ray Crockett, the Broncos' All-Pro defensive back, said there were two issues—the problem of African Americans becoming head coaches and black athletes bringing the issue before the public. "A lot of the players don't want to upset the coaches—or the owners—because they are playing for them," Crockett said. "And there's not enough representation of black coaches to defend them. If we put ourselves out there, our names on the line, and there's still a bunch of white coaches out there, of course you're intimidated. But I will say that if you're good enough to play this game, why can't we be good enough to coach it?"

Alfred Williams, a Denver defensive lineman with eight years of NFL experience, explained that the NFL's black majority is neutralized and held hostage. "Privately, we talk about it a little; it's never something we've met as a group about," Williams said. "In this league you can't just speak your mind and feel like it's going to go unnoticed. We play in a league with no guaranteed contracts."

Speaking publicly about controversial issues is one thing, doing something about it is another. Davis, the Broncos' All-Pro running back, said he was aware of the situation but was not sure about a solution. "Obviously, you can look around and see not that many head coaches, not that many offensive coordinators," he said. "Is it because people haven't applied, or is it because people just didn't hire them? I don't know. So what should I do—in the interview room say 'where are the black coaches?' without having any earthly idea about what I'm talking about, just because I don't see it?"

Cornelius Bennett, a Falcons linebacker, sees it. But "we can't do anything about it as players," he said. "We try to keep our comments to a minimum because—not that we're scared—there's nothing we can do. We can't go to them and demand—they're going to do what they have to do. You pay $300 million for a team; that pretty much gives you the right to do whatever you want to do."

Asked why players haven't been more vocal, Bob Whitfield, a Falcons offensive lineman, said: "You're the first one to ask me. I've never seen the process and how it worked out. But I definitely think there's something wrong when you have all these black players and none of them moves up to the ranks of head coach."

The racial issue leads to the more fundamental problem of devising performance standards for what it takes to become a head coach.

The anger and resentment directed at the league's owners are the imbalances in a system that painstakingly selects the best athletes while too often randomly hires coaches with questionable credentials. The NFL's challenge in the future will be to construct a new system that selects thoroughbred coaches as efficiently as it selects thoroughbred athletes. The competitive balance is at an all-time high: the distance between great teams, good teams and poor teams is razor thin.

The difference between great players and good players is marginal. The most glaring gap too often involves the head coaches whom owners hire to drive their Ferraris. Some are too inexperienced to drive, some are too old to drive. Some simply don't know how to drive a car with 72 percent super octane.

Without a better system, the NFL is creating an environment in which every white coach who is hired is seen as a crony, or an overseer to be field boss of the black majority. Every black hiring is an experiment.

Somewhere between fair play and equality lie objective standards. Find the best person and let's get on with it.

William C. Rhoden, "NFL's Silent Majority Afraid to Force Change," *New York Times,* January 29, 1999.

C

DISPATCHES FROM THE BUSINESS PAGE
AND SOME THOUGHTS FOR THE FUTURE

11. Venus Williams's Star Endorsements

On July 9, 2001, Venus Williams won her second straight Wimbledon title. Commentators noted the power of her play as well as her graciousness off the court. They also placed her triumph in historical context: not since 1957–58, when Althea Gibson had won back-to-back titles at Wimbledon, had an African American woman been dominant in the sport of tennis.

What occurred in the interval between Venus's two "All England" victories was perhaps even more momentous, however. She joined Michael and Tiger in gaining a huge endorsement package. Hers was with Reebok and it amounted to forty million dollars in all. "Reebok and Venus are shattering the glass ceiling in women's sports," said Sharon Barbano, a Reebok spokesperson. "Finally, women are on the same playing field as men."*

The media coverage of Venus and Serena Williams began with a focus on their well-honed athletic skills and the hard road they traveled to bring strength and technique together on the tennis courts. Their early years in the inner city featured prominently in those stories. So too did the presence of their imperious father, Richard—and the pressures he has placed on his daughters and the wisdom that he has imparted.** Increasingly, though, what sports fans have seen is poise under pressure and trophies held aloft. What's more, a far larger public now sees Venus Williams in advertisements, on the covers of magazines—where athleticism meets fashion and design. The victories on the tennis courts that many people predict for the future will be a significant contribution to the athletic record, but the breakthroughs now being reported on the business pages as well as in the sports section of our newspapers may also augur well for a better record of race relations in America.

——— ———

Venus Williams, who ruled the tennis world in 2000, capped off a season of triumphs with a reported $40 million Reebok endorsement deal, which the sporting apparel company said is the richest ever for a woman in sports.

"This is a big moment in my life," said the 20-year-old Williams, who last year won the Wimbledon, U.S. Open and Sydney Olympics titles during a brilliant win-

---

* *Miami Times*, January 2, 2001. This article mentions that the sum of her corporate endorsements is likely to exceed $70,000,000 over the next several years.

** See S. Roberts, "Williams Sisters"; Wertheim, *Venus Envy*.

Venus and Serena Williams (Allsport)

ning streak that stretched from summer into autumn. "It's been a journey," Williams, who grew up in the run-down Compton neighborhood outside Los Angeles and made a rapid rise to tennis stardom, said at a news conference. "For women of color, for my family. It's one dream coming true after another."

Specific terms of the deal were not announced, but Reebok's chief marketing officer, Angel Martinez, told the news conference that he would not deny reports that valued the deal at $40 million over five years. Williams also has endorsement deals with Avon, Wilson rackets and Wilson Leather. By comparison, the king of sports endorsements among male athletes—golfer Tiger Woods—is expected to rake in over $50 million a year from his various deals once his new Nike contract kicks in next August.

Williams, who is studying fashion design, has endorsed Reebok products on the court and in television and print ads since 1995, will also co-design the Reebok collections scheduled to debut in the 2002 tennis season. Besides designing, Williams recently took a turn at modeling in a cover layout with her sister, Serena, for *Elle Magazine.* The deal signed by Williams was lauded as a breakthrough for women in sports, particularly black women.

Uplifting Day

"It's a great day for her, but it is also an unbelievably, positively uplifting day for sports, especially women's sports," said former tennis champion Billie Jean King in a telephone hook-up from Arizona. "Its just fantastic the recognition for Venus and how versatile she is. She is fun to watch. Just her being on the court, it's a great pleasure," said King, who was captain of the U.S. team at the Sydney Olympics, where Williams also claimed the gold medal in doubles with her younger sister, Serena.

"I know that Althea Gibson is particularly happy today and Arthur Ashe is, in spirit," King said of the last two African Americans to win the coveted Wimbledon title. Donna Lopiano, executive director of the Women's Sports Foundation, also attended the news conference. "Venus is not only a symbol of skill and style but a woman of substance who stands tall," said Lopiano.

Williams said she hoped to improve on her ranking of third in the world, which suffered because she missed many early season tournaments because of injury. "Of course, I want to be number one," she said of the position now held by Switzerland's Martina Hingis, "but being happy and healthy is the most important thing."

Williams said she did not think her tennis rival, best friend and housemate Serena would be jealous over the new sponsorship deal. "But I guess I'll be doing all the shopping" she said with a beaming smile.

"New Deal Makes Venus Richest Female Athlete," *Jacksonville Free Press,* January 10, 2001.

12. Kenneth Shropshire / "The Next Millennium"

During the last decade of the twentieth century, a new generation of academicians and activists began expanding upon the agenda that had originally been set during the civil rights era. Scholars like Kenneth Shropshire, who teaches the business of sports at the prestigious Wharton School of the University of Pennsylvania, presently elaborate upon the issues that Harry Edwards and Jesse Jackson raised earlier. Today, concern about discrimination focuses less on the playing field itself, or on media characterizations of the athletic successes won by people of color, than on the significance of sport in broader social, economic, and cultural terms.

Here Shropshire echoes the hopes of the first muscular assimilationists, who believed that the thorough integration of athletic competition would facilitate the expansion of opportunities in other endeavors. This would include coaching and managerial positions, the fabled "front office" jobs, and the rapidly growing fields of sports law and administration. Despite some exceptions—Michael Jordan, for instance—Shropshire notes the continuing underrepresentation of African Americans in positions of real influence in corporate sports and beyond. Accounting for this problem, he deplores the ways that sports are "packaged" for black youth. Here, while he lauds such efforts as Midnight Basketball programs, he also shares the concerns of those educators and community leaders who believe that "hoop dreams" are too often unrealistic—damaging to the individual and to society.

More important still, Shropshire points to the unacknowledged but wide-ranging resistance by the dominant culture to discuss race relations in any meaningful way; "the creation of and compliance with antidiscrimination laws is not enough," he says. The sports industry ultimately lacks the will to pursue programs of real change. Beyond that, he sees relatively few high-profile athletes taking the risks that John Carlos and Tommie Smith did at the 1968 Olympic Games, or assuming the responsibility to act on behalf of genuine equal-

ity and opportunity. Though much of Shropshire's argument derives from his reading of the law and labor statistics, the scholar also knows his history: "'Power concedes nothing without a demand,'" he quotes Frederick Douglass. "'It never did and it never will.'"

———————

It's not my place to fight it, that's why we have a Jesse Jackson. I don't agree with discrimination or racism, but I'm not in the front office. I'm on the front line. I'm a black athlete who has been well taken care of.

—Barry Bonds, quoted in *Sports Illustrated*, April 5, 1993

Mention race relations to people in sports in any capacity, and the likely response is a shrug. Few volunteer to discuss the subject, and when it does come up, it's quickly brushed off.

—Frederick C. Klein, *Wall Street Journal* sports columnist, October 13, 1995

Would the Yankees hire a minority manager and general manager in the same year?

—*New York Times*, October 28, 1995

The Ideal Industry

In the movie *Mondo Cane,* New Guinean Aborigines built an airstrip, hoping to attract the planes that frequently passed overhead. They hoped to change the behavior of something they had no control over by putting all of the elements in place for the desired result—the landing of an aircraft. Antidiscrimination laws in the United States are often much like that airstrip. This is particularly true when the laws are interpreted to mean that color may not be a consideration in repairing racial inequities. A team, league, university, or sports management firm may not be violating any existing laws. Yet legislators put the present legal framework in place in the hope that equal rights and opportunity would come about for all races in all businesses. In some areas the planes still refuse to land; those at the controls have no desire to do so. A more positive characterization may be that those in the power positions in sports do not know how to bring about change or believe that enough is being done. The passage of antidiscrimination laws is unfortunately sometimes viewed as accomplishing equality because most formerly legal discrimination has been outlawed. As John Hope Franklin has written:

> Neither the courts nor the Congress nor the president can declare by fiat, resolution, or executive order that the United States is a colorblind society. They can only facilitate a movement in that direction by discharging their duties in a way that reflects their commitment to such a goal. From that point on, it is the people of all colors who must work in every possible way to attain that goal. Those who insist that we should conduct ourselves as if such a utopian state already existed have no interest in achieving it and, indeed, would be horrified if we ever approached it.

Along similar lines, some Supreme Court opinions have begun to point to the concept of choice as the explanation for why a statistical racial disparity exists in a particular industry. The argument is that although more African-Americans could be employed in a given industry, they are not because African Americans have chosen a different industry for employment, exercising their right of choice. That may be the case in some industries, but there are many qualified African-Americans who have chosen to work in sports and are not even being considered for positions.

In broad terms, there is a three-step progression to reaching the ideal of diverse management in the sports industry. Initially, there must be a recognition of the existence of racism, discrimination, and limited-access networks. Next, there must be a successful transition into a period where racial diversity is the standard. Diversity can be attained through affirmative action—affirmative action that focuses on opportunities for those with merit who have been ignored due to their race—affirmative action that focuses on breaking down the sports old boy network. The value of diversity must evolve to be appreciated. As this transition is completed, the accomplished goal would be multiculturalism—an industry with representation from across American society without racism, discrimination, or affirmative action programs. With that as the ultimate goal, one can see why the transition period of affirmative action programs as a means of striving for diversity may be with us for a while—if we can ever get there.

Former NFL commissioner Pete Rozelle tried to explain the lack of African-American head coaches by saying that picking a head coach is "like choosing a wife." The social impact of the phrase and the reasons for Rozelle's selection of it are almost haunting. Even though marriage between the races is now legal and accepted by most, some people still whisper when an interracial couple passes. In the case of Wedowee, Alabama, a high school principal attempted to cancel the school's 1994 prom because some interracial couples planned to attend. It is a permanent part of our consciousness. As John Hope Franklin has written, "The color line is alive, well, and flourishing in the final decade of the twentieth century."

How to Get There

Concerted Effort

It will take a concerted effort by many to bring about change in sports. Obviously, owners, commissioners, and anyone in the position to hire has the power to make an immediate impact in isolated situations. As one franchise executive maintained, the owner or chief executive officer has to believe in diversity: "That makes my job easier, when you have support from the top, and people realize that it's an area of importance and it's something we want to concentrate and focus our efforts on." Others, including the leaders of the NCAA, college presidents, athletic directors, and major sports management firms, must act as well. These people in power can hire or admit an African-American with no plan, program, or person compelling them.

To combat racism in sports, we must deal with both what America and sports in reality look and act like and the paragon of what they should look and act like in that ideal moment in the future. To get there, an intermediate period of transition is necessary. This transition period may well become permanent. The concept of permanence is not highly regarded by the courts in the current state of antidiscrimination jurisprudence as it relates to affirmative action programs. The law will continue to

Michael Jordan: The
Once and Future CEO
(Allsport)

wrestle with this problem, but currently, to be upheld, the plans must in all likelihood
have a termination date in order to pass judicial scrutiny. . . .

Changing the Focus of Youth

The saddest side of sports is that it serves as a magnet for young African-American
males but rejects them when their playing days are over. One portion of an ideal solution would be to remove sports as the brass ring in depressed communities and immediately replace the goal of athletic success with that of becoming something more
attainable, such as a businessperson, physician, engineer, attorney, or architect. In
1968, a Louisiana high school coach said, "A white kid tries to become president of the
United States, and all the skills and knowledge he picks up on the way can be used in a
thousand different jobs. A black kid tries to become Willie Mays, and all the tools he

picks up on the way are useless to him if he doesn't become Willie Mays." As the longest of long-term goals, this transition to a change in priorities is mandatory. To reach this point would require corporate advertisers, moviemakers, team owners, and fans to stop idolizing the athlete. Achieving this goal approaches the difficulty of eliminating racism itself. To suppress somehow the public knowledge of the salaries that the athletes receive is next to impossible. This would have to be done, at the same time making other routes to success more palatable. The task of deflating the fantastic status of sports in society is formidable. In short, it is not going to happen in the foreseeable future. . . .

The strangest irony is that even as the skewed role of sports in the African-American community is probably permanent, so too is racism. The focus on sports by African-Americans continues because of the good that sports can do. Not to be denied, there are the few financial success stories. There are also the stories of sports "keeping kids out of trouble." Midnight Basketball leagues are springing up in a number of cities as a late-night alternative activity to gang-banging. With all good intentions and probably little or no thought to invigorate professional contract dreams, Senator Carol Moseley Braun proposed a bill to provide 6 million dollars in federal funding for basketball leagues that begin play at 10 P.M. and later. Second to the ban on assault weapons, funding for Midnight Basketball may have been the most talked-about line item in the 1994 federal crime legislation. However, with all the good sports can do, athletics should not be held up as the ultimate way out for African-Americans. . . .

At the 1968 Olympics, probably the most dramatic and powerful demonstration by athletes was led on the field by two-hundred-meter sprinters John Carlos and Tommie Smith. On October 16, minutes after the two-hundred-meter dash, gold medalist Smith and bronze medalist Carlos stood in stocking feet on the victory platform, bowed their heads, listened to the U.S. national anthem, and raised black-gloved fists to the sky. As recounted by writer Kenny Moore:

> They meant their unshod feet to represent black poverty, Smith's black scarf and Carlos's beads to signify black lynchings, their fists to mean black unity and power. Any resemblance to Lady Liberty lifting her torch was ironic, for Smith and Carlos were taking U.S. society to task for having failed to extend liberty and justice to all.

The protest grew out of months of discussions through the Olympic Project for Human Rights. The demonstration was not just sports-related but focused on the condition of blacks worldwide. Carlos and Smith were truly on the "front line."

A number of whites competing at the 1968 Olympics wore buttons and spoke in support of the protest. Prominent among the supporters was the white second-place finisher in the two-hundred-meter sprint, Australian Peter Norman. He wore an Olympic Project for Human Rights button on his sweatsuit on the victory stand. Norman was later reprimanded by the Australian Olympic Committee. . . .

Those who feel strongly enough that something is wrong must take the same risks as have the athletes of the past. The legal rights that have been won for equal opportunity are important but are not the needed end result. . . .

The ideal is empowerment at representative levels for African-Americans. The creation of and compliance with antidiscrimination laws is not enough. Claims by the leagues or by our colleges and others that equal opportunity exists are not enough. Claims of color blindness must be recognized as rhetorical camouflage. The hearts, minds, ideas, and beliefs of sports leadership may change, but that will take time. Compared to simply changing the laws, bringing about real change is a longer, if not never-ending process. But the power that African-Americans rightfully deserve can be transferred in a much shorter time frame. Management, NCAA officials, and college presidents—the risks and sacrifices may vary among these entities, but they must be taken or the inequitable position of the African-American in sport will not change. In the words of Frederick Douglass, "Power concedes nothing without a demand. It never did and it never will." . . .

The difficulty in realistically discussing and bringing about change struck me in casual discussions after a presentation I gave to 350 sports lawyers, including sports executives. My topic was "Affirmative Action in Sports Franchise Front Offices." I asked if we accept that there is a problem, then what do we do? I emphasized that the sports industry today is what America will be in the future. The merit of African-Americans is not an issue in sports today. In other sectors of society, one can argue that the number of African-Americans with appropriate degrees, experience, or test scores is limited. Merit can be pointed to as an outstanding issue. But not in sports. So how can we deal with the problem unless we all take affirmative steps? At some point in the talk I said, quite a distance from my planned script, "Look around you, the composition of this audience is completely the opposite of those that play the game." I did see many members of the audience literally look around. I also saw a few nonchalant shoulder shrugs. The shrugs, and the conversations I had with many in the hallway after the presentation, were indicative of the general reaction: "You couldn't possibly be talking about me." The reality is that I am. Anyone who can have an impact on the business of sports has a responsibility to act, because the way sports addresses the issues says much about how other sectors will address inequality in the future.

Kenneth Shropshire, "The Next Millennium," *In Black and White: Race and Sports in America* (New York: New York University Press, 1996), 142–46, 157–59.

13. Gerald Early / "Performance and Reality: Race, Sports, and the Modern World"

How much of the progress in race relations in America derives from the efforts of black athletes, for example, Jackie Robinson, to make their way in national pastimes? To what extent did black champions in sport help African Americans in all walks of life to keep their eyes on the prize, to pursue civil rights as a "crusade"? How much "interracial education" actually occurred during Robinson's stint in major league baseball (or during the careers of Jesse Owens, Joe Louis, Muhammad Ali, "Magic," and Michael)? That is, how effective was sports

in persuading many white Americans to put away the racist baggage that for many genera-
tions sustained segregation and discrimination in custom and law?

Gerald Early's meditation on race and sports takes up these questions. He writes from a
different standpoint than that of Kenneth Shropshire and Harry Edwards, who seek, through
sport, to reinvigorate black activism or help solve some of today's problems encountered by
many black youth. As a cultural commentator, Early questions the efficacy of black athletes'
triumphs in transforming society. At one point, he addresses the anxieties of white athletes
in selected sports: there is a problem now, they are not winning. In another passage, Early
engages the pontifications of a white writer, John Hoberman, who assesses African Ameri-
can success on the playing fields as part of a black "fixation" on sport. Early deftly connects
these two concerns in the same terms used by earlier generations of black intellectuals: sport
has long offered highly visible opportunities for blacks to excel; what white critics make of
that is another matter. One man's "pathology" is another man's pride.

Ultimately, this essay makes common cause with the concerns of Henry Louis Gates Jr.,
bell hooks, and Nikki Giovanni about the deleterious aspects of high-level sport, even as it
renders athletic achievement as a significant part of a resilient black culture and conscious-
ness. Thus Early can celebrate Jackie Robinson as "an unambiguous athletic hero for both
races," then refer to Robinson's "sacrifice on the altar of racism." Elsewhere in his writings,
Early has shown his affinity for some of the insights offered by Ralph Ellison. Both writers
condemn injustice. At the same time, both understand paradox and try to explain the grim
ironies of American race relations. *

——— ———

[The] celebration of the fiftieth anniversary of Jackie Robinson's breaking the color
line in major league baseball was one of the most pronounced and prolonged ever
held in the history of our Republic in memory of a black man or of an athlete. It
seems nearly obvious that, on one level, our preoccupation was not so much with
Robinson himself—previous milestone anniversaries of his starting at first base for
the Brooklyn Dodgers in April 1947 produced little fanfare—as it was with ourselves
and our own dilemma about race, a problem that strikes us simultaneously as being
intractable and "progressing" toward resolution; as a chronic, inevitably fatal disease
and as a test of national character that we will, finally, pass.

Robinson was the man white society could not defeat in the short term, though
his untimely death at age 53 convinced many that the stress of the battle defeated him
in the long run. In this respect, Robinson did become something of an uneasy elegiac
symbol of race relations, satisfying everyone's psychic needs: blacks, with a redemp-
tive black hero who did not sell out and in whose personal tragedy was a corporate
triumph over racism; whites, with a black hero who showed assimilation to be a triumphant act. For each group, it was important that he was a hero for the other. All
this was easier to accomplish because Robinson played baseball, a "pastoral" sport of
innocence and triumphalism in the American mind, a sport of epic romanticism, a

---

* See Early, *Tuxedo Junction;* idem, *Culture of Bruising.*

sport whose golden age is always associated with childhood. In the end, Robinson as tragic hero represented, paradoxically, depending on the faction, how far we have come and how much more needs to be done.

Perhaps we reached back for Jackie Robinson . . . (just as we reached back for an ailing Muhammad Ali, the boastful athlete as expiatory dissident, the year before at the Olympics) because of our need for an athlete who transcends his self-absorbed prowess and quest for championships, or whose self-absorption and quest for titles meant something deeper politically and socially, told us something a bit more important about ourselves as a racially divided, racially stricken nation. . . .

What, indeed, is the place of black people in our realm? Perhaps, at this point in history, we are all, black and white, as mystified by that question as we were at the end of the Civil War when faced with the prospect that slave and free must live together as equal citizens, or must try to. For the question has always signified that affirmative action—a public policy for the unconditional inclusion of the African-American that has existed, with all its good and failed intentions, in the air of American racial reform since black people were officially freed, even, indeed, in the age of abolition with voices such as Lydia Maria Child and Frederick Douglass—is about the making of an African into an American and the meaning of that act for our democracy's ability to absorb all. We were struck by Jackie Robinson's story . . . because it was as profound, as mythic, as any European immigrant's story about how Americans are made. We Americans seem to have blundered about in our history with two clumsy contrivances strapped to our backs, unreconciled and weighty: our democratic traditions and race.

What makes Robinson so significant is that he seemed to have found a way to balance this baggage in the place that is so much the stuff of our dreams: the level playing field of top-flight competitive athletics. "Athletics," stated Robinson in his first autobiography, *Jackie Robinson: My Own Story* (ghostwritten by black sportswriter Wendell Smith), "both school and professional, come nearer to offering an American Negro equality of opportunity than does any other field of social and economic activity." It is not so much that this is true as that Robinson believed it, and that most Americans today, black and white, still do or still want to. This is one of the important aspects of modern sports in a democratic society that saves us from being totally cynical about them. Sports are the ultimate meritocracy. Might it be said that sports are what all other professional activities and business endeavors, all leisure pursuits and hobbies in our society aspire to be?

If nothing else, Robinson, an unambiguous athletic hero for both races and symbol of sacrifice on the altar of racism, is our most magnificent case of affirmative action. He entered a lily-white industry amid cries that he was unqualified (not entirely unjustified, as Robinson had had only one year of professional experience in the Negro Leagues, although on the other hand, he was one of the most gifted athletes of his generation), and he succeeded, on merit, beyond anyone's wildest hope. And here the sports metaphor is a perfectly literal expression of the traditional democratic belief of that day: If given the chance, anyone can make it on his ability, with no remedial aid or special compensation, on a level playing field. Here was the fulfillment of our American Creed, to use Gunnar Myrdal's term (*An American Dilemma* had appeared only a year before Robinson was signed by the Dodgers), of fair play and equal opportunity. Here was our democratic orthodoxy of color-blind competition realized. Here was an instance where neither the principle nor its application could be impugned. Robinson was proof, just as heavyweight champion Joe Louis and Olympic track star Jesse Owens had been during the Depression, that sports helped vanquish the stigma of race.

Sports may be among the most powerful human expressions in all history. So why could sports not serve the United States ideologically in whatever way people decided to define democratic values during this, the American Century, when we became the most powerful purveyors of sports in all history? . . . [And yet] since Robinson's arrival, sports have, in many respects, intensified race and racialist thinking or, more precisely, anxiety about race and racialist thinking.

Race is not merely a system of categorizations of privileged or discredited abilities but rather a system of conflicting abstractions about what it means to be human. Sports are not a material realization of the ideal that those who succeed deserve to succeed; they are a paradox of play as work, of highly competitive, highly pressurized work as a form of romanticized play, a system of rules and regulations that govern both a real and a symbolic activity that suggests, in the stunning complexity of its performance, both conformity and revolt. . . .

The Whiteness of the White Athlete

In a December 8, 1997, *Sports Illustrated* article, "Whatever Happened to the White Athlete?" S. L. Price writes about the dominant presence of black athletes in professional basketball (80 percent black), professional football (67 percent black), and track and field (93 percent of gold medalists are black). He also argues that while African-Americans make up only 17 percent of major league baseball players, "[during] the past 25 years, blacks have been a disproportionate offensive force, winning 41 percent of the Most Valuable Player awards." (And the number of blacks in baseball does not include the black Latinos, for whom baseball is more popular than it is with American blacks.) Blacks also dominate boxing, a sport not dealt with in the article. "Whites have in some respects become sports' second-class citizens," writes Price. "In a surreal inversion of Robinson's era, white athletes are frequently the ones now tagged by the stereotypes of skin color." He concludes by suggesting that white sprinter Kevin Little, in competition, can feel "the slightest hint—and it is not more than a hint—of what Jackie Robinson felt 50 years ago." It is more than a little ludicrous to suggest that white athletes today even remotely, even as a hint, are experiencing something like what Robinson experienced. White athletes, even when they play sports dominated by blacks, are still entering an industry not only controlled by whites in every phase of authority and operation but also largely sustained by white audiences. . . . Although blacks dominate the most popular team sports, they still make up only 9 percent of all people in the United States who make a living or try to make a living as athletes, less than their percentage in the general population.

What I find most curious about Price's article is that he gives no plausible reason for why blacks dominate these particular sports. He quotes various informants to the effect that blacks must work harder than whites at sports. "Inner-city kids," William

Ellerbee, basketball coach at Simon Gratz High in Philadelphia, says, "look at basketball as a matter of life or death." In a similar article on the black makeup of the NBA in the *Washington Post* last year, Jon Barry, a white player for the Atlanta Hawks, offers: "Maybe the suburban types of the white people have more things to do." Much of this is doubtless true. . . .

Nonetheless, these explanations do not quite satisfy. Ultimately, the discussion in both articles comes down to genetics. There is nothing wrong with thinking about genetic variations. After all, what does the difference in human beings mean and what is its source? . . . .

. . . [E]ven if it were true that blacks were athletically superior to whites, why then would they not dominate all sports instead of just a handful? There might be a more plainly structural explanation for black dominance in certain sports. This is not to say that genes may have nothing to do with it but only to say that, at this point genetic arguments have been far from persuasive and, in their implications, more than a little pernicious.

It is easy enough to explain black dominance in boxing. It is the Western sport that has the longest history of black participation, so there is tradition. Moreover, it is a sport that has always attracted poor and marginalized men. Black men have persistently made up a disproportionate share of the poor and the marginalized. Finally, instruction is within easy reach; most boxing gyms are located in poor neighborhoods, where a premium is placed on being able to fight well. Male fighting is a useful skill in a cruel, frontierlike world that values physical toughness, where insult is not casually tolerated and honor is a highly sensitive point.

Black dominance in football and basketball is not simply related to getting out of the ghetto through hard work or to lack of other amusements but to the institution most readily available to blacks in the inner city that enables them to use athletics to get out. Ironically, that institution is the same one that fails more often than it should in fitting them for other professions: namely, school. As William Washington, the father of a black tennis family, perceptively pointed out in an article last year in the *New York Times* discussing the rise of tennis star Venus Williams, "Tennis, unlike baseball, basketball or football, is not a team sport. It is a family sport. Your immediate family is your primary supporting case, not your teammates or the players in the locker room. . . . The experiences [of alienation and racism] start soon after you realize that if you play this game, you must leave your neighborhood and join the country club bunch. You don't belong to that group, and they let you know it in a variety of ways, so you go in, compete and leave." In short, because their families generally lack the resources and connections, indeed, because, as scholars such as V. P. Franklin have pointed out, black families cannot provide their members the cultural capital that white and Asian families can, blacks are at a disadvantage to compete in sports where school is not crucial in providing instruction and serving as an organizational setting for competition. When it comes to football and basketball, however, where school is essential to have a career, not only are these sports played at even the poorest black high schools they are also the dominant college sports. If baseball were a more dominant college sport and if there were no minor leagues where a player had to toil for several years before, maybe, getting a crack at the major leagues, then I think baseball would attract more young black men. Because baseball, historically, was not a game that was invented by a school or became deeply associated with schools or education, blacks could learn it, during the days when they were banned from competition with white professionals, only by forming their own leagues. Sports, whatever one might think of their worth as activities, are extremely important in understanding black people's relationship to secular institutions and secular, non-protest organizing: the school, both black and white; the independent, nonprofessional or semiprofessional league; and the barnstorming, independent team, set up by both whites and blacks.

Given that blacks are over-represented in the most popular sports and that young black men are more likely than young white men to consider athletics as a career, there has been much commentary about whether sports are bad for blacks. The March 24, 1997, issue of *U.S. News & World Report,* ran a cover story titled "Are Pro Sports Bad for Black Youth?" In February of that year Germanic languages scholar John Hoberman published *Darwin's Athletes: How Sport Has Damaged Black America and Preserved the Myth of Race,* to much bitter controversy. *The Journal of African American Men,* a new academic journal, not only published a special double issue on black men and sports (Fall 1996/Winter 1997) but featured an article in its Winter 1995/96 number titled "The Black Student Athlete: The Colonized Black Body," by Billy Hawkins. While there are great distinctions to be made among these works, there is an argument about sports as damaging for blacks that can be abstracted that tends either toward a radical left position on sports or, in Hawkins's case, toward a militant cultural nationalism with Marxist implications.

First, Hoberman and Hawkins make the analogy that sports are a form of slavery or blatant political and economic oppression. . . . The leftist critic condemns sports as a fraudulent expression of the heroic and the skilled in capitalist culture. The cultural nationalist critic condemns sports as an explicit expression of the grasping greed of white capitalist culture to subjugate people as raw resources.

On a more sophisticated level, the slavery analogy is used to describe sports structurally: the way audiences are lured to sports as a false spectacle, and the way players are controlled mentally and physically by white male authority, their lack of access to the free-market worth of their labor. (This latter point is made particularly about college players, since the breaking of the reserve clause in baseball, not by court decision but by union action, has so radically changed the status and so wildly inflated the salaries of many professional team players, regardless of sport.) Probably the most influential commentator to make this analogy of sport to slavery was Harry Edwards in his 1969 book, *The Revolt of the Black Athlete.* Richard Lapchick in his 1984 book, *Broken Promises: Racism in American Sports,* extends Edwards's premises. Edwards is the only black writer on sports that Hoberman admires. And Edwards is also cited by Hawkins. How convincing any of this is has much to do with how willing one is to be convinced, as is the case with many highly polemical arguments. . . .

The other aspects of the sports-damage-black-America argument, principally made by Hoberman, are that blacks are more likely to be seen as merely "physical," and thus inferior beings; that society's promotion of black sports figures comes at the expense of promoting any other type of noteworthy black person; that black overinvestment in sports is both the cause and result of black anti-intellectualism, itself the result of virulent white racism, meant to confine blacks to certain occupations. Implicit in Hoberman's work is his hatred of the fetishization of athletic achievement, the rigid rationalization of sports as a theory and practice. He also hates the suppression of the political nature of the athlete, and hates, too, both the apolitical nature of sports, mystified as transcendent legend and supported by the simplistic language of sportswriters and sports-apologist intellectuals, and the political exploitation of sports by ideologues and the powerful. As a critical theorist, Hoberman was never interested in proving this with thorough empiricism, and, as a result, was attacked in a devastatingly effective manner by black scholars, who blew away a good number of his assertions with an unrelenting empiricism. But he has got into deep trouble with black intellectuals, in the end, not for these assertions or for the mere lack of good empiricism. Hoberman, rather, has been passionately condemned for suggesting that blacks have a "sports fixation" that is tantamount to a pathology, a word that rightly distresses African-Americans, reminiscent as it is of the arrogance of white social scientists past and present who describe blacks as some misbegotten perversion of a white middle-class norm. . . .

In response to an article like *SI*'s "Whatever Happened to the White Athlete?" blacks are likely to ask, Why is it whenever we dominate by virtue of merit a legitimate field of endeavor, it's always seen as a problem? On the one hand, some blacks are probably willing to take the view expressed in Steve Sailer's August 12, 1996, essay in *National Review,* "Great Black Hopes," in which he argues that black achievement in sports serves very practical ends, giving African-Americans a cultural and market niche, and that far from indicating a lack of intelligence, blacks' dominance in some sports reveals a highly specialized intelligence: what he calls "creative improvisation and on-the-fly interpersonal decision-making," which also explains "black dominance in jazz, running with the football, rap, dance, trash talking, preaching, and oratory." I suppose it might be said from this that blacks have fast-twitch brain cells. In any case, blacks had already been conceded these gifts by whites in earlier displays of condescension. But black sports dominance is no small thing to blacks because, as they deeply know, to win is to be human.

On the other hand, what the *SI* article said most tellingly was that while young whites admire black athletic figures, they are afraid to play sports that blacks dominate, another example of whites leaving the neighborhood when blacks move in. This white "double-consciousness"—to admire blacks for their skills while fearing their presence in a situation where blacks might predominate—is a modern-day reflection of the contradiction, historically, that has produced our racially stratified society. To be white can be partly defined as not only the fear of not being white but the fear of being at the mercy of those who are not white. Whiteness and blackness in this respect cease to be identities and become the personifications not of stereotypes alone but of taboos, of prohibitions. Sports, like all of popular culture, become the theater where the taboos are simultaneously smashed and reinforced, where one is liberated from them while conforming to them. Sports are not an idealization of ourselves but a reflection. . . .

Postscript: O Defeat, Where Is Thy Sting?

My barber is a professional boxer. He fights usually as a light-heavyweight or as a cruiser-weight. He is 34 and would like to fight for a championship again one day, but time is working against him. He has fought for championships in the past, though never a world title. It is difficult to succeed as a boxer if you must work another job. A day of full-time work and training simply leaves a fighter exhausted and distracted. I have seen him fight on television several times, losing to such world-class fighters as Michael Nunn and James Toney. In fact, every time I have seen him fight he has lost. He is considered "an opponent," someone used by an up-and-coming fighter to fatten his record or by an established fighter who needs a tune-up. An opponent does not make much money; some are paid as little as a few hundred dollars a fight. My barber, I guess, is paid more than that. This is the world that most boxers occupy—this small-time world of dingy arenas and gambling boats, cramped dressing rooms and little notice. It is the world that most professional athletes occupy. He last fought on June 2 against Darryl Spinks for something called the MBA light-heavyweight title at the Ambassador Center in Jennings, Missouri. Darryl Spinks is the son of notorious St. Louis fighter and former heavyweight champion Leon Spinks. Spinks won a twelve-round decision, and my barber felt he was given "a hometown decision" in his own hometown, as he felt he decisively beat young Spinks. But Spinks is an up-and-coming fighter, and up-and-coming fighters win close fights. When I talked to my barber after the fight, he seemed to accept defeat with some equanimity. What upset him was that the local paper, or the local white paper, as it is seen by most blacks, the *St. Louis Post-Dispatch,* did not cover the fight. It was prominently covered by the *St. Louis American,* the city's black paper. I told him I would write a letter to the editor about that; he appreciated my concern. As things turned out, the fight was mentioned in the *Post-Dispatch* ten days later as part of a roundup of the local boxing scene. My barber's fight earned three paragraphs. It probably wasn't quite what he wanted, but I am sure it made him feel better. After all, a local fighter has only his reputation in his hometown to help him make a living. Nonetheless, I admired the fact that he took so well being unfairly denied something that was so important to him. Most people can't do that.

Gerald Early, "Performance and Reality: Race, Sports, and the Modern World," *The Nation,* August 10–17, 1998, 11–18.

14. Harry Edwards / "The Decline of the Black Athlete"

In 1903 the scholar and activist W. E. B. Du Bois intoned the prophetic words that the problem of the twentieth century would be "the problem of the color line." Before century's end, the preeminent African American historian of his era, John Hope Franklin, lamented that he foresaw the color line as the problem of the twenty-first century as well. After the desegregation of the playing fields during the civil rights revolution, the entry of some black sports figures into positions of ownership and corporate leadership, and the perception by many commentators that African American athletes—as widely admired cultural icons—have helped dissolve the racial antagonism over the last several decades, it comes as grim news indeed that the impact of racism remains the most troubling issue of our time.

As many scholars and journalists have noted, much of the problem lies in the fact that sporting glory (not just in the form of celebrity and fat paychecks) has largely been abstracted from everyday social and economic realities. The fame won by African American athletes may have transformed mainstream culture in significant ways, but it has not had a substantial influence on traditional patterns of income stratification or persuaded police officers to stop racial profiling. Neither has the "mainstreaming" of the top one thousand or so black athletes solved the problems of inner city black communities and the persistent alienation of black male youth.

In the following interview, Harry Edwards takes up the connection between sport and the concerns of the black community at the turn of the twenty-first century. Edwards has been on the front line of black activism in sport since the mid-1960s when he was among the first to advocate a boycott of the Olympic Games in protest of racism and discrimination in the United States. Since that time, he has been a conscientious critic of the ways racism (and sexism) inflect the relationship between sport and American society. One of his most compelling arguments over the years has been that professional sports offered a path too narrow and limited to accommodate the large numbers of ambitious and able black youth who desired to make their way out of impoverished backgrounds and into a new social and economic status. Moreover, he has asserted, that track has diverted black youth from the far more numerous and substantial opportunities afforded by higher education, which requires considerable preparation. To a significant extent, his thesis runs, the arena has become a lure or snare as much as a forum for the display of African American initiative and talent. The "single-minded pursuit of sports fame and fortune," he has written elsewhere, "has spawned an institutionalized triple tragedy in black society: the tragedy of thousands upon thousands of black youths in obsessive pursuit of sports goals that the overwhelming majority of them will never attain; the tragedy of the personal and cultural under-development that afflicts so many successful and unsuccessful black sports aspirants; and the tragedy of cultural and institutional under-development throughout black society at least in some part as a consequence of the drain in talent potential toward sports and away from other vital areas of occupational and career emphasis, such as medicine, law, economics, politics, education, and technical fields."*

In the present document, though, Edwards departs from some of the themes he has long emphasized, just as he parts company with other African American intellectuals, such as Henry Louis Gates Jr. and bell hooks. At one level, he discusses the highest echelons of sport and suggests that a decrease in opportunities for the development of black athletic talent has created a problem for the sporting industry. At a more fundamental level, Edwards wants to make connections between the NBA and the communities of East Oakland or the South Side of Chicago. The black youth who concern Edwards in this piece have not been persuaded that any programs of integrationism will work for them, that any kind of affirmative action has meaning. Instead of being a liability, or harmful distraction, for many black youth who might be spending time in the classroom or library, sports has become a necessary instrument, what

---

* Edwards, "Crisis of Black Athletes," 9. Edwards's autobiography offers considerable insight into his early years as an activist; see *The Struggle That Must Be*.

Harry Edwards (Courtesy Rick Rocamora/ *Colorlines*)

Edwards terms "a hook and a handle" to keep inner-city youth in basketball uniforms instead of prison garb. Where black activists like bell hooks lamented the "hoop dreams" of Arthur Agee and William Gates, here Harry Edwards speaks to the situation of many young males who felt left behind long before Agee and Gates scored their first lay-ups—and to the realities confronting those elders in the African American community who desire to help them.

———

After three decades in the spotlight, as sociology professor at the University of California, and as a consultant to the San Francisco 49ers, Dr. Harry Edwards remains one of the premier activists in sports. Lately, Dr. Edwards has been engaging another heated debate over the role of athletics in the black community. While black athletes have never been more visible or more culturally influential, Edwards now advances the provocative thesis that the "golden age" of black athletes is coming to an end. *Color-Lines* recently asked Edwards exactly what he means. Is he out of touch or on point? You decide.

ColorLines: A student of mine wrote a paper in which he juxtaposed the image of Tommie Smith and John Carlos in 1968 versus that of Charles Barkley and Michael Jordan during the 1992 Olympics—the raised black fist compared to a draping America flag strategically placed to cover up a Reebok label on their sweatsuits. What do these opposing images say about the last thirty years of black sports participation?

Edwards: Thirty years ago there would not have been any issue of them covering the Reebok logo because they would not have had the Nike contract that was in conflict with it. That would have gone to a white athlete. So what this change tells me is that black athletes are sufficiently integrated into the business matrix of sports. That there is something there, a business interest, which they feel obliged to protect.

ColorLines: In a number of spaces you have argued that we are currently witnessing the end of the "golden age of black athletes." Why is the "golden era" of blacks in sports coming to an end?

Edwards: Through societal processes, through institutional erosion, through the degradation of the black athletic pool, through disqualification, judicial procedures and deaths, we have so emaciated the black talent pool that we are beginning to see a drop-off in performance at every level, in all sports where blacks participate in numbers. We are simply disqualifying, jailing, burying, and leaving behind our black athletes, right along with our potential black doctors, black lawyers, and so forth.

Look at high school sports: an increasing number of high schools cannot even field a team. Last year, three San Francisco high schools could not field a football team. A number of years ago, Richmond High, which has produced many great black athletes in the Bay Area, had five people try out for the football team. Even if schools have enough players, they often times don't have the funds to put a team on the field.

You look at boxing and the same things are happening. I remember when you had Ali, Frazier, Ernie Shavers, Ernie Terrell, George Foreman, Floyd Patterson, Buster Mathis, and Sonny Liston. Now, you have Evander Holyfield, basically a puffed-up cruiser weight, and Mike Tyson, who spends more time in trouble out of the ring, when he is not getting in trouble in the ring. Where are the boxers? The boxers are in the cemetery, in jail, in gangs, and on the street. That is where the potential football, basketball, and baseball players are as well.

The talent pool in the black community has been so eroded that when you have a sport that is 80 percent black, like the NFL, or 88 percent, like the NBA, the fall-out is going to show up. In basketball this situation is crystal clear. In 1990, 27 out of 29 teams averaged over 100 points per game. In 1997 only four teams averaged more than 100 points, and last year only one team, the Sacramento Kings, was able to reach that level. Every statistic is down. You see the same statistical decline at the college level. The performance standards are down in free-throw average, points per game, rebound average, assist average.

Why? You just don't have as great an athlete today. We are jailing, burying, and academically disqualifying our potential point guards, wide-receivers, running backs, power forwards, centers, and so forth, at a very early age. If we look at it historically, literally from 1947, when Jackie Robinson broke into the major leagues, to 1997, those 50 years marked the golden age of the black athlete. Now we are seeing a precipitous drop-off, and the reasons are not inside sport; the reasons are in society, which are ultimately reflected in sport.

ColorLines: So what will the next thirty years look like?

Edwards: I think over the next thirty years we are going to continue to see a decline of black athletic participation.

More importantly, I think we are also going to see a phenomenal split within the black community: The black middle-class moving on to become doctors, lawyers, and engineers; the black masses not moving at all, being left behind. That is going to be an explosive situation.

The overwhelming majority of black athletes come out of the lower echelons of black society. I don't think it is accidental when you look at the inordinate number of blacks in jail and the proportionate number of blacks not on athletic teams. You are essentially looking at the same guy. They both have numbers; they are both in uniforms, and they both belong to gangs. Only they call one the Crips or the Bloods, while they call the other the 49ers, Warriors, Athletics, or the Giants. They are all in pursuit of respect. They all, at one level or another, keep score. The parallels are all there. It is the same guy.

But I think what you are looking at over the next thirty years is that the guy in the jail uniform is going to outstrip, in both numbers and impact, the guy in the athletic uniform. Increasingly he is going to be wearing a jailhouse number and a jailhouse uniform, instead of a sports team number and an athletic uniform.

ColorLines: So might the 21st century be the "Golden Age" of white athletics or the "Golden Age" of Latino athletics?

Edwards: I think that ultimately the 21st century will be a global sports age. The world is so small and sports is so international that I think you are going to see the same thing in American sports that you see in basketball and baseball today. When you look at athletes coming from Eastern Europe, Latin America, and other parts of the world, you see the future of sports. Right now, 40 percent of major league baseball players are foreign-born.

More generally, I believe sports are going to change. They are going to take on the hype of professional wrestling to cover the lack of quality of performance. I think sports will be hyped more and more as a business, and less and less as a performance craft. Rules changes will keep scoring up, but you won't see the caliber of players you saw in the past. You will still have the hitting, the dunks, but most importantly you will have the games being hyped and rules being changed, so that points keep going up, fans keep watching the games, and the money keeps rolling in.

ColorLines: Last year, *Sports Illustrated* featured a cover story entitled "What Ever Happened to the White Athlete?" Do you know what has happened to the white athlete?

Edwards: Well, the white athlete over the last 50 years has simply been displaced by a pool of largely untapped athletic talent, generated by a lack of alternative high-prestige occupational opportunities for masses of young black males, and increasingly, females. That is what happened to the white athlete in basketball, football, track, boxing, and to a certain extent in baseball.

But in 95 percent of American sports the white athlete is there in numbers and dominant: swimming, diving, water polo, golf, tennis, badminton, auto racing, horse racing. The white athlete is there in soccer, walking, gymnastics, and all the winter sports in dominant numbers. What happened to the white athlete? The white athlete is there, except in the few sports where blacks have had access.

The other thing that has happened is that blacks have changed the nature of some sports. Black culture, isolated from white society from slavery right up to integration, developed styles of playing sports that whites have had to learn or get out of the sport. So if you'd brought in a point guard who dribbled the ball through his legs and passed the ball behind this back, you better have a guy to guard him. What this generally meant was going into the black community to get someone who had played that kind of ball.

Whites have access to the full spectrum of sports, and the full spectrum of high-prestige occupational positions. They are not channeled into sports in disproportionately high numbers, and white talent is spread out across all sports and occupations. Well, blacks don't typically have those same opportunities.

ColorLines: Several years ago you argued that the black community's "singled-minded pursuit of sports" represented a severe problem within the black community. Looking back on this argument, do you still maintain this position, or have you changed your views on black athletic participation?

Edwards: There is still, thank God, a disproportionately high emphasis on sports achievement in black society, relative to other high-prestige occupational career aspirations. Given what is happening to young black people, who have essentially disconnected from virtually every institutional structure in society, sports may be our last hook and handle. They are unemployed in disproportionately high numbers, and increasingly they are unemployable. They drop out of school in disproportionately high numbers, and now they are not just uneducated and mis-educated, but often times diseducated. They have disengaged even from the black church. They are affiliated with the gangs, not the church. The street is their temple; the gang leader is their pastor. They don't seek the respect of anybody but each other. But they still want to be "like Mike."

That sports emphasis gives us a hook and a handle on them. Through midnight basketball, through Saturday football, or recreational facilities, we can put them back in contact with the clergy, mentors, health workers, counselors, government workers, with people from the economic and corporate sector.

Without that we have no way of getting to them at all, except through police and judicial action. I still maintain that there is a high and inordinate emphasis on sports in the black community. That emphasis has been transmuted, however, by the processes of the "end of the golden age of black athletics" from a liability to a virtue, in a sense that it may provide us with the last hook and handle that we have on a substantial proportion of this generation of young black people.

ColorLines: So you disagree with John Hoberman, whose book *Darwin's Athletes* argues that blacks should get out of sports, because such a singled-minded pursuit of sports has fueled societal racism and, therefore, historically hurt the black community?

Edwards: Yes! *Darwin's Athletes* is a classic case of intellectually picking up the ball and running the wrong way.

You cannot look at sport, where a certain level of opportunity has been opened up, and say that because of the racist spin that white society puts on achievement in that arena, that blacks should desist, not just from valuing that sports participation, from idealizing the people who participate in sports, but that we should get out of it all together. This is like saying, A, whites have cancer, therefore, B, let's treat black folks. The emphasis should be upon why white society puts that racist emphasis upon black sports achievement and, secondly, why is black achievement limited to sports in disproportionately high numbers, and not at least representative across the full spectrum of high-prestige occupational categories? These are the issues that Hoberman should have been dealing with.

ColorLines: What do you think will be the greatest challenge in sports over the next hundred years?

Edwards: Sports always recapitulates society, in terms of its character, dynamics, and the structure of human relations. Just as I believe emphatically that the challenge of the 21st century will be diversity in all of its guises, the challenge in sports is also going to be diversity. We are going to be looking at circumstances where we cannot separate out race from class, gender, sexuality, techno-class status, or age.

I worry about what is going to happen to this society. We are already in a situation where we are expecting children to play games that they cannot afford to watch. They, especially the classes that generate the athletes, can't afford the ticket to get into the stadium; they can't afford money for the pay-per-view. But, even as we attack them, we continue to expect them to be the athletes on our teams. Even as we jail them, even as we disqualify them from schools, even as we revoke the social services that support them, even as we eliminate the affirmative action that brings them to college campuses, we still want them to be on our teams. So as we look at the situation, it becomes very, very clear that we are headed for a set of crises, all of which revolve around diversity in sports, just as in society.

Dave Leonard, "The Decline of the Black Athlete: An Interview with Harry Edwards," *ColorLines* 30 (April 2000): 20–24.

CONCLUSION

Writing in the *Crisis* midway through the 1930s, Roy Wilkins offered a striking set of images to illustrate the relationship between sport and mainstream American culture and consciousness. Critically, Wilkins sought to capture the distinction between elite culture and popular culture in the minds of many Americans, and he did so by using the example of black athletic heroism and its potential "to prove equality." His premise was both simple and significant: then (as now) more people read the sports pages than book reviews. Thus he noted "that a Negro historian or editor or philosopher or scientist or composer or singer or poet or painter is more important than a great athlete." But none of those "worthy individuals" possessed more power or influence than the athlete. "Infinitesimal intellectual America," Wilkins declared rather optimistically, needed no conversion on the race problem:

> It is the rank and file, the ones who never read a book by Du Bois, or heard a lecture by James Weldon Johnson, or scanned a poem by Countee Cullen, or heard a song by Marian Anderson, or waded through a scholarly treatise by Abram L. Harris, Carter Woodson, Charles H. Wesley, or Benjamin Brawley. For those millions, who hold the solution of the race problem in their hands, the beautiful breasting of a tape by Jesse Owens and the thud of a glove on the hand of Joe Louis carry more "interracial education" than all the erudite philosophy ever written on race.*

Wilkins's assertion engaged a range of issues regarding the struggle for equality during the interwar years. What is more, it speaks now to the liberating potential of achievement made in athletic competition. How can we measure racial progress in the realm of sport during the years since the civil rights crusade? Has black athletic success been translated into more expansive opportunities for African Americans to participate fully in the political, social, and economic life of the nation? If not, what are the limitations of sport as an instrument for broad-based social change?

At a distance of two-thirds of a century from Wilkins's *Crisis* article, chroniclers of the African American experience have marked substantial improvements in race relations in the United States, just as they have acknowledged the role of athletic competition in remapping the social landscape. Since the era of Joe Louis and Jesse Owens and the years of Jackie Robinson's breakthrough in sport, the color line has been virtually erased with regard to the playing fields themselves. African Americans participate in a wide array of sports, at all levels of competition. Blacks constitute a dominant presence in high-profile venues: the Olympic stadium as well as the basketball arena, baseball

---

* Wilkins, "Joe Louis and Jesse Owens," 241.

diamond, and football gridiron. Beyond that, we can also point to the leading figures in men's golf and women's professional tennis at the turn of the twenty-first century and note that those sports were for many years not only rigidly segregated but also, because of the exclusive status and substantial expense associated with them, remote from the lives of the majority of African Americans.

Traversing difficult terrain—"the hard road to glory," in Arthur Ashe's ringing phrase—has required considerable sacrifice by black athletes, many of whom recall vividly the challenges they faced. It would be well to remind the present generation about the racism and discrimination that still shadows African American success in many areas of competition. Few observers of the sporting scene would be so smug as to proclaim that the ordeal of integration is over. Yet the huge popularity of big-time sport not just in the United States but around the world has helped make black champions into highly paid celebrities, welcome at the White House after a championship season, encouraged by city hall to participate in civic fund-raising activities, and pursued by sporting goods companies for their endorsements. Some black athletes are more widely recognized, both here and abroad, than most of the nation's leading political figures. This development represents a striking contribution to race pride and a testament to the fact that an increasing number of blacks are making it in America. The image of Michael Jordan in a business suit answering questions about player personnel suggests a key transition in the progress from the playing fields to positions of real authority.

That such images are still remarkable, though, indicates the distance that remains to be traveled in order to make the sporting realm a showcase of equal opportunity in the United States. What is more, although some social commentators have emphasized the point for decades now, our "national pastimes" employ relatively few people—whether as players, or coaches, or managers. The sports industry may be a high-profile, high-profit, high-pay enterprise, but in a market economy the supply of very talented athletes is much greater than the demand—and athletic careers are often brief and physically hazardous. This has become an issue of considerable concern, not merely because of the statistics about job opportunities, but also because many prospective athletes, especially young black athletes, have withdrawn from the classroom and library to make their way in sports and have been exploited by educational institutions at all levels. American popular culture renders the image of the stellar athlete as far more appealing than that of the corporate lawyer or the professor of economics, although preparation for those jobs opens up a much broader pathway to success.

Finally, one other obstacle lies in the way of a more thorough-going progress in American race relations. This is the perception, still largely held in mainstream culture, that black success in sports is exceptional or, even worse, that it derives from some natural ability. It is still the case that an African American man or woman walking through a college or university campus is sometimes mistaken for a member of a varsity team, or for a coach. This attitude may attest to the ways "muscular assimilationism" was a triumphant campaign at one level, but also too narrowly cast to transform prevailing notions of racial difference. Significantly, too, with regard to race relations, there are still many white Americans who project black athletic success *against* achievement in other endeavors. The descendants of the turn-of-the century scientific racists emerged in the early 1990s with "bell curve" charts describing black and white performance on IQ tests—not as an issue that requires social and political correctives but in terms of inherent cognitive differences. More recently, the resurgence of scientific racism has been manifest in bio-determinist, or genetic, explanations for black success in sports. Although evolutionary biologists and geneticists have thoroughly discredited these claims, such racial lore still tends to inflect popular consciousness, representing a considerable impediment to the striving by black Americans for success beyond the athletic arena.

Although there has been much to celebrate in recent years, such issues of concern should also make us wary about the future. At the very least, they should encourage us to examine the history of race relations with greater care and to discuss both the potential role as well as the limitations of sport in transforming the United States into a truly egalitarian society. In a wide-ranging book, *Rituals of Blood*, Orlando Patterson offers an intriguing appraisal of the recent past. "The essence of America's greatness as a culture," he writes, "the undeniable source of its claim to be the originator and propagator of any emerging global culture, is its astonishing capacity not simply to remake itself but to transcend its own limitations—in the process, converting flaws to assets, incorporating the once demonized, making insiders of outsiders, transforming evil into good—and often to do so against the will of its most powerful members."* Ultimately, while it is easy to share the sense of promise conveyed in these words, it also seems important to remember that the sporting experience for many black Americans has long been bound to paradox. In sporting terms, the longer race has not yet been won.

---

* Patterson, *Rituals of Blood*, 244.

BIBLIOGRAPHIC ESSAY AND LIST

Since at least the early nineteenth century, African Americans have participated in sport at various levels of competition and in a wide variety of settings. During the abolitionist crusade and the early campaigns for civil rights in the aftermath of the Civil War, athletic competition was not regarded by racial reformers as a part of the broader political struggle. Yet such competition became over the years an increasingly significant dimension of African American community life as well as a symbol of race pride.

The first person to trace these developments was Edwin Bancroft Henderson, a prominent physical educator and civil rights reformer during the middle years of the twentieth century. He did so initially in his articles about black pioneers in sport or the ordeals faced by African Americans on the playing fields. These appeared in the *Crisis, Opportunity,* and *The Messenger*—among the foremost journals of black commentary during the interwar years. Eventually, at the request of Carter G. Woodson—once dubbed the "father of Negro history"—Henderson wrote the frequently cited *Negro in Sports* (1939, 1949). Several decades later he authored, along with the editors of *Sport* magazine, *The Black Athlete: Emergence and Arrival* (1968). In the genealogy of athletics and activism, Henderson more than anyone else deserves the title "founder of African American sport history."

Henderson's books followed the pattern of several of Woodson's guiding texts: they highlighted black achievement and were meant to inspire African Americans; they sought to demonstrate the substantial contributions of black Americans to the national experience; and they placed those accomplishments within the context of the ongoing struggle against racial discrimination and inequality in American society. Many of the subsequent histories of black athletic participation, while sometimes varying in format and organization from Henderson's works, were also meant to instill a sense of pride and furnish examples of achievement in the face of white oppression. Included among this group are Andrew S. "Doc" Young's *Negro Firsts in Sports* (1963); Arna Bontemps's *Famous Negro Athletes* (1964); Jack Olsen's *Black Athlete: A Shameful Story* (1968); Jack Orr's *Black Athlete: His Story in American History* (1969); Wally Jones and Jim Washington's *Black Champions Challenge American Sports* (1972); Ocania Chalk's *Pioneers of Black Sport* (1975); Art and Edna Rust's *Art Rust's Illustrated History of the Black Athlete* (1985); and Arthur Ashe Jr.'s *Hard Road to Glory* (1988). (Full bibliographical information for all works mentioned in this essay is given in the list below.)

These formative works of scholarship and journalism on the African American experience have more recently informed wide-ranging interpretive texts on the history and sociology of sport. Some of the best works of this type are William J. Baker, *Sports in the Western World* (1988); Allen Guttmann, *A Whole New Ball Game* (1988); John A. Lucas and Ronald A. Smith, *Saga of American Sport* (1978); Benjamin G. Rader, *American Sports* (1983); Randy Roberts and James Olson, *Winning Is the Only Thing* (1989); Elliott J. Gorn and Warren Goldstein, *A Brief History of American Sports* (1993); Douglas A. Noverr and Lawrence E. Ziewacz, *The Game They Played* (1988); Richard O. Davies, *America's Obsession* (1994); Stephen Fox, *Big Leagues* (1994); Steven A. Riess, *Major Problems in American Sport History* (1997); Harry Edwards, *Sociology of Sport* (1973); Jay J. Coakley, *Sport in Society* (6th ed., 1998); Wilbert M. Leonard II, *A Sociological Perspective of Sport* (1993); D. Stanley Eitzen and two books by George H. Sage, *Sociology of North American Sport* (1993) and *Power and Ideology in American Sport* (1988).

Standing apart from the historical surveys and sociology texts are a number of more critical review essays, anthologies, and bibliographical works that provide overviews of African American participation in sport. The most thorough and thought-provoking review essay is Jeffrey T. Sammons's "'Race' and Sport: A Critical, Historical Examination" (1994). Other important works of this genre are David K. Wiggins, "From Plantation to Playing Field" (1986); Manning Marable, "Black Athletes in White Men's Games, 1880–1920" (1973); and Barry D. McPherson, "Minority Group Involvement in Sport" (1974). The best of the anthologies on African American participation in sport are David K. Wiggins, *Glory Bound* (1997); Dana Brooks and Ronald Althouse, *Racism in College Athletics* (2000); Gary Sailes, *African Americans in Sport* (1998); and Gerald Early, *Tuxedo Junction* (1989) and *The Culture of Bruising* (1994). Influential bibliographic works include Lenwood G. Davis and Belinda Daniels, comps., *Black Athletes in the United States* (1983); Dana Brooks and Ronald Althouse, *The African American Athlete Resource Directory* (1996); Lenwood G. Davis, *Joe Louis* (1983); David L. Porter, ed., *African-American Sports Greats* (1995); Laura Janis, "Annotated Bibliography on Minority Women in Athletics" (1985); Bruce L. Bennett, "Bibliography on the Negro in Sports"(1970) and "Supplemental Selected Annotated Bibliography on the Negro in Sports" (1970); and Grant Henry, "A Bibliography Concerning Negroes in Physical Education, Athletics, and Related Fields" (1973).

Important information on African American athletes can also be gleaned from their personal accounts. Although varying in quality, sometimes ghost written, and often fraught with inaccuracies, a number of autobiographies of African American athletes provide crucial insights into their own lives and the role of sport in both the black community and society at large. Some of the most interesting of these autobiographies are Jack A. Johnson, *Jack Johnson Is a Dandy* (1969); Marshall W. "Major" Taylor, *The Fastest Bicycle Rider in the World* (1971); Jackie Robinson, with Alfred Duckett, *I Never Had It Made* (1971); Joe Louis, with Edna and Art Rust Jr., *Joe Louis* (1978); Jesse Owens, with Paul Neimark, *Blackthink* (1970); Bill Russell, as told to William McSweeney, *Go Up for Glory* (1966); Bill Russell, with Taylor Branch, *Second Wind* (1974); Althea Gibson, *I Always Wanted to Be Somebody* (1958); Vincent Matthews, with Neil Amdur, *My Race Be Won* (1974); Woody Strode and Sam Young, *Goal Dust* (1990); Jim Brown, with Myron Cope, *Off My Chest* (1964); Jim Brown, with Steve Delsohn, *Out of Bounds* (1989); Charlie Sifford, with James Gallo, *Just Let Me Play* (1992); Rafer Johnson, with Phillip Goldberg, *The Best That I Can Be* (1998); Muhammad Ali, with Richard Durham, *The Greatest* (1975); Arthur Ashe and Arnold Rampersad, *Days of Grace* (1993); Chet Walker, with Chris Messenger, *Long Time Coming* (1995); Kareem Abdul-Jabbar and Peter Knobler, *Giant Steps* (1983); and Hank Aaron, with Lonnie Wheeler, *I Had a Hammer* (1991).

Recent memoirs tell haunting stories about the persistence of racism in the United States and just as many inspiring tales about the many ways black athletes have surmounted the obstacles that they have faced. In pursuing the historiography of the African American experience in sport, chronology is an instructive guide, for the narrative of black athletic accomplishment has largely followed the opportunities African Americans made for themselves to elaborate sports as a part of a distinctive culture and consciousness and at the same time as a means of claiming civil rights and unqualified participation in the social, economic, and political life of the nation.

The involvement of African Americans in sport prior to the Civil War was limited and sporadic at best. Slaves on farms and large southern plantations were sometimes able to transcend their horrible conditions and realize periods of leisure time as well as find opportunities to participate in recreation and sport. Free blacks nourished a vibrant community life, including participation in various sporting activities. A very select number of African American athletes during this period found success at the highest levels of sport, most notably Tom Molineaux, who fought twice in heavyweight championship bouts. Not unexpectedly, the scholarship on pre–Civil War topics is as limited and sporadic as the level of participation by African American athletes themselves. There are, however, a few studies that provide information on African Americans and sport prior to emancipation. In "The Play of Slave Children in the Plantation Communities of the Old South, 1820–1860" (1980) and "Sport and Popular Pastimes" (1980), David K. Wiggins furnishes insights into the leisure patterns and recreational activities of slaves. Additional information on this topic can be found in Wilma King, *Stolen Childhood* (1995), and Bernard Mergen, *Play and Playthings* (1982). The fighting career of Tom Molineaux, and in some cases that of his mentor Bill Richmond, is analyzed in Michael H. Goodman, "The Moor vs. Black Diamond" (1980); Carl B. Cone, "The Molineaux-Cribb Fight, 1810" (1982); Paul Magriel, "Tom Molineaux" (1951); Dennis Brailsford, *Bareknuckles* (1988); and Elliott J. Gorn, *The Manly Art* (1986).

In the latter half of the nineteenth century a number of elite African American athletes distinguished themselves in predominantly white organized sport at the highest levels of competition. Although much more research needs to be completed on these individuals, a number of important studies provide insights into the interconnection between African American athletes, white athletes, and this country's sport establishment. Jack W. Berryman's "Early Black Leadership in Collegiate Football" (1981) analyzes the involvement of African American football players at Amherst and other predominantly white institutions in Massachusetts. He concludes that a large number of African American football players, such as William H. Lewis and Matthew Bullock, were able to compete at predominantly white colleges in Massachusetts because of that state's more liberalized racial attitudes. David K. Wiggins takes a close look at the careers of Isaac Murphy, the great jockey from Kentucky, and the outstanding Australian boxer Peter Jackson in "Isaac Murphy" (1979) and "Peter Jackson and the Elusive Heavyweight Championship" (1985). Wiggins makes clear that Murphy and Jackson, though from different socioeconomic backgrounds and participants in different sports, both suffered the pangs of racial discrimination in a society steadily moving toward legalized segregation. Edward Hotaling provides detailed information on the earliest African American jockeys in *The Great Black Jockeys* (1999). Based on an impressive number of secondary sources and little-known primary materials, Hotaling tells the fascinating stories of such great riders as Isaac Murphy, Willie Simms, and Jimmy Winkfield. Andrew Ritchie's *Major Taylor* (1988) is a detailed and highly interesting account of the black bicyclist who found athletic success in both this country and foreign climes. Beyond Ritchie's attention to the details of championship cycling, perhaps his greatest contribution is his analysis of Taylor's experiences and race relations in comparative context: France was a very different place for African Americans in many respects. David W. Zang's *Fleet Walker's Divided Heart* (1995) is another intricate account of the triumphs and travails of an African American athlete in the late nineteenth century. Utilizing census records, newspaper accounts, and a number of other primary sources, Zang crafts the complicated story of a man of "mixed blood" who became not only major league baseball's first black player but also, intriguingly, an entrepreneur in America and a member of the back-to-Africa movement.

By 1900, most African American athletes would be excluded from predominantly white organized sport. With the notable exceptions of professional boxing and selected participation in predominantly white college sport and Olympic competition, African Americans were forced to organize their own teams and leagues as a result of Jim Crow laws and hardening racial policies. The most famous and most written about of these separate sporting organizations were the black baseball teams and leagues that sprang up in various parts of the country. Michael E. Lomax's "Black Baseball's First Rivalry" (1997) and "Black Entrepreneurship in the National Pastime" (1998) are important studies of baseball in the black community. So too is Lomax's expansive work on sport and economic self-help, *Operating by Any Means Necessary* (2003). Larry R. Gerlach takes a fascinating look at the first white American to play in the Negro Leagues in his "Baseball's Other 'Great Experiment'" (1998). Robert W. Peterson's classic study *Only the Ball Was White* (1970) has withstood the test of time and provides detailed information on the players and teams in black baseball. One of the significant contributions of Peterson's work was his reliance on theretofore little-used black newspapers. John Holway's *Voices from the Great Negro Baseball Leagues* (1975) and *Blackball Stars* (1988) and Stephen Banker's *Black Diamonds* (1989) provide interesting first-hand accounts of those who participated in black baseball. Both Donn Rogosin's *Invisible Men* (1987) and Mark Ribowsky's *Complete History of the Negro Leagues* (1995) offer expansive accounts of black baseball teams and players. Phil Dixon and Patrick J. Hannigan's *Negro Baseball Leagues* (1992) and Bruce Chadwick's *When the Game Was Black and White* (1992) present not only ex-quisitely rendered photographs in large format but also important analyses of black baseball. Neil Lanctot's *Fair Dealing and Clean Playing* (1994) is a relatively little known but valuable study of baseball and the economics of black entrepreneurship. G. Edward White offers significant insights into the development of black baseball in his *Creating the National Pastime* (1996). Janet Bruce's *Kansas City Monarchs* (1985) is a thoughtful and detailed case study of one of black baseball's most famous teams. William Brashler's *Josh Gibson* (1978) and Mark Ribowsky's *Power and the Darkness* (1996) and *Don't Look Back* (1994) are biographies of two of the best and most colorful players in black baseball, Josh Gibson and Satchel Paige. Rob Ruck's *Sandlot Seasons* (1987) remains the most innovative and impressive study in this field. It examines various black sporting organizations in Pittsburgh, including the highly successful Pittsburgh Crawfords and Homestead Grays, though perhaps Ruck's greatest contribution is his discussion of Cum Posey and Gus Greenlee, two of several great black entrepreneurs of sport still awaiting full biographies. For several memoirs see Buck O'Neil, with Steve Wulf and David Conrads, *I Was Right on Time* (1996) and Frazier Robinson, *Catching Dreams* (2000).

Far fewer scholarly studies have been completed on other professional sports in the African American community. Like the sport history field in general, football and basketball in the black community have received relatively little coverage from academicians and other writers. There are some exceptions, however. Rob Ruck's "Soaring above the Sandlots" (1982), an essay included in his *Sandlot Seasons,* is a rare look at an all-black football team, the Garfield Eagles. The essay is particularly good in illustrating how the Eagles contributed to a sense of racial pride and helped bring Pittsburgh's black community together to share in the excitement of sport. The two most famous black basketball teams, the Harlem Globetrotters and the New York Renaissance Five, are given space in Robert W. Peterson's *Cages to Jump Shots* (1990) and Nelson George's *Elevating the Game* (1992). Both authors place the Rens and the Globetrotters within the context of African American culture just as they assess the roles played by Robert Douglas and Abe Saperstein, the founders and organizers of the two clubs. Gerald R. Gems's "Blocked Shot" (1995) is an astute analysis of the growth of basketball in Chicago's black community.

Studies of amateur sport in the African American community are not much more plentiful than those about professional football and basketball. Information on interscholastic athletics is limited, with the notable exception of the data furnished on the famous Crispus Attucks High School basketball team in Randy Roberts's *But They Can't Beat Us!* (1999); Richard Pierce's "More than a Game" (2000); and Troy Paino's "Hoosiers in a Different Light" (2001). The works dealing with sport and historically black colleges are somewhat more numerous. Limited but worthwhile information on this topic can be found in such standard institutional histories as Clarence A. Bacote's *Story of Atlanta University* (1969); Benjamin Brawley's *History of Morehouse College* (1917); Rayford Logan's *Howard University, The First Hundred Years* (1969); Joe Richardson's *History of Fisk University* (1980); and George Woolfolk's *Prairie View* (1962). Three works intended for general readers that furnish information on various aspects of sport at historically black colleges are O. K.

Davis's *Grambling's Gridiron Glory* (1983); Michael Hurd's *Black College Football, 1892–1992* (1993); and Ted Chambers's *The History of Athletics and Physical Education at Howard University* (1986).

One view of African American women athletes and historically black colleges is provided in Gwendolyn Captain's "Enter Ladies and Gentlemen of Color" (1991). A more richly textured and insightful examination of African American women basketball players at one historically black college is provided in Rita Liberti's "'We Were Ladies, We Just Played Basketball Like Boys'" (1999). Liberti uses personal interviews and a host of other primary materials to explore the role of basketball among African American women at Bennett College and the changing interconnections between gender and class in American society. Liberti's work dovetails nicely with several chapters devoted to the black experience in Pamela Grundy's *Learning to Win* (2001).

A study that examines the ideology of sport and historically black colleges is Patrick B. Miller's "'To Bring the Race Along Rapidly'" (1995). Utilizing an impressive blend of secondary and primary sources emanating from the black community, Miller juxtaposes the quest for winning seasons at historically black colleges and the goal of assimilation and racial uplift promoted by "race men" like W. E. B. Du Bois.

The significance of sport in fostering African American community spirit and the struggle to raise the profile of black athletic accomplishment during the era of segregation remains a fertile field for historians to explore. Perhaps because of the fairly accessible source material and the fascination with interracial athletic contests, many scholars and journalists have, to date, concentrated on those African American athletes who triumphed in predominantly white organized sport at the national and international levels of competition during the first half of the twentieth century. Few athletes have fascinated scholars more than Jack Johnson, the great heavyweight champion who stirred considerable controversy as much by his refusal to acquiesce to the norms of the dominant culture as by his success in the ring. William H. Wiggins places Johnson within the context of hero types in African American folklore with his path-breaking article "Jack Johnson as Bad Nigger" (1971). Wiggins provides another interesting look at Johnson in his study "Boxing's Sambo Twins" (1988). This study offers an impressive analysis, not just of Johnson but of the interconnection between sport, race, and popular culture. Al-Tony Gilmore's *Bad Nigger!* (1975) is a study of public reaction to Johnson that owes much to the earlier work of Wiggins. Lawrence W. Levine's *Black Culture and Black Consciousness* (1977) and Gail Bederman's *Manliness and Civilization* (1995) provide insightful analysis of Johnson within the context of an American society obsessed with race and the meanings of masculinity. Randy Roberts's *Papa Jack* (1983) is the best full-scale biography of Johnson. Utilizing previously unused court documents from the National Archives and taking a far more critical approach to Johnson's autobiography than had previous scholars, Roberts weaves a fascinating story of Johnson's ring triumphs, personal life, and struggles against the U.S. government.

Far less controversial than Johnson were Jesse Owens and Joe Louis, two of the most renowned African American athletes in history. Owens, who achieved fame first at East Technical High in Cleveland, then at Ohio State University, and finally at the 1936 Berlin Olympics, has received relatively little attention from academicians. Although his extraordinary athletic exploits were accomplished under enormously trying circumstances, Owens has never captured the imagination of scholars. Fortunately, the one scholarly biography of Owens is an extremely well researched and superbly written study that furnishes substantial insight into Owens's mercurial career, especially after the Berlin Olympics. William J. Baker, in *Jesse Owens* (1986), recounts Owens's life from his earliest days in Alabama up through his four gold medal–winning performances in 1936 and in later years as a public speaker and goodwill ambassador. Drawing from the autobiographies Owens wrote with Paul Neimark, as well as a host of personal interviews and additional primary sources, Baker shatters several myths surrounding Owens's life and describes the philosophical differences between the famous Olympic hero and the younger breed of African American athletes of the late 1960s and early 1970s who were espousing a belief in black power and disrupting the "sacred" institution of sport.

Unlike Owens, Joe Louis has been the focus of several scholarly articles and books. Historians have been enthralled by Louis, a man who achieved heroic status in the African American community through his great triumphs in the ring against both black and white fighters. Anthony O. Edmonds provides an interesting look at the symbolism inherent in Louis's second fight with Max Schmeling in his "Second Louis-Schmeling Fight" (1973). Edmonds offers a much broader interpretation of Louis as cultural symbol in his *Joe Louis* (1973). This work, which depends heavily on Alexander J. Young's 1968 doctoral dissertation, "Joe Louis, Symbol," depicts the various responses to Louis as a boxer, African American, and cultural symbol. Jeffrey T. Sammons develops an intriguing analysis of the southern response to Louis in his "Boxing as a Reflection of Society" (1983). Sammons adds even more information on Louis and other black boxers, including Muhammad Ali, in his expansive study *Beyond the Ring* (1988). Al-Tony Gilmore's "The Myth, Legend and Folklore of Joe Louis" (1983) and Dominic J. Capeci Jr. and Martha Wilkerson's "Multifarious Hero" (1983) are two highly interpretative essays that emphasize Louis's role as a black boxer in racially torn American society. Chris Mead's *Champion* (1985) is perhaps the best and most thorough biography of Louis. The book, which began as a Yale senior thesis, examines Louis's life and career in great detail and with not a little passion. In addition to the above works, useful information on Louis can be found in such books as Gerald Astor's *And a Credit to His Race* (1974); Joe Louis Barrow Jr. and Barbara Munder's *Joe Louis: Fifty Years an American Hero* (1988); and Richard Bak's *Joe Louis: The Great Black Hope* (1996).

Ranging beyond the pantheon of black athletic heroes, historians have also engaged the experiences of African Americans who competed in predominantly white college sport between the two world wars. Through the use of NAACP documents, black and white newspapers, interviews, and a wide variety of archival sources, scholars have chronicled the triumphs of and the racial discrimination encountered by the select number of African American athletes who participated in college sport at such well-known institutions as Ohio State, Michigan, Harvard, Syracuse, and the University of California at Los Angeles (UCLA). The earliest study on this topic was John Behee's *Hail to the Victors!* (1974). Behee provides an insightful examination of Willis Ward, DeHart Hubbard, Cazzie Russell, and the other outstanding African American athletes who brought fame to the playing fields of the University of Michigan. David K. Wiggins's "Prized Performers but Frequently Overlooked Students" (1991) casts black athletic participation on predominantly white university campuses within a broad framework. Patrick B. Miller's "Harvard and the Color Line" (1991) relates the story of a Harvard lacrosse player who was denied the opportunity to compete against the U.S. Naval Academy on account of his color. The controversy occurred in 1941 and spilled over from athletic policy to discussions of politics and the war effort. More expansively, Miller examines the social and cultural background for changing racial negotiations and intersectional athletic contests in "Slouching toward a New Expediency" (1999). Donald Spivey and Tom Jones's "Intercollegiate Athletic Servitude" (1975) examines the role of African American athletes at the University of Illinois over a period of thirty-five years. Spivey's "End Jim Crow in Sports" (1988) is an interpretative case study of a significant student protest against New York University, which had barred Leonard Bates from competing against southern institutions because of the "gentlemen's agreements" that had long characterized northern participation in segregationist practices. John M. Carroll's *Fritz Pollard* (1992) is a good biography of the famous black running back from Brown University whose career included the early years of what would become the National Football League and various entrepreneurial ventures.

It would not be Pollard, however, or any of the legendary figures from Negro League baseball, who would be cast in the starring role in the desegregation of professional sports in the United States. The black heroes of diamond and gridiron, track oval and basketball arena, as well as those who made their marks in the ring, all played critical parts in opening up the sporting realm, but the process was subtle and never sure. With great skill and passion, a number of scholars have charted the uneven process of erasing the color line in professional sport. Not surprisingly, the reintegration of major league baseball, because of the sport's enormous popularity and its characterization as America's national pastime and most democratic of all games, has garnered the most attention from academicians. David K. Wiggins traces the nearly twelve-year campaign waged by the sportswriter Wendell Smith and the black *Pittsburgh Courier-Journal* against organized baseball's exclusionary policies in his "Wendell Smith, the *Pittsburgh Courier-Journal,* and the Campaign to Include Blacks in Organized Baseball, 1933–1945" (1983). Ronald A. Smith provides an interpretation of the differing philosophies of Jackie Robinson and Paul Robeson, including the latter's part in the struggle to end discrimination in baseball, in "The Paul Robeson–Jackie Robinson Saga and a Political Collision" (1979). William Simons discusses how the press perceived the shattering of the color line in baseball in "Jackie Robinson and the American Mind" (1985). In "'I Never Want to Take Another Trip like This One'" (1997), Chris Lamb describes the hardships Robinson experienced during his first spring training. Stephen H. Norwood and Harold Brackman chronicle very nicely the Jewish involvement in the signing of Robinson in their "Going to Bat for Jackie Robinson" (1999). Arnold Rampersad furnishes an intimate look at the life and career of Robinson in his *Jackie Robinson: A Biography* (1997). Joseph Dorinson and Joram Warmund provide a number of interesting essays on Robinson and baseball in their edited work *Jackie Robinson: Race, Sports, and the American Dream* (1998). Growing out of presentations given at Long Island University to commemorate the fiftieth anniversary of Robinson's signing with the Dodgers, the essays are generally quite informative, well written, and original. Jules Tygiel provides the definitive study on Jackie Robinson, the integration process, and the role of African American ballplayers in the 1950s in *Baseball's Great Experiment* (1983). He also has edited a nice collection of writings on Robinson's life and career, *The Jackie Robinson Reader* (1997). The less-publicized story of Larry Doby and the integration of the American League is told quite well in Joseph T. Moore's *Pride against Prejudice* (1988). Finally, Jack E. Davis marshals impressive evidence to offer a revisionist note in his look at the elimination of segregation at southern spring training sites in "Baseball's Reluctant Challenge" (1992).

The shattering of the color line in other professional sports has received far less coverage. By and large, scholars have not been as interested in uncovering the facts and recounting the integration process in football, basketball, and other sports. There are, however, notable exceptions to this general trend. Charles K. Ross provides much information and important details about the struggles of African Americans in their attempts to break the color line in professional football in his *Outside the Lines* (1999). Gerald R. Gems adroitly recounts the reintegration of professional football in his little-known study "Shooting Stars" (1988). Well written and full of important information, Gems's essay makes clear that the reintegration of professional football was very complex and the result of various political maneuvers. Thomas G. Smith's case study "Civil Rights on the Gridiron" (1987) and his more broadly based "Outside the Pale" (1988) detail the reintegration of professional football in an interesting fashion.

Studies on the integration of professional basketball are even less plentiful than those on football, but information on this topic can be found in Nelson George's *Elevating the Game* (1992) and Charles Salzberg's *From Set Shot to Slam Dunk* (1987). There is important information on the integration of professional golf in Calvin Sinnette's *Forbidden Fairways* (1998); John H. Kennedy's

A Course of Their Own (2000); Pete McDaniel's *Uneven Lies* (2000); and Marvin P. Dawkins and Graham C. Kinloch's *African American Golfers during the Jim Crow Era* (2000).

How the color line was breached in intercollegiate sport has been of great interest to some historians. Primarily, that interest has revolved around the integration of southern institutions and conferences. An early scholarly study on this topic is by Joan Paul and her colleagues, "The Arrival and Ascendance of Black Athletes in the Southeastern Conference, 1966–1980" (1984). The authors provide rich detail concerning the process of integration in one of the most famous yet rigidly segregated conferences in the country. Richard Pennington's *Breaking the Ice* (1987) is an informative, if not overly interpretative, work on the integration of the gridiron sport in the old Southwest Conference. Ronald E. Marcello's "The Integration of Intercollegiate Athletics in Texas" is a solid case study of integration at North Texas State College. Marked by its use of oral interviews, the study is largely concerned with the effects that integration of the North Texas athletics program had on the school's overall racial climate. No one, however, has contributed so much to the understanding of the complex processes of desegregation in college sport as Charles H. Martin, most notably in five solidly written and thoroughly researched essays: "Jim Crow in the Gymnasium" (1993), "Racial Change and Big-Time College Football in Georgia" (1996), "Integrating New Year's Day" (1997), "The Rise and Fall of Jim Crow" (1999), and "The Color Line in Midwestern College Sports, 1890–1960" (2002). These articles make clear that the integration process in southern college sport took place rather slowly and was fraught with much tension and controversy.

What is clear from Martin's careful studies is that the desegregation of college sports in the South was a critical component of civil rights reform. Just as significantly, African American athletes participated in a range of activist causes, from integration to the black power movement, during the late 1960s and early 1970s. Although not always politically savvy and sometimes reluctant to speak out on controversial issues for fear of jeopardizing their careers, African American athletes increasingly voiced their complaints about the racism in sport and the larger society. No African American athlete came to symbolize the struggle for equality more than Muhammad Ali, the charismatic and controversial fighter who inspired members of his race and a large portion of the dominant culture through his boxing exploits, membership in the Nation of Islam, and refusal to enter military service. Gerald Early's *Muhammad Ali Reader* (1998) is an eye-opening collection of writings about the meanings of Ali as boxer, African American hero, and avatar of a new age of racial understanding. Included in the collection are the writings of such people as Leroi Jones, Jackie Robinson, Norman Mailer, Joyce Carol Oates, and George Plimpton. Thomas Hauser, author of the well-known *Black Lights* (1986), is also the author of a nicely written book based on interviews with many of Ali's closest friends and associates, entitled *Muhammad Ali: His Life and Times* (1991). David Remnick in *King of the World* (1998) adds some detail to Sammons's discussions of Ali in *Beyond the Ring* and is particularly good at unraveling the complexity of Ali's life within the contexts of the boxing subculture and American society more generally. Perhaps the most important work on Ali, however, is *Muhammad Ali: The People's Champ* (1995), edited by Elliott J. Gorn. A collection of seven essays originally given as presentations at a special conference at Miami University in Ohio, the book is primarily concerned with Ali as a cultural symbol and what he meant to Americans—both black and white, boxing aficionados and nonfans alike—during one of the most tumultuous periods in this nation's history. Jose Torres's *Sting Like a Bee* (1971) and Ali A. Mazuri's "Boxer Muhammad Ali and Soldier Idi Amin as International Political Symbols" (1977) help enrich the subject.

Regarding the politics of sport, African American athletes exerted their greatest influence on the civil rights movement on predominantly white college campuses and in Olympic competition. Influenced by the examples set by professional athletes such as Ali, Bill Russell, Jim Brown, and others, young African American athletes staged protests and revolts at white institutions; additionally they took highly visible stands during both the 1968 and 1972 Olympic Games in an effort to expose the racial discrimination in sport and American society. David K. Wiggins examines the black athletic revolts on several predominantly white college campuses in "The Year of Awakening" (1992) and "The Future of College Athletics Is at Stake" (1988). Adolph Grundman explores the origins of black athletic involvement in the civil rights struggle in "Image of Intercollegiate Sports and the Civil Rights Movement" (1979). Donald Spivey analyzes African American activism in various Olympic protests in "Black Consciousness and Olympic Protest Movements, 1964–1980" (1985). Harry Edwards offers a largely firsthand account of the black athletic protests in *The Revolt of the Black Athlete* (1969). Two books that provide important insights into African American athletes and the black power movement are Richard Lapchick's *Broken Promises* (1984) and William Van Deburg's *New Day in Babylon* (1992).

Less visible than the male athletes who debated Olympic boycotts and campus protests, African American women athletes nevertheless continued to win victories in an increasing number of sports. Although no less race conscious than their male counterparts, African American women athletes did not become prominent figures in civil rights activism until later in the 1960s. One explanation for this is that, before the era of Title IX, women's sports did not receive the same media attention. Another reason is that many black male leaders of the movement (like their white counterparts) did not give full credit to the contributions of women as activists. This was a constant source of controversy during the civil rights era and beyond. Scholars have been slow to analyze the intersection of gender, race, and sport or to assess the record of black women's triumphs and travails in athletics, but they have recently begun to conduct thorough and sophisticated research on African American women athletes. Patricia Vertinsky and Gwendolyn Captain explore the historical construction of racist and sexualized myths surrounding African American female athletes in their insightful essay "More Myth than History" (1998). Susan Birrell provides an interesting sociological analysis of African American women and sport in "Women of Color, Critical Autobiography, and Sport" (1990). Linda Williams takes a look at the black press and African American women athletes in "Sportswomen in Black and White" (1994). Cindy Himes Gissendanner furnishes interpretive essays on sport and African American women athletes in her "African American Women and Competitive Sport, 1920–1960" (1993) and her "African American Women Olympians" (1996). Susan Cahn provides perhaps the most complete and thought-provoking analysis of African American women athletes in her well-known book *Coming on Strong* (1994). Through the use of oral interviews and other primary and secondary sources, Cahn discusses the status of African American women athletes in the black community and the influence of both race and gender on their sport participation. Yvonne Smith's "Women of Color in Society and Sport" (1992); Michael D. Davis's *Black American Women in Olympic Track and Field* (1992); Ellen Gerber and others, *The American Woman in Sport* (1974); Tina Sloan-Green and others, *Black Women in Sport* (1981); and Alfred Dennis Mathewson's "Black Women, Gender Equity and the Function at the Junction" (an article in a special 1996 issue of the *Marquette Sports Law Journal* entitled "Symposium on Race and Sports") are other works on African American women athletes that are worth consulting.

The last several years have brought what some commentators have termed an overrepresentation of African American athletes in certain sports and an underrepresentation in others. African American athletes have also dominated certain playing positions within team sports while finding fewer opportunities at others. It is apparent, moreover, that although the more blatant forms of racial discrimination have been eliminated from sport, African Americans continue to suffer racial slights and have limited access to coaching, managerial, and administrative positions within both college sport and professional sport. (For an ongoing survey of these issues, one might consult Northeastern University's Center for the Study of Sport in Society, which issues an annual report grading the opportunities offered by the sports industry for minorities and women. See the Web site at <http://www.sportinsociety.org>.)

Such issues as equal opportunity on the playing fields have been explored through a number of important qualitative and quantitative studies. John Loy and Joseph McElvoque's "Racial Segregation in American Sport" (1970); Donald Ball's "Ascription and Position" (1973); Greg Jones and others, "A Log-linear Analysis of Stacking in College Football" (1987); Wilbert M. Leonard's "Stacking in College Basketball" (1987); and Mark Lavoie's "Economic Hypothesis of Positional Segregation" (1989) are sociological studies dealing with "stacking" in sport, the overrepresentation of African Americans in certain playing positions. Gerald Scully's "Economic Discrimination in Professional Sports" (1973); Wilbert M. Leonard's "Salaries and Race/Ethnicity in Major League Baseball" (1989); and Robert Jiobu's "Racial Inequality in a Public Arena" (1988) are studies that explore race-based economic discrimination in sport. Timothy Davis's "Myth of the Superspade" (1995) and "African American Student-Athletes" (1996) and Robert Sellers's "African American Student-Athletes" (2000) examine the experiences of African American athletes in contemporary college sport. Dana D. Brooks and Ronald C. Althouse in their essay "African American Head Coaches and Administrators" (2000) discuss the status of black coaches in American sport.

Some of the most intriguing studies to have emerged in recent years deal with a distinctive black athletic style, not merely the moves African Americans bring to the basketball court, for instance, but also the cultural forms they have introduced during post-touchdown performances and other occasions for celebration. Richard Majors in "Cool Pose" (1990) argues that the "expressive lifestyle behaviors" (or what he terms the "cool pose") articulated by African American athletes have allowed them to realize, among other things, a sense of dignity, to gain recognition and prestige, and to exercise some control in a society marked by racial oppression and discrimination. Majors correctly points out, however, that the "cool pose" adopted by African American athletes can be "self-defeating" because it often takes away from a devotion to those pursuits that would challenge male hierarchies and white domination. Michael Eric Dyson's "Be Like Mike?" (1993) argues that Michael Jordan is a cultural hero who exemplifies the best in athletic skill and performance, expresses elements of style unique to African American culture, and is a product of market forces characteristic of a capitalistic society. Dyson notes that Jordan's approach to basketball reflects the "will to spontaneity," "stylization of the performed self," and "edifying deception" that are central to African American cultural expression. David Andrews furthers our understanding of Jordan in "The Fact(s) of Michael Jordan's Blackness" (1996) and his special issue of *Sociology of Sport Journal* entitled "Deconstructing Michael Jordan" (1996). James LeFlore's "Athleticism among American Blacks" (1982) claims that African American athletes, like many other blacks, interpret their social system through a specific and generalized pool of information. Therefore, they tend to gravitate toward those sports in which the larger society expects them to participate while avoiding those sports that foster disapproval from the white majority. William S. Rudman's "Sport Mystique in Black Culture" (1986); Richard Lapchick's *Five Minutes to Midnight: Race and Sport in the 1990's* (1991); and Larry E. Jordan's "Black Markets and Future Superstars" (1981) are other studies that examine various aspects of race, social structure, and sport participation patterns.

Black expressive style on the athletic field, leading to rules changes by the NFL, NBA, and NCAA, has generated considerable discussion concerning racial representation and role modeling. But those issues have not been nearly so controversial as the question of innate racial differences and sport performances. In the wake of alarming statements made by Al Campanis and Jimmy "the Greek" Snyder during the late 1980s about an alleged black athletic superiority (and an attendant lack of "the necessities" to manage or coach), a number of scholars and writers from a variety of disciplines have written about what mainstream culture has seemingly come to perceive as blacks' innate physiological gifts. David K. Wiggins provides a historical overview of the subject in his "'Great Speed but Little Stamina'" (1989). Through an examination of important secondary materials, Wiggins traces the debate from the latter half of the nineteenth century to the late twentieth century, bringing to light the views of such noteworthy individuals as Montague Cobb, Edwin Bancroft Henderson, and Harry Edwards. Laurel R. Davis examines the topic in "The Articulation of Difference" (1990). Well written and cogently analyzed, Davis's study delineates the reasons for the dominant culture's obsession with drawing links between supposedly innate physical gifts and black athletic performance.

Writing in the aftermath of the "bell curve" furor, John Hoberman examined the issue of the emphasis placed on sport, especially by African American intellectuals, in his *Darwin's Athletes* (1997). A work that has drawn much interest from academicians and the lay public alike, Hoberman's book offers a valuable introduction to the history and literature on medicine and biological differences, just as it delineates some features in the debate over black athletic superiority. Though the book attempts to come to terms with the broader ideological developments and policy ramifications bound to the concept of "race"—in sports studies as well as IQ studies—it largely seems to be a lecture about the responsibilities of black leaders for guiding African Americans into the most productive paths of community formation and economic development. That all but a handful of geneticists, evolutionary biologists, and physical anthropologists have in the last generation abandoned the notion of "race" as having any significant meaning in scientific terms is one of the themes raised by Patrick B. Miller in his "Anatomy of Scientific Racism" (1998). Another of Miller's concerns is that the racial lore that informed the measuring of bodies—like the attempts to measure intelligence—has long been used to reinforce hierarchies of subordination and to justify the oppression of people of color, not just in the present-day United States but throughout the modern history of imperialism and colonialism. The recent spate of bio-determinist polemics merely perpetuates the same kinds of stereotypes, he argues, as the more virulently racist works of the late nineteenth and early twentieth centuries. To a significant degree, Miller's essay anticipates Jon Entine's journalistic foray into racial science in *Taboo* (2000). Entine's argument, closely resembling some of the pronouncements advanced by J. Phillipe Rushton in *Race, Evolution, and Behavior* (1995), is that black athletes have achieved enormous success because of their superior genetic endowment. Seizing upon the records set by Kenyan distance runners while ignoring much of the recent literature on evolutionary biology, racial theory, and the social and cultural explanations for high-level athletic performance, Entine slickly packages biology as athletic destiny.

Despite the condescension that suffuses Hoberman's work on race and sport or the charlatanry that emerges from Entine's, an increasing number of cultural commentators have embraced the notion that athletic accomplishment has long represented a significant dimension of black culture and consciousness. In recent years, black theorists and social critics such as Orlando Patterson in *Rituals of Blood* (1999) and Paul Gilroy in *Against Race* (2000) have commented on the significance of sport in the construction of black masculinity and the overall imaging of people of color by mainstream cultures. What is more, an increasing number of history textbooks surveying African American life and race relations have incorporated discussions of sport into their broader analysis. These works, while offering basic information on black athletes, do something more: they demonstrate the enormous importance with which black Americans have endowed sport over the last century and they suggest the role that achievement in athletic competition played as part of the larger civil rights crusade. James Oliver Horton and Lois E. Horton, *Hard Road to Freedom* (2001), and Darlene Clark Hine, William C. Hine, and Stanley Harrold, *The African-American Odyssey* (2000), stand out in this regard; so too do Robin D. G. Kelley and Earl Lewis, eds., *To Make Our World Anew* (2000); and John Hope Franklin and Alfred A. Moss Jr., *From Slavery to Freedom* (2000). See also Henry Louis Gates Jr. and Cornel West, *The African-American Century* (2000).

In sum, the literature on African American athletes has increased in quantity and (generally) improved in quality over the last several decades. Scholars from various disciplinary perspectives, many of them taking their cues initially from Edwin Bancroft Henderson, have examined the involvement of African Americans in sport, both behind the walls of segregation and in integrated athletic contests at different levels of competition. Although much study remains to be done on this topic, it has been broadened significantly by painstaking research and analysis. In the process, we have realized a greater understanding of both race and American society.

Aaron, Hank, with Lonnie Wheeler. *I Had a Hammer: The Hank Aaron Story.* New York: Harper-Collins, 1991.

Abdul-Jabbar, Kareem, and Peter Knobler. *Giant Steps: The Autobiography of Kareem Abdul-Jabbar.* New York: Bantam, 1985.

Abrahams, Roger D. *Singing the Master: The Emergence of African American Culture in the Plantation South.* New York: Pantheon, 1992.

Ali, Muhammad, with Richard Durham. *The Greatest: My Own Story.* New York: Random House, 1975.

Allen, Maury. *Jackie Robinson: A Life Remembered.* New York: Franklin Watts, 1987.

Andrews, David. "The Fact(s) of Michael Jordan's Blackness: Excavating a Floating Racial Signifier." *Sociology of Sport Journal* 13 (1996): 125–58.

———, ed. "Deconstructing Michael Jordan: Reconstructing Postindustrial America." Special edition. *Sociology of Sport Journal* 13 (1996).

Andrews, William L., Frances Smith Foster, and Trudier Harris, eds. *The Oxford Companion to African American Literature.* New York: Oxford University Press, 1997.

Armstrong, Henry. *Gloves, Glory and God: An Autobiography.* Westwood, N.J.: Fleming H. Revell, 1956.

Arroyo, Eduardo. *"Panama" Al Brown.* Paris: J. C. Lattès, 1982.

Ashe, Arthur. "Don't Tell Me How to Think." *Black Sports* 5 (August 1975): 35–37.

———. *A Hard Road to Glory: A History of the African American Athlete.* 3 vols. New York: Warner Books, 1988.

———. "Send Your Children to the Libraries." *New York Times,* February 6, 1977, 2.

Ashe, Arthur, and Arnold Rampersad. *Days of Grace: A Memoir.* New York: Knopf, 1993.

Ashe, Arthur, with Frank Deford. *Portrait in Motion.* Boston: Houghton Mifflin, 1975.

Ashe, Arthur, with Neil Amdur. *Off the Court.* New York: New American Library, 1981.

Astor, Gerald. *And a Credit to His Race: The Hard Life and Times of Joseph Louis Barrow.* New York: Saturday Review Press, 1974.

Axthelm, Pete. *The City Game.* New York: Harper and Row, 1970.

Azevedo, Mario, and Jeffrey T. Sammons. "Contributions in Science, Business Film, and Sports." In *Africana Studies: A Survey of Africa and the African Diaspora,* edited by Mario Azevedo, 353–60. Durham, N.C.: Carolina Academic Press, 1993.

Bacote, Clarence A. *The Story of Atlanta University: A Century of Service, 1865–1965.* Atlanta: Atlanta University Press, 1969.

Bak, Richard. *Joe Louis: The Great Black Hope.* New York: Taylor, 1996.

Baker, William J. *Jesse Owens: An American Life.* New York: Free Press, 1986.

———. "Kings and Diamonds: Negro League Baseball in Film." *Journal of Sport History* 25 (Summer 1998): 303–8.

———. *Sports in the Western World.* Urbana: University of Illinois Press, 1988.

Ball, Donald. "Ascription and Position: A Comparative Analysis of 'Stacking' in Professional Football." *Canadian Review of Sociology and Anthropology* 10 (May 1973): 97–113.

Banker, Stephen. *Black Diamonds: An Oral History of Negro League Baseball.* Princeton: Visual Education Corporation, 1989.

Bankes, James. *The Pittsburgh Crawfords: The Lives and Times of Black Baseball's Most Exciting Team!* Dubuque, Ia.: Wm. C. Brown, 1991.

Barnett, C. Robert. "'The Finals': West Virginia's Black Basketball Tournament, 1925–1957." *Goldenseal* 9 (Summer 1983): 30–36.

Barrow, Joe Louis, Jr., and Barbara Munder. *Joe Louis: Fifty Years an American Hero.* New York: McGraw-Hill, 1988.

Bass, Amy. *Not the Triumph but the Struggle: The 1968 Olympics and the Making of the Black Athlete.* Minneapolis: University of Minnesota Press, 2002.

Bass, Amy B. "Flag on the Field: The Popular Construction of the Black Athlete." Ph.D. diss., State University of New York at Stony Brook, 1999.

Bederman, Gail. *Manliness and Civilization: A Cultural History of Gender and Race in the United States, 1880–1917.* Chicago: University of Chicago Press, 1995.

Behee, John. *Hail to the Victors! Black Athletes at the University of Michigan.* Ann Arbor, Mich.: Swink-Tuttle Press, 1974.

Bennett, Bruce L. "Bibliography on the Negro in Sports." *Journal of Health, Physical Education, and Recreation* 41 (September 1970): 77–78.

———. "Supplemental Selected Annotated Bibliography on the Negro in Sports." *Journal of Health, Physical Education, and Recreation* 41 (September 1970): 71.

Bennett, Lerone, Jr. *Before the Mayflower: A History of Black America.* Chicago: Johnson, 1982.

Berkow, Ira. *The Du Sable Panthers: The Greatest, Blackest, Saddest Team from the Meanest Street in Chicago.* New York: Athaeneum, 1978.

———. "The Minority Quarterback." In Berkow, *How Race Is Lived in America: Pulling Together, Pulling Apart,* 189–210. New York: Holt, 2001.

———. "They're Still Waiting for an NBA Payday: Choosing Draft over College Can Backfire." *New York Times,* June 24, 2001.

Berry, Bonnie, and Earl Smith. "Race, Sport, and Crime: The Misrepresentation of African Americans in Team Sports and Crime." *Sociology of Sport Journal* 17 (2000): 171–97.

Berryman, Jack W. "Early Black Leadership in Collegiate Football: Massachusetts as a Pioneer." *Historical Journal of Massachusetts* 9 (June 1981): 17–28.

Betts, John R. *America's Sporting Heritage: 1850–1950.* Reading, Mass.: Addison-Wesley, 1974.

Billet, Bret L., and Lance J. Formwalt. *America's National Pastime: A Study of Race and Merit in Professional Baseball.* Westport, Conn.: Praeger, 1995.

Birrell, Susan. "Women of Color, Critical Autobiography, and Sport." In *Sport, Men, and the Gender Order: Critical Feminist Perspectives,* edited by Michael A. Messner and Donald F. Sabo, 185–99. Champaign, Ill.: Human Kinetics, 1990.

Birrell, Susan, and Cheryl Cole, eds. *Women, Sport, and Culture.* Champaign, Ill.: Human Kinetics, 1993.

Blassingame, John W., ed. *Slave Testimony: Two Centuries of Letters, Speeches, Interviews, and Autobiographies.* Baton Rouge: Louisiana State University Press, 1977.

Bolland, Katherine, and John C. Walter. "The Black Quarterback." In *Proceedings of the North American Society for Sport History,* 90. University Park, Pa.: North American Society for Sport History, 1990.

Bontemps, Arna. *Famous Negro Athletes.* New York: Dodd, Mead, 1964.

Borish, Linda. "The Robust Woman and the Muscular Christian: Catharine Beecher, Thomas Higginson, and Their Vision of American Society, Health and Physical Activities." *International Journal of the History of Sport* (September 1987): 139–53.

Borries, Betty Earle. *Isaac Murphy, Kentucky's Record Jockey.* Berea, Ky.: Kentucky Imprints, 1988.

Boskin, Joseph. *Sambo: The Rise and Demise of an American Jester.* New York: Oxford University Press, 1986.

Boyd, Todd. *Am I Black Enough for You? Popular Culture from the 'Hood and Beyond.* Bloomington: Indiana University Press, 1997.

Brailsford, Dennis. *Bareknuckles: A Social History of Prize-Fighting.* Cambridge, Mass.: Lutterworth Press, 1988.

Brashler, William. *Josh Gibson: A Life in the Negro Leagues.* New York: Harper and Row, 1978.

Brawley, Benjamin. *History of Morehouse College.* Atlanta: Morehouse College, 1917.

Brooks, Dana D., and Ronald C. Althouse. *The African American Athlete Resource Directory.* Morgantown, W.Va.: Fitness Information Technology, 1996.

———. "African American Head Coaches and Administrators: Progress But . . . ?" In *Racism in College Athletics: The African American Athlete's Experience,* edited by Brooks and Althouse, 85–117. 2d ed. Morgantown, W.Va.: Fitness Information Technology, 2000.

———, eds. *Racism in College Athletics: The African American Athlete's Experience.* 2d ed. Morgantown, W.Va.: Fitness Information Technology, 2000.

Broome, Richard. "The Australian Reaction to Jack Johnson, Black Pugilist, 1907–09." In *Sports in History: The Making of Modern Sporting History,* edited by Richard Cashman and Michael McKerman, 343–63. St. Lucia, Australia: University of Queensland Press, 1979.

Brown, Jim. "How I Play Fullback." *Sports Illustrated,* September 26, 1960, 53–57.

Brown, Jim, with Myron Cope. *Off My Chest.* New York: Doubleday, 1964.

Brown, Jim, with Steve Delsohn. *Out of Bounds.* New York: Kensington, 1989.

Brown, Roscoe C. "The 'Jock-Trap': How the Black Athlete Gets Caught." In *Sport Psychology: An Analysis of Athlete Behavior,* edited by William F. Straub, 195–98. Ithaca, N.Y.: Movement Publications, 1978.

Brown, Roscoe C., Jr. "A Commentary on Racial Myths and the Black Athlete." In *Social Problems in Athletics,* edited by Daniel M. Landers, 168–73. Urbana: University of Illinois Press, 1976.

Brown, Sterling A. "Athletics and the Arts." In *The Integration of the Negro into American Society,* edited by E. Franklin Frazier, 117–24. Washington, D.C.: Howard University Press, 1951.

Bruce, Janet. *The Kansas City Monarchs: Champions of Black Baseball.* Lawrence: University Press of Kansas, 1985.

Bryant, Howard. *Shut Out: A Story of Race and Baseball in Boston.* New York: Routledge, 2002.

Cahn, Susan. *Coming on Strong: Gender and Sexuality in Twentieth-Century Women's Sport.* New York: Free Press, 1994.

Capeci, Dominic J., Jr., and Martha Wilkerson. "Multifarious Hero: Joe Louis, American Society, and Race Relations during World Crisis, 1935–1945." *Journal of Sport History* 10 (Winter 1983): 5–25.

Captain, Gwendolyn. "Enter Ladies and Gentlemen of Color: Gender, Sport, and the Ideal of African American Manhood and Womanhood during the Late Nineteenth and Early Twentieth Centuries." *Journal of Sport History* 18 (Spring 1991): 81–102.

Carroll, John M. *Fritz Pollard: Pioneer in Racial Advancement.* Urbana: University of Illinois Press, 1992.

———, ed. *The Black Military Experience in the American West.* New York: Liveright, 1971.

Cashmore, Ernest. *Black Sportsmen.* London: Routledge and Kegan Paul, 1982.

Chadwick, Bruce. *When the Game Was Black and White: The Illustrated History of Baseball's Negro Leagues.* New York: Abbeville, 1992.

Chalberg, John C. *Rickey and Robinson: The Preacher, the Player, and America's Game.* Wheeling, Ill.: Harlan Davidson, 2000.

Chalk, Ocania. *Black College Sport.* New York: Dodd, Mead, 1976.

————. *Pioneers of Black Sport: The Early Days of the Black Professional Athlete in Baseball, Basketball, Boxing, and Football.* New York: Dodd, Mead, 1975.

Chambers, Ted. *The History of Athletics and Physical Education at Howard University.* Washington, D.C.: Vantage, 1986.

Chass, Mark. "Campanis Is Out: Racial Remarks Cited by Dodgers." *New York Times,* April 9, 1987, B13–B14.

Coakley, Jay J. *Sport in Society: Issues and Controversies.* 6th ed. Boston: Irwin/McGraw-Hill, 1998.

Cobb, W. Montague. "Does Science Favor Negro Athletes?" *Negro Digest* 5 (May 1947): 74–77.

"Colored Athletes in the Famous Penn Relays." *The Competitor* 1 (June 1920): 73–75.

Cone, Carl B. "The Molineaux-Cribb Fight, 1810: Wuz Tom Molineaux Robbed?" *Journal of Sport History* 9 (Winter 1982): 83–91.

Corbett, Doris, and William Johnson. "The African American Female in Collegiate Sport: Sexism and Racism." In *Racism in College Athletics: The African American Athletic Experience,* edited by Dana D. Brooks and Ronald C. Althouse, 199–225. 2d ed. Morgantown, W.Va.: Fitness Information Technology, 2000.

Cottrell, Robert Charles. *The Best Pitcher in Baseball: The Life of Rube Foster, Negro League Giant.* New York: New York University Press, 2001.

Crawford, Scott A. G. M. "Tiger Flowers." In *Historical Dictionary of African Americans in Sport,* edited by David K. Wiggins. Armonk, N.Y.: M. E. Sharpe, forthcoming.

Creedon, Pamela J., ed. *Women, Media and Sport: Challenging Gender Values.* Thousand Oaks, Calif.: Sage, 1994.

Cronon, E. David. *Black Moses: The Story of Marcus Garvey and the Universal Negro Improvement Association.* Madison: University of Wisconsin Press, 1969.

Daniel, Walter C. *Black Journals of the United States.* Westport, Conn.: Greenwood, 1982.

Davies, Richard O. *America's Obsession: Sports and Society since 1945.* New York: Harcourt Brace, 1994.

Davis, Jack E. "Baseball's Reluctant Challenge: Desegregating Major League Spring Training Sites, 1961–1964." *Journal of Sport History* 19 (Summer 1992): 144–62.

Davis, John P. "The Negro in American Sports." In *The American Negro Reference Book,* edited by John P. Davis, 775–825. Englewood Cliffs, N.J.: Prentice-Hall, 1966.

Davis, Laurel R. "The Articulation of Difference: White Preoccupation with the Question of Racially Linked Genetic Differences among Athletes." *Sociology of Sport Journal* 7 (1990): 179–87.

Davis, Laurel R., and Othello Harris. "Race and Ethnicity in U.S. Sports Media." In *Media Sport,* edited by Lawrence R. Wenner, 154–69. New York: Routledge, 1998.

Davis, Lenwood G. *Joe Louis: A Bibliography of Articles, Books, Pamphlets, Records, and Archival Material.* Westport, Conn.: Greenwood, 1983.

Davis, Lenwood G., and Belinda Daniels, comps. *Black Athletes in the United States: A Bibliography of Books, Articles, Autobiographies, and Biographies on Professional Black Athletes, 1800–1981.* Westport, Conn.: Greenwood, 1983.

Davis, Michael D. *Black American Women in Olympic Track and Field: A Complete Illustrated Reference.* Jefferson, N.C.: McFarland, 1992.

Davis, O. K. *Grambling's Gridiron Glory: Eddie Robinson and the Tigers Success Story.* Rustin, La.: M&M Printing, 1983.

Davis, Timothy. "African American Student-Athletes: Marginalizing the NCAA Regulatory Structure." *Marquette Sports Law Journal* 6 (Spring 1996): 199–227.

————. "The Myth of the Superspade: The Persistence of Racism in College Athletics." *Fordham Urban Law Journal* 22 (November 3, 1995): 615–98.

————. "Race, Law and College Athletics." In *Racism in College Athletics: The African American*

Athlete's Experience, edited by Dana D. Brooks and Ronald C. Althouse, 245–65. 2d ed. Morgantown, W.Va.: Fitness Information Technology, 2000.

Dawkins, Marvin P., and Graham C. Kinloch. *African American Golfers during the Jim Crow Era.* Westport, Conn.: Greenwood Publishing Group, 2000.

Dent, David J. *In Search of Black America: Discovering the African American Dream.* New York: Simon and Schuster, 2000.

Dixon, George. *A Lesson in Boxing.* George Dixon and Co., 1893.

Dixon, Phil, and Patrick J. Hannigan. *The Negro Baseball Leagues: A Photographic Essay.* Mattituck, N.Y.: Ameon, 1992.

Dorinson, Joseph, and Joram Warmund, eds. *Jackie Robinson: Race, Sports, and the American Dream.* Armonk, N.Y.: M. E. Sharpe, 2002.

Duberman, Martin B. *Paul Robeson.* New York: Knopf, 1988.

Dunham, Elizabeth D. "Physical Education of Women at Hampton Institute." *Southern Workman* 53 (April 1924): 161–68.

Duval, Earl H., Jr. "An Historical Analysis of the Central Intercollegiate Athletic Association and Its Influence on the Development of Black Intercollegiate Athletics: 1912–1984." Ph.D. diss., Kent State University, 1985.

Durham, Philip, and Everett L. Jones. *The Negro Cowboys.* Lincoln: University of Nebraska Press, 1965.

Dyreson, Mark. "American Ideas about Race and Olympic Races from the 1890s to the 1950s: Shattering Myths or Reinforcing Scientific Racism?" *Journal of Sport History* 28 (Summer 2001): 173–215.

Dyson, Michael Eric. "Be Like Mike? Michael Jordan and the Pedagogy of Desire." *Cultural Studies* 7 (January 1993): 64–72.

———. "Crossing over Jordan." In Dyson, *Between God and Gangsta Rap: Bearing Witness to Black Culture,* 56–59. New York: Oxford University Press, 1996.

Early, Gerald. *The Culture of Bruising: Essays on Prizefighting, Literature, and Modern American Culture.* New York: Ecco Press, 1994.

———. *The Muhammad Ali Reader.* New York: Ecco Press, 1998.

———. *Tuxedo Junction: Essays on American Culture.* New York: Ecco Press, 1989.

Edmonds, Anthony O. *Joe Louis.* Grand Rapids: Eerdmans, 1973.

———. "Second Louis-Schmeling Fight: Sport, Symbol, and Culture." *Journal of Popular Culture* 7 (Summer 1973): 42–50.

Edwards, Harry. "Educating Black Athletes." In *Sport and Higher Education,* edited by Donald Chu, Jeffrey O. Seagrave, and Beverly J. Becker, 373–84. Champaign, Ill.: Human Kinetics, 1985.

———. "Crisis of Black Athletes on the Eve of the 21st Century." *Society* 37 (March/April 2000): 9–13.

———. "The Olympic Project for Human Rights: An Assessment Ten Years Later." *Black Scholar* 10 (March–April 1979): 2–8.

———. *The Revolt of the Black Athlete.* New York: Free Press, 1969.

———. *Sociology of Sport.* Homewood, Ill.: Dorsey Press, 1973.

———. "Sport within the Veil: Triumphs, Tragedies, and Challenges of African American Involvement." *Annuals of the American Academy of Political and Social Sciences* 44 (1979): 116–27.

———. *The Struggle That Must Be: An Autobiography.* New York: Macmillan, 1980.

Eisen, George, and David K. Wiggins, eds. *Ethnicity and Sport in North American History and Culture.* Westport, Conn.: Greenwood, 1994.

Eitzen, D. Stanley, and David C. Sanford. "The Segregation of Blacks By Playing Position in Football: Accident or Design? *Social Science Quarterly* 55 (March 1975): 948–59.

Eitzen, D. Stanley, and George H. Sage. *Sociology of North American Sport.* Dubuque, Ia.: Brown and Benchmark, 1993.

Elias, Robert, ed. *Baseball and the American Dream: Race, Class, Gender and the National Pastime.* Armonk, N.Y.: M. E. Sharpe, 2001.

Entine, John. *Taboo: Why Black Athletes Dominate Sports and Why We Are Afraid to Talk About It.* New York: Public Affairs Press, 2000.

Ewing, Addison A. "William H. Lewis." *Amherst Graduate Quarterly* 38 (February 1949): 118.

Fabre, Michel. *The Unfinished Quest of Richard Wright.* Translated by Isabel Barzun. New York: Morrow, 1973.

Fairclough, Adam. *Race and Democracy: The Civil Rights Struggle in Louisiana, 1915–1972.* Athens: University of Georgia Press, 1995.

Falkner, David. *Great Time Coming: The Life of Jackie Robinson from Baseball to Birmingham.* New York: Simon and Schuster, 1995.

Farish, Hunter Dickinson, ed. *Journal and Letters of Philip Vickers Fithian, 1773–1774: A Plantation Tutor of the Old Dominion.* Williamsburg, Va.: Williamsburg Restoration Historical Studies, 1943.

Farr, Finis. *Black Champion: The Life and Times of Jack Johnson.* Greenwich, Conn.: Fawcette 1969.

Festle, Mary Jo. *Playing Nice: Politics and Apologies in Women's Sports.* New York: Columbia University Press, 1996.

Fetter, Henry D. "Robinson in 1947: Measuring an Uncertain Impact." In *Jackie Robinson: Race, Sports, and the American Dream,* edited by Joseph Dorinson and Joram Warmund, 183–92. Armonk, N.Y.: M. E. Sharpe, 1998.

Fisher, Anthony Leroy. "The Best Way out of the Ghetto." *Phi Delta Kappan* 60 (November 1978): 240.

Fisk Collection. *Unwritten History of Slavery: Autobiographical Accounts of Negro Ex-Slaves.* Nashville: Social Science Institute, Fisk University, 1945.

Fitzpatrick, Frank. *And the Walls Came Tumbling Down: Kentucky, Texas Western, and the Game That Changed American Sports.* New York: Simon and Schuster, 1999.

Fleischer, Nat. *Black Dynamite: The Story of the Negro in the Prize Ring from 1782 to 1938.* New York: Ring Magazine, 1947.

Fletcher, Marvin E. *The Black Soldier and Officer in the United States Army, 1891–1917.* Columbia: University of Missouri Press, 1974.

———. "The Black Soldier Athlete in the United States Army, 1890–1916." *Canadian Journal of History of Sport and Physical Education* 3 (December 1971): 16–26.

Fox, Stephen. *Big Leagues: Professional Baseball, Football, and Basketball in National Memory.* New York: Morrow, 1994.

Franklin, John Hope, and Alfred A. Moss Jr. *From Slavery to Freedom: A History of African Americans.* 8th ed. New York: Knopf, 2000.

Fredrickson, George. *The Black Image in the White Mind: The Debate on Afro-American Character and Destiny, 1817–1914.* New York: Harper and Rowe, 1971.

Frey, Darcy. *The Last Shot: City Streets, Basketball Dreams.* Boston: Houghton Mifflin, 1994.

Gaddy, Charles. *An Olympic Journey: The Saga of an American Hero, Leroy T. Walker.* Glendale, Calif.: Griffin Publishing Group, 1998.

Gaines, Kevin K. *Uplifting the Race: Black Leadership, Politics, and Culture in the Twentieth Century.* Chapel Hill: University of North Carolina Press, 1996.

Gardner, Robert, and Dennis Shortelle. *The Forgotten Players: The Story of Black Baseball in America.* New York: Walker, 1993.

Gates, Henry Louis, Jr., and Cornel West. *The African-American Century: How Black Americans Have Shaped Our Country.* New York: Free Press, 2002.

Gems, Gerald R. "Blocked Shot: The Development of Basketball in the African American Community of Chicago." *Journal of Sport History* 22 (Summer 1995): 135–48.

———. "Shooting Stars: The Rise and Fall of Blacks in Professional Football." *Professional Football Research Association Annual Bulletin* (1988): 1–16.

Genovese, Eugene D. *Roll, Jordan, Roll: The World the Slaves Made.* New York: Vintage Books, 1976.

George, Nelson. *Elevating the Game: Black Men and Basketball.* New York: HarperCollins, 1992.

Gerber, Ellen, et al. *The American Woman in Sport.* Reading, Mass.: Addison-Wesley, 1974.

Gerlach, Larry R. "Baseball's Other 'Great Experiment': Eddie Klep and the Integration of the Negro Leagues." *Journal of Sport History* 25 (Fall 1998): 453–81.

Gibson, Althea. *I Always Wanted to Be Somebody.* New York: Harper, 1958.

Gildea, William. *Where the Game Matters Most.* Boston: Little, Brown, 1997.

Gilmore, Al-Tony. *Bad Nigger! The National Impact of Jack Johnson.* Port Washington, N.Y.: Kennikat, 1975.

———. "The Myth, Legend and Folklore of Joe Louis: The Impressions of Sport on Society." *South Atlantic Quarterly* 82 (Summer 1983): 256–68.

Gilroy, Paul. *Against Race: Imagining Political Culture beyond the Color Line.* Cambridge, Mass.: Belknap Press of Harvard University Press, 2000.

Giovanni, Nikki. "Black Is the Noun." In *Lure and Loathing: Essays on Race, Identity, and the Ambivalence of Assimilation,* edited by Gerald Early, 113–26. New York: Penguin, 1993.

Gissendanner, Cindy Himes. "African American Women and Competitive Sport, 1920–1960." In *Women, Sport and Culture,* edited by Susan Birrell and Cheryl Cole, 81–92. Champaign, Ill.: Human Kinetics, 1993.

———. "African American Women Olympians: The Impact of Race, Gender, and Class Ideologies, 1932–1968." *Research Quarterly for Exercise and Sport* 67 (June 1996): 172–82.

Goodman, Michael H. "The Moor vs. Black Diamond." *Virginia Cavalcade* 29 (Spring 1980): 164–73.

Gorn, Elliott J. *The Manly Art: Bare-Knuckle Prize Fighting in America.* Ithaca, N.Y.: Cornell University Press, 1986.

———, ed. *Muhammad Ali: The People's Champ.* Urbana: University of Illinois Press, 1995.

Gorn, Elliott J., and Warren Goldstein. *A Brief History of American Sports.* New York: Hill and Wang, 1993.

Gottlieb, Moshe. "The American Controversy over the Olympic Games." *American Jewish Historical Quarterly* 61 (March 1972): 181–213.

Gould, Stephen Jay. *The Mismeasure of Man.* New York: Norton, 1981.

Grant, William G. "Marshall Walter Taylor, The World Famous Bicycle Rider." *Colored American Magazine* (September 1902): 336–45.

Graves, Earl. "The Right Kind of Excellence." *Black Enterprise* 10 (November 1979): 4.

Graves, Joseph L., Jr. *The Emperor's New Clothes: Biological Theories of Race at the Millennium.* New Brunswick, N.J.: Rutgers University Press, 2001.

Greene, Bob. *Hang Time: Days and Dreams with Michael Jordan.* New York: Doubleday, 1992.

Greenfield, Jeff. "The Black and White Truth about Basketball." *Esquire,* October 1975, 170–71, 248.

Grombach, John W. *The Saga of Sock: A Complete Story of Boxing.* New York: A. S. Barnes, 1949.

Grundman, Adolph. "Image of Intercollegiate Sports and the Civil Rights Movement: A Historian's View." *Arena Review* 3 (October 1979): 17–24.

Grundy, Pamela. "From Amazons to Glamazons: The Rise and Fall of North Carolina Women's Basketball, 1920–1960." *Journal of American History* 87 (June 2000): 112–46.

———. *Learning to Win: Sports, Education, and Social Change in Twentieth-Century North Carolina.* Chapel Hill: University of North Carolina Press, 2001.

Gusky, Earl. "Two Friends, 10 Events: Johnson Outlasted Yang 30 Years Ago in Olympic Decathlon." *Los Angeles Times,* June 6, 1990, C1, C13.

Guttmann, Allen. *A Whole New Ball Game: An Interpretation of American Sports.* Chapel Hill: University of North Carolina Press, 1988.

Halberstam, David. *Playing for Keeps: Michael Jordan and the World He Made.* New York: Random House, 1999.

Hales, A. G. *Black Prince Peter: The Romantic Career of Peter Jackson.* London: Wright and Brown, 1931.

Harlan, Louis. *Booker T. Washington: The Making of a Black Leader, 1856–1902.* New York: Oxford University Press, 1972, 1983.

———, ed. *The Booker T. Washington Papers.* Vols. 2, 3, 10, 12, 13. Urbana: University of Illinois Press, 1972–89.

Harlan, Louis R. "Booker T. Washington and the *Voice of the Negro,* 1904–1907." *Journal of Southern History* 45 (February 1979): 45–62.

Harris, Francis C. "Paul Robeson: An Athlete's Legacy." In *Paul Robeson: Artist and Citizen,* edited by Jeffrey C. Stewart, 35–47. New Brunswick, N.J.: Rutgers University Press and the Paul Robeson Cultural Center, 1998.

Harris, Reed. *King Football: The Vulgarization of the American College.* New York: Vanguard, 1932.

Harrison, C. Keith. "Black Athletes at the Millennium." *Society* 37 (March/April 2000): 35–39.

Harrison, C. Keith, and Brian Lampman. "The Image of Paul Robeson: Role Model for the Student and Athlete." *Rethinking History* 5 (2001): 117–30.

Hart-Davis, Duff. *Hitler's Games: The 1936 Olympics.* New York: Harper and Row, 1986.

Hartmann, Douglas. *Golden Ghettos: Race, Culture, and the Politics of the 1968 African American Olympic Protest Movement.* Chicago: University of Chicago Press, forthcoming.

———. "The Politics of Race and Sport: Resistance and Domination in the 1968 African American Olympic Protest Movement." In *Everyday Inequalities,* edited by Jodi O'Brien and Judith A. Howard, 337–54. Cambridge: Blackwell, 1998.

———. "Rethinking the Relationships between Sport and Race in American Culture: Golden Ghettos and Contested Terrain." *Sociology of Sport Journal* 17 (2000): 229–53.

Hauser, Thomas. *The Black Lights: Inside the World of Professional Boxing.* New York: McGraw-Hill, 1986.

———. *Muhammad Ali: His Life and Times.* New York: Simon and Schuster, 1991.

Hawkins, Billy. *The New Plantation: The Internal Colonization of Black Student Athletes.* Winterville, Ga.: Sakiki, 2000.

Heintze, Michael R. *Private Black Colleges in Texas, 1865–1954.* College Station: Texas A&M University Press, 1985.

Henderson, Edwin B. *The Black Athlete: Emergence and Arrival.* New York: Publishers Company, 1968.

———. *The Negro in Sports.* Washington, D.C.: Associated Publishers, 1939, 1949.

———. "Physical Education and Athletics among Negroes." In Bruce L. Bennett, ed., *Proceedings of the Big Ten Symposium on the History of Physical Education and Sport.* Chicago: Athletic Institute, 1972, 67–83.

Henderson, Edwin B., and William A. Joiner, eds. *Official Handbook: Inter-Scholastic Athletic Association of Middle Atlantic States.* New York: American Sports Publishing, 1910–13.

Henry, Grant. "A Bibliography Concerning Negroes in Physical Education, Athletics, and Related Fields." *Journal of Health Physical Education, and Recreation* 44 (May 1973): 65–70.

Herskovits, Melville J. *The Myth of the Negro Past.* New York: Harper, 1941.

Hietala, Thomas R. *The Fight of the Century: Jack Johnson, Joe Louis, and the Struggle for Racial Equality.* Armonk, N.Y.: M. E. Sharpe, 2002.

Higginson, Thomas Wentworth. *Army Life in a Black Regiment.* 1869; New York: Norton, 1984.

Hill, Patrick. "The Harlem Globetrotters' Cold War: Basketball, Black Performance and the (Ex) Sporting of American Empire, 1950–1963." Ph.D. diss., University of Michigan, 2002.

Hine, Darlene Clark, William C. Hine, and Stanley Harrold. *The African-American Odyssey.* Englewood Cliffs, N.J.: Prentice Hall, 2000.

Hoberman, John. *Darwin's Athletes: How Sport Has Damaged Black America and Preserved the Myth of Race.* Boston: Houghton Mifflin, 1997.

Holt, Thomas. *The Problem of Race in the Twenty-first Century.* Cambridge, Mass.: Harvard University Press, 2001.

Holway, John. *Blackball Stars: Negro League Pioneers.* Westport, Conn.: Meckler, 1988.

———. *Voices from the Great Negro Baseball Leagues.* New York: Dodd, Mead, 1975.

Hoose, Philip M. *Necessities: Racial Barriers in American Sports.* New York: Random House, 1989.

Horton, James Oliver, and Lois E. Horton. *Hard Road to Freedom: The Story of African America.* New Brunswick, N.J.: Rutgers University Press, 2001.

Hotaling, Edward. *The Great Black Jockeys: The Lives and Times of the Men Who Dominated America's First National Sport.* Rocklin, Calif.: Forum, 1999.

Howe, Arthur. "Two Racers and What They Symbolize." *Southern Workman* (October 1932): 387.

Hurd, Michael. *Black College Football, 1892–1992: One Hundred Years of History, Education, and Pride.* Virginia Beach, Va.: Donning, 1993.

Jable, J. Thomas. "Sport in Philadelphia's African American Community, 1865–1900." In *Ethnicity and Sport in North American History and Culture,* edited by George Eisen and David K. Wiggins, 157–76. Westport, Conn.: Greenwood, 1994.

Janis, Laura. "Annotated Bibliography on Minority Women in Athletics." *Sociology of Sport Journal* 2 (September 1985): 266–74.

Jarvie, Grant, ed. *Sport, Racism and Ethnicity.* London: Falmer Press, 1991.

Jennings, Susan. "As American as Hot Dogs, Apple Pie and Chevrolet: The Desegregation of Little League Baseball." *Journal of American Culture* 4 (1981): 81–91.

Jiobu, Robert. "Racial Inequality in a Public Arena: The Case of Professional Baseball." *Social Forces* 67 (1988): 524–34.

Johnson, Jack A. *Jack Johnson Is a Dandy: An Autobiography.* New York: Chelsea House, 1969.

Johnson, Rafer, with Philip Goldberg. *The Best That I Can Be: An Autobiography.* New York: Random House, 1998.

Jones, Greg, et al. "A Log-linear Analysis of Stacking in College Football." *Social Science Quarterly* (March 1987): 70–83.

Jones, Norma R. "Robert Hayden." In *Dictionary of Literary Biography,* edited by Trudier Harris, 76:75–88. Detroit: Gale, 1988.

Jones, Wally, and Jim Washington. *Black Champions Challenge American Sports.* New York: David McKay, 1972.

Jones, William H. *Recreation and Amusement among Negroes in Washington.* 1927; Westport, Conn.: Negro Universities Press, 1970.

Joravsky, Ben. *Hoop Dreams: A True Story of Hardship and Triumph.* New York: HarperPerennial, 1996.

Jordan, Larry E. "Black Markets and Future Superstars: An Instrumental Approach to Opportunity in Sport Forms." *Journal of Black Studies* 11 (March 1981): 289–306.

Jordan, Pat. *Black Coach.* New York: Dodd, Mead, 1971.

Joyner-Kersee, Jackie, and Sonja Steptoe. *A Kind of Grace: The Autobiography of the World's Greatest Female Athlete.* New York: Warner Books, 1997.

Kahn, Lawrence M. "Discrimination in Professional Sports: A Survey of the Literature." *Industrial and Labor Relations Review* 44 (April 1991): 395–418.

Katz, Michael, and Thomas Sugrue, eds. *W. E. B. Du Bois, Race and the City: The Philadelphia Negro and Its Legacy.* Philadelphia: University of Pennsylvania Press, 1998.

Katz, William Loren. *The Black West: A Documentary and Pictorial History.* Garden City, N.Y.: Anchor Press/Doubleday, 1973.

Kaye, Andrew M. "'Battle Blind': Atlanta's Taste for Black Boxing in the Early Twentieth Century." *Journal of Sport History* 28 (Summer 2001): 217–32.

———. "The Canonization of Tiger Flowers: A Black Hero for the 1920s." *Borderlines: Studies in American Culture* 5 (1998): 142–59.

Kelley, Robin D. G. *Race Rebels: Culture, Politics, and the Black Working Class.* New York: Free Press, 1994.

Kelley, Robin D. G., and Earl Lewis, eds. *To Make Our World Anew: A History of African Americans.* New York: Oxford University Press, 2000.

Kennedy, John H. *A Course of Their Own: A History of African American Golfers.* Kansas City, Mo.: Andrews McMeel, 2000.

Keown, Tim. *Skyline: One Season, One Team, One City.* New York: Macmillan, 1994.

Kimball, Richard Ian. "Beyond the Great Experiment: Integrated Baseball Comes to Indianapolis." *Journal of Sport History* 26 (Spring 1999): 142–62.

King, C. Richard, and Charles Fruehling Springwood. *Beyond the Cheers: Race as Spectacle in College Sport.* Albany: State University of New York Press, 2001.

King, Peter. "Jim Brown." *Sports Illustrated,* September 19, 1994, 57–58.

King, Wilma. *Stolen Childhood: Slave Youth in Nineteenth-Century America.* Bloomington: Indiana University Press, 1995.

Kirkpatrick, Curry. "The Unlikeliest Homeboy." *Sports Illustrated* December 23, 1991, 70–75.

Kirsch, George B. *The Creation of American Team Sports: Baseball and Cricket, 1838–72.* Urbana: University of Illinois Press, 1989.

Krugel, Mitchell. *Jordan: The Man, His Words and His Life.* New York: St. Martin's, 1994.

Krüger, Arnd. "Fair Play For American Athletes: A Study in Anti-Semitism." *Canadian Journal of History of Sport and Physical Education* 9 (May 1978): 42–57.

Lacy, Sam, with Moses J. Newson. *Fighting for Fairness: The Life Story of Hall of Fame Sportswriter Sam Lacy.* Centreville, Md.: Tidewater, 1998.

LaFeber, Walter. *Michael Jordan and the New Global Capitalism.* New York: Norton, 2000.

Lamb, Chris. "I Never Want to Take Another Trip Like This One: Jackie Robinson's Journey to Integrate Baseball." *Journal of Sport History* 24 (Summer 1997): 177–91.

Lanctot, Neil. *Fair Dealing and Clean Playing: The Hilldale Club and the Development of Black Professional Baseball, 1910–1932.* Jefferson, N.C.: McFarland, 1994.

Lane, Roger. *Roots of Violence in Black Philadelphia, 1860–1900.* Cambridge, Mass.: Harvard University Press, 1986.

———. *William Dorsey's Philadelphia and Ours: On the Past and Future of the Black City in America.* New York: Oxford University Press, 1991.

Lansbury, Jennifer H. "'The Tuskegee Flash' and 'The Slender Harlem Stroker': Black Women Athletes on the Margin." *Journal of Sport History* 28 (Summer 2001): 233–52.

Lapchick, Richard. *Broken Promises: Racism in American Sports.* New York: St. Martin's, 1984.

———. *Five Minutes to Midnight: Race and Sport in the 1990's.* Lanham, Md.: Madison Books, 1991.

———. *The Politics of Race and International Sport: The Case of South Africa.* Westport, Conn.: Greenwood, 1975.

Lavoie, Mark. "The Economic Hypothesis of Positional Segregation: Some Further Comments." *Sociology of Sport Journal* 6 (1989): 163–66.

Lawson, Hal A. "Physical Education and Sport in the Black Community: The Hidden Perspective." *Journal of Negro Education* 48 (Spring 1979): 187–95.

Leckie, William H. *The Buffalo Soldiers: A Narrative of the Negro Cavalry in the West.* Norman: University of Oklahoma Press, 1967.

Lee, George L. *Interesting Athletes: Black American Sports Heroes.* New York: Ballantine, 1976.

LeFlore, James. "Athleticism among American Blacks." In *Social Approaches to Sport,* edited by Robert M. Pankin, 104–21. Toronto: Associated University Presses, 1982.

Lemon, Meadowlark, with Jerry B. Jenkins. *Meadowlark.* Nashville: Nelson, 1987.

Leonard, Wilbert M., II. "Salaries and Race/Ethnicity in Major League Baseball: The Pitching Component." *Sociology of Sport Journal* 6 (1989): 152–62.

———. *A Sociological Perspective of Sport.* New York: Macmillan, 1993.

———. "Stacking in College Basketball: A Neglected Analysis." *Sociology of Sport Journal* 4 (1987): 403–9.

Levine, Lawrence W. *Black Culture and Black Consciousness: Afro-American Folk Thought from Slavery to Freedom.* New York: Oxford University Press, 1977.

Lewis, David Levering. *W. E. B. Du Bois: Biography of a Race, 1868–1919.* New York: Holt, 1993.

Liberti, Rita. "'We Were Ladies, We Just Played Basketball Like Boys': African American Womanhood and Competitive Basketball at Bennett College, 1928–1942." *Journal of Sport History* 26 (Fall 1999): 567–84.

Lindholm, Karl. "William Clarence Matthews." *The National Pastime: A Review of Baseball History* 17 (1997): 67–72.

Lipsyte, Robert, and Peter Levine. *Idols of the Game: A Sporting History of the American Century.* Atlanta: Turning Publishing, 1995.

Litwack, Leon F. *Been in the Storm So Long: The Aftermath of Slavery.* New York: Vintage, 1980.

Lloyd, Craig. *Eugene Bullard: Black Expatriate in Jazz-Age Paris.* Athens: University of Georgia Press, 2000.

Logan, Rayford. *Howard University: The First Hundred Years, 1867–1967.* New York: New York University Press, 1969.

Lomax, Michael E. "Black Baseball's First Rivalry: The Cuban Giants versus the Gorhams of New York and the Birth of the Colored Championship." *Sport History Review* 28 (November 1997): 134–45.

———. "Black Entrepreneurship in the National Pastime: The Rise of Semiprofessional Baseball in Black Chicago, 1890–1915." *Journal of Sport History* 25 (Spring 1998): 43–64.

———. *Operating by Any Means Necessary: Black Baseball and Black Entrepreneurship in the National Pastime, 1860–1901.* Syracuse, N.Y.: Syracuse University Press, 2003.

Lombardo, Ben. "The Harlem Globetrotters and the Perpetuation of the Black Stereotype." *Physical Educator* 35 (May 1978): 60–63.

Longman, Jere, and Richard Lezin Jones. "Iverson: A Study in Contradictions." *New York Times,* July 21, 2002.

Lott, Eric. *Love and Theft: Blackface Minstrelsy and the American Working Class.* New York: Oxford University Press, 1993.

Louis, Joe, with Edna and Art Rust Jr. *Joe Louis: My Life.* New York: Harcourt Brace Jovanovich, 1978.

Lowenfish, Lee. "Sport, Race, and the Baseball Business: The Jackie Robinson Story Revisited." *Arena Review* 2 (Spring 1978): 2–16.

Loy, John, and Joseph McElvoque. "Racial Segregation in American Sport." *International Review of Sport Sociology* 5 (1970): 5–23.

Lucas, John A., and Ronald A. Smith. *Saga of American Sport.* Philadelphia: Lea and Febiger, 1978.

Lucas, Robert. "The World's Fastest Bicycle Rider." *Negro Digest,* May 1948, 10–13.

MacDonald, William W. "The Black Athlete in American Sports." In *Sports in Modern America,* edited by William J. Baker and John M. Carroll, 88–98. St. Louis: River City Publishers, 1981.

Magriel, Paul. "Tom Molineaux." *Phylon* 12 (December 1951): 329–36.

Majors, Richard. "Cool Pose: Black Masculinity and Sports." In *Sport, Men, and the Gender Order: Critical Feminist Perspectives,* edited by Michael A. Messner and Donald F. Sabo, 109–14. Champaign, Ill.: Human Kinetics, 1990.

Malcomson, Scott L. *One Drop of Blood: The American Misadventure of Race.* New York: Farrar, Straus and Giroux, 2000.

Mallory, William. *Old Plantation Days.* Hamilton, Ont.: n.p., n.d. Electronic edition, Chapel Hill, N.C.: Academic Affairs Library, University of North Carolina at Chapel Hill, 1999.

Malloy, Jerry, comp. *Sol White's History of Colored Base Ball with Other Documents on the Early Black Game, 1886–1936.* Introduction by Jerry Malloy. Lincoln: University of Nebraska Press, 1995.

Mandell, Richard D. *The Nazi Olympics.* Urbana: University of Illinois Press, 1986.

Mann, Horace Bond. *Education for Freedom: A History of Lincoln University, Pennsylvania.* [Lincoln, Pa.]: Lincoln University, 1976.

Marable, Manning. "Black Athletes in White Men's Games, 1880–1920." *Maryland Historian* 4 (Fall 1973): 143–49.

Marcello, Ronald E. "The Integration of Intercollegiate Athletics in Texas: North Texas State College as a Test Case, 1956." *Journal of Sport History* 14 (Winter 1987): 286–316.

Margolick, David. "Music: Only One Athlete Has Ever Inspired This Many Songs." *New York Times,* February 25, 2001.

Martin, Charles H. "The Color Line in Midwestern College Sports, 1890–1960." *Indiana Magazine of History* 48 (June 2002): 85–112.

———. "Integrating New Year's Day: The Racial Politics of College Bowl Games in the American South." *Journal of Sport History* 24 (Fall 1997): 358–77.

———. "Jim Crow in the Gymnasium: The Integration of College Basketball in the American South." *International Journal of the History of Sport* 10 (April 1993): 68–86.

———. "Racial Change and Big-Time College Football in Georgia: The Age of Segregation, 1892–1957." *Georgia Historical Quarterly* 80 (1996): 532–62.

———. "The Rise and Fall of Jim Crow in Southern College Sports." *North Carolina Historical Review* 76 (July 1999): 253–84.

Mathewson, Alfred Dennis. "Black Women, Gender Equity and the Function at the Junction." *Marquette Sports Law Journal* 6 (Spring 1996): 239–66.

Matthews, Vincent, with Neil Amdur. *My Race Be Won.* New York: Charterhouse, 1974.

Mazuri, Ali A. "Boxer Muhammad Ali and Soldier Idi Amin as International Political Symbols: The Bioeconomics of Sports and War." *Comparative Studies in Society and History* 19 (April 1977): 189–215.

McCallum, Jack. "Alone on the Mountaintop." *Sports Illustrated,* December 23, 1991, 64–69.

McDaniel, Pete. *Uneven Lies: The Heroic Story of African-Americans in Golf.* Greenwich, Conn.: American Golfer, 2000.

McKinney, G. B. "Negro Professional Baseball Players in the Upper South in the Gilded Age." *Journal of Sport History* 3 (Winter 1976): 273–80.

McMahon, David R. "Pride to All: African-Americans and Sports in Iowa." In *Outside-In: African American History in Iowa, 1838–2000,* edited by Bill Silag. Des Moines, Ia.: State Historical Society of Iowa, forthcoming.

———. "Remembering the Black and Gold: African-Americans, Sport, Memory, and the University of Iowa." *Culture, Sport, Society* 4 (Summer 2001): 63–98.

McPherson, Barry D. "Minority Group Involvement in Sport: The Black Athlete." *Exercise and Sport Science Reviews* 2 (1974): 71–101.

Mead, Chris. *Champion: Joe Louis, Black Hero in White America.* New York: Scribner's, 1985.

Meier, August. *Negro Thought in America, 1880–1915: Racial Ideologies in the Age of Booker T. Washington.* Ann Arbor: University of Michigan Press, 1963.

Meltzer, Milton, ed. *In Their Own Words: A History of the American Negro.* Vol. 1. New York: Crowell, 1964.

Mergen, Bernard. *Play and Playthings: A Reference Guide.* Westport, Conn.: Greenwood, 1982.

Messner, Michael A., and Donald F. Sabo, eds. *Sport, Men, and the Gender Order., Critical Feminist Perspectives.* Champaign, Ill.: Human Kinetics, 1990.

Miller, Patrick B. "The Anatomy of Scientific Racism: Racialist Responses to Black Athletic Achievement." *Journal of Sport History* 25 (Spring 1998): 119–51.

———. "Harvard and the Color Line: The Case of Lucien Alexis." In *Sports in Massachusetts: Historical Essays,* edited by Ronald Story, 137–58. Westfield, Mass.: Institute for Massachusetts Studies, 1991.

———. "The Nazi Olympics, Berlin, 1936." Review of exhibition, U.S. Holocaust Memorial Museum, Washington, D.C. *Olympika: The International Journal of Olympic Studies* 5 (1996): 127–40.

———. "Slouching toward a New Expediency: College Football and the Color Line during the Depression Decade." *American Studies* 40 (Fall 1999): 5–30.

———. "Sport as 'Interracial Education': Popular Culture and Civil Rights Strategies during the 1930s and Beyond." In *The Civil Rights Movement Revisited: Critical Perspectives on the Struggle for Racial Equality in the United States,* edited by Patrick B. Miller, Therese Frey Steffen, and Elisabeth Schäfer-Wünsche, 21–38. Hamburg: LIT Verlag, 2001.

———. "To 'Bring the Race Along Rapidly': Sport, Student Culture, and Educational Mission at Historically Black Colleges during the Interwar Years." *History of Education Quarterly* 35 (Summer 1995): 111–33.

———, ed. *The Sporting World of the Modern South.* Urbana: University of Illinois Press, 2002.

Mix, Ron. "Was This Their Freedom Ride?" *Sports Illustrated,* January 18, 1965, 24–25.

Moore, Joseph T. *Pride against Prejudice: The Biography of Larry Doby.* Westport, Conn.: Greenwood, 1988.

Morris, Willie. *The Courting of Marcus Dupree.* Garden City, N.Y.: Doubleday, 1983.

Nalty, Bernard C. *Strength for the Fight: A History of Black Americans in the Military.* New York: Free Press, 1986.

Nathan, Daniel A. "Sugar Ray Robinson, the Sweet Science, and the Politics of Meaning." *Journal of Sport History* 26 (Spring 1999): 163–74.

Nelson, Stanley. *The Black Press: Soldiers without Swords.* Videorecording produced and directed by Stanley Nelson. San Francisco: Half Nelson Productions, 1998. California Newsreel, distributor.

Nesfield, Carl. "Pride against Prejudice: Fritz Pollard Brown All-American Pre–World War I Vintage." *Black Sports,* December 1971, 81.

Norwood, Stephen H. "The Making of an Athlete: An Interview with Joe Washington." *Journal of Sport History* 27 (Spring 2000): 91–145.

Norwood, Stephen H., and Harold Brackman. "Going to Bat for Jackie Robinson: The Jewish Role in Breaking Baseball's Color Line." *Journal of Sport History* 26 (Spring 1999): 115–54.

Novak, Michael. *The Joy of Sports.* New York: Basic Books, 1976.

Noverr, Douglas A., and Lawrence E. Ziewacz. *The Games They Played: Sports in American History, 1865–1980.* Chicago: Nelson-Hall, 1988.

Oliver, Paul. *Aspects of the Blues Tradition.* New York: Oak Publications, 1970.

Olsen, Jack. *The Black Athlete: A Shameful Story.* New York: Time-Life Books, 1968.

O'Neil, Buck, with Steve Wulf and David Conrads. *I Was Right on Time.* New York: Simon and Schuster, 1996.

Oriard, Michael. *King Football: Sport and Spectacle in the Golden Age of Radio and Newsreel, Movies and Magazines, the Weekly and Daily Press.* Chapel Hill: University of North Carolina Press, 2001.

———. *Reading Football: How the Popular Press Created An American Spectacle.* Chapel Hill: University of North Carolina Press, 1993.

Orr, Jack. *The Black Athlete: His Story in American History.* New York: Lion Books, 1969.

Overmyer, James. *Queen of the Negro Leagues: Effa Manley and the Newark Eagles.* Lanham, Md: Scarecrow Press, 1998.

Owens, Jesse. "How I Learned Marching Is Sometimes More Important than Running." *Sepia,* December 1974, 26–29.

Owens, Jesse, with Paul Neimark. *Blackthink: My Life as Black Man and White Man.* New York: Morrow, 1970.

Paige, Leroy (Satchel), as told to David Lipman. *Maybe I'll Pitch Forever: A Great Baseball Player Tells the Hilarious Story behind the Legend.* Garden City, N.Y.: Doubleday, 1962.

Paino, Troy D. "Hoosiers in a Different Light: Forces of Change vs. the Power of Nostalgia." *Journal of Sport History* 26 (Spring 2001): 63–80.

Palmer, Arthur Judson. "The Fastest Man on Wheels." *Sports Illustrated,* March 14, 1960, 7–11.

Patterson, Orlando. *Ritual of Blood: Consequences of Slavery in Two American Centuries.* New York: Basic, 1998.

Paul, Joan, et al. "The Arrival and Ascendance of Black Athletes in the Southeastern Conference, 1966–1980." *Phylon* 45 (December 1984): 284–97.

Pennington, Richard. *Breaking the Ice: The Racial Integration of Southwest Conference Football.* Jefferson, N.C.: McFarland, 1987.

Peterson, Robert W. *Cages to Jump Shots: Pro Basketball's Early Years.* New York: Oxford University Press, 1990.

———. *Only the Ball Was White: A History of Legendary Black Players and All-Black Professional Teams.* Englewood Cliffs, N.J.: Prentice-Hall, 1970.

Phillips, Bob. "Still Carrying the Torch." *Scholastic Coach* 58 (August 1988): 38–40, 82–83.

Pierce, Richard B. "More Than a Game: The Political Meaning of High School Basketball in Indianapolis." *Journal of Urban History* 27 (November 2000): 3–23.

Platt, Anthony M. *E. Franklin Frazier Reconsidered.* New Brunswick, N.J.: Rutgers University Press, 1991.

Porter, David L., ed. *African American Sports Greats: A Biographical Dictionary.* Westport, Conn.: Greenwood, 1995.

Quercetani, Roberto L. *A World History of Track and Field, 1864–1964.* London: Oxford University Press, 1964.

Rader, Benjamin G. *American Sports: From the Age of Folk Games to the Age of Spectators.* Englewood Cliffs, N.J.: Prentice-Hall, 1983.

———. *Baseball: A History of America's Game.* 2d ed. Urbana: University of Illinois Press, 2002.

Rampersad, Arnold. *Jackie Robinson: A Biography.* New York: Knopf, 1997.

Rankin-Hill, Lesley M., and Michael L. Blakey. "W. Montague Cobb: Physical Anthropologist, Anatomist, and Activist." In *African American Pioneers in Anthropology,* edited by Ira E. Harrison and Faye V. Harrison, 101–36. Urbana: University of Illinois Press, 1999.

Rawick, George P., ed. *The American Slave: A Composite Autobiography.* Westport, Conn.: Greenwood, 1972.

Rayl, Susan J. "The New York Renaissance Professional Black Basketball Team, 1923–1950." Ph.D. diss., Pennsylvania State University, 1996.

Reed, Adolph, Jr. *W. E. B. Du Bois and American Political Thought: Fabianism and the Color Line.* New York: Oxford University Press, 1997.

Reed, Adolph L., Jr. *The Jesse Jackson Phenomenon: The Crisis of Purpose in Afro-American Politics.* New Haven: Yale University Press, 1986.

Reed, Harry A. "Not by Protest Alone: Afro-American Activists and the Pythian Baseball Club of Philadelphia, 1867–1869." *Western Journal of Black Studies* 9 (1985): 144–50.

Reisler, Jim. *Black Writers/Black Baseball: An Anthology of Articles from Black Sportswriters Who Covered the Negro Leagues.* Foreword by Don Newcombe. Jefferson, N.C.: McFarland, 1994.

Remnick, David. *King of the World: Muhammad Ali and the Rise of a Hero.* New York: Random House, 1998.

Ribowsky, Mark. *A Complete History of the Negro Leagues, 1884 to 1955.* New York: Birch Lane Press, 1995.

———. *Don't Look Back: Satchel Paige in the Shadows of Baseball.* New York: Simon and Schuster, 1994.

———. *The Power and the Darkness: The Life of Josh Gibson in the Shadows of the Game.* New York: Simon and Schuster, 1996.

Richardson, Joe. *A History of Fisk University, 1865–1946.* University: University of Alabama Press, 1980.

Riess, Steven A. *Major Problems in American Sport History.* New York: Houghton Mifflin, 1997.

Riley, James A. *The Biographical Encyclopedia of the Negro Baseball Leagues.* New York: Carroll and Graf, 1994.

Ritchie, Andrew. *Major Taylor: The Extraordinary Career of a Champion Bicycle Racer.* San Francisco: Bicycle Books, 1988.

Roberts, Randy. *But They Can't Beat Us! Oscar Robertson's Crispus Attucks Tigers.* Champaign, Ill.: Sports Publishing, 1999.

———. "Galveston's Jack Johnson: Flourishing in the Dark." *Southwestern Historical Quarterly* 82 (July 1983): 37–56.

———. "Heavyweight Champion Jack Johnson: His Omaha Image, a Public Reaction Study." *Nebraska History* 57 (Summer 1976): 226–41.

———. *Papa Jack: Jack Johnson and the Era of White Hopes.* New York: Free Press, 1983.

Roberts, Randy, and James Olson. *Winning Is the Only Thing: Sports in America since 1945.* Baltimore: Johns Hopkins University Press, 1989.

Roberts, Selena. "Williams Sisters Learned to Think off Court, Too." *New York Times,* July 3, 2000.

Robinson, Frazier, with Paul Bauer. *Catching Dreams: My Life in the Negro Baseball Leagues.* Syracuse, N.Y.: Syracuse University Press, 2000.

Robinson, Jackie, with Alfred Duckett. *I Never Had It Made.* New York: Putnam, 1972.

Rodman, Dennis, with Tim Keown. *Bad as I Wanna Be.* New York: Delacorte, 1996.

Rogosin, Donn. *Invisible Men: Life in Baseball's Negro Leagues.* New York: Athenaeum, 1987.

Rosaforte, Tim. *Raising the Bar: The Championship Years of Tiger Woods.* New York: St. Martin's, 2000.

Ross, Charles K. *Outside the Lines: African Americans and the Integration of the National Football League.* New York: New York University Press, 1999.

Ruck, Rob. *Sandlot Seasons: Sport in Black Pittsburgh.* Urbana: University of Illinois Press, 1987.

———. "Soaring above the Sandlots: The Garfield Eagles." *Pennsylvania Heritage* 8 (Summer 1982): 13–18.

Rudman, William S. "The Sport Mystique in Black Culture." *Sociology of Sport Journal* 3 (1986): 305–19.

Rudolph, Wilma. *Wilma.* New York: New American Library, 1977.

Russell, Bill, as told to William McSweeney. *Go Up for Glory.* New York: Conrad-McCann, 1966.

Russell, Bill, and Taylor Branch. *Second Wind: The Memoirs of an Opinionated Man.* New York: Random House, 1974.

Rust, Art, and Edna Rust. *Art Rust's Illustrated History of the Black Athlete.* Garden City, N.Y.: Doubleday, 1985.

Rutkoff, Peter M., ed. *The Cooperstown Symposium on Baseball and American Culture, 1997 (Jackie Robinson).* Jefferson, N.C.: McFarland, 1997.

Sage, George H. *Power and Ideology in American Sport: A Critical Perspective.* Champaign, Ill.: Human Kinetics, 1988.

Sailes, Gary. *African Americans in Sport.* New Brunswick, N.J.: Transaction, 1998.

Salzberg, Charles. *From Set Shot to Slam Dunk: The Glory Days of Basketball in the Words of Those Who Played It.* New York: Dutton, 1987.

Sammons, Jeffrey T. *Beyond the Ring: The Role of Boxing in American Society.* Urbana: University of Illinois Press, 1988.

———. "Boxing as a Reflection of Society: The Southern Reaction to Joe Louis." *Journal of Popular Culture* 16 (Spring 1983): 23–33.

———. "'Race' and Sport: A Critical Historical Examination." *Journal of Sport History* 21 (Fall 1994): 203–98.

Savage, Howard J., Harold W. Bentley, John T. McGovern, and Dean F. Smiley. *American College Athletics.* Carnegie Foundation for the Advancement of Teaching, Bulletin no. 23. New York: Carnegie Foundation for the Advancement of Teaching, 1929.

Scarupa, Harriet Jackson. "W. Montague Cobb: His Long, Storied, Battle-Scarred Life." *New Directions: The Howard University Magazine,* April 1988, 6–17.

Scott, Jack. *The Athletic Revolution.* New York: Free Press, 1971.

Scully, Gerald. "Economic Discrimination in Professional Sports." *Law and Contemporary Problems* 38 (Winter–Spring 1973): 67–84.

Sellers, Robert. "African American Student-Athletes: Opportunity or Exploitation?" In *Racism in College Athletics: The African American Athlete's Experience,* edited by Dana D. Brooks and Ronald C. Althouse, 143–74. 2d ed. Morgantown, W.Va.: Fitness Information Technology, 2000.

Shropshire, Kenneth L. *In Black and White: Race and Sports in America.* New York: New York University Press, 1996.

———. "Merit, Ol' Boy Networks, and the Black-Bottomed Pyramid." *Hastings Law Journal* 47 (January 1996): 455–72.

Sifford, Charlie, with James Gallo. *Just Let Me Play: The Story of Charlie Sifford, the First Black PGA Golfer.* Latham, N.Y.: British American Publishing, 1992.

Simons, William. "Jackie Robinson and the American Mind: Journalistic Perceptions of the Re-integration of Baseball." *Journal of Sport History* 12 (Spring 1985): 39–64.

Sinclair, Upton. *The Goose-Step: A Study of American Education.* Pasadena, Calif., 1923.

Sinnette, Calvin H. *Forbidden Fairways: African Americans and the Game of Golf.* Chelsea, Mich.: Sleeping Bear Press, 1998.

Sloan-Green, Tina, et al. *Black Women in Sport.* Reston, Va.: American Alliance for Health, Physical Education, Recreation, and Dance, 1981.

Smith, Maureen M. "Identity and Citizenship: African American Athletes, Sport, and the Freedom struggles of the 1960s." Ph.D. diss., Ohio State University, 1999.

Smith, Ronald A. "The Paul Robeson–Jackie Robinson Saga and a Political Collision." *Journal of Sport History* 6 (Summer 1979): 5–27.

———. *Sports and Freedom: The Rise of Big-Time College Athletics.* New York: Oxford University Press, 1988.

———, ed. *Big-Time Football at Harvard 1905: The Diary of Coach Bill Reid.* Urbana: University of Illinois Press, 1994.

Smith, Sam. *The Jordan Rules.* New York: Simon and Schuster, 1992.

Smith, Thomas G. "Civil Rights on the Gridiron: The Kennedy Administration and the Desegregation of the Washington Redskins." *Journal of Sport History* 14 (Summer 1987): 189–208.

———. "Outside the Pale: The Exclusion of Blacks from the National Football League, 1934–1946." *Journal of Sport History* 15 (Winter 1988): 255–81.

Smith, Yevonne R. "Sociohistorical Influences on African American Elite Sportswomen." In *Racism in College Athletics: The African American Athletic Experience,* edited by Dana D. Brooks and Ronald C. Althouse, 173–97. 2d ed. Morgantown, W.Va.: Fitness Information Technology, 2000.

Smith, Yvonne. "Women of Color in Society and Sport." *Quest* 44 (Summer 1992): 228–50.

Somers, Dale. *The Rise of Sports in New Orleans.* Baton Rouge: Louisiana State University Press, 1972.

Sperber, Murray. *Onward to Victory: The Crises That Shaped College Sports.* New York: Holt, 1998.

Spickard, Paul, and G. Reginald Daniel, eds. *Uncompleted Independence: Racial Thinking in the United States.* Notre Dame, Ind.: Notre Dame University Press, forthcoming.

Spivey, Donald. "Black Consciousness and Olympic Protest Movements, 1964–1980." In *Sport in America: New Historical Perspectives,* edited by Donald Spivey, 239–62. Westport, Conn.: Greenwood, 1985.

———. "'End Jim Crow in Sports': The Protest at New York University, 1940–1941." *Journal of Sport History* 15 (Winter 1988): 282–303.

———. "Sport, Protest, and Consciousness: The Black Athlete in Big-Time Intercollegiate Sports, 1941–1968." *Phylon* 44 (June 1983): 116–25.

Spivey, Donald, and Tom Jones. "Intercollegiate Athletic Servitude: A Case Study of the Black Illinois Student Athletes, 1931–1967." *Social Science Quarterly* 55 (March 1975): 939–47.

Steward, Austin. *Twenty-Two Years a Slave and Forty Years a Freeman.* Reading, Mass.: Addison-Wesley, 1969.

Streator, George. "Football in Negro Colleges." *Crisis* 39 (April 1932): 129, 141.

———. "Negro Football Standards." *Crisis* 38 (March 1931): 85–86.

Stout, Glenn. "Jim Crow Halfback." *Boston Magazine,* November 1987, 124–34.

Stovall, Tyler. *Paris Noir: African Americans in the City of Light.* New York: Houghton Mifflin, 1996.

Strode, Woody, and Sam Young. *Goal Dust: The Warm and Candid Memoirs of a Pioneer Black Athlete and Actor.* New York: Madison Books, 1990.

Taylor, Marshall "Major." *The Fastest Bicycle Rider in the World.* Battleboro, Vt.: Green-Stephen Press, 1971.

Telander, Rick. *Heaven Is a Playground.* Lincoln: University of Nebraska Press, 1995.

Thomas, Damion. "'The Good Negroes': African-American Athletes and the Cultural Cold War, 1945–1968." Ph.D. diss., University of California, Los Angeles, 2002.

Thompson, Richard. *Race and Sport.* London: Oxford University Press, 1964.

Torres, Jose. *Sting Like a Bee: The Muhammad Ali Story.* New York: Abelard-Schuman, 1971.

Tunis, John R. *$port$: Heroics and Hysterics.* New York: John Day Company, 1928.

Turco, Lewis. "Angle of Ascent: The Poetry of Robert Hayden." *Michigan Quarterly Review* 16 (Spring 1977): 199–219.

Tygiel, Jules. *Baseball's Great Experiment: Jackie Robinson and His Legacy.* New York: Oxford University Press, 1983.

———. *Extra Bases: Reflections on Jackie Robinson, Race, and Baseball History.* Lincoln: University of Nebraska Press, 2002.

———, ed. *The Jackie Robinson Reader: Perspectives on an American Hero.* New York: Penguin Dutton, 1997.

Van Deburg, William. *A New Day in Babylon: The Black Power Movement and American Culture, 1965–1975.* Chicago: University of Chicago Press, 1992.

Vecsey, George. "Retro Globetrotters Triumph by Losing." *New York Times,* February 11, 2001.

Vertinsky, Patricia, and Gwendolyn Captain. "More Myth than History: American Culture and Representations of the Black Female's Athletic Ability." *Journal of Sport History* 25 (Fall 1998): 532–61.

Wacquant, Loic. "The Social Logic of Boxing in Black Chicago: Toward a Sociology of Pugilism." *Sociology of Sport Journal* 9 (1992): 221–54.

Wade, Harold, Jr. *Black Men of Amherst.* Amherst, Mass.: Amherst College Press, 1976.

Walker, Chet, with Chris Messenger. *Long Time Coming: A Black Athlete's Coming-of-Age in America.* New York: Grove Press, 1995.

Walker, Moses Fleetwood. *Our Home Colony: A Treatise on the Past, Present, and Future of the Negro Race in America.* Steubenville, Ohio: Herald Printing Company, [c. 1908].

Wallechinsky, David. *The Complete Book of the Olympics.* New York: Viking, 1984.

Walton, Lester. "Search for a 'White Hope.'" *New York Age,* September 21, 1911.

Washington, Booker T. *Up from Slavery: An Autobiography.* New York: Doubleday, 1901.

Watkins, Ralph. "Recreation, Leisure and Charity in the Afro-American Community of Buffalo, New York: 1920–1925." *Afro-Americans in New York Life and History* 6 (July 1982): 7–15.

Watterson, John S. "The Gridiron Crisis of 1905: Was It Really a Crisis?" *Journal of Sport History* 27 (Summer 2000): 291–98.

Watterson, John Sayle. *College Football: History, Spectacle, Controversy.* Baltimore, Md.: Johns Hopkins University Press, 2000.

Weaver, Bill L. "The Black Press and the Assault on Professional Baseball's Color Line, October 1945–April 1947." *Phylon* 40 (Winter 1979): 303–17.

Welch, Paula. "Tuskegee Institute: Pioneer in Women's Olympic Track and Field." *The Foil* (Spring 1988): 10–13.

Wenn, Stephen R., and Jeffrey P. Wenn. "Muhammad Ali and the Convergence of Olympic Sport and U.S. Diplomacy in 1980: A Reassessment from behind the Scenes of the U.S. State Department." *Olympika: The International Journal of Olympic Studies* 2 (1993): 45–66.

Wertheim, L. Jon. *Venus Envy: A Sensational Season Inside the Women's Tennis Tour.* New York: HarperCollins, 2001.

White, G. Edward. *Creating the National Pastime: Baseball Transforms Itself, 1903–1953.* Princeton: Princeton University Press, 1996.

Whitfield, Mal. "Let's Boycott the Olympics." *Ebony,* March 1964, 95–96.

Wideman, John Edgar. *Hoop Roots: Basketball, Race, and Love.* New York: Houghton Mifflin, 2001.

Wiggins, David K. "Critical Events Affecting Racism in Athletics." In *Racism in College Athletics: The African American Athlete's Experience,* edited by Dana D. Brooks and Ronald C. Althouse, 23–49. 2d ed. Morgantown, W.Va.: Fitness Information Technology, 2000.

———. "Edwin Bancroft Henderson: Physical Educator, Civil Rights Activist, and Chronicler of African American Athletes." *Research Quarterly for Exercise and Sport* 70 (June 1999): 91–112.

———. "From Plantation to Playing Field: Historical Writings on the Black Athlete in American Sport." *Research Quarterly for Exercise and Sport* 57 (June 1986): 101–16.

———. "The Future of College Athletics Is at Stake: Black Athletes and Racial Turmoil on Three Predominantly White University Campuses, 1968–1972." *Journal of Sport History* 15 (Winter 1988): 304–33.

———. *Glory Bound: Black Athletes in a White America.* Syracuse, N.Y.: Syracuse University Press, 1997.

———. "'Great Speed but Little Stamina': The Historical Debate over Black Athletic Superiority." *Journal of Sport History* 16 (Summer 1989): 158–85.

———. "A History of Highly Competitive Sport for American Children." In *Children and Youth in Sport: A Biopsychosocial Perspective,* edited by Frank L. Smoll and Ronald E. Smith, 15–30. Dubuque, Ia.: Brown and Benchmark, 1996.

———. "Isaac Murphy: Black Hero in Nineteenth-Century American Sport, 1861–1896." *Canadian Journal of History of Sport and Physical Education* 10 (May 1979): 15–32.

———. "The 1936 Olympic Games in Berlin: The Response of America's Black Press." *Research Quarterly for Exercise and Sport* 54 (September 1983): 283–92.

———. "The Notion of Double-Consciousness and the Involvement of Black Athletes in American Sport." In *Ethnicity and Sport in North American History and Culture,* edited by George Eisen and David K. Wiggins, 133–53. Westport, Conn: Greenwood Press, 1994.

———. "Peter Jackson and the Elusive Heavyweight Championship: A Black Athlete's Struggle against the Late Nineteenth-Century Color Line." *Journal of Sport History* 12 (Summer 1985): 143–63.

———. "The Play of Slave Children in the Plantation Communities of the Old South, 1820–1860." *Journal of Sport History* 7 (Summer 1980): 21–39.

———. "Prized Performers, but Frequently Overlooked Students: The Involvement of Black Athletes in Intercollegiate Sports on Predominantly White University Campuses, 1890–1972." *Research Quarterly for Exercise and Sport* 62 (June 1991): 164–77.

———. "Sport and Popular Pastimes: The Shadow of the Slavequarter." *Canadian Journal of History of Sport and Physical Education* 11 (May 1980): 61–88.

———. "Wendell Smith, the *Pittsburgh Courier-Journal* and the Campaign to Include Blacks in Organized Baseball, 1933–1945." *Journal of Sport History* 10 (Summer 1983): 5–29.

———. "The Year of Awakening: Black Athletes, Racial Unrest, and the Civil Rights Movement of 1968." *International Journal of the History of Sport* 9 (August 1992): 188–208.

Wiggins, William H. "Boxing's Sambo Twins: Racial Stereotypes in Jack Johnson and Joe Louis Newspaper Cartoons, 1908 to 1938." *Journal of Sport History* 15 (Winter 1988): 242–54.

———. "Jack Johnson as Bad Nigger: The Folklore of His Life." *Black Scholar* 2 (January 1971): 4–19.

———. "Reflections on the Joe Louis Recordings." Liner notes for *Joe Louis: An American Hero,* compact disk compiled by Rena Kozersky. Rounder Records, 2001.

Wilkins, Roy. "Joe Louis and Jesse Owens." *Crisis* 42 (August 1935): 241.

Williams, Charles H. "Negro Athletes in the Tenth Olympiad." *Southern Workman* 61 (November 1932): 449–60.

Williams, Linda. "Sportswomen in Black and White: Sports History from an Afro-American Perspective." In *Women, Media and Sport: Challenging Gender Values,* edited by Pamela J. Creedon, 45–66. Thousand Oaks, Calif.: Sage, 1994.

Winters, Manque. *Professional Sports: The Community College Connection.* Inglewood, Calif.: Winnor Press, 1982.

Woods, Earl. *Playing Through: Straight Talk on Hard Work, Big Dreams and Adventures with Tiger Woods.* New York: Harper Collins, 1998.

Woolfolk, George. *Prairie View: A Study in Public Conscience, 1878–1946.* New York: Pageant Press, 1962.

Yetman, Norman R. "Positional Segregation and the Economic Hypothesis: A Critique." *Sociology of Sport Journal* 4 (1987): 274–77.

———, ed. *Voices from Slavery.* New York: Holt, Rinehart, and Winston, 1970.

Young, Alexander J., Jr. "The Boston Tarbaby." *Nova Scotia Historical Quarterly* 4 (September 1974): 277–93.

———. "Joe Louis, Symbol." Ph.D. diss., University of Maryland, 1968.

Young, Andrew S. "Doc." *Great Negro Baseball Stars and How They Made the Major Leagues.* New York: A. S. Barnes, 1953.

———. *Negro Firsts in Sports.* Chicago: Johnson Publishing, 1963.

Zang, David W. "Calvin Hill Interview." *Journal of Sport History* 15 (Winter 1988): 334–55.

———. *Fleet Walker's Divided Heart: The Life of Baseball's First Black Major Leaguer.* Lincoln: University of Nebraska Press, 1995.

Zimbalist, Andrew. *Unpaid Professionals: Commercialism and Conflict in Big-Time College Sports.* Princeton: Princeton University Press, 1999.

Zinkoff, David. *Go Man Go!: Around the World with the Harlem Globetrotters.* New York: Pyramid Books, 1958.

Zuckerman, Jerome, et al. "The Black Athlete in Post-bellum Nineteenth Century." *Physical Educator* 29 (October 1972): 142–46.

INDEX

David K. Wiggins teaches sport history at George Mason University. He is the author of *Glory Bound: Black Athletes in White America,* the editor of *Sport in America: From Wicked Amusement to National Obsession,* and a coeditor of *Ethnicity and Sport in North American History and Culture.* He has published many articles on the African American experience in sport and is the former editor of the *Journal of Sport History.*

Patrick B. Miller teaches history at Northeastern Illinois University in Chicago. He is the editor of *Sporting World of the Modern South* and coeditor of *The Civil Rights Movement Revisited: Critical Perspectives on the Struggle for Racial Equality in the United States.* He is also the author of numerous articles on sports, race relations, and American culture.

Sport and Society

The University of Illinois Press
is a founding member of the
Association of American University Presses.

Composed in 10.5/13 Minion
with Stone Sans display
by Jim Proefrock
at the University of Illinois Press
Designed by Paula Newcomb
Manufactured by Data Reproductions Corp.

University of Illinois Press
1325 South Oak Street
Champaign, IL 61820-6903
www.press.uillinois.edu